D0265927

Blackstone's Guide to the

ANTI-TERRORISM LEGISLATION

An update on developments to this legislation will be available from April 2004 on the Blackstone's Guides Series web site which is currently under construction. This can be found at the following location: http://www.oup.co.uk/law/practitioner/cws

WITHDRAWN
FROM
STOCK

100481572

Blackstone's Guide to the

ANTI-TERRORISM
LEGISLATION

Clive Walker

OXFORD
UNIVERSITY PRESS

100481572

KM
562.
22.
W24

OXFORD
UNIVERSITY PRESS

Great Clarendon Street, Oxford OX2 6DP

Oxford University Press is a department of the University of Oxford.
It furthers the University's objective of excellence in research, scholarship,
and education by publishing worldwide in

Oxford New York

Auckland Bangkok Buenos Aires Cape Town Chennai
Dar es Salaam Delhi Hong Kong Istanbul Karachi Kolkata
Kuala Lumpur Madrid Melbourne Mexico City Mumbai Nairobi
São Paulo Shanghai Taipei Tokyo Toronto

Oxford is a registered trade mark of Oxford University Press
in the UK and in certain other countries

Published in the United States
by Oxford University Press Inc., New York

© Clive Walker 2002

The moral rights of the author have been asserted
Database right Oxford University Press (maker)

First published 2002

Crown copyright material is reproduced with the permission
of the Controller of Her Majesty's Stationery Office

All rights reserved. No part of this publication may be reproduced,
stored in a retrieval system, or transmitted, in any form or by any means,
without the prior permission in writing of Oxford University Press,
or as expressly permitted by law, or under terms agreed with the appropriate
reprographics rights organization. Enquiries concerning reproduction
outside the scope of the above should be sent to the Rights Department,
Oxford University Press, at the address above

You must not circulate this book in any other binding or cover
and you must impose the same condition on any acquirer

British Library Cataloguing in Publication Data

Data available

Library of Congress Cataloging in Publication Data

Data available

ISBN 1-84174-183-3

5 7 9 10 8 6 4

Typeset by Style Photosetting Ltd
Printed in Great Britain
on acid-free paper by
Biddles Ltd., King's Lynn, Norfolk

Contents

An update on developments to this legislation will be available from April 2004 on the Blackstone's Guides Series web site which is currently under construction. This can be found at the following location: http://www.oup.co.uk/law/practitioner/cws

Preface

Two stories are related within this book. The work was commenced as a study of the Terrorism Act 2000 and was virtually concluded by autumn 2001. Dramatic events then conspired against completion. The attacks of the 11th September on the World Trade Centre, New York and the Pentagon, Washington DC, reinforced by subsequent apprehensions about assaults by anthrax and other horrifying weapons of mass destruction, produced a new agenda both for lawmakers and, consequently, for the author of this book. As far as officialdom was concerned, the result in no short time was the Anti-terrorism, Crime and Security Act 2001. That outcome was predictable. Legislation aimed against terrorism has been established in Great Britain for well over two decades. In Northern Ireland there have been successive measures which can be traced back for more than two centuries. Often, the laws have been prompted by a crisis and represent both a symbolic and practical response to a phenomenon which is seen as a grave menace to Liberal democracies and their citizenry. Given that history, the advent of the Anti-terrorism, Crime and Security Act 2001 could have been anticipated, though, as it followed hot on the heels of the coming into force (earlier the same year) of a comprehensive Terrorism Act 2000, it will be important to discern what is symbolic and what is practical in relation to combating terrorism. The new Terrorism Act 2000 is itself, on the face of it, also unremarkable, especially as the pre-existing legislation it replaced was time-limited and so required renewal and even re-enactment from time to time. However, the conjunction of the Terrorism Act 2000 with the most important political initiative in Northern Ireland since 1969 — commonly called 'the Peace Process' — does require some explanation, especially as the new Act is the most permanent and most comprehensive measure of its kind ever to be passed.

So, turning first to the Terrorism Act 2000, its importance can be judged both in terms of its role in preserving security and in terms of its wider place in criminal justice. The site of the Terrorism Act in criminal justice is in some ways distinct. Especially in Northern Ireland, the Act provides an almost self-contained complex which operates apart from normal processes. Indeed, it is important to realise that most official action against terrorism, aided above all by special policing powers, will be unseen intelligence-gathering, surveillance and countering actions, none of which is intended to be revealed in a public court process. Given their distinct nature, the anti-terrorism laws represent an early example of the fragmentation of the criminal justice process, in which successive offences or anti-social activities have been subjected to special regimes — whether serious frauds (as in the Criminal Justice Act 1987) or sex offenders (Sex Offenders Act 1997, as amended). However, this centrifugal force of specialisation (both in terms of laws and organisations) has now been subject to the check of the Human Rights Act 1998, whose norms provide universal standards for all aspects of state activity. Yet, in the context of legislation against terrorism, its rights norms have been interpreted in ways which allow flexibility, even to the point of indulgence.

As for preserving security, the incidence of terrorism has come to be seen as one of the major threats to security in western Liberal societies. These threats are perceived as burgeoning. They arise not only from what are depicted as small groups of, at best, political extremists or, at worst, ruthless fanatics but also from 'terrorist states' pursuing political objectives by surreptitious or surrogate means. The Cold War between the super-powers may have receded, but, in its place, there are believed to remain clear and present dangers. In a society beset by risk, a response is required to allay fears, to build confidence, and to impact on the risk by minimising its potential threat, but without any expectation that the threat will be eliminated. Terrorism is one such risk, taking its place alongside the likes of global warming, scares about food standards and new, untreatable diseases. Furthermore, the same factors creating pandemic risk, such as global networks and technological reliance, afford new vulnerabilities which terrorism can exploit. The modernist, nationalist terrorism, the prime exponent for most of the twentieth century and represented not only by Irish groups such as the Irish Republican Army (IRA) but also by the likes of ETA in Spain, has by no means disappeared, and the threats of globalisation will ensure that cultural and national causes remain vibrant. Networking has thereby presented opportunities to these nationalist terrorists — the IRA, for one, has demonstrated a capacity to operate not only in Ireland but also to garner logistical support in the continents of America and Africa (through the good offices of Libya) and to mount attacks throughout western Europe. The facility of communication and travel networks has also been utilised by interna-tional terrorism — especially Middle Eastern proponents who find the United Kingdom, and London in particular, a suitable venue for their fundraising, political and even military activities.

To these well-established bases for terrorism must now be added the prospect of what might be called, 'Third Millennium Terrorism' — terrorism emerging through non-national, global networks and with aspirations which are likewise distanced from place and time. Consequently, terrorism has developed new modes in line with the late modern age — based not on fixed territoriality and nationality but on motivating ideals or personalities spanning borders and yielding fluid networks without a clear core. The attacks and scares of autumn 2001 exemplified this emergent aspect of terrorism and again sharpened the desire for security. The resultant Anti-terrorism, Crime and Security Act 2001 is the response to 'a terrorist threat that is quite different from anything that we have previously faced' (HL Debs. vol. 629 col. 142, 27 November 2001, Lord Goldsmith), though, as a legislative vehicle, it also transported much else besides measures against any variant of terrorism.

Given the long history of anti-terrorist laws, it should be stated at the outset what are intended as the main impacts of the 2000 and 2001 legislation against terrorism.

As for the Terrorism Act 2000, some of the most eye-catching changes are structural. For the first time ever, anti-terrorism laws are stated comprehensively in one code, which draws together what was separate legislation for Great Britain, on the one hand, and Northern Ireland on the other. The legislation is intended to be not only comprehensive but also permanent, no longer requiring renewal or re-enactment save for one part relating exclusively to Northern Ireland. To a significant extent, these betterments have now been compromised by the Anti-terrorism, Crime and Security Act 2001, which is neither wholly permanent nor comprehensive and, since it in part amends the Terrorism Act, degrades some of its predecessor's finer design features.

In terms of substance, the picture is mixed. Parts of the pre-existing legislation have been dispensed with altogether. The most notable examples, confirming legislative changes made a couple of years previously, concern the power of exclusion (mainly involving the physical transfer of terrorist suspects from Great Britain to Northern Ireland) and the power of internment (detention without trial) in Northern Ireland. In other aspects, the laws have been expanded by both Acts — for example in relation to terrorist property, policing powers and terrorist-related offences, which the Anti-terrorism, Crime and Security Act 2001 expands even further into the fields of dangerous substances and acute vulnerabilities. The Anti-terrorism, Crime and Security Act 2001 also revives a form of detention without trial for specified foreign terrorist suspects. Overall, the picture from the second instalment of legislation is one of reinforcement rather than radical departures, hardly surprising in the light of the comprehensive array of anti-terrorism laws already in force before this legislation.

A constant theme of review of the terrorism legislation has hitherto concerned compliance with respect for human rights. This prerequisite can now be depicted in more concrete and forthright terms as a demand for compatibility with the terms of the Human Rights Act 1998, and, in this light, it is arguable that the interplay with individual rights has moved up the agenda for the terrorism legislation. Indeed, a significant goal in passing the Terrorism Act 2000 was to secure the withdrawal of the notice of derogation under Article 15 of the European Convention on Human Rights in respect of police detention powers under the previous legislation. This objective was achieved on the coming into force of that Act in February 2001, though whether the full content of the Act complies in every respect with the European Convention must remain a matter of considerable doubt. In addition, what the one Act gives, the other takes away. Thus, the Anti-terrorism,

Crime and Security Act 2001 has necessitated a new derogation as from December 2001, in respect of the power of detention without trial mentioned above.

In setting out the terrorism legislation in this book, a number of objectives are being pursued. The core aim is to describe and to analyse critically the legislation in detail, in context and in combination. Most of the detailed content is based around the wording of the Acts themselves (set out in Appendices 1 and 2). Further amplification will be drawn from their legislative history — Parliamentary debates, official reports, statistical sources and prior laws — and the context of the phenomenon of terrorism. Other lessons could be learnt from history and from foreign counterparts (such as the US Patriot Act (Uniting and Strengthening America By Providing Appropriate Tools Required To Intercept and Obstruct Terrorism, H.R. 3162, 2001)), but space does not allow for such an extended scrutiny. Consequently, the structure of the book's chapters (2 to 7) is reflective mainly of the parts of the Terrorism Act 2000, since it comprises the more codified instrument and since several parts of the Anti-terrorism, Crime and Security Act 2001 insert amendments by reference to it. Therefore, only two chapters (8 and 9) are shaped primarily on the basis of the 2001 Act. Indications will also be provided of how the legislation is being implemented (especially by the circular and codes — regrettably too voluminous to be reproduced here), and how it might be expected to be interpreted by the courts in the light of previous case-law. Finally, an eye will be kept on compatibility with the Human Rights Act 1998. In keeping with the format of other works in this series, referencing within the text is kept to a minimum, but, for the adventurous or curious, a comprehensive listing of source materials is provided in a bibliography at the end of the book.

It has been a demanding task to keep pace with the astonishing events which have unfolded during the writing of this book. To produce a scholarly commentary so soon after such sensational events therefore meant that the author required support and assistance. As usual, my colleagues at the Department of Law in the University of Leeds provided the closest support, but I should thank also a range of other sources or correspondents. They include the various officials at the Home Office and Northern Ireland Office, Dr Bill Norris and Trevor French of the office of the Independent Commissioner for Detained Terrorist Suspects, the respondents to a seminar paper presented to the Federalist Society meeting in New Orleans in January 2002 and various contributors (especially Peter Sommer) to the cyber-rights-UK mailing list (http://www.cyber-rights.org/mailing.htm). I also record my appreciation for the work of Ralph Smyth (see http://www.blagged.freeserve.co.uk/ta2000/fhome.htm) and of my research assistant, Vanda Pereira, who trawled for, and collected, many of the primary sources.

Clive Walker
Department of Law, University of Leeds
28 February 2002

Table of Cases

Table of Statutes

Table of Statutory Instruments

Table of International Treaties and Conventions

Chapter One
Background and introductory issues

1.1 THE HISTORY OF THE ANTI-TERRORISM LEGISLATION

Special laws against terrorism have provided a constant feature of political and legal life within the United Kingdom throughout most of the past century or more. The inventory of laws on both sides of the border in Ireland is especially substantial and prolonged, culminating in the Northern Ireland (Emergency Provisions) Acts 1973 to 1998 (see Donoghue, L.K., *Counter-Terrorism Law* (Irish Academic Press, Dublin, 2001); Hogan, G. and Walker C., *Political Violence and the Law in Ireland* (Manchester University Press, Manchester, 1989). Given that between 1966 and 1999, 3,636 deaths have occurred in Northern Ireland related to political violence (McKittrick, D., Kelters, S., Feeney, B., and Thornton, C., *Lost Lives* (Mainstream, Edinburgh, 1999), some kind of legislative response is not surprising, particularly as the rate of incidents is not inexorably decreasing, despite a Provisional IRA cease-fire since 20 July 1997 (see Table 1.1).

Even in Great Britain, where the equivalent figure for fatalities is 121 (Home Office and Northern Ireland Office, Legislation against Terrorism (Cm. 4178, London, 1998), para. 2.2), there has been a Prevention of Terrorism (Temporary Provisions) Act in continuous use since November 1974 (see Leigh, L.H., 'Comment' [1975] *Public Law* 1; Street, H., 'The Prevention of Terrorism (Temporary Provisions) Act' [1975] *Criminal Law Review* 192), while its predecessor, the Prevention of Violence Act 1939 persisted until 1954 (see Donoghue, L.K., *Counter-Terrorism Law* (Irish Academic Press, Dublin, 2001); Walker, C.P., *The Prevention of Terrorism in British Law* (2nd ed., Manchester University Press, Manchester, 1992). The anti-terrorist codes have taken on an air of permanence, not only because of the longevity of Irish irredentism but also because, during the 1980s, the Prevention of Terrorism Acts were extended following a report by Lord Jellicoe in 1983 to encompass terrorism from international (foreign) sources (Report of the Operation of the Prevention of Terrorism (Temporary Provisions) Act 1976, Cmnd. 8803, London, 1983; see Bonner, D., 'Combating terrorism: the Jellicoe approach' [1983] *Public Law* 224; Samuels, A., 'The legal response to terrorism: the Prevention of Terrorism (Temporary Provisions) Act 1984' [1984] *Public Law* 365; Walker, C.P., 'The Jellicoe Report on the Prevention of Terrorism (Temporary Provisions) Act 1976' (1983) 46 *Modern Law Review* 484; Walker, C.P., 'Prevention of Terrorism (Temporary Provisions) Act 1984' (1984) 47 *Modern Law Review* 704; Dickson, B., 'The Prevention of Terrorism (Temporary Provisions) Act 1989' (1989) 40 *Northern Ireland Legal Quarterly* 592).

Table 1.1   Northern Ireland Security situation

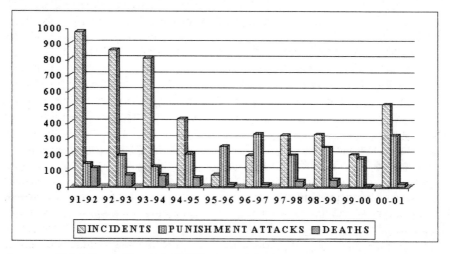

(*source: Chief Constable of the RUC, Annual Report for 2000–01 (Belfast 2001)*)

But the beguiling durability of these 'emergency' or 'temporary' laws became undermined by the close of 1999. The main legislation then in force in Northern Ireland, the Northern Ireland (Emergency Provisions) Acts 1996 to 1998, was set to expire on 24 August 2000, and so its replacement became an acute issue. Other factors then coming into play were the 'Peace Process' in Northern Ireland pursuant to the Belfast Agreement signed on Good Friday 1998 (British Irish Agreement reached in the multi-party negotiations (Cm. 3883, London, 1998)). It was a condition of the Agreement that security matters should be reviewed, and a review was also a crucial part of the arrangements for the decommissioning of terrorist weapons ((Mitchell) Report of the International Body on Decommissioning (http://www.britainUSA.com/nireland/law&order.asp, London, 1996), para. 53). Finally, the passage of the Human Rights Act 1998, incorporating into United Kingdom law large parts of the Articles of the European Convention on Human Rights and Fundamental Freedoms, made it advisable to conduct a more thorough rights audit of existing anti-terrorism provisions. A more general survey had in fact been underway since 1996, when a substantial review was produced by Lord Lloyd, assisted by Mr Justice Kerr in respect of Northern Ireland aspects of the laws and by a survey of terrorist threats produced by Professor Paul Wilkinson

(Inquiry into Legislation against Terrorism, Cm. 3420, London, 1996; see Ni Aolain, F., 'The fortification of an emergency regime' (1996) 59 *Albany Law Review* 1353). The government's broadly supportive response, Legislation Against Terrorism (Cm. 4178, London), appeared in December 1998.

A large part of the catalogue of laws just detailed has been shaped by dramatic and tragic events. The Emergency Provisions Acts emerged from a determination to change security policy in Northern Ireland away from the militaristic approach. The intervention of the British Army in 1969 had at its outset been in support of the civil power in the shape of the Royal Ulster Constabulary (RUC). But the scale of the violence grew beyond the capabilities of the latter, so by 1971, the Army had become the prime security force. Nevertheless, the emphasis upon a military strategy became at best distasteful and at worst shameful in the light of the internment without trial and ill-treatment of detainees and lethal confrontations such as Bloody Sunday in 1972. It in any event did not suit the needs of British politicians to distance the conflict by Ulsterisation. Therefore, in line with the assumption of responsibility by the UK government pursuant to 'Direct Rule' after March 1972, a review was quickly undertaken by Lord Diplock (Report of the Commission to consider legal procedures to deal with terrorist activities in Northern Ireland (Cmnd. 5185, London, 1972); see Fabian Tract No. 416, *Emergency Powers: A Fresh Start* (London, 1972); Twining, W.L., 'Emergency powers and the criminal process: the Diplock Report' [1973] *Criminal Law Review* 406) which formed the basis for the Emergency Provisions Act of 1973 and its core of special policing powers leading to special criminal justice processes. However, it was not until 1975 that the RUC, after a lengthy process of reform and reinforcement, were able to resume primacy.

The first Prevention of Terrorism Act was a swift response to the deaths in the Birmingham pub bombings in November 1974. The Criminal Justice (Terrorism and Conspiracy) Act 1998 likewise was the response to the outrage at those determined to perpetrate the Omagh bombing in August 1998 in the face of a communal craving for peace. Last, and freshest in the consciousness not only of the British polity but the whole world, are the attacks of 11 September 2001. These included the catastrophic attacks by hijacked aircraft on the twin towers of the World Trade Centre, New York, and Pentagon building in Washington DC, while a fourth crashed in Pennsylvania after passengers attempted to wrest control from the hijackers (*The Times*, 12 September 2001, p. 1). The loss of life was overwhelming, and, combined with the nature and scale of the attacks, conduced to an analysis that terrorism had indeed developed a new strand in the current millennium into a multi-faceted threat, unbounded by instrument or location. That change was personified by the Al Qa'ida group — a movement based on loose networks across national borders rather than tightly organised cells and a move- ment motivated by religious and cultural ideals rather than rooted in national self-determination or a particular political ideology (see Defence Select Commit- tee, The Threat from Terrorism (2001–02 HC 348-I), para. 24). It was the Al Qa'ida group on whom suspicion immediately fell, based on the identity of the

19 hijackers (see *The Times*, 15 September 2001, p. 1), 11 of whom had some links with the United Kingdom. Further incriminating evidence was claimed by the government soon after the attack, placing the blame on Al Qa'ida and linking it closely with the Taliban regime of Afghanistan (see Foreign and Commonwealth Office, Responsibility for the terrorist atrocities, http://www.fco.gov.uk/news/ dynpage.asp?Page = 10846&Theme = 34&Template = 999, 2001; Defence Select Committee, The Threat from Terrorism (2001–02 HC 348-I), para. 17). A legislative response was mooted within the week (*The Times*, 19 September 2001, p. 13). The Anti-terrorism, Crime and Security Act 2001 is one of the outcomes of those events. The first signal that the Government intended to introduce additional counter-terrorism legislation was given by the Home Secretary at the Labour Party Conference on the 3 October 2001 and later at the second recalled session of Parliament on the 4 October. The Bill was outlined to Parliament on the 15 October 2001 (HC Debs. vol. 372 col. 923) and was introduced on the 12 November 2001.

In contrast to these circumstances, the Terrorism Bill, which was presented to the House of Commons on 2 December 1999, potentially offered the opportunity for a new dispensation. Unlike the legislation of the past, which had too often been hastily drafted in circumstances of crisis and has remained fragmented as between the legislation applying to Great Britain and Northern Ireland, a new law could offer a more considered code constructed in a more considered, principled and comprehensive fashion (as recommended by Viscount Colville as long ago as 1990: Review of the Northern Ireland (Emergency Provisions) Acts 1978 and 1987 (Cm. 1115, London), para. 20.2). It could also present itself as an all-encompassing statement of laws and so avoid the 'incremental extension' that occurred over the previous decade or so (Fenwick, H., *Civil Rights* (Longman, Harlow, 2000), p. 65). Certainly, the period of gestation, which took over four years and goes back to the Lloyd Report (Lord Lloyd and Sir John Kerr, Inquiry into Legislation against Terrorism (Cm. 3420, London, 1996)) was impressive and contrasts starkly with that of the four weeks or so for the Anti-terrorism, Crime and Security Act 2001.

In the event, the Terrorism Act 2000 is only a partial success for three reasons. First, it cannot be said to be a clean break with the past, since its contents are mainly traceable to the legislation which it replaces. Some of the past it perpetuates is probably worth a new lease of life — including the measures against terrorist finances and aspects of the police investigative powers. Some of the past it discards deserves just that fate — such as the powers to exclude terrorist suspects from Britain to Northern Ireland and the offence of withholding information. Furthermore, there are also some significant and detailed improvements on prior formulations, such as the greater willingness to allow for judicial and independent scrutiny in areas like extended detentions, the proscription of organisations and the issuance of warrants for terrorist investigations. However, other parts of the contents remain disappointingly steadfast, especially the special measures (described in Chapter 7) relating to Northern Ireland.

Secondly, and even more disappointing, the Terrorism Act 2000 does not provide for the kind of structure to ensure the future democratic accountability for the operation of this type of law. The Home Secretary, Jack Straw, in introducing the legislation, adverted to the delicate conflict of objectives and values inherent in the Act (HC Debs. vol. 341 col. 152, 14 December 1999):

Although all crime to some degree plainly threatens the stability of the social and political order, terrorism differs from crime motivated solely by greed in that it is directed at undermining the foundations of government. It poses special difficulties for those of us who live in liberal democracies. Our sense of outrage is all the greater because in such democracies the overwhelming majority of the population believe that there are adequate non-violent means for expressing opposition and dissent. However, we will have handed the terrorists the victory that they seek if, in combating their threats and violence, we descend to their level and undermine the essential freedoms and rule of law that are the bedrock of our democracy.

The government claimed, pursuant to s. 19 of the Human Rights Act 1998, the Bill is compatible with European Convention rights. On paper, one might assess that compliance has largely been achieved, especially as the House of Lords has already indicated (in line with the view of the European Court of Human Rights: *Klass* v *Germany*, App. no. 5029/71, Ser. A. 28, paras 48–49, 59; *Brogan* v *United Kingdom*, App. nos. 11209, 11234, 11266/84, 11386/85, Judgment of Court Ser. A. 145-B, (1989) 11 EHRR 539 para. 48; *Fox, Campbell and Hartley* v *United Kingdom*, App. nos. 12244, 12245, 12383/86, Ser. A. 182, (1990) 13 EHRR 157 para. 44) that in 'reading down' statutory provisions in order to comply with the Convention, account must be taken of the special threat posed by terrorism. According to Lord Hope in *R* v *Director of Public Prosecutions, ex parte Kebilene* [1999] 3 WLR 972 at p. 1000:

Then there is the nature of the threat which terrorism poses to a free and democratic society. It seeks to achieve its ends by violence and intimidation. It is often indiscriminate in its effects, and sophisticated methods are used to avoid detection both before and after the event. Society has a strong interest in preventing acts of terrorism before they are perpetrated — to spare the lives of innocent people and to avoid the massive damage and dislocation to ordinary life which may follow from explosions which destroy or damage property.

Of course, each case depends on its fact, and proportion must also be shown in the actual exercise of powers (see Rowe, J.J., 'The Terrorism Act 2000' [2000] *Criminal Law Review* 527 at p. 530). But it is doubtful whether the Human Rights Act 1998 will immediately have 'dramatic' effect on anti-terrorism laws (compare Gearty, C., 'Terrorism and human rights' (1999) 19 *Legal Studies* 366 at p. 379).

Overall, one does not see any signs that as much new thinking has been devoted to constitutional governance as was given to the design of policing powers. So, in the context of legislation running to 131 sections and 16 schedules, the Act appears comprehensive, but the welter of detail should not bury the fact that not all areas have experienced due constitutional reform. Lord Lloyd in his review of the legislation in 1996 set four principles for the legislation to meet, and it is against these that it should be judged (Lloyd Report, Inquiry into Legislation against Terrorism (Cm. 3420, London, 1996), para. 3.1):

    (i)   Legislation against terrorism should approximate as closely as possible to the ordinary criminal law and procedure;

    (ii)   Additional statutory offences and powers may be justified, but only if they are necessary to meet the anticipated threat. They must then strike the right balance between the needs of security and the rights and liberties of the individual;

    (iii)   The need for additional safeguards should be considered alongside any additional powers;

    (iv)   The law should comply with the UK's obligations in international law.

One might argue in particular that there is no requirement for proof at any time of (i) and that (iii) has also not been observed. One might also suggest that Lord Lloyd's tests themselves are insufficiently demanding. As has been explained elsewhere (Walker, C.P., 'Constitutional governance and special powers against terrorism' (1997) 35 *Columbia Journal of Transnational Law* 1), full constitutional governance requires on a continuous basis:

    (a)   a 'rights audit' which means that the rights of individuals are respected according to traditions of the domestic jurisdictions and the demands of international law. The latter will include the periodic review of the very existence of any emergency or special measures;

    (b)   'democratic accountability' which includes attributes such as information, open and independent debate and an ability to participate in decision making; and

    (c)   'constitutionalism' — the subjection of government to norms, whether legal or extra legal (such as codes). More specific requirements in the field of special powers include the public articulation of reasons in support of particular actions taken for the public welfare, assurances through effective mechanisms that the crisis cannot be ended by normal means and that powers will not be used arbitrarily, and adherence to the overall purpose of the restoration of fundamental features of constitutional life. It also requires at a more individual level that excesses can be challenged, including through the courts.

Has the United Kingdom state lived up to these ideals? There are many who would claim not and that, especially in the context of Northern Ireland, there has been a dirty war on a par with Latin American experiences (see Dillon, M., *The Dirty War* (Hutchinson, London, 1990)). This problem is exemplified by the case of *Ireland* v *United Kingdom* (App. no. 5310/71, Ser. A. 25; (1979–80) 2 EHRR 25; see O'Boyle, M.P., 'Emergency situations and the protection of human rights' (1977) 28 *Northern Ireland Legal Quarterly* 160) in which allegations of degrading and inhuman treatment of IRA detainees were sustained. But whatever the excesses of the past, a slow process of scrutiny and reform has produced both the most extensive counter-terrorist code in western Europe but at the same time a diminished rate of abuse and complaint which does not prejudice or obviate the Peace Process being conducted at the same time.

The third shortcoming of the Terrorism Act 2000 is that it was not successful in averting the passage of the Anti-terrorism, Crime and Security Act 2001 (the nomenclature, 'Anti-terrorism', was simply to differentiate the legislation from its predecessor: HL Debs. vol. 629 col. 1290, 11 December 2001, Lord Rooker). That failure might in part be excusable if it could be convincingly concluded that there has emerged a wholly new phenomenon which could not be foreseen during the previous year nor countered by the measures then passed. To some extent, what has been called earlier in this book 'Third Millennium terrorism' does indeed bring into focus new modes of terrorist motivation and operation. To that extent, the Home Secretary, David Blunkett, was right when he claimed, 'On 11 September, families lost their loved ones, and the threat of terrorism touched us all. If we fail now to take the necessary action to protect our people, future generations will never forgive us.' (Home Office Press Release 250/2001, 15 October 2001). But in so far as there may have been gaps in other respects, the design of the Terrorism Act is at fault for failing to deliver a comprehensive package of laws either in respect of the issues it does cover (such as terrorist property) or in respect of its non-delivery of contingent powers (such as detention without trial). Perhaps it might be claimed that the Terrorism Act had partial success. After all, there was no immediate rush to legislation following the 11 September attacks, and the operation of the Terrorism Act did buy some time for reflection. Moreover, when the new legislation did appear, it was in fair part constructed around the Terrorism Act, rather than striking out in new and alarming directions such as military tribunals (see US Presidential Order, Detention, Treatment, and Trial of Certain Non-Citizens in the War Against Terrorism, 13 November 2001 (66 Federal Register 57831) section 4).

Yet, the result of the passage of the Anti-terrorism, Crime and Security Act 2001 is once again a legislative morass. Though that Act is in some ways an advance on the Terrorism Act by ensuring a full and independent review (by s. 122), the overall result is, once again, measures spread across two pieces of legislation and inconsistent timetables and forms of review. One must also doubt the effectiveness of the rights audit during the passage of the Anti-terrorism, Crime and Security Bill. There was no time for considered or sustained review. It is true that the Home Affairs Select Committee (Report on the Anti-terrorism, Crime and Security Bill 2001 (2001–02 HC 351)) and Joint Committee on Human Rights (Reports on the Anti-terrorism, Crime and Security Bill (2001–02 HL 37, HC 372) and (2001–02 HL 51, HC 420)) produced reports, but they are based on rather thin evidence and debate. Debate in the House of Commons was also severely curtailed by time-tabling motions. Furthermore, after Lord Rooker, the Minster of State at the Home Office, had made the statement that 'In my view the provisions of the

Anti-terrorism, Crime and Security Bill are compatible with the Convention rights'
(Home Office Explanatory Memorandum (London, 2001), para. 408), and the
Home Secretary had mused that a derogation 'may well' be necessary (HC Debs.
vol. 372 col. 924, 15 October 2001), the government later readily conceded that a
derogation under Article 15 was unavoidable because of the non-compliance with
Article 5 of the procedures of detention without trial under Part IIII, and so the
Bill was accompanied by a statement that it was in compliance with the Human
Rights Acts 1998, pursuant to s. 19 of that Act, subject to that derogation.

The derogation power is set out in Article 15 of the European Convention:

> In time of war or other public emergency threatening the life of the nation any
> High Contracting Party may take measures derogating from its obligations under
> this Convention to the extent strictly required by the exigencies of the situation,
> provided that such measures are not inconsistent with its other obligations under
> international law.

The derogation in connection with the 2001 legislation was issued domestically
under the Human Rights Act 1998 (Designated Derogation) Order 2001 (SI 2001
No. 3644). It concerns the extended power to detain a foreign national (see Chapter
8). In such cases, detention which lasts for more than a short period may be
incompatible with Article 5(1)(f) (which permits the lawful arrest or detention of
a person to prevent his effecting an unauthorised entry into the country or of a
person against whom action is being taken with a view to deportation or
extradition). It may even be doubtful whether the purpose of detention in those
circumstances, where deportation is not a lawful option, remains within Article
5(1)(f). The ground for the derogation is cited as the fact that:

> There exists a terrorist threat to the United Kingdom from persons suspected of
> involvement in international terrorism. In particular, there are foreign nationals
> present in the United Kingdom who are suspected of being concerned in the
> commission, preparation or instigation of acts of international terrorism, of being
> members of organisations or groups which are so concerned or of having links
> with members of such organisations or groups, and who are a threat to the
> national security of the United Kingdom.

This derogation was registered by the Council of Europe Secretariat on 18
December 2001. By way of further justification, the Minister of State (Beverley
Hughes), pointed to:

> . . . the events of 11 September; the two UN Security Council resolutions that
> pointed to the threat to international security and gave permission, as it were,
> for states to take measures to protect themselves; engagement in conflict in
> Afghanistan as a close ally of the United States; the presence of suspected
> terrorists here; further threats by Osama bin Laden and his supporters; and their

preparedness to use nuclear, chemical and biological weapons, and the material found during the conflict in Kabul. (HC Debs. vol. 375 col. 146, 19 November 2001)

The UN resolutions referred to were, first, on the 12 September 2001, Security Council Resolution 1368 (S/RES/1368) which called on all states to work together urgently to bring to justice the perpetrators, organisers and sponsors of the terrorist attacks and stated that those responsible for aiding, supporting or harbouring the perpetrators, organisers and sponsors of these attacks will be held accountable. The second was, on the 28 September, the General Assembly Resolution 1373 (A/RES/56/1), which required all states to prevent and suppress terrorist financing and to deny safe haven to those who finance, plan, support or commit terrorist acts. Further, in response to the criticism that no other Council of Europe member state has reacted in the same way (see Wadham, J., and Chakrabarti, S., 'Indefinite Detention Without Trial' (2001) 151 *New Law Journal* 1564), the Home Secretary claimed in evidence before the Joint Committee on Human Rights (Reports on the Anti-terrorism, Crime and Security Bill (2001–02 HL 51, HC 420)) that the evidence did point to the United Kingdom as being acutely at risk:

We are adjudged internationally to be more at risk than the Danes or other smaller European countries, we know that we are, and the steps we have taken since 11 September, in terms of civil contingencies and security protection, have reflected that heightened concern. Our position internationally and our support for the United States have increased that danger. Also, as the Germans and French are often pointing out, we have a larger host community of those who the Germans and French allege are organising for international terror.

By contrast, the Joint Committee on Human Rights (in its Report on the Anti-terrorism, Crime and Security Bill) expressed severe qualms about the legitimacy of the derogation:

Having considered the Home Secretary's evidence carefully, we recognise that there may be evidence of the existence of a public emergency threatening the life of the nation, although none was shown by him to this Committee. As no court in this country will be able to decide whether the derogation is justified against the criteria of Article 15 of the ECHR, it is especially important for each House to decide whether they are satisfied of the existence of a public emergency threatening the life of the nation. But even if it is accepted that there is such an emergency, the lack of safeguards built into the Bill, particularly in relation to detention powers, causes us to doubt whether the measures in the Bill can be said to be strictly required by the exigencies of the situation. (2001–02 HL 37, HC 372, para. 30)

We have concluded that, on the evidence available to us, the balance between freedom and security in the Bill before us has not always been struck in the right place. In particular, although we recognise the dilemma from which the Home Secretary sought to free himself by recourse to the derogation from Article 5, we are not persuaded that the circumstances of the present emergency or the exigencies of the current situation meet the tests set out in Article 15 of the ECHR. It is now for Parliament to draw its own conclusions, and for Members of both Houses to satisfy themselves that there are adequate safeguards to protect the rights of the individual citizen against abuse of these powers. (2001–02 HL 51, HC 420, para. 78)

The derogation was also attacked by Liberty in its briefing paper (see http:// www.liberty-human-rights.org.uk/, 2001):

There is no imminent threat of the complete breakdown of civil society in the UK. We have not reached this point as yet and although there are threats, the nation itself is not in jeopardy. That is why of the forty or so countries signed up to the Convention we are the only country indicating we want to opt out . . . given the nature of terrorist threats to European countries generally, the question will need to be asked as to why is it that the vast majority of the other forty or so countries signed up to the Convention do not feel that similar measures are so 'strictly required' in their countries.

The fundamental question is whether there is a sufficient degree of public emergency within the meaning of Article 15. It is true that there have occurred devastating attacks in the USA, resulting in British deaths. It is also true that there have for some years been present in the United Kingdom persons suspected of involvement in terrorism abroad, including alleged members of the organisations deemed responsible for the attacks. Recent examples include Khalid al Fawwaz, Ibrahim Eidarou and Adel Abdel Bary, who are awaiting extradition (*Al Fawwaz v Governor of Brixton Prison* [2001] 1 WLR 1234, 2 WLR 101), Zacarias Moussaoui (*The Times*, 12 December 2001, p. 3) and Richard Reid (*The Times*, 24 December 2001, p. 1), both under arrest in the USA for links to hijackings, and the approximately two dozen British citizens detained in Afghanistan or Guantanamo Bay, Cuba (see *The Times*, 28 January 2002, p. 1). But does this evidence justify a derogation? It must be noted that relevant organisations such as Al Qa'ida have never carried out attacks in the United Kingdom and have branches elsewhere in Europe. It must be borne in mind that, with the full panoply of the Terrorism Act 2000 in force, including the proscription of Al Qa'ida, extensive measures dealing with terrorism finances and offences about conspiracy and incitement to commit offences abroad, the United Kingdom was the most legally fortified country in Europe. Next, the number of arrests since 11 September has been very modest (many centred on Leicester (*The Times*, 19 January 2002, p. 12)) and many resulting in quiet releases without charge (*The Times*, 2 February 2002, p. 4). Can such a small cohort of people create an emergency sufficient to destabilise the rights regime of a powerful country like the United Kingdom? Finally, the abiding nature of the declared emergency is disturbing — if the war against terrorism is to be won by eradicating all terrorism in the world, then there can be no expectation that the emergency will ever end or the security state will ever be dismantled. An alternative strategy of policing by way of surveillance, calling in aid all the police powers in the Terrorism Act 2000 plus the Regulation of Investigatory Powers Act 2000 and elsewhere, would be more expensive. But it would be a feasible and more proportionate response. It might even be more productive. Exclusion orders under the Prevention of Terrorism Act were abolished finally in 2000 after the Home Office Consultation Paper argued that it was more profitable to keep suspects under surveillance and, where possible, to charge them with offences (Home Office and Northern Ireland Office, Legislation against Terrorism (Cm. 4178, London, 1998), para. 5.6).

As well as responding proportionately to the exigencies of the situation, the derogation must also be consistent with the United Kingdom's obligations under international law. The issue was raised in *Brannigan and McBride* v *United Kingdom*, App. nos. 14553/89, 14554/89, Ser. A. 258-B, (1994) 17 EHRR 539, where obligations under the United Nations International Covenant on Civil and Political Rights were raised in connection with the promulgation of a derogation. The Court accepted as sufficient for these purposes a statement to the Commons. One would suppose that the addition of a statutory instrument under the Human Rights Act 1998 further aids the claim to a formal and public declaration.

The House of Commons Defence Select Committee found that 'The position continues to be that there remains no intelligence of any specific threat to the UK at present', but it accepted that there is a continuing threat (The Threat from Terrorism (2001–02 HC 348-I), paras 43, 50). Even if there was such a threat towards the end of 2001 when that report was issued, whether that level of threat can be said to exist after the removal of the Taliban regime in Afghanistan, and after a thorough security trawl in the USA and Europe, must be doubted. It is also arguable that the derogation must also be used proportionately by limiting the detentions under Part IV to Al Qa'ida suspects and not to terrorist suspects of a different ilk.

1.2   THE NEED FOR ANTI-TERRORISM LEGISLATION

The broad approach implicit in the Terrorism Act 2000 is that there is a continuing need for extensive legislation against political violence now and for ever after. The Anti-terrorism, Crime and Security Act 2001 reinforces that stance, though there are in both Acts 'sunset' clauses which ensure that parts of the legislation must terminate after a set period. This fate applies to Part VII of the 2000 Act and to various parts of the 2001 Act (see Chapter 10). The legislation is therefore additional to 'normal' laws relating to police powers, such as those in the Police and Criminal Evidence Act 1984, and regular criminal offences (as well as crimes previously devised with terrorism in mind, such as the Explosive Substances Act 1883). Amongst the disadvantages of special laws are that they are unnecessary (either because of the level of threat of the existence of other powers), fear of abuse of the wide powers and concern about damage to the country's international reputation (Inquiry into Legislation against Terrorism (Cm. 3420, London, 1996), paras 5.6–5.9). Therefore, this claim to a need for distinct anti-terrorist laws should be examined at the outset. It can be answered at three levels.

The first level concerns the powers and duties of States. In principle, it is justifiable for Liberal democracies to defend their existence and their values, even if this defence involves some limitation of rights. In the words of one American judge, a democracy is not a suicide pact and measures can be taken against clear and present dangers (*Terminiello* v *Chicago* (1949) 337 US 1 at p. 37 per Douglas J). This point is also reflected in Article 17 of the European Convention on Human Rights:

> Nothing in this Convention may be interpreted as implying for any State, group or person any right to engage in any activity or perform any act aimed at the destruction of any of the rights and freedoms set forth herein or at their limitation to a greater extent than is provided for in the Convention.

It is also very much the point of the power of derogation from the Convention in time of emergency under Article 15. In the context of Northern Ireland, this derogation provision has been repeatedly invoked (see http://conventions.coe.int/Treaty/EN/CadreListeTraites.htm), and it has been upheld as applicable to the detention for up to seven days of terrorist suspects on police authority followed by authorisation by a Secretary of State, most notably in *Brannigan & McBride* v *United Kingdom*, App. nos. 14553/89, 14554/89, Ser. A. 258-B, (1994) 17 EHRR 539. However, it should be noted that one of the express purposes of the Terrorism Act 2000 (HC Debs vol. 341 col. 162, 14 December 1999, Jack Straw) was to allow the notice of derogation to be withdrawn because, in the view of the Home Secretary, the legislation is in compliance with the Convention. Accordingly, the previous notice of derogation (entered in 1988 and preserved for five years pursuant to the Human Rights Act 1998, sch. 3) was withdrawn for the United Kingdom territory on the 19 February 2001. It ceased effect on 26 February 2001, though not before the challenge in *Marshall* v *United Kingdom* (App. no. 41571/98, Judgment of Court 10 July 2001; see also *Kerr* v *United Kingdom*, App. no. 40451/98, Judgment of Court 19 July 2001), which found the derogation valid for the purposes of permitting what would otherwise have been a breach of Article 5(3) during February 1998 when 'the threat of terrorist outrage was still real and that the paramilitary groups in Northern Ireland retained the organisational capacity to kill and maim on a wide scale.' (pp. 12–13). The withdrawal only applies to United Kingdom territory and not the remaining British Islands (see further Chapter 10). Consequential amendments to the Human Rights Act 1998 are dealt with by the Human Rights Act (Amendment) Order 2001 (SI 2001 No. 1216). As indicated previously, a new derogation has now been entered in respect of the detention measures in Part IV of the Anti-terrorism, Crime and Security Act 2001.

Aside from the power to take action, there is a State responsibility to act against political or paramilitary violence. Each State has a duty, at least in international law, to safeguard the right to life of its citizens (as under Article 2 of the European Convention). In addition, States should more generally ensure the enjoyment of rights and democracy (under Article 1) and also must under United Nations instruments not harbour or condone terrorism (see, for example, United Nations General Assembly Resolutions 40/61 of 9 December 1985; 49/60 of 9 December 1994) (see also Donoghue, L.K., *Counter-Terrorism Law* (Irish Academic Press, Dublin, 2001), pp. 307–308).

The second level of justification is more morally grounded. This argument points to the illegitimacy of terrorism as a form of political expression — the fact that many of its emanations are almost certainly common crimes, crimes of war or crimes against humanity, even if the political cause of the terrorist is deemed legitimate.

Thirdly, there is the observation that terrorism is a specialised form of criminality which presents peculiar difficulties in terms of policing and criminal process — such as its remote organisation, capacity to intimidate and sophistication. It therefore demands a specialist response to overcome the difficulties posed for normal detection methods and processes within criminal justice.

These arguments, either singularly or cumulatively, have for many decades been convincing to the rulings élites within the United Kingdom (and most other Western States, including the Republic of Ireland). The 'end of the age of Liberal innocence' (Bernard Porter, *The Origins of the Vigilant State* (Weidenfeld & Nicolson, London, 1978), p. 192 — compare the different view of history in Gearty, C., 'Turning point' (2001) 145 *Solicitors' Journal* 426) can be dated as occurring around the 1880s — ever since then there has been a recognition by successive governments, and to a large degree an acceptance by the electorate, that organised political crime is a special threat to Liberality and democracy, though the strength of that threat has varied over the years. The belief in counter-terrorism laws extends to key members of the present United Kingdom government. Speaking in 1994, Tony Blair stated: '. . . it is not in dispute, and never has been, that we need anti-terrorist legislation' (HC Debs. vol. 239 col. 3000, 2 March 1994). There is an important proviso. Since it is the aim of terrorism to achieve political gains through violence, the prime point of counter-strategy for States to consider is whether there can be a response to those political gains which are sought. Can there be engagement of some kind which averts the need for violence? Liberal democracies have the capacity to be responsive to political demands, especially of minorities. This is demonstrated in Northern Ireland, where the Peace Process has reduced the rate of political violence, albeit to a point far from zero. The dialogue with the representatives of terrorism has many unpalatable aspects but must be considered alongside more security-oriented approaches.

Having established that States can and must take protective action against activities which seriously threaten the well-being of its citizens and its democracy (a conclusion also reached by the Inquiry into Legislation against Terrorism

(Cm. 3420, London, 1996), para. 5.15), one may ask next whether existing political or paramilitary violence falls into the category of 'serious threat'? Deaths and destruction from political or paramilitary violence in the United Kingdom do not occur at a very high rate. Even in Northern Ireland, the Chief Constable's Annual Report has often in recent years included a graph which demonstrates that deaths from road traffic accidents are more prevalent than deaths from terrorism (see, for example, Royal Ulster Constabulary, *Chief Constable's Annual Report for 1996* (Belfast, 1997), p. 85). But deaths and destruction from political or paramilitary violence have implications in two directions which road traffic mayhem does not.

First, its aim is to terrorise, and this outcome can have a widespread, destabilising impact. In Northern Ireland, communities are subject to deep social and political cleavages, and economic activity has been severely depressed. Some of these effects can reproduce in Britain, where the bombs in the City of London in 1992 and 1993 were designed to bring about a collapse of confidence, which was restored only by an extraordinary degree of security measures — the City's 'ring of steel' (see Kelly, O., 'The IRA threat to the City of London' (1993) 9 *Policing* 88, 'By all means necessary' (1994) 15 April *Police Review* 14) — and of reinsurance (see Reinsurance (Acts of Terrorism) Act 1993, which is largely unaffected by the Terrorism Act 2000). Normal crime can also have similar effects but is likely to be less severe, patterned or targeted.

Secondly, and arguably more seriously, political or paramilitary violence has an intended political impact — it is meant to be destructive of the political establishment — literally so if one takes as examples the Brighton bombing at the hotel being used by several Cabinet members of the Conservative Party government in 1984 and the mortar bombs fired in Downing Street in 1992. Once again, ordinary criminals do not possess the capacity or the inclination to strike at these targets, violence against which can create chronic instability and disruption to democratic political processes.

Assuming political and paramilitary violence can be viewed as a serious potential threat, should there be any legislative impact? In principle again, one must answer in the positive. Criminal laws and criminal procedures (including policing powers) are not monolithic. Just as variations have been adopted against, for example, rapists, serious fraudsters and drug traffickers (Sexual Offences (Amendment) Act 1976; Drug Trafficking Offences Act 1994; Criminal Justice Act 1987), so terrorists may warrant different treatment because of their atypical methods and targets.

This leads onto the last point — in what way(s) can groups engaged in political or paramilitary violence be said to be so different from ordinary criminal gangs as to justify special responses? Aside from their methods and impacts, the special attributes which hinder the re-establishment of public safety and democratic processes relate essentially to two features: the sophistication of the paramilitary groups in terms of organisation and training and the transnational scale of their activities in some cases; and (in Northern Ireland especially) the difficulty of obtaining assistance from paramilitary-affected communities because of the impact of paramilitary control either through intimidation or popularity or through the observance of counter-intelligence precautions.

From these factors, one can conceive it to be justifiable for a Liberal democracy to design and to employ special laws against groups engaged in political or paramilitary violence. This conclusion does not, however, entail allowing Liberal democracies *carte blanche* in response to how they react. There must be an adherence to limiting principles which reflect the values of individual rights, constitutionalism and democratic accountability.

It follows that recent United Kingdom governments have been correct to reject the call, inspired by events in Northern Ireland, 'No emergency, no emergency law' (Committee on the Administration of Justice, *No Emergency, No Emergency Law* (Belfast, 1995)). The main attractions of such a stance would be that it sends a clear political signal that the conflict is over, that reliance on military strength as the basis for non-conflict is unacceptable and that derogation under Article 15 is not to be tolerated. These are attractive ideals, but the following arguments might question the realism and the principle of the giving up of all special laws.

One can question the realism of the approach at two levels. First, is it realistic to assume that the conflict in Northern Ireland is over, especially in the absence of any assured degree of decommissioning by the main paramilitary groups, or that future military actions or preparations are unthinkable? In the light of the Omagh bombing in August 1998, these assumptions appear rather shaky. Secondly, is it politically realistic to assume that there will inevitably be overall political advantage to be gained from abruptly dropping special powers? Certainly it is a demand of some but not all the protagonists in Northern Ireland. There are two further concerns which should be introduced at this stage. One argument which the government clearly had in mind is that terrorism is not in any event confined to Ireland, and, as noted earlier, the focus of the Prevention of Terrorism Acts had in part been redirected towards 'foreign' terrorism. The Anti-terrorism, Crime and Security Act 2001 is wholly a facet of non-Irish terrorism. An even more sinister agenda for the Terrorism Act 2000 concerns other domestic groups —such as animal rights and environmental activists or other cultural, ethnic or nationalist groups (see Taylor, M., and Horgan, J., 'Future developments of political terrorism in Europe' (1999) 11(4) *Terrorism & Political Violence* 83; Monaghan, R., 'Terrorism in the name of animal rights' (1999) 11(4) *Terrorism & Political Violence* 159). The terms of the Terrorism Act 2000 expressly point in some of these new directions, even though it must be doubted whether international or non-Irish domestic terrorism is sufficiently serious or troublesome to justify having any special legislation actually in force. The Lloyd Report concluded that domestic terrorism is not currently a significant threat to society, though it could be in the future (Inquiry into Legislation against Terrorism (Cm. 3420, London, 1996), para. 1.24), while the subsequent Home Office Consultation Paper concluded Scottish and Welsh nationalist terrorism posed a diminished risk, though feared that animal rights violence was mounting (Home Office and Northern Ireland Office, Legislation against Terrorism (Cm. 4178, London, 1998), para. 3.10). The position in regard to international terrorism will be considered later. A rather more convincing fear is that total abolition of special legislation without replacement throws the baby out with the bath-water. In other words, safeguards and restraints, which have painstakingly been fought over, conceded and honed over a period of years, will be lost alongside more reviled instruments of coercion. As and when emergency powers are resurrected, one can be far from sure that the safeguards and restraints will likewise be resurrected, as is evident with the system of detention without trial under the Anti-terrorism, Crime and Security Act 2001 compared to that first produced in the light of the Gardiner Report (Report of a Committee to consider, in the context of civil liberties and human rights, measures to deal with terrorism in Northern Ireland (Cmnd. 5847, London, 1975)) in the Emergency Provisions Act 1975. The final stage in this argument is the proposition that one cannot be sure that there will never again be another crisis or emergency which will not precipitate the public and the government into panic, which may provide the legislative window of opportunity for Home Office repression. This stance may be mockingly depicted as 'determined pessimism', but it is rather less realistic to say that the conjured threats bear 'an air of unreality' (see Gearty, C., 'Finding an enemy' (1999) *London Review of Books* 15 at p. 26). The destruction of skyscrapers, biological warfare and sustained attacks on key computer networks are real enough even if, so far, most have either occurred elsewhere in the globe or have failed to cause the intended degree of destruction either because of bad luck or bad planning.

Assuming a new model of legislation, a stance of 'Break glass in case of emergency legislation' is to be preferred. It is illogical to oppose all conceivable forms of special laws on a platform of concerns for human rights. Rather our collective concern for human rights should lead us to the conclusions that we should do our utmost to protect citizens against either Zombie-like paramilitary organisations or maddened security forces and that to vacate the field to either faction is to abdicate rather than to exercise responsibility for the governance of special powers. This contingency model of a permanent legislative code reflects the philosophy of constitutionalism and democratic accountability — that the legislature can secure an important input if it can speak in advance in a way which cannot be drowned by the screams of a crisis. There is ample evidence to suggest that governments of wholly different complexions will, in a tight corner, wish to resort to much the same measures and react in much the same ways. Thus, if the legal field is left unattended, the power élite will very soon fill it with architecture which, in the circumstances of an emergency, will be rather ugly. One cannot coherently complain about 'panic' legislation but at the same time deny to the State the principled and refined means to defend itself and to allay its genuine fears (and often those of the majority of the general public and in Parliament). It is foolish not to plan for contingencies in this way, especially as the planning process can allow the legislature to have its say. Is it safe to imagine that there will never be again any emergency, whether from some Irish or Middle Eastern group, perhaps from racists attacking immigrant settlers or homosexuals such as the case of

David Copeland, who planted three nail bombs in 1999 and was found guilty of the murder of three people (*The Times*, 1 July 2000, p. 1; Wolkind, M., and Sweeney, N., '*R v David Copeland*' (2001) 41 *Medicine Science and Law* 185), or from some other, as yet unimagined, causes? In this way, the preferred stance reflects what the New Zealand Law Commission called sectoral emergency laws — legislation carefully tailored in detail to respond to each type of emergency (Report No. 12, *First Report on Emergencies* (Wellington, 1990); Report No. 22, *Final Report on Emergencies*, (Wellington, 1991)). Though the subtlety of having permanent laws available but not necessarily active may be unappealing to some (see Whitty, N., Murphy, T., and Livingstone, S., *Civil Liberties Law* (Butterworths, London, 2001), p. 126), there are several advantages flowing from this approach.

First, it can reduce the dangers of the passage of badly designed and dangerous emergency laws, so long as it contains within it mechanisms for continued scrutiny. The panic surrounding the Anti-terrorism, Crime and Security Act 2001 was bad enough but at least it was confined by the existence of the Terrorism Act 2000. More positively, one can seek to build upon the experience of permanent legislation and to impose effective scrutiny. This endurance of the Prevention of Terrorism Acts prompted US Supreme Court Justice Brennan to comment that ('The American experience', in Shimon Shetreet, *Free Speech and National Security* (Nijhoff, Dordrecht, 1991)):

Prolonged and sustained exposure to the asserted security claims may be the only way in which a country may gain both the discipline necessary to examine asserted security risks critically and the expertise necessary to distinguish the bona fide from the bogus.

The main danger associated with the permanent availability of special laws is the inclination towards overuse — that there will be too much smashing of the glass to take out the special laws. Therefore, three safeguards should be incorporated.

The first feature is to make debates about the legislation, especially in Parliament, more principled and informed and less emotional. This process could be aided by stating explicitly some of the desirable limiting principles adduced earlier. So, for each part of the special Act there should be expressed criteria by which to judge its value or dispensability and its proportionality so that there can be a distinct vote on each part. The next safeguard is to enforce observance of these preconditions. This vigilance should be undertaken not simply by Parliament, whose record in emergencies is uninspiring, but also by an independent permanent standing committee, which would investigate and report on any proposed institution of the legislation, its working while in force, its renewal and its compatibility with international obligations. Furthermore, the pronouncements of this body should be referred not only to the Home Secretary but also to a select committee, such as the Home Affairs Committee which could give further prominence and support to any proposals and in this way to internalise them within the

Parliamentary system. The third restriction is that, once invoked, the actual application of each special law should be subjected to judicial control so far as possible.

Civil libertarians can only hope to secure the principles of constitutionalism and democratic accountability if they confront, rather than ignore, future possibilities of emergency and apply to them all possible mechanisms of governance — executive, legislative and judicial. The simplistic repeal of all emergency laws abnegates the influence of the legislative and judicial branches and gifts absolute power to the executive, making the smash and grab of new powers an even greater danger than the precipitate smashing of glass to get at well conceived provisions already behind the glass. The alternative to principled security laws is to trust the Home Secretary to design his own laws and to produce them from his secret filing cabinet at a time when everyone (Parliament, the media and the public) will be too frightened to listen to civil liberties pleadings.

On this basis, it was right to pass a Terrorism Act — even in the very year that the Human Rights Act 1998 entered into force. But does it in detail contain the design qualities outlined above and should its provisions be immediately activated? There are substantial reservations on both grounds (see Gross, O., and Ni Aolain, F., 'To know where we are going we need to know where we are' in Hegarty, A., and Leonard, S., *Human Rights* (Cavendish, London, 1999), p. 113). The structural safeguards of formal and effective investigative review have not been instilled within the Terrorism Act 2000 (as described in Chapter 10), and *ex post facto* judicial review, even under the terms of the Human Rights Act 1998, cannot remedy this omission. As for necessity, it is submitted that for the most part, there is no sufficient emergency to warrant its use. There is no sufficient emergency from Irish sources, except in Northern Ireland itself, nor hitherto has there been sufficient threat from domestic or international terrorism. The position of other domestic terrorism has already been considered. As for international terrorism, the position before September 2001 was surely that the level of threat was insufficient to demand the invocation of special measures. The government had in fact accepted this point to some extent and had given an undertaking back in 1995 not to use the special powers of detention following arrest to their full extent against foreign suspects (House of Commons Debates vol. 256 col. 353, 8 March 1995, Mr M Howard). So, international political violence may be a legitimate target of legislative contingency provisions. But, with only 39 incidents during the past decade and 300 deaths between 1975 and 1995 (270 of which were at Lockerbie, a tragic event which could not in any way have been prevented by British legislation). With non-Irish domestic terrorism, there was at most a fear for the future (Home Office and Northern Ireland Office, Legislation against Terrorism (Cm. 4178, London, 1998), para. 3.12).

International terrorism as represented by the events of 11 September has taken on a much more threatening appearance, and the use of the Terrorism Act 2000 for a time in their aftermath is supportable. Those events have additionally prompted the passage of the Anti-terrorism, Crime and Security Act 2001. Parts of that Act justifiably respond to the incredible savagery now threatened by reference to dangerous substances and acutely vulnerable targets. Other parts (such as changes to the powers of the specialist police forces or to offences of bribery and corruption) amount to sensible law reform, and so the criticism of them relates more to the process of legislation and its hurried and selective nature. But other parts seem an inappropriate or disproportionate response to the problem. The atrocity of the World Trade Centre is despicable and claimed the lives of hundred of British citizens, but the perpetrators could be detected and prosecuted under existing domestic laws, whether of the United Kingdom or in the United States under the wide provisions already in existence, including those pertaining to aircraft security.

In summary, the legislation should most often remain behind the glass, but legislation there should be. Only in Northern Ireland are the circumstances clearly sufficient to justify longer-term special provisions, some to allow for transition, and others to deal with the continuing emanations of paramilitarism whether from the main protagonists or splinter groups. In terms of the overall design of counter-terrorism measures, the prime strategy to be reflected is a mixture of criminalisa-tion and risk management. As for international terrorism, there was crisis and panic, as governments were terrified, but that phase has surely passed. Criminal-isation should be the prime process by which the violence inherent in terrorism is addressed. While political engagement is important, Liberal democracies must not concede demands or methods which are wholly incompatible with their values. So it is proper to set standards to the modes of political engagement, including forms of policing action and ultimately punishment for acts of violence. Consequently, expressions like 'war on terrorism' are best avoided, at least in a domestic context. The process of criminalisation demands an emphasis on intelligence-gathering, through electronic surveillance, search powers, and also arrest and interrogation. However, the purpose is not simply to sustain convictions but often — probably much more often — to prevent, disrupt and counter and in this way to engage in risk management in response to the threat of terrorism. The difficult balance here will be to provide security and reassurance in ways which do not transform or disrupt legitimate activities, such as air travel or foreign currency transfers.

Even if the legislation does persist for some time, it may be predicted that it will continue to be largely peripheral in effect (see Walker, C.P., *The Prevention of Terrorism in British Law* (2nd ed., Manchester University Press, Manchester, 1992), ch. 11). More important factors in dealing with terrorism will comprise normal police powers and criminal offences and regular techniques of investigation and securitisation. These must operate alongside co-operation and vigilance on the part of the public who provide, even in terrorist cases where there is an emphasis on proactive intelligence-gathering, much of the policing capability of society. International co-operation is also of growing importance in response to more fluid and global vulnerabilities and Third Millennium terrorism. Above all, there must be a vibrant and inclusive democracy which can discern the difference between vituperative and politically immature hot air and violence with the potential to spill blood and which holds its nerve and its cherished values in the face of the heat and light of the terrorist spectacular.

1.3   THE NEW DEFINITION OF 'TERRORISM'

In political discourse, the definition of 'terrorism' is far from settled (but see Wilkinson, P., *Terrorism versus Democracy* (Frank Cass, London, 2000)). By contrast, law is able by its nature to provide authoritative, though not necessarily incontrovertible, definitions, but the danger then arises that politically motivated 'linguistic opportunism' will produce an overreaching denotation (Gearty, C., *Terror* (Faber & Faber, London, 1991), p. 2). The following version was advanced by s. 20(1) of the Prevention of Terrorism (Temporary Provisions) Act 1989:

> . . . 'terrorism' means the use of violence for political ends and includes any use of violence for the purpose of putting the public or any section of the public in fear.

The new definition (in s. 1 of the Terrorism Act 2000) states at greater length and detail as follows:

1.—(1)   In this Act 'terrorism' means the use or threat of action where—
(a)   the action falls within subsection (2),
(b)   the use or threat is designed to influence the government or to intimidate the public or a section of the public, and
(c)   the use or threat is made for the purpose of advancing a political, religious or ideological cause.
(2)   Action falls within this subsection if it—
(a)   involves serious violence against a person,
(b)   involves serious damage to property,
(c)   endangers a person's life, other than that of the person committing the action,
(d)   creates a serious risk to the health or safety of the public or a section of the public, or
(e)   is designed seriously to interfere with or seriously to disrupt an electronic system.
(3)   The use or threat of action falling within subsection (2) which involves the use of firearms or explosives is terrorism whether or not subsection (1)(b) is satisfied.
(4)   In this section—
(a)   'action' includes action outside the United Kingdom,
(b)   a reference to any person or to property is a reference to any person, or to property, wherever situated,
(c)   a reference to the public includes a reference to the public of a country other than the United Kingdom, and

(d) 'the government' means the government of the United Kingdom, of a Part of the United Kingdom or of a country other than the United Kingdom.

(5) In this Act a reference to action taken for the purposes of terrorism includes a reference to action taken for the benefit of a proscribed organisation.

The essence is in s. 1(1), which contains three conjunctive legs, all of which must normally be satisfied (subject to s. 1(3), as described below). The Anti-terrorism, Crime and Security Act 2001 largely relies upon the Terrorism Act 2000 definition, though variants may arise through its measures to enforce international law (see Chapter 6) or European Union Third Pillar obligations (see Chapter 10). It will be noted from s. 1(1)(b) that terrorism may be suffered either by the government (including its agents such as the police) or the public. A suggestion that attacks on the former might amount to political violence but not 'terrorism' (Whitty, N., Murphy, T., and Livingstone, S., *Civil Liberties Law* (Butterworths, London, 2001), p. 121) is at variance with a growing body of international law (such as the European Convention for the Suppression of Terrorism, ETS 90, 1977), with developments in extradition law (see Gilbert, G., *Aspects of Extradition Law* (Nijhoff, Dordrecht, 1991), ch. 6) and with the rationale for having anti-terrorism laws (which is to deal with forms of organised crime which cannot effectively be handled under 'normal' laws).

The official verdict in 1983 was that the predecessor formula in the Prevention of Terrorism (Temporary Provisions) Act 1989 (s. 20) 'has not given rise to any difficulties' (House of Commons Debates (HC Debs.) Standing Comm. D. col. 352, 8 December 1983, David Waddington) and did not, therefore, require amendment. But Lord Lloyd in his review in 1996 viewed it as too narrow, especially as it did not catch single issue or religious terrorism (Inquiry into Legislation against Terrorism (Cm. 3420, London, 1996), para. 5.22). Hence, s. 1 of the Terrorism Act 2000 is intended to expand both the forbidden activities and feared consequences. The origins of the new formulation lie in the *Lloyd Report* which expressed approbation for a working definition used by the FBI:

The use of serious violence against persons or property, or the threat to use such violence, to intimidate or coerce a government, the public or any section of the public, in order to promote political, social, or ideological objectives. (for a later version, see Federal Bureau of Investigation, *Terrorism in the United States, 1997 Report* (http://www.fbi.gov/library/terror/terroris.htm, 1998), p. 11)

However, it should be understood the definition of terrorism here cited is an administrative construct for jurisdictional, budgetary and other administrative purposes. It does not serve as a legal term of art on which liberty depends. By and large, relevant US legislation relies on listed offences as describing terroristic activities (see especially the (Federal) Omnibus Counterterrorism Act 1995, 18 USC ss. 1956(c)(7), 2331, 2332a(a), 2332b), rather than a more generic term which, because of vagueness (albeit that it requires violence or its threat in all cases), would probably fail to withstand constitutional challenge. Furthermore, even the Home Office viewed the inclusion of 'social' objectives as too broad, by including ordinary blackmail or extortion, while the definition was also too narrow by not covering property damage or serious disruption (Home Office and Northern Ireland Office, Legislation against Terrorism (Cm. 4178, London, 1998), para. 3.16). At the same time, s. 1(2) is not confined to trigger offences *per se*, though it may be that most of such activities will fall within the criminal law. However, the Home Office view is that to limit the application of the definition of terrorism to actions contrary to the criminal law will not suffice (House of Lords Debates (HL Debs.) vol. 611 col. 1484, 6 April 2000, Lord Bassam). It would cause uncertainties in dealing with international terrorism; the police might be unable to act unless and until they were sure that the action in question was contrary to the criminal law in the relevant country overseas. And there may be occurrences designed to terrify which are not unlawful — such as a refusal to perform a duty to keep others safe (HL Debs. vol. 614 col. 1448, 4 July 2000, Lord Bassam):

> For instance, an employee may advance a political cause and may deliberately omit to update a vital computer programme or omit to put a cleansing agent in a sewerage system, with the result that the health of a section of the public was severely put at risk. In our view that could be terrorism in certain circumstances.

However, a distinction was made between this kind of wrongdoing and the damage inflicted by collective industrial disputes (HC Debs. Standing Committee D col. 31, 18 January 2000, Charles Clarke):

> It is important that the definitions in the Bill should not catch actions in connection with industrial disputes, large demonstrations . . . or even politically motivated mass boycotts of major oil companies . . . To suggest, for instance, that the nurses' dispute could be a terrorist act is wrong. It would not cause a serious risk, nor would it be driven by a 'political, religious or ideological cause'. It would be a trade dispute, which is not a political, religious or ideological cause. . . . Many of the other provisions of the clause 1 definition cover some types of attack that terrorists might make with the aim of disrupting economic life. For example, bombing the stock exchange or hacking into the national grid computer system would both be caught under other definitions.

The differences between the formulations in the 1989 and 2000 Acts were the focus of much of the debate concerning the Terrorism Act. The general allegation is that s. 1 is significantly broader than its predecessor and will affect legitimate political activity as well as terrorism properly so called. In part, it is intentionally broad, as it is mainly the platform for investigative police powers where there must be some margin of error; it is not a term on which a criminal offence is based (HC Debs. vol. 346 col. 410, 15 March 2000, Charles Clarke). Overall, it is submitted that the changes in the terms of the definition are not tremendously significant.

Rather, it is the circumstance of how it is then applied later in the Terrorism Act 2000 — the remit — which is worrying. Neither is very satisfactory — relevant measures should instead be designed around a combination of the types of seriously threatening and destabilising offences being perpetrated and the nature of the collectives which carry them out and which render less capable normal criminal justice processes. In this way, the emphasis should be upon severe and collective political violence, rather than terrorism *per se*.

This overall verdict about the limited extent of terminological changes in 2000 can be justified by a comparison of the terms used in the definitions of 1989 and 2000.

In two respects s. 1 is expressly narrower than s. 20. One difference in the direction of restraint is that s. 1 demands a 'serious' level of violence (and also 'serious' damage or risks to health and safety or electronic disruption). 'Serious' here is comparable to 'grievous', as in the offence on s. 18 of the Offences against the Person Act 1861 (HL Debs. vol. 614 col. 166, 20 June 2000, Lord Bach). But s. 1 does also allow for endangerment of life without qualification, since any such endangerment can be viewed as a serious threat. This definition included, as originally drafted, protestors who only endanger their own lives — perhaps environmental protestors who dig hazardous tunnels are now the equivalent of suffragettes who threw themselves under race-horses except that they run the risk of being labelled as terrorists rather than malicious injurers or breachers of the peace. This interpretation was denied by government Ministers; according to Lord Bach, as regards:

. . . hunger strikers or the terrorist risking blowing himself up. We do not believe that that would be covered. It would not, by reason only that such a person endangered his own life, fall within what we believe is the obvious sense of [subsection (2)(c)]. That person would also have to put the public at risk. (HL Debs. vol. 614 col. 166, 20 June 2000)

But the criticism was eventually acceded to, and the words 'other than that of the person committing the action' were eventually added to subsection 2(c) (HL Debs. vol. 614 col. 1451, 4 July 2000, Lord Bassam). The critics did however point to some of the continuing uncertainties (House of Lords Debs. vol. 614 col. 1446, 4 July 2000, Lord Beaumont):

. . . there is a long and valuable tradition of non-violent civil disobedience in this country. The Green Party and many others regard it as most important that the legislation does not chip away at that tradition. It is part of the complex of thought which has since 1660 preserved the country from revolution.

Non-violent civil disobedience often entails the protestor risking his or her life and, particularly since suicide ceased to be a crime in this country, the action is not and should not be a crime, let alone terrorism. Therefore, I suggest that we should amend the Bill accordingly.

There are two complicating issues. One is where the person's action in committing suicide endangers other people's lives. One might call it the 'Emily Davison case', although no one, not even the horse, was seriously damaged except Emily herself. Only one jockey was hurt but no one was seriously damaged. Unfortunately, Emily Davison was not too efficient, having already tried to commit suicide at least twice and having been arrested once for stoning an innocent Baptist minister whom she mistook for Lloyd George.

The second issue relates to what one might call the 'Swampy case', where the protester may be thought to cause danger to other people because he tempts them to rescue him.

Next, as originally drafted, the Terrorism Bill entirely dropped the alternative objective in s. 20, 'putting the public or any section of the public in fear', which may sometimes result from a non-political cause and yet still amount to 'terrorism' such as hooliganism or individual acts of aggression (HC Debs. Standing Comm. col. 565, 17 January 1989, Douglas Hogg). However, as amended at Report Stage in the House of Lords, it is sufficient that the use or threat is 'to intimidate the public or a section of the public' (Terrorism Act 2000, s. 1(1)(b)). Nevertheless, this possibility is set alongside s. 1(1)(c), which requires some form of political, religious or ideological nexus not present in the 1989 Act.

Moving onto differences where s. 1 appears to have a broader coverage than the 1989 Act, the first issue focuses upon the word, 'violence'. Violence implies force which is unjustified and unlawful and usually entails criminal offences which involve a threat to, or endangerment of, personal safety. It was the view of some critics and indeed the concern of the Home Office that the FBI definition would not cover activities which might not be violent or even destructive but which can have a ruinous outcome. These might comprise disrupting key computer systems or interfering with the supply of water or power where life, health or safety may be put at risk on a broad scale (Home Office and Northern Ireland Office, Legislation against Terrorism (Cm. 4178, London, 1998), para. 3.16). The bombs in the City of London in 1992 and 1993 and in London Docklands in 1996 may be further illustrations. In a late modern society, the state is 'hollowed out' and power is diffused across both public and private sectors. Power relates more to finance, knowledge and security (see Castells, M., *The Information Age Vol. I: The Rise of the Network Society* (Blackwell, London, 1996); Giddens, A., *The Consequences of Modernity* (Polity Press, London, 1990), and so the likely targets of terrorists shift in line with the new centres of power and the new power-holders. Thus, it becomes less focused upon states and territories, while the terrorist groups themselves become more fluid and hybrid in objectives, forms and tactics (see Raufer, X., 'New world disorder and new terrorism' (1999) 11(4) *Terrorism & Political Violence* 30). In this light, s. 1(2) seeks to protect against risks to property, risks to safety and interference with computer systems.

Yet, it is not certain that the term 'violence' as a concept does not include attacks on property, and it is so defined in the Public Order Act 1986, s. 8. The use of the word 'violence' in connection with property may usefully carry the implication that trivial forms of damage (such as graffiti) cannot amount to 'terrorism' (HL Debs. vol. 613 col. 235, 16 May 2000, Lord Bassam). One exception is that the definition of terroristic attacks on property is expressly narrower in s. 57 since it expressly requires an endangerment of life. So, the general allegation that the definition of terrorism is being extended in this direction by s. 1(2)(b) to damage to property may not be strictly accurate since the term already covered this form of attack. In any event, according to the government, 'people have lost their lives in [property] attacks. It would be rash simply to exclude property, even though a terrorist organisation could say that its definition was not to threaten life' (HC Debs. Standing Committee D, col. 20, 18 January 2000, Charles Clarke). The debate on the meaning of violence in the context of property attacks was somewhat curtailed when, at the Report stage of the House of Lords, the government simply replaced the word 'violence' with the word 'damage' in s. 1(2)(b) (HL Debs. vol. 614 col. 161, 20 June 2000, Lord Bach). At the same time, there was the inclusion of s. 1(2)(e), which is designed to take account of cyber-terrorism — 'serious disruption to computer systems to advance a political, religious or ideological cause' (HL Debs. vol. 614 col. 160, 20 June 2000, Lord Bach). This aspect is a significant extension, and one which is also indicative of the development of a late modern, information, society: '. . . why assassinate a politician or indiscriminately kill people when attack on the electronic switching will produce far more dramatic and lasting results?' (Laqueur, W., 'Post-modern terrorism' (1996) 75(5) *Foreign Affairs* 35). Cyber-terrorism within s. 1(2)(e) covers various forms of hostile activity provided it is designed seriously to interfere with, or seriously to disrupt, an electronic system. This might involve not only direct threats to life, such as through interference with air traffic controls or hospital records but also defacing web-site text or images, the use of viruses or denial of service attacks through multiple key striking software — 'ping' engines — or through e-mail bombs, none of which causes physical damage but may fundamentally compromise the government provision of information and services (see Stephens, R.E., 'Cyber-biotech terrorism' in Kushner, H.W., *The Future of Terrorism* (Sage, Thousand Oaks, 1998); Denning, D.E., *Information Warfare and Security* (ACM Press, Addison-Wesley, New York, 1999); Valeri, L., and Knights, M., 'Affecting trust: terrorism, Internet and offensive information warfare' (2000) 12(1) *Terrorism & Political Violence* 15; Post, J.M., Ruby, K.G., and Shaw, E.D., 'From car bombs to logic bombs' (2000) 12(2) *Terrorism & Political Violence* 97; Mitliaga, V., 'Cyberterrorism' (2002) *Legal Executive* February p. 4; Infowar.com, http://www.infowar.com/class_3/class_3.shtml). Other forms of computer use by terrorist groups do exist (such as for internal communications, fund-raising, recruitment and propaganda — see Damphousse, K.R., and Smith, B.L., 'The Internet' in Kushner, H.W., *The Future of Terrorism* (Sage, Thousand Oaks, 1998)), but these can be tackled either as secondary aspects of proscription or as direct criminal offences (such as the new incitement offence in s. 59 of the Terrorism Act 2000). Next, s. 1 mentions the 'threat' as well as the use of violence, but this may not in reality be much difference from the use of violence for the purpose of putting the public in fear under the previous Act's s. 20.

Mention of 'political ends' in s. 20 emphasised that terroristic violence is a symbolic means to ulterior objectives, but those political ends were left wholly undefined by the 1989 Act. Consequently, the definition in s. 20 was equally applicable to revolutionary, counter-revolutionary, sub-revolutionary and State terrorism. However, the government has occasionally sought to establish a distinction between 'political ends' (within the legislation) and 'social objectives' (not within the legislation), such as might prompt animal liberationists or even factional fighting within Sikh extremist groups (HC Debs. Standing Committee B, cols. 570, 571, 17 January 1989, Douglas Hogg). It is submitted that this contrast, which seeks to carve out an uncertain area of sub-revolutionary terrorism from the scope of s. 20, is spurious because of the broad meaning of 'political ends'. Section 1 of the Terrorism Act 2000 now offers some clarification here in the intended direction of the wider uses of the term but with a similar emphasis on motive as a key feature in the definition of terrorism. The forbidden activities now comprise expressly religious or ideological causes, but whether this is really an extension again remains obscure (Edge, P., 'Religious organisations and the prevention of terrorism legislation' (1999) 4 *Journal of Civil Liberties* 194 at p. 198). First, the idea that there is a clear distinction between religion and politics belies thousands of years of history. Perhaps an example is intra-religion faction fighting not directed against the state (see Edge, P., 'Religious organisations and the prevention of terrorism legislation' (1999) 4 *Journal of Civil Liberties* 194 at p. 198). But any serious inter-ethnic or group conflict can easily be construed as political. Secondly, single issue ideological organisations such as 'eco-terrorists' or anti-abortion groups could also count as political campaigners even if their prime impact is upon private individuals (such as genetic crop farmers or abortionists in private clinics) rather than the State. The general extension towards non-State target was described as 'dangerous territory' in the Parliamentary debates (HC Debs. Standing Committee D, col. 10, 18 January 2000, Simon Hughes) and potentially net-widening for anti-terrorist legislation. A comparison might be made with the offence of terrorism in South Africa. Section 54(1) of the Internal Security Act 1982 forbids the commission of, or conspiracy or incitement to commit, any act or threat of violence with intent to overthrow or endanger the State, to achieve constitutional, political, industrial, social or economic change, to induce the government to do or abstain from doing anything, or to put in fear or demoralise the public or any section of it. The provision was much-reviled as an instrument of oppression whose impact can spread to political expression as well as to paramilitary violence (see Mathews, A., *Freedom, State Security and Rule of Law* (Juta, Cape Town, 1986), ch. 6). However, sectarian attacks in Northern Ireland have long been treated as within the definition of terrorism, and the use of Sarin gas by a quasi-religious cult, Aum Shinrikyo, in the Tokyo underground in March 1995 could be seen as likewise terroristic even if the target was the public at large rather than the State.

As for the feared consequences, it is welcome to note that these are limited in s. 1(1) to actions, and so cannot include the omissions, for example, of going on strike or passive forms of civil disobedience. A failure to define carefully here would have invited a return to the notion of 'subversion' which has fallen into disrepute under the Security Service Act 1989.

Overall, it is not the wording around the definition of 'terrorism' *per se* which should trouble the true believer in constitutionalism, and the threshold of the meaning of terrorism has not been significantly altered. Rather, it is the final decoupling of the Terrorism Act 2000 from its historical grounding in the conflict in Ireland and the consequent impact on the remit of the definition that raises the possibility of the use of draconian provisions in circumstances where ordinary policing and laws could easily respond to isolated or incompetent terrorists. Under the Prevention of Terrorism (Temporary Provisions) Act 1989, the legislative work done by the concept 'terrorism' was expressly restrained in all the contexts in which it had impact. In regard to proscription and exclusion, it was expressly confined to Irish terrorism. In respect of terrorist finances and policing powers, it could also apply to international terrorism. By contrast, the Terrorism Act 2000 moves away from the well-evidenced (and hitherto undoubtedly serious) menace from Irish paramilitaries and encourages a wider purview, not only domestically but also internationally, which does not guarantee the kind of danger or justification in terms of the protection of rights and democracy which inherently justifies special provisions. There were unsuccessful attempts in Parliament to confine the coverage of the Act to 'designated countries' — countries deserving of the protection of UK legislation rather than regimes which might be properly viewed as 'odious' (HC Debs. Standing Committee D, col. 26, 18 January 2000, David Lidington). But the implication of labelling some terrorism as officially acceptable was unpalatable to the government.

Consequently, if the legislation is to be disestablished from its Irish grounding in this way, then one ought to seek further qualifications to ensure that special powers really are needed and are a proportionate response. One reason why special powers might be justifiable is where the political violence occurs in the context of a secretive and organised group — it is the collective paramilitary nature which makes the action so threatening and difficult to police. Therefore, it should have been specified in s. 1 that the political violence must involve concerted action by a group of people acting in an organised and secretive way. Another factor is that the criminal violence is an attack on the collective. This condition is indeed recognised by s. 1(1)(b) — but is then subject to the exception of s. 1(3). The idea behind this exception is to allow for the label of 'terrorism' to be ascribed in all cases to attacks by explosives or firearms upon political or public figures, even if the purpose of the assailant is not clear and may even be personal rather than political: '. . . we do not want the police to feel hindered in any way from acting in situations that most, if not all of us would regard as terrorism — such as assassinations — because it was not clear that either of those elements was present' (HL Debs. vol. 614 col. 160, 20 June 2000, Lord Bach). However, this exception is still subject to the requirement of a purpose as in s. 1(1)(c), and it is limited to attacks with explosives or firearms whereas attacks by drowning, poisoning or strangulation would fall within s. 1(1)(b).

By contrast, both contexts are more clearly recognised in s. 2 of the Reinsurance (Acts of Terrorism) Act 1993:

2.—(1)   This Act applies to arrangements under which the Secretary of State, with the consent of the Treasury, undertakes to any extent the liability of reinsuring risks against—

(a)   loss or damage to property in Great Britain resulting from or consequential upon acts of terrorism; and

(b)   any loss which is consequential on loss or damage falling within paragraph (a) above; and to the extent that the arrangements relate to events occurring before as well as after an agreement of reinsurance comes into being, the reference in section 1(1) above to the obligations of the Secretary of State shall be construed accordingly.

(2)   In this section 'acts of terrorism' means acts of persons acting on behalf of, or in connection with, any organisation which carries out activities directed towards the overthrowing or influencing, by force or violence, of Her Majesty's government in the United Kingdom or any other government *de jure* or *de facto*.

(3)   In subsection (2) above 'organisation' includes any association or combination of persons.

It will be noted at the outset, returning to a previous point, that damage to property is not only included as a consequence of 'terrorism' but is the sole concern of the 1993 Act. This reflects its origins as response to massive IRA car-bombs in the City of London in 1992 and 1993. The main issue for present purposes is that the definition of an 'act of terrorism' under the 1993 Act does make clear that the acts of terrorism must be 'directed towards the overthrowing or influencing, by force or violence, of Her Majesty's government in the United Kingdom or any other government *de jure* or *de facto*'. This contrasts with the formulation in s. 20 of the Prevention of Terrorism (Temporary Provisions) Act 1989 and is even further distinct from s. 1 of the Terrorism Act 2000. Furthermore, the 1993 Act uses the phrase, 'persons acting on behalf of, or in connection with, any organisation', which eliminates any actions carried out by individuals with eccentric or singular purposes. What of anarchist groups for whom chaos and disorganisation is the goal and theoretically the *modus operandi*? Could a group of anarchists constitute an 'organisation'? Presumably they would be regarded as such, falling under the umbrella of an association provided their actions are in some way 'directed' against government policy but would not in so far as there is no discernible policy or pattern relevant to the United Kingdom (or foreign) State. A similar distinction would apply to animal rights or environmental protesters.

One should not, however, rest too much weight on this comparison with the 1993 Act. The wording is based on the Association of British Insurers circular to members (No. GIC 76/92, 12 November 1992), so it is clear that the government in drawing up the Reinsurance Act was reacting to the specific insurance situation (see Walker, C., and McGuinness, M., 'Risk, political violence and policing the

City of London' in Crawford, A., (ed.), *Crime, Insecurity, Safety and the New Governance* (Willan Publishing, 2002)). It demonstrates that the government was not legislating against terrorism directly, instead it was legislating for business. The focus of the 1993 Act was the reassurance, through reinsurance, of the business community first and foremost. In other words, the government was acting to mitigate the ramifications of terrorist activity in a particular sphere rather than take action against terrorists or terrorist acts themselves, as under the Terrorism Act 2000.

A more intractable problem than getting right the elements of the definition is that the continuing emphasis in the Terrorism Act 2000 upon the political motives of terrorist offenders could create problems in regard to extradition (see Gilbert, G., *Transnational fugitive offenders in international law* (Nijhoff, Hague, 1998)) and has added weight to claims for an amnesty or for special prison treatment for convicted terrorists. Certainly, the definition in the Terrorism Act 2000 is broader than most equivalents in international law. For example, Article 2.1(b) of the United Nations Convention for the Suppression of the Financing of Terrorism (Cm. 4663, London, 2000) delimits it to international crimes, such as hijacking, as well as:

Any other act intended to cause death or serious bodily injury to a civilian, or to any other person not taking an active part in the hostilities in a situation of armed conflict, when the purpose of such act, by its nature or context, is to intimidate a population, or to compel a government or an international organisation to do or to abstain from doing any act.

A further definitional problem raised during debates on the Bill was the 'Kosovo problem' — the concern that British soldiers fighting in conflicts abroad could be labeled as terrorists by reference to their very professional use of violence. The government's response to this point was rather unsatisfactory and relied on the alleged 'general principle in law that statutes do not bind the Crown unless by express provision or necessary implication' (HL Debs. vol. 613 col. 241, 16 May 2000, Lord Bach). In general, the law does tend to immunize the Crown in the way suggested. In *Lord Advocate* v *Dumbarton District Council* [1989] 3 WLR 1346 at 1360 (see also *Attorney-General* v *Hancock* [1940] 1 KB 427 in the context of the Courts (Emergency Powers) Act 1939), Lord Keith argued that:

I consider it to be no longer a tenable view that the Crown is in terms bound by general words in a statute but that the prerogative enables it to override the statute. As to the considerations which may be applicable for the purpose of finding a necessary implication that the Crown is bound, it is clear that the mere fact that the statute in question has been passed for the public benefit is not in itself sufficient for that purpose.

There is also some authority for this proposition in the context of terrorism provisions in the Court of Appeal's judgment in *Re Lockerbie Air Disaster The*

Times, 20 May 1992, in which the Court refused to order a former forensic scientist working for a Crown agency to comply with letters of request from a New York judge. Nevertheless, a more explicit statement about the use of force which is lawful under either domestic or international law by the Crown could have ended any doubts both about the exemption of soldiers properly going about their duties and the liability of soldiers who have abused their powers.

Because of these various problems, whether arising from uncertainty of scope and impact on rights to free expression or from the wider impact on criminal and penal policy, it would be desirable to avoid the establishment of legal measures (whether powers or offences) on the basis of an inevitably problematical definition of terrorism. A viable alternative (which was adopted by the Northern Ireland (Emergency Provisions) Acts 1973–96 and now lives on in Part VII of the Terrorism Act 2000 in relation to the allocation of cases for special, non-jury trials) is the 'scheduled offence' approach in which counter-terrorism provisions are designed by reference to the offences involved, making irrelevant the motives of the offender and underlining the criminal wrongdoing. Offences could be scheduled (and thereby become susceptible to special treatment) if existing criminal laws or procedures are demonstrated by a periodic review to be not reasonably adequate to secure the administration of justice in view of the organised and serious nature of that offence which is regularly being perpetrated against State agents, the public or any section of it. Challenges under the Human Rights Act 1998 would be far less likely if there could be instilled this closer correlation with criminality.

1.4   CONTENTS

1.4.1   Terrorism Act 2000

The 2000 Act is divided into eight parts (plus 16 schedules), with the six of them reflecting its substantive themes: proscribed organisations; terrorist property; terrorist investigations; counter-terrorism powers; miscellaneous offences; and extra measures confined to Northern Ireland. The details of these themes are contained in Chapters 2 to 7 of this book. Amongst the innovations are a new definition of 'terrorism' which leads into the application of many powers and offences to a much wider range of terrorism, including international and non-Irish domestic terrorism. There is also an attempt to subject a wider range of measures to judicial or quasi-judicial oversight — such as through a new commission to consider proscription orders and the judicial scrutiny of detention following arrest. Next, the laws in Britain and Northern Ireland are largely harmonised — save for a temporary extra inventory (Part VII) for Northern Ireland. One consequence is that some measures previously confined to Northern Ireland are now extended to Britain; on the other hand, the measures passed in 1998 to respond to Republican splinter groups have actually now been confined to Northern Ireland. There are some novel measures — such as the seizure of cash at borders — but these are relatively few and far between, and the Act was an occasion for clearer thinking rather than new thinking.

Conversely, it is as well to note what is absent. Though the Terrorism Act 2000 is not simply a consolidation measure and makes several substantial additions to the counter-terrorism laws, its passage was also the occasion to drop some measures.

One repeal concerns exclusion orders (see Bonner, D., 'Combating terrorism in Great Britain: the role of exclusion orders' [1982] *Public Law* 262; Walker, C.P., *The Prevention of Terrorism in British Law* (2nd ed., Manchester University Press, Manchester, 1992), ch. 5), which had in fact already lapsed in 1998. Lord Lloyd was in favour of dropping the power (Inquiry into Legislation against Terrorism (Cm. 3420, London, 1996), paras 16.2–16.4), as was the subsequent Consultation Paper (Home Office and Northern Ireland Office, Legislation against Terrorism (Cm. 4178, London, 1998), para. 5.7), the latter arguing that it was more profitable to keep suspects under surveillance. However, the notion of exclusion lingers on in English law. Section 42 of the Criminal Justice and Court Services Act 2000 empowers a police constable, in order to prevent harassment, alarm or distress to a resident, to order the reasonably suspected perpetrator to leave the vicinity and to remain at a distance as specified in the order.

Another notable absentee is the power of internment without trial. This power had always been controversial, even though it had not been in use since 1975 (see Lowry, D.R., 'Internment in Northern Ireland' (1976) 8 *Toledo Law Review* 169; Lowry, D.R., 'Draconian powers' (1976–77) 8-9 *Columbia Human Rights Law Review* 185; Spjut, R.J., 'Executive detention in Northern Ireland: the Gardiner Report and the Northern Ireland (Emergency Provisions) (Amendment) Act 1975' (1975) 10 *Irish Jurist* 272; Spjut, R.J., 'Internment and detention without trial in Northern Ireland 1971–75' (1986) 49 *Modern Law Review* 712). It was recommended for abolition as long ago as 1990 (following the recommendation of the (Colville) Review of the Northern Ireland (Emergency Provisions) Acts 1978 and 1987 (Cm. 1115, London, 1990), para. 11.10). Though a later reviewer recommended retention ((Rowe) Review of the Northern Ireland (Emergency Provisions) Act 1991 (Cm. 2706, London, 1995), para. 121), Lord Lloyd disagreed (Inquiry into Legislation against Terrorism (Cm. 3420, London, 1996), para. 16.8), and internment had long been looked on with great distaste by Labour Party spokespersons — 'internment is the terrorist's friend' (HC Debs. Standing Committee A col. 73, 25 November 1997, Adam Ingram). The power had actually been terminated by s. 3 of the Northern Ireland (Emergency Provisions) Act 1998 and now finds no place in the Terrorism Act 2000. Attempts to revive it were firmly resisted by the government, while 'It does not rule out for all time the introduction of the power to intern' (Home Office and Northern Ireland Office, Legislation against Terrorism (Cm. 4178, 1998), para. 14.2), it would be 'a significant backward step at a time when we are normalising the security situation in Northern Ireland' (HL Debs. vol. 613 col. 1054, 16 May 2000, Lord Falconer). Though the stance of the Labour Government against internment seemed very firm and principled, it has now been compromised by ss. 21 to 23 of the Anti-terrorism, Crime and Security Act 2001, as described in Chapter 8, which allow for the detention without trial of certain asylum-seekers. Moreover, in the context of the attacks on 11 September, the Home Secretary seemed more receptive to other categories of internment (HC Debs. vol. 372 col. 930, 15 October 2001):

> We do not intend to introduce internment, although if a major crisis arose from the terrorist threat, other specific measures would have to be introduced, as has always been the case since the Second World War. Governments have always held that in reserve.

The third non-appearance concerns the offence of withholding information (formerly in s. 18 in the Prevention of Terrorism (Temporary Provisions) Act 1989 and recommended for repeal by the Inquiry into Legislation against Terrorism (Cm. 3420, London, 1996), para. 14.24), and the Home Office Consultation Paper (Home Office and Northern Ireland Office, Legislation against Terrorism (Cm. 4178, London, 1998), para. 7.17), though a more focused offence dealing with financial institutions, formerly at s. 18A of the 1989 Act, is replicated as s. 19 of the Terrorism Act 2000. This particular omission was wholly reversed by s. 117 of the Anti-terrorism, Crime and Security Act 2001, as described in Chapter 4.

Fourth, the Criminal Justice (Terrorism and Conspiracy) Act 1998 provisions relating to specified organisations persist in Northern Ireland but are repealed in Britain.

It also remains a notable deficiency in a fundamental consolidation that no attention has been given to the victims of terrorism. There is a growing body of national precedents in France (see Loi no. 86-1021 of 9 September 1986, article 9, as amended), and the USA (see Victims of Terrorism Compensation Act 1986 (5 USC ss. 5569, 5570, 37 USC ss. 559, 1013), US Patriot Act: Uniting and Strengthening America By Providing Appropriate Tools Required To Intercept and Obstruct Terrorism, H.R. 3162, 2001, Title VI).

1.4.2 Anti-terrorism, Crime and Security Act 2001

This substantial legislative supplement (with 129 sections and 8 schedules) is organised into 14 Parts. The first three parts deal with terrorist property. Since this is also the subject of Part III of the Terrorism Act 2000, the additions will be set out alongside the 2000 Act provisions in Chapter 3. The overlap is substantial, as Part I of the Anti-terrorism, Crime and Security Act 2001 actually replaces ss. 24 to 31 of the Terrorism Act 2000, while Part II makes amendments to other Terrorism Act measures. Only Part III of the Anti-terrorism, Crime and Security Act 2001 treads into new territory, dealing with the freezing of foreign property held by United Kingdom institutions. Next, Part IV addresses immigration and asylum matters pertaining to terrorism. There are three elements here. The most controversial is the detention without trial of foreign persons denied asylum on national security grounds or because of their international crimes. In addition, there is an attempt to short-circuit any claim to asylum by making the tribunal focus upon the Secretary of State's reasons for denying the claim. Thirdly, Part IV deals with the retention of fingerprints in asylum and immigration case. Since these are new issues not contained in the Terrorism Act 2000, they are set out in a separate Chapter 8. Likewise in a distinct chapter (Chapter 9) are the measures in Parts VI to X, dealing with dangerous substances and acute vulnerabilities. The dangerous substances include weapons of mass destruction (Part VI) and pathogens and toxins (Part VII). The acute vulnerabilities are nuclear and aviation facilities (Parts VIII and IX). The measures bolstering their security also encompass the specialist police forces assigned to their protection (Part X, ss. 98 to 101). Other aspects of Part X (ss. 89 to 97), as well as extracts from Parts XI (ss. 102 to 107) and XIII, are translated in this book into either Chapter 4 (terrorist investigations) or Chapter 5 (counter terrorist powers), since they mainly consist of amendments to Terrorism Act 2000 measures. Next, there are various new criminal offences spread around the Anti-terrorism, Crime and Security Act 2001. Some are in Parts XI and XIII of the Act. More controversial is Part V, concerning religious hatred, which is related in this book within Chapter 6 (criminal offences). Finally, incorporated within Chapter 10 are miscellaneous matters such as the implementation of European Union obligations and structural matters (taken from Parts XIII and XIV of the Act).

The omissions from the 2001 legislation are again significant. Aside from changes during the passage of the Bill, one prominent non-appearance concerns the introduction of identity cards. Their utility had been considered by Lord Lloyd (Inquiry into Legislation against Terrorism (Cm. 3420, London, 1996), para. 16.31) but rejected because foreigners would not have them and because they are too easily forged or stolen. It is alleged that many of the perpetrators of the attacks on 11 September, foreign residents in the United States, had assumed false identities even though passport and travel documents are likely to be much more carefully scrutinised than identity cards. Earlier attempts to introduce such a system (see, for example, National Identity Card Bill 1988–89 HC 16) had also been rejected because the government was not persuaded that it would help to reduce crime. The administrative difficulties of not just issuing cards but in keeping the details up-to-date are also enormous. There are also worries that checks could result in racial harassment (Beck, A., and Broadhurst, K., 'National identity cards' (1998) 8 *Policing & Society* 40). After the attacks in September 2001, the Home Secretary professed himself as minded to introduce identity cards. However, there was never any provision in the Bill — the fear that such a controversial issue would unduly delay the Bill was a major factor, and there was an official announcement on the 8 November 2001 that the idea had been dropped (HC Debs. vol. 374 cols. 387–388w, Angela Eagle):

. . . the Government are considering whether a universal card which allowed people to prove their identity more easily and provided a simple way to access a range of public services would be beneficial. Such an entitlement card scheme could also help to combat illegal working which disproportionately affects the poorer sections of our society by undercutting the minimum wage and encouraging unscrupulous employers. It could also reduce fraud against individuals, public services and the private sector. The Government do not consider that an entitlement card scheme would have a significant effect in combating terrorism in the United Kingdom. The introduction of an entitlement card would be a major step and the Government would not proceed without consulting widely and considering all the views expressed very carefully.

Next, there is no product arising from the indications from the Home Secretary's statement that he was examining additional powers in relation to conspiracy, evidenced through training, providing goods and services or engaging in communications networks with those involved in terrorist activities. However, in evidence to the Home Affairs Committee, the Minister of State said that the conclusion was that the existing laws, including conspiracy to commit terrorist offences in the Criminal Justice (Terrorism and Conspiracy) Act 1998, were sufficient to deal with those situations (Report on the Anti-terrorism, Crime and Security Bill 2001 (2001–02 HC 351), para. 263).

Though changes were made to the laws relating to criminal hoaxes, especially to include the possible use of biological or chemical weapons following the anthrax cases in the United States (see s. 114, as described in Chapter 6), there was no retrospective increase in penalties for existing offences, contrary to some newspaper reports ('Hoaxers face seven years' jail from today', *Sunday Telegraph*, 21 October 2001) and so no apparent breach of Article 7 of the European Convention. This omission was welcomed by the Home Affairs Committee (Report on the Anti-terrorism, Crime and Security Bill 2001 (2001–02 HC 351), para. 64).

Finally, the issue of the criminalisation of mercenary activities emanated from reports that British Muslims had travelled to Afghanistan intending to fight for the Taliban regime. The law on mercenaries is not a blank page, though it is certainly not a page which carries a clear or wholly relevant message. Mercenary activities are regulated by the Foreign Enlistment Act 1870, s. 4, by which:

If any person, without the license of Her Majesty, being a British subject, within or without Her Majesty's dominions, accepts or agrees to accept any commission or engagement in the military or naval service of any foreign state at war with any foreign state at peace with Her Majesty, and in this Act referred to as a friendly state, or whether a British subject or not within Her Majesty's dominions, induces any other person to accept or agree to accept any commission or engagement in the military or naval service of any such foreign state as aforesaid, he shall be guilty of an offence. . .

It is also an offence under s. 5, to induce another to go abroad in order to accept any military commission or engagement. At the same time, the 1870 Act has its shortcomings in the modern age. The definition in section 4 of 'foreign State' includes any foreign prince, colony, province or part of any province or people, or any person or persons exercising or assuming to exercise the powers of government in or over any foreign country, colony, province, or part of any province or people. It does not include non-state groups like Al Qa'ida, and so the question arises as to whether any reforms would be helpful. The issue of private military companies, whether active or passive, was considered recently by the Legg Report (Report of the Sierra Leone Arms Investigation, 1997–98 HC 1016), though it mainly concerned their relationship with government (arising out of the role of Sandline (see http://www.sandline.com/) as a surrogate for British policy in Sierra Leone). Perhaps more relevant was the report on the Sierra Leone affair by the Foreign Affairs Committee (1998–99 HC 116; see also (Diplock) Report of the Committee of Privy Counsellors appointed to inquire into the recruitment of mercenaries (Cmnd. 6569, London, 1976) which pointed to the Foreign Enlistment Act 1870 as an 'antiquated piece of legislation . . . passed on the outbreak of the Franco-Prussian war' (para. 92). Apparently, there has never been a successful prosecution under the Act in connection with illegal enlistment or recruitment. The Report notes (para.93) that there is a UN Convention against the Recruitment, Use, Financing and Training of Mercenaries of 1989 (A/RES/44/34). However, the government regards the definition of 'mercenary' used in the Convention as impossible to use in British courts since it is too vague (for example, a 'mercenary' is one 'motivated to take part in the hostilities essentially by the desire for private gain') (Foreign Office, Private Military Companies: Options for Regulation (2001–02 HC 577), para. 68).

The government has now responded to these concerns by the publication of the a consultation paper, Private Military Companies: Options for Regulation (2001–02 HC 577), the focus of which is commercial military services and their uses and relations with governments and multi-national corporations.

1.4.3 Other anti-terrorism laws

The Terrorism Act 2000 was envisaged as the primary code relating to domestic counter-terrorism powers. In the press release accompanying the giving of Royal Assent, the Home Secretary, Jack Straw, commented that (Home Office Press Release, 21 July 2000):

> This new Act responds to the need for specific powers to combat the wide ranging and evolving threats from terrorism, yet properly ensures that the individual's rights are preserved.

However, the Terrorism Act 2000 was never intended as the only source of legislation against terrorism, nor does it operate in this way even in conjunction with the Anti-terrorism, Crime and Security Act 2001. Many of the offences directly relating to terrorist actions, whether in domestic law, such as the Explosive Substances Act 1883, or in international law, such as the Aviation and Maritime Security Act 1990 (see Wilkinson, P., and Jenkins, B.M., *Aviation Terrorism and*

Security (Frank Cass, London, 1999); Plant, G., 'Legal aspects of terrorism at sea' in Higgins, R., and Flory, M., (eds), *Terrorism and International Law* (Routledge, London, 1997)) remain unincorporated. There is a growing body of international process law. The trial of the Lockerbie suspects in the Netherlands shows the law against international terrorism cannot operate in isolation but may be moderated by the demands of politics and practicalities (see Klip, A., and Mackarel, M., 'The Lockerbie trial' (1999) 70 *Revue Internationale de Droit Penal* 777; Lockerbie Trial Briefing, http://www.ltb.org.uk/; Lockerbie Trial, http://www.thelockerbietrial.com/). The International Criminal Court, founded by the Rome Convention, cannot deal directly with 'terrorism' (see McGoldrick, D., 'The permanent International Criminal Court' [1999] *Criminal Law Review* 627; International Criminal Court Act 2001). The government views it as unsuitable because of difficulties of definition and the production of sensitive evidence (Government Response to the Foreign Affairs Committee, Foreign Policy and Human Rights (Cm. 4299, London, 1999), p. 3). Nevertheless, the deeds of terrorists may fall within admissible heads, such as crimes against humanity. Issues of sentencing are also found elsewhere (especially in the Northern Ireland (Remission of Sentences) Act 1995 and the Northern Ireland (Sentences) Act 1998 and in the practice of the courts in cases such as *R* v *Hindawi* (1988) 10 Cr App R (S) 104). There has been no response to the ideas put forward by Lord Lloyd of a clearer statement of deterrence in terrorist sentences and of the possibility of sentence discount for those who give information (Inquiry into Legislation against Terrorism (Cm. 3420, London, 1996) ch.15). Next, the laws relating to the use of force, especially lethal force, remain unchanged for the present, despite concerns from the European Court of Human Rights (*McCann, Savage and Farrell* v *United Kingdom*, App. no. 18984/91, Ser. A. vol. 324, (1996) 21 EHRR 97), but may face some reform whenever the Bloody Sunday Inquiry (http://www.bloody-Sunday-inquiry.org.uk/) produces its report (see also Ni Aolain, F., *The Politics of Force* (Blackstaff, Belfast, 2000); Walsh, D., *Bloody Sunday and the Rule of Law in Northern Ireland* (Gill & MacMillan, Dublin, 2000)). In addition, plans were afoot even at the time of passage of the Terrorism Act 2000 to strengthen counter-terrorism laws. For example, there were proposals to improve extradition procedures, especially in the context of western Europe (see Home Office, The Law on Extradition: A Review, London, 2001). These ideas were raised again at the time of the Anti-terrorism, Crime and Security Act 2001 (HC Debs. vol. 372 col. 675, 4 October 2001, Tony Blair), but again were not included, save that they may be implemented by order under s. 111 if agreed at a European level. Another Home Office paper, Animal Rights Extremism: A strategy document (London, 2001) promised further reforms to deal with tactics designed to intimidate the officers and employees of companies or units (such as at universities) involved in research which harms animals. These measures duly appeared in the Criminal Justice and Police Act 2001. By s. 42, the police are given broad powers to direct protestors (or perhaps journalists — see Hickman, L., 'Press freedom and new legislation' (2001) 151 *New Law Journal* 716) away from the residence of another where it is reasonably believed that the presence of the protestors amounts to harassment or is likely to cause alarm or distress. In this way, there is a summary police power to go alongside the more formal process of obtaining a court order under the Protection from Harassment Act 1997. Next, s. 45 allows for 'confidentiality orders' to be issued by the Secretary of State (for Trade and Industry) under an amendment to the Companies Act 1985. By an inserted s. 72B, the normal access to information about the addresses of directors and secretaries of companies on companies registers can be forbidden where the Secretary of State is satisfied that there is a serious risk that the officer will be subjected to violence or intimidation. In addition to these legal changes, there has been a reorganisation of policing of animal rights extremists by the setting up of a new unit in the National Crime Squad (*The Times*, 27 April 2001, p. 2).

1.5 CONCLUSIONS

None of the major political parties in Parliament opposed the passage of the Terrorism Act 2000 in principle, so the debates were rather low key and very few significant amendments were made. The Act received the Royal Assent on the 20 July 2000 and came into force on the 19 February 2001. It was further implemented by the Home Office, Circular 03/01: Terrorism Act 2000 (Home Office, London, 2001). By s. 2(1) it wholly replaces the Prevention of Terrorism (Temporary Provisions) Act 1989 and most of the Northern Ireland (Emergency Provisions) Act 1996 (see further Chapter 7) and so forms a permanent monument to the fragmented risk of terrorism in the late modern, globalised world.

By contrast, the Anti-terrorism, Crime and Security Bill produced some well-publicised debates, and some of its contents had to be dropped to secure an early passage through Parliament despite the handicap of severe time restraints on debate (see HC Debs. vol. 375 col. 121, 19 November 2001; vol. 376 col. 841, 12 December 2001). But it was again not opposed in principle, and the legislative process took just four weeks, so the extent of Parliamentary and public scrutiny should not be exaggerated.

It would be a fine development if, having been fortified with these sweeping powers, the United Kingdom Government and its security forces could have the confidence and ability to rely primarily on 'normal' policing powers and upon its extensive contingency planning and networks (see Civil Contingencies Committee and Secretariat, http://www.co-ordination.gov.uk/terrorism.htm). However, as they perceive themselves to live in threatening and troubled times, the legislation can probably look forward to a long and active life. Attention will now be turned towards its contents.

Chapter Two
Proscribed organisations

2.1 PROSCRIPTION IN GENERAL

Participation in terrorist organisations was an offence both in Britain, under s. 2 of the Prevention of Terrorism (Temporary Provisions) Act 1989, and in Northern Ireland under s. 28 of the Northern Ireland (Emergency Provisions) Act 1996. Organisations, which had to relate to terrorism concerned with Northern Ireland, became proscribed by listing in the primary legislation itself or by statutory order made by a Secretary of State. In essence, this system remains intact in Part II of the Terrorism Act 2000, but the legislation builds upon the existing features by allowing for non-Irish categories of groups to be added and by providing for a form of non-executive review of orders. It also combines the two sources together, with the effect of extending substantially the range of Northern Ireland groups proscribed in Britain. It may be noted that under s. 121, the interpretation of 'organisation' is that it includes any association or combination of persons, a phrase wide enough to encompass an affinity group or even an anarchistic 'disorganisation'.

2.2 PROSCRIBED GROUPS — IRISH AND OTHER DOMESTIC

In terms of groups covered, proscribed organisations under the previous legislation were exclusively Northern Ireland related. There were complaints that the process of selection of groups proscribed within that field betrayed political bias, especially in Northern Ireland with the failure to proscribe Sinn Féin (which was deproscribed in 1975) or the Ulster Defence Association, numerically the largest paramilitary group in Northern Ireland (which was eventually proscribed in 1992). No Loyalist group had ever been proscribed in Britain, but several Loyalists have convictions for fund-raising or gun-running, mainly in Scotland (*Hamilton* v *HM Advocate* 1980 SC 66; *Sayers* v *HM Advocate* 1982 JC 17; *HM Advocate* v *Copeland* 1987 SCCR 232; *Forbes* v *HM Advocate* 1990 SC (JC) 215; *Reid* v *HM Advocate* 1990 SCCR 83).

The new powers to proscribe in s. 3(3) (which operate by reference to the wider definitions in s. 1) first target Irish paramilitaries (see the Bibliography for further reading on these groups). The following are listed in sch. 2. The descriptions in the right-hand column are those of the author and are largely not contained within the schedule itself.

The Irish Republican Army	The leading Republican paramilitary group which has existed in one guise or another since 1919. The title appearing in sch. 2 is considered sufficient to cover the Provisional IRA (formed in 1970), the Official IRA (the residual group), the Real IRA (which emerged as a dissident faction opposed to the Peace Process in 1997) and the Continuity IRA (see below). Under s. 3(1)(b), an organisation is proscribed if it operates under the same name as an organisation listed in that schedule.
Cumann na mBan (Union of Women)	The Irish nationalist women's organisation was founded in 1914, and is now seen as an auxiliary section of the Provisional IRA.
Fianna na hÉireann (Warriors of Ireland)	The auxiliary youth section of the Provisional IRA (founded originally in 1909).
The Red Hand Commando	A Loyalist group formed in 1972 and linked to the Ulster Volunteer Force (below).
Saor Éire (Free Ireland)	A group founded originally in 1931 as the 'Revolutionary Workers' Party'; the name has been used occasionally since that time by various Republican factions.
The Ulster Freedom Fighters	The Loyalist UFF emerged from the Ulster Defence Association (below) in the early 1970s, often as a cover-name rather than a distinct grouping.
The Ulster Volunteer Force	The Loyalist UVF was formed initially in 1912 but was reconstituted in 1966.
The Irish National Liberation Army	The INLA emerged in 1974, mainly from ex-Official IRA activists.
The Irish People's Liberation Organisation	This name has been used by dissident INLA members from time to time.

The Ulster Defence Association	A loyalist paramilitary organisation, the UDA was created in 1971 as a militant mass movement to support Unionism and to some extent has operated as an umbrella organisation.
The Loyalist Volunteer Force	The LVF was formed in 1996 out of the mid-Ulster Ulster Volunteer Force (UVF) unit.
The Continuity Army Council	A splinter group formed in 1994 as the armed wing of Republican Sinn Fein (RSF), formed after the Provisional IRA announced a cease-fire. It also spawned the Continuity IRA.
The Orange Volunteers	Several Loyalist groups have used this name since the early 1970s, most recently in 1998.
The Red Hand Defenders	A Loyalist paramilitary group which began to operate in 1998, formed from dissident members of other paramilitary groups who oppose the Peace Process.

The groups listed above were all proscribed by the predecessor legislation, but the Terrorism Act 2000 brings about a substantial extension in one respect, namely, that prior to the Act, only the IRA and INLA were proscribed in Britain. It follows that all the other Irish groups are now proscribed in Britain for the first time. It was admitted during debates on the 2000 Act that some of the foregoing are at any one time more or less dormant but that it was felt necessary to continue proscription so as to deny the use of a potent title to dissidents (HC Debs. Standing Committee D, col. 76, 25 January 2000, Adam Ingram).

It was announced during the passage of the Bill that there are no plans to proscribe any (non-Irish) domestic groups (HC Debs. vol. 341 col. 227, 14 December 1999, Charles Clarke). Animal rights and environmental militants were thought by some critics of the legislation to be possible candidates for proscription (Gearty, C., 'Terrorism and human rights' (1999) 19 *Legal Studies* 366 at p. 370), but they do not in the main possess the sophistication, threat or strength to warrant proscription. Even those said to be linked to Islamic extremism have escaped this treatment (one candidate is said to be the Supporters of Sharia: *The Times*, 14 September 2001, p. 14).

2.3 PROSCRIBED GROUPS — FOREIGN

Unlike its predecessors, s. 3 can also apply to other domestic and to foreign groups. This change offers an opening not just for policing activity but also for added diplomatic responses. The United Kingdom has experienced a long history of pressure from foreign governments to take action against émigré groups. London is a natural magnate for foreign groups because of trade links, the concentration of media outlets and also a large student population. That pressure has been resisted, most notably in the nineteenth century when constant calls from the Russian secret police fell on deaf ears. Nevertheless, the United Kingdom Government rightly made an important concession to these demands in the shape of the Suppression of Terrorism Act 1978 which was based on the European Convention on the Suppression of Terrorism 1977 (ETS no. 90; see: Lowe, V., and Young, J., 'Suppressing terrorism under the European Convention' (1978) 25 *Netherlands International Law Review* 305). The latter especially provides for offences which are to be viewed as non-political *per se* and seeks to avoid judgments about the normative circumstances surrounding the commission of the act. The increased co-operation between Western European States, despite its shortcomings, has affected relationships elsewhere. Thus, extradition treaties between United Kingdom and both India and the United States have been amended along similar lines (see Suppression of Terrorism Act 1978 (Application of Provisions) (India) Order 1993 (SI 1993 No. 2533); Supplementary Treaty (1985) (Cmnd. 9862, London, 1986); USA (Extradition) (Amendment) Order 1986 (SI 1986 No. 2020)).

More recently, a range of foreign powers (Algeria, Egypt, France, India, Saudi Arabia and Tunisia amongst others) have lobbied to secure the curtailment of the political opposition by their nationals who are exiled in the United Kingdom (see *The Guardian*, 20 November 1997, p. 19; 26 August 1998, p. 3). Other factors at play have included a continuation of the general policy of combating all manifestations of terrorism, a policy which has been expressed at G8 summits in Birmingham and London during the UK's Presidency of the organisation (see Home Office Press Release 485/98, 8 December 1998) and had been signalled by, *inter alia*, support for United Nations General Assembly Resolution 51/210 on Measures to Eliminate International Terrorism of 17 December 1996 (Annex), which confirms that asylum-seekers must not be allowed to engage in terrorism. There was next some fright taken at developing case-law which suggested that while claims of terrorists to asylum could be rejected (*T v Secretary of State for the Home Department* [1996] AC 742), it might not be possible thereafter simply to deport the trouble-makers because of fears of persecution contrary to Article 3 in the receiving state (*Chahal v United Kingdom*, App. no. 22414/93, 1996-V, (1997) 23 EHRR 413, disagreeing with the Court of Appeal's view in *R v Secretary of State for the Home Department, ex parte Chahal* [1995] 1 WLR 526 which was that the Home Secretary had sufficient assurances as to future treatment of a Sikh nationalist from the Indian Government). So, the criminal law would have to be extended to curtail the activities of these unwelcome guests. The results of these developments were evidenced first by the Criminal Justice (Terrorism and Conspiracy) Act 1998, under which United Kingdom courts were given jurisdiction over acts of conspiracy and incitement in the United Kingdom relating to offences committed or intended to be committed abroad (see further Chapter 6). This part of the 1998 Act excited significant opposition because of the perceived undue curtailment of the activities of foreign dissidents who were seeking to overthrow repressive and undemocratic governments. The most frequent example given was of Nelson Mandela, who condoned acts of political violence against official property. But the Act was passed in emergency circumstances following the Omagh bombing in August 1998, and time did allow for the separation of these provisions from those directed against the Republican dissidents thought to be responsible for the bombing. Even these restraints on foreign extremists were not considered sufficient at the time of the Anti-terrorism, Crime and Security Act 2001, and therefore Part IV allows for their indefinite detention (see Chapter 8).

After the 1998 Act came into force, there were heightened police activities against Islamic fundamentalist groups. In September 1998, there were a number of arrests (though not under the Prevention of Terrorism (Temporary Provisions) Act 1989) of members of Al Qa'ida (see below). Khalid al Fawwaz, Ibrahim Eidarou and Adel Abdel Bary were charged with conspiracy to murder US citizens between 1993 and 1998, culminating in the bombing of the US embassies in East Africa. They are now awaiting extradition (*Al Fawwaz* v *Governor of Brixton Prison* [2001] 1 WLR 1234, 2 WLR 101). Some of the activities occurred through the 'Advice and Reform Committee' based in London. In January 1999, a number of British citizens were arrested in connection with alleged terrorist activities in Yemen and were alleged to be linked to a group based in Britain, the Supporters of Shariah, headed by Abu Hamza al Masri (*The Times*, 12 January 1999, p. 1; 16 January 1999, p. 5; 28 January 1999, p. 1; 10 August 1999, p. 1). The Yemeni authorities asked for his extradition, and he was briefly arrested but released without charge. The heightened profile of anti-terrorist legislation was also illustrated by the arrest under the 1989 Act of 77 Kurdish protesters, who occupied the Greek embassy in February 1999 after the capture of the leader of the PKK (see below), Abdullah Oçalan (*The Times*, 19 February 1999, p. 1). Next, Shafiq Ur Rehman became the first case to be heard under the Special Immigration Appeals Commission Act 1997 after the issuance of a deportation order relating to his alleged involvement with Lashkar e Tayyaba through the recruitment for training of British citizens and the raising of funds (*The Times*, 17 August 1999, p. 3). On appeal it was accepted that the process was proper and that the security interests of the United Kingdom could be affected by a threat to Pakistan (*Secretary of State for the Home Department* v *Rehman* [2001] 3 WLR 877). Finally, a number of prosecutions (which ultimately collapsed) for offences relating to terrorist preparations began against four Algerians (though their arrests arose in May 1997 and May 1998 and therefore well before the 1998 Act) (*R* v *Director of Public Prosecutions, ex parte Kebilene, The Times*, 31 March 1999; [1999] 3 WLR 972; *The Times*, 21 March 2000).

The joint Home Office-Northern Ireland Office consultation paper, *Legislation against Terrorism*, floated the notion that that proscription might be extended to all forms of terrorism, wherever based (para. 4.14), despite the obvious difficulties of keeping the list up-to-date and dangers of being seen to take sides in all manner of foreign disputes (para. 4.16). It would also embroil the police in foreign political issues arising often from speech which by definition in the context of a communication to intended perpetrators abroad hardly creates an immediate risk of unlawful serious violence. To take a commonly cited example, if the Terrorism Act 2000 had been in force a decade or so ago, 'Would the ANC have been deemed to be a terrorist organisation because of its obvious links with the struggle that Umkhonto we Sizwe was waging within South Africa?' (HC Debs. vol. 341 col. 194, 14 December 1999, Jeremy Corbyn).

Despite these concerns, the next step in the government campaign against foreign political dissidents based in the United Kingdom is the Terrorism Act 2000, Part II. The proscription powers can apply to foreign groups concerned in terrorism, and an early opportunity has been taken to activate this power. By the Terrorism Act 2000 (Proscribed Organisations) (Amendment) Order 2001 (SI 2001 No. 1261), which came into force on the 29 March 2001, the following 21 organisations are added to sch. 2 to the Terrorism Act 2000 (the descriptions in the right-hand column are those of the author and are not contained within the statutory instrument itself, but a fuller Home Office description was provided by a Press Release, dated the 28 February 2001 (also available through its web-site, http:// www.homeoffice.gov.uk); there are also some relevant commentaries in the Bibliography to this book):

Al-Qa'ida (The Base)	Its aim is to unite all Muslims and to establish a government which follows the rule of the Caliphs. It seeks to overthrow nearly all Arab governments and to eliminate Western influence. Usama bin Ladin, a multi-millionaire Saudi financier, is said to be a principal source of funding and direction. It is the group said to be responsible for the East African embassy bombings in 1998 and the 11 September 2001 attacks. The group has not made any attacks in the UK, and there is no overt representation in the UK. See http://www.ict.org.il/inter_ter/ orgdet.cfm?orgid = 74.
Egyptian Islamic Jihad (EIJ)	The group has existed since the 1973 and concentrates on armed attacks against Egyptian Government officials but also is alleged to have bombed the US Embassies in Dar es Salaam and Nairobi in August 1998. The group has not made any attacks in the UK, and there is no overt representation in the UK.

Al-Gama'at al-Islamiya (GI)	The Egyptian Islamic Group (GI) has been active since the late 1970s when it split from the EIJ. It seeks to overthrow the existing government by armed attacks against Egyptian security and other government officials, as well as Western targets such as tourists in Egypt (58, including six British citizens, were killed in Luxor in 1997). The group has not made any attacks in the UK, and there is no overt representation in the UK.
Armed Islamic Group (Groupe Islamique Armée) (GIA)	It seeks to overthrow the Algerian regime and replace it with an Islamic state. The GIA began its violent activities in early 1992 after the government prevented the electoral victory of the Islamic Salvation Front (FIS). The group has no overt representation here, but its UK members have allegedly provided logistical support.
Salafist Group for Call and Combat (Groupe Salafiste pour la Prédication et le Combat) (GSPC)	The group (also called the Hassan Hattab faction) emerged from the GIA in 1998, and aims to create an Islamic state in Algeria. The group has no overt representation here, but its UK members have allegedly provided logistical support.
Babbar Khalsa (BK)	The group fights for the liberation of Khalistan, the Sikh homeland in Punjab Province, which declared its independence in 1987. Attacks in India are mounted against Indian officials and facilities, as well as civilians. BK is alleged to use the UK as a base for fundraising, recruitment and co-ordination.
International Sikh Youth Federation (ISYF)	Also involved in the Khalistan conflict and drawing support from overseas Sikh communities, ISYF support is claimed to be spread across the UK.

Harakat ul Mujahideen (HK)	A militant group based in Pakistan and operating primarily in Kashmir, formed in 1993 (as Harakat ul-Ansar). Its prime goal is to oppose Indian security forces, but it has also attacked civilians and Western tourists. It is claimed that HK has supporters in several areas of the UK. See http://www. harkatulmujahideen.org/ and http://www. ummah.net.pk/harkat/.
Jaish e Mohammed (JeM)	The 'Army of Mohammed' is an Islamist group based in Pakistan and mainly concerned with attacks in Kashmir. It is claimed that JeM has supporters in the UK.
Lashkar e Tayyaba (LT)	A further Pakistani-based group (the 'Army of the Righteous') supporting the liberation of Kashmir from India. The political group associated is Markaz Dawa al Rishad, which is alleged to have a presence in the UK. See http://www.markazdawa.org/.
Liberation Tigers of Tamil Eelam (LTTE)	The LTTE was founded in 1972 and has become the most powerful group in Sri Lanka fighting for a distinct Tamil state. Armed conflict began in 1983 and has involved the occupation of territory in the north of Sri Lanka as well as attacks elsewhere. The LTTE's International Secretariat is based in the UK, and the UK is also alleged to be a source of funds for the LTTE. The LTTE declared a cease-fire in December 2001. See http://eelam.com/.

Hizbollah External Security Organisation (HESO)	Hizbollah (The Party of God) is the Lebanese-based Islamic movement founded after the Israeli military seizure of Lebanon in 1982. It seeks the creation of Iranian-style Islamic republic in Lebanon and removal of all Israeli and Western influences in the area, including by kidnappings and suicide bombs. There is said to be a small, overt Hizballah presence in the UK with extensive links to Hizballah's Foreign Relations Department (FRD), and also occasional External Security Organisation (ESO) terrorist-related activity in the UK. See http://www.hizballah.org/.
Hamas-Izz al-Din al-Qassem Brigades (HIDQ)	Various groupings emerged in the late 1980s to pursue the goal of establishing an Islamic Palestinian state in place of Israel. The related Izz el-Din al-Qassam (IDQ) Brigades have conducted many attacks against Israeli civilian and military targets. Hamas IDQ has no overt representation in the UK, but Hamas's political wing is represented by charitable organisations.
Palestinian Islamic Jihad — Shaqaqi (PIJ)	A variety of Shi'a groups formed in the 1970s and based in the Gaza Strip committed to the creation of an Islamic Palestinian state and the destruction of Israel. Like HESO, it is pro-Iranian. There is no overt representation in the UK, but it is alleged that there are some supporters.
Abu Nidal Organisation (ANO)	This Palestinian group formed out of the PLO in 1974, has operated against Israeli and Western targets since that time. Titles used by the group, which is mainly based in Lebanon and Libya, include the Fatah Revolutionary Council and Black September. There are admitted to be no known active supporters in the UK.
Islamic Army of Aden (IAA)	The group has been involved in acts of violence to fight secularism in Yemen and other Arab countries. This has involved the formation of the Aden-Abyan Islamic Army and attacks on Western tourists. There is no overt representation in the UK, but it is alleged that there are some supporters.

Mujahedin e Khalq (MeK)	This group, founded in 1965 and exiled in 1981, has become the largest and most active armed Iranian dissident group. It is also known as the People's Mujahedin of Iran (PMOI) and includes the National Liberation Army of Iran (NLA, the militant wing of the MEK) and the Muslim Iranian Student's Society (a front organisation used to garner financial support). The MeK has not attacked UK or Western interests. There is no acknowledged MeK presence in the UK, aside from its publication, *MOJAHED*. See http://www.iran-e-azad.org/english/; http://www.iran-e-azad.org/english/nla.html.
Kurdistan Workers' Party (Partiya Karkeren Kurdistan) (PKK)	The PKK was founded in 1974 and seeks an independent Kurdish state in south-eastern Turkey. It engaged in armed attacks from 1984 until after the capture of its leader, Abdullah Oçalan, following which a ceasefire was called for 1 September 1999. The PKK does not have any overt representation in the UK but undoubtedly has some support amongst Kurdish communities. See (in Turkish) http://www.pkk.org/ or (in English) http://burn.ucsd.edu/~ats/PKK/pkk.html.
Revolutionary Peoples' Liberation Party — Front (Devrimci Halk Kurtulus Partisi-Cephesi) (DHKP-C)	This Marxist Turkish group has origins going back to the 1970s. Its operations have been mainly confined to Turkish targets in Turkey. DHKP-C had an office in London which was engaged in overt political activity. See http://www.ozgurluk.org/dhkc/.
Basque Homeland and Liberty (Euskadi ta Askatasuna) (ETA)	The group was founded in 1959 to fight for an independent homeland principally in Spain's Basque region. ETA has no overt representation in the UK, although there may be present some sympathisers, including links through Irish Republican paramilitaries. See http://www.contrast.org/mirrors/ehj/html/freta.html.

17 November Revolutionary Organisation (N17)	A radical leftist group established in 1975 in Greece and opposing the Greek government and Western interests, especially those related to the US and NATO. In June 2000, N17 murdered Brigadier Stephen Saunders, the British Defence Attaché in Athens, but it has never operated in the UK.

The factors which shaped this list were enumerated by Lord Bassam in debates on the Bill (HL Debs. vol. 613 col. 252, 16 May 2000):

First, we would have to consider carefully the nature and scale of the group's activities; secondly, we would have to look at the specific threat that it posed to the United Kingdom and our citizens abroad, which is clearly a very important consideration, as well as the extent of its presence in this country. Indeed, the noble Lord drew our attention to one group which may, or may not, fall into that category. Thirdly, we would also have to consider our responsibility to support other members of the international community in the global fight against terrorism.

These factors were tabulated as follows in the Home Office press release of the 28 February 2001 which accompanied the listing above:

(a)   The nature and scale of an organisation's activities.
(b)   The specific threat that it poses to the United Kingdom.
(c)   The specific threat that it poses to British nationals overseas.
(d)   The extent of the organisation's presence in the United Kingdom.
(e)   The need to support other members of the international community in the global fight against terrorism.

The last factor allows a very wide range of action, and it is officially sanctioned by the UN Convention for the Suppression of Terrorist Bombings (A/RES/52/164, Cm. 4662, London, 1997) which demands under Article 15 that States take all practicable measures, including, if necessary, adapting their domestic legislation, prevent and counter preparations in their respective territories for the commission of those offences within or outside their territories, including measures to prohibit in their territories illegal activities of persons, groups and organisations that encourage, instigate, organise, knowingly finance or engage in the perpetration of specified terrorist offences.

By and large, it is acceptable to apply proscription in order to assist with serious offences committed in the course of campaigns against the United Kingdom's close allies in Europe and North America. Those States can be relied upon to be Liberal and democratic, and therefore terrorism is not a legitimate form of political opposition. This internationalisation is a trend both in anti-terrorism laws and also in asylum and immigration policy. For example, in *Secretary of State for the Home Department* v *Rehman* [2000] 3 WLR 1240; [2001] 3 WLR 877, the threat posed to Pakistan by a person with links to Lashkar e Tayyaba was sufficient to justify the refusal of a deportation order, without evidence of a direct threat to the security of the United Kingdom (compare *R* v *Secretary of State for the Home Department, ex parte Chahal* [1995] 1 WLR 526 at p. 531). Failure to react to terrorism also encourages strong States to engage in unilateral action, such as kidnapping, hijacking, or surrogate bombing, which can cause grave disruption in the international community. But the creeping abolition of the political offence exception runs the danger of ignoring individual human rights restraints which should apply to the treatment of criminal suspects and the right of peoples to self-determination or at least resistance to oppression. While any justification of the use of violence for political ends may be said to be 'specious' in regard to its use against the United Kingdom, French, US or Greek governments (Paul Wilkinson in Inquiry into Legislation against Terrorism (Cm. 3420, London, 1996) vol. II p. 4), do we necessarily say the same is true in regard to governments such as Iran, Iraq or North Korea which the President of the United States accuses of being part of an 'axis of evil' (http://www.whitehouse.gov/news/releases/2002/01/20020129-11. html, 2001)?

On a more practical level, one wonders whether the United Kingdom Government will look faintly ridiculous if it attempts to turn itself into the world's arbiter between 'terrorist' and 'freedom fighter'. It will also be difficult to keep the list up-to-date given the fluidity of such groups, and it would mean taking sides in all manner of foreign disputes, which is why the idea was doubted by the *Inquiry into Legislation against Terrorism* (Cm. 3240, London, 1996, para. 4.16). Examples of groups which have not been proscribed but which seem to fit the foregoing criteria include:

(a)   The Abu Sayyaf Group (ASG) is an Islamic extremist group operating in the southern Philippines which has engaged in kidnappings, including of Western tourists, in its efforts to promote an Iranian-style Islamic state in Mindanao.

(b)   The Revolutionary Armed Forces of Colombia (FARC), which was formed in 1964 as the military wing of the Colombian Communist Party. It has occupied a demilitarized zone, but its activities include guerrilla and conventional military action against Colombian political, military, and economic targets. It was alleged in 2001 that it has formed links with the Provisional IRA, following the charges brought against representatives of the latter in Bogota (*The Times*, 18 February 2002, p. 6).

The foregoing are designated as foreign terrorist groups by the US Government under the Antiterrorism and Effective Death Penalty Act 1996 (Pub L No. 104–132, 110 Stat. 1214, 8 USC s. 1181). One hopes that the United Kingdom Government will always require strong evidence (under criteria (b) and (d) of the Home Office press release cited above) of criminal activity within the

United Kingdom (including of universal offences) before making any order. To act otherwise will leave any order, and especially any form of criminal prosecution based on an order, open to challenge under Articles 10 and 11 of the European Convention. Especially in the case of dissidents who are exiles and unable to return to their homeland without a strong fear of persecution, they may have no other outlet for their political rights. However, the proscription orders have not been confined to groups active in the United Kingdom. For example, in regard to Al Qa'ida, it is accepted by the Home Office that the group has not made any attacks; some individuals from the United Kingdom have trained with Al Qa'ida in camps in Afghanistan but there is no overt representation here. The EIJ, GI, HIDQ, LT, JeM and PIJ have local members, though there is no overt representation and they have not attacked local targets directly nor even is there any allegation of fund-raising or planning activities.

It will be interesting to see how international political machinations shape the working of the legislation. Will an 'ethical' foreign policy (see HL Debs. vol. 580 col. 129, 15 May 1997, Baroness Symons) demand priority for the rantings of foreign dissidents or will healthy trade relations and smooth diplomacy carry the day?

2.4   PROSCRIPTION — MECHANISMS AND PROCEDURES

2.4.1   The Proscribed Organisations Appeal Commission

The Terrorism Act 2000 remains steadfastly executive in terms of the activation of proscription. By s. 3(3), the Secretary of State may by order (a) add an organisation to sch. 2; (b) remove an organisation from that schedule; (c) amend that schedule in some other way (such as in relation to notes within it which may be used to explain or qualify the effects of proscription — this is done in relation to the 'Orange Volunteers', and one possibility in the distant future might involve disapplying proscription to some variants of the 'Irish Republican Army' but not to others). Furthermore, the criteria remain subjectively worded — by s. 3(4) orders can be made against a group if 'he believes that it is concerned in terrorism', a belief which may be derived under s. 3(5) if an organisation (a) commits or participates in acts of terrorism, (b) prepares for terrorism, (c) promotes or encourages terrorism, or (d) is otherwise concerned in terrorism. Once an order has been made, there is no requirement that it be reviewed or renewed from time to time by the Secretary of State, though the Government has given the reassurance that proscribed organisations are kept under perpetual review: 'We do not put their names in a filing cabinet and forget about them' (HC Standing Committee D, col. 65, 18 January 2000, Charles Clarke).

While the Home Secretary of Northern Ireland retains the whip-hand, concern for the rights of those subjected to orders has resulted in two new procedures which, for the first time, expressly allow for challenges to orders. One envisages an application to the Secretary of State for the setting aside of an order. If there is a refusal, the second is an application for review by the Proscribed Organisations

Appeal Commission (POAC). Note that there is no possibility of direct application to POAC — the government wishes to consider the matter first and also to save possible expense (HL Debs. vol. 613 col. 262, 16 May 2000, Lord Bassam). As well as contesting an order for proscription when it is first made, the procedures may also be used to challenge the continuing viability of an order (HL Debs. vol. 613 col. 261, 16 May 2000, Lord Bassam):

> If a person thinks that an organisation is wrongly proscribed, the first step is to apply, as is understood, for deproscription. He may be able to present new information that was not available when the initial decision was taken, or he may have information which shows that an organisation which was at one time concerned in terrorism and was properly proscribed is no longer concerned in terrorism and should consequently be deproscribed.

Applications to the Secretary of State for deproscription arise under s. 4(1). An application may be made to the Secretary of State for the exercise of his power under s. 3(3)(b) to remove an organisation from sch. 2. The applicant may be either the proscribed organisation or any person affected by the proscription order. The phrase, 'person affected', appears in several other statutes. It was interpreted recently in *R* v *Broadcasting Standards Commission, ex parte British Broadcasting Corporation* [2000] 3 WLR 1327 to allow a complaint about an unwarranted infringement of the privacy of a body corporate on its own behalf to its employees being secretly filmed without cause contrary to the Broadcasting Act 1996, s. 110. This suggests that one group member may bring an action under s. 4 even if others (such as leaders) are more drastically affected. Likewise an action may be brought based on the impact on the group as an entity. This seems to follow from the case of *R* v *Broadcasting Complaints Commission, ex parte Owen* [1985] 1 QB 1153, in which the Leader of the Social Democratic Party complained in that capacity under s. 54 of the Broadcasting Act 1981 to the Broadcasting Complaints Commission that the party had received a disproportionately small amount of coverage and publicity from 13 February to 20 April 1984, having regard to the comparable number of votes received by the parties in the General Election of 1983 and subsequent by-elections.

Regulations relating to these proceedings shall be made under s. 4(3) and (4) and must include the giving of reasons. The Proscribed Organisations (Applications for Deproscription) Regulations 2001 (SI 2001 No. 107) allow for an application to be made in writing and with a statement of the grounds at any time after the organisation in question has been proscribed (reg. 3). Where the application is being made by the organisation, the application must also state under reg. 4(a) the name and address of the person submitting the application; and reg. 4(b) the position which he holds in the organisation or his authority to act on behalf of the organisation, and must be signed by him. Where the application is made by a person affected by the organisation's proscription, the application must be signed and must also state, under reg. 5(a) the manner in which the applicant is so

University of Ulster LIBRARY

affected; and by reg. 5(b), the applicant's name and address, and must be signed by him. By reg. 8, the Secretary of State shall determine an application within a period of 90 days from (but excluding) the day on which he receives the application. Where the Secretary of State refuses an application, he shall under reg. 9 immediately in writing inform the applicant of his refusal and notify the applicant of the procedures for appealing against the refusal to the POAC.

Where an application under s. 4 has been refused, the applicant may appeal to the POAC, set up under s. 5 and modelled on the Special Immigration Appeals Commission (see Special Immigration Appeals Commission Act 1997). This mechanism was suggested by the Lloyd Report (Inquiry into Legislation against Terrorism (Cm. 3420, London, 1996), para. 13.32). By s. 5(3), the POAC shall allow an appeal against a refusal to deproscribe an organisation if it considers that the decision to refuse was flawed when considered in the light of the principles applicable on an application for judicial review (possibly most authoritatively stated in *Council of Civil Service Unions* v *Minister for the Civil Service* [1985] AC 374). Where an order is made in favour of an applicant, the Secretary of State shall as soon as is reasonably practicable (a) lay before Parliament the draft of an order under s. 3(3)(b) removing the organisation from the list in sch. 2, or (b) make an order removing the organisation from the list in that schedule.

The constitution and procedures of the POAC are set out in sch. 3 and in statutory instrument. By sch. 3, para. 1, appointments to POAC, including that of the chairman, shall be made by the Lord Chancellor. Given that members 'shall hold and vacate office in accordance with the terms of his appointment', there is a distinct lack of statutory independence which may compromise the ability of the POAC to satisfy the requirements of Article 6 of the European Convention (the courts may consider the availability of judicial review sufficient to remedy any defect; compare, where there was an inevitable mixture of policy and judicial decision-making, *R (on the application of Alconbury Developments Ltd)* v *Secretary of State for the Environment, Transport and the Regions* [2001] 2 WLR 1389). Most other terms and conditions, including pay (para. 3) and sittings (para. 4), are also at the behest of the Lord Chancellor, though it is specified that each POAC panel must be three strong and must include at least one person who holds or has held high judicial office (within the meaning of the Appellate Jurisdiction Act 1876). Three judicial members have been appointed, all retired judges: Sir Murray Stuart Smith (chairman), Sir Harry Ognall and Sir Brian Smedley. There are also ten lay and other legal members. It is expected under para. 5 that the Lord Chancellor shall make rules regulating details of the appeal process, including by providing for proceedings before the Commission to be determined without an oral hearing in specified circumstances, for determining the burden of proof and admissibility of evidence, and for securing that information is not disclosed contrary to the public interest. Though legal representation is to be allowed, the procedural rules may provide for full particulars of the reasons for proscription or refusal to deproscribe to be withheld from the organisation or applicant concerned and from any person representing it or him or even to enable the Commission to exclude persons (including representatives) from all or part of proceedings. Where proceedings are brought by an organisation before the POAC, it may designate an individual to conduct those proceedings under para. 6, so as to avoid rival factions possibly duplicating or confusing the proceedings. In addition, under para. 7 and based on the Special Immigration Appeals Commission Act 1997, the relevant law officer may appoint a lawyer — a 'special advocate' — to represent the interests of an organisation or other applicant; such a lawyer is not to be responsible to the organisation or other applicant whose interests he is appointed to represent. By the Regulation of Investigatory Powers Act 2000, the Terrorism Act 2000 is amended in order to bring its procedures in line with the procedures under that Act. Surreptitious electronic surveillance is likely to be an important source of evidence in relation to proscription, and it can exceptionally be led before the POAC according to the Regulation of Investigatory Powers Act 2000, s. 18 (replacing rules in sch. 3 para. 8), but must still not be disclosed to the applicant, the organisation concerned (if different) or any representative of them.

Further details are provided by the Proscribed Organisations Appeal Commission (Procedure) Rules 2001 (SI 2001 No. 443). Aside from mundane details, such as delegation, methods of communication, forms of documents and notices, consolidation of appeals and procedural directions, r. 3 of the 2001 Rules reminds the POAC of its duty not to disclose information contrary to the public interest, and also requires under r. 7 an appeal to be made within 42 days. Rule 10 deals with the special advocate, whose function is to represent the interests of the appellant by representing the appellant in any proceedings from which the appellant and his representative are excluded. The POAC can regulate contacts between the special advocate and the appellant. Whatever is withheld from the appellant and his legal representative, the POAC will be provided by the Secretary of State with a summary of the facts relating to the decision being appealed and the reasons for that decision, the grounds on which he opposes the appeal, a statement of the evidence which he relies upon in support of those grounds, and an identification of any such evidence or other material disclosure of which would be unauthorised by virtue of s. 18(2)(b) of the Regulation of Investigatory Powers Act 2000. Where the Secretary of State objects to material being disclosed to the appellant or his representative, he must also (a) state the reasons for his objection; and (b) if and to the extent it is possible to do so without making a disclosure which is unauthorised by virtue of s. 18(2)(b) of the 2000 Act or which is contrary to the public interest, provide a statement of that material in a form which can be shown to the appellant; he must in any event make available to the special advocate, as soon as it is practicable to do so, the material which he has provided to the POAC. The consideration of the Secretary of State's objection to disclosure shall, under r. 12, take place in the absence of the appellant and his representative, but the special advocate must be invited to make written representations. Evidence may be oral or written and be required on oath, and, under r. 22, the POAC may receive evidence that would not be admissible in a court of law. It can also summons witnesses. At the end of the review, there will be a written determination under r. 25, though it may be predicted that these documents will be relatively unenlightening in view of the duty under r. 3.

Section 6 of the Terrorism Act 2000 preserves a right of further appeal on a question of law to (depending on jurisdiction) the Court of Appeal, the Court of Session or the Court of Appeal in Northern Ireland. An appeal may be brought only with the permission of the Commission, or the appeal court. According to r. 27 of the Proscribed Organisations Appeal Commission (Procedure) Rules 2001 (SI 2001 No. 443), an appeal shall be served on the Commission no later than 10 days from (but excluding) the day on which the appellant or, as appropriate, the Secretary of State has received written notice of the determination.

If an appeal is successful, then by s. 7 of the 2000 Act, any conviction which has been sustained in relation to activity which took place on or after the date of the refusal to deproscribe against which the appeal under s. 5 was brought, the person affected may without leave bring an appeal which shall be granted and compensation shall be payable under s. 133(5) of the Criminal Justice Act 1988. There is an onus on the affected person to make the appeal, but success is assured if there is an appeal. Given the certainty of the outcome, a group application by, say, the Attorney-General might have offered a fairer process.

The effect of the Proscribed Organisations Appeal Commission (Human Rights Act Proceedings) Rules 2001 (SI 2001 No. 127) is that the POAC becomes the appropriate tribunal for the purposes of s. 7 of the Human Rights Act 1998 in relation to proceedings under s. 7(1)(a) of that Act, where such proceedings relate to a refusal by the Secretary of State to deproscribe an organisation. Alongside s. 9, this allows for the special procedures and remedies of the POAC (including s. 7 of the Terrorism Act 2000) to prevail over normal (and more open) court procedures.

The establishment of the POAC under s. 5 of the Terrorism Act 2000 is in principle desirable and will offer the first non-executive scrutiny of proscription orders. However, the setting up of a special tribunal also reflects the unwillingness to put sensitive security evidence before the courts (HC Debs. Standing Committee D, col. 86, 25 January 2000, Charles Clarke). Further the system suffers from considerable weaknesses. One is that it is dependent on application by the organisation or any person affected. This is not to say group representatives will not apply. One notice of appeal has been lodged arising from the first wave of orders — in relation to Lashkar e Tayyaba (the Home Secretary has also mentioned an appeal by the International Sikh Youth Federation: HC Debs. vol. 378 col. 342, 21 November 2001). One might note in passing here the immunity in s. 10 from criminal proceedings for an offence under any of ss. 11 to 13, 15 to 19 and 56 of the 2000 Act arising from any submissions in an application to the Secretary of State or to the POAC. But even this concession is half-hearted. It does not relate to other offences, and it does not appear to apply to immigration related proceedings (HC Debs. Standing Committee D col. 111, 25 January 2000, Charles Clarke):

> The clause does not provide general immunity, and it would be wrong to do so. If, for instance, it emerged during proceedings that an individual had been involved in a bombing attack or had incited an act of terrorism abroad, immunity

in respect of criminal proceedings would not apply. That strikes the right balance. Offences involving weapons, articles, information and so on are omitted from the immunity provided in the clause because they do not relate directly to proscription.

One can imagine that a number of small crackpot groups would be delighted with the publicity if a Secretary of State were foolish enough to dignify them with proscription in the first place. What is less certain, however, is how effective their challenge will be given that a lot of the evidence will remain hidden from them. So it would be preferable if, akin to legislation like the Interception of Communications Act 1985, the POAC should take the role not only of appeal tribunal but also proactive review commission, and it should subject all orders to regular annual scrutiny — even those in sch. 2. The Lloyd Report likewise suggested an automatic annual review by a specially appointed advisory committee (Inquiry into Legislation against Terrorism (Cm. 3420, London, 1996), para. 13.32).

Another problem with the POAC is that (contrary to the marginal note to s. 5 — 'Deproscription: appeal') it is confined to the principles of judicial review: s. 5(3). Although this formula is wide enough to allow for the raising of points under the Human Rights Act 1998, the position is not much better than the degree of scrutiny applicable to a decision of the Secretary of State under the Prevention of Terrorism (Temporary Provisions) Act 1989. The POAC does not have full appeal powers, allowing it to consider the facts and reaching an independent judgment on the basis of them. Indeed, in these circumstances, judicial review in the courts might be preferred to judicial review by the POAC — court process is more open and more clearly independent, since the judges have forms of tenure not held by members of the POAC. Under the rules of administrative law, POAC procedures will have to be exhausted before turning to the Divisional Court (*R* v *Chief Constable of Merseyside, ex parte Calveley* [1986] 2 WLR 144; *R* v *Special Commissioner, ex parte Napier* [1988] 3 All ER 166; *R* v *Civil Service Appeal Board, ex parte Bruce* [1989] 2 All ER 907; *R* v *Birmingham CC, ex parte Ferraro Rocher* [1993] 1 All ER 550), but the POAC is unlikely to be the preferred forum. Furthermore, will judicial review be a sufficient degree of scrutiny to satisfy any degree of challenge under Article 13 of the European Convention? The European Court of Human Rights has been rather inconsistent on this matter; judicial review was sufficient to check the legality of detention in *Brogan* v *United Kingdom*, App. nos. 11209, 11234, 11266/84, 11386/85, Ser. A. 145-B, (1989) 11 EHRR 539, para. 65 but not in *Chahal* v *United Kingdom*, App. no. 22414/93, Report 1996-V, (1997) 23 EHRR 413, para. 130. Moreover, a combination of limited powers of scrutiny plus the limited involvement of the applicant in the process because of evidential sensitivity may trigger a breach of Article 6 (see Fenwick, H., *Civil Rights* (Longman, Harlow, 2000), p. 95).

2.4.2   Judicial review

Since the POAC is to apply principles of judicial review, the likely impact of that level of scrutiny should be considered further. In the main, the chances of meaningful litigation are remote because of the claims to national security which will doubtless be forthcoming both as a device to suppress evidence or as a persuasive argument to maintain a proscription order. The miserable performance of the courts has been demonstrated by cases such as *McEldowney* v *Forde* [1971] AC 632 (a rare example of direct challenge to a proscription order) and *R* v *Secretary of State for the Home Department, ex parte Brind* [1991] AC 696 (concerning the more indirect issue of the broadcasting ban applied in 1988 to representatives of Sinn Féin). In *R* v *Secretary of State for the Home Department, ex parte Cheblak* [1991] 2 All ER 319, the Court of Appeal rejected an application for judicial review and *habeas corpus* from a Lebanese employee of the Arab League in London since 1985. He had been served with a deportation order once the Gulf War had begun on grounds that his presence was not conducive to the public good because of national security considerations. The Home Office made vague allegations of links to an organisation involved in terrorism, but would not provide details to the applicant. The court held that the statement of the Home Secretary was sufficient for the purposes.

In *Re Williamson's Application for Judicial Review* [2000] NI 281, the applicant sought review of the decision in August 1999 under the Northern Ireland (Sentences) Act 1998, s. 3, by the Northern Ireland Secretary of State not to 'specify' the Provisional IRA as being connected with, or promoting or encouraging, terrorism and not maintaining a complete and unequivocal cease-fire. The Secretary of State was satisfied that the Provisional IRA was involved in arms smuggling from the United States and a murder during July 1999, and so the refusal then to specify the Provisional IRA was claimed to be in breach of administrative law by the applicant. The Northern Ireland Court of Appeal was prepared to review the facts on which a belief was based, but, as usual, ruled out any meaningful review of judgment on those facts. It was accepted that the Secretary of State possessed a high degree of knowledge and expertise and that her decisions required political judgment as well as analytical skills. Lord Chief Justice Carswell concluded:

> The area with which the 1998 Act is concerned is delicate and sensitive, and it is hardly surprising that strong views should be held on it or that decisions within this area should give rise to serious differences of opinion. It is part of the democratic process that such decisions should be taken by a minister responsible to Parliament, and so long as the manner in which they are taken is in accordance with the proper principles the courts should not and will not step outside their proper function of review.

Further evidence as to the likely approach of the courts may be demonstrated by their responses to challenges to the now repealed powers to issue exclusion orders under Part II of the Prevention of Terrorism (Temporary Provisions) Act 1989. An initial difficulty to be faced by litigants is justiciability — whether the courts will entertain complaints at any level. The issue arose in *R* v *Secretary of State for the Home Department, ex parte Stitt, (The Times*, 3 February 1987; see also: Hillyard, P., and Percy-Smith, J., *The Coercive State* (Pinter, London, 1988), p. 274), when Sean Stitt, a community worker from Belfast sought to overturn an order. In the leading judgment of Watkins LJ, three grounds advanced by the respondent were examined: the 'package' argument, a claim that national security and confidentiality made review inappropriate, and concern about delay in bringing the application. The first argument is that the statutory Adviser system under s. 7 of the Prevention of Terrorism (Temporary Provisions) Act 1989 provided 'a comprehensive package of rights' which renders common law judicial review impliedly unnecessary. The courts are often reluctant to accept this argument 'particularly when the statutory remedy is in the hands of an administrative body' (Wade, H.W.R., and Forsyth, C.F., *Administrative Law* (7th ed., Oxford University Press, 1994), p. 726), and no comment on it was offered by Watkins LJ. In addition, the POAC is not designated as a superior court of record (compare the title given to the Special Immigration Appeals Commission in s. 35 of the Anti-terrorism, Crime and Security Act 2001 — see Chapter 8). The second ground, national security, prevailed as 'powerfully persuasive' and 'the central issue'. Delay was said to be unimportant. The judgment of MacPherson J was more forthright on the package argument: 'I agree that Parliament prescribed in the [Prevention of Terrorism Acts] a defined package of rights for those who might be or have been excluded from this country'. Yet, delay and confidentiality are also cited by him for the rejection of review. Thus, the issue of sensitive information is the common basis for the decision, but this consideration, though relevant to many orders, need not arise in all challenges or prevent review without consideration of the evidence. However, the balance of *obiter* remarks also points towards acceptance of the 'package' argument, which is a more fundamental obstacle and was ominously echoed in the deportation case of *ex parte Cheblak*, in which the further, rather dubious, point was floated that the Home Secretary is accountable to Parliament and so judicial review is superfluous.

In summary, any decision by a Secretary of State to exclude (and likewise to proscribe) may be treated as non-justiciable (note that challenge based on European Union freedoms also failed in *R v Secretary of State for the Home Department, ex parte Adams* [1995] All ER (EC) 177 — see Douglas-Scott, S., and Kimbell, J.A., 'The Adams exclusion order case' [1994] *Public Law* 516). Nevertheless, it is arguable that the reluctance of the courts to intervene extends only to the substance of the decision by the Minister and not to other matters (such as procedures). This approach was effectively adopted by the Divisional Court in *R v Secretary of State for the Home Department, ex parte O'Neill*, 13 February 1992, unreported, and was expressly conceded by the Home Secretary in *R v Secretary of State for the Home Department, ex parte Gallagher*, 13 November 1992, EXIS (QBD); [1994] 3 CMLR 295 (CA); [1995] ECR I-4253 (ECJ); [1996] 2 CMLR 951 (CA).

O'Neill was born in Northern Ireland but also held Irish citizenship. He had lived intermittently in London since 1985 but was excluded in 1990. Following *ex parte Stitt*, Rose J felt that the substantive basis of the order could not be challenged, so reasons did not have to be provided. However, there was scrutiny of the procedures by which it had been made and whether representations from O'Neill had been properly considered, the judge being fully satisfied in all respects.

John Gerard Gallagher was an Irish citizen who had lived in Britain in periods between 1987 and 1991 in order to work. He had been arrested in September 1991; no charges were brought, but he was then excluded. The important concession was that 'the decisions [of the Home Secretary] are susceptible to review by this court, and that jurisdiction of this court is in no sense barred by any consideration of public security or claim relating to the interests of national security'.

Assuming that some review therefore remains possible, it will now be determined how far it might bite. There are various forms of error affecting jurisdiction which may trigger judicial intervention, such as where the competent authority has misdirected itself by applying the wrong legal test or by misunderstanding a matter in respect of which it must be satisfied. This form of review is relevant to proscription, but, as shall be described later, will be constrained by judicial unwillingness to seek out sensitive information.

As well as jurisdictional errors of substance, certain procedural errors may be reviewable. Thus, the courts might ensure that an order has actually been made and has been approved by the proper authority (Ministers of State can probably approve on behalf of their Secretary of State: *Government of Malaysia* v *Mahan Singh* [1975] 2 MLJ 155; *Najar Singh* v *Government of Malaysia* [1976] Ch 30; *McKernan* v *Governor of Belfast Prison and Another* [1983] NI 83. It is probable that civil servants can also act: *R* v *Secretary of State for the Home Department, ex parte Oladehinde* [1991] 3 WLR 797. Orders served should correspond with orders signed by the Minister: *R* v *Home Secretary, ex parte Budd* [1941] 2 All ER 749, [1942] 1 All ER 373, [1943] 2 All ER 452). Next, the formal requirements allowing for representations to the Secretary of State and a review by the POAC must all be considered mandatory.

Judicial review may next be triggered by abuses of discretion. By and large, evidential difficulties will ensure that challenges on the basis of irrationality have little impact or are non-justiciable, subject to some exceptions. First, if, contrary to its common practice, the executive reveals the information on which it acted, these reasons can be scrutinised (for example: *Attorney-General of Saint Christopher, Nevis and Anguilla* v *Reynolds* [1980] AC 637). The next forms of abuse of discretion are disregarding legally relevant, or taking into account legally irrelevant, considerations. For example, it would be improper for the Home Secretary to sign an order without reflection of any kind. However, the processing of a large number of orders in a short time does not raise such an inference (*Stuart* v *Anderson and Morrison* [1941] 2 All ER 665). Failure to specify any substantive reasons for proscription (that is beyond the civil servant drafted affidavits which are decidedly economical with the *verité*) will certainly not be deemed to be evidence of abuse in view of the sensitive nature of the evidence involved (*ex parte Stitt, loc. cit; ex parte Cheblak, loc. cit.*). Problems of proof are also the main hindrance to the final form of abuse of discretion, namely bad faith on the part of the decision-maker (see: *Sebe and others* v *Government of Ciskei* 1983 (4) SA 523 (CKSC)).

The final basis for judicial review is procedural impropriety. It is unlikely that the initial making of an order by the Secretary of State is at all affected. One reason is that the statutory POAC system rather than natural justice is available to remedy any errors at the earlier state. A second reason is that such prior notification of pending order could defeat the preventive aim of the Act (compare *Council of Civil Service Unions v Minister for the Civil Service* [1985] AC 374). By contrast, natural justice may be applicable to the POAC system. Personal impartiality is certainly demanded, both in reality and in appearance. For example, it was suggested by Farquharson LJ, somewhat impertinently, in *ex parte Gallagher* that the appointment of a Unionist politician would be tainted. Refusal to reveal the identity of the panel diminishes the chances of detection of such faults but was not seen as legally objectionable by the Court of Appeal in that case. Amongst the implied procedural requirements could be the giving of adequate notice of any hearing before POAC, so that the suspect may prepare a case. Similarly, reasonable requests for adjournments should be granted, for example, if a person wishes to obtain the statement of material witness. However, the recurrent problem of sensitive information makes it unlikely that the present practice of suppressing the adverse allegations or reasons for the Secretary of State's decision could be impugned, though the courts have regrettably also elided factual reasons with legal grounds and placed them equally behind the veil (compare: *Re McElduff* [1972] NI 1). Natural justice will also have a restricted impact on the procedures followed at the POAC procedures themselves, where the statutory procedures will probably be deferred to. In *ex parte Cheblak*, the court emphasised that the Advisory Panel was to be viewed as inquisitorial in nature, and so it, rather than the subject, should take the lead in amassing information. The same view would probably be taken of the POAC.

An obstacle to most forms of judicial review mentioned hitherto is the sensitive nature of the information involved (Shackleton Report (Review of the Operation of the Prevention of Terrorism (Temporary Provisions) Acts 1974 and 1976 (Cmnd. 7324, London, 1978)), para. 52, quoted with approval in *ex parte Stitt, loc. cit.*; see Schiff, D.N., 'Law and order — the British response to terrorism' (1979) 9 *Kingston Law Review* 121; Schiff, D.N., 'The Shackleton Review of the Operation of the Prevention of Terrorism Act' [1978] *Public Law* 352; Bates, T.St. J.N., 'The Shackleton Report on Terrorism' 1979 *Scottish Law Times* 205):

It is intelligence information, whose disclosure may involve unacceptable risks. Information which is specific about a person's participation in an act of terrorism may be known to only two or three people. It could, without difficulty, be traced back to its source if it became known to the subject of the exclusion order or to a wider circle of his associates and friends. From this might follow the death of the informant. The flow of information which can lead, and in many cases has led to convictions in the courts would be endangered.

Judicial aversion to security matters was the rock on which review in *ex parte Stitt* foundered. He complained that he had not been given 'the gist or the substance of the objection which is made to his presence' in Britain, so it was impossible to make cogent representations to the Adviser. However, Watkins LJ held that reasons could not be imparted since '[n]ational security is very much at stake in matters of this kind' especially the need to protect confidential sources. Similarly, in *ex parte Gallagher*, once Gallagher began voicing complaints about lack of reasons for the decision, the official defences were raised again by McCullough J:

> It is plain beyond argument that the whole reason for the Act was the consideration of public security, and it is clear that Parliament intended to leave to the Secretary of State the widest discretion in deciding what the public interest did and did not require.

Likewise, Farquharson LJ in the Court of Appeal seemed close to non-justiciability when he concluded that 'only the Home Secretary could form a judgment and appraise the risk'.

There was a more expansive inquisition into these issues in *R v Secretary of State for the Home Department, ex parte McQuillan* [1995] 4 All ER 400. No reasons were, as usual, forthcoming for the exclusion first imposed in 1987. McQuillan had no convictions for terrorist offences, but he had been a prominent official in the Irish Republican Socialist Party, which is allied to the proscribed Irish National Liberation Army. However, he claimed to have severed his connections in 1992. Sedley J was sympathetic to the administrative law challenge based on the failure to state the evidentiary basis for the decision (at p. 423):

> If the matter were free of authority, I would hold with little hesitation that the reasons of the [Home Secretary] do not necessarily amount to reasons of national security at all. They are, on the contrary, the straightforward and familiar reasons for the invocation of public interest immunity to protect sources of police information. If so, it would fall within the obligation of the court to scrutinise material, subject to proper safeguards, in order to decide whether the interests of justice called for its disclosure, notwithstanding its possible effects on informants.

This reasoning appears seriously confused in two respects. One is that Sedley J here confused the concept of national security as a substantive legal argument with national security as a procedural defence. The claim of the Home Office was based on national security as a factor to be weighed against the applicant's rights. Whether the jejune statement in support was sufficiently weighty is raised in the next point. However, it was not in any event a direct demand that the court should not investigate further. Had further and better particulars or discovery been demanded by the applicant in interlocutory proceedings, then a Public Interest Immunity Certificate (PIIC) might have been issued, but here the Court was asked to weigh the evidence as it stood and not as it might stand if all were revealed. The second confusion arises from the implication in the quoted passage that the courts must inquire into the assertion of national security in the context of a PIIC but not in the context of a supporting affidavit. As already described, it has not been universally accepted by the judiciary that supporting affidavits are wholly non-justiciable, nor equally is it certain that the grounds for a PIIC will be explored exhaustively.

From this experience, it may be predicted that judicial review of proscription will be largely sacrificed to the totem of security interests, which prove powerful not only in this context (see Livingstone, S., 'The House of Lords and the Northern Ireland conflict' (1994) 57 *Modern Law Review* 333 at p. 360). So long as the Home Office answers any complaints with an affidavit rehearsing satisfaction of the statutory grounds and setting out any reasons which can be disclosed without endangering security sources, the courts will not require more (compare: *Secretary of State for Defence* v *Guardian Newspapers Ltd* [1989] AC 359), and so domestic judicial review is unlikely to pick up anything other than disastrously and patently ill-founded or ill-argued cases (see Walker, C.P., 'Constitutional governance and special powers against terrorism' (1997) 35 *Columbia Journal of Transnational Law* 1 at p. 27). It is therefore important to note the changes in the Terrorism Act 2000 itself, which offers a more open, less executive-dominated proscription process, including the need for periodic review, should assist to demonstrate fairness, and this has become essential in the light of the guarantees to freedom of expression and association in Articles 10 and 11 of the European Convention (as implemented by the Human Right Act 1998). If challenged, it must be shown that total proscription, as opposed to other policing actions, is a proportionate response.

2.5 PROSCRIPTION — CRIMINAL OFFENCES

It should be emphasised that much of the purpose of proscription is symbolic — to express society's revulsion at violence as a political strategy as well as its determination to put a stop to it. This purpose is especially evident in Britain, where there have been no convictions since 1990 (though there have been 90 convictions in Northern Ireland between 1991 to 1998). So, the objective is largely achieved by the process of proscription itself, whether by Act or by order. But in case that message does not entirely get through, there are three offences which complete Part II of the Terrorism Act 2000. All are closely derived from the Prevention of Terrorism (Temporary Provisions) Act 1989 (ss. 2 and 3) and the Northern Ireland (Emergency Provisions) Act 1996 (ss. 30 and 31), though they are specified in greater detail. Within the context of these offences, proscription serves the purpose of short-circuiting the process of proof — the link is to the organisation rather than to specific activities (see Home Office and Northern Ireland Office, Legislation against Terrorism (Cm. 4178, London, 1998), para. 4.6).

By s. 11(1) of the Terrorism Act 2000, a person commits an offence if he belongs or professes to belong to a proscribed organisation. A defence is provided if it can be shown that membership has effectively lapsed by becoming entirely latent since the date of proscription (whether under the Terrorism Act 2000 or its predecessors). The prosecution must, of course, first establish membership, so this is not a case

of a reverse burden of proof (HC Debs. Standing Committee D, col. 117, 25
January 2000, Charles Clarke), but the defence is entirely for the defendant to
prove on the balance of probabilities and s. 118 (see further Chapter 6) does not
apply here. The maximum penalties are: (a) on conviction on indictment, to
imprisonment for a term not exceeding ten years, to a fine or to both, or (b) on
summary conviction, to imprisonment for a term not exceeding six months, to a
fine not exceeding the statutory maximum or to both.

Persons who cannot be shown directly to be members but have provided support
commit an offence under s. 12 of the 2000 Act. The commission can come about
through a number of distinct forms of involvement. First, forbidden by s. 12(1)
is the act of inviting support. It is declared that the support is not, or is not
restricted to, the provision of money or other property (since that activity is
expressly within the meaning of s. 15). Thus, the provision of labour and services
(such as helping with money laundering or digging a hole for weapons) could fall
into this category.

Secondly, by s. 12(2) of the 2000 Act, a person commits an offence if he
arranges, manages or assists in arranging or managing a meeting which he knows
is (a) to support a proscribed organisation, (b) to further the activities of a
proscribed organisation, or (c) to be addressed by a person who belongs or
professes to belong to a proscribed organisation. There is a defence under s. 12(4)
to charges under subsection (2)(c) if it can be shown that he had no reasonable
cause to believe that the address mentioned in subsection (2)(c) would support a
proscribed organisation or further its activities: 'That provides sufficient protection
for arranging genuinely benign meetings while still ensuring that subsection (2)(c)
will serve its basic purpose.' (HL Debs. vol. 614 col. 1453, 4 July 2000, Lord
Bassam). 'Benign' meetings might include meetings between government representatives and paramilitary leaders in order to end violence. The defence under
s. 12(4) is expressly confined to private meetings. In the words of the government
Minister:

> We accept that there could be a genuinely benign private meeting to be
> addressed by a member of a proscribed organisation — one could think of
> various examples — and it could therefore be legitimate to arrange such a
> meeting under the circumstances set out in our statutory defence. However, we
> cannot accept the arranging of public meetings to be addressed by members of
> proscribed organisations, even when the person arranging the meeting does not
> think that the address will support the organisation. (HC Debs. vol. 353 col. 655,
> 10 July 2000, Charles Clarke)

Because of concerns about a breach of Article 6 of the European Convention, this
defence must be read subject to s. 118(3): if evidence is adduced which is sufficient
to raise an issue, the court shall treat it as proved unless the prosecution disproves
it beyond reasonable doubt. This express declaration is to secure that the burdens
placed on the defendant are to be seen as evidential rather than persuasive or legal

burdens (HL Debs. vol. 613 col. 754, 16 May 2000, Lord Bassam) (see further Chapter 6).

Thirdly, by s. 12(3) of the 2000 Act, a person commits an offence if he addresses a meeting and the purpose of his address is to encourage support for a proscribed organisation or to further its activities. For these purposes, a 'meeting' means a meeting of three or more persons, whether or not the public are admitted, and a meeting is 'private' if the public are not admitted. The maximum penalties are (a) on conviction on indictment, to imprisonment for a term not exceeding ten years, to a fine or to both, or (b) on summary conviction, to imprisonment for a term not exceeding six months, to a fine not exceeding the statutory maximum or to both. The intention behind s. 12 is to take off the agenda of public debate any form of statement by an individual on behalf of a proscribed organisation: 'to drive it down, drive it down, drive it down' (HC Debs. Standing Committee D, col. 137, 25 January 2000, Charles Clarke). This stark aim does not quite reach the realms of the broadcasting ban imposed in 1988 (*R* v *Secretary of State for the Home Department, ex parte Brind* [1991] AC 696; Michael, J., 'Attacking the easy platform' (1988) 138 *New Law Journal* 786; Weaver, R.L., and Bennett, G.J., 'The Northern Ireland broadcasting ban: some reflections on judicial review' (1989) 22 *Vanderbilt Journal of Transnational Law* 1119; Henderson, L., Miller, D., Reilly, J., *Speak No Evil: The British Broadcasting Ban, The Media and the Conflict in Ireland* (Glasgow University Media Group, 1990)). But there is certainly a whiff of denying the oxygen of publicity. However, the proposed wider offence of addressing a meeting which a person knows is to be addressed by, 'a person who belongs or professes to belong to a proscribed organisation' was eventually taken out of the Bill (HL Debs. vol. 614 col. 182, 20 June 2000, Lord Bach). The activity of 'addressing' a meeting was felt to raise issues of freedom of speech in a rather more direct way than that of 'arranging' a meeting.

Perhaps the most flagrant breach of a proscription order (though not really the most serious) is to appear in public displaying some kind of allegiance with, or support for the impugned group. This behaviour is caught by s. 13(1) (formerly s. 3 of the Prevention of Terrorism (Temporary Provisions) Act 1989 or s. 31 of the Northern Ireland (Emergency Provisions) Act 1996). A person in a public place commits an offence if he (a) wears an item of clothing, or (b) wears, carries or displays an article, in such a way or in such circumstances as to arouse reasonable suspicion that he is a member or supporter of a proscribed organisation. The offence was felt to plug gaps in the relevant offences in the Public Order Act 1936 which were confined to the concept of a 'uniform' (see *O'Moran* v *DPP, Whelan* v *DPP* [1975] QB 864; Walker, C., 'Paramilitary displays and the PTA' 1992 *Juridical Review* 90). The offence is the least serious of those in Part II of the 2000 Act: it can only be tried summarily and the maximum penalty is (a) imprisonment for a term not exceeding six months, (b) a fine not exceeding level 5 on the standard scale, or (c) both. The penalty in Northern Ireland used to be up to one year imprisonment, but the lower precedent from Britain has been adopted partly because of lack of use of the offence (two prosecutions in Northern Ireland in the period 1992–1999 and none in Britain). As a result of these levels, a distinct power to arrest without warrant is granted in Scotland.

There have been very few prosecutions for these offences in Britain, where prosecutors have preferred either more serious, substantive charges or have deployed tried and tested mainstream public order offences. However, proscription in Northern Ireland is commonly used as an added charge in serious cases.

2.6 PROSCRIPTION — CONCLUSIONS

Picking up on the last point, proscription has been of marginal utility in combating political violence, to which the survival of the IRA over most of a century bears ample testimony. Paramilitary organisations cannot be abolished by legislative fiat, and proscription actually increases the difficulties of infiltration and monitoring so as to achieve the criminalisation of those members engaged in violence (see further Walker, C.P., *The Prevention of Terrorism in British Law* (2nd ed., Manchester University Press, Manchester, 1992), ch. 5). There are also objections in principle. There should be concern about the deployment of special offences when ordinary offences would suffice (they include the possession of weapons or conspiracy to carry out attacks, such as have been used in Scottish cases cited earlier or even more specialist offences (such as those concerning paramilitary displays under the Public Order Act 1936 and actually deployed against IRA sympathisers in *O'Moran* v *DPP*, *Whelan* v *DPP* [1975] QB 864)). Another concern is the curtailment of democratic expression. It seems inconsistent that the present UK Government should find powers of exclusion 'fundamentally objectionable' (Home Office and Northern Ireland Office, Legislation against Terrorism, (Cm. 4178, London, 1998), para. 5.6) because they interfere with freedom of movement but fails to see that proscription fundamentally interferes with freedom of expression, an equally important right. Furthermore, alongside proscription must be read other restrictions on political involvement in Northern Ireland (see Walker, C.P., 'Political violence and democracy in Northern Ireland' (1988) 51 *Modern Law Review* 605).

In answer to these points, the rationale for proscription has shifted in part to the 'presentational' (Report of the Operation of the Prevention of Terrorism (Temporary Provisions) Act 1976 (Cmnd. 8803, London, 1983), para. 207) — that it expresses the condemnation of the community and 'averts the danger of public outrage being expressed in public disorder' (Review of the Operation of the Northern Ireland (Emergency Provisions) Act 1978 (Cmnd. 9222, London, 1984), para. 414). But in view of the adequacy of regular public order laws, these presentational or public order grounds for proscription should be rejected. During the debates on the Terrorism Act 2000, the Government called in aid other grounds for proscription — symbolism was one, but deterrence and prosecution were others (HC Debs. Standing Committee D, col. 56, 18 January 2000, Charles Clarke):

There are three principal reasons why we think proscription is important. First, it has been, and remains, a powerful deterrent to people to engage in terrorist activity. Secondly, related offences are a way of tackling some of the lower-level support for terrorist organisations. The Hon. Member for Southwark, North and Bermondsey spoke about numbers: he is right that, broadly speaking, about 200 incidents have been dealt with since 1990 — as he said, usually on the second count of the charge. Without commenting on the details that he gave earlier, it is true that while that is a relatively small number, it is not insignificant. It has been a significant factor in dealing with some of the issues. Thirdly, proscription acts as a powerful signal of the rejection by the Government — and indeed by society as a whole — of organisations' claim to legitimacy. The points made by the Hon. Member for Aylesbury in that context were eloquent. It is important for society to state that certain activities are simply — I hesitate to use the phrase in this context — beyond the pale; I do not mean it in the Irish sense, but in the sense of the way in which civilised, democratic society operates. The legislation is a powerful symbol of that censure and is important. So I believe that the Government are right to continue with proscription and that the provision is justified.

In response, it is suggested that prosecution for ordinary crimes is the best way of achieving these objectives, especially as it allays doubts about the proportionality of proscription which have become more pressing since the Human Rights Act 1998 came into force. The protection of political speech, and indeed political association and religious manifestations, must be given special weight under Articles 9 to 11 of the European Convention (see, for example, *Lingens* v *Austria*, App. no. 9815/82, Ser. A. vol. 103, (1986) 8 EHRR 407; *Thorgeirson* v *Iceland*, App. no. 13778/88, Ser. A. vol. 239, (1992) 14 EHRR 843), and this precept has been applied to political parties which have faced restriction or ban without sufficient cause (see *United Communist Party of Turkey and Others* v *Turkey*, App. no. 19392/92, Reports 1998-I; *Socialist Party* v *Turkey*, App. no. 21237/93, Reports 1998-III). This privilege is even maintained in situations of unrest and conflict (see, for example, *Castells* v *Spain*, App. no. 11798/85, Ser. A. 236, (1992) 14 EHRR 445; *Zana* v *Turkey*, App. no. 18954/91, Reports 1997-VII; *Sürek* v *Turkey (No. 1, 2, 3, 4)* App. nos. 26682/95, 24122/94, 24735/94, 24762/94, Judgment of Court 8 July 1999; *Arslan* v *Turkey*, App. no. 23462/94, Judgment of Court 8 July 1999; *Baskaya and Okçuoglu* v *Turkey*, App. nos. 23536/94; 24408/94, Judgment of Court 8 July 1999; *Ceylan* v *Turkey*, App. no. 23556/94, Judgment of Court 8 July 1999; *Erdogdu and Ince* v *Turkey*, App. nos. 25067/94; 25068/94, Judgment of Court 8 July 1999; *Gerger* v *Turkey*, App. no. 24919/94, Judgment of Court 8 July 1999; *Karatas* v *Turkey*, App. no. 23168/94, Judgment of Court 8 July 1999; *Okçuoglu* v *Turkey*, App. nos. 24246/94, Judgment of Court 8 July 1999; *Polat* v *Turkey*, App. no. 23500/94, Judgment of Court 8 July 1999; *Sürek and Özdemir* v *Turkey*, App. nos. 23927/94; 24277/94, Judgment of Court 8 July 1999; *Association Ekin* v *France*, App. no. 39288/98, Judgment of Court 18 January 2000). This is not to say that the proscription powers under the Terrorism Act 2000 are bound to be unacceptable under the European Convention. Aside from arguments based on the illegitimate nature of terrorism (see *German Communist Party* v *Germany*, App. no. 350/57, 1 YBEC 222; *Retimag* v *Germany*, App. no. 712/60, 4 YBEC), the State's response may be held to be necessary for the purposes of national security, territorial integrity or public safety, for the prevention of disorder or crime (see *Brind and McLaughlin* v *United Kingdom*, App. nos. 18714/91, 18759/91, (1994) 77-A DR 42, (1994) 18 EHRR CD 82; (see also *In re McLaughlin's application* [1990] 6 NIJB 41; *Purcell* v *Ireland*, App. no. 15404/89, (1991) 70 DR 262); *O'Toole* v *RTÉ (No. 2)* (1993) 13 ILRM 458; *Brandon Books Publishers* v *RTÉ* [1993] ILRM 806; Hogan, G., 'The demise of the Irish broadcasting ban' (1995) 1 *European Public Law* 69). Furthermore, the European Commission has upheld restrictions by way of an exclusion order under the Prevention of Terrorism (Temporary Provisions) Act 1989 imposed upon Gerry Adams in 1983, leader of Sinn Féin. The order was held to be reasonably necessary in the interests of national security and the prevention of crime and disorder (*Adams and Benn* v *United Kingdom*, App. nos. 28999/95, 30343/96, European Commission 1997). Yet, under domestic legislation, the position appears incongruous; the values of free conscience and expression are given special weighting under ss. 12 and 13 of the Human Rights Act, whereas the Terrorism Act 2000, by singling out these motivations, seems to offer the reverse value judgment.

POSTSCRIPT

Though the judgment was delivered too late for detailed analysis in this book, readers are referred to the case of *R (on the application of the Kurdistan Workers' Party and Others)* v *Secretary of State for the Home Department*; *R (on application of the People's Mojahedin Organisation of Iran and Others)* v *Secretary of State for the Home Department*; *R (on the application of Nisar Ahmed)* v *Secretary of State for the Home Department* [2002] EWHC 644 (Admin). Three organisations (PKK, PMOI, and LT) sought to challenge their proscription under the Terrorism Act 2000. All failed on the principal ground that the POAC is to be treated as 'the forum of first resort' (para. 83) for challenges ahead of any resort to judicial review.

Chapter Three
Terrorist property

3.1 GENERAL STRATEGIES

It has long been recognised that 'money is a crucial factor in the continuance of terrorism' (Jellicoe Report, Report of the Operation of the Prevention of Terrorism (Temporary Provisions) Act 1976 (Cmnd. 8803, London, 1983), para. 213). Accordingly, Part III of the Prevention of Terrorism (Temporary Provisions) Act 1989 contained measures which both criminalised the donation and handling of assets for the benefit of terrorist groups and allowed the forfeiture of such assets when such persons are convicted of contravening the offences (see Walker, C., *The Prevention of Terrorism in British Law* (2nd ed., Manchester University Press, Manchester, 1992), ch. 7). There existed in addition even severer confiscation measures in Part VII of the Emergency Provisions Act 1991, but this 'morass of complex and overlapping legislative measures' (Dickson, B., 'The Prevention of Terrorism (Temporary Provisions) Act 1989' (1989) 40 *Northern Ireland Legal Quarterly* 592 at p. 621) has now been dropped in favour of the more regular Proceeds of Crime (Northern Ireland) Order 1996 (SI 1996 No. 1297, NI 9) as extended by the Financial Investigations (Northern Ireland) Order 2001 (SI 2001 No. 1866) (see Bell, R.E., 'Confiscation orders under the Proceeds of Crime legislation' (1998) 49 *Northern Ireland Legal Quarterly* 38). The Lloyd Report suggested a wide range of reforms in this field, given that the measures to date had produced limited impacts (Inquiry into Legislation against Terrorism (Cm. 3420, London, 1996), paras 13.18–19). So, what more does the Terrorism Act 2000 achieve, and what more could be achieved?

Part III of the Terrorism Act 2000 begins with a broad definition of 'terrorist property' in s. 14. It includes tangible property and money likely to be used for the purposes of terrorism, the proceeds of the commission of acts of terrorism, and the direct or indirect proceeds of acts carried out for the purposes of terrorism (including payments or other rewards in connection with its commission). The definition is especially wide in relation to proscribed organisations, where it can relate to any 'resources', which is deemed to mean any money or other property which is applied or made available, or is to be applied or made available, for use by the organisation. Thus, the property within the definition, where this expression is used, can range from resources used for bomb-making and the purchase of firearms to non-violent transactions such as paying rent and hiring cars.

Under Article 1 of the United Nations Convention for the Suppression of the Financing of Terrorism (A/RES/54/109, Cm. 4663, London, 1999), which the United Kingdom Government has ratified, there is reference to 'assets of every kind, whether tangible or intangible, movable or immovable, however acquired, and legal documents or instruments in any form, including electronic or digital, evidencing title to, or interest in, such assets, including, but not limited to, bank credits, travellers cheques, bank cheques, money orders, shares, securities, bonds, drafts, letters of credit' as well as to 'any funds derived from or obtained, directly or indirectly' through the commission of a relevant offence. Thus, the s. 14 definition appears wider, since it extends beyond assets and funds into resources.

There then follows in Part III of the Terrorism Act 2000 a series of offences, which can in turn trigger legal actions such as forfeiture and the seizure of tainted cash.

These strategies are supplemented by measures in the Anti-terrorism, Crime and Security Act 2001. Part I replaces the seizure of cash powers in the Terrorism Act 2000. The main variance is that the exercise of the power is no longer confined to internal or external borders. Section 3 and sch. 2 also amend other Parts of the Terrorism Act 2000 to ensure that investigative and freezing powers are more widely available. More original ideas in the 2001 Act concern the introduction of account monitoring orders will enable the police to require financial institutions to provide information on accounts for up to 90 days, and extra powers to freeze the assets of overseas governments or residents. The strategy behind these measures (and other besides) is set out in an Action Plan on Terrorist Financing (HC Debs. vol. 372 col. 940, 15 October 2001, Gordon Brown) and also includes a Terrorist Finance Team established within the National Criminal Intelligence Service; a multi-disciplinary task force which will enhance financial intelligence and investigate the use of underground banking systems in the transfer of criminal and terrorist assets; a new regulatory regime of supervision for bureaux de change, cheque cashiers and money transmission services (operated by Customs and Excise, the regime came into force on 12 November 2001); and consultation on whether companies should be required to disclose their beneficial ownership.

Overall, the purposes are to deter, detect, counter and criminalise any financial aid for terrorism and to attack and nullify the economic structures of terrorist enterprises.

3.2   OFFENCES

All stages of tangible support are covered by a series of offences. Thus, initial fund-raising or donations are forbidden by s. 15 of the Terrorism Act 2000, whether by inviting the contribution, by receiving it or by providing it:

(1)   A person commits an offence if he—

(a)   invites another to provide money or other property, and

(b)   intends that it should be used, or has reasonable cause to suspect that it may be used, for the purposes of terrorism.

(2)   A person commits an offence if he—

(a)   receives money or other property, and

(b)   intends that it should be used, or has reasonable cause to suspect that it may be used, for the purposes of terrorism.

(3)   A person commits an offence if he—

(a)   provides money or other property, and

(b)   knows or has reasonable cause to suspect that it will or may be used for the purposes of terrorism.

The aid can be provided by money or other property being given, lent or otherwise made available, whether or not for consideration. It will be noted that the *mens rea* for the offences in Part III requires, as alternatives, knowledge as to purposes or merely reasonable (rather than subjective) awareness. This basic offence ensures compliance with Article 2 of the United Nations Convention for the Suppression of the Financing of Terrorism (A/RES/54/109, Cm. 4663, London, 1999). It also covers the activities previously penalised by s. 9 of the Prevention of Terrorism (Temporary Provisions) Act 1989. But there is no specific reference in s. 15 which is equivalent to s. 10 of the 1989 Act to benefit to proscribed organisations, whether for terrorist purposes or not (the expression 'terrorist property' is not used here), and the burden of proof of absence of reasonable suspicion remains on the prosecution (unlike under s. 10).

The next stage involves the processing or laundering of the proceeds, and these activities are covered by three offences. By s. 16 of the 2000 Act (based on ss. 9(1)(c) and 10(1)(b) of the 1989 Act), a person commits an offence if he uses money or other property for the purposes of terrorism or possesses money or other property, and intends that it should be used, or has reasonable cause to suspect that it may be used, for the purposes of terrorism. More indirect involvement is covered by ss. 17 and 18. By s. 17 ('Funding arrangements' — similar to s. 9(2) of the 1989 Act), a person commits an offence if he enters into (in other words, is part of the initiation of), or becomes concerned in (in other words, joins in some existing relationship or transaction), an arrangement as a result of which money or other property is made available or is to be made available to another, and he knows or has reasonable cause to suspect that it will or may be used for the purposes of terrorism. By s. 18 ('Money laundering' — similar to s. 11 of the 1989 Act), a person commits an offence if he enters into or becomes concerned in an arrangement which facilitates the retention or control by or on behalf of another person of terrorist property. The 'arrangements' can involve concealment, by removal from the jurisdiction, by transfer to nominees, or otherwise. By use of the term, 'terrorist property', the section catches funding purposes which do not directly relate to terrorism, such as payments to the relatives of paramilitary prisoners. In respect of s. 18, proof of *mens rea* is even easier: the burden is switched to the defendant to prove that he did not know and had no reasonable cause to suspect that the arrangement related to terrorist property. Section 118 does not apply to this defence, so it is for the defendant to prove it on balance unassisted by any presumption in his favour (see further Chapter 6).

According to s. 22 of the Terrorism Act 2000, the maximum penalties under ss. 15 to 18 are (a) on conviction on indictment, to imprisonment for a term not exceeding 14 years, to a fine or to both, or (b) on summary conviction, to imprisonment for a term not exceeding six months, to a fine not exceeding the statutory maximum or to both. Despite the extensive web of offences, they are not often used in Britain. There have been just 11 charges under the equivalent to s. 15 following a detention under special powers before the coming into force of the Terrorism Act 2000 (source: Home Office statistics). However, in Northern Ireland, there have been 178 charges of contribution to terrorism under the Prevention of Terrorism (Temporary Provisions) Act 1989 and five charges of assistance in retention or control.

In order to assist the detection process, professional financial intermediaries are encouraged to report their suspicions to the authorities. By s. 19(1) of the 2000 Act (based on s. 18A of the 1989 Act), where a person believes or suspects that another person has committed an offence under any of ss. 15 to 18 on the basis of information which comes to his attention in the course of a trade, profession, business or employment, an offence is committed if he does not disclose to a police officer as soon as is reasonably practicable his belief or suspicion, and the information on which it is based. The width of the duty is striking; it is sufficient to have a subjective belief or suspicion which can only be safely suppressed if the intermediary has a 'reasonable excuse' under subsection (3) for not making the disclosure. This defence is not subject to s. 118 (see Chapter 6), consequently, the full legal and evidential burden fall on the defence. Furthermore, under s. 15(7), the duty has a global reach, since a person shall be treated as having committed an offence under one of ss. 15 to 18 if (a) he has taken an action or been in possession of a thing, and (b) he would have committed an offence under one of those sections if he had been in the United Kingdom at the time when he took the action or was in possession of the thing. At the same time, disclosure does not apply to legally privileged information, and it is expressly provided in s. 19(4) that the making of a disclosure by an employee to a higher authority (such as a Money Laundering Reporting Officer) within an organisation (rather than the police) which has established a set procedure for the purpose will provide a full defence. This defence (which is again not subject to s. 118) allows for bodies such as banks to perform collating and channelling functions for police organisations such as the Economic Crime Unit at the National Criminal Intelligence Service (NCIS) (see http://www.ncis.co.uk/ec.html for the relevant documentation). In 2000, 18,408 disclosures were made to NCIS's Economic Crime Unit (14,500 for 1999). Reports received in October 2001 alone numbered 4,387 (NCIS Press Release 46/01), and they are now referred to the Terrorist Finance Team (TFT), established as a sub-unit of the Economic Crime Unit within the NCIS in November 2001 with an initial staff of eight and a remit to track down terrorist funds (http://www.ncis.co.uk/press/ 46_01.html):

> The team is allowing the link between organised crime and terrorism to be analysed for the first time and is a key part of the UK strategy to combat terrorism. It has a multi-agency background, and combines counter-terrorist and financial intelligence analysis expertise. The majority of its intelligence is expected to be taken from the thousands of suspicious transaction reports (STRs) made to NCIS by UK financial institutions each year.

Extra discretion is afforded to officials listed under the Terrorism Act 2000 (Crown Servants and Regulators) Regulations 2001 (SI 2001 No. 192). The Regulations expressly disapply s. 19 of the Act in relation to the officials in organisations referred to in reg. 4, such as the Bank of England, the Financial Services Authority, and the Building Societies Commission, any recognised self-regulating organisation within the meaning of the Financial Services Act 1986 or any recognised professional body within the meaning of the Financial Services Act 1986. On the other hand, by para. 3, ss. 15 to 23 and 39 of the 2000 Act expressly apply to the Director of Savings and any person employed by or otherwise engaged in the service of the Director of Savings in circumstances where the Director or such a person is carrying on relevant financial business. There is a penalty on indictment under s. 19 of a term not exceeding five years, to a fine or to both.

The government was at pains to emphasise that s. 19 is not as wide as the previous duty to disclose under s. 18 of the Prevention of Terrorism (Temporary Provisions) Act 1989, which, having been the subject of vehement criticism from Lord Lloyd (Inquiry into Legislation against Terrorism (Cm. 3420, London, 1996), para. 14.24), was dropped from the Terrorism Act 2000. It has since been revived by the Anti-terrorism, Crime and Security Act 2001, s. 117, which is described in Chapter 6. By the former s. 18, a person was guilty of an offence if he failed to disclose to the police (or a procurator fiscal in Scotland or a soldier in Northern Ireland) information which he knows or believes might be of material assistance in dealing with terrorism (see Walker, C.P., *The Prevention of Terrorism in British Law* (2nd ed., Manchester University Press, Manchester, 1992), ch. 6). This wide duty of disclosure applied to a broad range of relationships, and the fact that it could demand that family members inform on each other gave it an unpalatable character redolent of totalitarian societies. Section 19 is more confined in two respects — it is limited to knowledge or suspicion of financial offences and it is limited to knowledge or suspicion arising from a professional or business relationship. However, the difference may not be as great as supposed, because family and private relations may still be involved in the context of small businesses (see Fenwick, H., *Civil Rights* (Longman, Harlow, 2000), p. 90). Another concern about the extent of s. 19 arises from the fact that journalism is considered a 'profession' for these purposes and so a reporter with knowledge of the preparations for an explosion might well have relevant information for the purposes of s. 19 (HC Debs. Standing Committee D, col. 155, 25 January 2000, Charles Clarke). There may be challenges here under Article 10 of the European Convention, because the chilling effect may be to deter journalists from investigating paramilitary activities or security force actions against them and may fail to reflect the encouragement to be given to investigative journalism in democratic politics (*Goodwin* v *United Kingdom*, App. no. 17488/90, Reports 1996-II, (1996) 22 EHRR 123). There was scant reassurance from the government Minister (Lord Bassam), who refused to accept any specific exemption for journalists (HL Debs. vol. 613 col. 653, 16 May 2000):

> If I may be a little more reassuring to those journalists who feel that the clause may restrain their legitimate activities, I must emphasise that the Government see the 'reasonable excuse' defence in subsection (3) as an important safeguard in this area. I cannot, of course, give a cast-iron assurance that protecting sources will always be a reasonable excuse; it would be wrong for me to do so. That would be for the courts to determine in any individual case. But protecting sources is clearly an important principle for journalists, particularly those working in this difficult area. However, money and other resources are the lifeblood of terrorist organisations. The offences in Part III are extremely important in deterring and disrupting the planning and execution of any act of terrorism, the more so where concerted terrorist campaigns are concerned.

A stricter duty to disclose in now imposed on the 'Regulated Sector' by sch. 2, pt 3 of the Anti-terrorism, Crime and Security Act 2001. This duty, under a new s. 21A, is applied instead of, and not additional to, s. 19 (sch. 2 para. 5(3), inserting s. 19(1A)). The 'Regulated Sector' is defined by a new sch. 3A inserted into the Terrorism Act 2000 as including a business accepting deposits (such as banks and building societies), a credit union, a bureau de change, investment institutions and brokers. Amongst the exclusions are activities carried on by the Bank of England. The 2001 Act then inserts a new offence as s. 21A of the Terrorism Act 2000. A person commits an offence if he knows or suspects or has reasonable grounds for knowing or suspecting, that another person has committed an offence under any of ss. 15 to 18, and the information came to him in the course of a business in the regulated sector, and he does not disclose the information or other matter to a constable or a nominated officer of his employer as soon as is practicable after it comes to him, unless there is reasonable excuse not to disclose or the information is subject to legal privilege. The objective standard is said to be justified by the '[g]reater awareness and higher standards of reporting in the financial sector' (Home Office, Regulatory Impact Assessment: Terrorist Property (2001), para. 8). Given the objective standard of criminal liability which is imposed, in deciding whether a person committed an offence under this section the court must consider whether he followed any guidance by the relevant supervisory body (which means the Bank of England, the Financial Services Authority, the Council of Lloyd's, the

Director General of Fair Trading, a body which is a designated professional body for the purposes of Part 20 of the Financial Services and Markets Act 2000 or the Secretary of State or the Treasury in relation to certain aspects of companies or insolvency or under the Financial Services and Markets Act 2000). This guidance has to be approved by the Treasury and published in a manner approved by the Treasury so as to bring it to the attention of persons likely to be affected by it. Though the guidelines are helpful, they do not readily answer criticisms that the impact of s. 21A is over-broad by applying equally to junior and senior staff, and there are also difficulties in distinguishing between the regulated sector and the non-regulated sector when some businesses (lawyers and accountants) carry out business in both sectors.

The offence has extra-territorial effect. By s. 21A(11): a person is to be taken to have committed an offence if (a) he has taken an action or been in possession of a thing, and (b) he would have committed the offence if he had been in the United Kingdom at the time when he took the action or was in possession of the thing. The penalties are on conviction on indictment, to imprisonment for a term not exceeding five years or to a fine or to both, and on summary conviction, to imprisonment for a term not exceeding six months or to a fine not exceeding the statutory maximum or to both.

Under s. 21B, any disclosure within s. 21A is not to be understood to breach any restriction on the disclosure of information (however imposed). This provision ensures that persons in the regulated sector can disclose information to the police which causes them to know or suspect, or gives them reasonable grounds to know or suspect, that an offence has been committed without risk of breaching any other legal restriction which would otherwise apply.

A very similar duty of disclosure will be applied to the regulated sector by the Proceeds of Crime Bill 2001–02 HC No. 31, clause 314, in respect of all forms of crimes involved in money laundering and not just those relating to drugs or terrorism.

As well as a duty to disclose, s. 20 of the Terrorism Act 2000 (based on s. 12 of the Prevention of Terrorism (Temporary Provisions) Act 1989) adopts a more permissive path to aiding law enforcement. It provides that a person may legally disclose to a constable a suspicion or belief (and its basis) that any money or other property is terrorist property or is derived from terrorist property or a belief or suspicion that arises in the course of a trade, profession, business or employment that a person has committed an offence under ss. 15 to 18. The disclosure may be made notwithstanding any restriction on the disclosure of information imposed by statute or otherwise (the 'otherwise' typically including contractual or other duties of confidentiality). Again, rather than disclosing directly to the police, a disclosure may be made to a designated officer of the employer. The provision is said to be used frequently ((Rowe) Report of the Operation in 1998 of the Prevention of Terrorism (Temporary Provisions) Acts (Home Office, London, 1999), para. 66).

The next strategy to assist law enforcement is contained in s. 21 of the Terrorism Act 2000 (based on s. 12 of the 1989 Act), which allows for more informal and ongoing cooperation with the police. In order to allow the police to investigate fully chains of transactions, arrangements, use or possession, a person does not commit an offence under any of ss. 15 to 18 if he is acting with the express consent of a constable or even if the person on his own initiative is involved in a transaction or arrangement but makes a disclosure as soon as is reasonably practicable. If the police intervene before the intended disclosure is made, s. 21(5) provides for a possible defence to the effect that the person intended to make a disclosure of the kind mentioned and there is reasonable excuse for his failure to do so up to that point. Section 118 does not apply to this defence — so the legal and evidential burden remain on the accused.

Perhaps the most significant impact of the Terrorism Act 2000 is a general extension of the financial offences under Part III and forfeiture to foreign terrorism, because foreign terrorism is now part of the standardised concept of terrorism in s. 1 (compare: the Inquiry into Legislation against Terrorism (Cm. 3420, London, 1996), paras.13.20, 13.24 and 13.31 and Home Office and Northern Ireland Office, Legislation against Terrorism (Cm. 4178, London, 1998), ch. 6). This builds upon the Prevention of Terrorism (Temporary Provisions) Act 1989, which could apply, under s. 9(3), not only to Northern Ireland terrorism but also to terrorism 'of any other description, except acts connected solely with the affairs of the United Kingdom or any part of the United Kingdom other than Northern Ireland'. However, so that the police and courts did not become too embroiled in overseas politics, s. 9(4) of the 1989 Act required a United Kingdom connection: the foreign terrorism being aided must either be committed in the United Kingdom or, if committed abroad, must constitute an offence triable in the United Kingdom. Given the limited extent of such offences, most groups supporting liberation movements outside Europe were not affected. In any event, the solicitation or donation had to occur in the United Kingdom. The extensions in the Terrorism Act 2000 are in the light of the United Nations Convention for the Suppression of the Financing of Terrorism (A/RES/54/109, Cm. 4663, London, 1999), article 7.

3.3   FORFEITURE

Pursuing terrorist assets reaches a crescendo with the compendious provisions allowing their forfeiture. This strategy is demanded by the United Nations Convention for the Suppression of the Financing of Terrorism (A/RES/54/109, Cm. 4663, London, 1999), article 8. Though there are many similarities with other confiscation codes in existence, such as under the Criminal Justice Act 1988, the Drug Trafficking Act 1994 and the Proceeds of Crime Act 1995, these provisions form a more draconian version reflecting that in sch. 4 of the Prevention of Terrorism (Temporary Provisions) Act 1989, though it is surprising that, where forfeiture does apply, there is still no assumption as to the ownership of property held in the last six years unlike under the other codes mentioned. It also remains the case that the powers are still categorised as criminal forfeiture — predicated upon the establishment of criminal offences *ad personam*. A number of changes to sch. 4 were made by sch. 2, pt 2, to the Anti-terrorism, Crime and Security Act 2001.

The power is set out initially in s. 23 of the Terrorism Act 2000. This provision is similar to s. 13(2) of the 1989 Act, though s. 23(6) is new. The court by or before which a person is convicted of an offence under any of ss. 15 to 18 may make a forfeiture order. It has been suggested that forfeiture should also apply to any terrorist type offence and not just those under Part III (Inquiry into Legislation against Terrorism (Cm. 3420, London, 1996), para. 13.24). However, Part III still demands a conviction under ss. 15 to 18. Arguably, the change is not necessary — forfeiture in respect of other offences can be achieved under the other legislation mentioned above (Home Office and Northern Ireland Office, Legislation against Terrorism (Cm. 4178, London, 1998), para. 6.21). Where a forfeiture order is imposed, it may extend to money or other property which the convict, at the time of the offence, had in his possession or under his control, and which, at that time, he intended should be used, or had reasonable cause to suspect might be used, for the purposes of terrorism. The wording is slightly altered to take account of the circumstances of ss. 15(3), 17 and 18. In respect of offences under ss. 17 and 18, there is no burden on the prosecution to show that the money or property was in the possession of the convicted person, or even, in the case of s. 18, that he has reasonable cause to suspect that it might be used for the purposes of terrorism. The court may also order under subsection (6) the forfeiture of any money or other property which wholly or partly, and directly or indirectly, is received by any person as a payment or other reward in connection with the commission of offences under ss. 15 to 18. This is a new measure and, while a terrorist finance offence must have been committed, it need not have been committed by the person holding the money or property. Thus, where an accountant prepared accounts on behalf of a proscribed organisation and was recompensed (see Home Office, Explanatory Notes to the Terrorism Act 2000 (London, 2000) para. 33), the payment can now be forfeited even though it was not intended or suspected for use in terrorism.

Section 23 says little about process — only in subsection (7) is there mention that a person other than the convicted person, who claims to be the owner of or otherwise interested in anything which can be forfeited by an order, shall be given an opportunity to be heard before making an order. Accordingly, the procedural details are set out at great length in sch. 4 to the Terrorism Act 2000, pt 1 relating to England and Wales, pt II to Scotland and pt III to Northern Ireland. These provisions (which reflect sch. 4 of the 1989 Act) will be described by reference to England and Wales, with only significant variations being mentioned for the other jurisdictions.

Schedule 4, para. 2 sets out the ancillary powers of the courts. A court may make such other provision as appears to it to be necessary for giving effect to the order, such as:

(a) requiring any of the forfeited property to be physically paid or handed over to a court officer (the justices' chief executive is specified under para. 4) or to a designated police officer;

(b) directing any of the forfeited property other than money or land to be sold or otherwise disposed of;

(c)   appointing a receiver to take possession and realise any assets;

(d)   directing a specified part of any forfeited money, or of the proceeds of the sale, disposal or realisation of any forfeited property, to be paid over to a third party claimant under s. 23(7).

In all cases the costs of sale, disposal or realisation may be deducted, and any receiver shall be paid remuneration out of the proceeds or, if insufficient, by the prosecutor; receivers are also given immunity from liability for loss or damage unless caused by negligence (para. 3).

Given that the criminal trial and also the forfeiture proceedings may take some time to complete, sch. 4, para. 5 seeks to avoid the interim dissipation of assets. Accordingly, the High Court may make a restraint order under this paragraph where a forfeiture order has already been made, or it appears to the High Court that a forfeiture order may be made, in the proceedings for the offence or even where the High Court is satisfied that a person is to be charged with an offence under any of ss. 15 to 18 and that a forfeiture order may be made in those proceedings. Especially in the latter case (which did not exist in previous legislation: Home Office and Northern Ireland Office, Legislation against Terrorism (Cm. 4178, London, 1998), para. 13.26), prosecutors may wish to avail themselves of the possibility under para. 5(4) to apply for a restraint order to a judge in chambers without notice. The Anti-terrorism, Crime and Security Act 2001, sch. 2, amends para. 5 to bring forward the bite of restraint orders. Under the amended version, they may also apply when a criminal investigation has been started with regard to an offence under any of ss. 15 to 18 and it appears to the High Court that a forfeiture order may be made in any proceedings for the offence. In this way, there is no need to wait for charges to be brought or even to be anticipated, and the forfeiture may arise in proceedings other than under sch. 4.

Lord Lloyd suggested that the restraint order procedure should be handled by the Crown Court so as to reduce the procedural complications for police and prosecutors and also up to five days before an arrest (Inquiry into Legislation against Terrorism (Cm. 3420, London, 1996), paras 13.26, 13.27). But there is no power of restraint order given to the Crown Court (Home Office and Northern Ireland Office, Legislation against Terrorism (Cm. 4178, London, 1998), para. 13.26) — the power is confined, unlike in Northern Ireland (see below) to the more remote High Court.

The effect of a restraint order is to prohibit a person to whom notice of it is given from dealing with the relevant property. To reinforce the powers of restraint, sch. 4, para. 7 allows a constable a summary power of seizure of any property subject to a restraint order for the purpose of preventing it from being removed from the jurisdiction, though the seizure should then be notified to the High Court which will give directions. The consequences of restraint orders in respect of land registration are covered by para. 8. Once an order is issued, notice must be given to any person affected by the order, and such person can apply for variation of the order (para. 6). A restraint order shall be discharged on such an application if the proceedings in respect of the offence are not instituted within such time as the High Court considers reasonable, or, in any event, if the proceedings for the offence have been 'concluded' as defined by para. 11 (though there may then be imposed a final forfeiture order).

Where a restraint order is discharged because proceedings are not instituted within a reasonable time or where proceedings for an offence under any of ss. 15 to 18 do not result in conviction for an offence or result in conviction which is subsequently pardoned or quashed, any person who had an interest in any property which was subject to the order may apply under para. 9 to the High Court for compensation (payable by the police or Director of Public Prosecutions, depending on the assignment of blame as below). However, the right to compensation is strictly confined by para. 9(4), by which the High Court must be satisfied:

(a) that there was a serious default on the part of a person concerned in the investigation or prosecution of the offence,

(b) that the person in default was or was acting as a member of a police force, or was a member of the Crown Prosecution Service or was acting on behalf of the Service,

(c) that the applicant has suffered loss in consequence of anything done in relation to the property by or in pursuance of the forfeiture order or restraint order, and

(d) that, having regard to all the circumstances, it is appropriate to order compensation to be paid.

Furthermore, by para. 9(5), the High Court shall not order compensation to be paid where it appears to it that proceedings for the offence would have been instituted even if the serious default had not occurred. A slightly more generous compensation provision is set out in para. 10, which applies where a forfeiture order or a restraint order is made in or in relation to proceedings for an offence under any of ss. 15 to 18, where the conviction is subsequently quashed on an appeal under s. 7(2) or (5); a person who had an interest in any property which was subject to the order may receive compensation if the High Court is satisfied the applicant has suffered loss and it is appropriate to order compensation to be paid (in this case by the Secretary of State).

Forfeiture or restraint orders made in Scotland or Northern Ireland may be enforced in England and Wales under sch. 4, para. 13. The same applies to orders made under corresponding legislation in the British Islands (Channel Islands and the Isle of Man) and even, under para. 14 in external jurisdictions specified by order. In these cases, the role of justices' chief executive shall be exercised by the appropriate officer of the High Court. Under the former Prevention of Terrorism (Temporary Provisions) Act 1989 (Enforcement of External Orders) Order 1995 (SI 1995 No. 760), the only external country where a cooperation arrangement was agreed was India. However, its replacement, the Terrorism Act 2000 (Enforcement of External Orders) Order 2001 (SI 2001 No. 3927), includes not only India but unilaterally extends the order to all European Union States and all G7 States. The prospects for actual cooperation depend on further agreements actually being signed, though some are being considered at European Union level (see Chapter 10).

Corresponding provisions for Scotland are set out in pt II of sch. 4 (paras 15 to 28). The powers are conferred principally upon the Court of Session. Applications for restraint orders shall be made by the Lord Advocate under para. 21.

Forfeiture in Northern Ireland is covered by pt III of sch. 4 (paras 29 to 40). By para. 32, the 'proper officer' of the court is defined as (a) where the forfeiture order is made by a court of summary jurisdiction, the clerk of petty sessions, and (b) where the forfeiture order is made by the Crown Court, the appropriate officer of the Crown Court. Applications for restraint orders are normally made by prosecutors under para. 33. However, an additional path is provided by para. 36, which allows the Secretary of State to make an order 'in any case in which it appears to him that the information which it would be necessary to provide in support of an application to the High Court or a judge under those provisions would, if disclosed, be likely to place any person in danger or prejudice the capability of members of the Royal Ulster Constabulary to investigate an offence under any of ss. 15 to 18'. It must be doubted whether this executive procedure (which was recommended for abolition in Inquiry into Legislation against Terrorism (Cm. 3420, London, 1996), para. 13.22) could withstand challenge under Article 6 of the European Convention, especially as other sensitive decisions under the Terrorism Act 2000 (such as the extension of detention) have been placed in independent judicial hands. Another special feature in Northern Ireland is that it is a specific offence under para. 37 to contravene a restraint order (punishable on indictment, to imprisonment for a term not exceeding 14 years, to a fine or to both, or on summary conviction, to imprisonment for a term not exceeding six months, to a fine not exceeding the statutory maximum, or to both). This offence is additional to the power of the High Court to deal with the contravention of a restraint order as a contempt of court (as would apply in England, Wales and Scotland). The offence has the advantage of allowing special pre-trial and trial processes to be applied. By para. 37(2). it is a defence to prove that there was a reasonable excuse for the contravention; s. 118 does not apply (see Chapter 6).

The final measures in sch. 4, pt IV (which applies throughout the United Kingdom), relate to the impact of forfeiture in the case of 'qualifying insolvency proceedings' (defined in para. 53). The effect is that an application can be made under paras 46 and 47 during the period of six months beginning with the making of a forfeiture order by an insolvency practitioner in respect of property which the insolvency practitioner would, but for the forfeiture order, exercise a function. In that case, the property shall cease to be subject to the forfeiture order and any ancillary order, and shall be dealt with in the insolvency proceedings as if the forfeiture order had never been made. In this way, the insolvency proceedings are given full priority. Nevertheless, under para. 48, the Secretary of State shall be taken to be a creditor in those proceedings to the amount or value of the forfeited property, albeit that he shall rank after the debts of all other creditors. Aside from applications against property known to be subject to forfeiture, insolvency practitioners are also given some relief under para. 51 from liability where they unwittingly seize or dispose of property which is subject to a forfeiture order or a restraint order, provided there is a reasonable belief that they are entitled to do so in the exercise of their functions, and they would be so entitled if the property were not subject to a forfeiture order or a restraint order. An Order in Council may be made under para. 52 to grant to insolvency practitioners in the Islands and designated countries corresponding rights under pt IV.

3.4 SEIZURE OF TERRORIST CASH

In the field of terrorist property, the most eye-catching change introduced in the Terrorism Act 2000 is the power of seizure of cash at borders — a form of civil, *in rem* forfeiture. This change is based around the recommendations of the Lloyd Report (Inquiry into Legislation against Terrorism (Cm. 3420, London, 1996), ch.13.33 — but note that the report called for powers to apply only to cash being taken out of the country and subject to a lower limit of £2,500 and with authorisation to hold for more that 48 hours being tested by a circuit judge). The powers are similar to those in the Drug Trafficking Act 1994, ss. 42 to 48, save that they affect not only external borders but also cash elsewhere (more akin to the pending Proceeds of Crime Bill 2001–02 HC no. 31 pt V). The powers first set out in the Terrorism Act 2000 were confined to borders (including between Britain and Northern Ireland) because of the historical precedents and presumably because borders provide a choke-point where effective interception can take place. Mainly because of the desire to remove this limitation, the opportunity was taken by s. 1 and sch. 1 of the Anti-terrorism, Crime and Security Act 2001 to replace wholesale ss. 24 and 31 of the Terrorism Act 2000. Consequential amendments to court process and public funding provisions are made by s. 2. As with drug trafficking, no criminal conviction is required.

According to s. 1(1) of the 2001 Act, the powers of forfeiture are to enable 'cash' which (a) is intended to be used for the purposes of terrorism, (b) consists of resources of a proscribed organisation, or (c) is, or represents, property obtained through terrorism, to be forfeited in civil proceedings before a magistrates' court or (in Scotland) the sheriff. It is emphasised under s. 1(2) that the powers conferred (under sch. 1) are exercisable in relation to any cash whether or not any proceedings have been brought for an offence in connection with the cash. Under sch. 1, para. 1 (previously s. 24 of the Terrorism Act 2000), 'terrorist cash' means cash within subsection (1)(a) or (b) of s. 1, or property earmarked as terrorist property. For these purposes, 'cash' includes coins and notes in any currency, postal orders, cheques of any kind, including travellers' cheques, bankers' drafts, bearer bonds and bearer shares (a category added in 2001) and such other kinds of monetary instrument as the Secretary of State may specify by order. Any amount, no matter how large or how small, may be seized (see Home Office and Northern

Ireland Office, Legislation against Terrorism (Cm. 4178, London, 1998), para.
6.28). Counterfeit 'cash' is not within para. 1 but could be seized under powers in
connection with the prohibition on import and export under ss. 20 and 21 of the
Forgery and Counterfeiting Act 1981 (HL Debs. vol. 629 col. 1049, 6 December
2001, Lord Rooker).

By sch. 1, para. 2 (formerly s. 25 of the Terrorism Act 2000), an 'authorised
officer' may seize and detain any cash to which this section applies if he has
reasonable grounds for suspecting that it is terrorist cash. The seizure may be
undertaken even if it is not reasonably practicable to seize only that part of the
cash believed to be terrorist cash. The cohort of 'authorised officers' comprises
constables, a customs officers and immigration officers, but the Code of Practice
for Authorised Officers Order 2001 (SI 2001 No. 425), art. 6, advises that the
powers should normally be exercised by the police.

Once seized, the cash must be released not later than the end of the period of 48
hours beginning with the time when it is seized. However, the detention period may be
extended under sch. 1, para. 3 (formerly s. 26 of the Terrorism Act 2000). An
authorised officer or the Commissioners of Customs and Excise (or in Scotland a
procurator fiscal) may apply to a magistrates' court (or in Scotland, the sheriff) for an
order which shall specify a period not later than the end of the period of three months
beginning with the date of the order. The court may grant the order only if satisfied that
there are reasonable grounds to suspect that the cash is terrorist cash, or the resources
of a proscribed organisation, or earmarked as terrorist property and, in whichever of
the three situations applies, that the continued detention of the cash is justified pending
completion of an investigation of its origin or derivation or pending a determination
whether to institute criminal proceedings (whether in the United Kingdom or
elsewhere) which relate to the cash or pending the conclusion of proceedings which
have been started. A court detention order may be renewed, but cash shall not be
detained by virtue of an order under this section after the end of the period of two years
beginning with the date when the first order was made in relation to it.

During its detention, the cash shall, under sch. 1, para. 4 (formerly s. 27 of the
Terrorism Act 2000), unless required as evidence of an offence, be held in an
interest bearing account. And the interest accruing on the cash shall be added to it
on its release or forfeiture.

Under sch. 1, para. 5 (formerly s. 27(2)), any person may apply to a magistrates'
court, or in Scotland to the sheriff, for a direction that seized cash be released. An
authorised officer, or, in Scotland, the procurator fiscal, may themselves take the
initiative to release cash if he is satisfied that its detention is no longer justified,
and he has notified the magistrates' court or sheriff who made the order by virtue
of which the cash is being detained. But no cash may be released while
proceedings on an application for its forfeiture under para. 6 (below) have not been
concluded, or while proceedings, whether in the United Kingdom or elsewhere,
which relate to the cash have not been concluded.

The next stage in the process will normally be forfeiture procedures under para.
6 (formerly s. 28 of the Terrorism Act 2000). This process is quite distinct from

that under s. 23, and it is regrettable that the same terminology is utilised for both. An authorised officer or the Commissioners of Customs and Excise may apply to a magistrates' court, or in Scotland the Scottish Ministers (formerly the procurator fiscal) may apply to the sheriff, for an order forfeiting detained cash. A magistrates' court or the sheriff may grant an application only if satisfied on the balance of probabilities that the cash is terrorist cash. The forfeiture can apply not only against the seized cash, but also in relation to any accrued profits (para. 15). By the former s. 28(5) of the 2000 Act, it was provided that the proceedings to the sheriff should be civil proceedings, perhaps implying that, aside from the standard of proof, proceedings before magistrates should be treated as criminal. However, s. 1(1) of the Anti-terrorism, Crime and Security Act 2001 now states that forfeiture is to take place in civil proceedings whether before magistrates or a sheriff.

Parties making a claim to ownership of detained cash may apply for release of the cash (or their share of it) under sch. 1, para. 9 during the proceedings or at any other time. Furthermore, the forfeiture will not apply against an excepted joint owner — a joint tenant who obtained the property in circumstances in which it would not (as against him) be earmarked as terrorist property (para. 6; 'property' is defined in para. 17). This idea of earmarking is explained further in paras 11 and 12 which ensure that forfeiture can apply to property obtained through terrorism, and property which represents property obtained through terrorism. By para. 11, a person obtains property through terrorism if he obtains property by, or in return for, acts of terrorism (such as carrying out a killing or explosion in return for payment) or acts carried out for the purposes of terrorism (for example, leasing a house to a terrorist cell). It is immaterial whether or not any money, goods or services were provided in order to put the person in question in a position to carry out the acts. Thus, property still counts as having been obtained through terrorism regardless of any investment in it. 'So if a person buys guns with honestly come by money, and sells them at a profit, the whole of the proceeds of the sale will count as having been obtained through terrorism, and not just the profit.' (Home Office, Explanatory Notes on the Anti-terrorism, Crime and Security Bill, London, 2001, para. 340.) And it is not necessary to show that the property was obtained through a particular act of terrorism if it is proven that the property was obtained through a range of terrorist acts, each of which would have been an act of terrorism, or acts carried out for the purposes of terrorism. Therefore, it will not matter, for example, if it cannot be established whether certain funds are attributable to extortion, customs evasion or armed robbery, provided that all those are acts of terrorism or acts carried out for the purposes of terrorism.

Having established that the property is obtained through terrorism in these ways, it is then 'earmarked as terrorist property' under sch. 1, para. 12. If earmarked terrorist property is disposed of (as defined by para. 18), it remains earmarked only if the recipient obtained it on a disposal from the person who obtained the property through terrorism or if the recipient himself is a person from whom the cash could be directly seized. Conversely, anyone who obtains terrorist property on disposal and does so in good faith, for value (which requires, under para. 18, the consideration to have been paid over or performed) and without notice that it was earmarked is immune from forfeiture (para. 16). Thus, a purchaser who paid full value for a car used in terrorism but unaware of its terrorist origins is exempt from forfeiture and the property is no longer earmarked, though the cash paid for the car then becomes earmarked. This immunity also applies to civil damages paid out of terrorist property or to payments of compensation or restitution orders under the Powers of Criminal Courts (Sentencing) Act 2000. But if the property remains earmarked, it can be traced through to property which represents the original terrorist cash (para. 13). Thus, if a person is given a car in return for carrying out an act of terrorism and then sells it, the cash so obtained will be property earmarked as terrorist property, as will property secured when the cash is spent. Mixed property can also be apportioned and the terrorist cash element forfeited (para. 14). Paragraph 15 provides that if profits accrue in respect of the property obtained through terrorism or traceable property, the profits are also to be treated as representative property. For these purposes, the definition of disposal in para. 18 encompasses where the property is dealt with in whole or part, including the creation or grant of an interest in the property, or where there is a payment, in cash or any other kind of property, to another, or where property changes hands on death.

The provisions on property earmarked as terrorist property apply under para. 18 to events occurring before commencement of the Act. So even if cash is obtained through terrorism before commencement of the schedule, it is still liable to seizure and forfeiture under the schedule. This retrospective application probably does not breach Article 7 of the European Convention. One should bear in mind that these proceedings are *in rem* and therefore may not be treated as being in the nature of a penalty pursuant to the proof of a criminal offence (compare *Welch* v *United Kingdom*, App. no.17440/90, Ser. A. 307-A, (1995) 20 EHRR 247).

Paragraph 7 of sch. 1 (formerly s. 29 of the 2000 Act) provides for an appeal by way of a rehearing (but only by a party to the hearing) within 30 days in England and Wales, to the Crown Court, or in Scotland to the Court of Session, or in Northern Ireland, to the county court. Under para. 7(4), the court hearing the appeal may make any order it thinks appropriate, which may allow it to order the release of part of the cash to meet reasonable legal expenses in connection with the appeal. The grant of public funding (as authorised by s. 2(1) of the Anti-terrorism, Crime and Security Act 2001) is important as the implications of being the possessor or owner of forfeited cash clearly raise criminal implications for the purposes of Article 6 of the European Convention.

If the cash is subject to a forfeiture order, then, by sch. 1, para. 8 (formerly s. 30 of the 2000 Act), it shall be paid into the Consolidated Fund (in other words, it is central government money and not available to local law enforcement agencies). If the cash is not subject to a forfeiture order, the person to whom it belongs or from whom it was seized may apply for compensation under para. 10. This right to compensation may arise from a failure to put the cash into an interest-bearing account and thereby the court is invited to award as compensation the amount that would have been accrued in interest (para. 10(2)) (interest may not have been earned under para. 4 if the cash is required as an exhibit in court). But compensation may also be granted for any 'exceptional' loss on top of any possible loss of interest (para. 10(4)).

Further rules concerning the roles of authorised officers are set out in s. 115 and sch. 14 to the Terrorism Act 2000. By para. 2 of sch. 14, an officer may enter a vehicle for the purpose of exercising any statutory functions conferred on him by virtue of this Act, and may, by para. 3, use reasonable force for the purpose of exercising a power. By para. 4, any information acquired by an officer may be supplied:

(a)   to the Secretary of State for use in relation to immigration;
(b)   to the Commissioners of Customs and Excise or a customs officer;
(c)   to a constable;
(d)   to the Director General of the National Criminal Intelligence Service or of the National Crime Squad;
(e)   to a person specified by order of the Secretary of State for use of a kind specified in the order.

Schedule 14, para. 6, also envisages the compilation of a code of practice for authorised officers. This has been issued pursuant to the Terrorism Act 2000 (Code of Practice for Authorised Officers) Order 2001 (SI 2001 No. 425) and is available at http://www.homeoffice.gov.uk/terrorism/copao.pdf. Suitable amendments to take account of the replacement of the powers by the Anti-terrorism, Crime and Security Act 2001 are allowed by order under ss. 1(5) and 2(4) to (7) of that Act. The power under s. 1(5) was considered to be excessive by the Delegated Powers and Regulatory Reform Select Committee (Report on the Anti-terrorism, Crime and Security Bill (2001–02 HL 45), para. 15).

The following desired practices emerge from the Code. The first (in para. 6) is that the powers to seize and detain cash under the Act should only be exercised by an immigration officer or customs officer exceptionally. If such officers do exercise the power, they should alert a police officer at the earliest opportunity in order to continue any investigation. Secondly, by para. 9, it is stated that:

'Reasonable grounds for suspecting' are likely to depend upon particular circumstances and the authorised officer should take into account such factors as how the cash was discovered, the amount involved, its origins, intended movement, destination, reasons given for a cash as opposed to normal banking transaction, whether the courier(s) and/or the owners of the cash (if different) have any links with terrorists or terrorist groups, whether here or overseas. Where the authorised officer has suspicions about the cash he/she should give the person who has possession of it a reasonable opportunity to provide an explanation on the details of its ownership, origins, purpose, destination and reasons for moving the amount in this way and to provide the authorised officer with supporting documentation. The authorised officer should make clear to the person that anything said will be noted and used in the event that the cash is seized and an application made to the court for its detention or forfeiture.

Thirdly, authorised officers are advised under para. 13 of the Code to give a written notification to the person from whom the cash is seized (including a statement of powers, value seized and rights); a copy should be given to the person from whom the money was taken and they should be asked to sign the copy kept by the officer.

Detailed rules of court are provided for under s. 31 of the Terrorism Act 2000. The Magistrates' Courts (Detention and Forfeiture of Terrorist Cash) (No. 2) Rules 2001 (SI 2001 No. 4013, replacing SI 2001 No. 194 (L. 6)) prescribe the procedures to be followed for applications to a magistrates' court and also prescribe the forms to be used. The Crown Court (Amendment) Rules 2001 (SI 2001 No. 193 (L.5)) amend the Crown Court Rules 1982 to establish appeal procedures to be followed under s. 28. Rule 2 requires the notice of appeal to state the grounds of appeal. Rule 3 provides for notice of the appeal to be given to persons with an interest in proceedings who may not have been joined as parties to the case in the magistrates' court.

It seems strange that magistrates' courts should handle forfeiture litigation under s. 28 of the 2000 Act. These disputes could well involve complex civil issues — much better put before a Crown Court. Attempts to make such a switch were defeated in the House of Lords on the basis that the corresponding jurisdiction in respect of drugs-related cash had not encountered any problems (HL Debs. vol. 629 col. 305, 28 November 2001; col. 1047, 6 December 2001, Lord Rooker). If applicable, a civil standard of proof is probably not *per se* contrary to Article 6 of the European Convention (see *Raimondo* v *Italy*, App. no. 12954/87, Ser. A. 281-A) but, as mentioned previously, a failure to grant public funding could cause problems (compare *Benham* v *United Kingdom*, App. no. 19380/92, Reports 1996-III). Enforcement problems may also exist at an earlier stage of the process as there has been just one case of seizure under the Terrorism Act 2000 during its first year (HL Debs. vol. 629 col. 307, 28 November 2001, Lord Rooker).

3.5   UN MEASURES IN RELATION TO AFGHANISTAN

The admixture of international and State-sponsored terrorism has allowed for international organisations like the United Nations to play a direct role against terrorist finances. This interplay has been most evident in regard to the Afghani government's support for Al Qa'ida. The process began with the UN Security Council Resolution, Sanctions Order 1267 on 15 October 1999 (S/RES/1267), and has been extended on 19 December 2000 with Order 1333 (S/RES/1333). Sanctions were then imposed for 12 months because of the Taliban support for international terrorism and their failure to hand over Usama bin Laden for trial in accordance with the demands of the Security Council in its resolution 1267. The sanctions included an arms embargo (backing a European Union embargo imposed by 96/726/CFSP of 17 December 1996); the closure of Taliban (non-diplomatic) offices overseas; the closure of Ariana Afghan Airlines offices overseas and a ban on all international flights to or from Taliban-controlled Afghanistan. There is also a freeze of Taliban funds as well as financial assets of Usama bin Laden and individuals and entities associated with him, including those in the Al Qa'ida network. In so far as necessary, the measures were implemented under the United Nations Act 1946 (see Afghanistan (United Nations Sanctions) Order 2001 (SI 2001 No. 396)). Further details were set out by the Bank of England in February 2001 (http://www.bankofengland.co.uk/afghan2001.pdf).

Enforcement became a more pressing matter after the 11 September attacks. The bank accounts of 160 Afghan nationals and seven corporations were frozen in the aftermath, though most related to the Taliban government and its agencies rather than Al Qa'ida (*The Times*, 25 September 2001, p. 4). Further measures were also passed. By the Terrorism (United Nations Measures) Order 2001 (SI 2001 No. 3365), issued on 10 October 2001 and implementing the further UN Security Council resolution 1373 of the 28 September (S/RES/1373), it was made an offence (additional to any in the Terrorism Act 2000) to make funds available for the benefit of terrorists (art. 3) or to facilitate such offences (art. 5). It is also made an offence to fail to disclose knowledge or suspicion of offences (art. 7). Offences must be prosecuted by the Secretary of State or with the consent of an Attorney-General (art. 10). The Treasury is also granted the powers to freeze funds (art. 4); this could be done without reference to any court order, though a person affected could then apply to court to set aside the order. The Treasury can also summarily demand the disclosure of financial information (art. 8).

3.6   FREEZING ORDERS

Though concerted action has been taken against Afghanistan through the United Nations, support from the international community for action against other non-United Kingdom based sites and forms of terrorism can be neither assured nor timely. Therefore, Part II of the Anti-terrorism, Crime and Security Act 2001 allows for action by the United Kingdom Government of a unilateral nature: 'If a decision to impose sanctions is taken at European Community level or under a United Nations Security Council resolution, it would not be appropriate to use the power.' (HL Debs. vol. 629 col. 353, 28 November 2001, Lord McIntosh). The purpose is to deny funds and assets to foreign terrorists, and this will be achieved by executive order and without scrutiny by the courts. As a result, such orders may be open to challenge on the basis of Article 6 and Article 1 of Protocol 1 of the European Convention. Pre-existing powers to prohibit financial transactions deemed to be threatening to the national economy were set out in s. 2 of the Emergency Laws (Re-enactments and Repeals) Act 1964 (as amended by s. 55 of the Finance Act 1968). Section 2 is repealed by s. 16 of the 2001 Act (but its demise does not affect any references to that provision in other subordinate legislation). The measures below are thought to be better tailored than the 1964 Act which was a relict from regulations during the Second World War. Under that

Act, the United Kingdom can freeze the assets of an overseas government and
overseas residents only if the country or the persons in question is (or are) acting
to the detriment of the United Kingdom economy. Under the Anti-terrorism, Crime
and Security Act 2001, there may also be a threat to the life or property of United
Kingdom nationals or residents.

By s. 4 of the Anti-terrorism, Crime and Security Act 2001, the Treasury may
make a freezing order if the following two conditions are satisfied:

> (2)   The first condition is that the Treasury reasonably believe that—
>
> (a)   action to the detriment of the United Kingdom's economy (or part of
> it) has been or is likely to be taken by a person or persons, or
>
> (b)   action constituting a threat to the life or property of one or more
> nationals of the United Kingdom or residents of the United Kingdom has been
> or is likely to be taken by a person or persons.
>
> (3)   If one person is believed to have taken or to be likely to take the action
> the second condition is that the person is—
>
> (a)   the government of a country or territory outside the United Kingdom,
> or
>
> (b)   a resident of a country or territory outside the United Kingdom.

'Nationals' and 'residents' are defined by s. 9. It should be noted that there is no
mention of terrorism, so s. 4 must be ascribed to the 'security' part of the Act. It
should also be noted that, by subsection (3), there must be a foreign perpetrator.

The procedure for making an order is set out in s. 10 of the 2001 Act. It is
exercisable by statutory instrument which must be laid before Parliament after
being made and is subject to the requirement of affirmative resolution within 28
days. As a matter of practice, the Bank of England will draw the attention of banks
to such orders (HL Debs. vol. 629 col. 362, 28 November 2001, Lord McIntosh).
Orders can be amended under s. 11 so as to change to names of the person or
persons (or any of the persons) to whom or for whose benefit funds are not to be
made available. In this case a statutory instrument containing the further order is
subject to annulment in pursuance of a resolution of either House of Parliament.
Likewise, by s. 12, a statutory instrument containing an order revoking a freezing
order (without re-enacting it) is subject to annulment in pursuance of a resolution
of either House of Parliament. On a technical point of Parliamentary process, s. 13
provides that freezing order instruments are not to be treated as hybrid, and so they
are not subject to procedures by which parties potentially affected must be afforded
the opportunity to make representations. By s. 14, an order under this Part may
include supplementary, incidental, saving or transitional provisions as well as
provisions directly relating to the freezing of assets.

The contents of freezing orders are related in s. 5 of the 2001 Act. A freezing
order is an order which prohibits persons from making funds available to or for
the benefit of a person or persons specified in the order. 'Funds' are defined as 'are
financial assets and economic benefits of any kind'. In sch. 3, para. 2, funds are

further defined as including 'gold, cash, deposits, securities (such as stocks, shares and debentures) and such other matters as the order may specify'. This definition will not cover all forms of property, but probably is sufficient to catch fungible assets within the financial sector. Though made in relation to foreign terrorism, the order will apply to all persons in the United Kingdom and to all persons elsewhere who are nationals of the United Kingdom or are bodies incorporated under the law of any part of the United Kingdom or are Scottish partnerships. Those placed under a duty must not make available funds to the person or persons reasonably believed by the Treasury to have taken or to be likely to take the action referred to in s. 4 or any person the Treasury reasonably believe has provided or is likely to provide assistance (directly or indirectly) to that person or any of those persons. By s. 15, it is expressly provided that a freezing order binds the Crown (save for Her Majesty in her private capacity), though no contravention by the Crown of a provision of a freezing order is to make the Crown criminally liable; but the High Court or in Scotland the Court of Session may, on the application of a person appearing to the Court to have an interest, declare unlawful any act or omission of the Crown which constitutes such a contravention.

Further details about the contents of freezing orders are introduced by s. 6 and set out in sch. 3 to the 2001 Act. By sch. 3, para. 3, a freezing order must explain the nature of the prohibition by including terms as to the meaning of making funds available to or for the benefit of a person. Normally, this will include transactions such as allowing a person to withdraw from an account, honouring a cheque, crediting a person's account with interest, releasing documents of title (such as share certificates), making available the proceeds of realisation of a person's property or making a payment to or for a person's benefit. Conversely, by para. 4, the order must allow for the granting of licences authorising funds to be made available (such as for basic living expenses or legal fees). Those handling the account may be required under para. 5 to provide information and documentation if required to do so and it is reasonably needed for the purpose of ascertaining whether an offence under the order has been committed. A further disclosure requirement may be imposed under para. 6 where:

(a)   the person required to disclose is specified or falls within a description specified in the order (such as an employee of a institution within the Regulated Sector), and

(b)   the person required to disclose knows or suspects, or has grounds for knowing or suspecting, that a person specified in the freezing order as a person to whom or for whose benefit funds are not to be made available is a customer of his or has been a customer of his at any time since the freezing order came into force or is a person with whom he has dealings in the course of his business or has had such dealings at any time since the freezing order came into force, and

(c)   the information came to him in the course of a business in the regulated sector (likely to be defined by reference to sch. 3A to the Terrorism Act 2000).

In those circumstances, the order will require disclosure to the Treasury as soon as is practicable, subject to a claim to legal privilege. Paragraph 7 envisages a range of offences, including:

(a) failure to comply with a prohibition imposed by the order or engaging in an activity knowing or intending that it will enable or facilitate the commission by another person of such an offence;

(b) failing without reasonable excuse to provide information, or to produce a document, in response to a requirement made under the order or providing false information or documentation.

The offences in (b) may be excused if the accused proves that he did not know and had no reason to suppose that the person to whom or for whose benefit funds were made available, or were to be made available, was the person (or one of the persons) specified in the freezing order as a person to whom or for whose benefit funds are not to be made available. The penalties specified are, for offences under (a), on summary conviction, to imprisonment for a term not exceeding six months or to a fine not exceeding the statutory maximum or to both or on conviction on indictment, to imprisonment for a term not exceeding two years or to a fine or to both, and for offences under (b) on summary conviction to imprisonment for a term not exceeding six months or to a fine not exceeding level 5 on the standard scale or to both. Paragraph 8 allows for the institution of proceedings to be restricted to the Treasury or the Director of Public Prosecutions or by their consent.

As for challenging such orders, by sch. 3, para. 10, an order may include provision for the award of compensation to or on behalf of a person on the grounds that he has suffered loss as a result of an order or the refusal of a licence. It must be shown that the claimant has behaved reasonably (which may include provision requiring him to mitigate his loss, for instance by applying for a licence). The conditions are also likely to require that the circumstances involve negligence or other fault. An application shall be made to the High Court or, in Scotland, the Court of Session. However, the legislation does not as such provide for substantive challenge or appeal or review, though, by para. 11, a person is specified in the order as a person to whom or for whose benefit funds are not to be made available, and he makes a written request to the Treasury to give him the reason why he is so specified, as soon as is practicable the Treasury must give the person the reason in writing. On the basis of these reasons, or on the basis of the procedures followed, an application for judicial review would be possible (HL Debs. vol. 629 col. 1060, 6 December 2001, Lord McIntosh), but the applicant is unlikely to succeed if the order has specifically been considered by Parliament which it will have been, given that it is subject to the affirmative procedure (see *R v Secretary of State for the Environment, ex parte Nottinghamshire CC* [1986] 2 WLR 1; *R v Secretary of State for the Environment, ex parte Hammersmith and Fulham LBC* [1990] 3 WLR 878).

By s. 7 of the 2001 Act, the Treasury must keep a freezing order under review, and, in any event, by s. 8, it must cease after two years.

3.7   CONCLUSIONS

Arguably, with the development of 'normal' laws — such as the Criminal Law Act 1988 and the Proceeds of Crime Act 1995 — and, more recently, the coming into force of the regulatory, investigative and prosecution powers of the Financial Services Authority (http://www.fsa.gov.uk/) under the Financial Services and Markets Act 2000, ss. 146, 165 and 402, the need for these special offences and powers is no longer so evident. It is interesting that the draconian powers in the Northern Ireland (Emergency Provisions) Act 1991 were not renewed in 1996 but were transferred (albeit not in their entirety) to the Proceeds of Crime (Northern Ireland) Order 1996. The Government admits that other powers are already relevant and important (Home Office and Northern Ireland Office, Legislation against Terrorism (Cm. 4178, London, 1998), para. 6.21). Consolidation would also have the advantage of avoiding some of the complexities faced by investigators. At very least, this consolidation could be considered in response to the work of the Home Office Working Group on Confiscation, *Third Report on Criminal Assets* (Home Office, London, 1998). Its recommendation of the benefits of a 'central confiscation agency would be to focus efforts in one place, build expertise and foster multi-disciplinary working' seems worthwhile and could take up the task from more limited liaison and specialist units (see Norman, P., 'The Terrorist Finance Unit and the Joint Action Group on Organized Crime' (1988) *Howard Journal* 375; RUC Chief Constable, Annual Report for 1998–99 (Belfast, 1999), p. 40). A central agency would surely be more energetic than the current authorities, whose efforts are dismissed in a report by the Cabinet Office Performance and Innovation Office, Recovering the Proceeds of Crime (http:// www.cabinet-office.gov.uk/innovation/2000/crime/recovering/default.htm, London, 2000, paras 1.36, 4.18, 4.31):

> The UK's anti-money laundering disclosure regime, under which financial institutions and others are required to disclose details of all suspicious transactions, generates an average of 15,000 disclosures each year, a small figure given the size of the UK's financial markets. And they are not received in equal measure from all types of institution required to disclose. There have been very few money laundering prosecutions and convictions. In 1995, there were 29 prosecutions for money laundering in the UK, compared with 538 in Italy and 2,034 in the USA . . .
>
> What little data exists shows that, despite legislation that provides for confiscation upon conviction for all crimes, the UK's confiscation track record is poor. Very little is ordered to be confiscated, even less is collected . . .
>
> The problem is both legislative and a matter of operational priority.

The Proceeds of Crime Bill 2001–02 (HC No. 31) will create a Criminal Assets Recovery Agency with the functions of the recovery of criminal assets through confiscation, civil recovery, the exercise of Revenue functions and the accreditation and training of financial investigators. It fits with the establishment of an Economic Crime Unit within the National Criminal Intelligence Service and the Terrorist Finance Team (TFT) as a sub-unit. There is no reason why these bodies should not have the task of pursuing terrorist funds as a priority. But until such wider institutional reforms take effect, one can predict that the impact of the measures outlined in this chapter will remain very limited.

The sphere of international co-operation is another area where further development is required. Prominent amongst the relevant organisations is the Financial Action Task Force on Money Laundering which is under the umbrella of the OECD (see http://www1.oecd.org/fatf/). Since its establishment following a G7 meeting in 1989 (and now with 29 member States), the FATF has pursued the objectives of the development and promotion of policies (especially its Forty Recommendations and Interpretive Notes), both at national and international levels, to combat money laundering (see Srivastava, A., 'Regulating money laundering to combat terrorism' (2001) 151 *New Law Journal* 1466 at p. 1467). It also monitors progress in implementing anti-money laundering measures, reviews money laundering techniques and counter-measures, and promotes the adoption and implementation of anti-money laundering measures.

At an extraordinary Plenary on the Financing of Terrorism held in Washington DC on 29 and 30 October 2001, the FATF expanded its mission beyond criminal money laundering so as to include terrorist financing. To this end it devised eight new Special Recommendations which demand that all States deny terrorists and their supporters access to the international financial system. The required steps include the implementation of the relevant United Nations instruments, the criminalisation of the financing of terrorism, the freezing and confiscation of terrorist assets, the reporting of suspicious transactions, and inter-State cooperation. All countries around the world have been invited to assess their performance on these standards and to formulate action plans, with the threat of counter-measures against those which fail to show sufficient response. It will be June 2002 before the picture becomes known, but the United Kingdom government believes it already meets the standards (Treasury press release 118/01, 31 October 2001). In legislative terms, that seems a fair assessment, but the execution of the laws still leaves much to be desired.

Chapter Four
Terrorist investigations

4.1 BACKGROUND

There is a considerable overlap between Part IV of the Terrorism Act 2000, 'Terrorist investigations', and Part V, 'Counter-terrorist powers'. In large part, the division is historical and relates to the origins in different legislation of the provisions now in Parts IV and V. In truth, all could be described as counter-terrorist powers, and all relate to countering, preventive or investigative purposes or a mixture of each. A more thorough codification would have been helpful. However, for present purposes, those responsible for drafting have utilised a technical definition of 'terrorist investigations' as a peg on which to hang various provisions within Part IV. The definition is set out in s. 32:

> . . . 'terrorist investigation' means an investigation of—
> (a) the commission, preparation or instigation of acts of terrorism,
> (b) an act which appears to have been done for the purposes of terrorism,
> (c) the resources of a proscribed organisation,
> (d) the possibility of making an order under section 3(3), or
> (e) the commission, preparation or instigation of an offence under this
> Act.

These terms will often cover not only investigations into possible criminal offences, but also other forms of preparatory work, such as in relation to proscription or transnational terrorism finances, might also be allowed.

4.2 CORDONS

The first set of powers in Part IV of the Terrorism Act 2000 is concerned with the setting up of cordons. These may or may not be connected with investigations. The typical scenario will be where the police suspect that a bomb has been planted or wish to take control over the vicinity of an actual explosion. The area may be cordoned off for protective purposes in the first case or to aid an investigation, especially forensic examinations, in the second case. These powers reproduce those in ss. 4 and 5 of the Prevention of Terrorism (Additional Powers) Act 1996 (incorporating section 16C and sch. 6A into the Prevention of Terrorism (Temporary Provisions) Act 1989), a response to reviews following the bombing in London Docklands and to fears of future attacks.

By s. 33 of the 2000 Act, a police officer (who by s. 34 must be of at least the rank of superintendent, unless there is urgency, in which case any constable may make a designation) can designate a 'cordoned area' if considered 'expedient for the purposes of a terrorist investigation'. The power is unusually broad, but is expressed in terms of expedience to cater for confused situations (HL Debs. vol. 613 col. 660, 16 May 2000, Lord Bassam):

> The police would not impose or maintain a cordon if they did not believe that to be the appropriate course of action in all the circumstances — and the involvement of a senior police officer in the process provides an adequate check on any tendency for over-use. However, that is not the same as requiring a reasonable belief that the cordon is necessary — which is what I take the amendment to mean. I am not sure that something which can be described as being 'reasonably necessary' achieves exactly that. However, I shall not over-egg that argument.
>
> An example might be where a bomb warning was imprecise, or the police believed it was inaccurate — deliberately or otherwise. In such a case the necessity for a cordon might be debatable, but it makes good sense to have one. Similarly, in the case of stop and search or parking restriction powers, there could be cases where a cordon might not be considered 'reasonably necessary' but could be to the general advantage. That is the important test. For instance, this might be the case if the alternatives, in the light of a terrorist threat to an event, were to authorise the use of the stop and search power or parking restrictions around the venue or to see the event cancelled altogether.

Because of the circumstances of grave emergency in which such operations arise, the designation may be oral in the first instance, but it must be confirmed in writing as soon as is reasonably practicable. It is not specified to whom the confirmation is to be given or where the written document is to be lodged, so the reality is that these remain matters under the control of the police unless challenged in court. Once an order has been issued under s. 33, the police are to demarcate the cordoned area, so far as is reasonably practicable by means of tape marked with the word 'police', or in such other manner as a constable considers appropriate. By s. 35, a designation under s. 33 has effect as specified in the order, but it must not endure longer than the end of the period of 14 days beginning with the day on which the designation is made, renewable for up to a further 14 days. While an area remains designated, any constable in uniform may, under s. 36(1):

(a)   order a person in a cordoned area to leave it immediately;

(b)   order a person immediately to leave premises which are wholly or partly in or adjacent to a cordoned area;

(c)   order the driver or person in charge of a vehicle in a cordoned area to move it from the area immediately;

(d)   arrange for the removal of a vehicle from a cordoned area;

(e)   arrange for the movement of a vehicle within a cordoned area;

(f)   prohibit or restrict access to a cordoned area by pedestrians or vehicles.

A person commits an offence if he fails to comply with an order, prohibition or restriction (the offence is punishable by summary conviction only to imprisonment for a term not exceeding three months, a fine not exceeding level 4 on the standard scale, or both). It is a defence under s. 36(3) for a person charged with an offence to prove that he had a reasonable excuse for his failure; lack of clear specification of the designated area might be one basis for the defence. Section 118 does not apply to this defence (see further Chapter 6).

Under the Anti-terrorism, Crime and Security Act 2001, sch. 7, para. 30, s. 34 of the 2000 Act is amended to allow the British Transport Police and Ministry of Defence Police, in certain circumstances, to designate areas in which cordons may be erected for the purposes of terrorist investigations.

One might accept that these are sensible, unobjectionable powers, though the cordoning power is associated with an alarming searching power which seems largely unregulated. The Government vaguely talked about common law powers being available anyway, but the common law power of exclusion is based on breach of the peace rather than forensic or protective purposes (as in the notable case of Alan Clark, MP (*The Times*, 14 June 1996, p. 5), who was fined £650 at Bow Street Magistrates' Courts for driving through a police cordon during a bomb alert in Piccadilly, London, the conviction being sustained on the basis of the offence of obstruction of the police in the execution of their duty). Consequently, there was a gap in the law, but it was not one which really caused any major practical problem.

4.3 COMPULSORY OBTAINING OF TESTIMONY AND EVIDENCE

Rather more related to terrorist investigations, and derived from the part of the Prevention of Terrorism (Temporary Provisions) Act 1989 to have originally used that term (in s. 17 and sch. 7), is s. 37 of the Terrorism Act 2000 which introduces the measures in sch. 5 by which testimony and documentary evidence may be obtained under compulsion. The schedule offers a series of powers and procedures which are variants upon the search warrants and production orders under sch. 1 of the Police and Criminal Evidence Act 1984 (PACE) or the Police and Criminal Evidence (Northern Ireland) Order 1989 in Northern Ireland. The main differences are the triggering criteria, which relate broadly to 'terrorist investigations' rather than to specified offences (specified serious arrestable offences under sch. 1 to

PACE 1984), the powers so triggered and, in Northern Ireland, the issuing authorities. However, in many respects, the terminology of the PACE legislation is followed and, by sch. 5, para. 17, ss. 21 and 22 of PACE 1984 (seized material: access, copying and retention) are directly applied.

In so far as these powers (or any others in the Terrorism Act 2000) involve the search of premises, then they are subject to s. 116(1), by which a power to search premises conferred by virtue of the Act shall be taken to include power to search a container.

The first search power, to enter premises, to search the premises and any person found there, and to seize and retain any relevant material, is in sch. 5, para. 1(1): 'A constable may apply to a justice of the peace for the issue of a warrant under this paragraph for the purposes of a terrorist investigation.' To make an application, the constable must have reasonable grounds for believing that the evidence is likely to be of substantial value to a terrorist investigation, and that it must be seized in order to prevent it from being concealed, lost, damaged, altered or destroyed. In turn, the justice may grant an application under this paragraph only if satisfied under para. 1(5):

(a)   that the warrant is sought for the purposes of a terrorist investigation,

(b)   that there are reasonable grounds for believing that there is material on premises specified in the application which is likely to be of substantial value, whether by itself or together with other material, to a terrorist investigation and which does not consist of or include excepted material (within the meaning of paragraph 4 below), and

(c)   that the issue of a warrant is likely to be necessary in the circumstances of the case.

Any searches are also subject to the bounds of legal privilege. Paragraph 1 includes in the definition of 'terrorist investigation' anything likely to be of substantial value to 'a' terrorist investigation and not 'the' terrorist investigation. This is designed to avoid the situation where a police officer finds material relevant to a different terrorist investigation and would otherwise have to return to court for a further warrant. A corresponding change is made throughout the rest of the schedule. The power to seize and retain materials attracts additional powers to seize and retain articles for sifting elsewhere enabled under the Criminal Justice and Police Act 2001, ss. 50, 51 and 55 (a response to the judgment in *R* v *Chesterfield Justices and Chief Constable of Derbyshire, ex parte Bramley* [2000] 2 WLR 401).

Greater latitude is allowed in the second search power, in para. 2, because the application is made by a police officer of at least the rank of superintendent, and especially because the application does not relate to residential premises. There is no equivalent to this power in PACE 1984. In this case, the justice to whom the application is made need not be concerned that the issue of a warrant is likely to be necessary in the circumstances of the case. The purpose is to allow for mass searches, such as of lock up premises in a given area where it is suspected that bomb-makers are active but without sufficient knowledge as to the location of their premises. Such a warrant is exercisable only within the period of 24 hours beginning with the time when the warrant is issued.

The third search power relates to cordoned areas, including residential premises. There is no equivalent to this power in PACE 1984. Given the likely circumstances of dire emergency, sch. 5, para. 3 allows a police officer of at least the rank of superintendent, provided he has reasonable grounds for believing that there is material to be found on the premises, by a written and signed authority to authorise a search of specified premises which are wholly or partly within a cordoned area. And if that does not deal with the situation, perhaps within the first few minutes of cordoning off, any constable may give an authorisation (presumably to himself) if he considers it necessary by reason of urgency. The search may be repeated at any time during designation. However, the limitations as to materials which may be seized are the same as in para. 1 and relate to legally privileged and excepted material (as defined in the PACE legislation). The power to seize and retain materials attracts additional powers to seize and retain articles for sifting elsewhere enabled under the Criminal Justice and Police Act 2001, ss. 50, 51 and 55. It is a summary offence wilfully to obstruct a search under para. 3 (the penalty is up to three months' imprisonment or a fine not exceeding level 4 on the standard scale, or both).

The fourth power deals with the production of, or access to, excluded and special procedure material. It is notable that, unlike under the PACE legislation, excluded material is potentially accessible, though solely under this paragraph. Special procedure material may be also seized under the other three powers described so far, but if it is intentionally sought, then para. 5 should be the chosen path. The powers under the Prevention of Terrorism (Temporary Provisions) Act 1989 have certainly been used for this purpose, especially to obtain journalistic materials (see *R v Middlesex Guildhall Crown Court, ex parte Salinger* [1993] 2 WLR 438; *R v Antrim Crown Court, ex parte Moloney* (1999) *Belfast Telegraph* 7). The powers also differ from PACE 1984 in that they are constructed in relation to terrorist investigations and not specified serious arrestable offences. By para. 5, a constable may apply to a Circuit judge (or in Northern Ireland, a Crown Court judge — substituted for a county court judge by the Anti-terrorism, Crime and Security Act 2001, s. 121, to bring it in line with the Proceeds of Crime Bill 2001–02 HC No. 31) for an order in respect of excluded or special procedure material (including, under para. 7, material coming into existence within 28 days) for the purposes of a terrorist investigation. There is no requirement that notice be given to the possessor of the materials or that the material must be potential 'evidence' for a court case and the application may also relate to material expected to come into existence under para. 7 (unlike under sch. 1 to PACE 1984). If an order is granted, it may require a specified person normally within seven days:

(a)   to produce to a constable within a specified period for seizure and retention any material which he has in his possession, custody or power and to which the application relates;

(b) to give a constable access to any material of the kind mentioned in (a) within a specified period;

(c) to state to the best of his knowledge and belief the location of material to which the application relates if it is not in, and it will not come into, his possession, custody or power within the period specified under (a) or (b).

An order may also order any other person who appears to the judge to be entitled to grant entry to the premises to allow any constable to enter the premises to obtain access to the material. The Circuit judge may grant an order (which under para. 10 is treated as if it were an order of the Crown Court, or, in Northern Ireland, the Crown Court — substituted for a county court by the Anti-terrorism, Crime and Security Act 2001, s. 121) if satisfied under either of two criteria in para. 6:

(2) . . .

(a) the order is sought for the purposes of a terrorist investigation, and

(b) there are reasonable grounds for believing that the material is likely to be of substantial value, whether by itself or together with other material, to a terrorist investigation.

[or]

(3) . . . there are reasonable grounds for believing that it is in the public interest that the material should be produced or that access to it should be given having regard—

(a) to the benefit likely to accrue to a terrorist investigation if the material is obtained, and

(b) to the circumstances under which the person concerned has any of the material in his possession, custody or power.

Only legally privileged material is exempt from the clutches of sch. 5, including, according to para. 8, the powers under para. 5. But para. 5 powers override all other statutory restrictions, and may also apply under para. 9 in relation to material in the possession, custody or power of a government department. Schedule 5 powers can also be used to obtain journalistic material, though the impact of s. 12(4) of the Human Rights Act 1998 (which requires particular regard for the importance of freedom of expression before any order is granted) remains to be determined. Over 100 production orders are issued per annum ((Rowe) Report of the Operation in 1998 of the Prevention of Terrorism (Temporary Provisions) Acts (Home Office, 1999), para. 70).

Should an order under sch. 5, para. 5 for production or access be viewed as inadequate for the purposes of the investigation (perhaps because it would tip off a potential terrorist collaborator), then under para. 11, a constable may apply to a Circuit judge (or in Northern Ireland, a Crown Court judge — substituted for a county court judge by the Anti-terrorism, Crime and Security Act 2001, s. 121) for the issue of a warrant (permitting entry, search and seizure) for the purposes of a terrorist investigation. This fifth procedure may be selected where, under para. 12, a Circuit judge is satisfied that an order made under para. 5 in relation to material on the premises specified in the application has not been complied with or where satisfied that there are reasonable grounds for believing that it is not appropriate to make an order under para. 5 because:

(a) it is not practicable to communicate with any person entitled to produce the material;

(b) it is not practicable to communicate with any person entitled to grant access to the material or entitled to grant entry to the premises on which the material is situated; or

(c) a terrorist investigation may be seriously prejudiced unless a constable can secure immediate access to the material.

The power to seize and retain materials attracts additional powers to seize and retain articles for sifting elsewhere enabled under the Criminal Justice and Police Act 2001, ss. 50 and 51.

The sixth investigative power follows on from, and is ancillary to, the foregoing. By sch. 5, para. 13, a constable may apply to a Circuit judge (or in Northern Ireland, a Crown Court judge — substituted for a county court judge by the Anti-terrorism, Crime and Security Act 2001, s. 121) for an order requiring any person specified in the order to provide an explanation of any material seized, produced or made available. There is no equivalent to this power in PACE 1984, and it has in practice again been used against journalists (see *DPP* v *Channel 4 & Box Productions, The Times* 1, 14 September 1992; Costigan, R., 'Further dispatches' (1992) 142 *New Law Journal* 1417). Though the usual exception as to legal privilege applies, a lawyer may be required to provide the name and address of his client. It is an offence under para. 14 knowingly or recklessly to make a false or misleading statement (punishable on conviction on indictment, to imprisonment for a term not exceeding two years, to a fine or to both, or on summary conviction, to imprisonment for a term not exceeding six months, to a fine not exceeding the statutory maximum or to both). By para. 13(4)(b), a statement by a person in response to a requirement imposed by an order under this paragraph may be used in evidence against him only on a prosecution for an offence under para. 14 (but not for any other offence — compare para. 6(3)(b) in the Prevention of Terrorism (Temporary Provisions) Act 1989). Thus, it has now been recognised in sch. 5 (in contrast to para. 6 of sch. 7 to the 1989 Act) that wider use as evidence would almost certainly contravene Article 6 of the European Convention (see *Saunders* v *United Kingdom*, App. no. 19187/91, Reports 1996-VI, (1997) 23 EHRR 313; *Funke* v *France*, App. no. 10828/84, Ser. A. 256-A; *Salabiaku* v *France*, App. no. 10519/83, Ser. A. 141-A, (1988) 13 EHRR 379; *Murray (John)* v *United Kingdom*, App. no. 18731/91, Reports 1996-I, (1996) 22 EHRR 29; *Serves* v *France*, App. no. 20225/92, Reports 1997-VI (1999) 28 EHRR 265). Whatever the concerns about legality, over 100 production orders are issued per annum ((Rowe) Report of the Operation in 1998 of the Prevention of Terrorism (Temporary Provisions) Acts (Home Office, London, 1999), para. 72).

The seventh investigative power, under sch. 5, para. 15, deals with cases of urgency. A police officer of at least the rank of superintendent may give written authority equivalent to a warrant or order under para. 1 or 11. The officer must have reasonable grounds for believing that the case is one of great emergency, and that immediate action is necessary. The condition in para. 7(1) of the Prevention of Terrorism (Temporary Provisions) Act 1989, that the action must be 'in the interests of the State', has been dropped because the Act applies to international terrorism directed against another country. Where an order is made under this paragraph, particulars of the case shall be notified as soon as is reasonably practicable to the Secretary of State, though no particular response is then required. Wilful obstruction of a search is an offence (punishable on summary conviction to imprisonment for a term not exceeding three months, a fine not exceeding level 4 on the standard scale, or both). There is no defence of reasonable excuse in this case but the requirement that the obstruction be 'wilful' performs part of its job. The power to seize and retain materials attracts additional powers to seize and retain articles for sifting elsewhere enabled under the Criminal Justice and Police Act 2001, ss. 50, 51 and 55.

Likewise, there is an emergency equivalent to the compulsory disclosure power under sch. 5, para. 13 for materials under para. 15. By para. 16, if a police officer of at least the rank of superintendent has reasonable grounds for believing that the case is one of great emergency he may by a written notice signed by him require any person specified in the notice to provide an explanation of any material seized in pursuance of an order under para. 15. It is an offence to fail to comply with a notice (punishable on summary conviction to imprisonment for a term not exceeding six months, a fine not exceeding level 5 on the standard scale, or both). One variant here is that it is a defence for a person charged with such an offence to show that he had a reasonable excuse for his failure (perhaps relating to the difficulty of accessing or amassing information within a required time scale); s. 118 does not apply (see Chapter 6).

A ninth power is available only in Northern Ireland. Under sch. 5, para. 19, the Secretary of State may by a written order which relates to specified premises give to any constable in Northern Ireland an equivalent authority to a search warrant under para. 1 or 11. The power to seize and retain materials attracts additional powers to seize and retain articles for sifting elsewhere enabled under the Criminal Justice and Police Act 2001, ss. 50, 51 and 55. Because of the lack of judicial oversight, the breadth of the power is confined in two respects. An order shall not be made under this paragraph unless:

(2)   . . .
     (a)   it appears to the Secretary of State that the information which it would be necessary to provide to the court in support of an application for a warrant would, if disclosed, be likely to place any person in danger or prejudice the capability of members of the Royal Ulster Constabulary to investigate an offence under any of sections 15 to 18 or under section 56, and

(b) the order is made for the purposes of an investigation of the commission, preparation or instigation of an offence under any of sections 15 to 18 or under section 56.

Given that applications can be made *ex parte*, the paragraph suggests a considerable distrust in courts and court officials. It is an offence wilfully to obstruct a search (punishable on summary conviction by imprisonment for a term not exceeding three months, a fine not exceeding level 4 on the standard scale, or both). The very unusual nature of the measure, wholly contrary to the separation of powers and, possibly, the requirement of independent scrutiny under Article 6 of the European Convention, and therefore seen as wrong in principle by the Lloyd Report (Inquiry into Legislation against Terrorism (Cm. 3420, London, 1996), para. 13.22) means that the paragraph is temporary on the same basis as Part VII of the 2000 Act.

The tenth power, under sch. 5, para. 20, is also confined to Northern Ireland and allows the Secretary of State to exercise the power to make an order under para. 5 in relation to any person in Northern Ireland. It must appear to the Secretary of State that the information which it would be necessary to provide to a Crown Court judge (substituted for a county court judge by the Anti-terrorism, Crime and Security Act 2001, s. 121) in support of an application for an order under para. 5 would, if disclosed be likely to place any person in danger, or be likely to prejudice the capability of members of the Royal Ulster Constabulary to investigate an offence under any of ss. 15 to 18 or under s. 56. A person commits an offence if he contravenes an order (the penalties are: on conviction on indictment, to imprisonment for a term not exceeding two years, to a fine or to both, or on summary conviction, to imprisonment for a term not exceeding six months, to a fine not exceeding the statutory maximum or to both). The time-limits on the life of this paragraph again apply as under paragraph 19.

Next, sch. 5, para. 21 affords the Secretary of State for Northern Ireland a power to issue a written order to require any person in Northern Ireland who is specified in the order to provide an explanation of any material seized in pursuance of an order under para. 19, or produced or made available to a constable in pursuance of an order made by virtue of para. 20. Time-limits again apply to this paragraph.

Part II of sch. 5 provides for Scottish powers equivalent (but not extra) to those in England and Wales. Powers equivalent to the first are set out in para. 28, by which the procurator fiscal may apply to the sheriff to grant a warrant for the purposes of a terrorist investigation. There is no direct equivalent to the second or third search powers. However, similar to the fourth power, by para. 22, the procurator fiscal may apply to the sheriff for a production order which can relate to material of any specified description (the concepts of special procedure and excluded materials not being part of Scottish law). Explanations, as in the sixth power, can be required under para. 30 on application by the procurator fiscal to the sheriff. Police powers, dealing with urgent situations, are granted by paras 31 (equivalent to the seventh power) and 32 (equivalent to the eighth power).

4.4   ADDITIONAL DISCLOSURE POWERS IN CONNECTION WITH FINANCIAL INSTITUTIONS

Though powers under sch. 5 to the Terrorism Act 2000 can be used in connection with financial investigations (as well as other inquiries), further powers (not previously existing in Britain under the Prevention of Terrorism (Temporary Provisions) Act 1989) to assist financial investigations are granted by s. 38 of the 2000 Act and are set out in sch. 6. The essence of these powers is to provide a quick method of obtaining the identities of the holders of accounts with financial institutions. These measures were added at the Report stage in the House of Commons (HC Debs vol. 346 col. 329, 15 March 2000) and are modelled on certain powers of financial investigators under sch. 2 to the Proceeds of Crime (Northern Ireland) Order 1996 (SI 1996 No. 1299). However, sch. 6 does apply in Northern Ireland since it facilitates investigations into not just crime proceeds but into terrorist property. The Anti-terrorism, Crime and Security Act 2001, s. 3 and sch. 3, inserts a new s. 38A and sch. 6A into the Terrorism Act 2000 and thereby allows for account monitoring orders.

These powers will be activated in relation to 'financial institutions', as defined in sch. 6, para. 6 to the 2000 Act, and similar to the Money Laundering Regulations 1993 (SI 1993 No. 33). The Anti-terrorism, Crime and Security Act 2001 adopts the same definition (sch. 6A, para. 1(5)), but it amends sch. 6 by allowing the measures to be extended to other financial institutions (including specified financial institutions) by order (sch. 2, para. 6).

4.4.1   Account holder information

At the core of sch. 6 to the Terrorism Act 2000 is a disclosure order which can be authorised under para. 3 by, in England and Wales, a Circuit judge, in Scotland, by the sheriff, or, in Northern Ireland, a Crown Court judge — substituted for a county court judge by the Anti-terrorism, Crime and Security Act 2001, s. 121. The application is made under para. 2 by, in England and Wales or Northern Ireland, a police officer of at least the rank of superintendent, or, in Scotland, the procurator fiscal. They must be satisfied under para. 5 that:

(a)   the order is sought for the purposes of a terrorist investigation,

(b)   the tracing of terrorist property is desirable for the purposes of the investigation, and

(c)   the order will enhance the effectiveness of the investigation.

If an order is granted, then by para. 1, a constable may require a financial institution to provide 'customer information' for the purposes of a terrorist investigation, notwithstanding any restriction on the disclosure of information imposed by statute or common law. An institution which fails to comply with a requirement under this paragraph shall be guilty of an offence and shall be liable on summary conviction to a fine not exceeding level 5 on the standard scale (the liability of the institution and its officers is further explained in para. 8). But it is a defence for an institution to prove that the information required was not in the institution's possession, or that it was not reasonably practicable for the institution to comply with the requirement (such as where there would be an enormous amount of information to convey: HC Debs. vol. 346 col. 331, 15 March 2000, Charles Clarke). Customer information is defined in para. 7 to include information whether a business relationship exists or existed between the financial institution and a particular person and then, assuming that there is a relationship, the date when it began and ended and identifying data such as account number, name, date of birth, address, evidence of identity, and co-account holders.

In line with the requirements of Article 6 of the European Convention, sch. 6, para. 9 provides that customer information provided by a financial institution under this schedule shall not be admissible in evidence in criminal proceedings against the institution or any of its officers or employees (save for a prosecution for an offence of non-compliance under para. 1 or 8).

As mentioned earlier, the schedule reflects powers in Northern Ireland which are officially viewed as very effective, and it is envisaged that operational practice there will also be replicated under the Terrorism Act 2000. In this way, rather than having individual applications, a so-called general bank circular will be authorised on one occasion by a circuit judge or equivalent (the idea was put forward for Northern Ireland by the (Rowe) Review of the Northern Ireland (Emergency Provisions) Act 1991 (Cm. 2706, London, 1995), para. 145). The 'circular' will allow the police to inquire of financial institutions whether they hold accounts in particular names. The financial institution only has to say whether it holds accounts in the names given but cannot be required to provide any details of what is in the account. If the police want such information, they would need to seek a production order under sch. 5. Perhaps because sch. 6 might obviate more costly investigations, it is claimed that 'the banks were generally supportive and supplied helpful information on compliance costs and other practical issues' (HC Debs. vol. 346, col. 329, 15 March 2000, Charles Clarke). Whether the judges will be quite so approving remains to be seen; it is arguable that a blanket authorisation of the kind envisaged does not adequately protect rights to privacy under Article 8 of the European Convention; it would certainly be difficult to show proportionality when particular cases have not been subject to any independent oversight (compare *Chappell* v *United Kingdom*, App. no. 10461/83, Ser. A. 152-A).

4.4.2 Account monitoring information

The Anti-terrorism, Crime and Security Act 2001, s. 3 and sch. 3, inserts a new s. 38A and sch. 6A into the Terrorism Act 2000 to provide for account monitoring orders (an idea also present in the pending Proceeds of Crime Bill 2001–02 HC no. 31 cl. 360). These differ from sch. 6 in two major effects: they relate to transactions rather than customer identity, and they can allow for real-time

disclosure rather than a response to a request. As with customer information, the
idea is that the more limited nature of the intrusion into private financial affairs
should not require a full warrant or production order procedure. There are no limits
on the information so gathered, including accounts relating to legal matters, for
'we cannot see any occasion when such information would be legally privileged'
(HL Debs. vol. 629 col. 345, 28 November 2001, Lord Rooker).

By sch. 6A, para. 2, a judge may, on an application made to him by an
appropriate officer, make an account monitoring order if he is satisfied that the
order is sought for the purposes of a terrorist investigation, the tracing of terrorist
property is desirable for the purposes of the investigation, and the order will
enhance the effectiveness of the investigation. If an order is made, then the
financial institution specified in the application for the order must for the period
specified in the order (which must not exceed 90 days), in the manner so specified,
at or by the time or times so specified, and at the place or places so specified,
provide information of the description specified in the application to an appropriate
officer. These proceedings will (by para. 1) be conducted before a circuit judge
sitting in the Crown Court or, in Scotland, the sheriff. The judge may hear the
application *ex parte* in chambers (para. 3). The 'appropriate officer' who makes
the application will be a police officer or, in Scotland, the procurator fiscal. In view
of the breadth of the powers, it is surprising that a police officer of any rank can
apply, though in practice, senior detectives are the likely participants. Applications
to vary or discharge may be made by an authorised officer or by any person
affected by the order (para. 4).

Though it is reassuring that a judge is the arbiter of such orders, it is wrong that
the test for an order is subjectively worded, a stance which may also conduce to
breach of Article 8 of the European Convention (compare *Chappell* v *United
Kingdom*, App. no. 10461/83, Ser. A. 152-A, para. 60). An amendment to require
reasonable suspicion was rejected in the House of Lords on the grounds that 'the
requirement to have reasonable grounds would preclude the use of this investigatory tool at an early stage in the investigation when it might not be possible to
establish such reasonable grounds' (HL Debs. vol. 629 col. 344, 28 November
2001, Lord Rooker).

If an order is granted, then by para. 6, in England and Wales and Northern
Ireland, it has effect as if it were an order of the court (so its breach is therefore a
contempt of court), and it takes effect in spite of any restriction on the disclosure
of information (including the doctrine of breach of confidence). Because of its
compulsory nature, a statement made by a financial institution in response to an
account monitoring order may not be used in evidence against it in criminal
proceedings (para. 7), save for proceedings for contempt of court, or in the case of
proceedings under s. 23 of the Terrorism Act 2000 where the financial institution
has been convicted of an offence under any of ss. 15 to 18 or on a prosecution for
an offence where, in giving evidence, the financial institution makes a statement
inconsistent with a prior statement, provided the financial institution has raised an
issue in relation to the statement.

4.5   ADDITIONAL DISCLOSURE POWERS IN CONNECTION WITH PUBLIC AUTHORITIES

Just as financial institutions are seen as holding potentially key information about terrorism, so public authorities are another pre-eminent source of information. The belief in both cases is that any notable terrorist group with activities in the United Kingdom cannot avoid the use of financial institutions nor cannot easily avoid providing information to public bodies, whether for national insurance, social security, driving license, or other purposes. Therefore, Part III of the Anti-terrorism, Crime and Security Act 2001 grants HM Customs and Excise and the Inland Revenue a general power to disclose information held by them for law enforcement purposes and to the intelligence services. The 2001 Act more generally increases the circumstances in which public authorities (which, by s. 20, has the same meaning as in s. 6 of the Human Rights Act 1998) may volunteer information to agencies involved in criminal investigations and proceedings. These powers are, by ss. 17(6) and 19(10), additional to powers of disclosure already set out. Though welcomed without argument by the Home Affairs Committee (Report on the Anti-terrorism, Crime and Security Bill 2001 (2001–02 HC 351), para. 55), it should be emphasised at the outset that these powers are not directly linked or confined to 'terrorist investigations', itself a criticism of them, but are located in this chapter as akin to other powers which are.

The new powers are additional to considerable powers of disclosure allowed by the Data Protection Act 1998. Normally, under the 1998 Act, electronic personal data cannot be divulged by one government department or agency to the police unless that purpose is specified in the Register of Data Users or falls clearly within s. 29 of the Act. Section 29 of the 1998 Act provides an exemption to non-disclosure where the disclosure is for the prevention or detection of crime or the apprehension or prosecution of offenders. This exemption was considered inadequate for anti-terrorism purposes because:

(a)   it requires a pre-disclosure assessment of the legality of disclosing the information on the part of the possessor of data, whereas, sometimes, the full picture is held by the requesting authority; and

(b)   the Data Protection Act 1998 provides that personal data is not to be transferred outside the European Economic Area unless the country in question ensures an adequate level of protection for data processing, whereas terrorism involves several countries which in general have inadequate data protection regimes.

Whether the latter is an effect of s. 17 is not clear. The Government emphasised on several occasions during debate that the Data Protection Act 1998 did apply under s. 17, such as by restricting the transfer of information outside the European Economic Area (HL Debs. vol. 629 col. 418, 28 November 2001, Lord McIntosh). However, s. 17 itself is silent on the matter (unlike section 19(7) below). Section 17(6) preserves other powers of disclosure but there is no mention of any statutory restrictions applying in priority to s. 17. In practical terms, the problem may not arise too much — the pathway for most disclosures will be from domestic public authority to a United Kingdom police or security agency, and in so far as they disclose to overseas counterparts, one would expect adequate data protection to be in place.

There are some other statutory sharing arrangements (affecting HM Customs and Excise under s. 127 of the Finance Act 1972 and the Department of Social Security under the Social Security Administration Fraud Act 1997 and the Finance Act 1997), otherwise, one official body has no authority to inform another of merely suspicious activity or simply on request and there may be offences if disclosure is made outside these bounds. In particular, the Finance Act 1989, s. 182, makes it an offence for the staff of the Inland Revenue or Customs to make an unauthorised disclosure, and the Inland Revenue has historically only offered disclosure in cases of the most serious crimes and has only responded to requests if the other agency can demonstrate reasonable grounds. However, this historical position has been modified in recent years in regard to law enforcement agencies, with a much freer system of disclosure to the National Criminal Intelligence Service's Economic Crime Unit.

The core reform in the Anti-Terrorism, Crime and Security Act 2001 is brought about by s. 17 which reinterprets a range of provisions, as listed in sch. 4, to have effect in relation to the disclosure of information by or on behalf of a public authority, as if the purposes for which the disclosure of information is authorised by that provision included the purposes of any criminal investigation which is being or may be carried out or which have been or may be initiated, whether in the United Kingdom or elsewhere, including the purposes of the initiation or bringing to an end of any such investigation or proceedings or determining whether any such investigation or proceedings should be initiated or brought to an end. The information may have been created or gathered before the commencement of the Act (s. 17(7)).

The list in sch. 4 to the 2001 Act includes 66 provisions, including, ironically, s. 59(1) of the Data Protection Act 1998, by which the Information Commissioner and members of the Commissioner's staff are otherwise forbidden to disclose information obtained by, or furnished to, the Commissioner under or for the purposes of the 1998 Act and which relates to an identified or identifiable individual or business, though disclosure may be made for the purposes of any proceedings, whether criminal or civil. By s. 17(3), this list may be changed by the Treasury by statutory instrument (subject to affirmative resolution, a procedure which was inserted after criticism from the Delegated Powers and Regulatory Reform Select Committee, Report on the Anti-terrorism, Crime and Security Bill (2001–02 HL 45), para. 17).

Because the s. 17 power can be used by public authorities to aid foreign investigations and proceedings, a restraint provision is inserted by s. 18. The implication is that it may not be in the United Kingdom national security interests to entrust information to every foreign power that seeks it, or even to some friendly powers which are treading on the toes of British security operations. The restraint will take the form of a direction from the Secretary of State, who can specify any overseas proceedings or any description of overseas proceedings and can prohibit a disclosure either absolutely or on conditions. It must appear to the Secretary of State that the overseas proceedings relate or would relate to a matter which could more appropriately be carried out by a court or other authority within the United Kingdom or of a third country. Directions cannot apply to any disclosure by a Minister of the Crown or by the Treasury — they have concurrent authority to make their own decisions as to the public interest. Any person who, knowing of any direction under this section, discloses any information in contravention of that direction shall be guilty of an offence and liable (a) on conviction on indictment, to imprisonment for a term not exceeding two years or to a fine or to both, or (b) on summary conviction, to imprisonment for a term not exceeding three months or to a fine not exceeding the statutory maximum or to both.

These disclosure powers are very controversial. It is clear that they cover a very wide range of highly confidential information which is often provided under compulsion (distinct from the financial information dealt with elsewhere in the terrorism legislation). Much of the information can have little relevance to terrorism — the sch. 4 list includes, for example, the Merchant Shipping (Liner Conferences) Act 1982 and the Diseases of Fish Act 1983. On the other hand, some sensitive health information can be disclosed by virtue of the Health Act 1999 whereby the Audit Commission can demand certain patient records, though normally in general statistical form rather than relating to individual patients. Furthermore, the powers are not confined to terrorism investigations but relate to crimes in general. Indeed, the definition of 'criminal investigation' in s. 20 means not only an investigation of any criminal conduct, including an investigation of alleged or suspected criminal conduct, but also an investigation of whether criminal conduct has taken place. An attempt at Commons Committee stage to confine the power to terrorism rather than crime (HC Debs. vol. 375 col. 791, 26 November 2001) failed, since the government wanted 'to make it simple for public officials to understand what they are supposed to disclose' by the expedient of allowing disclosure in virtually all circumstances (col. 794, Ruth Kelly). Reversing a Lords' amendment (see HL Debs. vol. 629 col. 972, 6 December 2001; col. 1432, 13 December 2001), the Home Secretary, David Blunkett, gave an example still no more related to terrorism (HC Debs. vol. 376 col. 898, 12 December 2001:

Take an employment agency that is being inspected. The inspectors come across information relating to an individual seeking to take up a particular, sensitive job. It is discovered that that person has claimed large amounts of benefit. Let us call him Mr AQ, just as an example of someone who might seek to do that. According to the framing of the House of Lords proposal [to restrict the power to terrorism], it would not be possible for that information to be shared. No one outside the House would thank us if we so restrained information giving and the

sharing of concerns that Mr AQ continued to draw benefits. It would be illegal
to pass on the information required.

Of course, it may turn out that Mr AQ is a terrorist and that benefit fraud is a
precursor to terrorism and part of the jigsaw of evidence against him, but that is a
very long shot and is no more likely than for any motorist stopped for defective
tyres or a TV licence defaulter.

In addition, the criteria for disclosure are not set very highly or very clearly. As
a nod in the direction of concerns for privacy under Article 8 of the European
Convention, by s. 17(5), no disclosure of information shall be made by virtue of
this section unless the public authority by which the disclosure is made is satisfied
that the making of the disclosure is proportionate to what is sought to be achieved
by it. This wording was added under pressure from the House of Lords (vol. 376
col. 1108, 13 December 2001). But there is no requirement that the disclosure be
considered necessary in the public interest (compare the Data Protection Act 1998,
s. 59) or that it be subjected to independent oversight or even a senior level of prior
review or subsequent audit within the relevant organisation. And the attempt in the
House of Lords to impose prior judicial control was firmly resisted on grounds of
practicality:

> If we have delay of the kind involved in prior judicial control, we will lose the
> scent; we will lose the information; we will lose the opportunity to deal with
> potential terrorists. It has to be done immediately. (HL Debs. vol. 629 col. 390,
> 28 November 2001, Lord McIntosh)

As a result, the Joint Committee on Human Rights, reiterating the criticism of the
Information Commissioner, was very critical of these measures (Report on the
Anti-terrorism, Crime and Security Bill (2001–02 HL 51, HC 420), para. 24), albeit
that general requirements such as respect for privacy under the Human Rights Act
1998 remain relevant considerations for the public authority. Very similar measures
were encouraged by a study (not yet reported) from the Performance and
Innovations Unit of the Cabinet Office (Privacy and Data, http://www.cabinet-
office.gov.uk/innovation/2000/privacy/datascope.shtml, 2000) and by its proposals
in relation to the proceeds of crime by the Inland Revenue (see Recovering the
Proceeds of Crime, http://www.cabinet-office.gov.uk/innovation/2000/crime/crime.
shtml, 2000, p. 95). Yet these came under fire in Parliament and were removed
from Part II of the Criminal Justice and Police Bill 2000–01 (2000–01 HC 31) at
the Report Stage in the House of Lords (see HL Debs. vol. 625 col. 1036, 9 May
2001).

Next, there were concerns that information might be disclosed to assist foreign
investigations into activities (such as anti-competitive practices) which are not
crimes within the United Kingdom and that there is no judicial oversight, no
requirement of senior administrative authorisation and an insufficient evidential
standard of proof (see HC Debs. Standing Committee F col. 412 *et seq.*, 6 March

2001). It may be noted that some attempt has been made to answer the first concern in the interpretive clause in s. 20(2), by which, 'Proceedings outside the United Kingdom shall not be taken to be criminal proceedings for the purposes of this Part unless the conduct with which the defendant in those proceedings is charged is criminal conduct or conduct which, to a substantial extent, consists of criminal conduct'. In addition, by s. 20(3), 'criminal conduct' must comprise either criminal offences under the law of a part of the United Kingdom; or must correspond to conduct which, if it all took place in a particular part of the United Kingdom, would constitute one or more offences under the law of that part of the United Kingdom.

Another problem is the issue of self-incrimination is not addressed. Some of the measures listed in sch. 4, as amended by the Youth Justice and Criminal Evidence Act 1999, ss. 58 and 59, and in the light of the adverse judgment in *Saunders* v *United Kingdom*, App. no. 19187/91, Reports 1996-VI, (1997) 23 EHRR 313, do provide restraint on the use of evidence obtained under threat of prosecution of the various financial offences but only in respect of those financial offences. However, s. 17 of the 2001 Act affords privileges rather than compulsion in respect of disclosure and so is probably distinguishable; 'There is no question of public officials being obliged to make disclosures. It is up to them to decide whether to do so.' (HL Debs. vol. 629 col. 367, 28 November 2001, Lord McIntosh).

Part III may have made some sense if designed around the concept of 'terrorist investigations' under s. 32, but the current draft is explicitly wider and betrays another legislative history and purpose which the 2001 Act should not have been commandeered to serve. As the briefing paper by Liberty argued (see http://www. liberty-human-rights.org.uk/, 2001):

The police will not need reasonable suspicion that the file contains evidence of a crime merely that it is useful in an investigation. The police will not need to go to a magistrate or court for authorisation and they will be able to access files without subsequent checks or audits. The subject of these investigations is unlikely ever to be told the police have rifled through their files and there will be no real remedy if the police are mistaken, over-zealous or plain malicious. Is this a proportionate response to the current situation?

Even more sweeping disclosure powers are granted by s. 19 in respect of information which is held by or on behalf of the Commissioners of Inland Revenue or the Commissioners of Customs and Excise within their records for 32 million individuals and 1.1 million companies or other organisations (see House of Commons Library, Research Paper 01/98, London, 2001, p. 12). Accordingly, rather than disapplying a specific list of prohibitions on disclosures, subsection (2) simply asserts that 'No obligation of secrecy imposed by statute or otherwise prevents the disclosure' for the purpose of facilitating the carrying out by any of the intelligence services of any of that service's functions or for the purposes of any criminal investigation whatever which is being or may be carried out, whether in the United Kingdom or elsewhere. The attempt by the House of Lords to confine the power to terrorism and security matters (HL Debs. vol. 629 col. 976, 6 December 2001) was again reversed. But because of privacy concerns, it is again stated that the disclosure must be proportionate to what is sought to be achieved by it. In addition, there is senior administrative oversight in this case — by s. 19(4), the information must be disclosed by the General or Special Commissioners. The Commissioners should also ensure that there will not be further disclosure except for a purpose mentioned (which do not include intelligence purposes) or by express consent of the Commissioners. However, the purposes under s. 19 are wider than under s. 17 and include the facilitation of the purposes of the intelligence services and not just of criminal investigations. There is also a reminder that nothing in this section authorises the making of any disclosure which is prohibited by any provision of the Data Protection Act 1998 (subsection (7)). The absence of this reminder from s. 17 should not be viewed as a green light for disclosure but reflects the more restrained power in that provision; conversely, the presence of the provision in s. 19 also reflects a similar idea in the failed clause 45 of the Criminal Justice and Police Bill.

4.6   OFFENCE OF WITHHOLDING INFORMATION

One of the vaunted reforms brought about by the Terrorism Act 2000 was the dropping of the offence of withholding information (formerly in s. 18 in the Prevention of Terrorism (Temporary Provisions) Act 1989). In the light of persistent unease about the principle of a duty to help the police, including by informing on friends and family and by pressurising investigative journalists (see Curtis, L., *Ireland: the Propaganda War* (Pluto Press, London, 1984); Walker, C.P., *The Prevention of Terrorism in British Law* (2nd ed., Manchester University Press, Manchester, 1992), ch. 7), the offence had been recommended for repeal by the Inquiry into Legislation against Terrorism ((Cm. 3420, London, 1996), para. 14.24) and the Home Office Consultation Paper (Home Office and Northern Ireland Office, Legislation against Terrorism (Cm. 4178, 1998), para. 12.7). As noted earlier in this chapter, a more focused offence dealing with financial institutions, formerly at s. 18A of the 1989 Act, is replicated as s. 19 of the Terrorism Act 2000. Despite this considered and principled outcome, the offence of withholding information has been revived by s. 117 of the Anti-terrorism, Crime and Security Act 2001, which inserts the offence as s. 38B into the Terrorism Act 2000. The wording of s. 38B and the former s. 18 of the 1989 Act is largely identical. The main difference between the two is that s. 18 was confined to acts of terrorism in Northern Ireland. In line with the policy of the Terrorism Act 2000 and in the light of the nature of the attacks of 11 September, the new offence has no such geographical limitation.

The offence is committed under s. 38B(2) of the 2000 Act if a person, without reasonable excuse, fails to disclose information falling within s. 38B(1), which is information which he knows or believes might be of material assistance in preventing the commission by another person of an act of terrorism, or in securing the apprehension, prosecution or conviction of another person, in the United

Kingdom, for an offence involving the commission, preparation or instigation of an act of terrorism. Since the offence is inserted into the 2000 Act, the definition of 'an act of terrorism' is that laid out in s. 1 of the Terrorism Act 2000 and therefore applies both to domestic and international terrorism. Section 38B(3) lists the officials to whom disclosure should be made — to a constable, or in Northern Ireland to a constable or a member of Her Majesty's forces. It is not sufficient to contact other persons in authority, such as magistrates or Members of Parliament, unless perhaps they are requested and agree to pass on the information to an authorised recipient or are known to be certain to do so automatically and promptly. As for the *actus reus*, a person may commit this offence through total inactivity (by not answering police questions or by not volunteering information), through the partial suppression of information or by relating a false account when the true facts are known. The information must be of a kind which is, or is believed to be, 'of material assistance'. This means that a person reasonably aware of their situation would consider that it ought to be disclosed, whereas information garnered through vague rumour or gossip would not trigger the duty. To prove this issue of fact, the police may have to describe their investigations up to that point, which obviously limits the attractiveness of s. 38B until their inquiries are exhausted. The *mens rea*, 'knows or believes', means that it is not enough that the defendant strongly suspects the possession of material information or thinks it probable or that a reasonable person would have been put on inquiry. Provided the defendant does genuinely believe the information is relevant, an offence is committed even if it is neither material nor accurate, though one would hope that a prosecution would not be necessary in such a case.

At the same time, there really must be an act of terrorism somewhere in the background, whatever the belief of the defendant. In *Attorney-General's Reference (No. 3) of 1993* [1993] NI 50, the defendant believed that a murder was an act of terrorism but was acquitted on the ground that the Crown had failed to prove that the murder was an offence of a terrorist nature as required by s. 18. The Attorney-General argued that the word 'believes' in s. 18(1) governed the whole of para. (b), so that an offence was committed if the defendant believed that an act of terrorism had been committed, and that if Parliament had intended that a substantive offence should first have been committed, it would have expressly so provided as under s. 5(1) of the Criminal Law Act (Northern Ireland) 1967. The Northern Ireland Court of Appeal rejected this argument. The Crown had to prove that an actual terrorist offence had in fact been committed, not merely that the defendant believed such an offence to have been committed. The difference in wording from s. 5(1) was explained by the fact that s. 18 applied to the withholding of information about future offences.

By s. 38B(4), it is a defence for a person charged with an offence under subsection (2) to prove that he had a reasonable excuse for not making the disclosure. The defence of reasonable excuse will often relate to fears of reprisal or reaction going beyond the defence of duress, but it does not excuse one who simply does not wish to 'get involved'. The operation of this defence gives rise to considerable uncertainties in three contexts.

The first is where there is a close personal relationship between the person involved in terrorism and the person with knowledge of it, such as a husband and wife. One might argue that the sanctity of personal ties must give way to the public interest in safety and so should be pierced. Though the latter result has caused some anguish in Parliament, the uncompromising view of the sponsor of the original s. 18 (HC Debs. vol. 882 col. 929, 28 November 1974, George Cunningham) and of the Government was that it is right, even in such hard cases, that 'when dealing with foul and disgusting deeds, someone who knows that someone else is likely to be threatened and imperiled has not only a moral duty to tell the police, but a legal one as well' (HC Debs. Standing Committee D col. 243, 24 November 1983, David Waddington). However, in order to appease those expressing disquiet, the police were advised by circular in 1989 that:

> A relative of a terrorist who is not involved in terrorism himself should not be put under strain by being reminded in a routine manner of the provisions of section [18]. This use of section [18] can only be justified in extreme cases — where the withholding of information might lead to death, serious injury or the escape of a terrorist offender. (Home Office Circular No. 90/1983, para. 9; see also Home Office Circular No. 27/1989, para. 7.4)

The Home Office Circular 7/2002 (p. 5) makes no allowance: 'having a legal or familial relationship with someone does not constitute immunity from the obligation to disclose information as defined in subsection (1)'.

Secondly, and equally problematical, is the existence of a potentially privileged relationship, such as between a lawyer and his terrorist client. Some light may be shed on whether these links provide a 'reasonable excuse' not to disclose by examining the analogous position under the common law misdemeanour of misprision of felony. Until abolished in 1967, misprision comprised an offence to conceal, or to procure concealment of, a felony known to have been committed (see Allen, C.K., 'Misprision' (1962) 78 *Law Quarterly Review* 40; Glazebrook, P., 'Misprision of felony' (1964) 8 *American Journal of Legal History* 189, 283, 'How long, then, is the arm of the law to be?' (1962) 25 *Modern Law Review* 301; Criminal Law Revision Committee Seventh Report: Felonies and Misdemeanours (Cmnd. 2659, London, 1965), para. 37). In *Sykes* v *Director of Public Prosecutions* [1962] AC 528, the defendant was convicted after he tried to supply stolen firearms to the IRA. The House of Lords provided a number of *dicta* on the two problems under scrutiny. Lord Denning's view was that a solicitor, doctor or clergyman who received information in confidence would have a defence but that close personal ties would not suffice (at p. 564). The position adopted in *Sykes'* case should, it is submitted, be reproduced under s. 38B. On the one hand, a party to a normally privileged relationship, such as a lawyer, should have a reasonable excuse for not disclosing the confidences of his client. The Government conceded the existence of some form of privilege in 1989 but sought to distinguish between (unprivileged) information which may prevent terrorism and (privileged) information which may assist the prosecution of terrorists (HL Debs. vol. 504 cols. 980–981, 28 February 1989). It is submitted that this contrast is unwarranted by the wording of s. 38B, though it is reflected in guidance from the Law Society that a solicitor may reveal information which 'he believes necessary to prevent the client from committing a criminal act that the solicitor believes on reasonable grounds is likely to result in serious bodily harm' (*The Guide to the Professional Conduct of Solicitors* (1990), para. 12.04). Accountants do not believe they have any privilege (Institute of Chartered Accountants, *Guidance for Members in Practice*, s. 1.306, para. 10). It is unfortunate that there is no advice in the Home Office Circular 7/2002 concerning professional advisers.

The third situation which has caused misgivings is whether one's privilege against self-incrimination provides a reasonable excuse for remaining silent. This issue was partly settled for the former s. 18 by an amendment which provided that the information being suppressed must concern terrorist involvement by 'any other person' (see Jellicoe Report, Review of the Operation of the Prevention of Terrorism (Temporary Provisions) Act 1976 (Cmnd. 8803, London, 1983), para. 233). This wording also appears in s. 117. However, it does not directly resolve the problem; if a person's evidence implicates both himself and another, it must be disclosed when the self-damning details cannot be severed. Therefore, it must still be determined whether the so-called 'right to silence' provides a defence of reasonable excuse in those circumstances. It was very remiss of Parliament not to resolve this long-standing and complex uncertainty in 2001.

The issue was considered in relation to the former s. 18 in *H.M. Advocate* v *Von* 1979 SLT (Notes) 62. This prosecution arose out of fund-raising activities on behalf of the UVF in Scotland. During the first day of his interrogation, the suspect was reminded of the requirements of s. 18. The following day, he stated that he:

> . . . wished to make a statement and to tell of his own involvement but that he would not name anyone. At this stage police officers realising that he was about to make a statement implicating himself, advised him that what he said could be used in evidence.

The accused made an inculpatory statement but claimed at his trial that it should be excluded because he had not been informed that 'he could reasonably be excused from not disclosing information if the information would be self-incriminating'. The presiding judge (Lord Ross) held (at p. 64):

> If . . . the accused had been given the usual full caution or had been informed that he was not obliged to give information which could incriminate himself and he had then made a statement, I would have thought that that statement would have been admissible as being a statement made in response to pressure or inducement or as a result of other unfair means . . . So far as the evidence goes, the accused was left in total ignorance of the fact that he was not obliged to incriminate himself.

Accordingly, the statement was excluded. However, this judgment rested on the premis that Von did not have to make incriminating statements to avoid the commission of an offence under s. 18. The reasons given for this assumption will now be examined.

One point was that a frequently used statutory duty to disclose, which does impliedly override the right to silence, was thought to be distinguishable. By s. 172 of the Road Traffic Act 1988, a vehicle owner may be obliged to provide the police with the identity of any driver of it, even if this entails the disclosure of an offence. Lord Ross opined that this was materially different from s. 18 since the owner 'is not in normal circumstances even suspect' (at p. 63). However, questioning under s. 172 may often lead to the owner being prosecuted for an offence either in that capacity or as the driver (see *Brown* v *Stott (Procurator Fiscal, Dunfermline) and another* [2001] 2 All ER 97). The second argument adduced by Lord Ross was that (at p. 64), 'if Parliament had intended to make statements of suspects admissible against them in the event of their being subsequently charged I would have expected Parliament to have made that clear'. However, examples already given, including s. 172 itself, demonstrate that the privilege may be impliedly excluded when necessary to avoid frustrating the object of legislation. On that basis, obtaining information about a suspect's own crimes might be just as important as coercing from him knowledge about others' misdeeds.

On balance, the danger of self-incrimination was probably not envisaged by the architects of the former s. 18 as a reasonable excuse. However, given the precedent of *Von's* case, the courts are unlikely to curtail the normal right to silence just because the suspect's knowledge also implicates others. The further argument which now arises, not available at the time of *Von's* case, is the impact of Article 6 of the European Convention, as imported by the Human Rights Act 1998. It is submitted that, on the precedent of cases such as *Saunders* v *United Kingdom*, App. no. 19187/91, Reports 1996-VI, (1997) 23 EHRR 313 (see Nash, S., and Furse, M., 'Self-incrimination, corporate misconduct and the ECHR' [1995] *Criminal Law Review* 854; Munday, R., 'Inferences from silence and the European Human Rights law' [1996] *Criminal Law Review* 370), where the defendant was forced to disclose information about corporate dealings which inevitably reflected upon his own role as chief executive, a strong steer has been given away from demanding self-incriminatory information backed directly by the threat of criminal sanction.

A further complication concerns the inter-relationship between s. 38B and the laws allowing inferences to be drawn from silence in response to police questioning, the Criminal Evidence (Northern Ireland) Order 1988 (SI 1988 No. 1987) and the Criminal Justice and Public Order Act 1994 (ss. 34 to 38). The interrelationship between the Order and s. 18 of the Prevention of Terrorism (Temporary Provisions) Act 1989 is complex. When the suspect has committed an offence and remains silent, there is no infringement of s. 38B, but art. 3 of the 1988 Order/s. 34 of the 1994 Act may penalise silence if a criminal prosecution is mounted. Thus, the statutory provisions do not overlap, but the police's incantation of a complex caution under the other legislation together with a recitation of s. 38B may sow great confusion. Conversely, where the subject knows about another's wrongdoing but is not personally implicated, an offence may be committed under s. 38B. It follows that silence in response to questioning about that offence may also trigger inferences under the 1988 Order or 1994 Act. Consequently, silence could be damning twice over: it forms the *actus reus* of s. 38B and then leads to the adverse inference that the person has suppressed relevant information and is guilty of the offence. Thus, s. 38B can pull itself up by its own boot straps with the aid of the other legislation.

A final concern about the relationship between s. 18 and the privilege against self-incrimination is that, even to the extent that it is preserved, suspects may be unaware of their legal position. This problem did not pertain to Scotland since 'the *Von* decision led to the adoption of guidelines to the police which require them to inform a suspect specifically that the provisions of section [18] do not oblige him to incriminate himself' (Jellicoe Report, para. 233). The dangers of confusion were also been reduced by circulars issued to all police forces in 1983 which emphasised the Jellicoe Report's recommendation that the offence of withholding information should only be recited when the police believe a person possesses information 'which would if revealed prevent acts of terrorism or lead to the apprehension of terrorists offenders', (Home Office Circular No. 90/1983, para. 9). Thus, the circulars discouraged the duty to disclose being brandished against possessors of very low-level intelligence, but a more apposite reform would be to allow the citation of s. 38B whenever it might elicit information but always subject to the special Scottish caution. Advice on the 2001 version is regrattably absent from the Home Office Circular 7/2002, and so the former safeguards in Scotland have lapsed.

Moving to process issues, the penalties for the offence are, on indictment, imprisonment for up to five years, or a fine or both; or on summary conviction, imprisonment for up to six months or a fine not exceeding the statutory minimum or both. Section 38B(6) allows proceedings for an offence under this section to be taken in any place where the person to be charged is or has at any time been since he first knew or believed that the information might be of material assistance as mentioned in subsection (1). This provision as to venue allows a person present in the United Kingdom to be charged with the offence even if he was outside the United Kingdom at the time he became aware of the information. According to Home Office Circular 7/2002, p. 5:

> For example, information about an act to be carried out in Greece could come to the attention of a UK resident while that person was in Spain — if the information were not disclosed and the act took place, that person could be charged in the UK or elsewhere, if evidence of deliberate non-disclosure were established.

In Great Britain, charges under the former s. 18 were very infrequent, and the results suggest that it has been invoked mostly on weak evidence and against those on the fringes of terrorism. Between 1984 and 1999, there were just 15 charges, resulting in just one finding of guilt. By contrast, the offence has figured slightly more prominently in Northern Ireland, with 58 charges between 1974 and September 2000. In Northern Ireland, the offence is additional to s. 5(1) of the Criminal Law Act (Northern Ireland) 1967:

> . . . where a person has committed an arrestable offence, it shall be the duty of every other person, who knows or believes—
>
>   (a)   that the offence or some other arrestable offence has been committed; and
>
>   (b)   that he has information which is likely to secure, or to be of material assistance in securing, the apprehension, prosecution or conviction of any person for that offence;
>
> to give that information, within a reasonable time, to a constable and if, without reasonable excuse, he fails to do so he shall be guilty of an offence . . .

Section 38B remains distinct in that the information must relate to 'terrorism' rather than an 'arrestable offence' and may concern future as well as past activities. However, it is submitted that neither difference excuses the considerable duplication between the two offences and any police claim that the offence will 'play an important role in countering terrorism and bringing terrorists to justice by reminding the public of their obligation to help protect their fellow citizens' (HL Debs. vol. 629 col. 625, 3 December 2001, Lord Rooker) must be doubted.

Charges under s. 38B can be relevant in four situations. The first is that, where the evidence of involvement in terrorism as an accomplice, conspirator or member of a proscribed organisation is relatively weak, s. 38B may be used as an additional, 'back-stop' count. Next, where the police have successfully detected active terrorists, those suspected of being less deeply implicated may be prosecuted under s. 38B. The third type of case is where a police investigation into a terrorist plot has largely failed, but evidence against some minor participants has been unearthed. The fourth target, persons who have been coerced into aiding terrorists (especially by loaning their cars), arises exclusively in Northern Ireland. The main objective is to motivate victims to contact the police automatically so that any planned outrage may be thwarted.

Justification of s. 38B must in part depend on whether it can clearly be distinguished from pre-existing, 'normal' crimes. Necessity in this sense has already been examined, and it was concluded that, while it has no close rival in British law, s. 38B is largely unnecessary in Northern Ireland.

Turning to the wider question of whether an offence of withholding information in any guise is acceptable in principle, the main advantage is claimed to be that it will 'create an atmosphere in which it [is] respectable to provide . . . information'. Given this objective, rates of prosecution and conviction are not decisive. The real value of the measure is to influence people to volunteer information; the prosecution of recalcitrant minor participants after violence has occurred is a second-best.

Reviewing all the available evidence, the Jellicoe Report concluded that 'the section is of significant value to the police service, but that service could operate without it if required to do so . . . however, the section should lapse only if the difficulties it causes or may cause in terms of abuse and of damage to civil liberties are genuinely serious and irremediable' (para. 222). In view of this half-hearted support, the defects associated with the offence should be catalogued in order to decide whether they outweigh the supposed benefits.

The drawbacks in principle were highlighted by Lord Shackelton (Review of the Operation of the Prevention of Terrorism (Temporary Provisions) Acts 1974 and 1976 (Cmnd. 7324, London, 1978), paras 132, 133) who recommended the abolition of the then s. 18 at least in Britain, since, 'there are genuine doubts about its implications in principle and about the way it might be used in the course of interviewing someone . . . it has an unpleasant ring about it in terms of civil liberties'. His verdict was rightly attacked in Parliament as hardly 'persuasive rationally' (HC Debs. vol. 969 col. 1662, 21 March 1979, George Cunningham), but more precise arguments for and against may be formulated.

The first justification for s. 38B might be that offences involving withholding information are familiar to our legal system. As well as misprision of felony and s. 5(1) in Northern Ireland, other closely related provisions include s. 6(2) of the Explosive Substances Act 1883, s. 6(1) of the Official Secrets Act 1920 and the common law misdemeanour of misprision of treason. As a result, there is authority for the view that, in exceptionally dangerous situations, society may compel its citizenry to provide succour. The contrary view of Viscount Colville, that there is nothing 'special' in withholding information about terrorism and so there is no good reason for the offence (at least outside Northern Ireland) is thus controverted. The *raison d'être* for the offence is surely that terrorism involves extraordinarily dangerous activities and may accordingly give rise to exceptional duties.

Section 38B conforms to established precedents, but those precedents might themselves be unsound because they unnecessarily conflict with the accepted policy of policing by consent. Thus, the former s. 18 has been decried for creating the sort of 'informer's society which exists in totalitarian states' (HC Debs. vol. 904 col. 475, 28 January 1976, Ian Mikado). Yet, s. 38B might still be a justifiable aim if it is viewed as exceptional. Given that this special offence has attracted substantial attention and support in Parliament, it may legitimately be concluded that 'in the case of terrorism, which is almost by definition criminal activity aimed at society as a whole, it seems . . . reasonable that there should be more than a merely moral duty to assist the police' (Jellicoe Report, para. 101). Another theoretical objection to s. 38B is that it should not form part of the criminal law as it does not penalise any action undertaken by the defendant or any dishonest intention on his part. In reply, having decided that it is acceptable to impose a legal, as well as a moral, duty to help the police to combat terrorism, it follows that an omission to fulfil that duty may properly incur legal sanctions. This is consistent with the view that failure to impart evidence is wicked because of the especially dangerous nature of terrorism.

Two important drawbacks arise from the practical application of s. 38B. The first is that there is no clear evidence that it has achieved its central goal of increasing the flow of information to the police, and it seems improbable that it will ever do so. It is presumably not claimed that s. 38B carries much clout with hardened terrorists, so it must be primarily aimed against those on the periphery of terrorism. Yet, even such soft targets are likely either to be more intimidated by terrorists than by s. 38B or to provide to the police false information, in order to obtain their release. The result seems to be that as the police recognise there is little advantage in prosecuting petty offenders; there is a great deal more to be gained by keeping them under surveillance and following the leads they provide.

The second practical drawback concerns the effect of s. 38B on the media. A reporter may discover information about terrorism by interviewing a terrorist leader or by witnessing a paramilitary display. Arranging, attending or reporting such events may implicate the journalist in various offences, but the former s. 18 became most threatening of all, and its effects have been felt in two directions. First, the offence contributes to a 'chilling' effect on the reporting of terrorism. Correspondents can expect close attention from the police and hostility and special restrictions from their own superiors. The second effect is via the direct threat of prosecution. A number of skirmishes occurred under the former s. 18 between the journalistic ethic to protect confidential sources and the demand of s. 18 to disclose them (see Walker, C.P., *The Prevention of Terrorism in British Law* (2nd ed., Manchester University Press, Manchester, 1992), pp. 141–143). The overall effect of s. 18 on the media was that coverage of Irish terrorism abounded with difficulties, and the subject was to some extent suppressed as 'guilty secrets' (Curtis, L., *Ireland: the Propaganda War* (Pluto Press, London, 1984), p. 275) without at the same time having much chance of actually coercing evidence from journalists.

In principle, there is value in having an offence of withholding information about serious offences, provided it is recognised that much of its value is superficial and that it carries grave dangers. To be acceptable in practice, s. 38B should be further limited to information about specified serious offences and should deal more explicitly and generously with suspects, lawyers and journalists.

4.7   ANCILLARY OFFENCES OF DISCLOSURE

Since terrorist investigations may involve not just police officers, who are subject to disciplinary codes as well as parts of the Official Secrets Act 1989 (see especially s. 4) but also civilians such as accountant and lawyers, s. 39 provides for two offences to discourage or penalise disclosures which may damage the effectiveness of ongoing terrorist investigations (corresponding to s. 17(2)–(6) of the Prevention of Terrorism (Temporary Provisions) Act 1989). However, the offences are not confined to those conducting the investigations, and others, such as journalists, who come by the information may also be threatened with prosecution. The possible stifling effect on investigations into the police's actions against terrorism could give rise to a challenge under Article 10 of the European Convention.

The first offence, under s. 39(2), arises whenever a person knows or has reasonable cause to suspect that a constable is conducting or proposes to conduct a terrorist investigation; he commits an offence if he (a) discloses to another anything which is likely to prejudice the investigation, or (b) interferes with material which is likely to be relevant to the investigation.

The second offence, under s. 39(4), arises where, knowing or having reasonable cause to suspect that a disclosure has been or will be made to the authorities under any of ss. 19 to 21 or s. 38B, he (a) discloses to another anything which is likely to prejudice an investigation resulting from the disclosure under that section, or (b) interferes with material which is likely to be relevant to an investigation resulting from the disclosure under that section.

Under either offence, it is a defence to prove either (a) that he did not know and had no reasonable cause to suspect that the disclosure or interference was likely to affect a terrorist investigation, or (b) that he had a reasonable excuse for the disclosure or interference. This defence must be understood in the light of s. 118, by which if the person adduces evidence which is sufficient to raise an issue with respect to the matter, the court or jury shall assume that the defence is satisfied unless the prosecution proves beyond reasonable doubt that it is not. The idea is to make express provision for the burdens placed on the defendant to be seen as evidential rather than persuasive or legal burdens (HL Debs. vol. 613 col. 754, 16 May 2000, Lord Bassam) (see further Chapter 6). Disclosures which are made for the purposes of legal advice or proceedings by a professional legal adviser are also excused.

The penalties for the offence are (a) on conviction on indictment, to imprisonment for a term not exceeding five years, to a fine or to both, or (b) on summary conviction, to imprisonment for a term not exceeding six months, to a fine not exceeding the statutory maximum or to both.

Chapter Five
Counter-terrorist powers

5.1 INTRODUCTION

The provisions in Part V of the Terrorism Act 2000 are probably its most controversial. As already indicated, there is a considerable overlap with Part IV — we are still considering various forms of policing powers. However, the catalogue in Part V more often involves direct action against individuals rather than, say, impersonal financial institutions or public authorities. The personalised nature of Part V is reflected in the use of the term 'terrorist', around which the substantive provisions are drawn. By s. 40(1), 'terrorist' means a person who (a) has committed an offence under any of ss. 11, 12, 15 to 18, 54 and 56 to 63, or (b) is or has been concerned in the commission, preparation or instigation of acts of 'terrorism' (as defined by s. 1) whether before or after the passing of the Act. The common conception of a 'terrorist' is that in the second leg part (a) allows action to be taken mainly against identified secondary helpers, whether in financial institutions or otherwise. In this respect, the Terrorism Act 2000 develops the prior definition of 'terrorist' in s. 58 of the Northern Ireland (Emergency Provisions) Act 1996. A further development is that the definition, by referring to 'preparation or instigation' as well as 'commission', covers both 'passive' and 'active' forms of terrorism, which may resolve the uncertainty created in the decision in *McKee* v *Chief Constable for Northern Ireland* [1984] 1 WLR 1358 as to whether passive terrorism, such as membership of a proscribed organisation, was sufficient to trigger counter-terrorist powers (see Walker, C.P., 'Emergency arrest powers' (1985) 36 *Northern Ireland Legal Quarterly* 145).

The powers granted in this Part of the Terrorism Act 2000 (and indeed elsewhere) are not meant to be exclusive. By s. 114, a power conferred by virtue of the Act on a constable is additional to powers which he has at common law or by virtue of any other enactment and shall not be taken to affect those powers. Further general provisions under s. 114 are that a constable may if necessary use reasonable force for the purpose of exercising a power conferred on him under the Act (with the exception of the powers to question someone at a port or border area under sch. 7, paras 2 and 3). Finally, where anything is seized under a power conferred by virtue of this Act, it may be retained for so long as is necessary in all the circumstances. These provisions are required as additions to those in s. 3 of the Criminal Law Act 1967 or s. 117 of PACE 1984 (and their equivalents elsewhere) since not all security operations are conducted in relation to specified criminal offences.

A key role in the operation of Part V powers in Britain is played by the National Joint Unit (NJU) at New Scotland Yard, which is the police group made up of officers from the Metropolitan Police Special Branch plus seconded officers from elsewhere. The NJU deals with applications for extensions of detentions, receives inquiries from ports and checks suspects against databases (there were 51,956 such checks in 1998) and generally provides training and advice (see (Rowe) Report of the Operation in 1998 of the Prevention of Terrorism (Temporary Provisions) Acts (Home Office, 1999), Appendix F). These roles are undertaken by the RUC alone in Northern Ireland.

5.2   ARREST WITHOUT WARRANT

The controversy surrounding Part V of the Terrorism Act 2000 is most sharply focused upon s. 41, which deals with arrest without warrant. Section 41 is the successor to s. 14(1)(b) of the Prevention of Terrorism (Temporary Provisions) Act 1989 and is arguably the most important single provision in the Act. Arrest under s. 41 is the starting point of many investigations, for the interviewing of the suspect and the collection of forensic evidence from the detainee have been two prime sources of evidence in most cases, especially those passing through the 'Diplock' non-jury criminal courts in Northern Ireland. The apparent attractions for investigators include the broad grounds for arrest in the first place, the limited disclosure to the suspect of the reasons for the arrest, and the longer than normal period of detention. In accordance with the wishes of the government (Home Office and Northern Ireland Office, Legislation against Terrorism (Cm. 4178, London, 1998), paras 7.9, 8.24), the powers remain largely unaltered, but some of the rules surrounding the treatment of detainees have been significantly amended. There may be three reasons for a special power of arrest of this kind.

The leading purpose is to interrogate suspects so as to uncover admissible evidence sufficient to put before a court or, and perhaps more common in the light of the low charging rate, to gather background intelligence information, aided by the extraordinarily lengthy period of detention following an arrest (see below) and aided by the fact that no detailed reasons for arrest on suspicion of terrorism need be offered at the point of arrest (see *Forbes* v *HM Advocate* 1990 SC (JC) 215; *Brady* v *Chief Constable for the RUC* [1991] 2 NIJB 22; *Oscar* v *Chief Constable of the RUC* [1992] NI 290). This purpose is allied to the idea that the threat of terrorism demands an early police intervention at the preparatory stages whether to interrogate or simply to disrupt. It is too dangerous to allow the terrorists to move very far towards their objectives (see especially *R* v *Cullen, McCann &*

Shanahan, The Times, 1 May 1990). But the differences from 'ordinary' policing are in fact narrowing because of two factors. One is the influence of the mainstream police practices under PACE legislation on policing practices in connection with terrorism. This is pervasive and incremental. The general impact, summed up by the notion of 'Investigative Interviewing' (Home Office Circular 72/1992, *Investigative Interviewing* (London, 1992)), is far better planned and brisker interview sessions — interviewing with a purpose — rather than more speculative and rambling sessions which rely more on fright than guile. Conversely, there is now greater importance in 'normal' interviewing attached to developing broader themes akin to those prevalent in terrorist cases, themes such as the importance of developing intelligence and informers (see Ericson, R.V., and Haggerty, K.D., *Policing the Risk Society* (Clarendon Press, Oxford, 1997)).

A second growing reason for the special arrest and detention powers is to facilitate the carrying out of searches. These are of two types. One is the search of premises on arrest. More relevant is the increasing emphasis upon forensic testing, despite its occasional lapses in standards (see (May Inquiry), Report of the Inquiry into the circumstances surrounding the convictions arising out of the bomb attacks in Guildford and Woolwich in 1974, Interim Report (1989–90 HC 556), Second Report (1992–93 HC 296), Final Report (1993–94 HC 449); (Caddy Report), Assessment and Implications of centrifuge Contamination in the Trace Explosive Section of the Forensic Explosives Laboratory at Fort Halstead (Cm. 3491, London, 1996)).

The third reason for s. 41, very particular to Britain, is to deal with the special problems posed by international terrorism — not only might there be dangerous and cohesive groups, but the police face difficulties over proof of identity, translation and liaison with foreign security agencies (see Report of the Operation of the Prevention of Terrorism (Temporary Provisions) Act 1976 (Cmnd. 8803, 1983), paras 13, 23, 75–78).

The process begins with the actual arrest which is simply provided for by s. 41(1): 'A constable may arrest without a warrant a person whom he reasonably suspects to be a terrorist.' Reasonable suspicion is a familiar concept, and it is accepted that it will fall short of proof beyond reasonable doubt (see *O'Hara* v *United Kingdom*, App. no. 37555/97, *The Times*, 13 November 2001, which followed an unsuccessful civil claim: *O'Hara* v *Chief Constable of the RUC* [1997] 2 WLR 1). It must be established as both a genuine suspicion in the mind of the arrestor which is justified on objective grounds, but it will be common in the context of anti-terrorist arrests for the evidence of informants to be in part suppressed and for it to be formed on the basis of second-hand information via briefings rather than events or information received first-hand by the arresting officer (see further *McKee* v *Chief Constable for Northern Ireland* [1984] 1 WLR 1358, Walker, C., 'Emergency arrest powers' (1985) 36 *Northern Ireland Legal Quarterly* 145; *Petticrew* v *Chief Constable, RUC* [1988] NI 192; *Stratford* v *Chief Constable of the RUC* [1988] NI 361; *Clinton* v *Chief Constable of the RUC* [1991] 2 NIJB 53; *Brady* v *Chief Constable of the RUC* [1991] 2 NIJB 22; Hunt, A., 'Terrorism and reasonable suspicion by "proxy"' (1997) 113 *Law Quarterly Review* 540).

The s. 41 formulation differs from normal arrest powers in that there is no need for there to be any specific offence in the mind of the arresting officer. Nor does the definition of terrorism itself refer to a schedule of offences. The result is to allow the police wider discretion in carrying out investigations — they are not bounded by the need to state on arrest or subsequently the offences which may be in mind.

Another extensions is that, given the wider definition of 'terrorism' in s. 1, terrorists may arise now from three sources: Irish, non-Irish domestic (a new category) or international. Hitherto, Irish arrests have provided the mainstay (85% according to Brown, D., *Detention under the Prevention of Terrorism Act* (Home Office Research and Planning Unit paper 75, London, 1993), p. 6), and the same study also found that most were male (91%) and aged 17–31 (61%); 26% were detained at ports; 31% of arrests occurred in London. There are signs of a current willingness to use extensively the special arrest power, which is seen as practically important by the police, more so than powers of proscription. For example, the pro-Kurdish demonstrators who occupied the Greek embassy in London following the capture of Abdullah Öcalan, the PKK leader, whose capture in Kenya with some alleged connivance by Greek officials triggered the occupation, were eventually arrested *en masse* under s. 14 of the Prevention of Terrorism (Temporary Provisions) Act 1989 (*The Times*, 19 February 1999, p. 1). This precedent may suggest that domestic animal rights and ecological protestors may also now be at risk, the point being to build up intelligence on the group and not simply to calm the scene, which can be achieved under public order laws. But since the Act came into force, there is no reported evidence of such an extended application.

Terrorist plots and attacks usually do entail serious offences, and this convergence has prompted the European Court of Human Rights to accept 'terrorism' as within the European Convention's notion of an 'offence' for the purposes of Article 5 (see *Brogan* v *United Kingdom*, App. nos. 11209, 11234, 11266/84, 11386/85, Ser. A. 145-B, (1989) 11 EHRR 539, para. 50; see also *Ireland* v *United Kingdom*, App. no. 5310/71, Ser. A. 25, (1979–80) 2 EHRR 25, para. 196). At the same time, any decision of the European Court of Human Rights must be seen in the light of the facts of the case, and in that case specific offences of membership of a proscribed organisation were in mind. This point was emphasised by Lord Lloyd in debates on the Bill (HL Debs. vol. 613 col. 677, 16 May 2000):

. . . the case did not decide what I think the Minister believes that it decides. The whole point of that case was that the applicants there were suspected of being members of a proscribed organisation, which is a specific offence, and suspected of various other specific offences. They were not suspected of being involved generally in acts of terrorism, as the Government were at great pains to point out. It was not on that ground that the European court decided at that point in favour of the United Kingdom. Perhaps I may read briefly from the judgment since the case was referred to by the Minister at Second Reading. At page 130 it states:

'In this connection, the government pointed out that the applicants were not in fact suspected of involvement in terrorism in general, but of membership of a proscribed organisation and involvement in specific acts of terrorism, each of which constituted an offence under the law of Northern Ireland and each of which was expressly put to the applicants during the course of their interviews following their arrests'.

Therefore, if the Government still rely on [*Brogan*] in support of that defence of Clause 40 as it currently stands, I suggest that they are on very weak ground.

The solution in Lord Lloyd's mind was to enact an offence of 'terrorism' (echoing the conclusion in his earlier report, Inquiry into Legislation against Terrorism (Cm. 3420, London, 1996), para. 8.16). In response, the Government was unmoved (HL Debs. vol. 613 col. 681–682, 16 May 2000, Lord Bassam; see also Home Office and Northern Ireland Office, Legislation against Terrorism (Cm. 4178, 1998), para. 7.16):

The noble and learned Lord, Lord Lloyd of Berwick, proposes an offence of terrorism primarily, it seems, because of his quite understandable concern that the arrest power under the Bill would not otherwise comply with Article 5(1)(c) of the ECHR, which provides that a person's arrest must be effected for the purpose of bringing the person before a competent legal authority on reasonable suspicion of having committed an offence. With the greatest respect, the Government take a different view.

In *Brogan* v *UK* in 1988 the Government argued successfully that it was not necessary to have arrested someone under the Prevention of Terrorism Act arrest power in connection with a specific offence in order to be compliant with Article 5(1)(c) of the convention. They argued that the way the arrest power was formulated in terms of being concerned in the commission, preparation or instigation of acts of terrorism should be regarded for convention purposes as a power of arrest for an offence.

The Court accepted that submission, saying that the arrest and subsequent detention of the applicants were based on a reasonable suspicion of an offence within the meaning of Article 5(1)(c).

While the Government recognise that no particular case can settle an ECHR point for all time — that has to be the case — and that the Court underlined that the particular circumstances of the *Brogan* case influenced the decision it took, the Government continue to be of the view that a terrorist arrest power, without an explicit link to a specific offence, is compatible with the ECHR and Article 5(1)(c) in particular. It was on that basis that the section 19(1)(a) Human Rights Act certificate was signed.

It may be further noted that a wide view was again taken of the nature of an 'offence' in connection with the meaning of 'breach of the peace' in *Steel and*

Others v *United Kingdom*, App. no. 24838/94, Reports 1998-VII, *The Times*, 1
October 1998. There is also the likelihood that the European Court will view
terrorist activity as especially threatening to rights and as especially difficult to
combat and therefore will allow some departure from strict interpretations of
Article 5 (see *Klass* v *Germany*, App. no. 5029/71, Ser. A. 28). In conclusion,
while each case will depend on its facts, especially in relation to the indicators as
to specific offences in the questioning, the arguments and precedents do seem to
point against Lord Lloyd's contention in this respect.

A final, unusually broad feature of the arrest power is that, by s. 41(9), a
constable in one part of the United Kingdom may exercise the power in any other
part of the United Kingdom.

In some respects, s. 41 appears narrower than the previous s. 14 of the 1989 Act,
which afforded specific powers to arrest for offences of membership and financial
support; however, this difference is explained by the fact that the term 'terrorist'
is defined to include these offences (compare Home Office and Northern Ireland
Office, Legislation against Terrorism (Cm. 4178, London, 1998), para. 7.10).
Equally, there is no counterpart to s. 3(1) of the Criminal Justice (Terrorism and
Conspiracy) Act 1998, allowing for arrest without warrant in Britain for offences
of membership of organisations proscribed only in Northern Ireland. Since the
proscription lists are now national, this power is no longer required.

The detention allowed subsequent to arrest under s. 41 departs substantially from
the rules and practices under the PACE legislation (Scottish laws are less precise
but may be taken to be similar in substance for these purposes). The purpose is
again to afford the police wider powers of investigation than would normally be
the case. Thus, instead of an initial 36-hour period on police discretion followed
by extensions by magistrates to a total of four days, s. 41(3) allows for detention
of up to 48 hours from either the time of arrest or examination at a port (as
described below). The detention period may then be extended for a further five
days according to the forms of review and authorisation laid down in sch. 8 to the
Act. This period is contrary to the recommendation of Lord Lloyd that four days
should be the maximum, though this limit was predicated upon the success of the
Peace Process in Northern Ireland (Inquiry into Legislation against Terrorism (Cm.
3420, London, 1996), paras 9.10, 9.22).

The most important form of review of the need for prolonged detention arises
at the 48-hour point. The person may be detained pending the making of, and
conclusion of the deliberation upon, an application (s. 41(5), (6)), and even the
refusal of an application does not prevent continued detention in accordance with
the unexpired detention period within 48 hours (s. 41(8)). The authorisation rules
are set out in pt III of sch. 8; whenever successful, the person's detention may
continue as specified (s. 41(7)). The process involves an application for a 'warrant
of further detention' under para. 29 of sch. 8 by a police officer of at least the rank
of superintendent. If granted, a warrant of further detention may allow for the
holding of the person for a specified period which shall expire not later than the
end of the period of seven days beginning with the time of his arrest under s. 41,

or examination under the port control powers (below). The form of warrant is set out in the Magistrates' Courts (Forms) (Amendment) Rules 2001 (SI 2001 No. 166). It is emphasised that the application is to 'a judicial authority'. The definition of a 'judicial authority' is (a) in England and Wales, the Senior District Judge (Chief Magistrate) or his deputy, or a District Judge (Magistrates' Courts) who is designated for the purpose of this Part by the Lord Chancellor; (b) in Scotland, the sheriff; and (c) in Northern Ireland, a county court judge, or a resident magistrate who is designated for the purpose of this Part by the Lord Chancellor. The selection of judicial personnel represents a major departure from the position under the Prevention of Terrorism (Temporary Provisions) Act 1989, according to which the Secretary of State reviewed these applications. The absence of judicial oversight in this way sparked the successful challenge which arose before the European Court of Human Rights in *Brogan and others* v *United Kingdom*. In its judgment of 29 November 1988, the European Court of Human Rights held that there had been a violation of Article 5(3) in respect of each of the applicants, all of whom had been detained under the 1989 Act. The Court held that even the shortest of the four periods of detention concerned, namely four days and six hours, fell outside the constraints as to time permitted by the first part of Article 5(3) (see further Livingstone, S., 'A week is a long time in detention' (1989) 40 *Northern Ireland Legal Quarterly* 288; Roche, P. M., 'The UK's obligation to balance human rights and its anti-terrorist legislation' (1989–90) 13 *Fordham International Law Review* 328; *O'Hara* v *United Kingdom*, App. no. 37555/97, *The Times*, 13 November 2001). In addition, the Court held that there had been a violation of Article 5(5) in the case of each applicant. The legal consequence was the unsatisfactory invocation of a derogation under Article 15. The recourse to a derogation was upheld as valid in *Brannigan and McBride* v *United Kingdom* (App. nos. 14553/89, 14554/89, Ser. A. 258-B, (1994) 17 EHRR 539; see also *McEldowney and others* v *United Kingdom*, App. no. 14550/89, Res DH(94) 31), albeit that the Court's judgment must be seen as taking a narrow view of its appropriate role in terms of assessing the options available to a State as well as relying heavily upon its usual margin of appreciation applied to the exigencies of the situation (see Roche, P. M., 'The UK's obligation to balance human rights and its anti-terrorist legislation' (1989–90) 13 *Fordham International Law Review* 328; Marks, S., 'Civil liberties at the margins' (1995) 15 *Oxford Journal of Legal Studies* 69).

The desire to avoid continued reliance upon the palliative of derogation in respect of detention following arrest under s. 41 has now been met. Lord Lloyd's blueprint (Inquiry into Legislation against Terrorism (Cm. 3420, London, 1996), para. 9.20) was to employ the Chief Stipendiary Magistrate (now the Senior District Judge (Chief Magistrate)) or Scottish Sheriff Principal, and this suggestion has been adapted by sch. 8. The coming into force of the Terrorism Act 2000 coincided, as noted in Chapter 1, with the withdrawal of the notice of derogation in respect of the United Kingdom. An unheralded outcome of the withdrawal of the derogation notice will be to extend the permissible period of detention for international terrorist suspects. Since the derogation notice was justifiable only in the case of the situation of Northern Ireland, it became the practice not to detain international suspects for more than four days (HC Standing Committee D, cols 182, 183, 25 January 2000, Charles Clarke). However, given the insertion of judicial oversight, the seven day detention power can be applied to all categories of suspects.

A new derogation notice, issued in December 2001, seeks to authorise the detention of international terrorist suspects who cannot be deported and are therefore held under Part IV of the Anti-terrorism, Crime and Security Act 2001. This distinct detention power is dealt with in Chapter 8.

The mechanisms by which a warrant of further detention may be obtained are also contained in pt III of sch. 8 of the 2000 Act. By para. 30, an application for a warrant, which may be written or oral, must be made within 48 hours or within six hours of the end of that period (provided in the latter case that the judicial authority does not consider that it would have been reasonably practicable to make it within 48 hours). The consideration by the judicial authority must likewise take place within those time limits (para. 35), so in practice an application must be made significantly inside the 48 hour mark. When making an application, a notice must be given to the detainee and it must state the grounds upon which further detention is sought (para. 31). It can be expected that the reference to 'grounds' rather than 'reasons' means that set formulas will be used which do not go into the details of an individual investigation (see *R* v *Officer in charge of Police Office, Castlereagh, ex parte Lynch* [1980] NI 126; see Walker, C.P., 'Arrest and rearrest' (1984) 35 *Northern Ireland Legal Quarterly* 1). However, the discretion of the judicial authority to grant an extension is limited to some extent by para. 32. The judicial authority must be satisfied that (a) there are reasonable grounds for believing that the further detention of the person to whom the application relates is necessary to obtain relevant evidence (relating to proof that he is a 'terrorist' within s. 40) whether by questioning him or otherwise or to preserve relevant evidence, and (b) the investigation in connection with which the person is detained is being conducted diligently and expeditiously. The statement of these criteria is an improvement over the predecessor legislation (which contained none), though they remain opaque compared to the 'Colville criteria' — a listing of reasons originally appearing in the Colville Report (Review of the Operation of the Prevention of Terrorism (Temporary Provisions) Act 1984 (Cm. 264, London, 1987), para. 5.16) and then promulgated to police forces as a guide (Home Office Circular No. 27/1989: Prevention of Terrorism (Temporary Provisions) Act 1989, para. 4.11). They were not comprehensive (interrogation of the detainee is not mentioned) but included:

1. Checking of fingerprints.
2. Forensic tests.
3. Checking the detainee's replies against intelligence.
4. New lines of enquiry.
5. Interrogation to identify accomplices.
6. Correlating information obtained from one or more other detained person in the same case.

7.   Awaiting a decision by the DPP.
8.   Finding and consulting other witnesses.
9.   Identification parade.
10. Checking an alibi.
11. Translating documents.
12. Obtaining an interpreter and carrying out the necessary interview with his assistance.
13. Communications with foreign police forces sometimes across timezones and language difficulties.
14. Evaluation of documents once translated and further investigated.

The criteria in the Terrorism Act 2000 are expressed in sch. 8, paras 23 and 34. A further procedural improvement in the 2000 Act, and one again in keeping with Article 5(3) of the European Convention, is that by para. 33, the detainee shall be given an opportunity to make oral or written representations to the judicial authority and shall be entitled to be legally represented at the hearing (the Advice and Assistance (Assistance by Way of Representation) (Scotland) Amendment (No. 2) Regulations 2001 (SSI 2001 No. 43) make assistance by way of representation available for proceedings in connection with an application for a warrant of further detention, or for extension of such a warrant). It should be noted that this formulation means that the detainee is not given a right to a hearing in person, which not only may diminish the power of the representations and the ability to instruct the lawyer representative but also foregoes an opportunity for an independent judicial officer to check on the welfare of a vulnerable prisoner.

The courts take seriously the right to make representations. In *Re Quigley's Application* [1997] NI 202, it was warned by the Northern Ireland High Court that failure to take account of representations might result in the quashing of a decision to extend detention by judicial review. But there was in this case sensitive information on which the decision was based, and the Court was satisfied that information of that kind was such that the representations could not under any circumstances have dissuaded the Minister. Some thought could be given to strengthening this safeguard — for example, to adopt a presumption that the detainee should appear unless contrary to the administration of justice; it is arguable that this is required to meet the demands of Article 5 of the European Convention. In fact, later amending legislation has made the prospect of appearance in person much less likely. By s. 75 of the Criminal Justice and Police Act 2001, the judicial authority may, after giving an opportunity for representations to be made by, or on behalf of, the applicant and the person to whom the application relates, direct that the hearing and all representations must be effected by suitable communications links and not in the physical presence of the detainee or of any legal representative. Any representations about the undesirability of such a direction are also subjected to the same facilities that will be used if the judicial authority decides to give a direction. A video link is in frequent use in Northern Ireland. Though the power to make a direction is worded in permissive terms —

'may' — para. 33(9) now provides that: 'If in a case where it has power to do so a judicial authority decides not to give a direction under sub-paragraph (4), it shall state its reasons for not giving it.'

Another procedural limit is that mainly (but not exclusively) because of security considerations, the judicial authority may exclude the detainee or any representative from any part of the hearing. The judicial authority may also, under sch. 8, para. 34, on an application of the police, withhold information from either or both of them on the grounds that disclosure could lead to evidence being interfered with or harmed, relevant property (subject to possible investigation or forfeiture or confiscation) being removed or lost, other suspects being alerted, other persons being interfered with or injured or, and these grounds are not in equivalent PACE legislation, the prevention of an act of terrorism becoming more difficult as a result of a person being alerted or the gathering of information about the commission, preparation or instigation of an act of terrorism being interfered with. The detainee and any representative are automatically excluded from the hearing of an application under para. 34. One wonders whether this blanket rule is consistent with concerns expressed by the European Court of Human Rights about the operation of Public Interest Immunity proceedings (*Rowe and Davis* v *United Kingdom*, App. no. 28901/95, *The Times*, 1 March 2000; *The Times*, 20 July 2000 (CA)), though it could be argued that the consequence of any unfairness more directly relates to a trial than here (compare *Schiesser* v *Switzerland*, App. no. 7710/76, Ser. A. 34). The process of application to a judicial authority may be repeated (para. 36), since in practice warrants are not usually granted for a full five days. Given this practice, it would have been better to specify that a warrant should not last more than 48 hours in one stretch.

The insertion of a form of independent judicial scrutiny is to be welcomed. Its importance is diminished by the absence of an appearance in person, but it is still worthwhile to have outside scrutiny and, of course, to be able to lift the notice of derogation. Not all have applauded the change — the Official Opposition felt (HC Debs. vol. 341 col. 172, 14 December 1999, Ann Widdecombe):

. . . unconvinced that it is legitimately a judicial function, rather than an Executive one. The decision to extend detention under existing legislation is usually based on intelligence material in the hands of the Executive that cannot be considered appropriate for judicial consideration. The information is often of such a sensitive nature that it cannot be disclosed to a detainee or his legal adviser without compromising the source of the intelligence, thus endangering lives or impeding an investigation.

By giving that power to a judicial authority, the judiciary would inevitably be seen as part of the investigation and prosecution process, which could bring its independence into question.

These views correlate closely with the arguments of the United Kingdom Government in *Marshall* v *United Kingdom*, App. no. 41571/98, Judgment of Court

10 July 2001, p. 8, in which its representative found it convenient to proffer the argument that 'the involvement of judges in the approval of extended detentions in terrorists cases could give rise to the risk that they would be perceived to be part of the process of investigation and prosecution, the more so since such decisions would require to be taken on the basis of materials which could not be disclosed, for security reasons, to the suspect or his lawyer'. However, the idea that judges cannot handle sensitive intelligence evidence and cannot operate without full disclosure to the accused is belied by their deployment as reviewers in other intelligence matters (under the Security Service Act 1989 and the Intelligence Services Act 1994) and by the compromises made everyday in the courts under the doctrine of Public Interest Immunity.

As well as the judicial form of authorisation, the police themselves must conduct formal reviews and thereafter keep the validity of the detention under constant review. In these aspects there are again parallels with the PACE legislation but also some important differences.

By way of the formal police reviews under pt II of sch. 8, para. 21 requires periodic checks by a 'review officer'. By para. 24, the review officer shall in any event be an officer who has not been directly involved in the investigation in connection with which the person is detained. For reviews within the first 24-hour period, the review officer shall be an officer of at least the rank of inspector (but if an investigative officer of a higher rank gives directions which the lower ranking review officer views as at variance with his duties, the matter of review shall be referred at once to an officer of at least the rank of superintendent); after 24 hours, an officer of at least the rank of superintendent must act as reviewer. The reviews must be carried out in person by an officer present at the police station where the detainee is held (see *R* v *Chief Constable of Kent Constabulary, ex parte Kent Police Federation Joint Branch Board and another, The Times*, 1 December 1999); there is no equivalent measure to s. 73 of the Criminal Justice and Police Act 2001, which allows for telephone and video links to be used in the corresponding reviews under s. 40 of PACE 1984. The first review shall be carried out as soon as is reasonably practicable after the time of the person's arrest. Subsequent reviews shall be carried out at intervals of not more than 12 hours (compared to nine-hourly reviews under the PACE legislation, and thereby suggesting that the Government preferred a scheme which permits the greatest degree of police discretion). The reviews may be postponed so as to avoid a prejudicial interruption of the questioning, if no review officer is readily available, or if it is otherwise not practicable for any other reason to carry out the review (para. 22). The grounds for continued detention are stated in para. 23; the review must be satisfied that it is necessary: (a) to obtain relevant evidence (that the person is a 'terrorist') whether by questioning him or otherwise, (b) to preserve relevant evidence, (c) pending a decision whether to apply to the Secretary of State for a deportation notice to be served on the detained person, (d) pending the making of an application to the Secretary of State for a deportation notice to be served on the detained person, (e) pending consideration by the Secretary of State whether to serve a deportation notice on the detained person, or (f)) pending a decision whether the detained person should be charged with an offence. The review officer must also be sure that the investigations (under (a) or (b)) or the processes (under (c) to (f)) are being conducted diligently and expeditiously. Grounds (a) and (b) are in practice the most common (88% according to Brown, D., *Detention under the Prevention of Terrorism Act* (Home Office Research and Planning Unit paper 75, London, 1993), p. 47). It is provided by s. 41(4) that if the review officer does not authorise continued detention, the person shall (unless detained under any other power) be released.

In conducting the review, certain procedural rights must be observed. First, before determining whether to authorise a person's continued detention, a review officer shall give an opportunity to make representations about the detention either to the detained person, or a solicitor representing him who is available at the time of the review (para. 26 — but very few solicitors do attend — 6% according to Brown, D., *Detention under the Prevention of Terrorism Act* (Home Office Research and Planning Unit paper 75, London, 1993), p. 47). Secondly, by para. 27, where a review officer decides to authorise continued detention he shall inform the detained person of any of his rights to have a person informed of his whereabouts or to see a solicitor (under paras 6 and 7, as below) which he has not yet exercised, and if the exercise of any of his rights is being delayed, of the fact that it is being so delayed (in which case the review officer must also reconsider whether delay continues to be necessary). By para. 28, the review officer shall make a written record of the outcome of the review and, as relevant, the grounds upon which continued detention is authorised, the reason for postponement of a review, the fact that the detained person has been informed as required under para. 27 and the review officer's reconsideration of the delay and the outcome, and the fact that the detained person is being detained pending the making of, or conclusion on, an application under s. 41. The review officer shall make the record in the presence of the detained person, and inform him at that time whether the review officer is authorising continued detention, and, if he is, of his grounds (there are exceptions when the detainee is incapable of understanding what is said to him, violent or likely to become violent, or in urgent need of medical attention).

This system of formal police reviews must come to an end under para. 22(4) after a warrant extending detention has been issued under pt III of sch. 8 (so there is no question of the police authorising a review period beyond 48 hours — compare Fenwick, H., *Civil Rights* (Longman, Harlow, 2000), p. 242). It is regrettable that in this respect the Terrorism Act 2000, unlike the PACE legislation, does not recognise the need not only for very occasional judicial oversight but also more formal police vigilance over the behaviour of investigative officers who are often working under considerable pressure and tension. However, the 2000 Act does at least insert a duty of constant, background police review, as set out in para. 37. A person detained by virtue of a warrant issued under this Part shall (unless detained in accordance with s. 41(5) or (6) pending the making or determination of an application for a warrant or under any other power outside the 2000 Act) be released immediately if the officer having custody of him becomes aware that any of the grounds under para. 32(1)(a) and (b) upon which the judicial authority authorised his further detention have ceased to apply. In addition, it has been found in practice that police 'welfare' checks may continue after 48 hours (Brown, D., *Detention under the Prevention of Terrorism Act* (Home Office Research and Planning Unit paper 75, London, 1993), p. 46).

As well as detention periods, sch. 8 (pt I) also governs the treatment of persons detained on the authority of s. 41; the commitment to apply PACE rules more fully has not really been observed (compare Home Office and Northern Ireland Office, Legislation against Terrorism (Cm. 4178, London, 1998), para. 8.50). The application of the rules is assisted by the fact that the places of detention are limited by designation under para. 1, and any person arrested under s. 41 must be taken as soon as is reasonably practicable to the designated place. In practice, a number of police stations in Britain have been equipped to hold terrorist suspects in conditions of sufficient security — most notably at Paddington Green Police Station in London. Additionally, some detentions occur at ports, and high security prisons could also be designated, though these places have the disadvantage that fingerprints and samples may not be taken and taping of interviews does not occur (HC Standing Committee D, cols 173, 174, 25 January 2000, Charles Clarke). In Northern Ireland, 'Holding Centres' in Armagh, Belfast and Londonderry have been most commonly used, but Castlereagh in Belfast, Gough Barracks in Armagh and Strand Road in Londonderry have all closed (see Independent Commissioner for the Holding Centres, 8th Annual Report (Belfast, 2001)), leaving a temporary unit in Lisburn as the sole special centre for the holding of terrorist suspects in Northern Ireland, though a custom-built centre is to be built in Antrim by 2003. Persons may be removed from the designated place only for the purposes of examination (or to establish nationality or to arrange removal from the country) under sch. 7. Once at the designated place of detention, sch. 8, pt I, provides for both policing powers (some investigative and some for routine processing purposes) and for rights to fair treatment.

Amongst the policing provisions is the power to take steps reasonably necessary to identify the individual (sch. 8, para. 2). This may be accomplished by photographing, measuring or otherwise identifying the detained person. The 'other steps' could include, for example, voice recognition tests, but expressly do not include fingerprints, non-intimate samples or intimate sampling since they are dealt with in para. 10 (with records being required under para. 11). The equivalent provisions in Scotland are in para. 20. Fingerprints and non-intimate samples (compare: Prevention of Terrorism (Temporary Provisions) Act 1989, s. 15(9) and Northern Ireland (Emergency Provisions) Act 1996, s. 48) may be taken with the appropriate consent given in writing, or, without consent, where a superintendent authorises the fingerprints or samples to be taken or where the person has been convicted of a recordable offence. In the case of intimate samples, there must be the appropriate consent given in writing in all cases, as well as authorisation by a superintendent. Authorisations can only be given under para. 10 where the officer reasonably suspects that the person has been involved in an offence under any of the provisions mentioned in s. 40(1)(a), and the officer reasonably believes that the fingerprints or samples will tend to confirm or disprove his involvement, or in any case, the officer is satisfied that the taking of the fingerprints or samples from the person is necessary in order to assist in determining whether he falls within s. 40(1)(b). Furthermore (under para. 12), if non-intimate samples prove insufficient for forensic purposes, an authorisation may be given in respect of a person since released from detention, provided again that the person also consents to the sampling. Under para. 11, the detainee shall be informed of the purposes of the process and the reasons for taking it by consent or the grounds (including the nature of the suspected offence) on which an authorisation has been given. It will be noted that intimate samples must in all cases be taken with consent. One reason is that they require the cooperation of non-police personnel whose ethical codes require the consent of their patients. An intimate sample other than a sample of urine may be taken only by a registered medical practitioner, while an intimate sample which is a dental impression may only be taken by a registered dentist (para. 13). Where appropriate consent is refused without good cause, in any proceedings against that person for an offence, inferences may be drawn from the refusal (para. 13).

Though the powers to take and retain fingerprints and samples are wider than under the PACE legislation, the purposes for which they can be utilised were limited by para. 14 in that they may be used only for the purpose of a terrorist investigation and not for routine criminal checks under s. 63A(1) of PACE 1984. However, the position has since been changed by s. 84 of the Criminal Justice and Police Act 2001. First, it allows the subsequent use not only for the purposes of a terrorist investigation but also for purposes related to the prevention or detection of crime, the investigation of an offence or the conduct of a prosecution. Secondly, the exclusion of checks against the fingerprints or samples under s. 63A or its Northern Ireland equivalent is diminished since the purposes of the prevention or detection of crime, the investigation of an offence or the conduct of a prosecution are again allowed. Thirdly, the relevant criminal investigations may relate to offences outside the United Kingdom.

Further amendments have been made by s. 89 of the Anti-terrorism, Crime and Security Act 2001 by specifying that fingerprints can be taken from those detained under the Terrorism Act 2000 in order to ascertain their identity. Though sch. 8, para. 2 is apparently worded in wide terms ('an authorised person may take any steps which are reasonably necessary for . . . (c) identifying him'), it was asserted that these powers could only be exercised to establish if he has been involved in certain offences under the Act or to establish if he has been concerned in the commission, preparation, or instigation of acts of terrorism. Given other, non-criminal forms of disposal now possible under ss. 21 to 24 of the 2001 Act (detention without trial), wider purposes must be specified simply to 'facilitate the ascertainment of that person's identity'. Accordingly, two new sub-paragraphs are inserted into para. 10 of sch. 8 of the 2000 Act. Sub-paragraph (6A) allows an officer of at least superintendent rank to authorise the taking of fingerprints of a person detained at a station without the person's consent if the officer is satisfied that the fingerprints will enable the identification of the person, and that the person has refused to identify himself or the officer reasonably believes that he has given a false identity. Sub-paragraph (6B) allows the powers to be used to show that a person is not a particular person (where there is a belief of a false identity). Subsection (3) makes corresponding amendments to s. 18(2) of the Criminal Procedure (Scotland) Act 1995 and also allows under subsection (4) (along the lines elsewhere of the Criminal Justice and Police Act 2001) the police to examine fingerprints or DNA samples retained under Terrorism Act 2000 powers when investigating a crime that, at that stage, is apparently non-terrorist. 'For example, a van may be stolen for use as a bomb, but recovered without any evidence of its intended terrorist use' (HL Debs. vol. 629 col. 711, 4 December 2001, Lord Rooker). Before this change, those records could be searched only if the police were investigating a suspected terrorist offence: 'There is therefore a risk that they will miss connections between ordinary criminal offences, which may be committed as precursors to terrorist activity, and terrorist suspects' (HC Debs. vol. 375 col. 742, 26 November 2001, Beverley Hughes).

Along the same lines, ss. 90 (England and Wales) and 91 (Northern Ireland) extend other search powers to allow them to be used specifically to establish identity. Such powers comprise:

(a)   section 54(6) of PACE 1984 which allows a custody officer to authorise a detained person to be searched to ascertain and record everything in the possession of a detainee. By an added s. 54A, such searches, if authorised by an inspector and provided the suspect withholds consent to an examination for a mark or it is not practicable to seek such consent, may also relate to 'any mark that would tend to identify him' or 'for the purpose of facilitating the ascertainment of his identity' where the person has refused to identify himself or the officer has reasonable grounds for suspecting that that person is not who he claims to be. Photographs may be taken of such bodily marks. In effect, what might otherwise have been considered an intimate search (a search of body orifices other than the mouth) under s. 55 of PACE 1984 can now be undertaken for purposes of identification rather than the investigatory or safety purposes allowed under s. 55. It is expressly forbidden to use s. 54A for the purposes of intimate searches within s. 55 (s. 54A(8)), but then it is expressly permitted under s. 54A(9) to use or disclose a photograph taken under this section for any purpose related to the prevention or detection of crime, the investigation of an offence or the conduct of a prosecution. There is no corresponding power for Scotland;

(b)   sections 27 and 61 of PACE 1984 which allow the taking of fingerprints without consent where, *inter alia*, there are reasonable grounds to suspect their involvement in a criminal offence and that fingerprints would tend to confirm or disprove that involvement. Where fingerprints are authorised to be taken to confirm or disprove a person's involvement in a crime, the prints can only be taken if a police superintendent rank (amended to inspector rank on implementation of s. 78 of the Criminal Justice and Police Act 2001) authorises them to be taken. Fingerprints could not previously be taken where the question is about identity. Accordingly, the effect of s. 90(2) is to provide an additional power in PACE 1984 to take fingerprints from an arrested person to establish or check their identity. Once taken, fingerprints taken for identification purposes will be retained in the same way in which fingerprints taken in order to prove or disprove commission of a crime are now retained. Thus, fingerprints will be retained whether or not the person is proceeded against or convicted, but can be used only for the purposes of the prevention or detection of crime, the investigation of an offence or the pursuit of a prosecution.

In further pursuance of the establishment of identity, s. 92 (s. 93 in Northern Ireland) inserts a new s. 64A after s. 64 of PACE 1984 which affords a power to photograph a person who is detained at a police station with the appropriate consent or, where consent is withheld, without it. Again, though photographing is allowed already under sch. 8, para. 2(a), s. 92(2) expressly allows the police to require the removal of any item or substance, such as face paint, worn on or over the whole or any part of that person's face or head and if the person does not comply, may use force under s. 117 of PACE 1984. While the purpose of the new measure is mainly identification, subsection (4) does allow for photographs to be used by or disclosed to any person for the purpose related to the prevention or detection of crime, the investigation of an offence or the conduct of a prosecution and for them subsequently to be retained, but then only used for a related purpose.

While ss. 92 and 93 deal with the photographing of suspects inside the police station for identification purposes, the photographing of suspects outside a police station is not closely regulated. Some target suspects may fall within the Regulation of Investigatory Powers Act 2000, otherwise one is left with the vague notion of 'private life' under Article 8 of the European Convention, which may not be very censorious of a process of photographing persons in a public place (see *Friedl* v *Austria*, App. no. 15225/89, Ser. A. 305B). Nevertheless, ss. 94 and 95 (in Northern Ireland) extend powers to gather information about identity. They extend to more situations the power in s. 60(4A) of the Criminal Justice and Public Order Act 1994 to require the removal of face coverings worn for the purpose of concealing identity. The basic s. 60 allows a blanket power to stop and search for offensive weapons and dangerous implements in a given locality and for a given period, provided an authorisation is given by a senior officer on the basis of a reasonable belief that incidents of serious violence may take place in the locality and that it is expedient to give an authorisation to prevent their occurrence. Section 60 did not extend to Northern Ireland, so, using the 'valuable opportunity' of the 2001 Act but also in the light of the use of knives in the 11 September hijackings (HC Debs. vol. 375 col. 765, 26 November 2001, Jane Kennedy), s. 96 first inserts a new art. 23B into the Public Order (Northern Ireland) Order 1987 (SI 1987 No. 463 (NI 7)) (the retention of things seized being dealt with under art. 23C, inserted by s. 97).

Having set the scene, ss. 94 and 95 provide that in relation to the power to require the removal of face coverings only, an authorisation (in the form required by subsection (6)) may also be given (under s. 60AA) where a senior officer reasonably believes activities may take place in the locality involving the commission of offences and that it is expedient to give such an authorisation to prevent or control those activities. The authorisation triggers these extra powers for a period of 24 hours, extendable for 24 hours at a time. The police will be expected (see HL Debs. vol. 629 col. 736, 4 December 2001, Lord Rooker) to conform to the advice in the PACE Code A, para. 1AA that:

> Where there may be religious sensitivities about asking someone to remove a face covering using the powers in Section 25 of the Crime and Disorder Act 1998, for example in the case of a Muslim woman wearing a face covering for religious purposes, the officer should permit the item to be removed out of public view. Where practicable, the item should be removed in the presence of an officer of the same sex as the person and out of sight of anyone of the opposite sex.

The Forum against Islamophobia and Racism is not reassured and objects in the strongest terms to these powers, especially in relation to their impact on Muslim women (Submission to the Home Affairs Committee, London, 2001, para. 6). A person who fails to remove an item when required to do so by a constable in the exercise of his power under this section is liable, on summary conviction, to imprisonment for a term not exceeding one month or a fine not exceeding level 3 on the standard scale. But there is no power to remove force to compel the removal of face coverings; presumably, if the police decide to arrest the person, there is then the possibility of using the powers in ss. 92 and 93.

Even in Northern Ireland, there is no revival of the offence formerly in the Northern Ireland (Emergency Provisions) Act 1996, s. 35, of wearing a mask or hood in a public place for the purpose of concealing identity. There is also to be no equivalent in Scotland because of an allegedly lukewarm reaction by the Association of Chief Police Officers in Scotland (HC Debs. vol. 375 col. 764, 26 November 2001), and it is admitted that the motivation behind the legislation is not terrorism but 'because the police believe that the tactic of wearing face coverings has become increasingly widespread during all kinds of events that could lead to public disorder' (HC Debs. vol. 375 col. 760, 26 November 2001, Beverley Hughes).

The Joint Committee on Human Rights believed that the extension of police powers entailed by the Bill would trigger issues of proportionality and respect for private and family life (Report on the Anti-terrorism, Crime and Security Bill (2001–02 HL 37, HC 372, para. 62)). Further safeguards were demanded, especially in regard to the removal of face coverings which might engage cultural and religious sensitivities (para. 64 of the Report). One might argue more generally that identification powers already existed in sch. 8, para. 2, and that in cases of doubt, further detention powers could be granted (including the refusal of bail after charge). Next, the powers in regard to the removal of items of clothing is not confined to suspected terrorists or those suspected of terrorist crime but will apply automatically to all those in the designated locality. Further, the offence does not provide a defence of 'reasonable excuse' for refusal and might cause problems in dealing with the ethnic minority communities for whom veils and head coverings are normal, though this point might be answered by a lack of intention to conceal (HC Debs. vol. 375 col. 761, 26 November 2001, Beverley Hughes). Finally, few of these provisions are actually limited to terrorism, though the Minister of State argued that it would be impractical so to confine them:

> Let us take the example in which someone has been brought into a police station and detained because he was trespassing on the property of a public utility, and has refused to divulge his identity. Clearly, the reasons for his trespassing could be many and varied. They could involve a range of criminal offences, sabotage or the planting of a bomb on those premises in relation to a terrorist activity.
>
> At that point, because the police do not know who the person is, they cannot begin to identify the kind of person with whom they are dealing or what that person might have been seeking to do. It is, therefore, critical that the identity of the person should be discovered in the shortest possible time, and that the police should have the powers to enable them to establish that identity. If, in that example, someone had already planted a bomb, time would be of the essence. The police would be doing many things at that point, but one thing that they would surely need to do would be to establish the identity of that person. (HC Debs. vol. 749, 26 November 2001, Beverley Hughes)

Returning to the processing of persons within police stations, amongst the rights to fair treatment might be included sch. 8, para. 3 which deals with the audio and video recording of interviews provided they take place in a designated police station (which means that interviews at ports will not be taped). Statutory orders and codes of practice have to be issued to ensure the audio recording of interviews, but the making of an order requiring the video recording of interviews is a matter of discretion (but if issued, a code of practice is required). This division reflects established practice, whereby audio recording has been established throughout the United Kingdom: in Northern Ireland, commencing in January 1999 under the Northern Ireland (Emergency Provisions) Act 1998, s. 5 (in harmony with the recommendation in the Review of the Northern Ireland (Emergency Provisions) Act 1991 (Cm. 2706, London, 1995), para. 131); in England and Wales (but not in Scotland), under a Home Office circular issued in 1992. The Terrorism Act 2000 (Code of Practice on Audio Recording of Interviews) Order 2001 (SI 2001 No. 159) allows for a code of practice in connection with the audio recording. The Terrorism Act 2000 (Code of Practice on Audio Recording of Interviews) (No. 2) Order 2001 (SI 2001 No. 189) demands that any interview shall be audio recorded in accordance with the audio code. But video-recording has only recently been required and only in Northern Ireland (beginning with overhead silent videos under the Northern Ireland (Emergency Provisions) Act 1996, s. 53 and then under the 1998 Act, s. 4; there is no routine video recording in Britain). Because of this history, an overlapping power in relation to video recording in Northern Ireland subsists in s. 100 (see Chapter 7). The Terrorism Act 2000 (Video Recording of Interviews) Order 2000 (SI 2000 No. 3179) provides for interviews only in Northern Ireland to be recorded by video, and the Terrorism Act 2000 (Code of Practice on Video Recording of Interviews) (Northern Ireland) Order 2001 (SI 2000 No. 402) allows for a code of practice in connection with the video recording with sound of any interview. It will be noted that these codes have been issued under paras 3 and 4 of sch. 8 and not s. 100. The video recording commenced in Northern Ireland in February 2001. A failure by a constable to observe a provision of a code shall not of itself make him liable to criminal or civil proceedings, but an infraction of a code shall be admissible in evidence and shall be taken into account by a court or tribunal in any case in which it appears to the court or tribunal to be relevant (presumably its main relevance will be to standards of admissibility of evidence such as under s. 78 of PACE 1984).

The Code of Practice on the audio recording of interviews under the Terrorism Act 2000 provides for rules about the recording and sealing of master tapes, the conduct of taping during interviews, interview records, tape security and tape destruction. In particular, the following might be noted. By para. 2.1, the audio recording of interviews shall be carried out openly so as to instill confidence in the integrity of the tape as an impartial and accurate record of the interview. By para. 3.3, the whole of each interview shall be audio recorded, including the taking and reading back of any statement. In this way, there is no provision for 'off-the-record' conversations, though there is no definition of 'interview' and it may be that intelligence-gathering which is not envisaged as leading to any possible proceedings against the detainee may not be considered to be part of the 'interview'. Under para. 5, an accurate record must be made of each interview with a detained person. The record must be made during the course of the interview, unless in the investigating officer's view this would not be practicable or would interfere with the conduct of the interview, and must constitute either a verbatim record of what was said or, failing this, an account of the interview which adequately and accurately summarises it. Unless it is impracticable, the person interviewed must be given the opportunity under tape recorded conditions to read the interview record and to sign it as correct or to indicate the respects in which he considers it inaccurate. By para. 8, at the conclusion of criminal proceedings, or in the event of a direction not to prosecute, the contents of a working copy of the tape shall be completely erased.

Drawing further upon the PACE precedents, ss. 56 and 58, for England and Wales, the Law Reform (Miscellaneous Provisions) Act 1985, s. 35, for Scotland and the Northern Ireland (Emergency Provisions) Act 1996, ss. 46 and 47, rights to have a person informed of the detention and to have access to a legal adviser are granted by paras 6 and 7 of sch. 8 of the Terrorism Act 2000. In Scotland, these rights are set out in para. 16. For Northern Ireland, para. 7 is more generous by far than previous formulations in that the right is to consult privately and at any time — not, as previously, once every 48 hours and always outside the interview room. It was confirmed in debates that the admission to the interview room in Northern Ireland was indeed intended, even though contrary to the views of a previous reviewer (Review of the Northern Ireland (Emergency Provisions) Act 1991 (Cm. 2706, London, 1995), para. 130) and of the courts (see especially *R v Chief Constable of the RUC, ex parte Begley* [1997] 1 WLR 1475; *Re Floyd's Application and related applications* [1997] NI 414). Lord Bassam explained the change as follows (HL Debs. vol. 613 col. 701, 23 May 2000):

> . . . we propose to ensure that once a person has been granted access to a solicitor, that solicitor may, save in the most exceptional of circumstances, be able to be present at all interviews. That is already the position in England and Wales under paragraph 6.8 and following of PACE Code C. It is our intention, also by code, to make that the position too in Northern Ireland. For Scotland, where no equivalent of the PACE Code exists, that position is achieved already by paragraph 21 of schedule 8. Currently, this provision is in force only in England and Wales, and again our records suggest that it has not been used in terrorist cases in recent times.

The Chief Constable of the RUC had already announced on the 29 September 2000 that solicitors would be allowed to sit in on interviews with terrorist suspects with immediate effect. The position is now confirmed in the Code of Practice (para. 6.7) under s. 99 (the Terrorism Act 2000 (Code of Practice on the Exercise of Police Powers (Northern Ireland) Order 2001 (SI 2001 No. 401) brings into force a code covering the exercise by police officers of the powers of detention and identification). As for Scotland, in the absence of primary legislation or case law, this aspect of the right is expressly dealt with by para. 19: the Secretary of State shall, by order, make provision to require that the solicitor shall be allowed to be present at any interview. The details have appeared as the Terrorism (Interviews) (Scotland) Order 2001 (SI 2001 No. 428 (S1)). Article 3 expressly allows the solicitor to be present at any interview carried out in connection with a terrorist investigation or for the purposes of sch. 7 (port and border controls) — unless, by para. 4, the solicitor's behaviour during the interview will interfere with, or obstruct, the conduct of the interview. Under the Home Office, Circular 03/01: Terrorism Act 2000 (Home Office, London, 2001, para. 17.24), it is recommended that Chief Officers in Scotland should look to ensure also that if the officer was of the view that a solicitor's conduct was such as to cause him to require the solicitor to leave the interview, then the police superintendent should also consider seriously whether there is also a need to inform the Law Society of Scotland of the solicitor's conduct. Where the solicitor concerned is a duty solicitor, the report should be both to the Law Society and to the Scottish Legal Aid Board.

In practice in England and Wales, around 49% of detainees take legal advice, a higher rate than under PACE and one which rises with the seriousness of the charges and length of detention (Brown, D., *Detention under the Prevention of Terrorism Act* (Home Office Research and Planning Unit paper 75, London, 1993), pp. 9–10, 21–22). As regards notification, 43% have availed themselves of this right (p. 23).

Delays to the exercise of these rights may be authorised by a superintendent for up to 48 hours, rather than the normal 36 hours (see (Jellicoe) Report of the Operation of the Prevention of Terrorism (Temporary Provisions) Act 1976 (Cmnd. 8803, London, 1983), para. 108). The grounds for doing so are equivalent to those in the PACE legislation, save that the following extra grounds are added (in para. 8 or para. 17 in Scotland): interference with the gathering of information about the commission, preparation or instigation of acts of terrorism; the alerting of a person and thereby making it more difficult to prevent an act of terrorism; and the alerting of a person and thereby making it more difficult to secure a person's apprehension, prosecution or conviction in connection with the commission, preparation or instigation of an act of terrorism. Writing materials and access to the telephone may be refused on the same grounds (PACE Code C, para. 5.6). In Northern Ireland, the courts had set their face against the provision of writing materials (*Re Floyd's Application and related applications* [1997] NI 414), but new rights to writing materials are set out in the Code of Practice, para. 3G(e) but only for the purpose of making representations about continued detention). Where delay is authorised, the detained person shall be told the reason for the delay as soon as is reasonably practicable, and the reason shall be recorded as soon as is reasonably practicable; once the reason for authorising delay ceases to subsist there may be no further delay in permitting the exercise of the right in the absence of a further authorisation.

A further qualification, particular to the Terrorism Act 2000, to the exercise of the right of access to a lawyer under sch. 8, para. 7 is that a direction may be given under para. 9 (para. 17 in Scotland) to the effect that a detained person may consult a solicitor only in the sight and hearing of a 'qualified officer' (an inspector) (see Report of the Operation of the Prevention of Terrorism (Temporary Provisions) Act 1976 (Cmnd. 8803, London, 1983), para. 111). This is a serious intrusion into normal due process rights and so must be authorised by an officer of at least the rank of Commander or Assistant Chief Constable and only if the officer giving it has reasonable grounds for believing that, unless the direction is given, the exercise of the right by the detained person will have any of the consequences specified as for delay. Even with these restraints, it is very doubtful whether access to legal advice under these circumstances can meet the standards of Article 6 of the European Convention. In *Brennan* v *United Kingdom* (App. no. 39846/98, *The Times*, 22 October 2001), the presence of the police during a consultation session with the detainee's solicitor amounted to a breach of Article 6. If there is concern about either intentional collusion or the relaying of unwitting messages, then some kind of firewall must be inserted between the lawyer-client consultation and the police, rather than allowing oversight (as recently permitted in US prisons by the Attorney-General's order regarding monitoring of confidential attorney-client communications, 66 Fed. Reg. 55062, 31 October 2001). But this is very difficult to achieve, since the intermediary (such as, say, a magistrate or assigned counsel, called in the United States a 'privilege' or 'taint' team) will either be unaware of the details of the investigation and will therefore not be able to recognise any danger signals or will chill the inclination to have a full and frank consultation between attorney and client.

Legal advice is, as the Court of Appeal declared in *R* v *Samuel* [1988] 2 WLR 920, a fundamental right under English law, and it has been treated likewise under the European Convention on Human Rights. In the context of denial of access to a solicitor of persons detained under anti-terrorism laws in Northern Ireland, the leading case is *Murray (John)* v *United Kingdom*, (App. no. 18731/91, Reports 1996-I, (1996) 22 EHRR 29; see further Walker, C., and Fitzpatrick, B., 'Holding Centres in Northern Ireland, the Independent Commissioner and the rights of detainees' [1999] *European Human Rights Law Review* 27; Flaherty, M.S., 'Interrogation, legal advice and human rights in Northern Ireland' (1997) 27 *Columbia Human Rights Law Review* 1). The European Court of Human Rights concluded that it would be incompatible with the right to silence to base a conviction solely or mainly on the accused's silence or on a refusal to answer questions, or to give evidence himself. However, the applicant's failure to answer questions put to him in custody did not expose him to the threat of penal sanctions, and he was not convicted solely or mainly on account of his silence but on the basis of forensic and other circumstantial evidence. Accordingly, there were no breaches of Article 6(1) and (2) of the European Convention arising from the drawing of adverse inferences — the reliance upon such inferences did not reverse the burden of proof. However, breaches of Article 6(1) in conjunction with Article 6(3)(c) of the Convention were sustained in *Murray's* case, arising from denial of access to a lawyer for 48 hours — the Court spoke of the 'paramount importance for the rights of the defence that an accused has access to a lawyer at the initial stages of police interrogation' (para. 66). Breaches were also sustained in *Averill* v *United Kingdom*, App. no. 36408/97, *The Times*, 20 June 2000 and *Magee* v *United Kingdom*, App. no. 28135/95, *The Times*, 20 June 2000. In *Magee*, the applicant was deprived of legal assistance for over 48 hours, while he was interviewed in five sessions prior to his confession, and the incriminating statements were crucial evidence in the prosecution's case and were the basis of the conviction. In *Averill*, the applicant was denied a solicitor for a period of 24 hours. He maintained his silence, and the trial judge consequently drew adverse inferences against him. The applicant's complaint under Article 6(1) in conjunction with Article 6(3)(c) of the Convention was upheld. Access to lawyers before, after and during interviews is the most vital safeguard against abuse and is also a requirement of fairness in an adversarial system. Increasingly, any denial of access may breach the Human Rights Act 1998 and jeopardise the admissibility of statements, results which will provide a powerful incentive to grant access. In line with this warning, the Government expects deferment to be limited to 'exceptional cases' (HC Debs. vol. 346 col. 375, 15 March 2000, Charles Clarke).

Deferment of these rights, especially to legal advice, is becoming uncommon. During the early 1990s in England and Wales, delay of legal access was authorised in 26% of cases, a far higher figure than under PACE 1984 (where the rate is now negligible), the grounds often being multiple, and the average length of delay was 16 hours (Brown, D., *Detention under the Prevention of Terrorism Act* (Home Office Research and Planning Unit paper 75, London, 1993), pp. 17–18). In notification cases, delay ran at 30% (p. 28). However, access has not been deferred in any terrorist case in Britain between 1997 to 1999. In Northern Ireland, notification to family is delayed in about 9% of cases, a figure which has not altered much over the decade. However, there has been a major change in practice in regard to access to solicitors (see Table 5.1). A refusal rate of 59% from 1987 to 1990 (see Walker, C.P., *The Prevention of Terrorism in British Law* (2nd ed., Manchester University Press, Manchester, 1992), p. 172) has now been substantially reduced (to zero in 2000). One factor has been a series of legal challenges to police practices, none of which was successful but which did serve to prompt police reflection on their practices (see *Moore* v *Chief Constable, Royal Ulster Constabulary* [1988] NI 456; *R* v *Harper* [1990] NI 28; *Re McNearney*, September 1991, unreported; *Re Duffy* [1991] 7 NIJB 62; *R* v *Chief Constable, ex parte McKenna and McKenna* [1992] NI 116; *R* v *Chambers* [1994] NI 170; *R* v *Cosgrove and Morgan* [1994] NI 182; *In re Russell* [1996] NI 310; *R* v *McWilliams* [1996] NI 545; *In re Begley* [1997] 1 WLR 1475; *Re Floyd's Application and related applications* [1997] NI 414. A second was pressure from outside organisations such as the European Commission for the Prevention of Torture (see Report to the UK Government on the Visit to Northern Ireland carried out by the European Commission for the Prevention of Torture etc. 1993 (CPT/Inf (94) 17, 1994); Response of the UK Government (CPT/Inf (94) 18, 1994)). A possible third reason is the influence of 'normal' practices under PACE 1984 and the police acceptance of the compatibility of solicitors within the police working environment. The latter may not, however, be a universal sentiment, and there are allegations of police collusion in the murders of two prominent Northern Ireland lawyers, Pat Finucane in 1989 and Rosemary Nelson in 1999 (see Flaherty, M., 'Human rights violations against defence lawyers: the case of Northern Ireland' (1994) 7 *Harvard Human Rights Journal* 87; Flaherty, M.S., 'Interrogation, legal advice and human rights in Northern Ireland' (1997) 27 *Columbia Human Rights Law Review* 1; Murphy, M.R., 'Northern Ireland policing reform and the intimidation of defense lawyers' (2000) 68 *Fordham Law Review* 1877). Charges were brought in the Finucane case against William Stobie, an Ulster Defence Association member, but the trial collapsed and he was murdered soon afterwards (*The Guardian*, 27 November 2001, p. 10; *The Times*, 13 December 2001, p. 11).

Whether deferment does in fact breach Article 6 of the European Convention will depend on the circumstances of the case; if no admissions or inferences result from the period of refusal, then there may be no breach (*Brennan* v *United Kingdom*, App. no. 39846/98, *The Times*, 22 October 2001). A problem remains with the accessibility of lawyers even after access has been formally granted.

However, the proposal to institute a full time Legal Advice Unit at the holding centres put forward by the Independent Commissioner has not found favour (see Walker, C., and Fitzpatrick, B., 'Holding Centres in Northern Ireland, the Independent Commissioner and the rights of detainees' [1999] *European Human Rights Law Review* 27).

Table 5.1: Access to lawyers in Northern Ireland

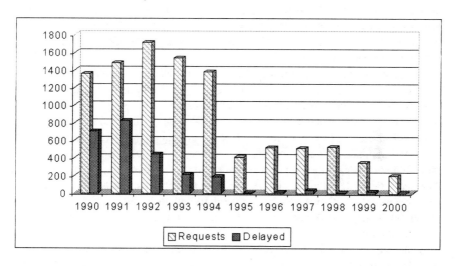

(*source: Northern Ireland Office*)

The treatment of lawyers contrasts curiously on paper with the broad rights of foreigners (including, for these purposes, Irish citizens detained in Britain) to communicate and consult with consular officials (see PACE Code C, para. 7; (Colville) Review of the Operation of the Prevention of Terrorism (Temporary Provisions) Act 1984 (Cm. 264, London, 1987), paras 6.2.1, 6.2.2; Colville Annual Report on the Operation in 1990 of the Prevention of Terrorism (Temporary Provisions) Acts (Home Office), para. 4.2). These arise pursuant to treaty arrangements (especially the Vienna Convention on Consular Relations 1963 (Cmnd. 2113, London, 1963), Article 36.1, as implemented by the Consular Relations Act 1968), but corresponding rights in Northern Ireland do not extend to Irish citizens. In reality, few diplomats (other than Irish officials) actually respond to the calls from terrorist suspects. In a study in England and Wales, it was found that the police often do not inform the detainee or embassy in relevant Irish cases (perhaps because of doubts over nationality), and few detainees wish to exercise the right. Delay was authorised in 26% of cases, the grounds often being multiple, and the average length of delay was 16 hours (Brown, D., *Detention under the Prevention of Terrorism Act* (Home Office Research and Planning Unit paper 75, London, 1993), pp. 38–39).

Alongside these special rules as to treatment, it should be borne in mind that normal rules under the PACE codes of practice (especially Code C) are applicable unless expressly disapplied. This has long been the position in England and Wales, but becomes also the position in Northern Ireland by virtue of pt II of sch. 16 to the Terrorism Act 2000. However, for the present, a special code is continued in Northern Ireland. Pursuant to s. 99 (previously s. 52 of the Northern Ireland (Emergency Provisions) Act 1996), the Terrorism Act 2000 (Code of Practice on the Exercise of Police Powers) (Northern Ireland) Order 2001 (SI 2001 No. 401) brings into force a code covering the exercise by police officers of the powers of detention and identification (replacing a code made under the Northern Ireland (Emergency Provisions) Act 1991, s. 61).

Overall, it should be questioned why this special power of arrest should be preserved in force. The police view is that it has proved the most 'critical' (Inquiry into Legislation against Terrorism (Cm. 3420, London, 1996), para. 4.14) provision in successive anti-terrorist legislation. Another view is that it is unacceptable as presently designed and executed since it allows excessive intelligence-gathering and oppressive interrogations and detentions, which have caused great damage on balance to the criminal justice system through miscarriages of justice. In addition, persons suspected of serious arrestable offences such as bombers, murderers and money launderers (at least outside of Scotland) can be detained for up to 96 hours under the PACE legislation, so why should terrorists be detained for any longer? In the circumstances of England and Wales post cease-fire, some special powers may be justifiable in principle, but it is very dubious on current usage whether the powers can be said to be necessary in the exigencies of the situation in Britain, as the following statistics reveal:

Table 5.2: Special detention powers in Britain

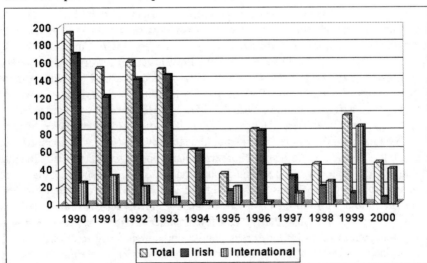

(*source: Home Office*)

In practice, the total average interviewing time is around 3 hours 8 minutes and the total average detention length is 28 hours 23 minutes (Brown, D., *Detention under the Prevention of Terrorism Act* (Home Office Research and Planning Unit paper 75, London, 1993), pp. 31, 50), with 22% being held for more than 48 hours (with a higher rate in international cases: Home Office Statistics). These rates are much longer than PACE 1984 (where the figures are around one hour and six hours respectively), but not of themselves a justification for seven days of detention. Most detainees are released without charge or any other action being taken (69%: p. 49), which may not entirely vitiate the intelligence-gathering purpose but is certainly a much higher rate than under PACE 1984 and so, at least, does not create a good impression of overall police astuteness and, at worse, confirms the perception of many detainees that they are detained 'primarily because they are Irish' (Hillyard, P., *Suspect Community* (Pluto Press, London, 1993), p. 7). As already indicated, it may be predicted that the conditioning of the PACE regime will lead to more and more detentions being governed by that regime in practice.

As might be expected, the statistics relating to use in Northern Ireland reveal a higher usage rate (though the rate of extension beyond 48 hours is similar at 25%), but a decline is clearly evident both in absolute terms an in comparison to the approximately 26,000 arrests under PACE 1984 per annum (source: Northern Ireland Office Statistics and Research Branch, *Digest of Information on the Northern Ireland Criminal Justice System*, Belfast, 1998):

Table 5.3: Special detention powers in Northern Ireland

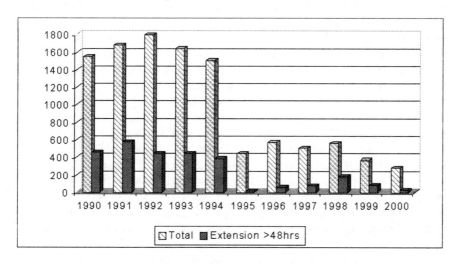

(*source: Northern Ireland Office*)

During a period of lengthy police detention, augmented safeguards for the prisoner are essential to avert the opportunities for abuse and ill-treatment. One should also question whether the Terrorism Act 2000 has achieved sufficient progress to meet this challenge. Many of the safeguards have been implemented in Northern Ireland pursuant to the Bennett Report (Report of the Committee of Inquiry into Police Interrogation Procedures in Northern Ireland (Cmnd. 9497, London, 1979)), including measures such as record-keeping, closed circuit television and regular medical checks. Later refinements have included, as already noted, video and audio recording. Though these are to be retained, few are demanded or even specified by legislation. It follows that there should be a clearer and more directly enforceable code of practice governing detention, and some of the measures in Northern Ireland (such as medical checks under para. 9.2, 9.3 of the s. 99 Code of Practice) should apply in Britain. The confinement of prisoners for up to seven days can have all kinds of psychological and physical effects, perhaps unintended perhaps not, which do not arise on what is on average just five or six hours of detention under PACE 1984 (Bucke, T., and Brown, D., *In Police Custody* (Home Office Research Study No. 174, London, 1997)). In a study in England and Wales, it was found that 46% of Prevention of Terrorism (Temporary Provisions) Act 1989 detainees saw a doctor, and virtually all of these contacts were initiated by the police. Delay was authorised in 26% of cases, the grounds often being multiple, and the average length of delay was 16 hours (Brown, D., *Detention under the Prevention of Terrorism Act* (Home Office Research and Planning Unit paper 75, London, 1993), p. 35).

Openness is an important part of constitutional governance. It is a value which continues to be neglected or even denied in regard to Terrorism Act detentions. The continuous independent oversight of detention conditions could allow much clearer differentiation between what are the unintended or unthinking consequences of designing out the consequences of a bomb attack on police facilities and designing in 'a significant risk of psychological forms of ill-treatment' as alleged by the European Torture Committee in regard to the Castlereagh Holding Centre in Belfast (CPT/Inf(94) 17, 1994, para. 109). This point was rejected by the Government (at CPT/Inf(94) 18 q36), but the Centre closed on 31 December 1999 and the two other special holding centres have also closed, leaving just a temporary facility in operation. It follows that lay visitors have a role to play here (Dickson, B., and O'Loan, N., 'Visiting Police Stations in Northern Ireland' (1994) 45 *Northern Ireland Legal Quarterly* 210). Lay visitors may provide not only a safeguard against abuse but also confidence in the police. The Patten Report (Patten Commission (The Independent Commission on Policing for Northern Ireland), *A New Beginning: Policing in Northern Ireland* (Northern Ireland Office, Belfast, 1999), para. 8.16) endorsed the advantages of video recording (already described) and also called for lay visiting to interrogation centres.

In addition the Independent Commissioner for the Holding Centres (an office held by Sir Louis Blom Cooper from 1993–2000 and now by Dr Bill Norris) has had an important and beneficial influence (see Walker, C. and Fitzpatrick, B., 'The Independent Commissioner for the Holding Centres: a review' [1998] *Public Law* 106; Walker, C., and Fitzpatrick, B., 'Holding Centres in Northern Ireland, the

Independent Commissioner and the rights of detainees' [1999] *European Human Rights Law Review* 27), and it is disappointing that this office is still not mentioned in the Act. This office should become the special inspector of Terrorism Act detainees and detention facilities throughout the United Kingdom. Why is the Independent Assessor of Military Complaints Procedures in Northern Ireland enshrined in s. 98 of the Terrorism Act 2000, a job which has been more or less done and dusted given the current absence of military patrolling and policing in Northern Ireland, whereas the inspector of terrorist detentions is nowhere to be seen? The Independent Commissioner has done a good job and should be helped with formal powers and a remit to cover the whole of the United Kingdom, and Parliament should forge relations with him through its select committee system. As is related in Chapter 7, the office, redesignated as the Independent Commissioner for Detained Terrorist Suspects in 2001, should become the special inspector of Terrorism Act detainees and cover detention facilities throughout the United Kingdom.

The courts have now rejected one possible further sanction — that the detention should become unlawful (and thereby subject to the payment of damages) if there occur serious assaults or forms of maltreatment. The Northern Ireland Court of Appeal was at first attracted to the idea (*Re Gillen's Application* [1988] NI 40) but has now rejected it (*Cullen* v *Chief Constable of the RUC* [1999] NI 237) in the light of House of Lords' jurisprudence (*R* v *Deputy Governor of Parkhurst Prison, ex parte Hague* [1992] 1 AC 58).

A further unaddressed aspect affecting the detention regime concerns the rules (previously in s. 12 of Northern Ireland (Emergency Provisions) Act 1996) as to the admissibility of evidence in Northern Ireland. This point will be considered in Chapter 7.

In conclusion, a clear message on how to view this area of the Prevention of Terrorism (Temporary Provisions) Act 1989 came from the May Inquiry Final report (1989–90 HC 558, 1992–3 HC 296):

> If all the safeguards of PACE are necessary to avoid miscarriages of justice then it must be recognised that in terrorist cases greater risks of injustice are accepted than in the ordinary course of criminal cases.

The omissions described in this commentary suggest that the legislators have had insufficient regard to the many of the past lessons from miscarriage of justice cases or to the future lessons to be meted out under the Human Rights Act 1998. The gathering of intelligence is a 'crucial' strategy in dealing with terrorism (Wilkinson, P., *Terrorism versus Democracy* (Frank Cass, London, 2000), p. 105), and it may in any event be difficult to disentangle intelligence-gathering from forensic interrogation (Review of the Northern Ireland (Emergency Provisions) Act 1991 (Cm. 2706, London, 1995), para. 126). Nevertheless, the case for affording seven days to complete the task is not easily sustainable. Furthermore, not enough has been done to regulate detention. Time and again, independent inquiries have found evidence of ill-treatment (see European Commission for the Prevention of Torture and Inhuman and Degrading Treatment, *Report to the UK Government on the Visit to Northern Ireland carried out by the European Commission for the Prevention of Torture etc. 1993* (CPT/Inf (94) 17, 1994), *Report on UK* (CPT/Inf (2001) 6, May 2001); *Report on the Mission of the Special Rapporteur to the United Kingdom of Great Britain and Northern Ireland* (E/CN.4/1988/39/Add.4, Geneva, 1998)). There have been considerable advances in the last couple of years with the closure of most of the holding centres, the introduction of taping with sound (see European Commission for the Prevention of Torture and Inhuman and Degrading Treatment, *Report to the UK Government on the Visit to Northern Ireland carried out by the European Commission for the Prevention of Torture etc. 1999* (CPT/Inf (2001) 6, May 2001), para. 122, 124) and the admission of solicitors to the interview room in Northern Ireland. But more detailed rules are needed as to matters such as furniture in cells, toiletries, clothing, reading and writing materials, exercise, natural light, and clocks, as well as closed-circuit surveillance and medical checks.

5.3   SEARCH OF PREMISES

Added to the various complex search provisions in Part V of the Terrorism Act 2000 is a more traditional-sounding power under s. 42, by which a justice of the peace (or a sheriff in Scotland) may on the application of a constable issue a warrant in relation to specified premises if he is satisfied that there are reasonable grounds for suspecting that a person whom the constable reasonably suspects to be a 'terrorist' is to be found there. In this way, the power (redolent of s. 15(1) of the Prevention of Terrorism (Temporary Provisions) Act 1989) is really a search for persons rather than a search of premises and links to the arrest power in s. 41. In practice, most arrest operations under s. 41 are conducted without warrant, and so ancillary searches can be brought within enabling powers such as PACE 1984, s. 17.

5.4   SEARCH OF PERSONS

The search of persons is dealt with by s. 43 of the Terrorism Act 2000 (compare s. 15(3) of the Prevention of Terrorism (Temporary Provisions) Act 1989). By s. 43(1), a constable may stop and search a person whom he reasonably suspects to be a 'terrorist' to discover whether he has in his possession anything which may constitute evidence that he is a terrorist. Presumably, this power can apply in public and private places, provided in the case of the latter, there is some other legal basis for entry. Likewise, those already arrested under s. 41 may also be searched — in this situation, as a matter of routine, since reasonable suspicion has already been established for the arrest.

   Stop and search powers in s. 43, and elsewhere in the Act are subject to s. 116(2), by which a power to stop a person includes power to stop a vehicle (other than an aircraft which is airborne). By s. 116(3), a person commits a summary offence if he fails to stop a vehicle when required to do so.

The power to seize and retain materials under s. 43(4) on reasonable suspicion that they may constitute evidence that the person is a terrorist attracts additional powers to seize and retain articles for sifting elsewhere enabled under the Criminal Justice and Police Act 2001, s. 51 (a response to the judgment in *R* v *Chesterfield Justices and Chief Constable of Derbyshire, ex parte Bramley* [2000] 2 WLR 401).

Various safeguards apply to these searches. In particular, under s. 43(3), a search of a person under this section must be carried out by someone of the same sex.

5.5   STOP AND SEARCH

The powers of search in s. 44 of the Terrorism Act 2000 can be more randomly exercised than the foregoing. It allows any constable in uniform to stop a vehicle in an area or at a place specified in the authorisation and to search the vehicle; the driver of the vehicle; a passenger in the vehicle; anything in or on the vehicle or carried by the driver or a passenger. It also extends to a pedestrian or anything carried by him in a specified area. Section 44 is the descendant of a number of additions to the Prevention of Terrorism (Temporary Provisions) Act 1989 (ss. 13A and 13B) brought about first by the Criminal Justice and Public Order Act 1994. The changes were expressly designed to deal with vehicle bombs and smaller devices carried by individuals by allowing chance interceptions or disruption of plans (Inquiry into Legislation against Terrorism (Cm. 3420, London, 1996), paras 10.14, 10.21). The first amendment was made by s. 62 of the 1994 Act, responding to concerns following bombs in the City of London. Further measures were invoked by the Prevention of Terrorism (Additional Powers) Act 1996, a response to reviews following the London Docklands bombing and to future fears. The powers had been used 29 times in five police areas (22 in London alone) up to 1996 (Inquiry into Legislation against Terrorism (Cm. 3420, London, 1996), para. 10.16).

Section 44 is amended (by the Anti-terrorism, Crime and Security Act 2001, sch. 7, para. 31) to allow the British Transport Police and Ministry of Defence Police, in certain circumstances, to specify areas or places in which for up to 28 days the relevant officers can stop and search vehicles, their occupants and pedestrians for the prevention of terrorism. An assistant chief constable, or higher officer, may authorise any uniformed constable to stop and search pedestrians or vehicles. The Secretary of State must confirm these orders within 48 hours.

It is made clear in s. 45(1) that this can be a random or blanket search — it may be exercised whether or not the constable has grounds for suspecting the presence of articles of that kind. The absence of reasonable suspicion must put into question its compatibility with Article 8 of the European Convention (and Article 5 given that the constable may also detain for such time as is reasonably required to permit the search to be carried out), but the pre-conditions for exercise, the limited nature of the search and the nexus to combating terrorism may save the day.

ιe pre-conditions for exercise include the requirement of an authorisation ςh may be given only if the person giving it considers it 'expedient' for the prevention of acts of terrorism. An authorisation, which can endure for up to 28 days under s. 46 of the 2000 Act and can be renewed, may be given by a police officer for the area who is of at least the rank of assistant chief constable or commander of a London force. Section 46 requires the police to inform the Secretary of State as soon as is reasonably practicable, and, to continue, the authorisation must be confirmed within 48 hours (this new safeguard follows the recommendation in the Inquiry into Legislation against Terrorism (Cm. 3420, London, 1996), para. 10.25 and the Home Office and Northern Ireland Office, Legislation against Terrorism (Cm. 4178, London, 1998), para. 9.13). Furthermore, where the Secretary of State confirms an authorisation, he may substitute an earlier date or time; alternatively he may cancel an authorisation with effect from a specified time. Though it is good in principle that there is review of the police decision, it is odd that the review is executive in nature rather than judicial, the reform path followed by s. 41. According to the Home Office, Circular 03/01: Terrorism Act 2000 (Home Office, London, 2001), para. 5.6.2, each authorisation should specify whether it applies across the entire force area, across a particular part of the force area, or only at a particular place (forces are asked to consider providing supporting intelligence on potential targets where the powers are restricted to a particular place). It must also specify the period for which the authorisation has effect, up to a maximum of 28 days. The National Joint Unit (NJU) will be responsible for sending to the Home Office any application for the Secretary of State's confirmation of an authorisation.

The limited nature of the search is also specified in s. 45 of the 2000 Act. Searches may be exercised only for the purpose of searching for articles of a kind which could be used in connection with terrorism, and may not involve a person being required to remove any clothing in public except for headgear, footwear, an outer coat, a jacket or gloves. A further safeguard is that where a driver or pedestrian applies within 12 months for a written statement as to the legal basis for a stop, it shall be provided.

A person commits an offence under s. 47 if he:

(a)   fails to stop a vehicle when required to do so by a constable in the exercise of the power conferred by an authorisation under s. 44(1);

(b)   fails to stop when required to do so by a constable in the exercise of the power conferred by an authorisation under section 44(2);

(c)   wilfully obstructs a constable in the exercise of the power conferred by an authorisation under s. 44(1) or (2).

The penalties are on summary conviction to imprisonment for a term not exceeding six months, a fine not exceeding level 5 on the standard scale, or both.

Given these further limitations in these powers, it is possible that they do not contravene the European Convention. On the other hand, there is no requirement for reasonable suspicion (compare *McVeigh, O'Neill and Evans* v *United Kingdom*, App. nos. 8022, 8025, 8027/77; DR 18 p. 66 (admissibility), DR 25 p. 15 (final report), (1981) 5 EHRR 71; *Murray (Margaret)* v *United Kingdom*, App. no. 14310/88, Ser. A. 300-A, (1994) 19 EHRR 193; *Fox, Campbell and Hartley* v *United Kingdom*, App. nos. 12244, 12245, 12383/86, Ser. A. 182, (1990) 13 EHRR 157) and the rate of arrests is extremely low (see HC Debs. vol. 275 col. 211, 2 April 1996, Michael Howard), which, taken together, may be interpreted as falling foul of Article 5.

5.6   PARKING RESTRICTIONS

Section 5 of the Prevention of Terrorism (Additional Powers) Act 1996 (incorporating s. 16D into the Prevention of Terrorism (Temporary Provisions) Act 1989) gave the police a power to impose parking prohibitions and restrictions and to remove vehicles. This has now been translated into s. 48 of the Terrorism Act 2000. The power allows an authorisation to empower any constable in uniform to prohibit or restrict the parking of vehicles on a specified road (and to use reasonable force under s. 114). The authorisation can be given by an assistant chief constable or police commander in London only if the person giving it considers it expedient for the prevention of acts of terrorism. By s. 50, the authorisation can endure for up to 28 days (and can be renewed), but there is no oversight by the Secretary of State in this case. The effect of authorisation is that the police will under s. 49 place a traffic sign on the road concerned, suspend any existing parking places and impose parking restrictions. A person commits an offence under s. 51 if he parks a vehicle in contravention of a prohibition or restriction (punishable on summary conviction to a fine not exceeding level 4), or if he is the driver or other person in charge of a vehicle which has been permitted to remain at rest in contravention of any prohibition or restriction, or if he fails to move the vehicle when ordered to do so by a constable in uniform (punishable on summary conviction to imprisonment for a term not exceeding three months, or a fine not exceeding level 4 on the standard scale, or both). It is a defence under s. 51(3) for a person charged with an offence under this section to prove that he had a reasonable excuse for the act or omission in question (s. 118 does not apply here — see further Chapter 6), but possession of a current disabled person's badge shall not itself constitute a reasonable excuse.

5.7   PORT AND BORDER CONTROLS

The final measure in Part V of the Terrorism Act 2000 concerns port controls involving the scrutiny of travellers (especially between Britain and Ireland) under s. 53. These controls have been in existence since the first Prevention of Terrorism Act in 1974 (see Walker, C.P., *The Prevention of Terrorism in British Law* (2nd ed., Manchester University Press, Manchester, 1992), ch. 8) and were latterly granted by s. 16 and sch. 5 to the Prevention of Terrorism (Temporary Provisions) Act 1989. The main reforms are that the maximum period that a person may be

detained at a port for questioning, whether or not the examining officer has a
reasonable suspicion that the person is or has been concerned in the commission,
preparation or instigation of acts of terrorism, is reduced from 12 hours to nine
hours (para. 6) and captains of aircraft carrying passengers other than for reward
may permit their passengers to embark from, or disembark at, non-designated
airports provided they give 12 hours' notice to an examining officer (para. 12)
(see Home Office and Northern Ireland Office, Legislation against Terrorism
(Cm. 4178, London, 1998), para. 11.17). The port controls are additional to the
general principles regulating entry into and staying in the United Kingdom under
the Immigration Act 1971.

Further changes are brought about by s. 118 of the Anti-terrorism, Security and
Crime Act 2001. The effect is to allow an examining officer to exercise the port
controls in relation not just to traffic entering the United Kingdom or between
Northern Ireland and Britain but also to persons whose presence at a port is
believed to be connected with their travelling on a flight within Great Britain or
Northern Ireland or to a person on a ship or aircraft that has arrived at any place
in Great Britain or Northern Ireland whether from within or outside Great Britain
or Northern Ireland.

The details are set out in sch. 7 of the Terrorism Act 2000 (as amended by
ss. 118 and 119 of the Anti-terrorism, Security and Crime Act 2001), though
changes are possible, because s. 53(2) allows the Secretary of State to order the
repeal of 'carding' (the routine collection of information from individual travellers). In addition, this provision must in the first place be activated by affirmative
order (sch. 7, para. 16). The explanation is that this represents a facet of the
Northern Ireland Peace Process and the expectation that anti-terrorism measures
affecting Irish people should be less intrusive in the future. According to Lord
Bassam (HL Debs. vol. 613 cols 736–737, 23 May 2000):

. . . the power has been the source of some concern in certain quarters. Indeed,
Members of the Committee have expressed that concern this evening. Objections
have included that its use can delay journeys on occasions and that it can appear
to be used disproportionately against Irish people. Mindful of these sensitivities
and the availability of passenger information provisions, the Bill provides that
the carding power will have to be explicitly 'switched on' by the affirmative
resolution procedure rather than being permanently available, as is currently the
case. We envisage that one of the main factors that will be taken into account
when deciding whether an order should be laid is the prevailing security
situation. Even when a carding order is in force, that is not to suggest that
blanket carding of all flights and sailing will take place simply as a matter of
course.

In the event, the promise of restraint was not met, and the Terrorism Act 2000
(Carding) Order 2001 (SI 2001 No. 426) maintains carding in force on much the
same basis as before (in other words, in relation to those passengers who disembark

or embark at a sea or air port in Great Britain or Northern Ireland from or, as the case may be, on a ship or aircraft travelling between Great Britain, Northern Ireland, the Channel Islands, the Isle of Man, or the Republic of Ireland). Furthermore, no such promise is made in relation to the even more intrusive powers of detention pursuant to an examination, though the nine hours of maximum detention represents a useful reduction from 12 hours (though not as low as the six hours suggested by Lord Lloyd; see Home Office and Northern Ireland Office, Legislation against Terrorism (Cm. 4178, London, 1998), para. 11.15). Moreover, it is surprising that the facility of low-level intelligence gathering involved in carding should be given up so readily, given that 'The police have found it to be an extremely useful tool in tackling terrorism' (HL Debs. vol. 613 col. 736, 16 May 2000, Lord Bassam) and that there are 'sound strategic reasons to carry out checks at ports' (col. 746).

In terms of the details under sch. 7, the process of controls begins under para. 2, whereby an 'examining officer' (meaning a constable, an immigration officer, or a designated customs officer) may question a person for the purpose of determining whether he appears to be a 'terrorist'. Rather like s. 44, it is made clear that examining officers may exercise their powers under this paragraph whether or not they have grounds for suspicion against any individual. This power can be applied to a person entering or leaving Great Britain or Northern Ireland at a port or airport or (under para. 3) in the border area (within one mile of border between Northern Ireland and the Republic of Ireland or wherever is the first stop of a train from the Republic). By s. 118 of the Anti-terrorism, Security and Crime Act 2001, an examining officer may also exercise the port controls in relation not just to traffic entering the United Kingdom or between Northern Ireland and Britain but also to persons whose presence at a port is believed to be connected with their travelling on a flight within Great Britain or Northern Ireland or to a person on a ship or aircraft that has arrived at any place in Great Britain or Northern Ireland whether from within or outside Great Britain or Northern Ireland. The powers can also be supplemented in Northern Ireland by s. 97, under which the Secretary of State may by order provide for members of Her Majesty's Forces to perform specified functions conferred on examining officers and may also supplement or modify sch. 7, about entering or leaving Northern Ireland by land. It should be noted that under s. 114, a constable may not use reasonable force for the purpose of exercising a power under paras 2 and 3 of sch. 7. Presumably, those who fail to cooperate will often give rise to suspicion sufficient for a s. 41 arrest.

For the purpose of satisfying himself whether there are any persons whom he may wish to question under para. 2 an examining officer may under para. 7 search a ship or aircraft, search anything on a ship or aircraft or search anything which he reasonably believes has been, or is about to be, on a ship or aircraft. In order to carry out an examination, an examining officer may under para. 6 stop a person or vehicle, authorise the person's removal from a ship, aircraft or vehicle or detain a person. The conditions of detention are broadly covered by sch. 8, save that the length of detention must not exceed nine hours; the detention may then be authorised by an arrest but not for the purposes of consideration of the case (compare *Breen* v *Chief Constable of Dumfries and Galloway, The Times,* 24 April 1997). Nine hours represents a reduction from 12 in the Prevention of Terrorism (Temporary Provisions) Act 1989 (though Lord Lloyd had recommended six hours and most persons are released within four hours).

A person who is questioned under paras 2 or 3 must, under para. 5:

(a)   give the examining officer any information in his possession which the officer requests;

(b)   give the examining officer on request either a valid passport which includes a photograph or another document which establishes his identity (the alternative is necessary because travel between Ireland and Britain does not require the production of a passport);

(c)   declare whether he has with him documents of a kind specified by the examining officer; or

(d)   give the examining officer on request any document which he has with him and which is of a kind specified by the officer.

The person, and any ship or aircraft carrying him (or vehicle in Northern Ireland), may also be searched under para. 8 by an examining officer (or a person authorised by an officer under para. 10). There is also a wide power to search unaccompanied baggage and goods under para. 9 (taken from s. 3 of the Prevention of Terrorism (Additional Powers) Act 1996). Section 118(4) of the 2001 Act amends para. 9 by applying the powers to examine goods which have arrived in or are about to leave Great Britain or Northern Ireland on a ship or vehicle and goods which have arrived at or are about to leave any place in Great Britain or Northern Ireland on an aircraft whether the place they have come from or are going to is within or outside Great Britain or Northern Ireland. Property may be seized for further investigation for a period of seven days under para. 11.

In order to aid the process of scrutiny of traffic, the legislation allows for the regulation of entry and exit points and facilities, so that it becomes more predictable where the port controls can be effectively imposed. The first step is that, by para. 12, carriers of passengers for reward involved in journeys to or from Great Britain, the Republic of Ireland, Northern Ireland or any of the Islands, must call at a designated port or in circumstances specifically approved by an examining officer. Aircraft which are not carrying passengers for reward must either call at a designated port or give at least 12 hours' notice in writing to the police. This measure represents a compromise between the Prevention of Terrorism (Temporary Provisions) Act 1989 position of requiring permission from the police and Lord Lloyd's recommendation that no restriction should exist (Inquiry into Legislation against Terrorism (Cm. 3420, London, 1996), para. 10.57). No regulations apply to non-passenger boat movements, though coastguard monitoring does apply. A list of designated ports is scheduled — it does not include those ports without Irish connections, such as Dover, creating an obvious route for evasion of the port controls though possibly not normal border checks. But the controls (in the Channel Tunnel (International Arrangements) Order 1993 (SI 1993 No. 1813)) are supplemented in respect of the Channel Tunnel system by the Channel Tunnel (International Arrangements) (Amendment) Order 2001 (SI 2001 No. 178). Within designated ports, the Secretary of State may order ship or aircraft operators to designate 'control areas' (para. 13) in which passengers are expected to embark or disembark. and may order port managers to provide specified facilities within them (para. 14). According to the Home Office, Circular 03/01: Terrorism Act 2000 (Home Office, London, 2001), para. 16.18, it is hoped that the Home Secretary will not have to give formal notice designating control areas and that it will prove possible to agree appropriate arrangements at a local level without having to invoke the power. Where problems are encountered, the National Co-ordinator of Ports Policing will be a source of advice.

Operators must routinely ensure that passengers and crew are subject to examination (para. 15) and must provide passenger information if an examining officer makes a written request (para. 17). The provision only applies under the 2000 Act to the Common Travel Area (journeys between Great Britain, Northern Ireland, the Republic of Ireland and the Islands). Section 119 of the 2001 Act extends the duty to a ship or aircraft which (a) arrives or is expected to arrive in any place in the United Kingdom (whether from another place in the United Kingdom or from outside the United Kingdom), or (b) leaves or is expected to leave the United Kingdom. A new order-making power requires the Secretary of State to define the information required, but no order has yet been issued (compare the Passenger Information Order 2000 (SI 2000 No. 912), under the Immigration Act 1971), as discussions are continuing (Home Office, Regulatory Impact Assessment: Terrorism Act 2000 Passenger Information (2001), para. 17). As mentioned earlier, s. 53(2) of the 2000 Act allows the Secretary of State to order the repeal of 'carding', and it was hoped that the routine provision of extensive passenger information would remove the need for carding (Home Office and Northern Ireland Office, *Legislation against Terrorism* (Cm. 4178, London, 1998), para. 11.20). But in the meantime, carding is currently allowed by order under para. 16. The essence is that passengers may be required by an examining officer to complete and produce to the officer a card (currently supplied by the officer, though the order could require it to be supplied by the carrier) containing information about their identity. The designs of the cards themselves are set out in the Terrorism Act 2000 (Carding) Order 2001 (SI 2001 No. 426).

Further details of the powers of examining officers are set out in s. 115 and sch. 14 to the 2000 Act (which makes provision about the exercise of functions by examining officers for the purposes of sch. 7). By para. 2 of sch. 14, an officer may enter a vehicle for the purpose of exercising any statutory functions conferred on him by virtue of this Act, and may, by para. 3, use reasonable force for the purpose of exercising a power (apart from paras 2 and 3 of sch. 7). By para. 4, any information acquired by an examining officer may be supplied:

(a) to the Secretary of State for use in relation to immigration;

(b)   to the Commissioners of Customs and Excise or a customs officer;

(c)   to a constable;

(d)   to the Director General of the National Criminal Intelligence Service or of the National Crime Squad;

(e)   to a person specified by order of the Secretary of State for use of a kind specified in the order.

Conversely, under para. 4(2) information acquired by a customs officer or an immigration officer may be supplied to an examining officer. No similar powers exist for freight manifests.

Schedule 14, para. 6, also envisages the issuance of a code of practice for authorised officers (following the Consultation Paper, Home Office and Northern Ireland Office, Legislation against Terrorism (Cm. 4178, London, 1998), para. 11.14). This has been issued pursuant to the Terrorism Act 2000 (Code of Practice for Examining Officers) Order 2001 (SI 2001 No. 427). Whether it is perceived as achieving one of its aims, the avoidance of stereotyping (see Hillyard, P., *Suspect Community* (Pluto Press, London, 1993), p. 60; HC Standing Committee D, col. 239, 1 February 2000, Charles Clarke) remains to be seen. Amongst the provisions in the Code are, under para. 6, that only in exceptional circumstances should an immigration officer or customs officer exercise functions under the Act and only when a police officer is not readily available; or if specifically requested to do so by a police officer of the rank of sergeant or above. Pursuant to a recommendation of the Lloyd Report (Inquiry into Legislation against Terrorism (Cm. 3420, London, 1996), para. 10.57), the exercise of powers is dealt with in para. 10 as follows:

Examining officers should therefore make every reasonable effort to exercise the power in such a way as to minimise causing embarrassment or offence to a person who has no terrorist connections. The powers to stop and question a person should not be exercised in a way which unfairly discriminates against a person on the grounds of race, colour, religion, creed, gender or sexual orientation. When deciding whether to question a person the examining officer should bear in mind that the primary reason for doing so is to maximise disruption of terrorist movements into and out of the United Kingdom.

Note for guidance on paragraph 10: The selection of people stopped and examined under the port and border area powers should, as far as is practicable given the circumstances at the port or in the area, reflect an objective assessment of the threat posed by various terrorist groups active in and outside the United Kingdom. Examining officers should take particular care not to discriminate unfairly against minority ethnic groups in the exercise of these powers. When exercising the powers examining officers should consider such factors as:

- *known and suspected sources of terrorism*
- *any information on the origins and/or possible location of terrorist groups*

- *the possible nature of any current or future terrorist activity*
- *the means of travel (and documentation) which a group of individuals could use*
- *local circumstances, such as movements, trends at individual ports or parts of the border area.*

It must be appreciated that though the powers of examination can be applied randomly, police strategy demands some targeting otherwise either police resources will be overwhelmed or potential suspects will pass by unnoticed amongst the millions of travellers.

It is an offence under sch. 7, para. 18 wilfully to fail to comply with a duty, to contravene a prohibition, or to obstruct or to frustrate a search or examination under the port controls. To give some reassurance to hard-pressed commercial operators, the offence was amended during passage to require wilful default rather than just knowing default: 'so, if a carrier makes every effort to collect the requested information but it is simply not possible for some reason, even within a reasonable time-scale, the courts could take the view that no offence had been committed' (HL Debs. vol. 614 col. 1457, 4 July 2000, Lord Bach). The penalties are on summary conviction, imprisonment for a term not exceeding three months, a fine not exceeding level 4 on the standard scale, or both.

The transitory nature of these checks probably allows them to remain within the exception to the right to liberty for a stated legal 'obligation' under Article 5(1)(b) of the European Convention. This verdict has been reached on previous occasions by the European Commission in regard to travellers from the Irish Republic in the *McVeigh* case (see *McVeigh, O'Neill and Evans* v *United Kingdom*, App. nos. 8022, 8025, 8027/77; DR 18 p. 66 (admissibility), DR 25 p. 15 (final report), (1981) 5 EHRR 71); (see Warbrick, C., 'The Prevention of Terrorism (Temporary Provisions) Act 1976 and the European Convention on Human Rights: the McVeigh case' (1983) 32 *International & Comparative Law Quarterly* 757). The same view was adopted in regard to passengers between Britain and Northern Ireland in *Harkin, X, Lyttle, Gillen and McCann* v *United Kingdom*, (App. nos. 11539, 11641, 11650, 11651, 11652/85, (1981) 9 EHRR 381) since Article 5(1)(b) can apply to the regulation of passage over a clear geographical boundary within a state. While these decisions can be doubted both for their reasoning and level of authority, it is notable that the Terrorism Act 2000 now provides for a shorter period of detention pursuant to these powers than previously (though not as short as the six hours maximum suggested by the Inquiry into Legislation against Terrorism (Cm. 3420, London, 1996), para. 10.57). It is doubtful that the attempted restrictions in the foregoing code of practice will make much difference to this debate, since they are not 'law' for the purposes of the Convention (compare Rowe, J.J., 'The Terrorism Act 2000' [2000] *Criminal Law Review* 527 at p. 536).

The other legal threat to border checks of this kind arises from the policy of open borders pursued by the European Union. The Schengen Agreement (OJ L 239, 2000, 22.9.2000) demands the progressive removal of frontier checks. While the United Kingdom Government has now agreed to join the system to some extent (see Chapter 10), it has always contended that free movement rights do not affect the rights of States to institute security measures (Fire, Safety and Policing of the Channel Tunnel, Cm. 1853, London, 1992), and the European Court of Justice has also declared that targeted police checks may be acceptable (*Re Belgian Passport Controls* [1990] 2 CMLR 492; *Re Entry into Dutch Territory: EC Commission* v *Netherlands* [1993] 2 CMLR 389).

Compared to the numbers of passengers passing through the relevant ports, very few detentions are made. For example, in 1995, out of around 170 million travelers, just 720,000 were examined, 60% in the Common Travel Area (in other words, between the United Kingdom and Ireland) (Inquiry into Legislation against Terrorism (Cm. 3420, London, 1996), paras 10.26, 10.38). During 2000, only 521 persons (mostly Irish) were examined for more than one hour (Home Office Statistics). Furthermore, many of the resultant arrests relate to non-terrorist matters which have been discovered incidentally — such as the possession of stolen goods or drugs or the execution of an outstanding arrest warrant (Inquiry into Legislation against Terrorism (Cm. 3420, London, 1996), para. 10.40). This suggests that, if there is utility in the exercise at all, it must be to gather low-level intelligence (see Home Office, Regulatory Impact Assessment: Terrorism Act 2000 Passenger Information (2001), para. 3) or, as the Code of Practice for Examining Officers puts it in blatant terms:

> When deciding whether to question a person the examining officer should bear in mind that the primary reason for doing so is to maximise disruption of terrorist movements into and out of the United Kingdom.

Another aspect of the value of port controls may be to ward off more pervasive and intrusive techniques such as identity cards and registration of residence.

5.8   RETENTION OF COMMUNICATIONS DATA

Several deeply-seated factors have tended to impel policing agencies in late modern societies towards techniques of surveillance. One is that information technologies have developed enormously and pervade the economies and societies in western States (see Akdeniz, Y., Walker, C., and Wall, D., *The Internet, Law and Society* (Longman, London, 2000). Their uses are both for good and ill, the latter being the subject of policing. At the same time, the technologies provide both a new site for policing activity and also furnish a variety of opportunities for surveillance which would not previously have been feasible (see Dandeker, C, *Surveillance, Power and Modernity* (Polity Press, Cambridge, 1990); Lyon, D., *The Electronic Eye: The Rise of Surveillance Society* (Polity Press, Cambridge, 1994); Davies, S., *Big Brother: Britain's Web of Surveillance and the New Technological Order* (Pan, London, 1996); Banisar, D., *Privacy & Human Rights: An International Survey of Privacy Laws and Developments* (EPIC, Washington DC, 2000)).

They may allow 'investigators for example to establish links between suspected conspirators (itemised bill) or to ascertain the whereabouts of a given person at a given time, thereby confirming or disproving an alibi (cell site analysis)' (Home Office, Regulatory Impact Assessment: Anti-terrorism, Crime and Security Bill (2001)). The trend next represents part of a fundamental switch away from the reactive policing of incidents to the proactive policing and management of risks (see Ericson, R.V. and Haggerty, K.D., *Policing the Risk Society* (Clarendon Press, Oxford, 1997)).

In line with these impulses towards greater police attention to information and communications technologies, the National Hi-Tech Crime Unit (NHTCU) was launched within the National Criminal Intelligence Service in April 2001 (see NCIS Press release 18/010). The NHTCU is tasked with the key role in the response to cyber-crime, especially as practiced by serious and organised crime using IT. The NHTCU comprises of four main divisions — Investigation, Intelligence, Support and Forensic Retrieval.

Given the process of the 'hollowing out' of the State (see Jessop, B., 'Post-Fordism and the State' in Amin, A., (ed.), *Post-Fordism: A Reader* (Blackwell, London 1994), p. 251), one cannot expect that all the important information will conveniently be held by compliant public authorities. Rather, a great deal of computer data will be in the clutches of private company Communications Service Providers (CSPs) who sign up customers in return for e-mail and world wide web access and facilities. At the same time as these positive trends, there are conversely negative trends from the law enforcement perspective (Home Office, Home Office Regulatory Impact Assessment: Retention of Communications Data (2001), para. 6):

> Changes to the business model are leading to a reduction in the amount of data which is needed for billing purposes (e.g. pre-pay/ subscription/ 'always on'). Combined with pressure from the privacy lobby, this is leading to a decrease in data retention overall.

Hence, Part XI of the Anti-terrorism, Crime and Security Act 2001 seeks to ensure that CSPs will retain communications data for an investigatory rainy day. The idea is that it must be held for a specified period. If access for investigatory purposes is then required, attention must be turned to the Regulation of Investigatory Powers Act 2000, and the Anti-terrorism, Crime and Security Act 2001 itself grants no further provisions about access, disclosure or utilisation.

Despite this limit, Part XI was criticised as excessive. Rather like Part III of the 2001 Act, it may have been easier to stomach if designed around the concept of 'terrorist investigations' under s. 32, but the current draft is explicitly wider and allows mass snooping. While confined to 'communications data', the effect can be to provide a complete dossier on private life — who you contact, what are your interests and habits and where you are, go, and have been. The measure suggests a certain failure on the part of those authorities tasked to collect intelligence and to combat terrorism that the entire population must be treated as potentially suspect. And like Part III, it betokens earlier and wider origins than the combating of terrorism. In this case, the idea may be traced to lobbying from the National Criminal Intelligence Service (on behalf of the police, HM Customs and Excise, the Security Service, Secret Intelligence Service and GCHQ) as the next step on from the passage of the Regulation of Investigatory Powers Act 2000 and to ensure that it is effective in implementation (Gaspar, R., NCIS Submission to the Home Office; Looking to the Future: Clarity on Communications Data Retention Law (see http://cryptome.org/ncis-carnivore.htm, 2000), para. 6) which called for communications data to be retained by the communications service provider for a minimum period of 12 months, and then to be archived for retention, either in-house or by a Trusted Third Party agency or contractor, and retained for a further six-year period. According to the Report, the retention of communications data has great value to law enforcement:

> 1.2.1   Communications data is crucial to the business of the Agencies. It is pivotal to reactive investigations into serious crime and the development of proactive intelligence on matters effecting not only organised criminal activity but also national security. At the lower level, it provides considerable benefit to the detection of volume crime. The four principle requirements for communications data are: Primary Evidence — e.g. often the only evidence to locate the proximity of a mobile phone user to a crime scene and the sole eyewitness account in Hi-Tech crime. Corroborative Evidence — e.g. proof of association between criminal elements through telephone contact. Intelligence — e.g., identifying and tracing associates and locating places of significance. Post-trial Evidence — e.g. accuracy of digital data to support appeals against conviction and investigations into miscarriages of justice. Short term retention and then deletion of data will have a disastrous impact on the Agencies' intelligence and evidence gathering capabilities.
>
> 1.2.2   Communications data is becoming increasingly important to provide evidence to establish innocence. Premature deletion will seriously compromise the interests of justice. Communications data has a unique value to promoting a safe and free society. This provides the overriding justification for longer-term retention.

This progeny is officially denied (HL Debs. Vol. 629 col. 770, 4 December 2001, Lord Rooker). The retention of communications data was next alleged to be part of the demands for enhanced security written by the US President to the European Commission on the 16 November 2001, including the call for the moderation of data protection principles 'in the context of law enforcement and counterterrorism imperatives' (http://www.statewatch.org/news/2001/nov/06uslet.htm).

In detail, Part XI of the 2001 Act establishes that, under s. 102, the Secretary of State can issue a voluntary code of practice relating to the retention of 'communications data' by 'communications providers' (by s. 107, meaning a person who provides a postal service or a telecommunications service). No distinction is made between public and private communication service providers (see HL Debs. vol. 629 col. 756, 4 December 2001, Lord Rooker), such as the United Kingdom universities' JANET network (see http://www.ja.net/) or the Parliamentary Data and Video Network (http://www.adaptwestminster.co.uk/html/HoCDepts/ PDVNGuidInfo.htm), though one hopes that purely domestic networks operated for personal, family or household affairs will be exempt. 'Communications data' has the same meaning as in s. 21(4) in Chapter 2 of Part I of the Regulation of Investigatory Powers Act 2000, which means it is data relating to the mode and nature of telephone, Internet and postal communications, but it does not include the contents of the communications itself. The Telecommunications (Data Protection and Privacy) Regulations 1999 (SI 1999 No. 2093; note also the European Proposal for a Directive of the European Parliament and of the Council concerning the processing of personal data and the protection of privacy in the electronic communications sector (Brussels, 12 July 2000, COM(2000)385)) currently regulate the retention of such data by communication service providers. Such data can only be retained for certain specific commercial purposes (such as to send a bill to a customer), otherwise it must be erased or made anonymous. Whilst the Regulations permit the retention of communications data on national security and crime prevention grounds, there is currently no general guidance as to when these might apply or for how long. It is also the case that several Data Protection Principles in the Data Protection Act 1998, including the First (having a legitimate basis for processing), Third (to ensure that data are relevant and not excessive in relation to the purpose for processing) and Fifth (a data controller should not hold personal data for longer than necessary for its own purpose for processing the data) would almost certainly forbid the blanket storage of logs recording such details as web-sites browsed or e-mail addresses. Other data, such as the length of the link to the CSP, may be kept so long as it is relevant to billing or fraud control, as permitted by the Telecommunications Regulations of 1999 which introduce more specific provisions relating to traffic and billing data held by communications providers; the need for retention would be judged against the continued necessity for its business purposes such as for sending out a bill, dealing with a disputed matter or ensuring the security of the network.

Therefore, Part XI will give guidance to communications providers as to the basis for retaining on national security and crime prevention grounds communications data beyond the period that they require it for their own business purposes. The code will apply to communications data that the communications providers have generated or otherwise possess. Further agreements with specific communications providers (especially those with direct access to the Internet structure rather than those renting from the major half dozen operators) will provide greater detail as to the type of data to be retained and the conditions of retention and retrieval. The partnership approach followed a meeting, on 24 October 2001, involving representatives of the Home Office and the Department of Trade and Industry, the Internet Services Providers Association (ISPA), the London Internet Exchange

(LINX), the CBI and telecommunications companies. The sector as a whole includes around 280 public telecommunications operators, 570 international simple voice resale providers and 300 Internet Service Providers (Home Office Regulatory Impact Assessment: Retention of Communications Data (2001) paras 21–23).

The core measure is in s. 102(3) of the 2001 Act, by which the code and any agreements may contain provisions necessary to safeguard national security, to prevent or detect crime and to prosecute offenders, additional to, and without prejudice to, the communication provider's own business purposes. The width of the purposes should be noted. It was said to be impractical to limit the measure to terrorism data (HL Debs. vol. 629 col. 774, 4 December 2001, Lord Rooker), and a Lords amendment to this effect was reversed (HL Debs. vol. 629 col. 981, 6 December 2001; col. 1479, 13 December 2001). In devising the code, there are three stages under s. 103. First, there must be consultation with the communications providers and the Information Commissioner; secondly, the code must be published in draft, allowing for public representations; thirdly, the code must be authorised by a statutory instrument approved by Parliament (HL Debs. vol. 629 col. 1282, 11 December 2001, Lord Rooker). Under s. 106, there may be government payments in order to compensate communications providers (similar to the largesse provided for by the Regulation of Investigatory Powers Act 2000, s. 24). It is emphasised that the code will be voluntary, and there are no legal penalties for non-compliance, though the code or any specific agreement can be invoked in legal proceedings brought against a communications provider by a person whose communications data they hold. This proviso is intended to prevent a communications provider incurring civil liability for acting data in accordance with the code. In all likelihood, retention for a period of 12 months will be required (Home Office Regulatory Impact Assessment: Retention of Communications Data (2001), para. 11).

If, 'after reviewing the operation of any requirements contained in the code of practice and any agreements under s. 102, it appears to the Secretary of State that it is necessary to do so', then, by s. 104, the Secretary of State can issue compulsory directions. So, compulsion can apply if the CSPs 'don't volunteer enough' ('The net's eyes are watching', *The Guardian Online*, 15 November 2001). Precise criteria on which to judge success of failure are not set out in the 2001 Act but are expected to be detailed in the voluntary code of practice (HL Debs. vol. 629 col. 800, 4 December 2001, Lord Rooker). Mandatory directions may apply to all communications providers, a particular type of communications providers, or one or several specific communications providers. Some consultation is again required (including with the CSPs and the Information Commissioner), as well as approval of a statutory instrument by Parliament. Payments under s. 106 may be made. While some internet service providers already keep data for a year (and therefore have expressed some acceptance of these measures: Internet Service Providers Association (ISPA) Council Statement, http://www.ispa.org.uk/html/statement_2510dp.htm, 26 October 2001), others delete it just days after the traffic has occurred and so will incur costs. The ISPA has estimated costs at around £20m, the Government says at least £9m (Home Office Regulatory Impact Assessment: Retention of Communications Data (2001), para. 27). Phone companies keep detailed records of traffic data in order to calculate customers' bills, and the main provider, BT, retains it for seven years; by contrast, ISPs do not charge by traffic volume, and so do not need to keep the information that long (AOL retains e-mail traffic data for three months, Freeserve for 90 days and Claranet for two weeks: *The Guardian Online*, 15 November 2001). In the light of this pattern, there is worry that the burdens will fall upon smaller or niche-market firms and will more widely affect international competitiveness (Home Office, Home Office Regulatory Impact Assessment: Retention of Communications Data (2001), paras 9, 10). In the event of non-compliance by the communications providers, the Secretary of State may bring civil proceedings for an injunction or other appropriate relief.

The absence of criminal sanctions demonstrates how hesitant Parliament felt about the grant of these powers. This apprehension is also evidenced by s. 105, by which any mandatory scheme under s. 104 will itself lapse after two years unless renewed (which can occur more than once) by affirmative order.

It may be seriously doubted whether Part XI of the 2001 Act will achieve its expressed effect. With standard e-mail programs (Pegasus or Outlook), the e-mail address and name of the person being contacted is logged by the system. But by the expedient of either using web-based (and foreign-based) e-mail systems such as Hotmail or Yahoo or by the use of more sophisticated anonymised systems (such as Anonymizer.com or Hushmail.com) or encryption (such as Pretty Good Privacy), it is relatively easy to render the retention of communications data fairly pointless. In the main, Part XI is conceived with switched telephony in mind, and it was forlornly admitted by one Government Minister that 'e-mail is more difficult . . . I do not fully understand the details of headers and so forth. I have never used hotmail, although I have used Internet and e-mail services' (HL Debs. vol. 629 cols 757, 781, 4 December 2001, Lord Rooker). So much more likely is it that trained terrorists will know how to cover their tracks — such as by the use of public Internet booths (increasingly common in shopping malls or libraries) or by pre-paid mobile phones. One is therefore left with the worry that the Government was as much engaged in an exercise of flexing muscles against the allegedly anarchic Internet as combating terrorism as in actually garnering useful information. In the process, one can expect damage to the principles of individual rights, especially respect for individual privacy (Article 8) (see Mohammed, E.A., 'An examination of surveillance technology and their implications for privacy and related issues' (1999) (2) *Journal of Information, Law & Technology*; Schwartz, P. M., 'Privacy and democracy in cyberspace' (1999) 52 *Vanderbilt Law Review* 1609). In her comments on the Bill, the Information Commissioner has stated that the proposed provisions 'could have a significant impact on the privacy of individuals whose data are retained' and suffer from a 'lack of proportionality such as to render the prospective legislation incompatible with Convention rights' (Information Commissioner news release, Information Commissioner contributes to scrutiny of anti-terrorism bill http://www.dataprotection.gov.uk/dpr/dpdoc1.nsf,

13 November 2001). Alongside the ethical emphasis on individual autonomy must be set democratic and legal accountability, not easy to square with private power-holders such as communications providers.

In addition to practical difficulties, there are also legal difficulties. It left unspecified what is the relation between Part XI and the Data Protection Act 1998. Presumably, that Act will override any codes or even statutory regulations which ask for retention of data on an excessive scale (by reference either to time or type). One must also assume that Part XI is subject to the Human Rights Act 1998 (such as the test of proportionality under Article 8) but should be seen as overriding the Telecommunications Data Protection Directive.

As mentioned above, if access to retained communications data for investigatory purposes is then required, attention must be turned to the Regulation of Investigatory Powers Act 2000 (see Akdeniz, Y., Taylor, N., and Walker, C., 'Regulation of Investigatory Powers Act 2000: Bigbrother.gov.uk' [2001] *Criminal Law Review* 73). Communications data can be a useful tool for law enforcement agencies and if held by a communications provider may be accessible by an investigative authority under Chapter II of Part I of the Regulation of Investigatory Powers Act 2000 (RIPA) which is yet to come into force (though there is a draft code of practice: Home Office, Accessing Communications Data Draft Code of Practice, http://www.homeoffice.gov.uk/ripa/pcdcpc.htm, August 2001); the fact that it is not in force suggests strongly again that these measures in the 2001 Act were not as vital as alleged. Under s. 21 of RIPA 2000, there is a distinction between (a) interceptions of communications, including their contents, in the course of their transmission, which falls under chapter I of Part I of RIPA 2000, and (b) conduct involving the obtaining or disclosure of 'traffic data' or other information about usage or provision of telecommunications or postal services. Examples of 'communications data' include equipment and location details, telephone subscriber details, itemised telephone bill logs, e-mail headers, Internet Protocol addresses, and information on the outside of postal items.

Data of these kinds may be obtained under s. 22(2) of RIPA 2000 where necessary, *inter alia*:

  (a)   in the interests of national security;
  (b)   for the purpose of preventing or detecting crime or of preventing disorder;
  (c)   in the interests of the economic well-being of the United Kingdom;
  (d)   in the interests of public safety;
  (e)   for the purpose of protecting public health . . .

Any action taken must be proportionate and necessary (s. 23(8)).

Where authorisation is given for obtaining and disclosure of the data, then the operator can be compelled (if necessary by civil proceedings) to provide it, though the issuing authority may decide (for example to maintain secrecy or because of superior technical capabilities) to obtain the data itself (s. 22(3)). Authorisation will be in writing and must define the conduct authorised and the data to be obtained; the authorisation remains valid for one month (s. 23). The issuing authority under Chapter II is not the Secretary of State but will be an office-holder designated by statutory order within the police, intelligence services, Customs and Excise, Inland Revenue, or any other public authority specified by order.

RIPA 2000 is an improvement on the previous free-for-all, but it potentially empowers an alarmingly large range of public agencies to snoop, ranging from the Egg Inspectorate to GCHQ, and for a rambling array of reasons. And most serious of all, it allows intervention on the basis of standards and procedures which are intentionally lax on the grounds that interception is a much greater intrusion than the collection of traffic data (see Home Office, *Interception of Communications in the United Kingdom* (Cm. 4368, London, 1999), para. 10.9). The Data Protection Commissioner (now the Information Commissioner) was also critical, contending that 'access to traffic and billing data should also be made subject to prior judicial scrutiny' (Data Protection Commissioner, Briefing For Parliamentarians on RIP, http://www.fipr.org/rip/DPCparlRIP. htm, 2000) and feared that the lack of precision and foreseeability in legislation might not comply with Article 8 (privacy rights) under the European Convention (News Release, 13 November 2001).

5.9   ELECTRONIC SURVEILLANCE

Though electronic surveillance is an important counter-measure against terrorism, it appears only fleetingly in the legislation. The Terrorism Act 2000 says little about it, and resistance to the idea that the fruits of such surveillance should become admissible as evidence has persisted (see Chapter 1). However, in addition to the retention of communications data required by the Anti-terrorism, Crime and Security Act 2001 (under the previous heading), s. 116 amends the Intelligence Services Act 1994 so as to ensure the full powers of the secret State can effectively be brought to bear against foreign terrorist threats.

Section 116 first amends and extends to the Government Communications Headquarters (GCHQ; see http://www.gchq.gov.uk/) the authorisation procedure which currently applies only to the Secret Intelligence Service (SIS) under s. 7 of the Intelligence Services Act 1994. Section 7 sets out the authorisation procedure for acts necessary for the activities of the SIS which take place abroad. The amendment extends this authorisation procedure to GCHQ.

Subsection (2) also allows both GCHQ and SIS to be authorised under s. 7 to act in this country provided the intention is for those actions to have an effect only on apparatus located outside the British Islands or on material originating from such apparatus. Before this change, any authorised acts had to take place abroad.

Some other, more minor housekeeping changes are made by s. 116 of the 2001 Act. Subsection (3) provides for the meaning of the prevention and detection of crime as set out in s. 81(5) of the Regulation of Investigatory Powers Act 2000 to be applied to the Secret Intelligence Service. The same definition applies to the Security Service in the Security Service Act 1989 (see http://www.mi5.gov.uk/).

The impact is to ensure that the Secret Intelligence Service can act in support of evidence-gathering activities.

The decisive step in explicitly allowing the secret agents into the world of policing was taken a decade ago when the increased threat from terrorism and organised crime prompted shifts in power. Before that time, for the most part MI5 dealt with matters of internal security and MI6 those pertaining to overseas, with Special Branch having responsibility for responding to internal criminal and terrorist matters. But the high level of IRA activity in Britain in the early 1990s, particularly the sustained bombing campaign in London, led to MI5 taking over Special Branch's role as the lead intelligence-gathering agency in 1992. Next, the Security Service Act 1996 provided the Security Service with a greater profile in combating serious crime. Further reforms in the Police Act 1997 have strengthened the role of the National Criminal Intelligence Service and have reformed the Regional Crime Squads into an elite National Crime Squad. Overall, the trend is away from local policing towards national agencies and, increasingly, away from police agencies to intelligence agencies. The trend has implications not only for the strategies being employed but also for issues such as democratic accountability. The tasking of externally-oriented secret service agencies in ways which can involve activity within the United Kingdom is further evidence of these worrying trends.

Chapter Six
Criminal offences

6.1 INTRODUCTION

Many offences in the Terrorism Act 2000 have already been encountered. They mainly relate to forms of obstruction to, or non-compliance with, the powers already outlined. Furthermore, most of the offences relating to terrorism are not in the 2000 Act at all. It is part of a criminalisation approach which has been adopted since 1975 that terrorists should not be treated as offenders or prisoners with political motivations which mark them out as extraordinary (see Wharam, A. 'Treason and the terrorist' (1976) 126 *New Law Journal* 428) or afford them special status or treatment (Walker, C.P., 'Irish Republic prisoners, political detainees, prisoners of war or common criminals?' (1984) 19 *Irish Jurist* 189) but should be depicted as common criminals. Accordingly, offences of homicide and other offences against the person, and even more directly applicable explosives offences (such as under the Explosive Substances Act 1883) are the common diet of terrorist trials, though modifications have been made both to the offences and the criminal process over the years, especially in Northern Ireland, rendering claims to commonality or normality less tenable. The offences in Part VI of the Terrorism Act 2000, unhelpfully entitled 'Miscellaneous', are therefore in many senses peripheral, adding to the margins rather than the core of criminalisation. The government rightly resisted Lord Lloyd's call for an offence of terrorism (see Chapter 5) which would have undermined the policy of criminalisation (HL Debs. vol. 611 col. 1487, 6 April 2000, Lord Bassam). Further offences were added by the Anti-terrorism, Crime and Security Act 2001, some of which fit closely with those established in the Terrorism Act 2000 (such as several relating to dangerous substances and the revived offence of non-disclosure of information), others striking out in new directions (such as race and religious hatred or bribery and corruption abroad).

6.2 WEAPONS TRAINING

Some of the offences in Part VI of the Terrorism Act 2000 are included in order to extend slightly the ambit of the existing catalogue of 'normal' offences referred to above. This interpretation may be taken in respect of s. 54, which deals with weapons training. A person commits an offence if he provides instruction or training in the making or use of (a) firearms, (aa) radioactive material or weapons designed or adapted for the discharge of any radioactive material, (b) explosives, or (c) chemical, biological or nuclear weapons (as amended by s. 120 of the Anti-terrorism, Crime and Security Act 2001, which added (aa)). The offence has its origins in successive Northern Ireland (Emergency Provisions) Acts (latterly s. 34 of the 1996 version), but it is now extended throughout the United Kingdom, despite the recommendation otherwise by Lord Lloyd (Inquiry into Legislation against Terrorism (Cm. 3420, London, 1996), para. 14.28). One wonders whether the case of David Copeland, who carried out a series of three bombings in London in 1999 out of racist and homophobic motives, strengthened the case for extension to Britain (*The Times*, 1 July 2000, p. 1). Part of the evidence at his trial was that he had obtained the information on how to make bombs (*The Terrorists' Handbook* and *How To Make Bombs Book Two*) from the Internet. These and other relevant materials (for instance, *The Anarchist's Cookbook* and *The Big Book of Mischief*), are readily available through any search engine, though it turned out he could not assemble the necessary ingredients (Wolkind, M., and Sweeney, N., '*R* v *David Copeland*' (2001) 41 *Medicine Science and Law* 185 at p. 190). It might also be added that library books can also supply such data (see for example: Grivas-Dighenis, G., *Guerrilla Warfare and EOKA's Struggle* (Longmans, London, 1964).

Bearing in mind incidents such as the use of Sarin by the Aum Shinrikyo cult in Tokyo in 1995 as well as threats and scares following the 11 September attacks, the offence has been extended beyond conventional firearms and explosives. The enlargement was envisaged by the Home Office Consultation Paper (Home Office and Northern Ireland Office, Legislation against Terrorism (Cm. 4178, London, 1998), para. 12.13), and these new terms are described in s. 55 of the Terrorism Act 2000, as amended by s. 120(2) of the Anti-terrorism, Crime and Security Act 2001, so that the current definitions are as follows:

(a)   'biological weapon' means a biological agent or toxin (within the meaning of the Biological Weapons Act 1974) in a form capable of use for hostile purposes or anything to which s. 1(1)(b) of that Act applies;

(b)   'chemical weapons' are (i) toxic chemicals and their precursors, (ii) munitions and other devices designed to cause death or harm through the toxic properties of toxic chemicals released by them, (iii) equipment designed for use in connection with munitions and devices falling within paragraph (ii) (Chemical Weapons Act 1996, s. 1);

(c)   'radioactive material' means radioactive material capable of endangering life or causing harm to human health.

The definition of 'nuclear weapon' in s. 55 (by reference to the Nuclear Material (Offences) Act 1983, schedule) is now omitted, presumably because the meaning of radioactive material is wider still.

Quite why this offence could not be translated into the regular explosives and firearms codes is not clear, save that there is one reference to the term 'terrorism'. This appears in s. 54(5) of the 2000 Act, by which it is a defence for a person charged with an offence to prove that his action or involvement was wholly for a purpose other than assisting, preparing for or participating in terrorism. This formulation is curious. One would have expected a more positive burden on the prosecution to demonstrate that the training was not for a lawful purpose or was not otherwise lawful. The defence is actually much wider and would allow, for example, a gangster training others in the use of explosives to rob a bank to escape the clutches of s. 54. In addition, s. 118 applies, so if the accused adduces sufficient evidence to raise the issue, the defence is satisfied unless the prosecution proves beyond reasonable doubt there is no defence. This provision is explained more fully later in this chapter.

It is correspondingly an offence under s. 54(2) to receive instruction or training, or, under s. 54(3) to invite another to receive instruction or training contrary to subsection (1) or (2) even if the activity is to take place outside the United Kingdom. In this way, the offence also now pertains to recruitment for training as well as the training itself, arising mainly from concerns about groups seeking (often through the Internet) to recruit British Muslims for military training in madrassas (Islamic religious schools) in Afghanistan, Pakistan and elsewhere. By way of interpretation, under s. 54(4), 'instructions' and 'invitations' can be general (such as by a pamphlet or via the Internet) or to one or more specific persons. In this way, and in contrast with its predecessor in the Northern Ireland (Emergency Provisions) Act 1996, no identifiable recipient is needed for the offence to be committed. Perhaps because of these very varied circumstances, the penalties are wide ranging: on conviction on indictment, there may be imprisonment for a term not exceeding ten years, a fine or both; or on summary conviction, imprisonment for a term not exceeding six months, a fine not exceeding the statutory maximum or both. The court may also forfeit items in the person's possession for purposes connected with the offence (subject to hearing the claims of owners or persons otherwise interested in the items).

6.3 DANGEROUS SUBSTANCES

Just as the offence of weapons training has been extended to cover chemical, biological and nuclear weapons and materials, so ss. 113 to 115 of the Anti-terrorism, Crime and Security Act 2001 extend offences relating to uses of weapons and threats and hoaxes concerning them from traditional areas such as firearms and explosives to chemical, biological and nuclear weapons and materials.

By s. 113(1), it becomes an offence for a person to use or threaten to use a noxious substance or thing to cause serious harm in a manner designed to influence the Government or to intimidate the public. The serious harm is defined further by subsection (2) as comprising: (a) causes serious violence against a person anywhere in the world; (b) causes serious damage to real or personal property anywhere in the world; (c) endangers human life or creates a serious risk to the health or safety of the public or a section of the public; or (d) induces in members of the public the fear that the action is likely to endanger their lives or create a serious risk to their health or safety; but any effect on the person taking the action is to be disregarded. The latter caters for the situation where the attack has been disrupted before it has had chance to take effect, 'for example, where the police intercept a package of anthrax spores designed to kill the recipient before it reaches its target' (HL Debs. vol. 629 col. 1162, 10 December 2001, Lord Rooker). The list overall is reflective of s. 1(2) of the Terrorism Act 2000, save that there is understandably no reference to electronic systems. By s. 113(3), it is an offence to make a threat to carry out an action which constitutes an offence under subsection (1) with the intention to induce in a person anywhere in the world the fear that the threat is likely to be carried out. Offences under this clause carry a wide range of sentences — up to 14 years and a fine on indictment and up to six months and a fine on summary process.

Section 114 deals with hoaxes with reference to 'a noxious substance or other noxious thing'. The law as it stood before the 2001 Act, in s. 51 of the Criminal Law Act 1977 (as amended by the Criminal Justice Act 1991), made it an offence for someone to place or send any article intending to make another person believe that it is likely to explode or ignite and thereby cause personal injury or damage to property (see Walker, C.P., *The Prevention of Terrorism in British Law* (2nd ed., Manchester University Press, Manchester, 1992), ch.12). It was also an offence under s. 51 for someone to communicate any information which he knows or believes to be false intending to make another person believe that a bomb is likely to explode or ignite. There were corresponding offences in Scotland (s. 63) and in Northern Ireland (Criminal Law (Amendment) (Northern Ireland) Order 1977 (SI 1977 No. 1249), art. 3). A related offence is food contamination contrary to s. 38 of the Public Order Act 1986 (see Watson, S., 'Consumer terrorism' (1987) 137 *New Law Journal* 84; Watson, S., 'Product contamination' (1987) 84 *Law Society's Gazette* 7 January, p. 13). It is an offence under subsection (1) to intend to cause alarm, injury or loss by contamination or interference with goods or by making it appear that goods have been contaminated or interfered with in a place where goods of that description are consumed, used, sold or otherwise supplied. It is also an offence to make threats or claims along these lines (s. 38(2)) or to possess materials with a view to the commission of an offence (s. 38(3)). Section 38 responded to a small number of well-publicised incidents of consumer terrorism, a minority of which involved animal liberationists.

It follows that there was a substantial range of offences in existence before 2001, but it was felt that there remained gaps. The offences in s. 51 related only to hoax devices which are 'likely to explode or ignite'. The s. 38 offences protected only the integrity of goods. Post-September 11, the scare arose from the posting of anthrax powder in the USA and the fear that groups like Al Qa'ida had possession of other biological or nuclear materials which could be extremely dangerous and harmful not just in the consumer chain but through any form of contact or distribution.

Accordingly, s. 114(1) widens the offence by extending the *actus reus* to placing or sending 'any substance or article intending to make others believe that it is likely to be or contain a noxious substance or thing which could endanger human life or health'. In the circumstance post-September 11, relevant actions might include 'scattering white powder in a public place or spraying concentrated water droplets around in an Underground train' (Home Office Circular 7/2002, p. 4). By subsection (2), it is an offence for a person to falsely communicate any information to another person anywhere in the world that a noxious substance or thing is or will be in a place and so likely to cause harm or to endanger human life or health. The offence may be tried either way; the maximum penalty on indictment is imprisonment for up to seven years (but there is no provision for the retrospective effect which was at one time threatened — see Chapter 1 and the Home Affairs Committee, Report on the Anti-terrorism, Crime and Security Bill 2001 (2001–02 HC 351) para. 64).

For the purposes of both ss. 113 and 114, s. 115 makes clear that 'substance' includes any biological agent and any other natural or artificial substance (whatever its form, origin or method of production). The word 'noxious' is not defined, but it is possible that the meaning will follow that given to the word in the context of the an offence under s. 23 of the Offences against the Person Act 1861 (to administer a noxious thing to endanger life). Whether a substance is 'noxious' requires the jury to consider 'quality and quantity' and to decide as a question of fact and degree in all the circumstances whether that thing was noxious (see Archbold, *Criminal Pleading Evidence and Practice* (49th ed., Sweet & Maxwell, London, 2001), para. 19–229). Section 115 also specifies that for a person to be guilty of an offence under s. 113(3) or 114 it is not necessary for him to have any particular person in mind as the person in whom he intends to induce the belief in question. Thus, threats and hoaxes issued to the whole world, such as via the Internet, can be penalised.

The difficulties of detection remain formidable, so more effective counteractions against hoaxes has consisted of more sophisticated telephonic exchanges which allow quicker tracing, new packaging technology, stock records and consumer awareness.

6.4 DIRECTING A TERRORIST ORGANISATION

By s. 56(1) of the Terrorism Act 2000, a person commits an offence if he directs, at any level, the activities of an organisation which is concerned in the commission of acts of terrorism. Section 56 has its origins in the late 1980s in Northern Ireland, when there was growing concern about terrorist 'godfathers' who escaped liability under other offences since they did not directly involve themselves at the sharp end of death and destruction (see Walker, C., and Reid, K., 'The offence of directing terrorist organisations' [1993] *Criminal Law Review* 669). The first appearance was in s. 27 of the Northern Ireland (Emergency Provisions) Act 1991 (latterly s. 29 of the Northern Ireland (Emergency Provisions) Act 1996), but s. 56 now applies throughout the United Kingdom and is not expressly restricted to Irish terrorist organisations. Section 56 overlaps with the offences relating to proscribed organisations (see Chapter 2). But it takes account of the fluidity of terrorist groupings by avoiding reference to proscription, though the involvement must be in commission and not promoting or encouraging terrorism. It follows that s. 56 could be applied to organisations which have resorted to political violence but have not (yet) been proscribed — say, to animal liberation groups. A better approach would have been to require the organisation under s. 56 to be both proscribed and concerned in the commission of terrorism (as suggested in HC Debs. vol. 187 col. 403, 6 March 1991). Another important relationship to proscription is that s. 56 imposes a more severe penalty (a mandatory sentence of imprisonment for life) than any other in the Terrorism Act 2000.

All 'directions' are penalised, even if lawful and, indeed, even if desirable. For example, it would be an offence for an IRA commander to direct others to surrender, to observe a cease-fire or to help in fund-raising for prisoners' wives. However, it is not easy to confine the offence without taking away its sting. For example, it is designed to catch the IRA commander who orders the IRA quartermaster to buy a gross of balaclavas. Such a purchase is not (apart from s. 56) 'terrorism' but is clearly one which the framers of the offence would wish to catch. The consent of the DPP to any prosecution may be a necessary safeguard here. For example, one would presume the DPP would not sanction the prosecution of an RUC officer who 'directs' the occupants of a house, known to contain a cornered IRA unit, to surrender. Often, one would expect to see evidence in the shape of what might be called 'predicate crimes' before a prosecution can be successfully launched.

There was a great deal of debate in Parliament in 1991 about what is meant by 'directs at any level'. The Minister of State at the Northern Ireland Office emphasised that 'directing' has its ordinary, common-sense meaning and that the reference to 'any level' is designed to catch not so much minor members of the terrorist group as regional and local (as well as headquarters) leaders (HC Debs. vol. 187 col. 404, 6 March 1991). Thus, it is not a fair criticism that the concept, 'directs', is contradicted by the qualification, 'at any level', or that the IRA's kitchen staff would be guilty under s. 56 by 'directing' the washing up of the IRA's dirty dishes (HL Debs. vol. 528 col. 1394, 13 May 1991). In law, to 'direct' has been defined more narrowly than is implied by such examples. It seems to embody the attributes of being able to order other people and of commanding some obedience from them (see *Bolton Engineering* v *T.J. Graham* [1957] 1 QB 159; *Dudderidge* v *Rawlings* (1912) 108 LT 802). Thus, direction 'embraces the notion of a controlling influence on the activities in question' (HL Debs. vol. 528 col. 1396, 13 May 1991, Lord Belstead).

There have been very few convictions under the forerunner to s. 56, but the Home Office Consultation Paper claimed that, when sustained, they did have 'a major impact' (Home Office and Northern Ireland Office, Legislation against Terrorism (Cm. 4178, London, 1998), para. 12.9). The most notable case has been that of Johnny Adair, a prominent Loyalist in the Shankill area of Belfast (see *The Irish Times*, 7 September 1994, p. 8).

6.5   POSSESSION FOR TERRORIST PURPOSES

The offence of possession of items for terrorist purposes in s. 57 had been an offence in Northern Ireland since the time of s. 30 of the Northern Ireland (Emergency Provisions) Act 1991 and was latterly set out in s. 32 of the Northern Ireland (Emergency Provisions) Act 1996. The offence originated pursuant to the recommendation of the Review of the Northern Ireland (Emergency Provisions) Acts 1978 and 1987 (Cm. 1115, London, 1990, para. 2.9), though the idea was there confined to possession in public places. Then, the Criminal Justice and Public Order Act 1994, s. 63, extended a possession offence to Britain by way of s. 16A of the Prevention of Terrorism (Temporary Provisions) Act 1989. Continuance was supported by Lord Lloyd as allowing early police intervention (Inquiry into Legislation against Terrorism (Cm. 3420, London, 1996), para. 14.6), and so the offence now appears as s. 57 of the Terrorism Act 2000 for the whole of the United Kingdom. It proved to be one of the most controversial debating points during its passage, even though it is unchanged largely since 1994.

By s. 57(1) a person commits an offence if he possesses an article in circumstances which give rise to a reasonable suspicion that his possession is for a purpose connected with the commission, preparation or instigation of an act of terrorism. The penalties are the same as for s. 54. There is no need for any proof of a terrorist purpose in the mind of the possessor. It is notable that there is again no link to proscribed organisations, so the perpetrators may include, in accordance with the definition in s. 1, animal liberation activists seeking to attack a laboratory. The articles concerned will be lawful in themselves and even commonplace; in this s. 57 differs markedly from offences such as possession of an offensive weapon or going equipped for theft. There is no need for s. 57 to deal with those caught red-handed in possession of explosives and firearms. Rather, items such as wires, batteries, rubber gloves, scales, electronic timers, overalls, balaclavas, agricultural fertilizer and gas cylinders, especially in conjunction, are the menu for s. 57. The wide range of articles which may attract suspicion highlights the problematic nature of s. 57. The actions of the suspects at this stage are highly equivocal — persons with overalls and balaclavas may be preparing for an attack on a police patrol or on a rabbit warren. In this way, there is an extension of the criminal law to put people in the dock for activities which do not require activities directly related to terrorism or with the intention of being involved in terrorism.

Proof of 'possession' is aided by subsection (3): if it is proved that an article (a) was on any premises at the same time as the accused, or (b) was on premises of which the accused was the occupier or which he habitually used otherwise than as a member of the public, the court may assume that the accused possessed the article, unless he proves that he did not know of its presence on the premises or that he had no control over it.

Recognising the possible overreach of s. 57, subsection (2) offers a defence for a person charged with an offence to prove that his possession of the article was not for a purpose connected with the commission, preparation or instigation of an act of terrorism. In addition, under s. 57(3) it is open to the defendant to show he did not know of the presence of the item on the premises or had no control over it. It has been argued that this defence does not alleviate the unfairness of the offence and in fact perpetrates another by switching the burden of proof to the defence, contrary to Article 6(2) of the European Convention.

The meaning of the offence and its possible breach of Article 6(2) by undermining the presumption of innocence have been considered by the House of Lords in *R v Director of Public Prosecutions, ex parte Kebilene* [1999] 3 WLR 972. Their Lordships ultimately decided the case on the technical ground of the non-reviewability of prosecution decisions, but opinions were divided between the House of Lords and Court of Appeal on the complaint of a breach of Article 6(2). An illuminating analysis of the problem was provided in the speech of Lord Hope: (at pp. 992–993):

> It is necessary in the first place to distinguish between the shifting from the prosecution to the accused . . . the 'evidential burden', or the burden of introducing evidence in support of his case, on the one hand and the 'persuasive burden,' or the burden of persuading the jury as to his guilt or innocence, on the other. A 'persuasive' burden of proof requires the accused to prove, on a balance of probabilities, a fact which is essential to the determination of his guilt or innocence. It reverses the burden of proof by removing it from the prosecution and transferring it to the accused. An 'evidential' burden requires only that the accused must adduce sufficient evidence to raise an issue before it has to be determined as one of the facts in the case. The prosecution does not need to lead any evidence about it, so the accused needs to do this if he wishes to put the point in issue. But if it is put in issue, the burden of proof remains with the prosecution. The accused need only raise a reasonable doubt about his guilt.
>
> Statutory presumptions which place an 'evidential' burden on the accused, requiring the accused to do no more than raise a reasonable doubt on the matter with which they deal, do not breach the presumption of innocence. They are not incompatible with article 6(2) of the Convention. They take their place alongside the common law evidential presumptions which have been built up in the light of experience. They are a necessary part of preserving the balance of fairness between the accused and the prosecutor in matters of evidence. It is quite common in summary prosecutions for routine matters which may be inconvenient or time-consuming for the prosecutor to have to prove but which may reasonably be supposed to be within the accused's own knowledge to be dealt with in this way. It is not suggested that statutory provisions of this kind are objectionable.
>
> Statutory presumptions which transfer the 'persuasive' burden to the accused require further examination. Three kinds were identified by the applicants in their written case. . . . First, there is the 'mandatory' presumption of guilt as to an essential element of the offence. As the presumption is one which must be applied if the basis of fact on which it rests is established, it is inconsistent with the presumption of innocence. This is a matter which can be determined as a preliminary issue without reference to the facts of the case. Secondly, there is a

presumption of guilt as to an essential element which is 'discretionary.' The tribunal of fact may or may not rely on the presumption, depending upon its view as to the cogency or weight of the evidence. If the presumption is of this kind it may be necessary for the facts of the case to be considered before a conclusion can be reached as to whether the presumption of innocence has been breached. In that event the matters cannot be resolved until after trial.

The third category of provisions which fall within the general description of reverse onus clauses consists of provisions which relate to an exemption or proviso which the accused must establish if he wishes to avoid conviction but is not an essential element of the offence . . .

These provisions may or may not violate the presumption of innocence, depending on the circumstances.

Two further important points need to be made about this classification. The first is that this is not an exact science. The provisions vary so widely in their detail as to what the prosecutor must prove before the onus shifts, and their effect on the presumption of innocence depends so much on circumstances. These matters may not be capable of being fully assessed until after the trial. The best that can be done, by way of a preliminary examination, is to see whether the legislative technique which has been adopted imposes a persuasive or merely an evidential burden, whether it is mandatory or discretionary and whether it relates to an essential element of the offence or merely to an exception or proviso. The second is that, even if the conclusion is reached that prima facie the provision breaches the presumption of innocence, that will not lead inevitably to the conclusion that the provision is incompatible with Article 6(2) of the Convention. The European jurisprudence, which I shall examine later, shows that other factors need to be brought into consideration at this stage.

In this way, it is desirable to ensure that the interpretation of the provision is that it imposes an evidential burden (a requirement to raise evidence in support of an issue in a case) on the defence but thereafter the burden is taken up by the prosecution to disprove there is any defence and to emphasise that the final burden of proof of guilt beyond reasonable doubt, including proof of all essential facts (possession and reasonable suspicion of a terrorist purpose), remains on the prosecution. Such restraint is more likely to satisfy Article 6(2) as interpreted in the jurisprudence of the European Court of Human Rights, which does allow for some flexibility in the issue of proof, especially where it could be shown that important social concerns are at stake and where the defendant has ready access to the information required for the defence (see *Salabiaku* v *France*, App. no. 10519/83 Ser. A. 141-A (1988) 13 EHRR 379; *Brown* v *Stott (Procurator Fiscal, Dunfermline) and another* [2001] 2 All ER 97; *R* v *Benjafield* [2001] 3 WLR 75; *R* v *Lambert* [2001] 3 WLR 206).

In the light of these concerns and conflicting factors, the Government was at first content simply to reenact the existing offences without change. However, in the light of the onslaught from critics, which singled out s. 57 above all other similar provisions, s. 118 was added to the 2000 Act and affects both s. 57(2) and 57(3). By s. 118, if evidence is adduced which is sufficient to raise an issue, the court shall treat it as proved unless the prosecution disproves it beyond reasonable doubt. This formula was intended to be merely declaratory (HL Debs. vol. 613 col. 754, 16 May 2000, Lord Bassam). But in so far as it does impact on the problem, it would seem to avoid s. 57 placing any 'legal' or 'persuasive' burden upon the defendant by ensuring that, once raised, the issue remains for the prosecution to prove, and it may also slightly ease the evidential burden placed on the defendant by requiring simply the issue to be raised for it to negate the presumption in the statute unless the prosecution can prove otherwise (see Rowe, J.J., 'The Terrorism Act 2000' [2000] *Criminal Law Review* 527 at p. 540; Emmerson, B., and Ashworth, A., *Human Rights and Criminal Justice* (Sweet & Maxwell, London, 2001), para. 9–59).

The offence has been charged 30 times in Britain before the coming into force of the Terrorism Act 2000, though no convictions have yet been sustained (source: Home Office statistics).

6.6   COLLECTION OF INFORMATION

The offences of the collecting or recording or possessing information of a kind likely to be useful to a person committing or preparing an act of terrorism have existed in Northern Ireland for some time (latterly in the Northern Ireland (Emergency Provisions) Act 1996, s. 33). They were also translated into Britain by the Criminal Justice and Public Order Act 1994, s. 63, and inserted as s. 16B of the Prevention of Terrorism (Temporary Provisions) Act 1989. Now they are set out in s. 58 of the Terrorism Act 2000, though there remains an added offence for Northern Ireland alone relating to the protection of specified security force personnel and other public officials (now in the Terrorism Act 2000, s. 103, as described in Chapter 7). A 'record' includes photographic or electronic formats as well as writings and drawings, but mental notes and knowledge which are not recorded in any form are not covered. The penalties are the same as for s. 54.

Once again, the main controversy surrounding s. 58 concerns the equivocal nature of the actions involved and the fact that it is left to the defendant to prove as a defence, under subsection (3), that he had a reasonable excuse for his action or possession. In *R* v *McLaughlin* [1993] NI 28, a radio enthusiast was able to show reasonable excuse for possessing a list of RUC radio frequencies. Section 118 is applicable. The indeterminate range of the offence has also given rise to alarm on the part of journalists: 'What journalist worth his or her salt does not have a contacts book? A cuttings file? A file on the activities and personal details of prominent public figures?' (Hickman, L., 'Press freedom and new legislation' (2001) 151 *New Law Journal* 716). Indeed, one could add that a wide range of people, including academic scholars, can become effective investigators and collators of information, including through Internet sources such as the web site, 192.com, and through documents freely available through the web, such as *The*

Terrorist's Handbook and *The Big Book of Mischief*. It follows that it is not necessary to show that the information was obtained or held in breach of law; the possession of army manuals was the basis for conviction in *R v Lorenc* [1988] NI 96.

6.7   INCITING TERRORISM OVERSEAS

The remaining offences in Part VI of the Terrorism Act 2000 are more concerned with the establishment or extension of jurisdiction over criminal offences rather than the extension of the formulation of offences or the creation of wholly new offences. This observation certainly applies to ss. 59 to 61, which seek to give United Kingdom courts jurisdiction over offences of incitement of terrorism abroad. This notion of extended jurisdiction is not new and follows especially the extension of conspiracy offences. Sections 5 to 7 of the Criminal Justice (Terrorism and Conspiracy) Act 1998 give the courts jurisdiction over acts of conspiracy in the United Kingdom relating to offences committed or intended to be committed abroad. The 1998 Act covers all types of offences, not just serious arrestable offences, nor just offences against the person (compare the US Anti-Terrorist Act 1996, s. 702 (18 USC s. 2332b) which is limited to persons who kill, maim, kidnap, cause serious bodily injury or assault with a deadly weapon), nor just acts of 'terrorism' nor offences scheduled to the Suppression of Terrorism Act 1978. There remains some protection for political asylum in that the 1998 Act does not breach the principle of extra-territoriality: if the conspiracy as well as the substantive offence takes place outside the jurisdiction, the conspirators cannot be prosecuted. In view of their application to non-terrorist cases, these offences have not been incorporated into the Terrorism Act 2000 (though they were considered in that context by the Inquiry into Legislation against Terrorism (Cm. 3420, London, 1996), para. 12.39).

By comparison, ss. 59 to 61 of the Terrorism Act 2000, which followed a Government review (Home Office and Northern Ireland Office, Legislation against Terrorism (Cm. 4178, London, 1998), paras 4.18, 4.19) does potentially require the United Kingdom to protect every crazy government in the world. By s. 59, a person commits an offence if (a) he incites another person to commit an act of terrorism wholly or partly outside the United Kingdom, and (b) the act would, if committed in England and Wales, constitute one of the offences listed in subsection (2). The listed offences are (a) murder, (b) an offence under s. 18 of the Offences against the Person Act 1861 (wounding with intent), (c) an offence under s. 23 or 24 of that Act (poison), (d) an offence under s. 28 or 29 of that Act (explosions), and (e) an offence under s. 1(2) of the Criminal Damage Act 1971 (endangering life by damaging property). It may be notable that the latter offence is narrower than the reference in s. 1 to serious damage to property. However, the Government Minister, Lord Bach, has denied that there is any substantial difference (HL Debs. vol. 613 col. 760, 16 May 2000):

Our intention in this provision, which essentially fills in gaps in UK law, is to outlaw the incitement here of very serious acts with a terrorist motive overseas.

So, in relation to property crime, the relevant offence is to incite the endangering of life by damaging property. It is not a case of one definition of 'terrorism' for here and a narrower one for abroad; it is the same definition for all acts, whether here or abroad. We are applying the definition in Clause 1 to specify existing offences, to ensure that incitement here to commit certain acts abroad — which, if committed here, would constitute one of those specified offences — will be caught.

By subsection (4) it is expressly immaterial whether or not the person incited is in the United Kingdom at the time of the incitement. The only relief is in subsection (5) by which any person acting on behalf of, or holding office under, the Crown cannot be liable — members of the security services or Government may be allowed to assassinate and so on. This statement is considered to be an express version of the immunity of the Crown from offences which would otherwise impliedly cover both s. 59 and other offences in the Act (Home Office, Circular 03/01: Terrorism Act 2000 (Home Office, London, 2001), para. 6.7). Corresponding offences to s. 59 are set out in s. 60 for Northern Ireland and s. 61 for Scotland.

Sections 59 to 61 turn certain offences into universal crimes when they are not recognised as such elsewhere and in relation to foreign States which are not within the scope of the Suppression of Terrorism Act 1978. Within the context of an incitement from the United Kingdom to intended perpetrators within a foreign country, how can it be said that the 'incitement' possibly creates an immediate risk of unlawful serious violence? The immediacy and causal link are diminished from what one normally thinks of as incitement. It is suggested that the offences should at least be confined in two ways. First, in terms of persons, the scope should relate to either the activities of British citizens or incitements to persons who are in the United Kingdom. This would leave a wide offence — given the indiscriminate nature of the Internet and other modern means of communications. Secondly, in terms of actions, the list of offences should be more clearly politically related and should not go much beyond such internationally recognised offences as hijacking, attacks on internationally protected persons (which already provide for universal jurisdiction for incitement offences) and perhaps even the wider range of terrorist bombing offences under s. 62 (below). They would then more clearly reflect the core of terrorism than the offences listed.

In response, the Home Secretary has argued that ss. 59 to 61 resolve anomalies. The aim of the incitement offences is to deter those who seek to use the United Kingdom as a base from which to promote terrorist acts abroad. It is claimed that under the Suppression of Terrorism Act 1978, there is already extra-territorial jurisdiction over a number of serious offences including murder, manslaughter, kidnapping, wounding with intent, and causing explosions, and incitement to any of those offences. It is then argued that, given the limitations of the treaty, 'There is no obvious justification for incitement to commit murder in Turkey or India to be an offence in the UK, whereas incitement to commit murder in Japan or

Australia is not an offence' (HC Debs vol. 341 col. 163, 14 December 1999, Jack Straw). But, as already mentioned, the incitement of many designated terrorist offences (hijacking and so on) already carry universal jurisdiction. Further, one wonders how may cases of incitements have resulted in prosecution instead of extradition under the 1978 Act? From reported cases at least, the answer would appear to be zero, and this is also the figure given in debates by the Minister (HC Standing Committee D, col. 262, 1 February 2000, Charles Clarke).

There will also arise evidential difficulties, whereby dissident groups will find it difficult to adduce evidence from overseas as to their true nature and intentions (see JUSTICE, *Response to Legislation against Terrorism* (London, 1999), paras 3.6, 3.7). On the other hand, repressive regimes will be able to present evidence obtained by all kinds of unconscionable means.

The Government was of the view that there was a need to balance free speech interests against the unacceptability of 'encouraging and glorifying acts of terrorism' (Home Office and Northern Ireland Office, Legislation against Terrorism (Cm. 4178, London, 1998), para. 4.19). However, this is one of the areas where a mature democracy should have maintained its patience with the politically immature and intemperate. Any prosecutions under ss. 59 to 61 will be open to challenge under Article 10 of the European Convention, especially if made by a person who could be designated as a politician and especially if made against a Government (see *Castells* v *Spain*, App. no. 11798/85, Ser. A. 236, (1992) 14 EHRR. 445; *Incal* v *Turkey*, App. no. 22678/93, Reports 1998-IV, (2000) 29 EHRR 449).

6.8   UNITED NATIONS TERRORIST BOMBING AND FINANCE OFFENCES

Over several decades, international treaties have been developed to respond to terrorism. They relate to hijacking and attacks upon aircraft, ships and related installations (see Aviation Security Act 1982, Aviation and Maritime Security Act 1990), diplomats (see the Internationally Protected Persons Act 1978), hostages (the Taking of Hostages Act 1982), nuclear installations and materials (the Nuclear Material (Offences) Act 1983) as well as dealing with procedural consequences such as extradition (see the Suppression of Terrorism Act 1978). This list has now been added to by two further UN treaties, the UN Convention for the Suppression of Terrorist Bombings (A/RES/52/164, Cm. 4662, London, 1997) and the United Nations Convention for the Suppression of the Financing of Terrorism (A/RES/54/109, Cm. 4663, London, 1999). In so far as their implementation is not already dealt with elsewhere in the Terrorism Act 2000, it is the subject of ss. 62 to 64 which basically allow for the prosecution in the United Kingdom for, or the extradition in respect of, terrorism activities committed abroad and which fall within the terms of the Conventions. In this way, the usual international law responses of extradition or prosecution can be appeased.

Pursuant to Articles 4 and 6 of the UN Bombing Convention (which entered into force on the 23 May 2001 and was ratified by the United Kingdom on the 7 March 2001), if a person does anything outside the United Kingdom as an act of terrorism or for the purposes of terrorism, and his action would have constituted the commission of a specified offence (causing explosions under ss. 2, 3 or 5 of the Explosive Substances Act 1883, the use of biological weapons or chemical weapons under s. 1 of the Biological Weapons Act 1974 or s. 2 of the Chemical Weapons Act 1996) if it had been done in the United Kingdom, he shall be guilty of the offence of terrorist bombing under s. 62(1) of the Terrorism Act 2000 and the relevant penalty from the UK Act will apply. There is no need for any special designation of the foreign territory — unlike under, say, the Suppression of Terrorism Act 1978. Extradition (Article 9) or more or less universal criminal jurisdiction (Article 6) can apply automatically. It follows that terrorists can be tried in the United Kingdom even though the action was conceived, prepared and perpetrated abroad and involved no British citizens whether as perpetrators or victims. As a limit on s. 62, it is expressed Government policy that extradition should be preferred to extra-territorial prosecution wherever possible (HC Debs. Standing Committee D, col. 309, 8 February 2000, Charles Clarke).

Section 62 of the 2000 Act goes well beyond the terms of the UN Bombing Convention, though by Article 6.5, that Convention does not exclude the exercise of any criminal jurisdiction established by a State party in accordance with its domestic law. In particular, the specified offences are not linked to any particular targets or victims. But, by Article 2, the Convention is confined to bombings in official or specified public places:

1.   Any person commits an offence within the meaning of this Convention if that person unlawfully and intentionally delivers, places, discharges or detonates an explosive or other lethal device in, into or against a place of public use, a State or government facility, a public transportation system or an infrastructure facility:

(a)   With the intent to cause death or serious bodily injury; or

(b)   With the intent to cause extensive destruction of such a place, facility or system, where such destruction results in or is likely to result in major economic loss.

2.   Any person also commits an offence if that person attempts to commit an offence as set forth in paragraph 1 of the present article.

3.   Any person also commits an offence if that person:

(a)   Participates as an accomplice in an offence as set forth in paragraph 1 or 2 of the present article; or

(b)   Organizes or directs others to commit an offence as set forth in paragraph 1 or 2 of the present article; or

(c)   In any other way contributes to the commission of one or more offences as set forth in paragraph 1 or 2 of the present article by a group of persons acting with a common purpose; such contribution shall be intentional and either be made with the aim of furthering the general criminal activity or purpose of the group or be made in the knowledge of the intention of the group to commit the offence or offences concerned.

For these purposes under Article 1:

1. 'State or government facility' includes any permanent or temporary facility or conveyance that is used or occupied by representatives of a State, members of Government, the legislature or the judiciary or by officials or employees of a State or any other public authority or entity or by employees or officials of an intergovernmental organization in connection with their official duties.

2. 'Infrastructure facility' means any publicly or privately owned facility providing or distributing services for the benefit of the public, such as water, sewage, energy, fuel or communications.

3. 'Explosive or other lethal device' means:

(a) An explosive or incendiary weapon or device that is designed, or has the capability, to cause death, serious bodily injury or substantial material damage; or

(b) A weapon or device that is designed, or has the capability, to cause death, serious bodily injury or substantial material damage through the release, dissemination or impact of toxic chemicals, biological agents or toxins or similar substances or radiation or radioactive material.

4. 'Military forces of a State' means the armed forces of a State which are organized, trained and equipped under its internal law for the primary purpose of national defence or security, and persons acting in support of those armed forces who are under their formal command, control and responsibility.

5. 'Place of public use' means those parts of any building, land, street, waterway or other location that are accessible or open to members of the public, whether continuously, periodically or occasionally, and encompasses any commercial, business, cultural, historical, educational, religious, governmental, entertainment, recreational or similar place that is so accessible or open to the public.

6. 'Public transportation system' means all facilities, conveyances and instrumentalities, whether publicly or privately owned, that are used in or for publicly available services for the transportation of persons or cargo.

Next, pursuant to the UN Terrorism Financing Convention, which is not yet in force but was ratified by the United Kingdom on the 7 March 2001, s. 63 allows for jurisdiction over forms of financial activities which would fall under any of ss. 15 to 18 if they had been done in the United Kingdom but are actually performed wholly outside the jurisdiction. The penalties are to be those for the Terrorism Act 2000 offences. In this way, action can be taken against non-proscribed groups which are engaged in Part III offences outside the United Kingdom.

As under the UN Bombing Convention, it is arguable that s. 63 goes beyond the confines of the UN Terrorism Financing Convention in that the definition of 'terrorism' used in ss. 15 to 18 is wider that the definition in Article 2 of the Convention:

1.   Any person commits an offence within the meaning of this Convention if that person by any means, directly or indirectly, unlawfully and wilfully, provides or collects funds with the intention that they should be used or in the knowledge that they are to be used, in full or in part, in order to carry out:

(a)   An act which constitutes an offence within the scope of and as defined in one of the treaties listed in the annex; or

(b)   Any other act intended to cause death or serious bodily injury to a civilian, or to any other person not taking an active part in the hostilities in a situation of armed conflict, when the purpose of such act, by its nature or context, is to intimidate a population, or to compel a government or an international organization to do or to abstain from doing any act.

The offences referred to in Article 2.1(a) are those in the international hijacking and other treaties referred to earlier. So the problem lies in the definition in (b) where there is no reference, for example, to serious damage to property, or interference with an electronic system.

By s. 64 of the 2000 Act, and reflecting Article 9 of the UN Bombing Convention and Article 11 of the UN Terrorism Financing Convention, the Extradition Act 1989, s. 22, is amended to allow for the foregoing Conventions to serve as general extradition arrangements for the purposes of s. 3 of that Act (or to allow for the relevant offences to be added by order to established bilateral arrangements under the Extradition Act 1870). It is also provided that the terms of s. 1 of the Suppression of Terrorism Act 1978 are to apply to the offences covered by either Convention, which means, in accordance with Article 11 of the UN Bombing Convention and Articles 6 and 14 of the UN Terrorism Financing Convention, that they are not to be regarded as offences of a political character (they are also not to be regarded as fiscal offences under Article 13 of the UN Terrorism Financing Convention).

The UN Bombing Convention requires further liaison under Article 15, by which the States parties shall cooperate in the prevention of the offences set forth in Article 2, particularly by exchanging accurate and verified information and by consultations on the development of standards for marking explosives in order to identify their origin in post-blast investigations, exchange of information on preventive measures, cooperation and transfer of technology, equipment and related materials. Corresponding forms of cooperation are required by Articles 12 and 18 of the UN Terrorism Financing Convention. Such exchanges no doubt occur, though are not reflected in the legislation.

6.9   RACE AND RELIGIOUS HATRED

At this point, attention will be turned to the offences in the Anti-terrorism, Crime and Security Act 2001. The list begins with those dealing with race and religion. The essence of the change, contained in Part V of the 2001 Act, is to widen the concept of race hatred and to add the concept of religious hatred for the purposes of some relevant criminal offences. The presence of Part V is perhaps explained, if not justified, on two grounds — one looking inward to violent attacks and incitements within the jurisdiction, the other looking more outward as a signal that action against terrorism is not motivated by racial hatred (HC Debs. vol. 375 col. 703, 26 November 2001, David Blunkett):

> Two factors affected my thinking on whether to include religion . . . the first of which was internal reassurance. Since 11 September, people in this country have had a genuine fear, which was articulated earlier this afternoon, that individuals would seek to attack or abuse people, not because of their race but because they are Muslims. Similarly, there is a fear that those who sought to stir up hate against those whom they described as the infidel were equally untouchable under the existing law.
>
> The second factor was international provision. In the past 11 weeks, consider-able attention has been focused on the United Kingdom by other countries, particularly Arab countries. In satellite broadcasts and interviews, it became patently clear that the commitment on religion made on 3 October had a significant impact on people living in and viewing satellite broadcasts in certain countries, including interviewers. They appreciated that that particular change had an impact; they perceived that we were prepared to protect people whom they were told we did not care about and in whom we had no interest because, prima facie, the intention was to damage their religion. Those serious issues deserve serious consideration for the reassurance, resilience and social cohesion of our own community; it is important to be able to contribute to that.

Incidents under the first heading included the closure of the first State-funded Islamic school, the Islamia Primary School, in Brent after threatening telephone calls (HL Debs. vol. 629 col. 1190, 10 December 2001, Lord Goldsmith).

The legislation in Bill form ambitiously extended the offence of incitement to racial hatred to religious hatred. Thus, clause 38 of the original version of the Bill inserted a definition of religious hatred after s. 17 of the Public Order Act 1986. Religious hatred was defined as hatred against a group of persons defined by reference to religious belief or lack of religious belief. The hatred may relate to the religion (or lack of it) prevalent amongst the group or the fact that the group does not share the religion of another group. This definition was designed to encompass a wide range of religious beliefs but did not define either what amounts to a religion or a religious belief. The group must be defined by reference to religion, so a group identified by any other factors, such as political opinion, would not be caught, save that it might often be difficult to separate religion and politics. However, after fierce debate in Parliament, some of which sought to distinguish stirring hatred on the basis of a human attribute such as race from attacks on the basis of more elective beliefs (which shade into legitimate freedom of expression), these wider aspects were dropped at the very last gasp so as to ensure passage of the Bill after contrary votes in the House of Lords (HC Debs. vol. 376 col. 1112,

13 December 2001). The Government accepted the need for further and calmer debate on the subject, particularly after it was found difficult to offer convincing guidelines on prosecution policy (an idea put forward by the Attorney-General (HL Debs. vol. 629 col. 1163, 10 December 2001, Lord Goldsmith) and which temporarily contented the House of Lords (col. 1463, 13 December 2001). The Attorney-General's draft (and ultimately redundant) guidance relating to freedom of expression stated (col. 1452, 13 December 2001):

> Given the high threshold tests set by these offences it is not easy to foresee circumstances in which legitimate methods of religious debate will justify a prosecution. So, expressions of, or indeed criticism of, one's own or another's religious beliefs or practices, even when robustly expressed, or satirising or poking fun at or making comical representations of religion, people who are religious or who follow particular religions are unlikely to offend the statute. Legitimate expressions of religious belief which, taken within their context, time and the wider national and international arena, could not be construed as anything other than the expression of a religious tenet are, similarly, not likely to amount to an offence of incitement to religious hatred.

The defeat also followed prompting by the Home Affairs Committee (*Report on the Anti-terrorism, Crime and Security Bill 2001* (2001–02 HC 351) para. 61):

> We have not seen sufficient evidence to justify the proposition that extending the law of incitement to include religious as well as racial hatred will work in practice. The proposals in the Bill would be difficult to enforce. We note in particular the evidence from a group of distinguished Muslim organisations and individuals: 'we have grave reservations about the extension of this criminal power to cover religious groups at this particular time'. We therefore see no reason for this measure to be included in this emergency terrorism Bill.

It may be noted that the extension would not be such a dangerous step into the unknown as it was presented to be during the debates. Incitement to religious hatred has been an offence for some decades in Northern Ireland, where it is now contained in art. 13 of the Public Order (Northern Ireland) Order 1987 (SI 1987 No. 463 (NI 7); see Hadfield B., 'The prevention of incitement to religious hatred — an article of faith?' (1984) 35 *Northern Ireland Legal Quarterly* 231). The offence has produced just a few prosecutions, though they are very controversial (*R* v *McKeague, Belfast Telegraph*, 28 June, 14 December 1971; *R* v *Seawright, The Times*, 30 November 1984, p. 2). It might also be argued that the protection of religious susceptibilities in this way is required by Article 20 of the UN International Covenant on Civil and Political Rights, by which 'any advocacy of national, racial or religious hatred that constitutes incitement to discrimination, hostility or violence shall be prohibited by law'. More indirectly, Article 14 of the European Convention on Human Rights forbids discrimination on any ground, including religion, in connection with the exercise of freedom of expression, freedom of thought, conscience and religion, and freedom of assembly and association. However, one strongly suspects that the passage of such an offence in Britain would be more likely in the atmosphere prevailing after 11 September to provoke prosecutions of Muslims than of those speaking against their faith. As a Liberty briefing paper suggested (see http://www.liberty-human-rights.org.uk/, 2001):

> In our view, the creation of the new offence could be particularly divisive and counter-productive at a time when free religious discourse (both within and between faiths) may be more important than ever. In our view, a climate of religious freedom and tolerance will not be created by criminal censorship. It could be extremely dangerous to provide a form of martyrdom for religious extremists of whatever faith by driving their speech underground. Further, the possibility of Muslims themselves facing prosecution (at the complaint of other Muslims or members of other faiths) cannot be ruled out. In any event, perceptions of prosecution contrary to free speech would be extremely counter-productive to the aim of social cohesion.

As evidence of the danger, the only prosecution for hate speech related to the 11 September events has concerned Abdullah el-Faisal, who has been charged with soliciting to murder (*The Times*, 19 February 2001, p. 1). Alternatively, it might be predicted that any new law would be a dead-letter, just as offences of race hatred under Part III of the Public Order Act 1986 have been exceedingly rare (Source: HC Debs. vol. 373 col. 851, 1 November 2001):

Table 6.1: Usage of Part III of the Public Order Act 1986

	1997	1998	1999	2000	2001 (1 Nov)
No. of applications to prosecute	12	2	4	7	7
Withdrawn	-	1	-	-	-
Not granted	2	-	-	-	-
Prosecuted	10	1	4	7	7
Convicted	9	1	3	4	-

In terms of what the 2001 Act does achieve, Part V begins by extending the existing concept of racial hatred as used, in connection with the offences of incitement to racial hatred, in s. 17 of the Public Order Act 1986 and the corresponding art. 8 of the Public Order (Northern Ireland) Order 1987 (see generally Wolffe, W.J., 'Values in Conflict' [1987] *Public Law* 85; Bradney, A., *Religions, Rights and Laws* (Leicester University Press, 1993); Coliver, S. (ed.), *Striking a Balance* (Article 19, London, 1992)). The extension is to remove the

limit on protection which could only apply to a group of persons in Great Britain
or Northern Ireland, as the case may be. By means of this change, it becomes an
offence under ss. 37 and 38 to stir up hatred against identifiable racial groups
abroad. The meaning of a 'racial group' under s. 3 of the Race Relations Act 1976
('a group of persons identified by reference to colour, race, nationality or ethnic
or national origins') has been the subject of litigation over the years. It can overlap
with religious groups, if the circumstances of discrimination also affects an
identifiable nationality, race or ethnic group — as in the case of Sikhs in *Mandla*
v *Dowell Lee* [1983] 2 AC 548, Pakistani or Indian Muslims in *Malik* v *British*
Home Stores (1980) CRE Report p. 78, Jews in *Seide* v *Gillette Industries Ltd*
[1980] IRLR 427, *Tower Hamlets LBC* v *Rabin* [1989] ICR 693 or gypsies in
Commission for Racial Equality v *Dutton* [1989] 1 All ER 306 but not Rastafarians
in *Crown Suppliers (PSA)* v *Dawkins* [1993] ICR 517. But the express extension
of the definition to religious groups was rejected in 2001, just as it was in 1976,
when the Government argued that there would have to be extensive consideration
of the extent to which religious discrimination would have to be allowed to protect
religious freedom (HC Debs. Standing Committee A cols 84–118, 29 April and
4 May 1976).

In addition to these changes in definition, ss. 40 and 41 of the 2001 Act increase
the maximum penalties for race hatred offences from two to seven years.

Next, and more boldly, s. 39 of the Anti-terrorism, Crime and Security Act 2001
allows a religious motivation to be treated as an aggravating factor in charging
offenders under the Crime and Disorder Act 1998, s. 28 and then sentencing them
under s. 153 of the Powers of Criminal Courts (Sentencing) Act 2000 (previously
in s. 82 of the Crime and Disorder Act 1998). In this way, if a court is considering
the seriousness of an offence and finds that it is aggravated by either race or
religion, it is required to treat this as increasing the seriousness of the offence and
to state in open court that the offence is found to be aggravated. This applies to
nine specified offences in ss. 29 to 32 of the Crime and Disorder Act 1998 and
relating to assaults, criminal damage, public disorder and harassment (see generally
Home Office Consultation Paper, *Racial Violence and Harassment* (London,
1997)). The effect is to advance the indirect protection against religious attacks
granted by s. 28 of the Crime and Disorder Act 1998. In defining 'racially
aggravated', by subsection (3) 'it is immaterial . . . whether or not the offender's
hostility is also based, to any extent, on . . . the fact or presumption that any person
or group of persons belongs to any religious group'. Under the 2001 Act, the
predicate offence will become an aggravated offence under the 1998 Act provided
there is evidence of hostility towards the victim of that offence by the offender at
the time of committing the offence or immediately before or after doing so and
that hostility is caused by the victim's membership of a racial or religious group.
In addition, an offence will be aggravated if evidence is adduced that it was
motivated by hostility towards members of a racial or religious group. The
requirement of an independent offence provides some restraint on the use of s. 39,
but the fact that one of those listed is harassment under s. 2 of the Protection from

Harassment Act 1997 (which may involve no more that 'alarming the person or causing the person distress') may result in pressure to take action against offensive speech than anticipated by Parliament.

Corresponding to the unsuccessful clause 38, a 'religious group' is defined by reference to a person's particular religious belief, lack of a particular religious belief, or lack of any religious belief or where the hostility is based on the fact that the victim does not share the particular religious beliefs of the offender. This phraseology encompasses traditional organised religions, but also the subjective beliefs of an individual or a small group of individuals, such as The First Church of Jesus Christ, Elvis (http://jubal.westnet.com/hyperdiscordia/sacred_heart_elvis. html) or indeed a person's atheist 'non-belief'.

By s. 42, Part V of the 2001 Act does not apply to anything done before it came into force.

6.10 BRIBERY AND CORRUPTION

Even less closely connected with the expected subject-matter of combating terrorism is Part XII of the Anti-terrorism, Crime and Security Act 2001, which addresses aspects of the laws relating to bribery and corruption in relation to foreign governments and officials. Once again, the 2001 Act provided a convenient vessel for proposals, contained in the Government White Paper, Raising Standards and Upholding Integrity: the Prevention of Corruption (Cm. 4759, London, 2000), which otherwise might have experienced a lengthy shelf-life. The Minister of State (Beverley Hughes) valiantly argued that there was a link to terrorism on the ground that 'corrupt Governments help to create the conditions that engender terrorism and we need to make it clear that the bribery of foreign officials is just as unacceptable as the bribery of United Kingdom officials' (HC Debs. vol. 375 col. 418, 21 November 2001). On the same ground, one would expect to see in the Act general laws which outlaw dealings with foreign governments which fail to respect rights or spend too much on military hardware and not enough on medicines or generally breach international law. Other pending reforms concerning bribery and corruption (see the wide-ranging Law Commission report, Legislating the Criminal Code: Corruption (Report No. 248) and the Government Response to the Sixth Report from the Committee on Standards in Public Life (Cm. 4817, London, 2000), mainly focused on standards in relation to British public life) were presumably too controversial or too unripe to be included.

By s. 108(1) of the 2001 Act, the common law offence of bribery is extended to persons holding public office outside the United Kingdom. This change is in line with the recommendation of the Law Commission (para. 7.15) which sought the inclusion of bribery within Group A offences under the Criminal Justice Act 1993. There are also changes to the Public Bodies Corrupt Practices Act 1889, the Prevention of Corruption Act 1906 and the Prevention of Corruption Act 1916 to attach the relevant offences to the bribery and corruption of foreign public officials, as well as those in the private sector, irrespective of whether the offences are committed in the United Kingdom. The Law Commission was likewise hostile to the distinction between public and private sectors (para. 3.34). The Government White Paper (para. 2.19) concurred and was especially enthusiastic about the dilution in territorial jurisdiction in order to meet international obligations to root out corruption (such as the Council of Europe's Criminal Law Convention on Corruption (ETS No. 173, 1999), the European Union's Corruption Convention (OJ C 195, 25 June 1997) and the Corruption Protocol to the European Union Fraud Convention (OJ C 313, 23 October 1996) and the OECD Convention on Combating Bribery of Foreign Public Officials in International Business Transactions, 1997). The effect goes further than the indication in the courts that, provided a substantial measure of activities take place in the home jurisdiction, the corruption of foreign officials could be prosecuted here. It is now made clear in s. 109 that a national of the United Kingdom or a body incorporated under the law of any part of the United Kingdom commits a relevant offence if an act is committed in a country or territory outside the United Kingdom, and the act would, if done in the United Kingdom, constitute a corruption offence. In other words, s. 109 establishes extra-territorial offences based on nationality. This goes further than the Government White Paper aim of putting beyond doubt an ability to prosecute where the *actus reus* does not occur 'wholly within the United Kingdom's jurisdiction' (para. 2.19) and reflects the more ambitious idea of jurisdiction based on nationality (para. 2.23).

Section 110 ensures that the presumption of corruption contained in s. 2 of the Prevention of Corruption Act 1916 does not apply any more widely as a result of the two previous sections. Following a recommendation of the Law Commission (para. 4.78), accepted by the Government in its White Paper (para. 2.9), the intention is to abolish the presumption completely.

Prosecutions under the 1889 Act, as amended by the 1916 Act and the 1906 Act, require the consent of the Attorney-General, which is also required under ss. 108 and 109 because they operate in effect by way of amending those Acts. The common law offence of bribery does not require the consent of the Attorney-General, but 'where a common law offence is being brought to avoid one of the issues in the statutory offence . . . it is the practice of the Crown Prosecution Service to ensure that they are brought to the attention of the Law Officers' (HL Debs. vol. 629 col. 822, 4 December 2001, Lord Goldsmith).

The total number of persons proceeded against under the relevant Acts in 2000 was 17. It is expected that these measures will result in five more prosecutions per year (HC Debs. vol. 375 col. 419, 21 November 2001), which suggests both major problems in the detection of a consensual crime and also considerable selectivity in the choice of accused.

Chapter Seven
Northern Ireland special measures

7.1 INTRODUCTION

Pending the successful resolution of the Peace Process in Northern Ireland, it was felt to be appropriate to keep in place most of the extra counter-terrorism measures which applied specifically to the Province under the Northern Ireland (Emergency Provisions) Act 1996 (as amended in 1998) (see Hogan, G., and Walker C., *Political Violence and the Law in Ireland* (Manchester University Press, Manchester, 1989); Dickson, B., 'Northern Ireland's emergency legislation' [1992] *Public Law* 529). As a result, they are translated with little change into the Terrorism Act 2000. But because of their intended transitory nature, they are kept distinct in Part VII and made subject to annual renewal by s. 112 (described in Chapter 10). As a result, there is some overlap between measures in Part VII and those in the remainder of the Act — presumably, Part VII will normally take precedence in Northern Ireland.

The situation is made even more complex by the fact that s. 2 (referring to sch. 10, preserved for one year (from the 24 August 2000), renewable by order for a further 12 months at a time, the Northern Ireland (Emergency Provisions) Act 1996 (as amended by the Prevention of Terrorism (Temporary Provisions) Act 1989, and s. 4 of the Criminal Justice (Terrorism and Conspiracy) Act 1998 (forfeiture orders). This transitional period was allowed until arrangements could be made for the coming into force of the whole of the Terrorism Act 2000. Not preserved in this way were the following provisions of the Northern Ireland (Emergency Provisions) Act 1996: s. 26(1)(b) (power of entry on authority of Secretary of State), s. 35 (wearing of hoods — see Inquiry into Legislation against Terrorism (Cm. 3420, London, 1996), para. 14.11), and s. 50 (licensing of explosives factories). These were dropped without further ado in 2000, as the advice from the RUC was that they were neither used nor needed (HC Standing Committee D, col. 48, 18 January 2000, Adam Ingram). At the same time, though the extended life was meant to be very finite, a number of relatively minor amendments were also made by sch. 1 (and also s. 118) to various provisions in the 1996 Act during the transition period. These related especially to the granting of appeals against decisions not to grant or to revoke a certificate for the provisions of private security services. Further transitional measures, especially relating to the detention of persons, are set out in s. 129. Much of this transitional complexity has now been resolved by the bringing into force in February 2001 of the body of the Terrorism Act 2000 (see further Chapter 10). After this time, there remain only those measures from the Northern Ireland (Emergency Provisions) Acts 1996 and 1998 preserved by Part VII for a further transitional period of up to five years. Of course, several other measures reemerge elsewhere in the Terrorism Act 2000, including forfeiture measures and the powers to regulate private security services.

The powers in Part VII are by s. 105 expressly additional to other powers under statute or at common law (including such powers as may exist akin to martial law under the prerogative).

7.2   SPECIAL CRIMINAL PROCESS

One of the major modifications brought about by the Northern Ireland (Emergency Provisions) Act 1973 was the institution of a special court to deal with terrorist cases, as well as a number of other pre-trial modifications. These changes were made pursuant to the Report of the Commission to consider legal procedures to deal with terrorist activities in Northern Ireland (Cmnd. 5185, London, 1972), and, taking their name from the chairman, became known as the 'Diplock courts'. Though there is a commitment to phase out the Diplock system (Home Office and Northern Ireland Office, Legislation against Terrorism (Cm. 4178, London, 1998), para. 13.8), it lives on for the present.

Subjected to these special processes are persons who are charged with 'scheduled offences', which are listed in s. 65 and sch. 9 to the Terrorism Act 2000 (previously s. 1 and sch. 1 of the Northern Ireland (Emergency Provisions) Act 1996, as amended by s. 2 of the Northern Ireland (Emergency Provisions) Act 1998). The list is long, and includes common law offences, such as homicides, and many statutory offences, relating to offences against the person, explosives, firearms, breaches of prison security as well as offences under the Terrorism Act 2000 itself. In addition to these offences which are commonly associated with terrorism, there are several other offences which are frequently committed outside the context of paramilitary activity (see Walsh, D.P.J., *The Use and Abuse of Emergency Legislation in Northern Ireland* (Cobden Trust, London, 1983)). These include offences under the Theft Act (Northern Ireland) 1969, such as robbery and aggravated burglary, and offences under the Computer Misuse Act 1990. As a result, these offences may be filtered out of the 'Diplock' process, by the Attorney-General for Northern Ireland certifying that it is not to be treated as a scheduled offence. An addition to the list of offences which may be certified out concerns any extra-territorial offence under the Criminal Jurisdiction Act 1975 (as recommended by the (Rowe) Report on the Operation in 1998 of the Northern Ireland (Emergency Provisions) Acts (Northern Ireland Office) (Belfast, 1999), para. 44).

There has long been a debate as to whether there should be 'certifying in' by the Attorney-General rather than the current possibility of certifying out. The argument in favour is that switching the process in this way to certifying in might assist in the return to normal criminal justice processes, and as the security situation in Northern Ireland improves, so could the proportion of cases being entrusted to jury trial (Inquiry into Legislation against Terrorism (Cm. 3420, London, 1996), para. 16.16). The change has been resisted for various reasons. One is that scrutiny of each case would be practically difficult. It would put pressure on the Law Officers to investigate and reach conclusions about a case in its early stages and allow for disruptive legal challenges at that stage (HC Debs. Standing Committee A col. 60, 25 November 1997, Adam Ingram). However, it should be noted that the rate of certifying out has increased substantially during the past decade, and so the extra workload and pressure may not be as great as it first appears.

Table 7.1: Certifying out of scheduled mode of trial by the AG for NI

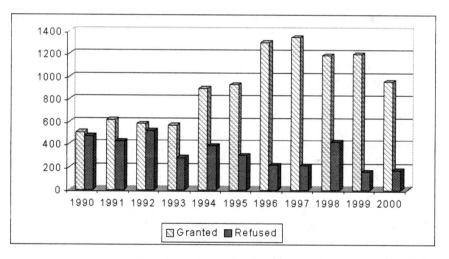

(source: Northern Ireland Office)

The second is that the Attorney-General is to be seen in principle as granting relief from repressive measures and not imposing them, though how this squares with his role as a prosecutor is not clear. Thirdly, it is seen as preferable for Parliament to take a blanket decision, rather than leaving it to a case-by-case basis (Rowe Report on the Emergency Provisions Acts, Review of the Northern Ireland (Emergency Provisions) Act 1991 (Cm. 2706, London, 1995), para. 36), which would also raise problems of challenge and the use of Public Interest Immunity (Diplock Review: Report (Belfast, 2000), p. 13).

Whether certifying in or out is adopted, either may be vulnerable to challenge on the ground that reasons are not given for a decision which results in unequal treatment in criminal justice process (Dickson, B., 'The Prevention of Terrorism (Temporary Provisions) Act 1989' (1989) 40 *Northern Ireland Legal Quarterly* 592 at p. 607). This argument was raised in *Kavanagh* v *Ireland*, CCPR/C/71/D/819/ 1998, 4 April 2001 before the UN Human Rights Commission in connection with corresponding measures in the Republic of Ireland's Offences against the State Act 1939. The (Hederman) Interim Report of the Committee to Review the Offences against the State Acts 1939–1998 (Irish Government, Dublin, 2001) has recommended that the decision of the DPP should be subject to independent counsel and review by a Supreme Court judge (para. 11.12).

Having defined and selected a scheduled offence, the special processes begin with s. 66 of the Terrorism Act 2000 (previously s. 2 of the Northern Ireland (Emergency Provisions) Act 1996), by which proceedings before a magistrates' court for a scheduled offence shall, if the prosecution so requests, be by way of a preliminary inquiry under the Magistrates' Courts (Northern Ireland) Order 1981 (SI 1981 No. 1675 (NI 26)). Unlike in normal law, there is no need for agreement from the defence. This process avoids a preliminary investigation, which might be delayed by non-recognition of the court system by Republican defendants (see (Gardiner) Report of a Committee to consider, in the context of civil liberties and human rights, measures to deal with terrorism in Northern Ireland (Cmnd. 5847, London, 1975) or which might involve the calling of witnesses who could then be subject to intimidation.

Likewise, restrictions are also placed on the powers to grant bail under s. 67 of the 2000 Act (previously s. 3 of the Northern Ireland (Emergency Provisions) Act 1996) unless the scheduled offence is to be tried summarily. An application for bail (for the purposes of which a lawyer may be assigned to assist the applicant) may only be granted by a judge of the High Court or the Court of Appeal (or by the trial judge rather than by a magistrate), and there is no presumption in favour of bail. In 2000, 602 out of 1059 (57%) of bail applications were granted (source: Northern Ireland Office). This is considerably lower than the figure for non-scheduled offences which is around 80% (Northern Ireland Office Statistics and Research Branch, *Digest of Information on the Northern Ireland Criminal Justice System* (Belfast, 1998)). Legal aid applications in connection with bail are referred under s. 68 of the 2000 Act (previously s. 4 of the 1996 Act) directly to the High Court rather than the Legal Aid Department of the Law Society. If bail is not granted, then the maximum period of remand in custody according to s. 69 (previously s. 5 of the 1996 Act) shall be not more than 28 days beginning with the day following that on which the accused is remanded. Special restrictions are also applied under ss. 70 and 71 (previously ss. 6 and 7 of the 1996 Act) to young persons who are charged with a scheduled offence and have been remanded or committed for trial and not released on bail; they may be held in custody in such prison or other place as may be specified in a direction given by the Secretary of State (usually the secure Young Offenders Centre, at Hydebank Wood in south Belfast). Under ordinary law, most young persons would be remanded to rather less secure destinations, such as a training school or remand home.

Given the complexity and seriousness of many terrorist trials, there are often concerns about the length of the pre-trial process, which can take on the appearance of a form of *de facto* internment. These concerns reached a height during the trials based on informer evidence ('supergrasses') from 1981 and 1985 (see (Baker) Review of the Operation of the Northern Ireland (Emergency Provisions) Act 1978 (Cmnd. 9222, London, 1984); Bonner, D., 'The Baker Review of the Northern Ireland (Emergency Provisions) Act 1978' [1984] *Public Law* 348; Bonner, D., 'Combating terrorism: Supergrass trials in Northern Ireland' (1988) 51 *Modern Law Review* 23; Greer, S., 'Supergrasses and the legal system in Britain and Northern Ireland' (1986) 102 *Law Quarterly Review* 189; Greer, S.C, *Supergrasses* (Clarendon Press, Oxford, 1995)). Therefore, the Secretary of State was empowered to impose maximum periods either for specific processes or for the overall period of custody on remand. These provisions are now in ss. 72 and 73 of the 2000 Act (previously ss. 8 and 9 of the Northern Ireland (Emergency Provisions) Act 1996) but have never been activated because the dire consequences of failure to meet the deadlines — that the accused shall be treated for all purposes as having been acquitted of the offence to which the proceedings relate — are seen as unacceptable. There are administrative targets for time limits, which have been operating since 1992. A total of 48 weeks is allowed (Review of the Northern Ireland (Emergency Provisions) Act 1991 (Cm. 2706, London, 1995), para. 52), but the failure to meet that target is not subject to any legal sanction. A more flexible power, allowing for different time limits to be set for different offences has been called for but not enacted (Review of the Northern Ireland (Emergency Provisions) Act 1991 (Cm. 2706, London, 1995), para. 54). The Government has also failed to keep its promise to apply time limits through normal laws (Home Office and Northern Ireland Office, Legislation against Terrorism (Cm. 4178, 1998), para. 13.17). During 2000, the average processing times were 33.3 weeks from remand to committal; 4.5 weeks from committal to arraignment; and 7.9 weeks from arraignment to hearing (source: Northern Ireland Office).

The key provisions of the 'Diplock' process are in ss. 74 and 75 of the 2000 Act (previously ss. 10 and 11 of the 1996 Act). The trial of a scheduled indictable offence is centred upon the Crown Court at Belfast, which is a highly secure and relatively convenient location for lawyers and security force witnesses, though after the Baker Report (Review of the Operation of the Northern Ireland (Emergency Provisions) Act 1978 (Cmnd. 9222, London, 1984), paras 197–181) proposals were implemented, it became possible to hold terrorist trials elsewhere. Under s. 75, the trial shall be conducted before a single judge, sitting without a jury. The judge is a regular member of the judiciary. It is some 40 years since military officers have sat in trials in either part of Ireland (in contrast to the US Presidential Order, Detention, Treatment, and Trial of Certain Non-Citizens in the War Against Terrorism, of the 13 November 2001 (66 Federal Register 57831) s. 4) (see further, House of Commons Library, Research Paper 01/112: *The Campaign against International Terrorism* (London, 2001), p. 48).

In order to compensate in part for the loss of the jury, where the court trying a scheduled offence convicts the accused of that or some other offence, it shall give a judgment stating the reasons for the conviction at, or as soon as is reasonably practicable after, the time of conviction. This requirement under s. 75(7) is to facilitate the bringing of an appeal. In addition, under s. 75(8), a person convicted of an offence on a 'Diplock' trial may, notwithstanding ss. 1 and 10(1) of the Criminal Appeal (Northern Ireland) Act 1980, appeal to the Court of Appeal without the leave of the Court of Appeal or a certificate of the judge of the court of trial. In 1990–1996, 53% of all criminal appeals were in respect of scheduled offences, even though they represent less than 20% of persons tried (Northern Ireland Office Statistics and Research Branch, *Digest of Information on the Northern Ireland Criminal Justice System* (Belfast, 1998) p. 89). In 1990–1996, 13% were successful, compared to 29% in non-scheduled cases (p. 91); scheduled defendants were also less likely to abandon the appeal: 38%:58%.

In the light of experience and corresponding experience in the Republic (a Special Criminal Court has existed in Dublin since 1972: Hogan, G., and Walker, C., *Political Violence and the Law in Ireland* (Manchester University Press, Manchester, 1989), ch. 10), the existence of a special trial system in Northern Ireland is unremarkable. No doubt, some defendants even prefer the more incisive and reasoned verdict of a judge to that of the Delphic jury verdict (likewise, a non-jury court was agreed to in the Lockerbie trial (see, for the verdict *The Times*, 1 February 2001)). Moreover, there have been few claims of miscarriages of justice (see Dickson, B., 'Miscarriages of justice in Northern Ireland' in Walker, C., and Starmer, K., *Miscarriages of Justice* (Blackstone Press, London, 1999)). However, the nature of special trials and the facility with which they can be applied rightly cause concern about prejudice to the defendant from 'case-hardened' judges (Inquiry into Legislation against Terrorism (Cm. 3420, London, 1996), paras 16.16–18). These misgivings are especially felt amongst Catholics in Northern Ireland. The Northern Ireland Office Statistics and Research Branch, *Digest of Information on the Northern Ireland Criminal Justice System* (Belfast, 1998) reports 75% of Protestants expressing confidence in criminal justice compared to 63% of Catholics. There are many intermediate arrangements between the cherished trial by jury and the unloved single-judge court, and some are both practicable and preferable (see Jackson, J.R., Quinn, K., and O'Malley, T., 'The jury system in contemporary Ireland' (1999) 62 *Law & Contemporary Problems* 203). The most acceptable compromise would be to employ a judge to deal with legal issues accompanied by three lay assessors of fact, who would retain the elements of common sense and freshness normally imparted by a jury (see Greer, S., and White, A., *Abolishing the Diplock Courts* (London: Cobden Trust 1986); Review of the Operation of the Northern Ireland (Emergency Provisions) Act 1978 (London: Cmnd. 9222 HMSO 1984) paras 108–129). There is less enthusiasm for a three judge court because of staffing difficulties and because in principle, it is no nearer to a jury (Review of the Northern Ireland (Emergency Provisions) Act 1991 (Cm. 2706, London, 1995), paras 62–64). Even before a special court is activated, attention should be given to alternative steps which might preserve the jury system. Amongst the possible strategies are extra protections for jurors or witnesses such as by suppression of their identities (and various other measures in the case of witnesses: Review of the Northern Ireland (Emergency Provisions) Act 1991 (Cm. 2706, London, 1995), ch. 14) or of publicity concerning the trial and a change of venue. A range of protections for victims and witnesses have been conjured in 'normal' cases in the Youth Justice and Criminal Evidence Act 1999. There should be some movement towards normality — it is not acceptable simply to reproduce at this stage in the peace process the 'Diplock courts' of 1973. However, these ideas were rejected by the Northern Ireland Office's Diplock Review: Report, which was published in May 2000. Though the government's view is that 'there is nothing to show that the system has produced perverse judgments or that it has lowered standards' (HC Debs. vol. 301 col. 173, 18 November 1997, Adam Ingram), at the same time, it is accepted in principle that there should be a return to jury trials (Diplock Review: Report, p. 2), the time is not ripe, mainly because of the risk of intimidation which is ineffectively countered through measures such as jury anonymity (Diplock Review: Report, pp. 6, 16; see further Mullin, J., 'The trying game' *The Guardian*, 20 January 1998, p. 17).

In recent years, the number of Diplock trials has declined sharply (and represents under 20% of all Crown Court trials in Northern Ireland). The effective acquittal rate (percentage pleading not guilty found not guilty) has remained variable (ranging from 29% in 1993 to 100% in 1998, reflecting low numbers of defendants who plead not guilty), but for 1990–98 averaged 40% which is below the rate for non-scheduled trials (source: Northern Ireland Office).

Table 7.2: Diplock trials in Northern Ireland

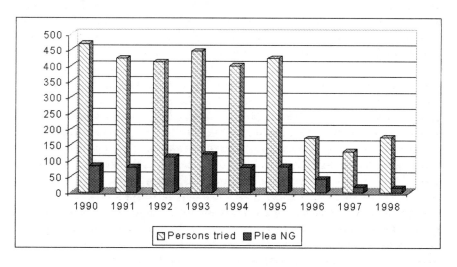

(*source: Northern Ireland Office*)

There are a number of ways in which the absence of a jury affects the dynamics of the trial process, including by encouraging more interventions by the judges and focusing more on the legal issues rather than on more emotional advocacy (see Jackson, J.R., and Doran, S., 'Conventional trials in unconventional times' (1993) 4 *Criminal Law Forum* 503; Jackson, J.R., and Doran, S., *Judge without Jury* (Oxford: Clarendon Press, 1995)). There is also a heightened reliance upon silence as evidence (Jackson, J.D., Quinn, K., and Wolfe, M., *Legislating against Silence* (Northern Ireland Office, Belfast, 2001)). But by far the most important intentional alteration is set out in s. 76 of the 2000 Act (previously s. 12 of the Northern Ireland (Emergency Provisions) Act 1996). It provides that if the prosecution gives or proposes to give a statement made by the accused in evidence, '(b) prima facie evidence is adduced that the accused was subjected to torture, inhuman or degrading treatment, violence or the threat of violence in order to induce him to make the statement, and (c) the prosecution does not satisfy the court that the statement was not obtained in the manner mentioned in paragraph (b)', the court shall either exclude the statement, or direct that the trial be restarted before a differently constituted court (before which the statement shall be inadmissible). The rule about violence reflects the judicial assertion in *R* v *O'Halloran* [1979] NI 45 at p. 47 that it is difficult for the court to envisage the admission of any statement obtained in circumstances involving any form of physical violence. It is sufficient that the threat is from a third party rather than directly by the police (*R* v *Howell* [1987] 5 NIJB 10). However, the wording of s. 76 does require the intent to cause ill-treatment and violence and with the purpose of inducing a statement (*R* v *McGrath* [1980] NI 91). In addition to the specific exclusions, there is a residual discretion in s. 76(6) for the court to exclude or ignore a statement, or direct a trial to be restarted, where the court considers it appropriate in order to avoid unfairness to the accused or otherwise in the interests of justice. This residual discretion builds upon earlier cases which recognised its existence, though which warned that it should affect the reliability of the statement and should not reassert common law tests of voluntariness: (*R* v *McBrien and Harman* [1984] NI 280; *R* v *Dillon* [1984] NI 292). In total, these grounds for exclusion are significantly narrower than those under arts 74 and 76 of the Police and Criminal Evidence Order (Northern Ireland) 1989 (SI 1989 No. 1341 (NI 12)) (see *R* v *Latimer* [1992] NI 45). In particular, the possibility of exclusion on grounds of oppressive treatment do not apply because the circumstances of the interrogation process in Northern Ireland are arguably intended to be inherently oppressive (see *R* v *Gargan* [1972] May NIJB; *R* v *Flynn and Leonard* [1972] May NIJB; *R* v *McBrien and Harman* [1984] NI 280; Taylor, P., *Beating the Terrorists?* (Penguin, London, 1980); European Committee for the Prevention of Torture, *Report on Conditions in Castlereagh* (Strasbourg: 1995), paras 75, 110). The courts have also held that the offer of an inducement does not necessarily require exclusion (*R* v *Cowan* [1987] NI 338), and that foul language does not constitute degrading treatment (*R* v *Mullan* [1988] 10 NIJB 36). In view of the increased regulation of interrogation processes since the time of the Bennett Report (Report of the Committee of Inquiry into Police Interrogation Procedures in Northern Ireland (Cmnd. 9497, London, 1979)), one would suppose that the time has arrived for 'normalising' these rules on admissibility, and this reform seemed to have been endorsed by the Lloyd Report (Inquiry into Legislation against Terrorism (Cm. 3420, London, 1996), para. 16.22 — subject to the success of the Peace Process), the Government Consultation Paper (Legislation against Terrorism (Cm. 4178, 1998), para. 13.8) and the Northern Ireland Office Diplock Review: Report (p. 9). However, for the purposes of the Terrorism Act 2000, the Government concluded that the change would also stop what it viewed as effective anti-terrorist action (HC Debs. Standing Committee D, col. 273, 3 February 2000, Adam Ingram):

> Prolonged and robust questioning, which is habitual in scheduled offences, might rank as oppression, and it would be difficult for the court to accept evidence obtained in such circumstances. That would be an undesirable end to the process.

Another evidential change is set out in s. 77 of the 2000 Act (previously s. 13 of the Northern Ireland (Emergency Provisions) Act 1996) which applies to a trial on indictment for a scheduled offence where the accused is charged with possessing explosives or firearms contrary to any offence listed in subsection (3). In those circumstances, if it is proved that the article (a) was on any premises at the same time as the accused, or (b) was on premises of which the accused was the occupier or which he habitually used otherwise than as a member of the public, the court may assume that the accused possessed (and, if relevant, knowingly possessed) the article, unless he proves that he did not know of its presence on the premises or that he had no control over it. This switch in proof departs from the previous position (see *R* v *Whelan* [1972] NI 153). The Northern Ireland judges have limited the impact of the special provisions (see Hogan, G., and Walker C., *Political Violence and the Law in Ireland* (Manchester University Press, Manchester, 1989), p. 115). In *R* v *Killen* [1974] NI 220, it was made clear that a conviction should not be sustained unless there is proof beyond reasonable doubt, even though the measure can assist to establish a *prima facie* case. And in *R* v *Lavery* [1976] NI 148, it was suggested that the provision is designed for cases where there almost certainly exists, out of a number of defendants, one who is guilty but not all; if a conviction against any can be sustained, it should not be used against the remainder. Likewise in *R* v *McLernon* [1992] NI 168, a very suspicious set of circumstances justified the invocation of the power. The provision must now be considered in the light of the Human Rights Act 1998. In *R* v *Lambert* [2001] 3 WLR 206, the House of Lords concluded that this type of formula appeared to impose a legal or persuasive burden of proof contrary to Article 6 of the European Convention. However, because of the impact of s. 3 of the Human Rights Act 1998, the courts should interpret it as an evidential burden, meaning that it remains for the prosecution to prove the offence in all respects. The interpretation in *R* v *Killen* in effect already reaches this result — the presumption could be described as discretionary rather than mandatory and plays an evidentiary role, for it is made clear that the ultimate burden in all essential facts is upon the prosecution. Furthermore, this evidential interpretation is imposed by s. 118 of the Terrorism

Act 2000 itself: if evidence is adduced which is sufficient to raise an issue, the court shall treat it as proved unless the prosecution disproves it beyond reasonable doubt. The idea is to make express provision for the burdens placed on the defendant to be seen as evidential rather than persuasive or legal burdens (HL Debs. vol. 613 col. 754, 16 May 2000, Lord Bassam). Lord Lloyd called for the abolition of what is now s. 77, subject to the proven establishment of peace in Northern Ireland (Inquiry into Legislation against Terrorism (Cm. 3420, London, 1996), para. 16.22).

A further vital evidential change is the drawing of adverse inferences from silence under the Criminal Evidence (Northern Ireland) Order 1988 (SI 1988 No.1987). Since this amounts to 'normal' law, applicable to every suspect and accused, even though it was conceived in relation to terrorist cases, it will not be discussed further here (but see Jackson, J.D. 'Curtailing the right to silence' [1991] *Criminal Law Review* 404, 'Inferences from silence' (1993) 44 *Northern Ireland Legal Quarterly* 103; 'Interpreting the silence provisions' [1995] *Criminal Law Review* 587; *R* v *Murray* [1994] 1 WLR 1; *Murray (John)* v *United Kingdom*, App. no. 18731/91, Reports 1996-I, (1996) 22 EHRR 29; *Averill* v *United Kingdom*, App. no. 36408/97, *The Times*, 20 June 2000 and *Magee* v *United Kingdom*, App. no. 28135/95, *The Times*, 20 June 2000; compare *Heaney and McGuinness* v *Ireland*, App. no. 34720/97, Judgment of Court 21 December 2000, finding a violation of art. 6(1) and (2) arising from the application of the Republic of Ireland's Offences against the State Act 1939, s. 52, by which it is an offence to fail to answer questions about movements and actions when detained on suspicion). Likewise, the use of informant evidence is of importance, but, unlike during the period from 1981 to 1985 when trials based on the testimony of 'supergrasses' dominated the criminal justice scene, this type of evidence has receded again to the background and is not often aired in court (see Greer, S., 'Supergrasses and the legal system in Britain and Northern Ireland' (1986) 102 *Law Quarterly Review* 189; Greer, S.C, *Supergrasses* (Clarendon Press, Oxford, 1995)).

As well as a special trial process, some alterations are made to penal provisions by ss. 78 to 80 of the 2000 Act. First, by s. 78 (previously s. 14 of the Northern Ireland (Emergency Provisions) Act 1996), where a child (a person under 17) is convicted on indictment of a scheduled offence (and 68% of scheduled offenders compared to 51% of non-scheduled offenders sentenced by the Crown Court receive custodial punishments: Northern Ireland Office Statistics and Research Branch, *Digest of Information on the Northern Ireland Criminal Justice System* (Belfast, 1998) p. 63), forms of detention can be imposed where the sentence is for five years or more (normally 14 years or more). Secondly, under s. 79 (previously s. 15 of the 1996 Act), the remission granted under prison rules in respect of a sentence of imprisonment passed for a scheduled offence shall not, where it is for a term of five years or more, exceed 33% of the term (instead of the previous 50%, a level introduced in 1976 as compensation for the phasing-out of special category status and the absence of any substantial pre-release parole programme — see Walker, C.P., 'Irish Republic prisoners, political detainees, prisoners of war or common criminals?' (1984) 19 *Irish Jurist* 189). Section 79, which was introduced by the Prevention of Terrorism (Temporary Provisions) Act 1989 at a time of severe violence in Northern Ireland, has in part been overridden by the Northern Ireland (Remission of Sentences) Act 1995. That Act provides for the release on licence of relevant prisoners half way through their sentences. While on licence, such prisoners may be recalled up until the two-thirds point if they are considered likely to commit further offences or if their continued liberty could threaten the safety of the public. After the two-thirds point they may be granted remission. In reality, almost all paramilitary offenders have now been released well before the normal point of remission pursuant to the 'Peace Process' under the terms of the Northern Ireland (Sentences) Act 1998. Next, under s. 80 (previously s. 16 of the 1996 Act), if a person is sentenced to imprisonment or a term of detention in a young offenders centre for a period exceeding one year (other than life imprisonment), is released on remission and is then convicted on indictment of a scheduled offence during the period of remission, the court must order the person's return to prison for the unexpired term of original imprisonment consecutively to any new term of imprisonment for the second offence and it must be served in full (this had some bite before most prisoners were released under the 1998 Act: Review of the Northern Ireland (Emergency Provisions) Act 1991 (Cm. 2706, London, 1995), para. 77).

7.3 SPECIAL POLICING POWERS

The Northern Ireland (Emergency Provisions) Acts, as the successors to the Civil Authorities (Special Powers) (Northern Ireland) Acts 1922–43, contained a startling array of special powers granted to the security forces. These still find a berth in Part VII and overlap with those elsewhere in the Terrorism Act 2000.

The overlap is especially evident in regard to s. 81 of the 2000 Act (previously s. 17 of the Northern Ireland (Emergency Provisions) Act 1996), by which a constable may enter and search any premises if he reasonably suspects that a terrorist, within the meaning of s. 40(1)(b), is to be found there. The constable may use reasonable force under ss. 95 and 114. This adds to the power under s. 42 to search premises for terrorists on the foot of a judicial warrant or powers of entry under the PACE legislation. Section 17 caters for the theoretical gap in that PACE relates to offences and not terrorism (see HC Debs. Standing Committee B col. 162, 30 January 1996, Sir John Wheeler).

Rather more distinct are a number of powers which are worded around the concept of 'scheduled offences' rather than 'terrorist' or 'terrorist investigation'. Thus, by s. 82 of the 2000 Act (based on s. 18 of the Northern Ireland (Emergency Provisions) Act 1996), a constable may arrest without warrant any person if he reasonably suspects that the person is committing, has committed or is about to commit (a) a scheduled offence, or (b) a non-scheduled offence under the Terrorism Act 2000. The power is considered necessary in order to allow for a power of arrest without further condition in respect of such scheduled offences under the Terrorism

Act 2000 as they are not 'arrestable' in PACE terms (see HC Debs. Standing Committee B col. 169, 30 January 1996, Sir John Wheeler). This claim to necessity may be somewhat doubted in the light of the fact there have been no arrests whatsoever under this power between 1991 and 2000 (source: Northern Ireland Office). The constable may also enter and search any premises where the person is or where the constable reasonably suspects him to be and seize and retain relevant evidence. The power to seize and retain materials under subsection (3) attracts additional powers to seize and retain articles for sifting elsewhere enabled under the Criminal Justice and Police Act 2001, s. 50. In the execution of these various powers, the constable may use reasonable force under ss. 95 and 114.

There are also several broader powers. One such is s. 83 of the 2000 Act (previously s. 19 of the 1996 Act), which reflects the history of the conflict in Northern Ireland by recognising the role of soldiers. Normally, soldiers have no special legal powers but are, literally, citizens in uniform. Given their enhanced policing function in Northern Ireland, it has been necessary to enhance their legal status. Therefore, s. 83 allows a member of Her Majesty's forces on duty who reasonably suspects that a person is committing, has committed or is about to commit any offence to (a) arrest the person without warrant, and (b) detain him for a period not exceeding four hours. The breadth of the power is remarkable in that it applies to any offence, even very trivial offences where police officers would also have to show that 'general arrest conditions' also apply under PACE 1984. However, the latitude is afforded in the light of the lack of legal training of soldiers, though it does also raise the possibility of a lack of proportionality and thereby a breach of Article 5 of the European Convention. Equally reflecting a lack of legal training is the further provision in s. 83, by which a soldier making an arrest under this section is deemed to comply with any rule of law requiring him to state the ground of arrest if he states that he is making the arrest as a member of Her Majesty's forces. But the requirements of Article 5(2) of the European Convention are preserved under subsection (6) and therefore must be observed (as explained in *Fox, Campbell and Hartley* v *United Kingdom*, App. nos. 12244, 12245, 12383/86, Ser. A. 182 (1990) 13 EHRR 157, paras 40–42; see Finnie, W., 'Anti-terrorist legislation and the European Convention on Human Rights' (1991) 54 *Modern Law Review* 288). This requirement on the face of it seems to negate effectively the impact of subsection (2), but the *Fox* case did accept that reasons can be inferred from questions put to a suspect, so, in other words, it might still be possible to comply with Article 5(2) without giving a formal recitation of reasons. The House of Lords also accepted in *Murray* v *Ministry of Defence* [1988] 2 All ER 521 (see Walker, C.P., 'Army special powers on parade' (1989) 40 *Northern Ireland Legal Quarterly* 1; *Murray (Margaret)* v *United Kingdom*, App. no. 14310/88, Ser. A. 300A, (1994) 19 EHRR 193) that the reason-giving process can be postponed until the scene is made secure. The powers of entry and search for the purpose of making an arrest under s. 83 are broad and can be exercised not only to arrest a person for any offence but also because it is reasonably suspected that a person is a 'terrorist'. As well as a power of arrest, there is also granted by s. 83(5) a power of seizure of items for a period not exceeding four hours of anything which he reasonably suspects is being, has been or is intended to be used in the commission of an offence under s. 93 or 94 (relating to interference with road closures).

It should be noted that the use of s. 83-type powers has virtually died out since the time that the Peace Process began. A reduction in army visibility is an important part of that process. Thus, between 1990 and 1994, there were 362 arrests; from 1995 to 2000, there were just 49 (source: Northern Ireland Office).

Further broad powers granted to soldiers and police officers are set out in ss. 89 and 90 of the 2000 Act. By s. 89 (previously s. 25 of the 1996 Act), both may exercise a power to stop and question any person. Force may be used under s. 114. The purpose is to ascertain:

(a)   his identity and movements; or
(b)   what he knows about a recent explosion or another recent incident endangering life; or
(c)   what he knows about a person killed or injured in a recent explosion or incident.

The incidental detention may persist 'for so long as is necessary'. It will normally be a matter of minutes, such as at a vehicle check-point, but a detention of one hour 25 minutes was upheld as lawful in *Mooney* v *Ministry of Defence* [1994] 8 BNIL n28. This phrase must be read as subject to reasonable limitations, but an attempt to impose a specific time-limit (such as 15 minutes) failed during the parliamentary debates (HC Debs. Standing Committee D, col. 282, 3 February 2000, Adam Ingram). It is an offence to fail to stop or to refuse to answer a question or to fail to answer to the best of his knowledge and ability (as suggested by the Review of the Northern Ireland (Emergency Provisions) Act 1991 (Cm. 2706, London, 1995), para. 93). The breadth of the power to stop and detain — without any requirement of reasonable suspicion — may fall foul of Article 5 of the European Convention, depending on whether, in any individual case, there was reasonable suspicion and depending on the length of the detention (compare: *McVeigh, O'Neill and Evans* v *United Kingdom*, App. nos. 8022, 8025, 8027/77; DR 18 p. 66 (admissibility), DR 25 p. 15 (final report), (1981) 5 EHRR 71; *Murray (Margaret)* v *United Kingdom*, App. no. 14310/88, Ser. A. 300A, (1995) 19 EHRR 193; *Fox, Campbell and Hartley* v *United Kingdom*, App. nos. 12244, 12245, 12383/86, Ser. A. 182, (1990) 13 EHRR 157). Furthermore, though only punishable by summary conviction (at level 5), the breadth of the possible questioning, the absence of any legal advice and the possible seriousness of the issues involved surely cast doubt on whether the requirements under (b) and (c) can withstand challenge under article 6(2) as a breach of the privilege against self incrimination in the event that evidence from questioning were to be presented in court (see *Murray (John)* v *United Kingdom*, App. no. 18731/91, Reports 1996-I, (1996) 22 EHRR 29; *Quinn* v *Ireland*, Judgment of Court App. no. 36887/97, 21 December 2000).

Section 90 of the 2000 Act (based on s. 26 of the 1996 Act but without the alternative justification of 'authorisation' by the Secretary of State) deals with powers of entry if considered 'necessary in the course of operations for the preservation of the peace or the maintenance of order'. Again, the wording of the power does little to discourage disproportionate intrusions into property and privacy. Though the power has long existed in Northern Ireland and is widely used, the British police have not asked for such a power (HL Debs. vol. 613 col. 732, 16 May 2000, Lord Bach).

The remaining powers deal with more specific problems. Searches for munitions and transmitters by police and soldiers are covered by s. 84 and sch. 10 (previously ss. 20 and 21 of the 1996 Act), though the Terrorism Act 2000 is wider as the definition of 'wireless apparatus' in para. 1 of sch. 10 covers scanning receivers as well as transmitters. Police officers and soldiers may enter premises under para. 2 to carry out searches on a random or routine basis, but dwellings may only be entered on the authorisation of commissioned officers or police inspectors and only where there is reasonable suspicion of the presence of the unlawful munitions or any wireless apparatus. In practice, a team of police and/or soldiers will carry out a search, and authorisation of team members must be explicit, if not precise (*Kirkpatrick* v *Chief Constable of the RUC* [1988] NI 421). Reasonable force may be used under s. 95. Following case-law (see *R* v *Murray* [1994] 1 WLR 1; *Murray (Margaret)* v *United Kingdom*, App. no. 14310/88, Ser. A. 300A, (1995) 19 EHRR 193; *Kirkpatrick* v *Chief Constable of the RUC* [1988] NI 421), sch. 10, para. 4 allows officers to take action for up to four hours (extendable for a further four hours by a police superintendent) to prevent searches from being frustrated. Thus, para. 4 provides that if a member of Her Majesty's forces or constable carrying out a search believes that it is necessary to do so for the purpose of effectively carrying out the search or of preventing the frustration of its object, he may require any person who when the search begins is on, or during the search enters, the premises or other place where the search is carried out to remain in, or in a specified part of, that place, to refrain from entering a specified part of it or to go from one specified part of it to another specified part. He may require any person who is not resident in the place of search to refrain from entering it; and he may use reasonable force to secure compliance with any such requirements. Records must be kept of searches under para. 8, unless it is not reasonably practicable. In practice, records are likely to be made of searches of dwelling-houses and of any damage caused by the search, and the owner is asked to sign these records (see for a description, Walker, C.P., 'Army special powers on parade' (1989) 40 *Northern Ireland Legal Quarterly* 1). As well as searches of premises, there are also powers under para. 6 to stop and search a person for the relevant items. If exercised in a public place, the power may be exercised randomly and routinely; but otherwise the officer must have reasonable suspicion of possession. Failing to comply with requirements or obstruction are offences under paras 10 and 11. By s. 85 (previously s. 22 of the 1996 Act), explosives inspectors may enter and search premises (except dwellings) for unlawfully held explosives and may also stop and search persons in a public place; 'This power is primarily intended for use by those who provide security at court premises, since the powers of an explosives inspector under the Explosives Act 1875 do not extend to public places.' (Home Office, Explanatory Notes to the Terrorism Act 2000, London, 2000, para. 74.) There are no specific penalties for non-compliance, but, no doubt, enforcement can be arranged through liaison with the security forces.

These powers have been used on an enormous scale over the years of the conflict, though the operations have now been scaled back, especially on the part of the army which carried out just 19 such operations in 1999 and 20 in 2000:

Table 7.3: Searches for munitions

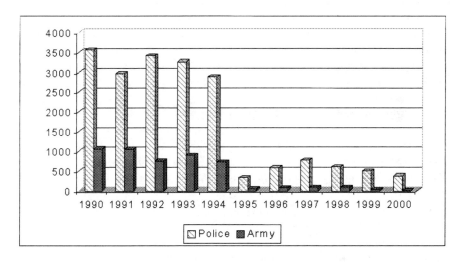

(source: Northern Ireland Office)

A similar set of powers to search premises exists under s. 86 of the 2000 Act (previously s. 23 of the 1996 Act) in relation to a person who, it is reasonably believed, is unlawfully detained in such circumstances that his life is in danger. The requirement of reasonable belief of the detention is a change from 1996, but there is still no requirement for reasonable suspicion in relation to the detained person being located in the premises to be searched — it follows that area searches are still possible under s. 86. The absence of reasonable suspicion and judicial oversight must render the power vulnerable to challenge under Article 8 of the European Convention.

According to s. 87 of the 2000 Act (previously s. 24 of the 1996 Act), a consequence of any search operation under Part VII of the Terrorism Act 2000 may be the examination and removal for further study for up to 48 hours, which can be extended for a further period of up to 48 hours on the authorisation of a police inspector, of any document or record (unless it is an item subject to legal privilege). This controversial power was first granted by s. 22 of the Northern Ireland (Emergency Provisions) Act 1991. A record must be made of such examinations and a copy passed to the holder. Further regulations are set out in

s. 88. There is no requirement of reasonable suspicion or judicial oversight, which may again give rise to challenges under Article 8, though it may be more doubtful that the use in court of seized documentary evidence would be deemed unfair under Article 6 (*Funke* v *France*, App. no. 10828/84, Ser. A. 256-A). Such seizures may provide the evidence which gives rise to charges under s. 58 or 103 of the 2000 Act, and the purposes of seizure under s. 87 must be limited to those offences.

The application of the various special policing powers (both policing powers and the security operation powers set out next) is detailed in s. 95 of the 2000 Act, which includes powers to use reasonable force and an application of the powers to enter premises to vehicles (with an offence in subsection (4) of failing to stop a vehicle). The expression, 'reasonable force' remains undefined, and there is no response in law to the Patten Commission's call for the greater regulation of the use of plastic baton rounds (The Independent Commission on Policing for Northern Ireland, *A New Beginning: Policing in Northern Ireland* (Northern Ireland Office, Belfast, 1999), para. 9.20).

7.4   SECURITY OPERATIONS

Part VII of the Terrorism Act 2000 next contains a number of provisions which range well beyond the scope of what would normally be conceived as policing powers. Their purpose is to allow for security operations, as well as more permanent installations relating to the offensive or defensive capabilities of the security forces. Pursuant to the Peace Process, military and security installations are gradually being dismantled (especially army bases) and many cross-border roads have been reopened.

The most sweeping component is s. 96 of the 2000 Act (previously s. 49 of the Northern Ireland (Emergency Provisions) Act 1996), by which the Secretary of State may by regulations make provision for promoting the preservation of the peace and the maintenance of order. It is a summary offence to fail to comply. The last set of regulations to be issued were the Northern Ireland (Emergency Provisions) Regulations 1991 (SI 1991 No. 1759).

Slightly more precise is s. 91 of the 2000 Act, which allows the Secretary of State, if he considers it necessary for the preservation of the peace or the maintenance of order, to authorise a person to take possession of land or other property or to carry out works on land (or even to destroy property). The previous s. 26 of the 1996 Act gave more discretion to the security forces; s. 91 requires in all cases authority from the Secretary of State on the basis of necessity which may better ensure compliance with rights to private property under Article 1 of Protocol 1 of the European Convention. This power has been used to allow the building of military structures (such as watchtowers) as well as clearing structures which are identified as threatening to military bases and also to provide protection for residents at sectarian interfaces. Given the ongoing Peace Process, there has been more use in recent times of de-requisitioning (115 from 1990–2000) than of requisitioning orders (97):

Table 7.4: Requisition/de-requisition orders

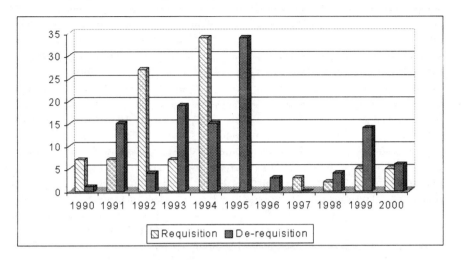

(*source: Northern Ireland Office*)

More specific powers are granted by s. 92 of the 2000 Act (previously s. 26 of the Northern Ireland (Emergency Provisions) Act 1996) to allow for road restrictions, diversions and closures. The diversion or closure may be ordered by any officer for the immediate preservation of the peace or the maintenance of order, but a more permanent direction must be issued by the Secretary of State under s. 94 (previously s. 27 of the 1996 Act). These interventions are undertaken for defensive purposes (both to benefit the security forces and vulnerable communities) or to make movement more detectable, such as around the border with the Republic. In that setting, they have been very controversial, often causing considerable inconvenience for local inhabitants. Some residents, especially in rural communities, have sought physically to remove the obstacles or filling in cratered roads by use of building and farming equipment. An array of offences relating to interferences and the creation of by-passes is therefore set out in ss. 93 and 94 (these began life in the Northern Ireland (Emergency Provisions) Act 1991). Section 93 deals with interferences; it is a defence to show reasonable excuse but s. 118 does not apply. Section 94(3) forbids the execution of by-passes and even the possession of construction equipment within 200 metres of road closure works, unless under subsection (4) there is reasonable excuse (again, s. 118 does not apply).

Compensation is provided whenever (a) real or personal property is taken, occupied, destroyed or damaged, or (b) any other act is done which interferes with private rights of property under the terms of s. 102 and sch. 12 of the 2000 Act (previously, ss. 55 and 56 of the Northern Ireland (Emergency Provisions) Act 1996 — see Hogan, G., and Walker C., *Political Violence and the Law in Ireland*

(Manchester University Press, Manchester, 1989), pp. 71–73). The nature of 'private rights' has been explained in *R (McCreesh) v County Court Judge of Armagh* [1978] NI 164 and in *R (Secretary of State for Northern Ireland) v County Court Judge for Armagh* [1981] NI 19. The cases demonstrate that special loss (such as to business profits) arising from interference with a public right (such as a road closure) is not recoverable. Under sch. 12, para. 3, claims must be brought within 28 days (previously four months), and they are determined at the first instance by the Secretary of State (para. 4), with an appeal as to refusal to pay or the amount of payment to the county court (para. 5). Compensation may be refused or reduced where false statements are made or there is not full disclosure (para. 6 — these actions may also be offences under para. 12). In addition, compensation may be refused on public policy grounds under para. 9 in respect of an act done in connection with, or revealed evidence of the commission of, a scheduled offence or a non-scheduled offence under the Terrorism Act 2000 for which the claimant is convicted. It is arguable that the width of this disqualification is not proportionate to the needs of public policy under Article 1 of Protocol 1 of the European Convention. For example, why should a person convicted of an offence of attempting to create a by-pass contrary to s. 94(3) be refused compensation for land occupied as a result of the road blocks? Is not the fine for the offence sufficient?

Payments under sch. 12 of the 2000 Act and its predecessors have been substantial:

Table 7.5: Compensation payments

(*source: Northern Ireland Office*)

7.5 CONTROLS OVER SPECIAL POWERS

In accordance with the trend firmly set by the PACE legislation, the various security powers are subjected to regulation by codes of practice (these have been in existence since the issuance by the Northern Ireland Office of the Guide to the Emergency Powers in 1990 which was superseded by codes issued in 1994 and 1996 (SI 1993 No. 2788, SI 1996 No. 1698) under s. 61 of the Northern Ireland (Emergency Provisions) Act 1991). The procedures for their making are in s. 101 of the 2000 Act. They are introduced by s. 99, by which the Secretary of State may make codes of practice in connection with any power exercised by police officers or by members of Her Majesty's forces (the hesitant 'may' was inserted while the Government considered the sufficiency of codes under the Police and Criminal Evidence Order — HC Debs. Standing Committee D, col. 284, 3 February 2000, Adam Ingram). A more specific power, in relation to requiring the silent video recording of interviews and the issuance of a code of practice about it, is allowed by s. 100 (previously s. 53 of the Northern Ireland (Emergency Provisions) Act 1996 and following the recommendation of the Review of the Northern Ireland (Emergency Provisions) Acts 1978 and 1987 (Cm. 1115, London, 1990), para. 4.5; the Patten Report (Patten Commission (The Independent Commission on Policing for Northern Ireland, *A New Beginning: Policing in Northern Ireland* (Northern Ireland Office, Belfast, 1999), para. 8.16) equally endorsed the advantages of video recording). According to s. 101, the status of codes under ss. 99 and 100 is the same as in the PACE legislation: a failure to comply with a provision of a code shall not of itself make the officer liable to criminal or civil proceedings, but it shall be admissible in evidence and shall be taken into account.

Pursuant to s. 99 of the 2000 Act (previously s. 52 of the Northern Ireland (Emergency Provisions) Act 1996), the Terrorism Act 2000 (Code of Practice on the Exercise of Police Powers) (Northern Ireland) Order 2001 (SI 2001 No. 401) brings into force a code covering the exercise by police officers of the powers of detention and identification (replacing the code made under s. 61 of the Northern Ireland (Emergency Provisions) Act 1991).

Pursuant to s. 100 of the 2000 Act, no code has been issued. However, codes have been issued under paras 3 and 4 of sch. 8 and not s. 100 (see Chapter 5). The Terrorism Act 2000 (Video Recording of Interviews) Order 2000 (SI 2000 No. 3179) provides for interviews only in Northern Ireland to be recorded by video, and the Terrorism Act 2000 (Code of Practice on Video Recording of Interviews) (Northern Ireland) Order 2001 (SI 2001 No. 402) allows for a code of practice in connection with the video recording with sound of any interview. Video recording commenced in Northern Ireland in February 2001 (see Chapter 5).

Finally, in addition to s. 87, s. 104 of the 2000 Act requires the Chief Constable of the Royal Ulster Constabulary to make arrangements for securing that a record is made of each exercise by a constable of a power under Part VII. This is a new safeguard which follows a recommendation of the Patten Commission (The Independent Commission on Policing for Northern Ireland, *A New Beginning:*

Policing in Northern Ireland (Northern Ireland Office, Belfast 1999), para. 8.14), but it is subject to the large proviso that it must be reasonably practicable to implement in the circumstances.

7.6 INDEPENDENT ASSESSOR OF MILITARY COMPLAINTS

Broadening the theme of controls over special powers, the office of Independent Assessor of Military Complaints Procedures in Northern Ireland was instituted on a non-statutory basis following Viscount Colville's report in 1990 (Review of the Northern Ireland (Emergency Provisions) Acts 1978 and 1987 (Cm. 1115, London, 1990), ch. 5) and was first recognised in statute in the Northern Ireland (Emergency Provisions) Act 1991, s. 60 (later the Northern Ireland (Emergency Provisions) Act 1996, s. 51 and sch. 4). The first annual report appeared in 1993 (1993–94 HC 369). While the Secretary of State has a power (rather than a duty) to appoint an Assessor, 'the Government has said that the position will remain while the army is needed to act in support of the police in Northern Ireland.' (Home Office, Explanatory Notes to the Terrorism Act 2000, London, 2000, para. 84.) The post is now set out under s. 98 of the Terrorism Act 2000, which requires the office-holder to 'keep under review the procedures adopted by the General Officer Commanding Northern Ireland for receiving, investigating and responding to complaints'. It will be noted that the Assessor may not receive or investigate complaints, but stands one step back and audits the process. The closest to direct intervention is that the Assessor may require the General Officer Commanding to review a particular case. Further details of the system are set out in sch. 11.

Accountability and openness are important aspects of constitutional governance. It follows that the Assessor has performed an important task and has certainly improved the processes by which the army investigates complaints against itself. However, the impact is limited to the system and so cannot match the impact which an Ombudsman-type model can have (compare the Police (Northern Ireland) Act 2000, Part VIII). In addition, the task has thankfully declined in importance given the current absence of military patrolling and policing in Northern Ireland. By contrast, an arguably more important and prominent form of inspection has been undertaken since 1993 by the Independent Commissioner for the Holding Centres (see Walker, C., and Fitzpatrick, B., 'The Independent Commissioner for the Holding Centres: a review' [1998] *Public Law* 106; Walker, C., and Fitzpatrick, B., 'Holding Centres in Northern Ireland, the Independent Commissioner and the rights of detainees' [1999] *European Human Rights Law Review* 27). The office (which was filled by Sir Louis Blom Cooper until 2000 and is now held by Dr Bill Norris), has had an important influence, and it is disappointing his office is not even mentioned in the Act. This office, which was redesignated as the Independent Commissioner for Detained Terrorist Suspects in 2001, should become the inspector of Terrorism Act detainees and cover detention facilities throughout the United Kingdom. In addition, there should be a legislative grant of formal powers, and Parliament should forge relations with the Commissioner through its select committee system.

The Patten Report (*A New Beginning: Policing in Northern Ireland* (Northern Ireland Office, Belfast, 1999), para. 8.16) argued that, assuming the end of the Holding Centres, the role of the Commissioner should cease and that the office should be replaced by lay visitors. Though lay visitors should not be precluded from terrorist cases, the Commissioner does have significant advantages in terms of frequency of coverage and expertise in a specialist regime of policing.

7.7 SPECIAL OFFENCES

As noted in Chapter 6, there is an offence of collecting or recording or possessing information of a kind likely to be useful to a person committing or preparing an act of terrorism set out in s. 58 of the Terrorism Act 2000. This is augmented for Northern Ireland by s. 103 (previously s. 33 of the Northern Ireland (Emergency Provisions) Act 1996) which relates to the protection of specified security force personnel and other public officials. For example, the possession of army manuals was the basis for conviction in *R v Lorenc* [1988] NI 96 and planning and training materials in *Re Kerr's Application* [1997] NI 225.

Though the penalties are the same, s. 103 is wider than s. 58 in several respects. The *actus reus* includes publishing, communicated or attempting to elicit as well as collecting or recording. As with s. 58, the main controversy concerns the equivocal nature of the actions involved and the fact that it is left to the defendant to prove as a defence, under subsection (5), that he had a reasonable excuse for his action or possession. In *R v McLaughlin* [1993] NI 28, a radio enthusiast was able to show reasonable excuse for possessing a list of RUC radio frequencies. There is the further presumption in subsection (4) that if it is proved a document or record (a) was on any premises at the same time as the accused, or (b) was on premises of which the accused was the occupier or which he habitually used otherwise than as a member of the public, the court may assume that the accused possessed the document or record, unless he proves that he did not know of its presence on the premises or that he had no control over it. By s. 118, which applies to both subsection (4) and (5), if evidence is adduced which is sufficient to raise an issue, the court shall treat it as proved unless the prosecution disproves it beyond reasonable doubt. Materials may be forfeited on conviction, but third parties interested in the property must first be heard (s. 103(8) — a new provision which was not in the Northern Ireland (Emergency Provisions) Act 1996).

Section 35 of the Northern Ireland (Emergency Provisions) Act 1996 made it an offence in Northern Ireland to wear a hood in public places. This offence is not replicated in the 2000 Act. The issue of face coverings is dealt with under powers described in Chapter 5, and further measures were said to be not needed according to the police (HC Standing Committee D, col. 48, 20 January 2000, Adam Ingram).

7.8 PRIVATE SECURITY SERVICE

Fund-raising activities of paramilitary groups in Northern Ireland have included the provision of private security services, sometimes amounting to little more than extortion, sometimes on a more subtle basis. To ensure that terrorist-connected firms or individuals could be filtered out of the industry, and long before the Private Security Industry Act 2001 was conceived, the Northern Ireland (Emergency Provisions) Act 1987 required providers of private security services to be licensed by the Northern Ireland Office. The process of licensing could then be used to check backgrounds and standards. These measures (latterly in ss. 37 to 44 of the Northern Ireland (Emergency Provisions) Act 1996) are continued in place by s. 106 and sch. 13 of the Terrorism Act 2000, despite the government commitment to translate them into normal laws (Home Office and Northern Ireland Office, Legislation against Terrorism (Cm. 4178, London, 1998), para. 13.16).

By sch. 13, para. 1 of the 2000 Act, 'security services' means the services of one or more individuals as security guards (whether or not provided together with other services relating to the protection of property or persons). This formula allows a much broader sweep than the Private Security Industry Act 2001 which will proceed by way of the designation of specified activities. To enforce the regulatory system, it is an offence to provide or offer (para. 2) or to advertise (para. 3) unlicensed services or to pay for them (para. 4). There is a defence under paras 3 and 4 to the effect that the person reasonably believed the other party was in fact licensed (s. 118 does not apply). The Northern Ireland Office remains the licensing authority (para. 6), and licenses will be denied to those representing a proscribed organisation or even if 'closely associated' with a proscribed organisation (para. 7). New powers are given under para. 7 to impose conditions on granting a licence in order to ensure that a defined organisation does not benefit from the business. Individual security guards must also be notified to the Northern Ireland Office, as well as other change of personnel within the service (paras 13, 14). An appeal against refusal, conditions imposed or revocation may be made to the High Court (para. 10), a new mechanism not available under the Northern Ireland (Emergency Provisions) Act 1996 and which reflects concerns about the impact of the European Convention, Article 6 and Article 1 of Protocol 1 (see Home Office, Circular 03/01: Terrorism Act 2000 (Home Office, London, 2001), para. 22.10). However, where the Secretary of State issues a certificate under para. 11 that the refusal of a licence relates to paramilitary connections (and so is likely to involve sensitive information), the appeal will instead be heard by the Tribunal under s. 91 of the Northern Ireland Act 1998. Licenses are normally valid for one year at a time (para. 8), and the police may carry out inspections to check records (para. 16).

Between 1990 and 2000, 2,674 certificates have been issued or renewed, with just 23 being refused, cancelled or revoked (source: Northern Ireland Office).

The private security is by no means the only source of paramilitary funding in Northern Ireland. Similar concerns about Mafia-type extortion have been expressed about other sectors (see especially Northern Ireland Office, Terrorist Exploitation of the Construction Industry in Northern Ireland (Belfast, 1993)), but in so far as specific counter-measures have been taken, they have been outside the terrorism legislation and no similar licensing requirement has been imposed. Furthermore,

Lord Lloyd called for the abolition of what is now s. 106 of the 2000 Act, subject to the proven establishment of peace in Northern Ireland (Inquiry into Legislation against Terrorism (Cm. 3420, London, 1996), para. 16.27).

7.9   SPECIFIED ORGANISATIONS

The Criminal Justice (Terrorism and Conspiracy) Act 1998 was passed primarily as a reaction to the challenge to the 'Peace Process' as represented by the Real IRA, the Republican dissident group responsible for the Omagh bombing on 15 August, 1998, when a large car-bomb exploded in the centre of the town, killing 28 persons and injuring at least 220 (see further Walker, C.P., 'The bombs in Omagh and their aftermath: the Criminal Justice (Terrorism and Conspiracy Act 1998)' (1999) 62 *Modern Law Review* 879; Campbell, C., 'Two steps backwards' [1999] *Criminal Law Review* 941; Kent, K., 'Basic rights and anti-terrorism legislation' (2000) 33 *Vanderbilt Journal of Transnational Law* 221). The overall impact of the 1998 legislation was officially admitted, and indeed intended, to be 'Draconian' (repeating the epithet used by the Home Secretary, Roy Jenkins, when introducing the original Prevention of Terrorism legislation in 1974 (HC Debs. vol. 882 col. 35, 25 November 1974)). (The word was first used by the Irish Taoiseach, Bertie Ahern (*The Times*, 20 August 1998, p. 1) and was then repeated by Prime Minister Tony Blair on a visit to Omagh (*The Daily Telegraph*, 26 August 1998, p. 1)). Echoing the legislative history of the 1974 Act and also the more recent Prevention of Terrorism (Additional Powers) Act 1996, the legislative process leading to the 1998 Act entailed not only parliamentary passage within a remarkably short space of time (two days) but also the extraordinary recall of both Houses of Parliament during the summer recess. There was also corresponding legislation in the Republic of Ireland in the form of the Offences against the State (Amendment) Act 1998 (No. 39).

The measures duly enacted in ss. 1, 2 and 4 of the 1998 Act affected suspected and proven offences of membership of proscribed organisations, but a distinction had to be made between those proscribed organisations which were seen as abiding for the most part by the Peace Process and were observing a ceasefire (including the Provisional IRA) and those, like the Real IRA which were evidently prepared to use violence. A further list, of 'specified' organisations, had already been devised under the Northern Ireland (Sentences) Act 1998, dealing with the early release of paramilitary prisoners, in order to signal which proscribed organisations are viewed as not being committed to the current or future use of exclusively democratic and peaceful means and to co-operation with the official arms decommissioning process (under the Northern Ireland Arms Decommissioning Act 1997). More precisely, s. 3(8) of the 1998 Act cited two grounds for the specification of an organisation: that it is concerned in terrorism and that it has failed to establish or maintain an unequivocal ceasefire. Evidence for the latter includes the organisation's commitment to democratic and peaceful means, in-volvement in acts of violence or preparations for them (including punishment beatings) and the degree of cooperation with the decommissioning body (HC Debs. vol. 313 col. 1084, 10 June 1998, Marjorie Mowlam). Those 'specified organisations' were at the time of enactment of the 1998 Act — the Continuity IRA, the INLA, the LVF and the 'Real' IRA (Northern Ireland (Sentences) Act 1998 (Specified Organisations) Order 1998 (SI 1998 No. 1882)). The LVF declared a cease-fire in May 1998 (and even handed in some weapons in December 1998) and so was removed from the original list by the Northern Ireland (Sentences) Act (Specified Organisations) (No. 2) Order 1998 (SI 1998 No. 2869), which came into force in November 1998. A further Order, made in March 1999 (SI 1999 No. 1152), removed from the list the INLA, which has been observing a cease-fire since 22 August 1998, but at the same time added two Loyalist groups, the Orange Volunteers and the Red Hand Defenders. The Ulster Defence Association, Ulster Freedom Fighters and Loyalist Volunteer Force were specified in October 2001 (SI 2001 No. 3411). It is solely membership of these various specified organisations which was affected by the 1998 Act. The concentration upon 'specified' organisations does not mean that the law entirely distinguishes 'good' from 'bad' terrorists (HC Debs. vol. 317 col. 885, 2 September 1998, William Ross), since groups such as the IRA remain proscribed and otherwise criminalised. However, there are now arguably 'bad but redeemable' terrorists as opposed to 'bad and damnable terrorists'.

For the purposes of the 1998 Act, the provisions concerning specified organisations applied equally both in Great Britain and Northern Ireland. However, under the Terrorism Act 2000, these extra measures apply solely in Northern Ireland. The definition of a 'specified organisation' is dealt with by s. 107, which simply continues to rely on listing for the purposes of s. 3(8) of the Northern Ireland (Sentences) Act 1998 (subject to the group also being a proscribed organisation for the purposes of the Terrorism Act 2000). The organisations currently specified for the purposes of s. 107 are confined to the Continuity IRA, the Loyalist Volunteer Force, the Orange Volunteers, the Real IRA, the Red Hand Defenders, the Ulster Defence Association, and the Ulster Freedom Fighters. Despite all the detail which follows, no charges have ever been brought which rely on these provisions (HC Debs. Standing Committee D, col. 291, 3 February 2000, Adam Ingram).

In *Re Williamson's Application for Judicial Review* [2000] NI 281, the applicant sought review of the decision in August 1999 under the Northern Ireland (Sentences) Act 1998, s. 3 by the Northern Ireland Secretary of State not to 'specify' the Provisional IRA as being connected with, or promoting or encouraging, terrorism and not maintaining a complete and unequivocal ceasefire. The Northern Ireland Court of Appeal interpreted s. 3 as requiring the exercise of a subjective judgment — a belief was sufficient without necessarily reasonable grounds to believe. As related in Chapter 2, the Court rejected the application.

7.9.1 Evidential changes

Section 108 of the Terrorism Act 2000 (formerly ss. 1 and 2 of the Criminal Justice (Terrorism and Conspiracy) Act 1998) concerns the admissibility of police opinions and inferences to be drawn from the silence of the accused in prosecutions concerning membership of specified organisations. It is declared in s. 113(6) that these measures do not apply to statements made or failures to mention facts which occur before the date of Royal Assent of the 1998 Act (4 September 1998). It would be contrary to notions of fairness (under Article 6 of the European Convention) to apply retrospective significance to forms of evidence which did not legally warrant any kind of defence challenge when originally made. However, the special measures can apply to statements or failures after Assent in connection with events (such as the Omagh bombing) before the Assent date (compare *Quinn* v *United Kingdom*, App. no. 23496/94, declared admissible in part 21 October 1996, decision of Commission 11 March 1997).

The first strategy adopted by this part of the 2000 Act is to admit into evidence the opinion of a senior police officer for the purposes of convicting someone of being a member of a specified organisation. The effect is to turn the police officer into an expert witness who becomes entitled to give opinions based on experience and judgement rather than being confined to the testimony of first-hand facts. No doubt, the officer would claim that the proffered opinions are based on firm evidence, but it is likely to be a much wider range of sources than first-hand evidence, including hearsay evidence (such as evidence gathered from a range of other officers or security agencies), inadmissible evidence (such as prior convictions and evidence from telephone tapping normally excluded under the Regulation of Investigatory Powers Act 2000, s. 17) and sensitive evidence (such as from other forms of electronic surveillance or from agents or informants).

In pursuance of this strategy, s. 108 provides that where a person is charged with the offence under s. 11 (belonging or professing to belong to a proscribed organisation), an oral statement of a police officer of, or above, the rank of superintendent that in his opinion the accused belongs to a proscribed organisation which is specified, or belonged at a particular time to an organisation which was then specified, the statement shall be admissible as evidence of the matter stated. But a person cannot be committed for trial, found to have a case to answer or convicted solely on the basis of the police officer's statement (s. 108(3)(b)). The police officer will normally be from the RUC, but British and Scottish police can also make use of the strategy (s. 108(4)) when conducting inquiries within the jurisdiction of Northern Ireland and in connection with prosecutions being brought in Northern Ireland. It will be noted that the only offence covered is one of 'belonging or professing to belong' contrary to s. 11; other offences under ss. 12 and 13 (such as soliciting or arranging or addressing support meetings) are not affected, and the Government was resistant to such extensions as it is proof of membership *simpliciter* where evidence is currently absent (HL Debs. vol. 593 col. 98, 3 September 1998, Lord Williams). The impact of this form of evidence will be highly problematic for three reasons.

First, the evidential weight of a statement of opinion which is not backed by the reasoning or sources which support it must be very slight indeed. Just as the courts would pay little attention to the evidence of a forensic scientist who said that he

believed a sample taken from under the defendant's fingernails had tested
positively for Semtex, but he could not explain what tests had been carried out or
why that conclusion was derived from them, so the courts should not be impressed
by a raw statement of police opinion. According to Lord Lloyd, 'it will carry no
weight whatever' (HL Debs. vol. 593 col. 37, 3 September 1998), and one might
suggest that for a court in Northern Ireland especially to act otherwise would be
highly contentious, given the negative perceptions of Royal Ulster Constabulary
credibility in nationalist communities. This remained the view of Lord Lloyd
during the debates on the Terrorism Bill (HL Debs. vol. 613 col. 1080, 16 May
2000):

> . . . no judge in Northern Ireland . . . would take account of the opinion of a
> police office, however senior, as to whether an accused was a member of
> a specified organisation unless he could back up that opinion with some
> evidence. Without evidence it is mere opinion, and mere opinion is worthless in
> a court of law except when it is given on expert grounds; and on this a police
> officer is not an expert. The only evidence which a police officer could use to
> back up his opinion of the membership of an accused of a specified organisation
> would almost certainly be the evidence of an informer or other evidence from
> some secret source which could not be given in court. Therefore there could be
> no effective, meaningful cross-examination of the police officer on the opinion
> he had expressed.

Secondly, such weight as the opinion might be able to muster can be easily
negatived. Thus, it was found in relation to the Offences against the State
(Amendment) Act 1972, s. 3, that once Republican suspects began to contest police
claims of membership (which they did after 1975), the courts would not convict
on this basis — the opinion remained admissible but carried little evidential weight
unless the evidence behind it could be tested in court (Hogan, G., and Walker C.,
Political Violence and the Law in Ireland (Manchester University Press, Manchester, 1989) ch. 11). So, as the Lord Advocate admitted during debates on the 1998
Act, 'any criminal worth his salt will realise that the way round [s. 108] is to deny
that he is a member of the organisation' (HL Debs. vol. 593 col. 105, 3 September
1998, Lord Hardie). There is then no silence from which to draw any inference.
To demand more from the suspect — that he positively helps the prosecution case
in some way — would surely breach the presumption of innocence protected by
Article 6(2) of the European Convention.

Thirdly, if the statement is to be admitted in evidence, then it is potentially open
to cross-examination. If the evidence behind the opinion is based on the statement
or conduct of the accused, then a trial judge might readily conclude that such
evidence ought to be heard at trial. But, more likely, there will arise problems of
disclosure by the police, who may well wish to claim public interest immunity to
protect their sensitive sources and investigative techniques which have also been
used to justify the statement. However, if the claim to Public Interest Immunity is

sustainable, then the trial judge (or indeed the prosecutor) may well conclude that it will not be fair to allow the trial to proceed. If the trial is allowed to continue, then there could be a breach of Article 6(1) of the European Convention in that a significant part of the prosecution evidence is not being heard and tested in open court (compare *Edwards v United Kingdom*, App. no. 13071/87, Ser. A. 247-B, (1992) 15 EHRR 417; *Rowe and Davis v United Kingdom*, App. no. 28901/95, *The Times*, 1 March 2000 and see Court of Appeal at *The Times*, 20 July 2000). Alternatively, if the statement is admitted and allowed to carry weight, then the limits on effective cross-examination would breach Article 6(3)(d) of the European Convention ((Rowe) Report of the Operation in 1998 of the Prevention of Terrorism (Temporary Provisions) Acts (Home Office, 1999), para. 18).

The second strategy, in s. 109 of the 2000 Act (formerly in ss. 1 and 2 of the Criminal Justice (Terrorism and Conspiracy) Act 1998), is to allow an inference of guilt to be drawn from the refusal to mention any material facts to a police officer whether before or after charge under s. 11. This provision builds upon, and is expressly additional to, other changes to 'the right to silence' in recent years (see Walker, C., and Starmer, K., *Miscarriages of Justice* (Blackstone Press, London, 1999), ch. 5). These changes include the Criminal Evidence (Northern Ireland) Order 1988 (SI 1988 No. 1987), which allows the courts to draw whatever inferences would be proper from the fact that an accused person remained silent in four different specified situations: during police questioning (art. 3), at trial (art. 4), concerning substances or marks on his clothing (art. 5), and concerning presence at a particular place (art. 6). The 'right of silence' was also modified along very similar lines for England and Wales by the Criminal Justice and Public Order Act 1994. It permits inferences to be drawn in certain circumstances from an accused person's failure to mention facts when questioned or charged (s. 34), silence at trial (s. 35), a failure or refusal to account for particular objects, substances or marks (s. 36), or a failure or refusal to account for physical presence at a particular place (s. 37).

In comparison to the foregoing, s. 109 is both wider and narrower. It is wider in the sense that it allows an inference of guilt not only to be drawn from a failure to mention something that is later relied upon in defence, but also it allows an inference of guilt to be drawn from any failure 'to mention a fact which is material to the offence and which he could reasonably be expected to mention'. Thus, the fact of silence becomes admissible whether a defence is raised or not. But s. 109 is narrower in that only the first three of the four situations covered by the 1988 Order and the 1994 Act appear here. The omission of any provision about silence at trial presumably arises because of concern that the judiciary would be hostile (as they had been in relation to the previous legislation). A further condition is that the detainee must have been permitted to consult a solicitor (s. 109(2)(b)). This requirement is an express acknowledgement of the judgment of the European Court of Human Rights in the case of *Murray (John) v United Kingdom*, App. no. 18731/91, Reports 1996-I, (1996) 22 EHRR 29, where the drawing of inferences under the 1988 Order breached Article 6 of the European Convention in circumstances where access to a solicitor had been refused. However, there is no requirement, either in that judgment or in the Act that the questioning takes place in the presence of the solicitor.

The presentation as evidence of silence is a matter for the discretion of the trial judge. It is provided that, subject to any directions by the court in a specific case, evidence tending to establish a failure to mention material facts can be adduced before or after evidence tending to establish the fact which the accused is alleged to have failed to mention (s. 109(5)). Any inference may be subject to other arguments as to inadmissibility (such as under PACE 1984, s. 78) — s. 110(1)(a).

An accused person cannot be committed for trial, or found to have a case to answer, or convicted, solely on the basis of the inferences drawn from his failure to mention material facts (s. 109(4)(b)). This replicates the limitation in regard to evidence arising from the oral statement from a police superintendent under s. 108. But there is nothing to stop both ss. 108 and 109 acting in tandem (that is, a police statement and any inferences from silence) being capable of leading to a committal for trial, a finding that a person has a case to answer, or a conviction. This combination may be viewed as 'a case of nought plus nought equalling one' (HL Debs. vol. 593 col. 77, 3 September 1998, Lord Donaldson), but that indeed is 'the fundamental thrust of the legislation' (HC Debs. vol. 317 col. 881, 2 September 1998, Adam Ingram). In addition, it is expressly permissible to use as further evidence inferences from silence under the 1988 Order or the 1994 Act (s. 110(1)(b)), though these relate only to the weight of a defence. However, it is more doubtful whether the two sufficient pieces of evidence could be derived from two opinions from two separate police officers. It is probably implicit in s. 108 that only one police officer can give evidence in this way in a given case.

Since the 1998 Act differed from previous instances in law of inferences from silence, it required a new form of police caution to be devised. This was issued in each relevant jurisdiction. For example, a letter from the Security Policy and Operations Division, Northern Ireland Office to Chief Officers of Police makes clear that there should be a 'special warning' immediately following the standard caution:

> . . . telling the suspect in ordinary language:
> - that he is being investigated for belonging or professing to belong to a [specified] proscribed organisation . . .
> - that this organisation is also a specified organisation . . .
> - that a court may draw an inference if he fails to mention any fact which is material to this offence (after he has been permitted to consult a solicitor before being questioned); and
> - that a record is being made of the interview and that it may be given in evidence if he is brought to trial.

These matters are unfortunately omitted from the Code of Practice on the Exercise of Police Powers issued under s. 99 (Terrorism Act 2000 (Code of Practice on the Exercise of Police Powers) (Northern Ireland) Order 2001 (SI 2001 No.401)).

The prime concern is that these various changes, either singly or cumulatively, subvert the delivery of criminal justice, especially of an adversarial type. Even the seminal Report of the Commission to consider legal procedures to deal with terrorist activities in Northern Ireland (the 'Diplock Report' (Cmnd. 5185, London, 1972), para. 22) had rejected the idea of admitting police opinions as too much in conflict with the concept of a 'regular' criminal trial. In particular, there is concern that the legislation contravene rights to fairness and the presumption of innocence under Article 6 of the European Convention (see *Saunders* v *United Kingdom*, App. no. 19187/91, Reports 1996-VI, (1997) 23 EHRR 313). Some would say that internment without trial would be a more honest strategy (Hogan, G., 'Internment preferable to laws that fail tests', *The Irish Times*, 19 August 1998), though it is doubtful whether a derogation notice could be sustained in the uneasy non-conflict situation of Northern Ireland. A further concern is that, while reflecting almost universal determination and support, ss. 108 and 109 of the 2000 Act appear to have little prospect of success in terms of convictions and have in any event not been used (see (Rowe) Report on the Operation in 1998 of the Northern Ireland (Emergency Provisions) Acts (Northern Ireland Office, 1999), paras 61, 64).

The Home Office Consultation Paper of 1998 also considered a range of further changes to the laws of evidence — including the admissibility of accomplice statements as evidence against a co-accused, the automatic admissibility of previous convictions for 'terrorist' offences and changing the burden of proof in possession cases to a civil standard or making proof of possession conclusive and not just prima facie evidence (Home Office and Northern Ireland Office, Legislation against Terrorism (Cm. 4178, London, 1998), para. 14.3). The Government was dubious about most of these suggestions, and it also rejected, mainly on European Convention grounds, the further suggestion that there be an offence of refusing to answer questions after an arrest on suspicion of involvement in terrorism. This proposal is contrasted with the adverse inferences from silence currently permitted by the 1998 Act, the clear inference being that the Government considers the 1998 Act compatible with the European Convention, practically desirable and indeed uncontroversial.

7.9.2 Confiscation of assets

The effect of s. 111 of the Terrorism Act 2000 (formerly s. 4 of the Criminal Justice (Terrorism and Conspiracy) Act 1998) is to apply some of the forfeiture penalties under Part III of the 2000 Act (including all of the powers and processes in sch. 4) to persons convicted of membership and other offences under ss. 11 and 12 provided that at the time of their offences they belonged to organisations which are 'specified organisations'. By s. 111(2), the money or property may be forfeited if the convicted person had it in his possession or under his control at the time of the offence and it has been used in furtherance of or in connection with the activities of the specified organisation, or the court believes it may be so used unless forfeited. In this way, and contrary to the recommendations of the Lloyd Report

(Inquiry into Legislation against Terrorism, para. 13.24), the Act concentrates on the usage rather than the origins of the money or property. In line with a number of provisions in other statutes concerning the confiscation and forfeiture of the proceeds of crime (such as the Criminal Justice Act 1988, s. 71(7A) and the Drug Trafficking Act 1994, s. 2(8)), the standard of proof required to determine whether the convicted person belonged to the specified organisation, whether he had it under his possession or control at the time of his offence and whether it had been used in connection with the activities of the specified organisation is to be that applicable in civil proceedings (s. 111(4)). If a person other than the convicted person claims to be the owner or to be otherwise interested in anything which is liable to forfeiture under this provision, it is intended that he or she should be given an opportunity to be heard (s. 111(3)). Restrictions on retrospective effect of forfeiture provisions apply under the European Convention, Article 7 (*Welch* v *United Kingdom*, App. no. 17440/90, Ser. A. 307-A, (1995) 20 EHRR 247).

7.9.3   Comment

Much of the Criminal Justice (Terrorism and Conspiracy) Act 1998 is in reality a dead-letter. But as it is the recent progeny of the Government also sponsoring the Terrorism Act 2000, it is perhaps too soon to admit that parliamentary time had been wasted. May be a lesson was learnt by September 2001 — that a rush to legislation does not always produce helpful answers. One should harbour the desire that Part VII as a whole will also fade away, but much more active steps will have to be taken in order to restore confidence in the criminal justice system than are currently evident. The Northern Ireland Office has managed a major Criminal Justice Review (Criminal Justice Review Group, Review of the Criminal Justice System in Northern Ireland, http://www.nio.gov.uk/pdf/mainreport.pdf, 2000), which should have a confidence-building impact once the implementation plan is actioned (see http://www.nio.gov.uk/issues/justice.htm). At that point at the latest, there must be a much fuller and more determined effort to phase out special criminal process than the meagre Diplock Review: Report (Belfast, 2000).

Chapter Eight
Immigration and asylum

8.1 INTRODUCTION

Part IV of the Anti-terrorism, Crime and Security Act 2001 contains measures concerned with the interface of immigration and asylum procedures and the public interest in security and the prevention of terrorism (for the general position in regard to asylum, see Home Affairs Committee, Border Controls 2000–01 HC 163, 375; Home Office, *Secure Borders, Save Havens* (Cm. 5387, London, 2002), ch. 4). There are three responses. The first is to extend powers to detain foreign nationals who are suspected international terrorists (ss. 21 to 33). The second blocks the consideration of the substance of an asylum claim made by certain people whose removal from the United Kingdom has already been deemed to be conducive to the public good (ss. 34 and 35). Without any hint of conceit, the Explanatory Notes which refer to the Anti-Terrorism, Crime And Security Bill as brought from the House of Commons on 26 November 2001 (HL Bill 29, para. 71) state that these measures 'are fairly narrow in their focus'. That is a fair description in so far as a very limited range of persons is affected. But the implications of enactment are far reaching. The result is the reintroduction of a form of detention without trial which has necessitated a further derogation from the European Convention under Article 15. The third measure allows the Secretary of State to retain fingerprints taken in asylum and certain immigration cases which were previously destroyed within a specified time.

8.2 DETENTION OF SUSPECTED INTERNATIONAL TERRORISTS

8.2.1 Background

As described more fully in Chapter 1, the power of internment without trial was omitted from the Terrorism Act 2000, and it had not been in force in Northern Ireland since 1975. Most reviewers had called for the repeal, including Lord Lloyd (Inquiry into Legislation against Terrorism (Cm. 3420, London, 1996), para. 16.8), and the power (latterly in s. 36 and sch. 3 of the Northern Ireland (Emergency Provisions) Act 1996) had actually been terminated by s. 3 of the Northern Ireland (Emergency Provisions) Act 1998 (having lapsed in 1980). It was said by the Labour Government that 'internment is the terrorist's friend' (HC Debs. Standing Committee A col. 73, 25 November 1997, Adam Ingram), though the Home Office Consultation Paper 'does not rule out for all time the introduction of the power to intern' (Home Office and Northern Ireland Office, Legislation against Terrorism (Cm. 4178, London, 1998), para. 14.2). It must also be accepted that the debate was very much fixated upon internment in Northern Ireland and the care not to balk the Peace Process. Nevertheless, it was a major reversal of policy when detention without trial was announced as part of the Anti-terrorism, Crime and Security Bill.

The explanation for these new powers of detention derives from a perceived dangerous mismatch between the threat of foreign terrorism and the compulsory protection required by international laws relating to either asylum or human rights of foreign dissidents. Whether they can be excluded or expelled consistent with international asylum refugee law is debatable. The debate turns upon the UN Convention relating to the Status of Refugees 1951 (189 UNTS 150) and the 1967 Protocol (606 UNTS 267) (the 'Refugee Convention'). Governments call in aid two provisions, the interpretation of which is far from settled (see Kalin, W., and Kunzli, J., 'Article 1F(b): freedom fighters, terrorists, and the notion of serious non-political crimes' (2000) 12 Supp. *International Journal of Refugee Law* 46; Shah, P., *Refugees, race and the legal concept of asylum in Britain* (Cavendish, London, 2000); Harvey, C.J., *Seeking asylum in the UK* (Butterworths, London, 2000); Hathaway, J.C. and Harvey, C.J., 'Framing refugee protection in the New World Disorder' (2001) 34 *Cornell International Law Journal* 257).

The first is Article 1(F) of the Refugee Convention which applies:

With respect to whom there are serious reasons for considering that:
    (a) he has committed a crime against peace, a war crime or a crime against humanity, as defined in the international instruments drawn up to make provision in respect of such crimes;
    (b) he has committed a serious non-political crime outside the country of refuge prior to his admission to that country as a refugee;
    (c) he has been guilty of acts contrary to the purposes and principles of the United Nations.

Such persons are unworthy of refugee status and can be denied entry on this preliminary ground alone.

As for the meaning of a serious non-political crime outside the country of refuge under (b), there is no need for the crime to be committed in relation to the asylum state or its citizens, or for formal proof of any previous crime (UN High Commission for Refugees, Handbook on Procedures and Criteria for Determining Refugee Status under the 1951 Convention and the 1967 Protocol relating to the

Status of Refugees (HCR/IP/4/Eng/REV1, Geneva, 1992, para. 149)). Exploring the meaning of 'serious', the advice from the UN High Commission for Refugees' Handbook (para. 155) is that 'minor offences punishable by moderate sentences' are not grounds for exclusion and that all the exclusionary grounds should be applied in restrictive manner (para. 180). Further guidance on what is 'serious' arises from court interpretations which tie it to the contracting meaning of 'political offence' under extradition law. In *T* v *Secretary of State for the Home Department* [1996] AC 742, refugee status was denied to an Algerian member of FIS because of his part in bombing the civilian Algiers airport which could not be counted as a 'political' act according to acceptable norms of behaviour (a finding now echoed by the UN Convention for the Suppression of Terrorist Bombings (A/RES/52/164, Cm. 4662, London, 1997)). However, according to other sources, the hijacking of aircraft in order to escape from persecution should not result in automatic exclusion but should be considered on a case by case basis (UN High Commission for Refugees' Handbook, para. 161).

As for the grounds of international law under (a) or (c), it may be noted that UN Terrorism Declaration of 1997 (Measures to Eliminate International Terrorism, GA Res.51/210), which may be said to be declarative of the purposes and principles of the United Nations, does seek to limit the grant of asylum and so has been called in aid as showing that terrorism in general (or perhaps at least those forms of terrorism clearly contrary to an international law, such as hijacking) is a ground for refusal of asylum. By Article 3:

The States Members of the United Nations reaffirm that States should take appropriate measures in conformity with the relevant provisions of national and international law, including international standards of human rights, before granting refugee status, for the purpose of ensuring that the asylum-seeker has not participated in terrorist acts, considering in this regard relevant information as to whether the asylum-seeker is subject to investigation for or is charged with or has been convicted of offences connected with terrorism and, after granting refugee status, for the purpose of ensuring that that status is not used for the purpose of preparing or organizing terrorist acts intended to be committed against other States or their citizens . . .

In addition, Article 3(3) of UN Security Council Resolution 1373 (S/RES/1373), passed on 28 September 2001, requires States to:

Take appropriate measures in conformity with the relevant provisions of national and international law, including international standards of human rights, for the purpose of ensuring that the asylum-seeker has not planned, facilitated or participated in the commission of terrorist acts.

Next, those persons who have been admitted as refugees may not normally then be expelled under Article 32 'save on grounds of national security or public order'. The limits on return in those circumstances are explained further by Article 33:

> 1. No Contracting State shall expel or return ('refouler') a refugee in any manner whatsoever to the frontiers of territories where his life or freedom would be threatened on account of his race, religion, nationality, membership of a particular social group or political opinion.
> 2. The benefit of the present provision may not, however, be claimed by a refugee whom there are reasonable grounds for regarding as a danger to the security of the country in which he is, or who, having been convicted by a final judgment of a particularly serious crime, constitutes a danger to the community of that country.

Hence, the focus here is on activities in the country of refuge rather than prior acts abroad. However, on the first ground of a threat to national security, foreign terrorists will readily fall within this heading since it was accepted that the security interests of the United Kingdom could be affected by a threat to a foreign country such as Pakistan in *Secretary of State for the Home Department* v *Rehman* [2001] 3 WLR 877 without proof of a distinct threat to the country of asylum.

Yet, whatever, the position in asylum law, there is a further bar to State action under international human rights law (see Lambert, H., 'Protection against refoulement in Europe' (1999) 48 *International & Comparative Law Quarterly* 543). If these troublesome individuals seek asylum in the United Kingdom (or any other Council of Europe contracting State), and their presence is deemed not conducive to the public good because of their terrorism links, nevertheless their expulsion could then be forbidden in international law. The ground is that they would be subjected to torture when returned to their country of origin contrary to Article 3 of the European Convention on Human Rights (see *Chahal* v *United Kingdom*, App. no. 22414/93, Reports 1996-V, (1996) 23 EHRR 413). These concerns override those of security and safety of the asylum State. Though the bar is confined to protection against Article 3 type abuses on return and not others (such as arbitrary detention) and therefore does not fill all the ground of refugee status protection against 'persecution', it does provide considerable pause for thought in terrorist cases.

The situation is made more difficult for asylum States since continued, indefinite detention is also forbidden under the European Convention (and is considered no better than refoulement under asylum law: Conference of Plenipotentiaries on the Status of Refugees and Stateless Persons (UN Doc.A/CONF.2/SR16 at p. 8)). Article 5(1)(f) of the European Convention permits the detention of a person with a view to deportation only in circumstances where 'action is being taken with a view to deportation', according to *Chahal* v *United Kingdom*, App. no. 22414/93, Reports 1996-V, (1996) 23 EHRR 413 at para. 112. Therefore, detention will cease to be permissible under Article 5(1)(f) if deportation proceedings are not being prosecuted with due diligence (or at all) and if the duration of the deportation proceedings becomes extensive (para. 113). Lengthy detention is also forbidden in domestic law. Persons can be arrested and detained under the Immigration Act 1971 pending their removal or deportation (facilities for detention exist at Harmondsworth near Heathrow Airport, Yarl's Wood (Bedfordshire — the centre was badly damaged in a fire in February 2002), and Dungavel (Lanarkshire). Many immigration detainees have hitherto been held in prisons, but this practice is intended to be ended in 2002 with the creation of up to 4,000 secure places in Removal Centres (some of which are being 'converted' from prisons: Home Office, *Secure Borders, Save Havens* (Cm. 5387, London, 2002), paras 4.75, 4.78).

Under sch. 2, para. 16(1) to the Immigration Act 1971: 'A person who may be required to submit to examination under paragraph 2 above may be detained under the authority of an immigration officer pending his examination and pending a decision to give or refuse him leave to enter'. Next, sch. 3 to the Immigration Act 1971 (as amended) provides that people who are subject to deportation orders may be detained at the Secretary of State's direction. Where a person has been recommended for deportation by a court but is not detained in connection with a criminal sentence imposed by a court and has not been bailed by a court, they will — unless the court or the Secretary of State directs otherwise — be detained pending the making of a deportation order. However, the courts in the United Kingdom have ruled that this power of detention can only be exercised during the period necessary, in all the circumstances of the particular case, to effect removal and that, if it becomes clear that removal is not going to be possible within a reasonable time, detention will become unlawful (see *R* v *Governor of Durham Prison, ex parte Singh* [1984] 1 All ER 983). Likewise, in *R (on the application of Saadi and others)* v *Secretary of State for the Home Department* [2001] 4 All ER 961, the Court of Appeal gave judgment in the case of four Kurds who had come to the United Kingdom to seek asylum. They had been detained for a period not exceeding ten days in Oakington reception centre under para. 16 of sch. 2 (see Home Office, *Secure Borders, Save Havens* (Cm. 5387, London, 2002), para. 4.69). It held that a short period of detention was lawful and proportionate to the needs of the authorities to organise the practical details of the alien's repatriation or while his application for leave to enter the territory in order to be afforded asylum was considered. According to Lord Phillips: 'A short period of detention is not an unreasonable price to pay in order to ensure the speedy resolution of the claims of a substantial proportion of this influx. In the circumstances such detention can properly be described as a measure of last resort' (para. 27). By contrast, indefinite detention which goes well beyond the week mentioned in that case (para. 67) and to ensure public safety rather than the processing of the case (though it is not necessary to show that detention is necessary to prevent unlawful immigration) cannot possibly meet these standards of legality.

The problem of dangerous aliens is far from new (see Cotter, C.P., 'Emergency detention in wartime: the British experience' (1954) 6 *Stanford Law Review* 238; Gillman, P., and Gillman, L., *Collar the Lot* (Quartet Books, London, 1980); Cesarani, D., and Kushner, T. (eds.), *The Internment of Aliens in 20th Century*

Britain (Frank Cass, London, 1993)), but seems to have become more acutely felt in recent years. The conundrum can be illustrated by a couple of cases.

The first case to reach prominence was that of the Saudi dissident, Dr Muhammad al-Masari, who, while not alleged to be a terrorist, caused diplomatic friction between the Saudi and British governments. Having been refused asylum within the United Kingdom, Dr al-Masari was then ordered to be deported to Dominica, his return to his homeland being out of the question because of well-founded fear of persecution (which would breach Article 3 of the European Convention) (see *The Times*, 5 January 1996). The deportation order was later set aside by the Immigration Appeals Tribunal (see *The Times*, 6 March 1996) since it appeared that an attempt had been made to circumvent the United Nations Convention on Refugees for 'diplomatic and trade reasons' and because the Home Secretary had failed to establish that Dominica was a safe third country. The deportation order was then lifted and exceptional leave to remain and then permanent residency were granted (see *The Times*, 19 April 1996 and *Mail on Sunday*, 3 July 2001), leaving him free to conduct his embarrassing campaign against the Saudi Government.

Even more pertinent to the treatment of terrorists is the *Chahal* case. Chahal, an Indian Sikh, settled illegally in the United Kingdom in 1971 but was granted indefinite leave to remain in 1974. During a visit to Punjab in 1984, he was detained and tortured. On his return to Britain, he became a prominent activist in favour of an independent Sikh homeland, Khalistan. He was twice charged but acquitted of criminal offences. In 1990, a deportation order was issued on grounds of national security arising from his alleged fund-raising activities and intimidation of moderate Sikhs. His request for political asylum was rejected in 1992, and his legal challenge to that decision failed (*R* v *Secretary of State for the Home Department, ex parte Chahal* [1995] 1 WLR 526). The European Court of Human Rights, however, concluded there was a risk of torture if he were to be deported (*Chahal* v *United Kingdom*, App. no. 22414/93, Reports 1996-V, (1996) 23 EHRR 413) and that it would therefore be a breach of the Convention to send him back to India. Other cases have followed along similar lines (such as the cases of Mukhtiar Singh and Paramjit Singh, alleged Sikh terrorists allowed to remain in the United Kingdom because of the fear of prosecution (*The Guardian*, 1 August 2000, p. 5).

Although there are powers to detain people where the intention is to remove them, case law suggests that if removal is not going to be possible within a reasonable period of time, detention will be unlawful. Likewise, the European Court of Human Rights has pronounced that Article 5(1)(f) of the European Convention permits the detention of a person only in circumstances where action is being pursued to bring about deportation. If the person cannot be removed in the foreseeable future, then he cannot be held in detention.

The problem was noted by Lord Lloyd (Inquiry into Legislation against Terrorism (Cm. 3420, London, 1996), para. 12.19), but he suggested exclusion or deportation subject to new international agreements — easier said than done. More ominously, he also called for contingency plans for detention (para. 18.14). No drafts were published, but it did not take long to produce them in autumn 2001, given the vast range of experience of internment lurking in the corridors of British power.

The design of detention without trial now adopted seems to derive from a number of sources. Many of the procedures are closely related to the Special Immigration Appeals Commission (SIAC) under the Special Immigration Appeals Commission Act 1997. This Act represented the latest attempt to solve the perennial problem of squaring procedural safeguards for the individual with the national security interests of the State. An earlier model, introduced in 1969, had involved a non-statutory hearing before a panel of three advisers (see HC Debs. vol. 819 col. 376wa, 15 June 1971), a process which withstood challenge in domestic administrative law in *R v Secretary of State for the Home Department, ex parte Hosenball* [1977] 3 All ER 452; *NSH v Secretary of State for the Home Department* [1988] Imm AR 389. Two additional advisers were appointed at the time of the Gulf War of 1991, when some 160 Iraqis and Palestinians were detained pending deportation on national security grounds; see *R v Secretary of State for the Home Department, ex parte Cheblak* [1991] 2 All ER 319. But it was thought that the system would be open to challenge under the European Convention, and so it proved in *Chahal's* case, where it was accepted that the panel was not a 'court' for the purposes of Articles 5(4) and 13. There were also strong doubts that, even if it could so qualify, its procedures would have been counted as 'fair' within Article 6. So, the 1997 Act is the response to the *Chahal* judgment. A Special Immigration Appeals Commission (SIAC) is established under s. 1, with a senior judge and Immigration Appeal Tribunal member as two of the panelists plus a third member who usually is from a security background. It has jurisdiction to allow an appeal (and not simply to advise the Secretary of State) where the decision was not in accordance with law or with immigration rules or where discretion should have been exercised differently (s. 4). An important procedural feature is the power under s. 6 to appoint a security-vetted 'special advocate' to represent the appellant's interests when the appellant and his legal representative are excluded from the proceedings (as may occur on grounds of national security under s. 5). There is a further appeal on law to the Court of Appeal (Court of Session in Scotland) (s. 7). The system was commended by the House of Lords in *Secretary of State for the Home Department v Rehman* [2001] 3 WLR 877, para. 62.

Some of the ideas behind Part IV of the Anti-Terrorism, Crime and Security Act 2001 seem to have derived from the Northern Ireland precedents mentioned earlier. Their format was latterly set by the Gardiner Report (Report of a Committee to consider, in the context of civil liberties and human rights, measures to deal with terrorism in Northern Ireland (Cmnd. 5847, London, 1975); see Spjut, R.J., 'Executive detention in Northern Ireland: the Gardiner Report and the Northern Ireland (Emergency Provisions) (Amendment) Act 1975' (1975) 10 *Irish Jurist* 272; Lowry, D.R., 'Internment in Northern Ireland' (1976) 8 *Toledo Law Review* 169; Hogan, G., and Walker C., *Political Violence and the Law in Ireland* (Manchester University Press, Manchester, 1989) ch. 3; Spjut, R.J., 'Internment and detention without trial in Northern Ireland 1971–75' (1986) 49 *Modern Law Review* 712) and were first published in the Northern Ireland (Emergency Provisions) (Amendment) Act 1975. That system involved an interim detention order (para. 4). If the detention was to last more than 14 days, the case had to be referred to an Adviser, who had to determine whether the person was engaged in terrorism and whether the detention was necessary for the protection of the public (para. 7). If the Secretary of State was satisfied on the same grounds, then a Detention Order could be made under para. 8. A detained person could request a review of the detention every six months (para. 9). There were detailed rules as to the treatment of detainees, though it must be said that the physical conditions of detention facilities were never good (see McGuffin, J., *Internment* (Anvil Press, Tralee, 1973)).

Thirdly, there seems to be some borrowing from the US Patriot Act (Uniting and Strengthening America By Providing Appropriate Tools Required To Intercept and Obstruct Terrorism, HR 3162, 2001), whereby, under s. 412, the detention of more than 1,000 foreign suspects has been a major plank of security policy, despite constitutional doubts (*Zadvydas* v *Davis*, 121 S. Ct. 2491 (2001)). However, the US system is distinct in that the Alien Terrorist Removal Court has not been activated (see Antiterrorism and Effective Death Penalty Act 1996, 18 USC s. 1531).

It was occasionally argued that the Anti-terrorism, Crime and Security Act 2001, does not contain a true power of internment since it will be open to a detainee to end his detention at any time by agreeing to leave the United Kingdom. Hence, the official nomenclature is 'detention' and not 'internment' (HL Debs. vol. 629 col. 480, 29 November 2001, Lord Rooker). This choice was supported as long ago as the Diplock Report (Report of the Commission to consider legal procedures to deal with terrorist activities in Northern Ireland (Cmnd. 5185, London, 1972), para. 28). However, it will often be practically impossible for the detainee to find a suitable country willing to accept him. Therefore, internment is a fair description — there is no criminal conviction and no intention to sustain one nor is there any prospect of any other legal processing which would end the need for detention. Whatever the classification, these measures attracted considerable controversy and argument. Aside from reviving the notion of internment, the early drafts of the Bill sought to exclude judicial review. Added to those arguments was the undoubted and unpalatable consequence of a new derogation from the European Convention on Human Rights. In the light of these reservations, the Home Affairs Committee gave only grudging support to this Part of the Act (Report on the Anti-terrorism, Crime and Security Bill 2001 (2001–02 HC 351), para. 34):

We are concerned that the power of detention is exercised only as a last resort, i.e., in circumstances where it is clearly not possible to proceed with prosecution, extradition or deportation. The Committee understands that, in some cases, prosecutions do not proceed because certain types of intelligence, such as telephone intercepts, cannot be admitted in court. We believe that within the law enforcement community there is a variety of views on whether such evidence should be used in court. We suggest that the Government conduct a review of the law and procedure relating to the admissibility of intercept evidence in court, with a view to extending the circumstances in which such evidence could be admitted.

8.2.2   Operative measures

The process commences with the issuance of a certificate by the Secretary of State under s. 21 of the Anti-terrorism, Crime and Security Act 2001. The criteria are that the Secretary of State reasonably (a) believes that the person's presence in the United Kingdom is a risk to national security, and (b) suspects that the person is a terrorist. It will be noted that the exercise of the power is couched in objective terms, though, as described fully in Chapter 2, the impact of sensitive security evidence will hamper effective challenge. There is said to be a significant difference between 'believes' and 'suspects' (HL Debs. vol. 629 col. 459, 29 November 2001, Lord Rooker):

> If there were a reasonable belief that someone was an international terrorist, then under the terms of the Terrorism Act, the police already have powers. For that reason, the clause as drafted is designed to cover cases where insufficient admissible evidence can be brought forward that points to a person being a terrorist. Indeed, that is the point of the clause. Our aim throughout has been that our first priority would be to prosecute alleged terrorists; secondly, if we cannot prosecute them, to remove them; and thirdly, failing the opportunity, wherewithal and appropriate circumstances to remove such people, to detain them. Those are the three routes of action.

However, the claim that the standard of 'reasonable belief' allows for police action is inaccurate, for s. 40 actually refers to 'reasonable suspicion' for an arrest. A standard of neither reasonable suspicion nor reasonable belief allows for prosecution and there is in any event no offence of being a terrorist. More assuredly, it is asserted that a suspicion is less firm than a belief (col. 463; *Johnson* v *Whitehouse* [1984] RTR 38).

It should also be noted that the definition of 'terrorist' is much broader than that in s. 40 of the Terrorism Act 2000 (see Chapter 5). By s. 40, there is a close link either to the commission of terrorist offence or to being concerned in the commission, preparation or instigation of acts of terrorism. By contrast, s. 21(2) defines a 'terrorist' as a person who:

(a)   is or has been concerned in the commission, preparation or instigation of acts of international terrorism,

(b)   is a member of or belongs to an international terrorist group, or

(c)   has links with an international terrorist group.

The confinement to international terrorism (which was overturned once in the House of Lords: (HL Debs. vol. 629 col. 483, 29 November 2001) is understandable in the circumstances. The legislation is based within immigration, and the circumstances of the particular emergency of 11 September, including the terms of the derogation, related to international and not domestic terrorism. But the final leg, subsection (2)(c), appears to represent an unpalatable reliance upon guilt by association, though, by s. 21(4), a person has 'links' with an international terrorist group only if he supports or assists it, suggesting a more active form of involvement than merely being socially or professionally associated with persons who happen to be terrorists. In this way, 'Osama bin Laden's distant family relatives, about ten times removed, do not have a sufficient "link" ' (HL Debs. vol. 629 col. 502, 29 November 2001, Lord Rooker). The definition is also very broad in the sense that, by s. 21(3), an 'international terrorist group' is any group subject to the control or influence of persons outside the United Kingdom which the Secretary of State suspects is concerned in the commission, preparation or instigation of acts of international terrorism. There is no requirement that the group should be proscribed under the Terrorism Act 2000, so the objectivity of the prime power under s. 21(1) is somewhat undermined by this subjective designation. There was some further indication during debates that the link to proscription offences is not precise and that the evidence required for certification may actually be more demanding: 'the judgment will depend not on whether people turn up to a PKK rally in Stoke Newington but on whether they pose a risk' (HC Debs. vol. 375 col. 379, 21 November 2001, David Blunkett).

By s. 21(6) of the 2001 Act, where the Secretary of State issues a certificate under subsection (1) he shall as soon as is reasonably practicable (a) take reasonable steps to notify the person certified, and (b) send a copy of the certificate to the Special Immigration Appeals Commission. This allows the triggering of the review mechanisms described below.

Once a certificate has been issued, subject to challenge, it is enforced under the terms of ss. 22 and 23 of the 2001 Act. Section 22 details the counter-measures which may be taken in respect of a suspected international terrorist despite the problem that those measures cannot for the time being result in the actual removal of that suspect because either a point of law relating to an international agreement or a practical consideration prevents removal. A 'practical consideration' might involve the unavailability of routes to the country of intended removal or, more likely, a lack of acceptable travel documentation (Home Office, Explanatory Notes on the Anti-terrorism, Crime and Security Bill (London, 2001) para. 80). The measures include refusing leave to enter, recommending deportation or making a deportation order, or giving directions for a person's removal. The section cannot achieve the desired removal, but it allows measures to be taken with a view to future removal which, unless the person had been certified as a suspected international terrorist, the courts could set aside. In addition, the immigration detention powers in s. 23 are tied to such measures. Subsection (3) provides that where a certificate is made under s. 21 after one of the measures listed in subsection (2) has been taken, that measure is to be treated as having been taken again after certification. The purpose is to ensure that a court cannot set aside any of those measures once a certificate has been made (other than as a consequence of cancelling the certificate itself).

The core detention power is set out in s. 23. A suspected international terrorist may be detained under para. 16 of sch. 2 to the Immigration Act 1971 (detention of persons liable to examination or removal), and para. 2 of sch. 3 to that Act (detention pending deportation). The detention is permitted despite the fact that his removal or departure from the United Kingdom is prevented (whether temporarily or indefinitely) by a point of law which wholly or partly relates to an international agreement or by a practical consideration (such as travel difficulties or perhaps illness). Section 24 envisages that the person may be released on bail, and the procedures will be determined by rules of procedure under the Special Immigration Appeals Commission Act 1997. Otherwise, the 2001 Act is disturbingly silent about the conditions of detention. Even the US Presidential Order, Detention, Treatment, and Trial of Certain Non-Citizens in the War Against Terrorism, of the 13 November 2001 (66 Federal Register 57831, s. 3) specifies that the affected individuals shall be 'treated humanely, without any adverse distinction based on race, color, religion, gender, birth, wealth, or any similar criteria; afforded adequate food, drinking water, shelter, clothing, and medical treatment; allowed the free exercise of religion consistent with the requirements of such detention; and detained in accordance with such other conditions as the Secretary of Defense may prescribe'. As for the conditions under the 2001 Act, the plans are mentioned only in the Parliamentary debates (HL Debs. vol. 629 col. 508, 29 November 2001, Lord Rooker):

The chances are that persons detained under the new procedure will be in high security prisons. Such persons will be suspected international terrorists. They will not be people who have absconded from the Immigration Service, but those who are 'copper-bottom' suspected of major offences. If they choose not to leave the country or cannot do so and are detained, they will be locked up in a suitable institution — a prison.

Though there is a promise that, while in prison, the detainees will be treated as if on remand, the lack of a legal regime and their detention alongside convicts leave much to be desired (see Harding, A.J., and Hatchard, J., *Preventive Detention and Security Law* (Nijhoff, Dordrecht, 1993), pp. 10, 13).

As far as legal challenges are concerned, s. 21(8) and (9) of the 2001 Act provide that a decision of the Secretary of State in connection with certification or with an action pursuant to it may be questioned in legal proceedings only under s. 25 or 26 or (in connection with pursuant actions) s. 2 of the Special Immigration Appeals Commission Act 1997. By s. 25, a suspected international terrorist may appeal within three months (or longer by leave) to the SIAC against his certification under s. 21. The SIAC must cancel the certificate if (a) it considers that there are no reasonable grounds for the Secretary of State's belief or suspicion or (b) it considers that for some other reason the certificate should not have been issued.

These review periods were considered insufficiently frequent by the Joint Committee on Human Rights to comply with Article 5(4) of the European Convention (Report on the Anti-terrorism, Crime and Security Bill (2001–02 HL 51, HC 420), para. 17). Detention without review for a period longer than around 14 days may still be viewed as disproportionate even in a situation of emergency (*Aksoy* v *Turkey*, App. no. 21987/93, Reports 1996-VI).

In addition to an appeal initiated by the detainee, the SIAC must on its own initiative under s. 26 of the 2001 Act hold a first review of each certificate issued under s. 21 as soon as is reasonably practicable after the expiry of the period of six months of the issuance of the certificate or of the final determination of an appeal under s. 25 and then after a further three months. In addition, the SIAC may hold additional reviews if the person certified applies for a review, and the Commission considers that a review should be held because of a change in circumstance. The SIAC's powers on review are more restricted than on appeal. It may set aside the certificate if it considers that there are no reasonable grounds for a belief or suspicion of the kind referred to in s. 21(1)(a) or (b) but otherwise, may not make any order (save as to leave to appeal) (s. 26(5)). The Joint Committee on Human Rights was concerned that (Report on the Anti-terrorism, Crime and Security Bill (2001–02 HL 51, HC 420), para. 15):

> there is a significant risk that [the provision] could permit a person to be detained indefinitely after new evidence or a change of circumstances led to a situation in which the suspicion or belief under [s. 21], while reasonable, was shown to be mistaken. This seems unlikely to represent the intention of the Government, and would be likely to give rise to a violation of Article 5(4) of the ECHR.

However, the view of the Government is that 'the current wording does require SIAC to take account of all relevant information up to the time that it hears the review, and that it is compliant with Article 5(4) of the European Convention on Human Rights' (HL Debs. vol. 629 col. 1242, 11 December 2001, Lord Rooker). The omission of the extra basis to set aside certificates under s. 25(2)(b), where it considers that for some other reason the certificate should not have been issued, is said to be unnecessary since it exists:

> to enable the SIAC to cancel a certificate where there has been some form of procedural irregularity. That issue will not arise at the review stage as, if there had been any irregularity in making the s. 21 certificate, the matter would already have been considered by SIAC at the appeal stage. (col. 1242)

By s. 27(9) of the 2001 Act, cancellation by the Commission of a certificate issued under s. 21 shall not prevent the Secretary of State from issuing another certificate, whether on the grounds of a change of circumstance or otherwise. The Joint Committee on Human Rights expressed concern at the possibility of abuse or oppression and called for tighter wording (Report on the Anti-terrorism, Crime and Security Bill (2001–02 HL 51, HC 420), para. 18):

> This could result in cases being batted backwards and forwards indefinitely between the Secretary of State and the Commission, and would not offer adequate protection for detainees against arbitrary interference with their right to liberty under Article 5 of the ECHR. . . .
>
> The Secretary of State could be enabled to issue a new certificate if, and only if, (a) there is fresh evidence, (b) the original certificate was quashed on technical grounds rather than because there were insufficient grounds for making it, or (c) there has been a material change of circumstances justifying the making of a new certificate.

The explanation given in Parliament is that one of the reasons for the words 'or otherwise' is to deal with the following cases (HL Debs. vol. 629 col. 544, 29 November 2001, Lord Rooker):

> First, if there is a change in circumstances and matters have moved on from the time when the original certificate was made, there may be new reasons for considering that a person now qualifies as a suspected international terrorist, notwithstanding SIAC's decision. Secondly, the same basic case against an individual may exist, but new evidence may come to light which substantiates a previous suspicion or belief. For example, there may have been a belief that a person was a member of a proscribed organisation but SIAC may have concluded that there were no reasonable grounds for that belief. New information may subsequently emerge which strongly supports the original contention, and that may justify a fresh certificate. Thirdly, there are technical matters where the certificate was cancelled for procedural shortcomings. Fourthly, a higher court might reverse a decision of SIAC, which would mean a fresh certificate being issued unless that higher court resurrected the certificate itself.

Appeals and reviews are by s. 27 of the 2001 Act subject to several features of the SIAC, including, by s. 6 of the Special Immigration Appeals Commission Act 1997, the assignment of an advocate to represent the detainee's interest and, under s. 7, the restriction of any further appeal (to the Court of Appeal or Court of Session) and rules under s. 7A pending an appeal. There must also be written reasons for the detention provided to the SIAC by the Secretary of State under r. 10 of the Special Immigration Appeals Commission (Procedure) Rules 1998 (SI 1998 No. 1881) and it must, under r. 23, promulgate and publish its determination, subject to not publishing to the applicant sensitive information. It is also provided that for the purpose of the application of s. 26(2) and (3) of the 2001 Act, the determination by the SIAC of the appeal or review in connection with which the further appeal is brought shall be treated as a final determination. The SIAC also can make the final determination where the Secretary of State notifies the Commission that in his opinion the further appeal under s. 7 of the Special Immigration Appeals Commission Act 1997 is confined to calling into question one or more derogation matters within the meaning of s. 30 of this Act.

Under earlier versions of the Bill (clause 29 as introduced, and clause 30 as amended in Committee), an attempt was made to exclude any other form of legal oversight. Not only would the SIAC be the first venue to hear any challenges (as is now provided for by s. 21), but it was also specified that the decisions of SIAC could not be entertained in any court or tribunal (except as provided by s. 27):

(1) No court or tribunal may, except as provided by a provision of this Part, entertain proceedings for questioning—

(a) a decision or action of the Secretary of State in connection with certification under section 21 or a provision of sections 21 to 31, or

(b) a decision or action of the Special Immigration Appeals Commission taken by virtue of or in connection with a provision of sections 21 to 27.

(2) No court or tribunal other than the Special Immigration Appeals Commission may entertain proceedings for questioning an action of the Secretary of State taken in reliance on section 22 or 23.

(3) A certificate of the Secretary of State that specified action is taken in reliance on section 22 or 23 shall be conclusive of the matter certified.

Given that there have in fact only been three legal challenges (all appeals) to the SIAC, the Home Affairs Committee actually supported the clause (Report on the Anti-terrorism, Crime and Security Bill 2001 (2001–02 HC 351), paras 49, 53). Nevertheless, the clause was removed after substantial Parliamentary opposition (HL Debs. vol. 629 col. 1014, 6 December 2001).

Even if it had been passed, its effect might have been less sweeping than intended, since the judges are wary of such exclusion clauses. The lonely voice of opposition of Lord Atkin in *Liversidge* v *Anderson* [1942] AC 206 at p. 244 has now been echoed forcefully by many judicial bretheren (see, for example, *Nakkuda Ali* v *MF de S Jayaratne* [1951] AC 66; *Anisminic Ltd* v *Foreign Compensation Commission* [1969] 2 AC 147), as discussed at greater length in Chapter 2. In any event, the European Court of Human Rights has asserted that it is a violation of Article 5(4) to allow national authorities to be 'free from effective control by the domestic courts whenever they choose to assert that national security and terrorism are involved' (*Chahal* v *United Kingdom*, App. no. 22414/93, Reports 1996-V, (1996) 23 EHRR 413, at para. 131).

Likewise, the European Court of Justice has demanded that any form of restraint on the movement of European Union 'workers' would require independent review in accordance with Directive 64/221 (*R* v *Secretary of State for the Home Department, ex parte Gallagher*, [1995] I-4253; *R* v *Secretary of State for the Home Department, ex parte McQuillan* [1995] 4 All ER 400; *R* v *Secretary of State for the Home Department, ex parte Shingara*, *The Times*, 23 June 1997; Prevention of Terrorism (Exclusion Orders) Regulations 1996 (SI 1996 No. 892)). Of course, the SIAC, with its judicial profile and power to override (and not simply 'advise' the Secretary of State) is itself intended to supply the requisite independent scrutiny without the need for further judicial intervention, though there might remain arguments under Article 6 of the European Directive that a person, who is being removed on grounds of public policy, public security or public health, should be informed of those grounds — 'unless this is contrary to the interests of the security of the State involved'. Furthermore, Article 9 requires not just independence of decision-making but also 'rights of defence and of assistance or representation'. Extra grounds for challenge may exist under the (Maastricht) Treaty on European Union of 1992 (Cm. 1934, HMSO, London, 1992, as implemented by the European Communities (Amendment) Act 1993) by virtue of the more expansive rights of all European Union citizens to move and reside within member States, as granted by Article 8a of the Treaty. However, a challenge in respect of an exclusion order mounted by Gerry Adams (*R* v *Secretary of State for the Home Department, ex parte Adams* [1995] All ER (EC) 177 — see Douglas-Scott, S., and Kimbell, J.A., 'The Adams exclusion order case' [1994] *Public Law* 516) fell foul of the 'the limitations and conditions laid down in this Treaty and by measures adopted to give it effect' imposed in relation to Article 8a. In particular, by Article 223(1)(a) of the Treaty of Rome, 'no Member State shall be obliged to supply information the disclosure of which it considers as contrary to the essential interests of its security'. While further arguments remained, in the light of the revocation of the order against Adams, the High Court withdrew its references to the European Court of Justice in April 1995, and so the case has ground to an unresolved halt (see further Walker, C.P., 'Constitutional governance and special powers against terrorism' (1997) 35 *Columbia Journal of Transnational Law* 1).

At the same time, the discussion in Chapter 2 also suggests this trend against judicial self-abnegation is far less sure-footed within the security field than outside it (as signalled in *Council of Civil Service Unions* v *Minister for the Civil Service* [1985] AC 374 and *R* v *Secretary of State of the Home Department, ex parte Cheblak* [1991] 2 All ER 319). In the current crisis, one is struck by the self-abasing statement of Lord Hoffman on behalf of the judiciary (similar to the disconcerting addendum of Justice Frankfurter in *Korematsu* v *United States*, 323 US 214 (1944)), which he offered in *Secretary of State for the Home Department* v *Rehman* ([2001] 3 WLR 877):

62. *Postscript.* I wrote this speech some three months before the recent events in New York and Washington. They are a reminder that in matters of national security, the cost of failure can be high. This seems to me to underline the need for the judicial arm of government to respect the decisions of ministers of the Crown on the question of whether support for terrorist activities in a foreign country constitutes a threat to national security. It is not only that the executive has access to special information and expertise in these matters. It is also that such decisions, with serious potential results for the community, require

a legitimacy which can be conferred only by entrusting them to persons responsible to the community through the democratic process. If the people are to accept the consequences of such decisions, they must be made by persons whom the people have elected and whom they can remove.

There remains an effective back-door exclusion clause in s. 35 of the Anti-terrorism, Crime and Security Act 2001. As an amendment to the Special Immigration Appeals Commission Act 1997 it is provided that a decision of the Commission shall be questioned in legal proceedings only in accordance with s. 7 of that Act or s. 30 of the 2001 Act (dealing with challenges to the derogation notice). But the criticisms of this measure by judicial figures were in part met by the further statement in s. 35 which expressly constitutes the SIAC as a superior court of record, which was seen as enhancing its status 'on a par with the Administrative Court' (HL Debs. vol. 629 col. 1436, 13 December 2001, Lord Goldsmith), putting it on a status equivalent to the Court of Appeal, High Court and Crown Court (see Supreme Court Act 1981, ss. 15, 19, 45) and affording it powers at least as great as judicial review (HC Debs. vol. 376 col. 919, 12 December 2001, David Blunkett). According to *A v B, ex parte News Group Newspapers Ltd* [1998] ICR 55 at p. 63:

> Superior court is to be construed historically and it connotes a court having an inherent jurisdiction to administer justice according to law, as and being a part of, or descended from, and as exercising part of the power of, the Aula Regia, established by William I, which had universal jurisdiction in all matters of right and wrong throughout the kingdom, and over which, in its early days, the king presided in person.

It has powers to correct its own irregular actions and judgments: *Isaacs v Robertson* [1985] 1 AC 97. A more insidious result is that its express designation as a superior court of record almost certainly means the SIAC cannot be subjected to review by the High Court (compare *R v Cripps, ex parte Muldoon* [1984] 1 QB 68), though the Home Secretary was perhaps too polite to mention this facet of the new-found status. The status of the SIAC is further bolstered by the fact that for the purposes of appeal or review under the 2001 Act, all (25) High Court judges currently nominated to hear cases in the administrative court will also be appointed to SIAC, plus the Lord Chief Justice and four Lords Justices (HL Debs. vol. 629 col. 994, 6 December 2001, Lord Goldsmith).

Given the SIAC's judicial nature and the width of its scrutiny, it must be doubted whether judicial review would have added anything in the circumstances. The Attorney-General confidently asserted that 'there is nothing that SIAC cannot do that judicial review could do' (HL Debs. vol. 629 col. 560, 29 November 2001, Lord Goldsmith). It is true that judicial review could involve neither the range of evidence before the SIAC nor the range of grounds for challenge, and so on those criteria it is not effective, save that a fresh look in addition to the SIAC after some time for reflection is a way of signalling the vital interests at stake — the interests of individual rights and the rule of law (see HL Debs. vol. 629 col. 1003, 6 December 2001, Lord Donaldson).

In conclusion, it is interesting to compare the provisions in the Anti-terrorism, Crime and Security Act 2001 with the more considered process which produced the Northern Ireland (Emergency Provisions) Act 1975. Certainly the Gardiner Report (Report of a Committee to consider, in the context of civil liberties and human rights, measures to deal with terrorism in Northern Ireland (Cmnd. 5847, London, 1975)) pointed to a number of safeguards which were not adequately considered in 2001. They included the criterion for detention that the detainee should not only be involved in terrorism but also a danger to the public (para. 166). Differences could arise relating to charges of terrorism based on membership and association, and the further requirement ensures that detention is preventive and never punitive. In addition, the Gardiner Report was insistent that the power to sign order detention should be confined to the Secretary of State in person (para. 159). On the other hand, the 1975 system was decidedly executive in format, and a greater level of independent judicial scrutiny now applies on the precedent of the 1997 Act.

8.2.3 Derogation

The Bill was accompanied by a statement that it was in compliance with the Human Rights Acts 1998, pursuant to s. 19 of that Act, subject to one derogation. The derogation was issued domestically under the Human Rights Act 1998 (Designated Derogation) Order 2001 (SI 2000 No. 3644) which was made under powers in s. 14(1) and (6) of the Human Rights Act 1998 on 11 November 2001 in anticipation of the making of a proposed derogation. It was approved by resolutions passed by each House of Parliament following debates on 19 November 2001. It concerns the extended power to detain a foreign national where it is intended to remove or deport that person from the United Kingdom because the Secretary of State believes that his presence is a risk to national security and suspects him of being an international terrorist, but where such removal or deportation is not currently possible because it is not legally acceptable to take action with a view to deportation, for example, if deportation would result in treatment contrary to Article 3 of the European Convention. As already described, detention which lasts for more than a short period may be incompatible with Article 5(1)(f) (which permits the lawful arrest or detention of a person to prevent his effecting an unauthorised entry into the country or of a person against whom action is being taken with a view to deportation or extradition). It may even be doubtful whether the purpose of detention in those circumstances, where deportation is not a lawful option, remains within Article 5(1)(f). The ground for the derogation is said to be the fact that:

There exists a terrorist threat to the United Kingdom from persons suspected of involvement in international terrorism. In particular, there are foreign nationals present in the United Kingdom who are suspected of being concerned in the commission, preparation or instigation of acts of international terrorism, of being members of organisations or groups which are so concerned or of having links with members of such organisations or groups, and who are a threat to the national security of the United Kingdom.

The derogation was registered by the Council of Europe Secretariat on 18 December 2001.

There may be a number of questions relating to the validity of this derogation, as further explained in Chapter 1, where it was also argued that, even if a sufficient threat exists, the derogation must also be used proportionately by limiting the detentions under Part IV to Al Qa'ida suspects and not to terrorist suspects of a different ilk. Whether the derogation is justifiable or not will ultimately be decided in the Strasbourg court. Section 30 of the Anti-terrorism, Crime and Security Act 2001 is concerned with domestic proceedings which to any extent challenge the derogation from Article 5 or the designation under s. 14(1) of the Human Rights Act 1998 which reflects that derogation. These are referred to as a 'derogation matter'. Where a derogation matter is raised, the SIAC will be the sole appropriate venue for hearing the proceedings, including those brought under s. 7 of the Human Rights Act 1998. An appeal against the decision of SIAC is routed to the Court of Appeal (or the Court of Session in Scotland). The special advocate may also appear at that level under the inherent jurisdiction of the court (*Secretary of State for the Home Department* v *Rehman* [2000] 3 WLR 1240). This exclusive jurisdiction is similar to the use of the Proscribed Organisations Appeal Commission and for similar reasons relating to the admission of sensitive evidence (see Chapter 2).

8.2.4   Duration and review

Because of the extraordinary nature of detention without trial and the consequent reliance upon a derogation notice, Parliament insisted on limits on the duration of the powers plus an extra tier of scrutiny for these measures. These time-limits were in line with recommendations of the Home Affairs Committee (Report on the Anti-terrorism, Crime and Security Bill 2001 (2001–02 HC 351), para. 40) which asked for a 'sunset' provision so that any revival or continuance of the detention and other powers would then depend on the full parliamentary debate on a renewal Bill.

By s. 29 of the Anti-terrorism, Crime and Security Act 2001, the duration initially set is the period of 15 months beginning with the day on which the Act is passed. The Secretary of State may by statutory order repeal ss. 21 to 23 at an earlier date. Conversely, if the measures are about to expire, have expired or have been repealed, the Secretary of State may by order continue in force or revive those sections for a period not exceeding one year. The order is subject to affirmative resolution of Parliament. But any new lease of life is subject to a 'sunset' clause in s. 29(7) (ss. 21 to 23 shall by virtue of this subsection cease to have effect at the end of 10 November 2006).

Turning to the issue of review, by s. 28 of the 2001 Act, the Secretary of State is required to appoint a person to review the operation of ss. 21 to 23. The review must take place not later than 14 months after the passage of the Act, and one month before the expiry of any revived period of operation. A copy of any report shall be laid before Parliament as soon as is reasonably practicable but there is no requirement for debate. The reviewer is to be Lord Alex Carlile of Berriew (a Liberal Democrat lawyer and an ex-MP) (HL Debs. vol. 629 col. 460, 29 November 2001, Lord Rooker).

These measures are to be welcomed as ensuring that extraordinary intrusions into liberty are kept under control by subjecting them to independent scrutiny. The express review is an improvement on the extra-statutory concessions in the Terrorism Act 2000. The special time-limits are also warranted by the contents and special circumstances of this legislation. The main critical point to be voiced is that, while ss. 21 to 23 are the most severe incursions into individual rights, they are not unique within the Act in requiring the closest scrutiny.

8.2.5 Extent

By s. 32 of the 2001 Act, an Order in Council may direct that ss. 21 to 31 shall extend, with such modifications as appear appropriate, to any of the Channel Islands or the Isle of Man. This extension of jurisdiction is unusual for, by and large, as explained in Chapter 10, these British Islands have their own separate legislation, albeit often very similar to the United Kingdom model.

8.2.6 Comment

The policy of 'break glass in the case of emergency' contingency legislation (see Chapter 1) was not followed in the case of detention without trial by the Terrorism Act 2000. The Lloyd Report (Lord Lloyd and Sir John Kerr, *Inquiry into Legislation against Terrorism* (Cm. 3420, London, 1996), para. 18.14) had recognised that 'in planning, there may be a case for considering a power, on the lines of Northern Ireland (Emergency Provisions) Act 1996, s. 36, to detain terrorist suspects in time of emergency'. The point was made more forcefully by Andrew McKay (HC Debs. vol. 301 col. 181–182, 18 November 1997):

Governments should consider invoking the power only if there were a serious deterioration in the security situation. It would be self-defeating to spell out the precise circumstances in which that would happen, but the facts that the power has not been used since 1975 and that it has technically lapsed, are not compelling reasons to warrant its removal altogether from the statute book.

While contingent enactment would not have changed greatly the shape of the powers actually produced in Part IV, it could have done more to avert the attempts at exclusion of judicial review and the extra time would surely have permitted more attention to detail of the conditions of detention.

A more straightforward detention power, not predicated upon immigration and nationality, could also avert any allegations of discrimination (see Joint Committee on Human Rights, Report on the Anti-terrorism, Crime and Security Bill (2001–02 HL 37, HC 372), para. 39). After all, why is it only foreigners who are treated in this way, when British citizens, who might be equally suspect, equally cannot be deported (and no longer even excluded) from vulnerable areas? As the Immigration Law Practitioners' Association submission concerning the Bill warns (para. 3):

> It is important to note that this means that many Muslims who have been settled in the UK for many years could be affected by these measures, not only those who are here as visitors or for other short-term purposes.

Likewise, a detention power properly so called would avoid the 'dilemma' that the detainee under Part IV, this dangerous individual whose liberty is unthinkable, is free to leave the country at any time and wreak havoc (see HC Debs. vol. 375 col. 383, 21 November 2001, David Blunkett).

8.3   REFUGEE PROCEEDINGS

While asylum seekers can be detained without trial according to the foregoing provisions, there may still be asylum or immigration proceedings to transact either in relation to terrorist suspects who cannot be returned to their country of origin (and are therefore detained) or to persons who can be removed for the public good. The Anti-terrorism, Crime and Security Act 2001 seeks to simplify and foreshorten those proceedings which fall within s. 2 of the Special Immigration Appeals Commission Act 1997. The Act raises as a preliminary, decisive issue the status of suspected terrorists as potential refugees under Articles 1(F) (because there are serious grounds for considering that they have committed an offence or action listed in that Article) or 33(2) (because of reasonable grounds for regarding the refugee as a danger to the security of the country) of the Refugee Convention (the contents of which were described above). Accordingly, by s. 33(1) of the 2001 Act, the Secretary of State may certify that a person is excluded from refugee status under Article 1(F) or not entitled to the protection of Article 33(1) and that his removal from the United Kingdom would be conducive to the public good. Where such a certificate is made, the SIAC must, in deliberating upon the asylum appeal, consider only the statements made in that certificate, and will not be able to go on to consider whether a person has a sustainable claim to refugee status on the basis of a well-founded fear of persecution.

Where the SIAC upholds the Secretary of State's certificate, it must dismiss any aspect of the appeal which amounts to a claim for asylum. If there are other aspects to the appeal the SIAC can still proceed to deliberate upon those elements. Conversely, should the SIAC allow the appeal, the case would be referred back to the Secretary of State who would have to consider the substance of the asylum claim. If the claim was still rejected, any appeal would lie to the Immigration Appellate Authority in the normal way under the Immigration and Asylum Act 1999, unless a public interest provision were asserted (in which event the appeal would be routed to SIAC).

Appeals against decisions of SIAC must be made to the Court of Appeal (or the Court of Session in Scotland). Unlike in relation to the internment provisions, there remains an exclusion clause in s. 33(8), by which:

No court may entertain proceedings for questioning—

(a) a decision or action of the Secretary of State in connection with certification under subsection (1),

(b) a decision of the Secretary of State in connection with a claim for asylum (within the meaning given by section 167(1) of the Immigration and Asylum Act 1999) in a case in respect of which he issues a certificate under subsection (1) above, or

(c) a decision or action of the Secretary of State taken as a consequence of the dismissal of all or part of an asylum appeal in pursuance of subsection (4).

The effect of this exclusion in relation to judicial review is uncertain, as already explained.

Corresponding to s. 32, s. 33 may with appropriate modifications, be extended by Order in Council to any of the Channel Islands or the Isle of Man (s. 33(10)).

By s. 34 of the 2001 Act, in considering whether or not Article 1(F) or Article 33(2) applies, there is no requirement to consider the gravity of the fear of persecution the person may have or the threat to their life or freedom they may face if removed from the United Kingdom. Consideration of whether a person comes within the scope of Article 1(F) or Article 33(2) will be determined solely by reference to the appropriate Article.

The prioritisation of these issues under Article 1(F) or Article 33(2) does not comply with the advice in the UN High Commission for Refugees, Handbook on Procedures and Criteria for Determining Refugee Status under the 1951 Convention and the 1967 Protocol relating to the Status of Refugees (HCR/IP/4/Eng/ REV1, Geneva, 1992), para. 156. At least in regard to applying the ground under Article 1(F)(b), it suggests that it is necessary to strike a balance between the nature of the offence and the degree of feared persecution. Therefore, the offence should not be considered in isolation. More directly and generally, the Handbook notes that applicants for refugee status may have committed acts of violence as part of organised groups. Nevertheless, the application must be considered (paras 176, 177):

. . . from the standpoint of the inclusion clauses . . . Where it has been determined that an applicant fulfils the inclusion criteria, the question may arise as to whether, in view of the acts involving force or violence committed by him, he may not be covered by the terms of one or more of the exclusion clauses . . .

8.4 FINGERPRINTS

The final measure in Part IV of the Anti-terrorism, Crime and Security Act 2001 allows for the retention of fingerprint records of asylum-seekers. This is achieved by s. 36 which amends s. 143 of the Immigration and Asylum Act 1999. The history and explanation is as follows.

The Asylum and Immigration Appeals Act 1993 created a power to require asylum seekers and their dependents to provide fingerprints. Under s. 3(2), any fingerprints which are taken have to be destroyed within a month of the person being given indefinite leave to remain in the United Kingdom or within 10 years if not. Section 141 of the Immigration and Asylum Act 1999 (which replaced s. 3(2)) provides that in addition to asylum-seekers that fingerprints may be taken in other circumstances, such as where the person's identity is in doubt or there is a suspicion that, if granted temporary admission, the asylum-seeker may not comply with immigration conditions. Section 143 stipulates that the destruction of the fingerprints must be brought about as soon as reasonably practicable after the person's identity as a British citizen or Commonwealth citizen with right of abode has been established or he has been given leave to enter or indefinite leave to remain in the United Kingdom or a deportation order against him has been revoked. Where the retention period is not otherwise specified, it is 10 years.

Section 36 now removes that time-limit both for prints on record and those yet to be taken. The main reason is the security threat from asylum-seekers and foreigners in general, who may turn out to be dangerous terrorists when checked against records or may evade suspicion on re-entry through the creation of multiple identities. In addition, the retention of records has become more viable and productive because of the development of a computerised fingerprint storage system in the Immigration and Nationality Directorate's records (HC Debs. vol. 374 col. 179w, 6 November 2001, Angela Eagle). However, whether indefinite detention, especially without any form of review, can meet the standards of the protection of privacy in Article 8 of the European Convention must be doubted. The Joint Committee on Human Rights was rightly hostile: 'It seems to us to risk stigmatizing immigrants who have no criminal connections. The provision has no clear connection with terrorism or security' (Report on the Anti-terrorism, Crime and Security Bill (2001–02 HL 37, HC 372), para. 52).

Chapter Nine
Dangerous substances and acute vulnerabilities

9.1 INTRODUCTION

Parts VI to IX of the Anti-terrorism, Crime and Security Act 2001 are lumped together for the purposes of this chapter as they deal with the related issues of dangerous substances and acute vulnerabilities. Their genesis resides in the shock from the ferocious attacks of 11 September, attacks which sought mass destruction and mass deaths. The implication that the new breed of Third Millennium terrorism is unbounded in terms of its desire to inflict harm, as well as its flexible nature and organisation, seemed to be confirmed by the discovery of anthrax in letters to key political figures and to the media in the United States. Certainly the Defence Select Committee perceived a risk (The Threat from Terrorism (2001–02 HC 348-I), para. 79). Accordingly, the reaction reflected in the 2001 legislation is that it is necessary to tighten the laws relating to weapons of mass destruction (Part VI) or the security surrounding the possession and use of pathogens and toxins of the most perilous variety (Part VII). It is also necessary to improve the security of the nuclear industry (Part VIII) and the aviation industry (Part IX). The measures appearing under these headings were cobbled together in a very short space of time from various sources. Not surprisingly, many had already been resting on the legislative stocks or were at least in the legislative drawing room before 11 September. The Anti-terrorism, Crime and Security Act 2001 provided a suitable vessel in which all could be launched with a much shorter deadline than originally envisaged. Strategies alongside the legislative have included the provision of information about the nature of the threat and practical counter-measures. For example, counteraction, including against biological attack through the post, is posted at the Home Office web-site, http://www.homeoffice.gov.uk/atoz/terrorists. htm.

In all, these legislative changes are mostly worthwhile reforms, though some are not sufficiently linked to terrorism or sufficiently developed to have been included in the 2001 Act. The impact is likely to be marginal, because administrative security in the United Kingdom was usually tight, and because international cooperation is just as vital as national efforts but is far from universal, even amongst Western States.

9.2   WEAPONS OF MASS DESTRUCTION

Within Part VI of the Anti-terrorism, Crime and Security Act 2001 are measures relating to biological agents and toxins and nuclear weapons. Part VI deals with offences relating to offences such as possession and transfer. Measures regarding their secure possession are set in Parts VII and VIII respectively. Threats and hoaxes about these types of materials have been considered in Chapter 6. (See further on weapons of mass destruction: Stern, J., *The Ultimate Terrorists* (Harvard University Press, Cambridge, Mass., 1999); Romano, J-A., 'Combating Terrorism and Weapons of Mass Destruction' (1999) 87 *Georgetown Law Journal* 1023; Laqueur, W., *The New Terrorism: Fanaticism and the Arms of Mass Destruction* (Oxford University Press, New York, 1999); Gurr, N., *The New Face of Terrorism: Threats from Weapons of Mass Destruction* (I.B. Tauris, London, 2000); Spiers, E.M., *Weapons of Mass Destruction: Prospects for Proliferation* (Macmillan Press, Basingstoke, 2000); Herring, E., *Preventing the use of Weapons of Mass Destruction* (Frank Cass, London, 2000).)

9.2.1   Biological agents and toxins and chemical weapons

The Anti-terrorism, Crime and Security Act 2001 builds upon the controls already set out in the Biological Weapons Act 1974 and the Chemical Weapons Act 1996. This earlier legislation is based on international treaties, namely, the Convention on the Prohibition of the Development, Production and Stockpiling of Bacteriological (Biological) and Toxin Weapons and on their Destruction, 1972 (the 'Biological and Toxin Weapons Convention', Cmnd. 5053, London 1972) and the Convention on the Prohibition of the Development, Production, Stockpiling and Use of Chemical Weapons and on their Destruction, 1993 (Cmnd. 2331, London 1993). The use of such materials in weapons is considered by the World Health Authority (see Health Aspects of Biological and Chemical Weapons, draft 2nd ed., Geneva, 2001, http://www.who.int/emc/pdfs/BIOWEAPONS_FULL_TEXT2.pdf).

The Biological Weapons Act 1974 implements in the United Kingdom the provisions of the Biological and Toxin Weapons Convention. The 1972 Convention supplements the Geneva Protocol of 1925 (Protocol for the Prohibition of the Use in War of Asphyxiating, Poisonous or other Gases, and of Bacteriological Methods of Warfare) which banned the use in war of chemical and biological weapons by banning in addition the development, production, stockpiling or acquisition of biological and toxin agents, as well as weapons or means of delivery designed to use such agents or toxins. In contrast to the Convention on the Prohibition of the Development, Production, Stockpiling and Use of Chemical Weapons and on their Destruction of 1993 (the 'Chemical Weapons Convention'), the Biological Weapons Convention contains no verification provisions to ensure compliance. The suspicion that Iraq had attempted to develop biological weapons created an impetus for negotiations on the development of an effective verification regime. However, in July 2001, the United States rejected the drafts of an Ad Hoc Group of States Parties which was established in 1996 to consider a verification protocol on grounds that the procedures could compromise biotechnology trade secrets and national security (see Defence Select Committee, *The Threat from Terrorism* (2001–02 HC 348-I), para. 66), and this stance was affirmed in the Fifth Review Conference in November 2001. As a result, there is no oversight body for biological weapons, though the World Health Organisation provides some assistance to States. At national level, it is monitored by the Department of Trade and Industry (http://www.dti.gov.uk/non-proliferation/bwcna/). See further on biological weapons: Spiers, E.M., *Chemical and Biological Weapons* (Macmillan, Basingstoke, 1994); McCuen, G.E., *Biological Terrorism & Weapons of Mass Destruction* (G.E. McCuen Pub., Hudson, Wis., 1999); Drell, S.D., Sofaer, A.D., Wilson, G.D., (eds.), *The New Terror: Facing the Threat of Biological and Chemical Weapons* (Hoover Institution Press, Stanford, 1999); Tucker, J.B. (ed.), *Toxic Terror: Assessing the Terrorist Use of Chemical and Biological Weapons* (MIT Press, Cambridge, Mass., 2000); Kellman, B., 'Biological terrorism' (2001) 24 *Harvard Journal of Law & Public Policy* 417; Parliamentary Office of Science and Technology, Report 166: *Bioterrorism* (London, http://www.parliament.uk/post/pn166.pdf, 2001).

The Chemical Weapons Convention banned the development, production, stockpiling, transfer and use of chemical weapons and, as noted above, provided for a verification regime (see http://www.dti.gov.uk/non-proliferation/cwcna/). Compliance is monitored by the Organisation for the Prohibition of Chemical Weapons (OPCW; http://www.opcw.nl/), which is based in The Hague and seeks to propose policies for the implementation of the Convention to the Member States of the OPCW and to develop and deliver programmes with and for them. It is responsible for verifying destruction programmes, inspecting military facilities and civilian plants producing chemicals that could be used for weapons and carrying out monitoring and checks. The US Government has again objected to parts of the inspection regime, especially challenge inspections (Foreign Affairs Committee, *Weapons of Mass Destruction* (1999–00 HC 407), para. 94 and Government reply (Cm. 4884, 2000). See further on chemical weapons: Krutzsch, W. and Trapp, R., *A Commentary on the Chemical Weapons Convention* (Martinus Nijhoff, Dordrecht, 1994); Fitzgerald, K.J., 'The Chemical Weapons Convention' (1997) 20 *Suffolk Transnational Law Review* 425; Bothe, M., Ronzitti, N., and Rosas, A. (eds.), *The New Chemical Weapons Convention* (Kluwer Law International, Hague, 1998); Hunt, C., 'The potential contribution of the Chemical Weapons Convention (1999) 20 *Michigan Journal of International Law* 523; Eshbaugh, M., 'The Chemical Weapons Convention' (2001) 18 *Arizona Journal of International and Comparative Law* 209; Tucker, J.B. (ed.), *Toxic Terror: Assessing the Terrorist Use of Chemical and Biological Weapons* (MIT Press, Cambridge, Mass., 2000); Parliamentary Office of Science and Technology, Report 167: *Chemical Weapons* (London, http://www.parliament.uk/post/pn167.pdf, 2001). At national level, regulation is overseen by the Chemical Weapons Convention National Authority within the Department of Trade and Industry.

Turning to the Anti-terrorism, Crime and Security Act 2001, by s. 43, the Biological Weapons Act 1974 is amended to make it an offence to transfer biological agents or toxins outside the United Kingdom or to assist another person to do so, provided the biological agent or toxin is likely to be kept or used (whether by the transferee or any other person) otherwise than for prophylactic, protective or other peaceful purposes and he knows or has reason to believe that that is the case. This offence is added as s. 1(1A), and it supplements the following offences already in s. 1:

> (1) No person shall develop, produce, stockpile, acquire or retain—
>   (a) any biological agent or toxin of a type and in a quantity that has no justification for prophylactic, protective or other peaceful purposes; or
>   (b) any weapon, equipment or means of delivery designed to use biological agents or toxins for hostile purposes or in armed conflict.
> (2) In this section—
>   'biological agent' means any microbial or other biological agent; and
>   'toxin' means any toxin, whatever its origin or method of production.

Biological agents and toxins are defined in s. 1 of the 1974 Act as 'any microbial or other biological agent' and 'toxin' means 'any toxin, whatever its origin or method of production'. There is no corresponding alteration to the Chemical Weapons Act 1996 because that Act already makes it an offence to 'participate in the transfer of a chemical weapon' under s. 2:

> (1) No person shall—
>   (a) use a chemical weapon;
>   (b) develop or produce a chemical weapon;
>   (c) have a chemical weapon in his possession;
>   (d) participate in the transfer of a chemical weapon;
>   (e) engage in military preparations, or in preparations of a military nature, intending to use a chemical weapon.

By s. 1 of that Act, 'chemical weapons' are (a) toxic chemicals and their precursors; (b) munitions and other devices designed to cause death or harm through the toxic properties of toxic chemicals released by them; (c) equipment designed for use in connection with munitions and devices falling within paragraph (b). In turn, a toxic chemical is 'a chemical which through its chemical action on life processes can cause death, permanent harm or temporary incapacity to humans or animals', and a precursor is 'a chemical reactant which takes part at any stage in the production (by whatever method) of a toxic chemical'.

Next, s. 44 extends United Kingdom jurisdiction over offences under s. 1 of the Biological Weapons Act 1974 carried out overseas by a United Kingdom person (defined by s. 56). The corresponding measure in relation to chemical weapons already exists under s. 3 of the 1996 Act. In addition, under s. 50 it becomes an offence (with a sentence of up to life imprisonment) for a United Kingdom person outside the United Kingdom to assist a foreigner to do an act which would (for a United Kingdom person) be contrary to s. 1 of the Biological Weapons Act 1974 or s. 2 of the Chemical Weapons Act 1996. These offences would not extend to either a United Kingdom-based foreign national, including an EU citizen, who, while abroad, commits an act that, if committed by a British person, would be an offence or someone who, although not a British subject, has exceptional leave to remain in this country, and who commits such an act while on a foreign trip (HC Debs. vol. 375 col. 719, 26 November 2001, Ben Bradshaw). It is not clear why a more universal jurisdiction was not asserted.

Further incidental matters are dealt with in ss. 45 and 46, by which the Customs and Excise Commissioners can enforce offences under the Biological Weapons Act 1974 and the Chemical Weapons Act 1996 (or under s. 50 of the Anti-terrorism, Crime and Security Act 2001 relating to biological weapons), in cases involving the development or production outside the United Kingdom of relevant materials or the movement of a biological or chemical weapon across a border. Officers of the Commissioners will be able to institute offences in England and Wales and Northern Ireland (provided the Attorney-General gives his consent under s. 2 of the 1974 Act and s. 31 of the 1996 Act). Sections 45 and 46 do not apply in Scotland.

9.2.2 Nuclear weapons

While the use of nuclear weapons would undoubtedly entail offences against the person and against property on an almost inconceivable scale, technically crude devices — 'dirty bombs' — and the preparatory stages of manufacturing a more sophisticated weapon were not, surprisingly enough, covered by any offence in force. The reason is that, though security was strongly associated with the civil nuclear programme, it tended to concentrate upon weapons grade plutonium. However, there was fear after 11 September that terrorists might resort to a radiological weapon or 'dirty' nuclear bomb — not only based on the ruthlessness of those attacks, but also on claims and some documentary evidence after the fall of Kabul that Al Qa'ida had indeed taken an unhealthy interest in nuclear materials (*The Times*, 15 November 2001). An independent reason for heightened concern about nuclear security arose from the government decision (announced on the 3 October 2001: DEFRA News Release 165/01) to grant permission for British Nuclear Fuels to reprocess nuclear fuel at Sellafield through its MOX (Mixed Oxide) plant, which is intended to make nuclear reactor fuel out of plutonium and uranium for export around the world. A side-effect is to increase the required movement of nuclear materials and therefore to exacerbate security problems.

Consequently, by s. 47(1) of the Anti-terrorism, Crime and Security Act 2001, it becomes an offence (punishable by life imprisonment) if a person (a) knowingly causes a nuclear weapon explosion; (b) develops or produces, or participates in the development or production of, a nuclear weapon; (c) has a nuclear weapon in his possession; (d) participates in the transfer of a nuclear weapon; or (e) engages in military preparations, or in preparations of a military nature, intending to use, or threaten to use, a nuclear weapon. Section 48 makes exceptions for actions carried out in the course of an armed conflict or for actions authorised by the Secretary of State (to prevent essential operational and maintenance activities of authorised persons connected to the United Kingdom's independent nuclear deterrent from being an offence: HC Deb. vol. 375 col. 721, 26 November 2001, Ben Bradshaw). It should be noted that the confinement to 'nuclear weapons', a phrase based on international law, would otherwise mean that radiological or 'dirty' bombs would not be covered by s. 47(1). The view was offered that other measures in the Act, such as those relating to noxious substances in s. 113, together with the Nuclear Material (Offences) Act 1983, provide sufficient legal sanctions against such activities (HL Debs. vol. 629 col. 643, 3 December 2001, Baroness Symons). However, by s. 47(6), 'nuclear weapon' is defined to include nuclear explosive devices not intended for use as a weapon — for example, nuclear material from the nuclear power industry may be released as a 'dirty' bomb where the explosive material is non-nuclear and the nuclear material is being used as a contaminant. The offences apply under s. 47 to acts outside the United Kingdom by a United Kingdom person. Furthermore, s. 50 applies to the s. 47 offence, so it is also an offence for a United Kingdom person outside the United Kingdom to assist a foreigner to do an act which would (for a United Kingdom person) be contrary to s. 47.

By s. 54 of the 2001 Act, there are offences in relation to obtaining an authorisation from the Secretary of State under s. 48 by fraud. Section 49 sets out defences for the absence of knowledge that an object was a nuclear weapon or for an attempt to inform the Secretary of State or a police officer as soon as practicable after discovering that an object was a nuclear weapon.

By s. 47(9), the offence of knowingly causing a nuclear weapon explosion will cease to have effect on the coming into force of the Nuclear Explosions (Prohibitions and Inspections) Act 1998. Because it contains a similar, internationally approved offence, it will replace s. 47(1)(a). The relevant offence is in s. 1 of the 1998 Act:

(1)   Any person who knowingly causes a nuclear weapon test explosion or any other nuclear explosion is guilty of an offence and liable on conviction on indictment to imprisonment for life.

(2)   Nothing in subsection (1) shall apply to a nuclear weapon explosion carried out in the course of an armed conflict.

The Comprehensive Test Ban Treaty is currently overseen by a Preparatory Commission until the establishment of the Comprehensive Nuclear-Test-Ban Treaty Organization (http://www.ctbto.org/) is triggered. The 1998 Act will come into force following the entry into force of the Comprehensive Test Ban Treaty (the Comprehensive Nuclear-Test-Ban Treaty adopted in New York on 10 September

1996 and the Protocol to that Treaty (Cm. 3665 and 4675, London, 1997, 2000)). The Comprehensive Test Ban Treaty is currently awaiting ratification by the USA but was ratified by the United Kingdom in 1998. An Additional Protocol (Cm. 4282, London, 1999) is implemented by the Nuclear Safeguards Act 2000 which relates to information which may be collected by the Secretary of State and passed to the International Atomic Energy Agency, which is also afforded rights of access, including to information on nuclear fuel cycle-related activities (such as the manufacture of specialised equipment, and research and development) even where nuclear material is not involved. See further: Koplow, D.A., *Testing a Nuclear Test Ban* (Dartmouth, Aldershot, 1996); Simpson, J., and Howlett, D., *The Future of the Non-Proliferation Treaty* (St. Martin's Press, New York, 1994).

9.2.3 Supplemental matters

Section 51 of the Anti-terrorism, Crime and Security Act 2001 supplements the offences under ss. 47 and 50 in so far as they relate to the acts of United Kingdom persons overseas. It is specified that the venue for trial may be anywhere in the United Kingdom. It is also possible to extend the coverage to bodies incorporated in the Channel Islands, the Isle of Man or any colony.

By s. 52, there are granted powers of entry under a justice's or sheriff's warrant to officers of the Secretary of State to search for evidence for the commission of an offence under ss. 47 and 50. There is no provision for the police to obtain a warrant directly (presumably these are considered to be matters beyond their expertise), but they may be permitted to accompany authorised officers. It is intended to preserve legal privilege under the order-making power in s. 124 (HL Debs. vol. 629 col. 640, 3 December 2001, Baronnes Symons).

By s. 53, the Customs and Excise Commissioners can enforce offences under ss. 47 and 50 in cases involving offences outside the United Kingdom or the movement of a nuclear weapon across a border. Officers of the Commissioners will be able to institute offences in England and Wales and Northern Ireland (assuming the Attorney-General gives his consent under s. 54). This section does not apply to the institution of proceedings in Scotland.

By s. 55, the Attorney-General's consent is required for prosecutions under ss. 47 and 50 in England and Wales and Northern Ireland.

By s. 57, Her Majesty may by Order in Council direct that any of the provisions of Part VI of the 2001 Act shall extend to any of the Channel Islands, the Isle of Man or to any British overseas territory.

9.2.4 Other measures

Beyond the Anti-terrorism, Crime and Security Act 2001, some other measures were taken to enhance nuclear safety. In particular, in the light of the hijackings of 11 September, which could cause catastrophic damage if applied against nuclear facilities (Edwards, E., 'What would happen if a passenger jet ploughed into a nuclear plant', *New Scientist*, 13 October 2001), it was announced (HC Debs. vol. 374 col. 540w, 12 November 2001) that restrictions were to be imposed which prohibit aircraft from flying over the Sellafield nuclear site below a height of 2,200 feet above mean sea level in a two nautical mile radius. Similar restrictions had operated around Magnox reactors on five sites owned by the State-owned British Nuclear Fuels Ltd. Flying restrictions have now been initiated around other nuclear plants owned by British Energy.

Pending before Parliament is the Export Control Bill 2001–02 (HL No. 20) which will replace the Import, Export and Customs Powers (Defence) Act 1939, as amended by the Import and Export Control Act 1990, taking account of the recommendations of the Scott Inquiry (Sir Richard Scott, Report of the Inquiry into the Export of Defence Equipment and Dual-Use Goods to Iraq and Related Prosecutions (1995–96 HC 115)) and the White Paper on *Strategic Export Controls* (Cm. 3989, London, 1998). The Bill includes powers to impose controls (by way of licensing) on exports, the transfer of technology and the provision of technical assistance overseas as well as controls on the acquisition, disposal or movement of goods or on activities which facilitate such acquisition, disposal or movement. Control orders may be imposed in order to prevent the carrying out of terrorism anywhere in the world (Schedule, para. 7E).

9.3   SECURITY OF PATHOGENS AND TOXINS

Part VII of the Anti-terrorism, Crime and Security Act 2001 is rather more self-contained than Part VI, for there is rather less in the way of international conventions or even domestic legislation in this field. However, as one would expect with deadly pathogens and toxins, there is some regulation, mainly through the office of the Advisory Committee on Dangerous Pathogens (ACDP). This non-statutory advisory body, based within the field of the Department of Health, has the task of advising the Health and Safety Commission, the Health and Safety Executive, Health and Agriculture Ministers and their counterparts under devolution in Scotland, Wales and Northern Ireland, on all aspects of hazards and risks to workers and others from exposure to pathogens (see http://www.doh.gov.uk/ acdp.htm). Advice on protecting the general population is available from the Department of Health (http://www.doh.gov.uk/epcu/epcu/). The Department of Health has also issued guidance to the NHS to help plan health service response in the event of deliberate release of biological and chemical agents (Deliberate Release of Biological and Chemical Agents, Department of Health, March 2000), as well as the Guide to a co-ordinated response to a hazardous material (HAZMAT) incident (http://www.doh.gov.uk/epcu/pdf/hazmat.pdf, 2000). The Public Health Laboratory Service (http://www.phls.co.uk/advice/index.htm) has issued a response to a deliberate release (http://www.phls.co.uk/facts/deliberate_releases.htm, http:// www.phls.co.uk/advice/smallpox_guidelines.pdf). Other aspects of contingency planning are dealt with by the Civil Contingencies Committee and Secretariat (http://www.co-ordination.gov.uk/terrorism.htm), which has issued a document,

Response to the Deliberate Release of Chemicals and Biological Agents: Guidance for Local Authorities (http://www.lga.gov.uk/Documents/Briefing/Our_Work/pub_prot/biological.pdf, 2001). The process continues; 'our duty is to go on planning for all eventualities' (HC Debs. vol. 372 col. 1049, 16 October 2001, Alan Milburn).

The ACDP produces information on pathogens and has established a ranking system (see *Categorisation of biological agents according to hazard and categories of containment*, 4th ed., HSE Books, Sudbury, 1995 — see http://www.hse.gov.uk/hthdir/noframes/agent1.pdf) which seeks to provide practical standards for the safe conduct of work with infectious biological agents in accordance with the Control of Substances Hazardous to Health Regulations 1999 (SI 1999 No. 437) which implement European Community Directives 90/679/EEC (on the protection of workers from risks related to biological agents at work) and 93/88/EEC (which contains a Community classification of biological agents).

There also exists guidance from the Health Services Advisory Committee (HSAC) on safe working in clinical laboratories (http://www.hse.gov.uk/hthdir/noframes/biolhaz.htm). Implementing the advisory standards is the Health and Safety Executive. The supply of pathogens to laboratories requires those laboratories to have suitable facilities for the containment of those pathogens (reg. 7 to the Control of Substances Hazardous to Health Regulations 1999), and such laboratories have to be notified to the HSE in order to be supplied with pathogens or to send them elsewhere (sch. 3, paras 12 and 13). The 1999 Regulations (sch. 3, para. 3(4)) define four levels of hazard from biological agents, and the ACDP defines four corresponding Containment Levels for laboratory work:

(a) Group 1: A biological agent unlikely to cause human disease.

(b) Group 2: A biological agent that can cause human disease and may be a hazard to employees; it is unlikely to spread to the community and there is usually effective prophylaxis or effective treatment available.

(c) Group 3: A biological agent that can cause severe human disease and presents a serious hazard to employees; it may present a risk of spreading to the community, but there is usually effective prophylaxis or treatment available.

(d) Group 4: A biological agent that causes severe human disease and is a serious hazard to employees; it is likely to spread to the community and there is usually no effective prophylaxis or treatment available.

Anthrax (Bacillus anthracis) is within Group 3, while smallpox (Variola virus) and Ebola viruses are Group 4. Most of the pathogens within Part VII of the Anti-terrorism, Crime and Security Act 2001 are within Groups 3 and 4.

While extensive, these existing controls focus largely on health and safety, especially in relation to laboratory employees (of whom there are estimated to be around 230,000, mainly working with Group 2 pathogens), rather than security. Safe containment will have implications for defence from attack, and the notification process should prevent the supply of pathogens to unacceptable recipients. But there is little said about unauthorised access and entry or approval or imposition of security arrangements in the approximately 50 laboratories (most of which are in the National Health Service or university sectors) (Home Office, Regulatory Impact Assessment: Security of Pathogens and Toxins (2001), para. 2).

These security concerns are the focus of Part VII of the Anti-terrorism, Crime and Security Act 2001, and it proceeds not by licensing but by compulsory audit (HL Debs. vol. 629 col. 650, 3 December 2001, Lord Bassam). It is necessary to define at the outset, in s. 58, the dangerous pathogens and toxins which will be brought within the controls set out in Part VII. The relevant materials are described as 'dangerous substances', and they include anything which consists of or includes a substance for the time being mentioned in sch. 5; or anything which is infected with or otherwise carries any such substance. The main threats are set out in sch. 5, chosen by reference to their degree of hazard as well as their availability and usefulness to terrorists (for the Hazard group, see http://www.hse.gov.uk/hthdir/noframes/agent1.pdf):

Table 9.1: Dangerous substances under Part VII

Nature	Substance	Hazard group
VIRUS (an organism that can only reproduce within the cells of other organisms)	Chikungunya virus	3
	Congo-crimean haemorrhagic fever virus	4
	Dengue fever virus	3
	Eastern equine encephalitis virus	3
	Ebola virus	4
	Hantaan virus	3
	Japanese encephalitis virus	3
	Junin virus	4
	Lassa fever virus	4
	Lymphocytic choriomeningitis virus	3
	Machupo virus	4
	Marburg virus	4
	Monkey pox virus	3
	Rift Valley fever virus	3
	Tick-borne encephalitis virus (Russian Spring-Summer encephalitis virus)	4
	Variola virus (Smallpox)	4
	Venezuelan equine encephalitis virus	3
	Western equine encephalitis virus	3
	Yellow fever virus	3

RICKETTSIAE (bacteria which cannot survive outside the cells of animals)	Bartonella quintana (Rochalimea quintana, Rickettsia quintana)	2
	Coxiella burnetii	3
	Rickettsia prowazeki	3
	Rickettsia rickettsii	3
BACTERIA (single celled organisms that multiply by cell division and do not possess a nucleus)	Bacillus anthracis (anthrax)	3
	Brucella abortus	3
	Brucella melitensis	3
	Brucella suis	3
	Burkholderia mallei (Pseudomonas mallei)	3
	Burkholderia pseudomallei (Pseudomonas pseudomallei)	3
	Chlamydophila psittaci	3
	Clostridium botulinum	2
	Francisella tularensis ((tularemia) Type A/Type B)	3/2
	Salmonella typhi	3
	Shigella dysenteriae (Type 1/other Types)	3/2
	Vibrio cholerae	2
	Yersinia pestis (Plague)	3
TOXIN (a poisonous agent, especially a poisonous substance produced by a living organism including a genetically modified organism)	Aflatoxins	Not applicable
	Botulinum toxins (Botulism)	
	Clostridium perfringens toxins	
	Conotoxin	
	Microcystin (Cyanginosin)	
	Ricin	
	Saxitoxin	
	Shiga toxin	
	Staphylococcus aureus toxins	
	Tetrodotoxin	
	Verotoxin	

The Secretary of State may, by order, modify the list provided the material is not simply dangerous but 'could be used in an act of terrorism to endanger life or cause serious harm to human health' (s. 58(3)).

Further details as to these substances may be found at the web-site of the Public Health Laboratory Service (http://www.phls.co.uk/facts/index.htm). There is also technical information available through the Centers for Disease Control and Prevention (http://www.bt.cdc.gov/Agent/Agentlist.asp), the lead Federal agency for protecting the health and safety within the umbrella of the US Department of

Health and Human Services. According to this agency, pathogens considered to pose the highest risk comprise: Bacillus anthracis (anthrax); Clostridium botulinum toxin (botulism); Francisella tularensis (tularemia); Variola major (smallpox); Viral haemorrhagic fever (Viral and Rickettsial diseases); Yersinia pestis (plague). These are depicted as 'Category A Diseases/Agents', high-priority agents include organisms that pose a risk to national security because they can be easily disseminated or transmitted from person to person; cause high mortality, and have the potential for major public health impact; might cause public panic and social disruption; and require special action for public health preparedness.

Building upon this framework, Part VII of the 2001 Act seeks to ensure that these substances are held in circumstances of high safety and security, out of harm's way as far as terrorism is concerned. Only in those prescribed conditions, likely to involve a small number of laboratories undertaking medical development and experimentation, may the substance be lawfully possessed. In this way, and in order to ensure that security regulation can be imposed, s. 59 places a duty on the occupiers of premises to notify the Secretary of State within one month before keeping or using any dangerous substance there. Further information can be demanded under ss. 60 and 61. By s. 60, the police can require occupiers to provide information about the presence and security of any dangerous substances kept or used on their premises. By s. 61, the police can request information about persons who have access to dangerous substances or to the premises in which they are kept or used. Section 61 also requires occupiers to ensure that other persons do not have access to the premises or substances. Where occupiers intend to give access to anyone else, notification must be given to the police, and access must be denied until 30 days following the notification unless otherwise agreed by the police. The police can also, under s. 65, enter relevant premises, following at least two days' notice, with any other persons, to assess security measures. In addition (for example, when there is urgency), under s. 66, a justice of the peace or sheriff may issue a search warrant where the police believe that dangerous substances are kept or used on premises for which no notification has been given, or where it is believed that the occupier may not be complying with directions.

Having carried out their checks on the premises and relevant persons, the police can, under s. 62, require the occupier of premises holding dangerous substances to make improvements to the security arrangements operating there. More drastic enforcement powers are given to the Secretary of State, who, under s. 63, can require the disposal of any dangerous substances kept or used on premises where security arrangements are unsatisfactory, and, under s. 64, can require that any specified person be denied access to dangerous substances or the premises in which they are held where exclusion is necessary in the interest of national security or public safety. It is assumed that 'national security' can include 'international security', presumably on the basis of the case of Secretary of State for the Home Department v Rehman [2001] 3 WLR 877 (HL Debs. vol. 629 col. 676, 3 December 2001, Lord Rooker).

By s. 67 of the 2001 Act, it is an offence for occupiers of premises to fail, without reasonable excuse, to comply with any duty or directions. A person guilty of an offence under this section is liable (a) on conviction on indictment, to imprisonment for a term not exceeding five years or a fine (or both); and (b) on summary conviction, to imprisonment for a term not exceeding six months or a fine not exceeding the statutory maximum (or both). Sections 68 and 69 deal with offences by bodies corporate, partnerships and unincorporated associations.

In view of the fact that personal employment, property and business rights might be severely constricted by these measures, a number of appeals mechanisms are set up. First, s. 70 of the 2001 Act establishes the Pathogens Access Appeal Commission (PAAC) to receive appeals made by any person denied access on the direction of the Secretary of State under s. 64. By subsection (3), the Commission must allow an appeal if it considers that the decision to give the directions was flawed when considered in the light of the principles applicable on an application for judicial review. A further appeal may be made with permission on a question of law under subsection (4) to the Court of Appeal or Court of Session.

Schedule 6 to the 2001 Act deals with the constitution and procedures of the PAAC. The Commissioners are appointed by the Lord Chancellor and shall hold and vacate office in accordance with the terms of the appointment (para. 1); whether this is sufficient independence for European Convention purposes is very doubtful. The PAAC shall normally sit as a panel of three, including one person who holds or has held high judicial office (within the meaning of the Appellate Jurisdiction Act 1876 (para. 4)). By para. 5, in line with the precedent of POAC (see Chapter 2), the rules of procedure may provide for full particulars of the reasons for denial of access to be withheld from the applicant and from any person representing him and enable the Commission to exclude persons (including representatives) from all or part of proceedings. Where evidence is kept secret in this way, sch. 6 follows the pattern established in the Special Immigration Appeals Commission Act 1997. A special advocate may be appointed under para. 6 by the relevant Law Officer.

Appeals aside from persons denied access (such as from occupiers of premises against directions relating to compliance with security directions, the disposal of dangerous substances or the provision of information about security arrangements) are provided for by s. 71. The person may appeal within one month to a magistrates' court (with a further appeal to the Crown Court) against the requirement on the ground that, having regard to all the circumstances of the case, it is unreasonable to be required to do that act. In Scotland, the route is the sheriff's court, to sheriff principal to Court of Session.

In relation to the various powers to issue statutory orders under Part VII of the 2001 Act, these are subject to the draft affirmative resolution procedure (in the case of orders amending sch. 5) and the negative resolution procedure (in other cases). As well as the power to amend the list of dangerous substances in sch. 5, s. 75 allows the Secretary of State to apply Part VII to a much wider range of substances, namely (a) toxic chemicals (within the meaning of the Chemical Weapons Act 1996) provided the Secretary of State is satisfied that the chemical could be used in an act of terrorism to endanger life or cause serious harm to human health; or

(b) animal pathogens, plant pathogens and pests, provided the Secretary of State is satisfied that there is a risk that the pathogen or pest is of a description that could be used in an act of terrorism to cause widespread damage to property, significant disruption to the public or significant alarm to the public. The power is subject to the affirmative procedure.

Initial surveys suggested that around a half of the relevant laboratories required some work (HC Debs. vol. 375 col. 723, 26 November 2001, Beverley Hughes).

9.4   SECURITY OF NUCLEAR INDUSTRY

Part VIII of the Anti-terrorism, Crime and Security Act 2001 deals with the security of the nuclear industry. It differs from Part VII, which protects against nuclear materials falling into the wrong hands, in that these measures deal more with organisations, installations and information rather than the materials themselves.

9.4.1   Organisations

Looking first at organisations, s. 75 of the 2001 Act seeks to bolster the position of the Atomic Energy Authority Constabulary. The Constabulary (see http://www.ukaea.org.uk/about/constab.htm), which had been formed in 1954 to take over from War Department and Admiralty Constabularies, is now regulated by the AEA (Special Constabulary) Act 1976 (see Mason, G., 'Nuclear police' (1991) 99 *Police Review* 2384; Johnston, L., 'Policing plutonium' (1994) 4 *Policing and Society* 53). Its officers, who have the status of special constable under s. 3 of the Special Constables Act 1923, are tasked to provide physical protection at designated nuclear sites, with the largest contingent (out of a total of around 500 officers) based at Sellafield in Cumbria. Thus, its jurisdiction is confined to these sites, a 15-mile radius around them, plus the transportation of nuclear materials. Aside from its rather remote system of accountability, the other notable feature of the AEA Constabulary is that a higher than normal proportion of officers are armed.

Section 75 extends its role in various ways. First, it extends the jurisdiction of officers to all nuclear sites that are not for the time being designated by deeming them to be premises under the control of the UK Atomic Energy Authority, in other words, those of the UKAEA (Dounreay, Harwell, and Winfrith), BNFL (Sellafield, Drigg, Chapelcross and Springfields) and Urenco Limited (Capenhurst). The Secretary of State may also by order designate defence and military nuclear sites which are not designated. Though these might receive the protection not only of military personnel but also the Ministry of Defence Police (see below), the expertise of the AEA Constabulary may prove useful at times. Next, these special constables are conferred with the powers and privileges (and are liable to the duties and responsibilities) of a regular constable anywhere within five kilometres of the limits of the nuclear sites and elsewhere when, for example, dealing with the transportation of nuclear material or the pursuit, arrest and custody of suspects. No doubt, existing protocols between the AEA Constabulary and local police, to ensure due notification of AEA Constabulary activities off-site, will be amended accordingly. The powers are in relation to 'nuclear material' which is defined narrowly in subsection (7) to include only fissile material, and not non-nuclear radioactive material, which is less sensitive and does not require AEA Constabulary escort.

The costs of the extra workload for the AEA Constabulary are said to be unquantifiable (Home Office, Regulatory Impact Assessment: *Security of Nuclear Industry, Security of Pathogens and Toxins* (2001), para. 14).

9.4.2 Installations

Security arrangements against the theft of nuclear materials and against attack on nuclear facilities which are power generating stations or are laboratories used for the examination of irradiated fuel are secured by the Nuclear Generating Station (Security) Regulations 1996 (SI 1996 No. 665), made under the Health and Safety at Work etc. Act 1974. The Regulations require there to be site security and transport plans approved by the Secretary of State and periodic security assessments. For the other sites the mechanism is based on Directions under the Atomic Energy Act 1954 and the Nuclear Installations Act 1965. The Office of Civil Nuclear Security (OCNS), which has been part of Department of Trade and Industry since 1 October 2000 (see http://www.consumers.gov.uk/nid/security. htm), is the security regulator. It is responsible for setting security standards and for enforcing compliance. Through the Standing Committee on Police Establishments (SCOPE), it vets personnel and reviews police numbers at licensed nuclear sites policed by the AEA Constabulary (see http://www.consumers.gov.uk/energy/ pdf/scope2.pdf). Further oversight and standard-setting is provided at an international level by the Convention on the Physical Protection of Nuclear Material (Cm. 2945, London, 1995) which came into force in 1987 under the sponsorship of the UN's International Atomic Energy Agency (http://www.iaea.org/). Most relevant is the IAEA's document, 'The Physical Protection of Nuclear Material and Nuclear Facilities' (INFCIRC/225/Rev4, http://www.iaea.org/worldatom/ Programmes/Protection/inf25rev4/rev4_content.html).

By s. 77 of the 2001 Act, the civil nuclear industry is subjected to added powers to demand security measures, and these replace (under s. 77) earlier powers in the Nuclear Installations Act 1965 and the Atomic Energy Authority Act 1971 (and also because employee vetting procedures are now set out in the Police Act 1997, Part V). The Secretary of State may make regulations (subject to negative resolution) for the purpose of ensuring the security of nuclear sites and premises, nuclear material and equipment, including material in transport, other radioactive material and sensitive nuclear information. The regulations may require the production of satisfactory security plans, compliance with any directions given by the Secretary of State and the creation of summary offences, and they can apply to acts done outside the United Kingdom by United Kingdom persons. For these purposes, 'sensitive nuclear information' means (a) information relating to, or capable of use in connection with, any treatment of uranium that increases the proportion of the isotope 235 contained in the uranium; or (b) information relating to activities carried out on or in relation to nuclear sites or other nuclear premises which appears to the Secretary of State to be information which needs to be protected in the interests of national security.

9.4.3 Information

It is vital to keep secure not only nuclear material itself but also information about nuclear technology. Accordingly, s. 79 of the 2001 Act makes it an offence to disclose any information or thing the disclosure of which might prejudice the security of any nuclear site or of any nuclear material either (a) with the intention of prejudicing that security; or (b) being reckless as to whether the disclosure might prejudice that security. Companies working in the nuclear industry are already subject to safety and security regimes, but s. 79 can also extend to individuals (Home Office, Regulatory Impact Assessment: *Security of Nuclear Industry, Security of Pathogens and Toxins* (2001), para. 41). The activities may be committed outside the United Kingdom, but only fall within the offence if they are done by a United Kingdom person. For these purposes, the relevant nuclear material is that held on a nuclear site within the United Kingdom or nuclear material anywhere in the world which is being transported to or from a nuclear site or carried on board a British ship. The penalty on conviction on indictment is imprisonment for a term not exceeding seven years or a fine (or both); and on summary conviction, imprisonment for a term not exceeding six months or a fine not exceeding the statutory maximum (or both). This is a remarkably broad offence which makes no reference to whether the information is in the public domain or whether it might be in the wider public interest to disclose it. Battles fought over the Official Secrets Act 1989 might have to be resumed here (see also Joint Committee on Human Rights, *Report on the Anti-terrorism, Crime and Security Bill* (2001–02 HL 51, HC 420), para. 26). However, the Government Minister (Lord Rooker) did give the following reassurance (HL Debs. vol. 629 cols.1277, 1279, 11 December 2001):

> . . . there is a great deal of information on nuclear transport that has no security implications. This is not in any way intended to be an attack on monitoring by environmental groups on where nuclear matter is moved around the country. People standing and observing on bridges and railway lines can hardly be prejudicing security because they are collecting public information. The same applies to the disclosure of information already in the public domain. The dissemination of that information is very unlikely to fall within the offence here. . . . I reiterate that it will not cover environmental monitoring or whistle-blowing on health and safety matters. It is about giving advance notice of transport movements that leaves them open to attack.

Next, s. 80 of the 2001 Act allows for the Secretary of State to make regulations (subject to the affirmative procedure) prohibiting the disclosure of information about the 'enrichment' of uranium (in other words, any treatment of uranium that increases the proportion of the isotope 235 contained in the uranium). Like s. 79, s. 80 can also extend to individuals as well as regulated companies (Home Office, Regulatory Impact Assessment: *Security of Nuclear Industry, Security of Pathogens and Toxins* (2001), para. 25). The regulations may provide for any prohibition to apply to acts done outside the United Kingdom by United Kingdom persons (as defined in s. 81). This wider jurisdiction is taken since 'this technology is highly attractive to proliferators . . . it can be easily adapted for use in developing nuclear weapons' (HL Debs. vol. 629 col. 685, 3 December 2001, Lord Sainsbury).

Breach of the regulations is made an offence under subsection (3), and the penalty is (a) on conviction on indictment, to imprisonment for a term not exceeding seven years or a fine (or both); and (b) on summary conviction, to imprisonment for a term not exceeding six months or a fine not exceeding the statutory maximum (or both).

Finally, the offences under ss. 79 and 80 may only be prosecuted by or with the consent of the Attorney-General (as regards a prosecution in England and Wales) and the Attorney-General for Northern Ireland (as regards a prosecution in Northern Ireland), except in Scotland (s. 81).

9.5 SECURITY OF AVIATION

Part IX of the Anti-terrorism, Crime and Security Act 2001 amends and supplements the already substantial body of international laws relating to aviation security (see McWhinney, E., *Aircraft Piracy and International Terrorism* (2nd ed., Nijhoff, Dordrecht, 1987); Fitzgerald, G.F, 'Aviation terrorism and the ICAO' (1988) XXV *Canadian Yearbook of International Law* 219; Alexander, Y., and Sochor, E., (eds.) *Aerial Piracy and Aviation Security* (Nijhoff, Dordrecht, 1990); St John, P., 'The role of international aviation organisations in enhancing security' (1998) 10 *Terrorism & Political Violence* 83; Abeyratne, R.I.R., *Aviation Security: Legal and Regulatory Aspects* (Aldershot: Ashgate, 1998); Wilkinson, P., and Jenkins, B.M., *Aviation Terrorism and Security* (Frank Cass, London, 1999); Wilkinson, P., *Terrorism versus Democracy* (Frank Cass, London, 2000), ch. 8). In the light of the hijackings on 11 September, aviation was concentrated upon as the form of transportation most vulnerable to terrorist attack, but that is not to say that other modes of travel have no protection (for example, see the Railways Act 1993, Part III, and the Channel Tunnel Security Order 1994 (SI 1994 No. 570)).

As far as domestic law is concerned, the most relevant measures were the Tokyo Convention Act 1967 (see Convention on offences and certain other Acts committed on board aircraft (Cmnd. 2261, London, 1961) which was replaced by s. 92(1) of the Civil Aviation Act 1982 (as supplemented by the Civil Aviation (Amendment) Act 1996)), the Hijacking Act 1971 (see Convention for the Suppression of

Unlawful Seizures of Aircraft (Cmnd. 4577, London, 1971)), replaced by the Aviation Security Act 1982, the Protection of Aircraft Act 1973 (see Convention for the Suppression of Unlawful Acts against the Safety of Civil Aviation (Cmnd. 4822, London, 1971)), replaced by identical provisions in the Aviation Security Act 1982, the Policing of Airports Act 1974, again replaced in 1982, and the Civil Aviation and Maritime Security Act 1990 (see Protocol for the Suppression of Unlawful Acts of Violence at Airports Serving International Civil Aviation (Cm. 378, London, 1988)). The effects fall into three parts.

First, Part I of the Aviation Security Act 1982 contains broad offences with wide jurisdiction dealing with hijacking, the destruction or endangerment of aircraft and the possession of dangerous articles. These offences are supplemented by s. 1 of the Aviation and Maritime Security Act 1990, which forbids the endangerment of life or property at aerodromes. Secondly, protective measures for aircraft and aerodromes may be required by directive from the Secretary of State for Transport, Local Governments and the Regions or his Airport Security Inspectorate under Part II of the 1982 Act (as amended in 1990) (see further Walker, C.P., *The Prevention of Terrorism in British Law* (2nd ed., Manchester University Press, Manchester, 1992), ch. 12). These reflect the International Civil Aviation Organisation's Standards and Recommended Practices (SARPs) for the safeguarding of international civil aviation. The SARPs relating to civil aviation security are contained in Annex 17 to the Chicago Convention (http://www.icao.org/cgi/goto_atb.pl?icao/en/atb/avsec/overview.htm). In summary, the emphasis is rightly upon ground security through the detection of explosives (see http://www.invision-tech.com/company/overview.html) and firearms, the scrutiny of passengers and passenger-baggage matching. The policing of airports is implemented further by Part III of the 1982 Act. Airports may be 'designated' under s. 25 so that the local police force may freely enter what is otherwise private property.

The changes effected by Part IX of the Anti-terrorism, Crime and Security Act 2001 mainly relate to the policing and protective measures. As regards policing, the story begins with s. 82, by which offences relating to unauthorised presence in the restricted zone of an airport or on an aircraft (ss. 21C(1) and 21D(1) of the Aviation Security Act 1982) and trespassing on a licensed aerodrome (s. 39(1) of the Civil Aviation Act 1982) are made 'arrestable' offences for the purposes of s. 24(2) of the Police and Criminal Evidence Act 1984 (PACE) (or art. 26 of Police and Criminal Evidence (Northern Ireland) Order 1989 (SI 1989 No. 1341 (NI 12)). The result is that the police can arrest without warrant even though the penalties for those offences would not normally bring them within the summary arrest powers in s. 24 of the 1984 Act. In the absence of a statutory code like PACE in Scotland, a statutory power of arrest without warrant is introduced by s. 82(3). Other relatively minor policing changes include, by s. 83, an increase in the penalty (from level 1 to level 3) for the offence of trespass on an aerodrome contrary to s. 39(1) of the Civil Aviation Act 1982, and by s. 84, the provision of a specific power for the police or aviation authority employees to use force to remove intruders on aerodrome restricted zones or aircraft whose presence is unauthorised under s. 21C of the Aviation Security Act 1982 (equivalent to s. 31(4) of the Aviation and Maritime Security Act 1990, as amended, for ports areas and under art. 31 of the Channel Tunnel Security Order 1994 (SI 1994 No. 570)). While the purported aim of these measures is to ensure the security of airports, it is almost certain they will be used primarily against environmental protesters. It is also envisaged that they will be used against journalists who 'probe' airport security (Home Office, Regulatory Impact Assessment: *Aviation Security*, 2001, para. 8). There are currently around 70 incidents per year (para. 9).

Next, s. 86 of the 2001 Act extends powers of the Aviation Security Inspectorate to bring them in line with provisions for the detention of ships and Channel Tunnel trains (s. 21 of the Aviation and Maritime Security Act 1990 and art. 27 of the Channel Tunnel (Security) Order 1994 (SI 1994 No. 570)). They may detain aircraft (as permitted by s. 60 of the Civil Aviation Act 1982 and art. 118 of the Air Navigation Order 2000 (SI 2000 No. 1562) not simply to carry out an inspection of airworthiness (under s. 20(3) of the 1982 Act) but also if 'of the opinion' that the standard of security uncovered by the inspection is inadequate because of a failure to comply with the Department's statutory Directions or an Enforcement Notice or because of threats or potential acts of violence. These powers are granted by a new s. 20B of the Aviation Security Act 1982. There are corresponding offences of failing to comply or obstruction; on summary conviction fines up to level 5 can be imposed, on indictment the penalty is a maximum of two years and or a fine. In 1999–2000, 898 inspections were made of airports and 1,199 to air cargo agents (see below) to check security; there were issued 175 Deficiency Notices and one Enforcement Notice (Home Office, Regulatory Impact Assessment: *Aviation Security*, 2001, para. 25).

New protective security measures are envisaged by ss. 85 and 87 of the 2001 Act. Section 85 inserts a new s. 20A into the Aviation Security Act 1982 in order to grant the Secretary of State extra powers under s. 21F of the 1982 Act. Under s. 21F, the Secretary of State for the Department of Transport, Local Government and the Regions (DTLR) may, by regulations, maintain a list of air cargo agents who are approved (on condition that they observe proper security standards pursuant to the Aviation Security (Air Cargo Agents) Regulations 1993 (SI 1993 No.1073), as amended by SI 1996 No. 1607, SI 1998 No. 1152) to offer secure air cargo services. These arrangements are now to be applied to other parts of the industry which provide security services to civil aviation — 'for example companies contracted by airports and airlines to provide passenger and baggage screening services, and companies and individuals who provide aviation security training services' (Home Office, Explanatory Notes to the Anti-terrorism, Crime and Security Bill (London, 2001) para. 189). Section 87 tightens the regulations relating to air cargo agents themselves. As noted above, by s. 21F, there is a list of security approved air cargo agents. However, there was no offence of pretending to have been approved by DTLR to operate as a security approved air cargo agent (even though at least two such cases have come to light: Home Office, Regulatory Impact Assessment: *Aviation Security*, 2001, para. 36). Accordingly, s. 87 enacts a new s. 21F, to create a new offence of issuing a document which falsely claims to come from a security approved air cargo agent (it is a summary offence (level 5)).

Finally, s. 88 of the 2001 Act allows these measures to be applied outside the United Kingdom to the Channel Islands, the Isle of Man and any colony along the lines already laid down by s. 108(1) and (2) of the Civil Aviation Act 1982 and s. 39(3) of the Aviation Security Act 1982.

It would be difficult to devise on paper a more stringent security system, but there is room for doubt as to whether it has been implemented as vigorously as possible. The Government has often sought to achieve voluntary co-operation and has therefore avoided use of formal, enforceable directives. The inspection of standards has been alleged to be inadequate, with a thin layer of Department of Transport inspectors in the Transport Security Division (TRANSEC) (see Malik, O., 'Aviation security before and after Lockerbie' (1998) 10 *Terrorism & Political Violence* 112) and no proper ICAO inspectorate (Wilkinson, P., *Terrorism versus Democracy* (Frank Cass, London, 2000), p. 169). It has also shirked any responsibility for the funding of security measures and wound up an Aviation Security Fund in 1983. At the same time, it should be remembered that for air travel to grind to a halt because of security restrictions would itself be a victory for terrorism. The Anti-terrorism, Crime and Security Act 2001 did not offer the occasion for a more thorough review of aviation security, nor did it encourage an update of related areas such as maritime security (see the Aviation and Maritime Security Act 1990, Parts II and III; see Ronzitti, N., (ed.), *Maritime Terrorism and International Law* (Nijhoff, Dordrecht, 1990)). There is plenty of work left to be done.

9.6   POLICING VULNERABLE SITES

In 9.4 above, it is mentioned that there exists an Atomic Energy Authority Constabulary (AEAC) which undertakes security duties in connection with atomic energy sites and whose role is extended under the Anti-terrorism, Crime and Security Act 2001. Likewise, the Ministry of Defence Police (MDP) and British Transport Police (BTP) are given added responsibility. Part X of the Anti-terrorism, Crime and Security Act 2001 extends their jurisdiction so as to maximise their expertise and policing impact.

9.6.1   Ministry of Defence Police

The MDP was formed in 1971 from the unification of distinct service constabularies and is now regulated by the Ministry of Defence Police Act 1987. The MDP is a civilian police force (with 3,443 officers as at 1 January 2001 in 16 area policing teams) exercising police powers in connection with military establishments; all uniformed officers are trained to use firearms (see http://www.official-documents.co.uk/document/cm38/3889/mod105.htm; Johnston, L., 'An unseen force' (1993) 3 *Policing and Society* 23). It became an MOD Agency in 1996. The MDP must be distinguished from the various other policing agencies, including the Ministry of Defence Guard Service (MGS) which undertakes a range of unarmed guarding tasks including access control and patrols; the Military Provost Guard Service of locally engaged Service personnel, who since 1997 have exercised a guarding, rather than full policing role; the Service Police (the military police forces, including the Royal Navy Regulating Branch; the Royal Marines Police; the Royal Military Police; and the Royal Air Force Police), which comprise Service personnel; and other private guards employed to provide security (see Defence Committee, The Physical Security of Military Installations in the United Kingdom (1983–84) HC 397-I; Security at Royal Ordnance Factories and Nuclear Bases (1984–85) HC 217; The Physical Security of Military Installations in the United Kingdom (1989–90) HC 171; Ministry of Defence Police and Guarding (1995–96) HC 189).

By s. 98 of the 2001 Act, there is an amendment to s. 2 of the Ministry of Defence Police Act 1987. By s. 98(3), the MDP jurisdiction in relation to defence personnel (which applies anywhere in the United Kingdom) is extended from the alleged commission of offences by defence personnel to offences against defence personnel (such as any attempt to incite or bribe defence personnel into committing offences revealing confidential information).

By s. 98(4), instead of being geographically confined to defence land and property within the United Kingdom and its territorial waters, the MDP is also enabled to operate beyond and with full 'normal' constabulary powers, whenever a constable of Home Department police force, the Police Service of Northern Ireland, the British Transport Police or the UK Atomic Energy Authority Constabulary has asked for assistance. Compared to the previous version, the new powers are restricted to the particular incident, investigation or operation in relation to which assistance is requested, but they are not restricted to the vicinity of the defence land. They will be exercisable within the police area of a requesting police force. In an emergency, an MDP officer in uniform (or with proof of office, such as a warrant card), may act without request if he (i) reasonably suspects that an offence is about to be committed, is being committed or has been committed, or where he reasonably believes that action is necessary to save life or prevent or minimise personal injury, and (ii) reasonably believes that waiting for such a request would frustrate or seriously prejudice the purpose of his action. It is expected that emergency circumstances will be narrowly conceived: 'Given the availability of modern radio communications, the effect will restrict its use to circumstances of genuine emergency when a virtually instant reaction is needed' (HC Debs. vol. 375 col. 775, 26 November 2001, Lewis Moonie). Examples might be where (col. 776):

Intelligence is received that a possible terrorist is near a defence base — perhaps a US base. The suspect is believed to be a member of an illegal organisation, or to have with him a stolen passport or a weapon. There may be no immediate threat of violence; the suspect is only scouting — carrying out reconnaissance. Under the Terrorism Act 2000, the MDP have the power to arrest members of illegal organisations. They have powers of arrest and stop and search related to stolen articles, but at present they could act only if two requirements are met: the suspect is 'in the vicinity' of the base on which the police are operating, and the local force agrees. The new powers in the Bill will allow the MDP to act if there is no time to bring in the local police — in other words, if there is an emergency.

To take a second case — an MDP officer in a street adjacent to defence property is approached by a woman who says, 'Stop that man, he has taken my purse'. That could happen up the road at the Ministry of Defence — our own officers patrol outside. The officer sees a man running away. Should he say, 'Sorry, can't help. Although I may look like a police officer, I am in the MDP and I have no jurisdiction'? Should the officer try to establish whether the man had or had not used violence in taking the purse — by which time the man will have made off? Should the officer try to contact the local police station to seek instruction? The result would be the same.

Additional to s. 98(4), s. 99 (inserting a new s. 2A into the 1987 Act) envisages that the MDP may also swing into action where another police force requires extra resources to meet a special burden. If offering such inter-force assistance (similar to the Police Act 1996, s. 24(3)), the MDP officers come under the direction of the chief officer of the force with which they are serving for the time being and have full powers of a constable of that force. Corresponding Scottish measures are in sch. 7, paras 1 to 7.

9.6.2 British Transport Police

The British Transport Police (BTP) was established under the Transport Acts 1962–92 under the British Railways Board (BRB) (see http://www.btp.police.uk/; Purnell, J., 'Banish bias against the BTP' (1992) 100 *Police Review* 200). The Railways Act 1993 transferred these powers direct to the Secretary of State, and the BRB were required to appoint a Committee to secure an adequate and efficient police service for the railway network. The Committee appoints and supervises the Chief Constable who is responsible for the administration of the force. The Strategic Rail Authority inherited the authority of the BRB under the Transport Act 2000. The BTP is the national police force for the public railways system throughout England, Scotland and Wales (but not Northern Ireland). The force is also responsible for policing the London Underground, the Docklands Light Railway, the Croydon Tramlink and the Midland Metro. Its main activities include public order policing and protecting from attack, damage and theft. The antecedent of the BTP go back to the building of the railways in the nineteenth century. There are currently just over 2,000 officers. Other than its national basis, the BTP is very similar in training, regulations and practices to Home Office maintained police forces.

Section 100 makes stipulations for the BTP to act outside their normal railways jurisdiction corresponding to those for the MDP. According to the Government Memorandum accompanying the Anti-terrorism Bill (para. 254):

BTP constables already have jurisdiction on, and in the vicinity of, the railways and elsewhere on railways matters. They need however to move between railway sites and often have a presence in city centres, and BTP officers are frequently called upon to intervene in incidents outside their 'railways' jurisdiction. It is estimated that some such 8,000 incidents occur each year. In these circumstances BTP officers only have the powers of an ordinary citizen, despite being police officers fully trained to the standards of a Home Office force, and despite routinely dealing with the same range of incidents in the course of their railway activities.

Therefore, similar to s. 98(4), s. 100(1) allows a BTP officer to assist other forces (and with the full powers of that force) on request in relation to a single incident, investigation or operation. The power can be exercised without request in an emergency, as under s. 98(4).

9.6.3 Both forces

Both the MDP and BTP are provided with a range of further policing powers in sch. 7. Most apply to the BTP and are in its case based on Chapter 6 of the Department of Transport, Local Government and the Regions' consultation document, *Modernising the British Transport Police* (http://www.railways.dtlr.gov.uk/consult/police/index.htm, 2001). Paragraphs 8 to 10 amend s. 54 of the Firearms Act 1968 so as to allow BTP officers and associated civilian employees (who are not Crown servants) to possess, purchase and acquire CS incapacitant sprays and ammunition used for such sprays (in line with the Consulation Paper, para. 6.33). Paragraphs 11 to 14 amend ss. 35 and 36 of PACE 1984 so as to allow the BTP's chief constable to designate police stations to be used to detain arrested persons and to appoint custody officers for these stations (Consultation Paper, para. 6.29). Paragraphs 15 and 16 amend s. 60 of the Criminal Justice and Public Order Act 1994 so as to allow a BTP officer of the rank of inspector or above, to authorise, in certain circumstances, the use of certain stop and search powers in, on and in the vicinity of premises policed by the BTP when it is reasonably believed that incidents of violence may take place or that persons are carrying dangerous weapons. The power is included even though the Consultation Paper (para. 6.17) foresaw its use in connection with 'policing football crowds and major demonstrations in London' rather than terrorism. Paragraphs 17 to 19 allow the BTP to make use of ss. 136, 137 and 140 of the Criminal Justice and Public Order Act 1994 so as to conduct cross-border operations between the jurisdictions of England, Wales or Scotland (see Walker, C., 'Internal cross-border policing' (1997) 56 *Cambridge Law Journal* 114). Again, football policing (as between Scotland and England) is the main reason behind this extension (Consultation Paper, para. 6.21). Paragraphs 20 to 28 deal with changes to the Police Act 1996, amending s. 23 of the Police Act 1996 to enable the BTP to enter collaboration agreements with other police forces; amending s. 24 to allow the BTP to provide aid to other police forces to meet special demands on those other forces; and amending s. 25 to allow the BTP to provide special police services to any person. These amendments are made not only for operational effectiveness but also to ensure budget accountability by charges to the requesting force (Consultation Paper, para. 6.11). There are also changes to ss. 90 and 91 of the Police Act 1996 to make it an offence to impersonate a BTP constable or cause disaffection in the BTP. There was hitherto no comparable legislation for the BTP on 'causing disaffection' (Consultation Paper, para. 6.15).

Finally, paras 29 to 33 amend the Terrorism Act 2000. Section 34 is amended (by para. 30) to allow the BTP and the MDP, in certain circumstances, to designate areas in which cordons may be erected for the purposes of terrorist investigations. It may be noted that since 1997, over half the terrorist attacks on the mainland have taken place on the railway and that the BTP is second only to the Metropolitan Police in responding to the various terrorist threats that are made within its jurisdiction (Consultation Paper, para. 6.5). Section 44 of the Terrorism Act 2000 is amended (by para. 31) to allow the BTP and MDP, in certain circumstances, to specify areas or places in which for up to 28 days the BTP or MDP can stop and search vehicles, their occupants and pedestrians for the prevention of terrorism. An assistant chief constable, or higher officer, may authorise any uniformed constable to stop and search pedestrians or vehicles (para. 6.6). The Secretary of State must confirm these orders within 48 hours.

9.6.4   Comment

Many of the proposals relating to the extension of the jurisdiction of the specialist police revive earlier overtures. The lack of time for proper consideration and for the insertion of effective safeguards is an inevitable criticism. The refusal to tie down the extensions to terrorist investigations or policing is a recurrent theme, which the Defence Minister, Lord Bach, sought valiantly to answer in this context (HL Debs. vol. 629 col. 643, 4 December 2001; see also cols. 1466, 1533, 13 December 2001):

> . . . what is it reasonable to assume is terrorism? What of the case of going equipped to commit criminal damage, or the use of a stolen car? Would it be reasonable for a Ministry of Defence police officer to assume that that constituted an act of terrorism? What of the possession of a stolen passport? Perhaps I may cite as an example an individual acting suspiciously and tampering with a vehicle. He may be attempting simply to steal it, which would not be an act of terrorism. Alternatively, he may be seeking to place a bomb under the car. Clearly that would be such an act.

If it is so impossible to distinguish terrorism from crime, then one wonders what is the value of the arrest power in s. 41 at the heart of the Terrorism Act 2000?

In the case of the MDP, similar ideas appeared in the Armed Forces Bill 2000–2001 (see Select Committee on the Armed Forces Bill, 2000–01 HC 154-I, xvi). It was felt by the Secretary of State for Defence that the greater mobility of the MDP and the encouragement of mutual aid between uniformed policing services made these changes advisable (para. 36, 13 March 2001). But, in response, the Select Committee was keen to avoid the preemption of local police forces and sought clearer local protocols to be agreed (paras 39, 46). The proposals were later withdrawn in order for the remainder of the legislation to receive Royal Assent before the pending General Election. The hostility to the MDP was based on the criticism that they lacked training to deal with the public (para. 52), on the fears that they could be used as a mobile paramilitary police on a national basis, and misgivings about their limited degree of accountability to the public, especially at a local level. The MDP is accountable to the Secretary of State, as a Ministry of Defence Agency (para. 40):

Day to day responsibility for the MDP is delegated to the Second Permanent Under Secretary who is the owner of the Agency and who chairs the Ministry of Defence Police Committee. The committee's membership includes senior Service and police personnel, MoD officials, and . . . three independent members, of whom one is a trade union representative, and another represents the Army Families Federation.

The Select Committee recommended that the MoD Police Committee should in future have at least a third of its members from outside the civil service, the police service or the Armed Services (para. 41). None of these concerns is addressed by the Anti-terrorism, Crime and Security Act 2001 (though three independent members have been added in practice to the MoD Police Committee, and there is an undertaking of further reforms (HC Debs. vol. 375 col. 779, 26 November 2001, Lewis Moonie). The idea of local protocols to decide geographic areas of operation has been rejected (HC Debs. vol. 375 col. 777, 26 November 2001, Lewis Moonie) in favour of tasking by request (see Defence Select Committee, The Ministry of Defence Police: Changes in Jurisdiction Proposed under the Anti-Terrorism, Crime and Security Bill 2001 (2001–02 HC 382), para. 18). National protocols continue to exist (Home Office Circular 17/1999, 25 March 1999; Scottish Police Circular 14/1999).

The Defence Select Committee (Defence Select Committee, The Ministry of Defence Police: Changes in Jurisdiction Proposed under the Anti-Terrorism, Crime and Security Bill 2001 (2001–02 HC 382)) supported much of the legislation. It viewed the powers to deal with emergencies as sensible and practicable (para. 23) but recognised the continuing defects in regard to accountability (para. 28) and a complaints system (para. 34) and inspections (para. 36). The Police Reform Bill 2001–02 (HL 48) Part V addresses the last two issues but not accountability.

As for the BTP, the Government announced its intention to introduce legislation about the BTP in 1998 in order, *inter alia*, to create an independent national police authority (it is proposed that the Authority would have 13 members who would be appointed by the Secretary of State and would represent the railways industry,

passenger groups, regional assemblies, the SRA, and other specialist and independent interests) and to give the BTP jurisdiction outside the railways in certain
circumstances. In October 2001 the Department of Transport, Local Government
and the Regions published a consultation document, *Modernising the British
Transport Police* (see http://www.railways.dtlr.gov.uk/consult/police/index.htm).
The consultation period was due to close in January 2002, but the Home Office
took on some changes as a matter of urgency. Chapter 5 of the consultation paper
identifies several of the issues now addressed in the 2001 Act, including the lack
of any jurisdiction for the BTP outside the railways (para. 5.1). It will be noted
that, once again, the extra powers (though not to act in response to a request from
the public — para. 5.2) have preceded the extra accountability.

The Government asserts that the MDP and other specialist forces should be
entrusted with wider policing duties:

> Anyone would think that members of the MDP police only ever deal with people
> in uniform. That is simply not the case; they police housing estates . . . They
> undergo the same basic training as any other constable. Their primary role is, in
> fact, to deal with civilians, dependants, contractors, trades people and visitors to
> our sites. The MDP police service football and rugby matches. They police
> public events, garrison areas, such as Colchester, Salisbury Plain, Aldershot and
> Catterick, and public roads open to and widely used by the general public. They
> run community initiatives in defence areas. . . . They are not amateurs; they are
> highly trained civilian police officers. They are not a military police force.
> However, I submit that they are as well trained as anyone in any other police
> force.' (HC Debs. vol. 375 cols. 778–779, 26 November 2001, Lewis Moonie)

However, the Joint Committee on Human Rights believed that the extension of BTP
and MDP powers does not offer adequate protection for human rights (Report on the
Anti-terrorism, Crime and Security Bill (2001–02 HL 37, HC 372), para. 68):

> The ordinary constabularies are subject to elaborate mechanisms designed to
> provide safeguards for those rights, including subjection to various Codes of
> Practice, recording requirements, complaints procedures, and training pro-
> grammes. These safeguards usually make it possible to say that the exercise of
> police powers which interfere with Convention rights will normally be justifiable
> within the terms of the [European Convention on Human Rights]. It is not clear
> how those safeguards will be applied to, and operated by, the Ministry of
> Defence Police, the British Transport Police, and the Atomic Energy Authority
> special constables. Until the extent to which the safeguards surrounding the
> procedures of Home Office police forces will apply to the Ministry of Defence
> Police, the British Transport Police, and the Atomic Energy Authority special
> constables in their new functions is clarified, we are unable to be confident that
> the Bill provides adequate safeguards against abuse of or interference in human
> rights.

Chapter Ten
Structural and other matters

10.1 COMMENCEMENT AND TRANSITION

10.1.1 Terrorism Act 2000

On assent (20 July 2000), only a few provisions of the Terrorism Act 2000 came immediately into force: ss. 129 to 131 and, by virtue of s. 128, ss. 2(1)(b) and (2) and 118 and sch. 1. Thereafter, ss. 99 (police and army powers: code of practice), 101 (codes of practice: supplementary) and parts of schs 8 (treatment of persons detained under s. 41 or sch. 7) and 14 (exercise of officers' powers) took effect on 12 October 2000 (Terrorism Act 2000 (Commencement No. 1) Order 2000 (SI 2000 No. 2800)). Further provisions took effect on the 31 October 2000, pursuant to the Terrorism Act 2000 (Commencement No. 2) Order 2000 (SI 2000 No. 2944): s. 4 (deproscription: application), subsections (3) and (4); (b) in s. 5 (deproscription: appeal), subsection (1), and subsection (6) in part; s. 24 (seizure of terrorist cash: interpretation), subsection (2)(e); s. 31 (seizure of terrorist cash: rules of court); s. 119 (Crown servants, regulators etc.); s. 123 (orders and regulations); sch. 3 (the Proscribed Organisations Appeal Commission), and parts of schs 4 (forfeiture orders), 5, 6 (financial information), 7 (port and border controls), and 8 (detention). The remainder of the Act came into force by order (Terrorism Act 2000 (Commencement No. 3) Order 2001 (SI 2001 No. 421)) on 19 February 2001 with the exception of s. 100 (code of practice relating to the video-recording of interviews in Northern Ireland). The Order also terminates the effect of the transitional provisions in sch. 1 relating to Northern Ireland, effectively replacing them with the transitional provisions in Part VII and ensures that their effect cannot be revived.

As described in Chapter 1, the Terrorism Act 2000 is meant to comprise a comprehensive and permanent code. It therefore follows that, by s. 2, the Prevention of Terrorism (Temporary Provisions) Act 1989, and the Northern Ireland (Emergency Provisions) Act 1996 (subject to transitional arrangements) cease to have effect. Section 125 introduces the large list of consequential amendments (sch. 15) and repeals (sch. 16). Amongst the repeals are the whole of the Prevention of Terrorism (Temporary Provisions) Act 1989 and its amending legislation (such as the Criminal Justice and Public Order Act 1994, ss. 81 to 83, the Prevention of Terrorism (Additional Powers) Act 1996 and the Criminal Justice (Terrorism and Conspiracy) Act 1998, ss. 1 to 4) as well as the whole of the Northern Ireland (Emergency Provisions) Acts 1996 and 1998. However, s. 2 and sch. 1 preserved certain sections of the 1996 Act, in some cases with amendment, for a transitional period. These preservations (which ended with the coming into force of the bulk of the Terrorism Act 2000 on 19 February 2001) are in addition to the incorporations on a temporary basis of the measures within Part VII of the Act (see Chapter 7). The impermanence of both is, of course, predicated upon the progress in the Northern Ireland Peace Process and the hope that it will be possible soon to dispense with these special measures.

It may be deduced from the foregoing discussion that ss. 5 to 7 of the Criminal Justice (Terrorism and Conspiracy) Act 1998 have taken on a life now independent of the Terrorism Act 2000.

In the event, the Terrorism Act 2000 allowed the Prevention of Terrorism (Temporary Provisions) Act 1989 to subsist until 19 February 2001 (having last been renewed on the 22 March 2000). The Northern Ireland (Emergency Provisions) Acts 1996 and 1998 (as renewed on the 8 and 14 June 2000) were given a lease of life beyond 24 August 2000 in a form subject to amendments in sch. 1, again until 19 February 2001.

10.1.2   Anti-terrorism, Crime and Security Act 2001

By s. 127, much of the Anti-terrorism, Crime and Security Act 2001 came into force on the date of assent (14 December 2001). This was the fate of Parts II to VI, Part VIII, except s. 78 (repeals relating to the nuclear industry), Part IX, except ss. 84 and 87 (which come into force after two months), ss. 89 to 97, ss. 98 to 100, except so far as they extend to Scotland, s. 101 and sch. 7, except so far as they relate to the entries in respect of the Police (Scotland) Act 1967, Part XI, Part XIII, except s. 121, and most of Part XIV except those measures impinging on the excepted measures. The Anti-terrorism, Crime and Security Act 2001 (Commencement No. 1 and Consequential Provisions) Order 2001 (SI 2001 No. 4019) brought s. 1, together with sch. 1, s. 2, s. 3, together with sch. 2, and Part 1 of sch. 8, as well as the code of practice under sch. 14 to the Terrorism Act 2000 (as modified) into force on 20 December 2001.

However, there are some delays. For example, Part VII (security of pathogens and toxins) requires some administrative infrastructure to be erected before it becomes operational. In addition, a number of powers and offences are delayed (for two months) while advice to the police or courts is produced, including the power of arrest without warrant under s. 82, and the increased penalty for trespass on an aerodrome under s. 83. A number of Scottish measures are delayed (to a date to be appointed) to allow consultation with the Scottish Ministers (ss. 98 to 100,

s. 101 and sch. 7, so far as they relate to the entries in respect of the Police (Scotland) Act 1967, s. 125 and sch. 8, so far as they relate to the entries in Part 6 of sch. 8 in respect of the British Transport Commission Act 1962 and the Ministry of Defence Police Act 1987, so far as those entries extend to Scotland) and so will enter into force by order.

10.2   DURATION AND SCRUTINY

10.2.1   Terrorism Act 2000

Since the Terrorism Act 2000 is meant to be a permanent code, responding to a permanent threat to national security and the right to life of individuals, there is no requirement for periodic renewal or re-enactment, in line with the wishes of Lord Lloyd (Inquiry into Legislation against Terrorism (Cm. 3420, London, 1996), paras 1.20, 17.6). According to Government Minister, Charles Clarke (HC Debs. vol. 346 col. 363, 15 March 2000):

> We have had so-called temporary provisions on the statute book for 25 years. The time has come to face the fact of terrorism and be ready to deal with it for the foreseeable future. We need to make the powers permanently available, although the fact that those powers are available does not mean that they have to be used.

An exception is Part VII (which is deemed for these purposes to include the extraordinary powers of the Secretary of State to issue restraint or search orders under paras 36 and 37 of sch. 4, and paras 19 to 21 of sch. 5). These are the extra measures for Northern Ireland whose demise awaits the more certain success of the Peace Process. For those measures alone, s. 112 provides for annual renewal by order of the Secretary of State. Furthermore, in line with the Northern Ireland (Emergency Provisions) Act 1996, renewal by order cannot persist beyond the period of five years. However, the statutory requirement of independent review for the measures relating to specified proscribed organisations (formerly in s. 8 of the Criminal Justice (Terrorism and Conspiracy) Act 1998) has been dropped. In the meantime, the undertaking has been given that (HC Debs. vol. 341 col. 226, 14 December 1999, Charles Clarke):

> Our whole approach to this part of the Bill is part of a process in which all our colleagues in Northern Ireland have participated. The Government are prepared to remove Part VII as soon as the assessed level of threat means that it is safe to do so. It is part of the process through which we have gone and to which both sides of the House are committed. We intend to be in tune with the process rather than being at odds with it. That is why the Bill has been introduced, and why we have dealt with these matters in this way.

While it is logical that there should be no requirement of renewal, the level of scrutiny applied otherwise to what are meant to be unusual incursions into the normal rights of individuals is disappointing, uninventive and fails to live up to the ideals of Lord Lloyd set out in Chapter 1 (for previous attempts, see Walker, C.P., 'The commodity of justice in states of emergency' (1999) 50 *Northern Ireland Legal Quarterly* 164). Section 126 (which was conceded at the Committee stage of the passage of the Act: HC Debs. Standing Committee D, col. 312, 8 February 2000, Charles Clarke) simply requires that the Secretary of State shall lay before both Houses of Parliament at least once in every 12 months a report on the working of this Act. It would seem that the report will relate primarily to the past working of the legislation rather than, as under previous arrangements, to the future need for it. Given that the Act is to be permanent (aside from Part VII), it cannot be contemplated that the latter issue should be considered at any length. But given that some measures are not meant to be permanent, especially Part VIII, but also proscription orders and carding at ports, it may be that the two issues will be considered in the future. Certainly, there were mixed messages on the extent of scrutiny from Government Ministers. On the one hand, the Home Secretary, when presenting the legislation, contended that 'it was hoped to do away with the need for annual debate' (HC Debs. vol. 327 col. 999, 16 March 1999, Jack Straw). Equally the Home Office Minister in the House of Lords stated that:

> The Government believe that the time has come for counter-terrorist powers to be made permanent, but they fully recognise the interest and concern in both Houses, and in the country more generally, in ensuring that these powers continue to be used fairly, proportionately and effectively. An annual independent report will allow those issues to be addressed. (HL Debs. vol. 611 col. 1433, 6 April 2000, Lord Bassam).

On the other hand, the Home Office Minister of State seemed to envisage a more extensive scrutiny:

> The assessor's annual reports on the legislation will remain in place. The debate under the affirmative procedure will allow full examination of the Government's decisions on the continuation of the legislation or removal of parts of it. (HC Debs. Standing Committee D col. 293, 3 February 2000, Adam Ingram)

A further extra-statutory concession was made during Parliamentary passage that the annual report will derive from an independent reviewer reporting to the Secretary of State who is then obliged to lay the report before Parliament (HC Debs. Standing Committee D, col. 315, 8 February 2000, Charles Clarke). Of course, this still represents a significant diminution in scrutiny — there is no certainty of a debate or proper, full public answers to queries raised by the reviewer or others. No concession was made that there would be a debate on the floor of the House — the Minister pointed rather to possible Select Committee scrutiny

(HC Debs. Standing Committee D, col. 315, 8 February 2000, Charles Clarke). This stance, though in accord with the Inquiry into Legislation against Terrorism (Cm. 3420, London, 1996, para. 17.6), means that an annual parliamentary review is no longer needed. Surely, the better approach is that extraordinary powers should be subjected to extraordinary scrutiny. An annual report could be strengthened by a number of devices. First, the invocation of powers should be subject to pre-announced and expressly invoked criteria, in order that the reviewers and Parliament can make judgments as to the desirability of the provisions. So, there should always be some kind of declaration of invocation based on stated facts relating both to the clear and present danger and the nature of the failure of existing laws. Secondly, there should be an independent standing committee, which would investigate and report on any proposed institution of the legislation, its working while in force, its renewal and its compatibility with international obligations. Thirdly, there should occur the subjection of the actual application of each special law to judicial control so far as possible; the Human Rights Act 1998 will probably allow for this, subject to standing and financial aid.

10.2.2 Anti-terrorism, Crime and Security Act 2001

A complex array of limits and reviews are contained in the 2001 Act. The overlapping and messy arrangements arise from the fact that the legislation was passed in haste, and so amendments were forced upon the Government without adequate time for reflection as to coherence. Such is the effect of s. 122, by which the Home Secretary shall appoint a committee to conduct a review of this Act. This idea was first planted at the House of Lords' Committee stage (HL Debs. vol. 629 col. 460, 29 November 2001, Lord Rooker) but did not reach fruition until the final stages of the Bill (col. 1532, 13 December 2001). The committee must comprise no fewer than seven members, all of whom must be Privy Counsellors. It was made clear by the Government that this is not meant to be an episodic review (HL Debs. vol. 629 col. 1536, 13 December 2001, Lord Rooker):

> It is true that there will be a report before two years, but our intention is that the review will start as soon as the Act comes into effect, so that there will be a constant period of review. We cannot say when, but the committee will be set up and proposals will be drawn up as soon as possible, early in the new year. It has never been our intention that everything should go to sleep and then, all of a sudden after two years, the committee will look at what has happened. Our intention has always been to have a constant review.

The committee shall complete the review and send a report to the Secretary of State not later than the end of two years beginning with the day on which this Act is passed. A copy must then be laid before Parliament. The establishment of a statutory form of review, based within Parliament, is to be welcomed, but the opportunity was not taken to afford the committee powers to take evidence and to

obtain documents; its effectiveness is therefore to a worrying degree at the behest
of the Home Secretary. On the other hand, it was granted under s. 123 one
fearsome weapon to grab attention. By s. 123, a report may specify that any
provision of this Act shall cease to have effect at the end of the period of six
months beginning with the day on which the report is laid before Parliament under
s. 122, unless in the meantime a motion has been made in each House of
Parliament considering the report.

Moving to more specific forms of limit and review under the 2001 Act, as
related in Chapter 8, because of the extraordinary nature of detention without trial
and the consequent reliance upon a derogation notice, Parliament insisted on limits
on the duration of the powers plus an extra tier of scrutiny for these measures. The
duration is dealt with by s. 29, which sets an initial period of 15 months beginning
with the day on which this Act is passed. The Secretary of State may by statutory
order repeal ss. 21 to 23 at an earlier date. Conversely, if the measures are about
to expire, have expired or have been repealed, the Secretary of State may by order
continue in force or revive those sections for a period not exceeding one year. The
order is subject to affirmative resolution of Parliament. Overall, ss. 21 to 23 are
subject to a 'sunset' clause in s. 29(7), by which they shall cease to have effect at
the end of 10 November 2006. As for review, by s. 28, the Secretary of State is
required to appoint a person to review the operation of ss. 21 to 23. The review
must take place not later than 14 months after the passage of the Act, and one
month before the expiry of any revived period of operation. A copy of any report
shall be laid before Parliament as soon as is reasonably practicable but there is no
requirement for debate.

Another limit as to duration applies in Part XI in connection with the retention
of communications data. If, 'after reviewing the operation of any requirements
contained in the code of practice and any agreements under section 102, it appears
to the Secretary of State that it is necessary to do so', then, by s. 104, the Secretary
of State can issue compulsory directions. However, the apprehension of Parliament
concerning the intrusiveness of these measures is evidenced by s. 105, by which
any mandatory scheme under s. 104 will itself lapse after two years unless renewed
(which can occur more than once) by affirmative order.

The next limit is in s. 111 which relates to the implementation of European
Union Third Pillar measures relating to terrorism (described later in this chapter).
In order to ensure that the wide powers to introduce legislation are not used much
beyond the needs of anti-terrorism measures, they are time-limited to the 1 July
2002 (see HL Debs. vol. 629 col. 1142, 10 December 2001, Baroness Symons).

As argued in Chapter 8, these measures are to be welcomed as ensuring that
extraordinary intrusions into liberty are kept under control by subjecting them to
independent scrutiny. But remaining powers and offences in the Act are not
subjected to the same degree of scrutiny, even though they contain many features
threatening to individual rights. An attempt to impose a one year limit on the Bill
as a whole was rejected at the Committee stage in the Commons (HC Debs.
vol. 375 col. 342, 21 November 2001) and again on consideration of Lords'

amendments (HC Debs. vol. 376 col. 952, 12 December 2001). The Government argued that there was universal agreement on certain Parts and so no need to revisit them. However, this is to overvalue the extent of the universal agreement (which does not comprise everything apart from Part IV) and to underestimate the value of full legislative scrutiny and participation. The idea of a general two year sunset clause was again resisted in the House of Lords: 'We are not convinced of the need for sunset clauses on what I would call the bread-and-butter precautionary anti-terrorist measures in this Bill' (HL Debs. vol. 629 col. 634, 3 December 2001, Lord Rooker). Such an amendment was carried in the House of Lords (HL Debs. vol. 629 col. 1205, 10 December 2001) but was later reversed (HC Debs. vol. 376 cols 1483, 1532, 13 December 2001).

10.2.3   Comment

In conclusion, the Government believes that 'there will be a continuing need for counter-terrorism legislation for the foreseeable future . . . regardless of the threat of terrorism related to Northern Ireland . . . It believes the time has come to put that legislation on a permanent footing' (Home Office and Northern Ireland Office, Legislation against Terrorism (Cm. 4178, London, 1998), para. 4). In principle, there may be good arguments to accept this judgement. But the wholesale continuation of most of the pre-2000 legislation, plus the addition of the 2001 legislation, all for the most part without independent scrutiny on a permanent basis is a serious defect if constitutional principles are to be preserved (see Walker, C., 'Constitutional governance and special powers against terrorism' (1997) 35 *Columbia Journal of Transnational Law* 1). It is to mechanisms such as independent review, NGOs and parliamentary lobbying that changes have been made to the legislation over the years, rather than through victories in court (Gearty, C., 'The cost of human rights' (1994) 47 *Current Legal Problems* 19 at p. 40). Given that Part VII of the 2000 Act and ss. 21 to 23 of the 2001 Act are subject not only to annual renewal but also to re-enactment after five years, and that the 2001 Act must be kept under review, it would not have inconvenienced the Government greatly to have allowed greater scrutiny by way of annual review, report, debate and vote of the whole of the legislation.

10.3   CONSENT TO PROSECUTION

By s. 117 of the Terrorism Act 2000, the consent of the relevant Director of Public Prosecutions is required in England and Wales or Northern Ireland for the prosecution of any offence under the Act other than the less serious offences under ss. 36 and 51, or para. 18 of sch. 7, para. 12 of sch. 12, or sch. 13. The appointment of this officer represents a departure from the position under the Prevention of Terrorism (Temporary Provisions) Act 1989, s. 19, whereby the relevant Attorney-General performed the role. However, the Attorney-General must act in the most sensitive cases where it appears to the Director of Public Prosecutions that an offence to which this section applies is committed for a purpose connected with the affairs of a country other than the United Kingdom. In addition, it is apparently the intention that the Director of Public Prosecutions will consult the Attorney-General in a much wider range of cases (HC Debs. Standing Committee D, col. 295, 3 February 2000, Charles Clarke).

10.4 CROWN SERVANTS, REGULATORS, &C.

By s. 119(1) of the Terrorism Act 2000 (formerly in s. 19A of the Prevention of Terrorism (Temporary Provisions) Act 1989, as inserted by the Criminal Justice Act 1993, s. 77 and sch. 4), the Secretary of State may make regulations providing for any of ss. 15 to 23 and 39 to apply to persons in the public service of the Crown. In other words, civil servants and employees of semi-autonomous State agencies may be subjected to the provisions relating to financial restraint and terrorist investigations and may not simply claim a defence of Crown privilege of any kind (HC Debs. Standing Committee D, col. 297, 3 February 2000, Charles Clarke):

> Its purpose is to ensure that Crown privilege cannot be used by public servants to avoid prosecution for money-laundering offences. An example would be Crown servants who work for National Savings, who should not be able to evade prosecution for their money-laundering offences by virtue of the fact that they are public servants. That is the intention.

In pursuance of this power, the Terrorism Act 2000 (Crown Servants and Regulators) Regulations 2001 (SI 2001 No. 192; see formerly SI 1994 Nos. 1758 and 1760), by reg. 3, ss. 15 to 23 and 39 of the 2000 Act expressly apply to the Director of Savings and any person employed by or otherwise engaged in the service of the Director of Savings in circumstances where the Director or such a person is carrying on relevant financial business. On the other hand, reg. 4 disapplies s. 19 from the persons in the following bodies:

(a)   the Bank of England;

(b)   the Financial Services Authority;

(c)   the Building Societies Commission;

(d)   a designated agency within the meaning of the Financial Services Act 1986;

(e)   a recognised self-regulating organisation within the meaning of the Financial Services Act 1986;

(f)   a recognised professional body within the meaning of the Financial Services Act 1986;

(g)   a transferee body within the meaning of the Financial Services Act 1986;

(h)   a recognised self-regulating organisation for friendly societies within the meaning of the Financial Services Act 1986;

(i)   the Council of Lloyds;

(j)   the Friendly Societies Commission;

(k)   the Chief Registrar of Friendly Societies;

(l)   the Assistant Registrar of Friendly Societies for Scotland;

(m) the Central Office of the Registry of Friendly Societies;

(n)   the Registrar of Credit Unions for Northern Ireland;

(o)   the Assistant Registrar of Credit Unions for Northern Ireland; and

(p)   any person who is employed by, or otherwise engaged in, the service of any person referred to above for the purpose of performing such functions.

The Secretary of State may also under s. 119(2) choose to exempt from duties of disclosure under s. 19 persons who are in his opinion performing or connected with the performance of regulatory, supervisory, investigative or registration functions of a public nature. Those persons are of course expected to tip off where appropriate, but do not require the sanction of a possible offence to encourage them to do so, nor, perhaps, would it be appropriate for them to answer in public for slip-ups. Or to put it more gently (HC Debs. Standing Committee D col. 297, 3 February 2000, Charles Clarke):

Subsection (2) is designed for people in roles in which the obligation to disclose suspicion could hamper the proper exercise of their functions. There is a real issue about regulatory and investigative functions. Our concern is to ensure that the obligation to disclose does not hamper the functions more generally.

Aside from the foregoing, there is no general assertion of exemption for the Crown from the Terrorism Act 2000. Nor is there a general saving, equivalent to the Northern Ireland (Emergency Provisions) Act 1996, s. 63(1), for 'Her Majesty's prerogative or any powers exercisable apart from this Act by virtue of any rule of law or enactment'. The only relevant provision is s. 105 of the 2000 Act, which preserves other powers under statute or at common law in relation to Part VII measures. This omission may strengthen the argument that the Terrorism Act 2000 is meant to be a comprehensive statement of the law, but the position is far from certain (see *Attorney-General* v *De Keyser's Royal Hotel* [1920] AC 508; *Laker Airways Ltd* v *Department of Trade* [1977] QB 643; *R* v *Secretary of State for the Home Department, ex parte Fire Brigades Union* [1995] 2 AC 513).

10.5   EVIDENCE

One of the most contentious issues in debates on the Terrorism Act 2000 concerned the several offences which seemed to shift onto the defence a burden of proof contrary to Article 6(2) of the European Convention on Human Rights. The arguments have been set out in Chapter 6 and so will not be repeated fully here. The purpose of s. 118 of the Terrorism Act 2000, in the light of the House of Lords decision in *R* v *Director of Public Prosecutions, ex parte Kebilene* [1999] 3 WLR 972, is:

(a)   to declare that provisions of this kind at most impose an evidential burden
on the defence to raise the issue of the defence, but thereafter the burden is taken
up in law by the prosecution to disprove there is any defence; and
   (b)   to emphasise that the final burden of proof remains on the prosecution.

Such restraint is more likely to satisfy Article 6(2) as interpreted in the jurisprudence of the European Court of Human Rights which does allow for some
flexibility in the issue of burden of proof, especially where it could be shown that
important social concerns are at stake and where the defendant has ready access
to the information required for the defence (see *Salabiaku* v *France*, App. no.
10519/83 Ser. A. 141-A (1988) 13 EHRR 379; *Brown* v *Stott (Procurator Fiscal,
Dunfermline) and another* [2001] 2 All ER 97; *R* v *Benjafield* [2001] 3 WLR 75;
R v *Lambert* [2001] 3 WLR 206).
   There are two situations where s. 118 is utilised. One relates to provisions where
'it is a defence for a person charged with an offence to prove a particular matter'
(s. 118(1) and (2) — such as ss. 12(4) or 39(5)(a)). The other are provisions where a
court '(a) may make an assumption in relation to a person charged with an offence
unless a particular matter is proved, or (b) may accept a fact as sufficient evidence
unless a particular matter is proved' (s. 118(3) and (4) — such as s. 57(1) and (3)).
In total, s. 118 is applicable to the following provisions: ss. 12(4), 39(5)(a), 54, 57,
58, 77 and 103 of this Act; and (until they were repealed) ss. 13, 32 and 33 of the
Northern Ireland (Emergency Provisions) Act 1996 (possession and information
offences). It follows that s. 118 does not affect: s. 11(2) (membership); s. 18(2)
(money laundering); s. 19(3) (disclosure); s. 21(5) (cooperation with the police);
s. 36(3) (breach of cordons); s. 51(3) (breach of parking restrictions); s. 93(2) (road
closures); sch. 4, para. 37 (forfeiture); sch. 5, paras 16 and 32 (explanation orders);
sch. 6, para. 1 (financial disclosures); sch. 13 paras 3, 4, and 16 (private security
services). Because of the balance referred to in the previous paragraph, one should
be hesitant to say these measures are bound to contravene Article 6(2), but it would
not be surprising if arguments were raised to that effect.
   Section 118 is additional to any other form of safeguard which the courts may
wish to insert in the interests of general fairness. For example, in interpreting what
is now s. 77 of the Terrorism Act 2000 (see further Chapter 7), the Northern Ireland
Court of Appeal in *R* v *Killen* [1974] NI 220 concluded that a conviction should not
be sustained unless there is proof beyond reasonable doubt, even though the
measure can assist to establish a *prima facie* case. And in *R* v *Lavery* [1976] NI 148,
it was suggested that the provision is designed for cases where there almost
certainly exists, out of a number of defendants, one who is guilty but not all; if a
conviction against any can be sustained, it should not be used against the remainder.
   As well as the general declaration concerning matters to be proven by a
defendant set out in s. 118, a further point of evidence is dealt with by s. 120 of the
Terrorism Act 2000, by which notices and directions from the Secretary of State are
deemed to be valid until the contrary is proved, while certificates shall be evidence
(or, in Scotland, sufficient evidence) of the document in legal proceedings.

10.6   INTERPRETATION

A list of interpretations is provided at s. 121 of the Terrorism Act 2000. One which has prompted some change over time is that 'property' includes property wherever situated and whether real or personal, heritable or moveable, and things in action and other intangible or incorporeal property (see Walker, C.P., *The Prevention of Terrorism in British Law* (2nd ed., Manchester University Press, Manchester, 1992), p. 110). Another already noted (in Chapter 2) is that an 'organisation' includes any association or combination of persons, a phrase wide enough to encompass an affinity group or even an anarchistic 'disorganisation'. The interpretations provided elsewhere in the Act are usefully indexed at s. 122.

10.7   SECONDARY LEGISLATION

10.7.1   Terrorism Act 2000

The Terrorism Act 2000 serves as the parent legislation for a wide variety of possible orders and regulations. Section 123 describes the processes by which they may be issued. Most of the statutory instruments will, by virtue of s. 123(2) be subject to the 'negative' procedure, that is, they shall be subject to annulment in pursuance of a resolution of either House of Parliament. However, there must be an affirmative resolution under s. 123(3) in the cases of (a) the first order to be made under para. 17(4) of sch. 7 (specification of passenger information in connection with port controls), and (b) the first order to be made under para. 19 of sch. 8 (consultation with a solicitor in Scotland). Positive scrutiny (a draft must be laid before and approved by resolution of each House of Parliament) is also required under s. 123(4) for orders relating to:

(a)   s. 3(3) (proscription);
(b)   s. 53(2) (the possible repeal of carding);
(c)   s. 65(3) (changes to scheduled offences);
(d)   s. 96 (preservation of the peace regulations);
(e)   s. 101(4) (security force codes of practice);
(f)   s. 112(2) (extension of Part VII);
(g)   para. 2(2) of sch. 1 (changes to transitional arrangements);
(h)   para. 6(2) or 7(3) of sch. 6 (financial institutions to be subject to the measures);
(i)   para. 16 of sch. 7 (mechanics of carding);
(j)   para. 3(2) of sch. 8 (recording of interviews);
(k)   para. 4(4) of sch. 8; (recording of interviews);
(l)   para. 4(1)(e) of sch. 14 (supply of information by an authorised or examining officer);
(m)   para. 7(3) of sch. 14 (codes of practice for authorised or examining officers).

In cases of urgency, an order or regulation may be made without a draft having been approved if the Secretary of State is of the opinion that it is necessary by reason of urgency; but it shall cease to have effect at the end of the period of 40 days, unless a resolution approving the order is passed by each House during that period.

By contrast, far less scrutiny applies to those instruments deemed less important. By subsection (7), an order under para. 8(3) of sch. 13 (length of licences issued to private security firms in Northern Ireland) shall merely be laid before Parliament. By subsection (8), several types of order need not be made by statutory instrument and therefore involve no oversight by Parliament or other formality. This process applies to orders under s. 94 (road closure in Northern Ireland), para. 36 of sch. 4 (restraint orders issued by the Secretary of State in Northern Ireland), paras 19 to 21 of sch. 5 (search authorities issued by the Secretary of State in Northern Ireland) and orders made under the authority of regulations made under s. 96.

There is no set process for 'directions', but it is mentioned in s. 124, that a direction given under the Act may be varied or revoked by a further direction.

10.7.2 Anti-terrorism, Crime and Security Act 2001

There are many powers to make secondary legislation in the 2001 Act but no central signpost equivalent to s. 123 of the Terrorism Act 2000. The most wide-ranging power is in s. 124, which reflects what appeared, at times, to be a chaotic legislative process which gave rise to concern that mistakes would be made which should later be corrected. By s. 124(1), a Minister of the Crown 'may by order make such incidental, consequential, transitional or supplemental provision as he thinks necessary or expedient for the general purposes, or any particular purpose, of this Act or in consequence of any provision made by or under this Act or for giving full effect to this Act or any such provision'. The power is not confined to matters of detail. By s. 124(2), it can extend to primary legislation, by amending, repealing or revoking any provision of, or made under, an Act passed before the 2001 Act or in the same Session or for making savings, or additional savings, from the effect of any repeal or revocation made by or under the 2001 Act. Despite their breadth, such orders are subject only to negative resolution.

As regards other orders, the 2001 Act adopts an array of processes. The affirmative procedure applies to: the making of freezing orders in s. 10; changes to the list of public authorities subject to additional disclosure powers under s. 17; the continuation or revival of detention without trial under ss. 21 to 23; orders under s. 75 to apply Part VII to a much wider range of substances or to amend sch. 5 (the lists of pathogens and toxins subject to Part VII); s. 80, which allows for the Secretary of State to make regulations prohibiting the disclosure of information about the 'enrichment' of uranium; the making of a code in connection with the retention of communications data under s. 103 and the renewal under section 105 of any mandatory scheme under s. 104. The negative procedure applies to: orders to amend or revoke freezing orders under ss. 11 or 12; remaining powers to issue statutory orders under Part VII (security of pathogens and toxins); and under s. 77, the powers of the Secretary of State to make regulations for the purpose of ensuring the security of nuclear sites and premises, nuclear material and equipment, including material in transport, other radioactive material and sensitive nuclear information. Reports from reviewers, whether under s. 28 with reference to ss. 21 to 23, or under s. 122 with reference to the whole Act, shall be laid before Parliament but there is no requirement for debate. No procedures are specified in relation to: the specification of other kinds of monetary instrument for the purposes of the seizure of terrorist cash under sch. 1, para. 1; the power to extend (sch. 6A, para. 1(5)) sch. 6 by allowing its measures to be extended to other financial institutions; and the power to extend s. 33 and Part VI (weapons of mass destruction) to any of the Channel Islands or the Isle of Man.

10.7.3 Third Pillar of the European Union

Omitted from the description under the previous heading is the power under s. 111 of the Anti-terrorism, Crime and Security Act 2001 to issue regulations:

(a)   for the purpose of implementing any obligation of the United Kingdom created or arising by or under any third pillar measure or enabling any such obligation to be implemented;

(b)   for the purpose of enabling any rights enjoyed or to be enjoyed by the United Kingdom under or by virtue of any third pillar measure to be exercised; or

(c)   for the purpose of dealing with matters arising out of or related to any such obligation or rights.

These controversial powers were at several stages threatened with parliamentary annihilation, but they survived after some reassurance. This did not include the confinement of their remit to terrorism issues, as sought by the Home Affairs Committee (Report on the Anti-terrorism, Crime and Security Bill 2001 (2001–02 HC 351), para. 67), since this would be 'to tie our hands when it comes to judicial co-operation on dealing with terrorist organisations' (HC Debs. vol. 375 col. 426, 21 November 2001, Angela Eagle). Here, as elsewhere, the Government advised that for practical reasons, it is not possible to divide terrorism from other serious crime especially in terms of the funding of terrorism (HL Debs. vol. 629 col. 599, 3 December 2001, Baroness Symons). However, the reassurance did include the insertion of a time limit in s. 111 of the 1 July 2002 so as to point the power in the direction of the existing European Union anti-terrorism proposals rather than future, unimagined measures (HL Debs. vol. 629 col. 1142, 10 December 2001); it also included the precise specification in s. 111(2) of the European sources of the pending legislation (col. 1160).

The Third Pillar, beginning in Article K.1 of the Treaty on European Union (The Maastricht Treaty, Cm. 1934, London, 1992) as cooperation in the area of Justice and Home Affairs and, after the Amsterdam Treaty, (entitled 'Provisions on police and judicial cooperation in criminal matters') is driven by the European Council and the Council of Ministers, with the Commission being merely 'associated' and the Parliament merely consulted and the Court of Justice largely excluded. During the five-year transitional period following the entry into force of the Treaty of Amsterdam in May 1999, the Council is to act unanimously on a proposal from the Commission or on the initiative of a Member State, and after consulting the European Parliament. After the transition, the Council may act (with unanimous agreement) on proposals from the Commission which will then acquire sole right of initiative. The Council shall consult the European Parliament, subject to the co-decision (which involves the ultimate right of veto in certain circumstances). The Treaty of Nice, whenever it comes into force, will make certain Articles in Title IV subject to Qualified Majority Voting once the Council adopts unanimously the necessary legislation laying down basic principles and common rules. These provisions will not affect the United Kingdom unless there is an opt-in under the relevant Protocols. In any event, the final decision on all such proposals remains in the hands of the Governments of the Member States, in a process which is more akin to the negotiation of Treaties than to a conventional legislative process.

Article K.1 of the Treaty on European Union (TEU) defined as 'matters of common interest' asylum policy, combating drug addiction and international fraud, external border controls, immigration policy, judicial cooperation in civil and criminal matters, customs cooperation and police cooperation in action against terrorism, drug-trafficking and other serious international crime. By Article K.2, Member States were to consult and exchange information and then adopt joint positions, draw up joint action and draft conventions for national adoption. Now, under Articles 29 to 42 of the Amsterdam Treaty, the revised Title VI covers fewer areas (since some were translated into an enforceable part of the European Communities Treaty — the former Third Pillar policies on asylum, visas, immigration and other policies connected with the free movement of persons). By Article 29 of Title VI of the (Amsterdam) Treaty on European Union (Police and Judicial Co-operation in Criminal Matters) (Cm. 3780, London, 1997), it becomes amongst the objectives of the European Union:

To provide citizens with a high level of safety within an area of freedom, security and justice by developing common action among Member States in the fields of police and judicial cooperation in criminal matters and by preventing and combating racism and xenophobia. That objective shall be achieved by preventing and combating crime, organised or otherwise, in particular terrorism, trafficking in persons and offences against children, illicit drug trafficking and illicit arms trafficking, corruption and fraud, through:

— closer cooperation between police forces, customs authorities and other competent authorities in the Member States, both directly and through the

European Police Office (Europol), in accordance with the provisions of Articles 30 and 32;

— closer cooperation between judicial and other competent authorities of the Member States in accordance with the provisions of Articles 31(a) to (d) and 32;

— approximation, where necessary, of rules on criminal matters in the Member States, in accordance with the provisions of Article 31(e).

Article 31 expands on these objectives:

Common action on judicial cooperation in criminal matters shall include:

(a)   facilitating and accelerating cooperation between competent ministries and judicial or equivalent authorities of the Member States in relation to proceedings and the enforcement of decisions;

(b)   facilitating extradition between Member States;

(c)   ensuring compatibility in rules applicable in the Member States, as may be necessary to improve such cooperation;

(d)   preventing conflicts of jurisdiction between Member States;

(e)   progressively adopting measures establishing minimum rules relating to the constituent elements of criminal acts and to penalties in the fields of organised crime, terrorism and illicit drug trafficking.

Much of the activity under the Third Pillar is in the nature of consultation, co-ordination and audit. However, various formal measures have arisen, some of which have required national implementation, including:

(a)   the 1995 Convention drawn up on the basis of Article K.3 of the Treaty on European Union on Simplified Extradition Procedure between the Member States of the European Union;

(b)   the 1996 Convention drawn up on the basis of Article K.3 of the Treaty on European Union relating to Extradition between the Member States of the European Union;

(c)   framework decisions adopted under Article 34 of the Treaty on European Union on the execution in the European Union of orders freezing property or evidence, on joint investigation teams, or on combating terrorism;

(d)   the Convention on Mutual Assistance in Criminal Matters between the Member States of the European Union, and the Protocol to that Convention, established in accordance with Article 34 of the Treaty on European Union;

(e)   the establishment of Europol (note also the Convention on Mutual Assistance and Cooperation between Customs Administrations (Cm. 5020, London, 2000)). The extension of the purview of Europol (see House of Lords Select Committee on the EC, Europol (1994–95 HL 51); Convention based on Article K.3 of the Treaty on European Union, on the Establishment of a European Police Office (Europol Convention) with Declarations (Cm. 3050, London, 1995, Cm. 4837,

London, 2000)) to terrorism was approved by the European Union Justice and Home Affairs Council in 1998 and began to be implemented in 1999 (see Marotta, E., 'Europol's role in anti-terrorism policing' (1999) 11 *Terrorism & Political Violence* 15). There has also been cooperation on extradition and judicial processes (see Gilbert, G., *Aspects of Extradition Law* (Nijhoff, Dordrecht,1991) ch. 6; Gueydan, C., 'Co-operation between Member States of the European Community in the fight against terrorism' in Higgins, R., and Flory, M., (eds), *Terrorism and International Law* (Routledge, London, 1997)).

The purpose of s. 111 is to avoid legislative delay in the implementation of new, and possibly urgent, counter-measures. Rather than primary legislation, there can be secondary legislation, roughly equivalent to the precedent in Common Market matters to s. 2(2) of the European Communities Act 1972. On the basis of s. 2(2), the scope of the regulation-making power is very wide — by s. 111(3) it includes 'any such provision (of any such extent) as might be made by Act of Parliament', but subject to a list of limitations in s. 111(4), which in particular rule out retrospective rules, the creation of any power to legislate, or the creation of a criminal offence beyond a specified severity (on indictment, for more than two years' imprisonment, or on summary process, more than three months). However, as regards the latter, s. 111(6) goes on to allow the creation of an offence punishable on conviction on indictment with imprisonment for a term of any length provided that term is required by an obligation specifically created or arising by or under any third pillar measure or where the offence is not committed in the United Kingdom but would, if committed in the United Kingdom be punishable on conviction on indictment with imprisonment for a term of that length.

Though s. 2(2) of the 1972 Act does stand as a precedent (and over 100 offences have been created pursuant to it), it is confined to economic and regulatory matters rather than the areas of policing and criminal justice which were considered so sensitive at the time of the 1972 Act that sch. 2 para. (1)(d) prevents the Government from implementing by way of affirmative instrument any Community obligation which creates 'any criminal offence punishable with imprisonment for more than two years or punishable on summary conviction with imprisonment for more than three months'. The Delegated Powers and Regulatory Reform Select Committee, Report on the Anti-terrorism, Crime and Security Bill (2001–02 HL 45) concluded that, in the light of the unprecedented nature of the s. 111 power and also the significant differences between legislative scrutiny under the First and Third Pillars (paras 11, 13):

> We do not consider it would be right for all proposals to be dealt with in this way . . . the Committee is of the view that the powers to implement by secondary legislation proposals under the third pillar should not be granted except to allow the implementation of a measure which the Government can demonstrate is a key element in its emergency proposals and yet not of such importance as to warrant primary legislation.

A number of supplemental provisions are set out in s. 112. In particular, the parent power can be exercised by any Secretary of State, the Lord Chancellor, the Chancellor of the Exchequer or by the Devolved Administrations where the powers relate to devolved issues. The secondary legislation will be subject to the affirmative procedure in Parliament. Scrutiny of Third Pillar documents has been problematic because of secrecy and speed involved in the European policy debates in these matters. Supervision is now under the wing of the Parliamentary European Scrutiny Committee (see House of Lords' European Communities Committee, Enhancing Parliamentary Scrutiny of the Third Pillar 1997–98 HL 25). Whether the affirmative procedure will provide adequate oversight must be doubted. There can be no substantial debate and no opportunity for amendment, even though framework decisions are usually far less precise than directives.

Following the attacks in the United States on 11 September, a series of meetings were held under the umbrella of the Justice and Home Affairs Council of the European Union to bolster existing measures against terrorism (on which, see Reinares, F. (ed.), *European Democracies Against Terrorism* (Ashgate, Aldershot, 2000)). It met on the 20 September and agreed two proposals for Council Framework Decisions. One, the Council Framework Decision on Combating Terrorism (Proposed Framework Decision on Terrorism from the Commission, COM (2001) 521), establishes minimum rules for the constituent elements of criminal acts and penalties depending on the circumstances of between not less than two years' and not less than 20 years' imprisonment. In this way, there is constituted an EU definition of terrorism, as follows:

Article 3 — Terrorist Offences
1.   Each Member State shall take the necessary measures to ensure that the following offences, defined according to its national law, which are intentionally committed by an individual or a group against one or more countries, their institutions or people with the aim of intimidating them and seriously altering or destroying the political, economic, or social structures of a country, will be punishable as terrorist offences:
   (a)   murder;
   (b)   bodily injuries;
   (c)   kidnapping or hostage taking;
   (d)   extortion;
   (e)   theft or robbery;
   (f)   unlawful seizure of or damage to state or government facilities, means of public transport, infrastructure facilities, places of public use, and property;
   (g)   fabrication, possession, acquisition, transport or supply of weapons or explosives;
   (h)   releasing contaminating substances, or causing fires, explosions or floods, endangering people, property, animals or the environment;
   (i)   interfering with or disrupting the supply of water, power, or other fundamental resource;

(j)   attacks through interference with an information system;

(k)   threatening to commit any of the offences listed above;

(l)   directing a terrorist group;

(m)   promoting of, supporting of or participating in a terrorist group.

2.   For the purpose of this Framework Decision, terrorist group shall mean a structured organisation established over a period of time, of more than two persons, acing in concert to commit terrorist offences referred to in paragraph (1)(a) to (1)(k).

Article 4 — Instigating, Aiding, Abetting and Attempting
Member States shall ensure that instigating, aiding, abetting or attempting to commit a terrorist offence is punishable.

Article 6 — Aggravating Circumstances
Without prejudice to any other aggravating circumstances defined in their national legislation, Member States shall ensure that the penalties and sanctions referred to in Article 5 may be increased if the terrorist offence:

(a)   is committed with particular ruthlessness; or

(b)   affects a large number of persons or is of a particular serious and persistent nature; or

(c)   is committed against Heads of State, Government Ministers, any other internationally protected person, elected members of parliamentary chambers, members of regional or local governments, judges, magistrates, judicial or prison civil servants and police forces.

Arguments about whether this definition of 'terrorism' is sufficiently limited or whether it might capture forms of public disorder arising from political protest echo those set out in Chapter 1. A serious degree of impact is required by Article 3, but not necessarily any form of organisation or sustainability. It may be an academic argument, for the Government has opined that 'the proposal does not go further than existing UK legislation, which is considered to be adequate and not to require change' (House of Lords Committee on the European Union, UK Participation in the Schengen Acquis 1999–00 HL 34, Appendix 3).

The second proposal, for a Council Framework Decision on a European arrest warrant (see Decision on a European Arrest Warrant from the Commission, COM (2001) 522), introduces a pan-European arrest and extradition procedure as follows (see further House of Lords Select Committee on the European Union, Counter-Terrorism: The European Arrest Warrant Procedure (2001–02 HL 34):

1.   the purpose of the European arrest warrant is the enforced transfer of a person from one Member State to another. The proposed procedure replaces the traditional extradition procedure. It is to be treated as equivalent to it for the interpretation of Article 5 of the European Convention on Human Rights relating to freedom and security;

2. it is a horizontal system replacing the current extradition system in all respects and, unlike the Treaty between Italy and Spain, not limited to certain offences;

3. the mechanism is based on the mutual recognition of court judgments. The basic idea is as follows: when a judicial authority of a Member State requests the surrender of a person, either because he has been convicted of an offence or because he is being prosecuted, its decision must be recognised and executed automatically throughout the Union. Refusal to execute a European arrest warrant must be confined to a limited number of hypotheses. The scope of the proposed text is almost identical to that of extradition: the European arrest warrant allows a person to be arrested and surrendered if in one of Member States he has been convicted and sentenced to immediate imprisonment of four months or more or remanded in custody where the offence of which he is charged carries a term of more than a year. Given that the mechanism is particularly binding for the person concerned, it is felt important to allow its use only in cases that are serious enough to justify it;

4. the procedure for executing the European arrest warrant is primarily judicial. The political phase inherent in the extradition procedure is abolished. Accordingly, the administrative redress phase following the political decision is also abolished. The removal of these two procedural levels should considerably improve the effectiveness and speed of the mechanism;

5. the European arrest warrant will take account of the principle of citizenship of the Union. The exception made for the nationals should no longer apply. The primary criterion is not nationality but the place of the person's main residence, in particular with regard to the execution of sentences. Provision is made for facilitating the execution of the sentence passed in the country of arrest when it is there that the person is the most likely to achieve integration, and moreover, when a European arrest warrant is executed, for making it possible to make it conditional on the guarantee of the person's subsequent return for the execution of the sentence passed by the foreign authority;

6. the cases of refusal to execute the arrest warrant are limited and are listed in order to simplify and accelerate the procedure. The principle of double criminal liability is abolished, as is the principle of speciality. But Member States have the possibility, if they wish, of drawing up a negative list of offences for which they will state that they refuse to execute the European arrest warrant on their territory. Similarly, it is possible to restore the requirement of the double criminal liability for cases in which the issuing State exercises extraterritorial authority;

7. the elements appearing in the European arrest warrant are standardised at the level of the Union. They must, in all but exceptional cases, enable the authority of the executing country to surrender the person without other controls being carried out;

8. the mechanism of the European arrest warrant is intended to replace, as between the Member States, the 1957 Convention, its two protocols of 1975 and

1978, the provisions concerning extradition of the terrorism Convention and the two Union Conventions of 1995 and 1996. Certain provisions of the Schengen Implementing Convention are also replaced.

In terms of substance, the 'European arrest warrant' will be used both for the purposes of arrest and surrender (unlike the normal two stages of extradition) and can in some circumstances also trigger search powers. The warrant travels between judicial authorities without any executive or diplomatic input. At most there is a judicial examination of the arrest warrant within 10 days of the arrest (Article 15) unless the requested person consents to 'surrender' to the issuing State. The decision must be given within 90 days (Article 20). The offences, as defined by the law of the issuing Member State, shall, under the terms of this Framework Decision and without any limitation as to double criminality, give rise to a surrender of the suspect pursuant to a European arrest warrant, include: membership of a criminal organisation, laundering of the proceeds of crime, high tech crime, murder, grievous bodily injury, kidnapping, illegal restraint and hostage-taking. It should be emphasised that there is no recognition whatever of any 'political offence' exception. A further effect of this measure will be to subject all extradition between the EU Member States (plus Norway and Iceland) to the jurisdiction of the European Court of Justice, though as regards references for a preliminary ruling, this jurisdiction will only apply in those Member States which have accepted the Court's jurisdiction over 'third pillar' matters (not including the United Kingdom). The framework decision must be applied by the end of 2002, by when it is hoped that concerns will be allayed about individual rights, whether the listed offences are specific enough, the position of the specialty rule, the absence of a presumption in favour of bail and rights of appeal (House of Lord Committee on the European Union, UK Participation in the Schengen Acquis 1999–00 HL 34, Appendix 3).

In addition to these two Framework decisions, the Justice and Home Affairs Council set in motion in September 2001 a whole range of other work (see SN 4019/01, SN 4019/1/01, 12579/01, 12800/01, and 12800/1/01 REV 1), including:

(a)   the implementation of Article 13 of the Mutual Legal Assistance Convention (Convention on Mutual assistance on criminal matters between the Member States of the EU (OJ 2000 C 197/1)) concerning joint investigation teams;

(b)   giving greater prominence to Eurojust, the EU's public prosecutions unit (see Decision 2000/799/JHA setting up a provisional Judicial Cooperation Unit (Eurojust) (OJ 2000 L 324/2), and Europol (there are within its staff of 224 only seven counter-terrorism specialists) at the centre of the EU's counter-terrorism programme;

(c)   requesting the Commission to submit proposals for law enforcement authorities access to communications data and calling for more urgent action on national contact points in the European Judicial Network. The European Judicial Network was created in July 1998 and links the mutual legal assistance units (Joint Action 98/428/JHA establishing a European Judicial Network (OJ L 191, 7.7.98));

(d) requesting the EU Police Chief's Operational Task Force (established in 1999) to organise an ad hoc meeting of heads of EU counter-terrorist agencies;

(e) requesting cooperation between military intelligence agencies;

(f) creating a new EU Intelligence Chief's Task Force to begin meeting regularly;

(g) instructing the Article 36 Committee to work out a simpler and quicker evaluation and assessment mechanism in order to find a procedure for assessing national anti-terrorist arrangements on the basis of legislative, administrative and technical procedures (following the Commission communication on cyber-crime (COM (2000) 890). Examples given are legislation on 'administrative telephone-tapping' and a 'list of terrorist organizations';

(h) instructing the EU Working Party on Terrorism to draw up an inventory of national measures to combat terrorism;

(i) drawing up a common list of proscribed groups by Europol, anti-terrorist units and intelligence agencies (further to the Joint action 98/733/JHA of 21 December 1998 adopted by the Council on the basis of Article K.3 of the Treaty on European Union, on making it a criminal offence to participate in a criminal organisation in the Member States of the European Union, Official Journal L 351, 29.12.1998);

(j) reviewing EC and EU financial legislation to ensure that banking systems comply with anti-terrorism investigations and automatic exchanges of information about terrorist funding; reviewing immigration and asylum legislation to be examined 'with reference to the terrorist threat'; seeking to devise a framework Decision on the execution of orders freezing assets or evidence and to widen its scope to terrorist offences, building upon the Council Recommendation of 9 December 1999 on cooperation in combating the financing of terrorist groups (Official Journal C 373, 23.12.1999).

The foregoing list of ongoing work (for updates, see http://europa.eu.int/news/110901/index.htm) would appear to encompass a substantial catalogue which may justify the Government's argument that s. 111 is necessary to avoid legislative overload. However, only four framework decisions have been agreed in over two and a half years since the Treaty of Amsterdam entered into force, with implementation deadlines averaging two years. In addition, UK legislation is often fully or wholly already in compliance with such instruments, and, in the field of crime and terrorism, the United Kingdom is usually not the last State to act. Many actions under the Third Pillar do not in any event require legislative action but are administrative in nature.

The Government has indicated that it will not implement the European Arrest Framework Decision by way of s. 111 but will resort to primary legislation (HL Debs. vol. 629 col. 1142, 10 December 2001, Baroness Symons). This leaves its main programme, as now specified in s. 111(2) (cols 1143, 1157, 1158), the 1995 and 1996 Conventions under Article K.3 on Extradition, the Framework Decision on Combating Terrorism, the Mutual Legal Assistance Convention, plus a possible

Framework Decision on asset freezing and a possible Framework Decision on setting up joint investigative teams.

Other measures relating to European Union cooperation in the fields of home affairs and policing include the Schengen Agreement (OJ L 239, 2000, 22.9.2000). The United Kingdom's relationship with the Schengen Agreement has been complex (see House of Lords Committee on the European Communities, Schengen and the United Kingdom's Border Controls 1998–99 HL 37). As part of the integration of the Schengen Agreement into the Treaty (TEU) and the abolition of internal border controls by the Amsterdam Treaty, the Schengen Protocol provides that the Schengen *acquis* applies only to the 13 States which have signed the Schengen Agreement. Under Article 4 of this Protocol the UK and Ireland 'may at any time request to take part in some or all of the provisions of this acquis', and if they do so request, the response will be determined by unanimous decision of the other 13 States. Protocol 3 recognises the special travel arrangements with Ireland and stipulates that the United Kingdom will continue to exercise border controls regardless of Article 14 of the TEU. Protocol 4 accepts that the United Kingdom (and Ireland) remain outside the existing Schengen arrangements, though they can opt in to measures concerning the EU external frontier and asylum, while remaining outside any arrangements made in future for EU internal frontiers. In 1999, the Government decided to opt in to various Schengen measures, though not to any that required the abandonment of border controls (HC Debs. vol. 327 cols 380-2wa, 12 March 1999, Jack Straw). A further official statement was made in 2001 (HL Debs. vol. 363 cols.152–153wa, 1 March 2001) to announce cooperation in a range of measures, including, on asylum and immigration regulations, a Commission proposal for a Council regulation concerning the establishment of 'Eurodac' for the comparison of the fingerprints of applicants for asylum and certain other aliens (its title was subsequently amended to 'Council Regulation concerning the establishment of "Eurodac" for the comparison of fingerprints for the effective application of the Dublin Convention'); in regard to proposed Directives: an Initiative of the French Republic for a Council Directive defining the facilitation of unauthorised entry, movement and residence; a Commission proposal for a Council Directive on minimum standards on procedures in Member States for granting and withdrawing refugee status; the Initiative of the French Republic for a Council Directive concerning the harmonisation of financial penalties imposed on carriers transporting into the territory of the Member States third country nationals not in possession of the documents necessary for admission; the Initiative of the French Republic for a Council Directive on mutual recognition of decisions concerning expulsion of third country nationals; a Commission proposal for a Council Directive on minimum standards for giving temporary protection in the event of a mass influx of displaced persons and on measures promoting a balance between Member States in receiving such persons and bearing the consequences thereof; a Commission proposal for a Council Decision establishing a European Refugee Fund. United Kingdom participation has yet to come into effect, as it is subject to a further unanimous decision of the Council that all the conditions for participation have been met (see House of Lord Committee on the European Union, UK Participation in the Schengen Acquis 1999–00 HL 34).

It may be noted that there is growing European co-operation in crime control aside from within the context of the European Union. For example, the Council of Europe's Cybercrimes Convention (ETS 185, Strasbourg, 2001) requires Member States to implement provisions related to interception of communications, preservation and disclosure of traffic data, production orders, search and seizure of stored computer data, real-time collection of traffic data, interception of content data, and mutual assistance.

10.8 JURISDICTION AND COVERAGE

10.8.1 Jurisdiction

The Terrorism Act 2000 extends to the whole of the United Kingdom as a general rule (s. 130). Indeed the consolidation of two partly overlapping codes, the Prevention of Terrorism (Temporary Provisions) Act and the Northern Ireland (Emergency Provisions) Acts, represents one of the undoubted benefits of the new Act. Of course, Part VII extends only to Northern Ireland, and there are also other sections which are expressly directed just to specified jurisdictions (ss. 59 to 61, and schs 4 and 5). The gain of consolidation has now been largely lost with the passage of the Anti-terrorism, Crime and Security Act 2001, which likewise applies throughout the United Kingdom.

The Anti-terrorism, Crime and Security Act 2001 correspondingly applies to the whole of the United Kingdom. However, some measures do not apply to Scotland. These include Part V (race and religion), which is disapplied because of the breadth of Scottish public order offences, above all, the common law offence of breach of the peace, and Part XII (bribery and corruption), which may be a matter for the devolved administration. As regards Northern Ireland, s. 76 (regarding the Atomic Energy Authority Constabulary) and s. 100 (the British Transport Police) are disapplied since these forces have no representation in Northern Ireland.

The jurisdictions of the Bailiwick of Jersey, the Bailiwick of Guernsey and the Isle of Man are not subject to the Terrorism Act 2000. By contrast, there are several impacts caused by the Anti-terrorism, Crime and Security Act 2001. By s. 32, an Order in Council may direct that ss. 21 to 31 (detention of foreign suspects) shall extend, with such modifications as appear appropriate, to any of the Channel Islands or the Isle of Man. Corresponding to s. 32, s. 33 (certification of exclusion from refugee status) may with appropriate modifications, be extended by Order in Council to any of the Channel Islands or the Isle of Man (s. 33(10)). Next, by s. 57, Her Majesty may by Order in Council direct that any of the provisions of Part VI shall extend to any of the Channel Islands, the Isle of Man or to any British overseas territory. By s. 88, Part IX of the Act can be applied by order to the Channel Islands, the Isle of Man or any colony.

Aside from these exceptions, the equivalent laws in these jurisdictions largely still rest on the model of the Prevention of Terrorism (Temporary Provisions) Act

1989 (see Walker, C.P., *The Prevention of Terrorism in British Law* (2nd ed., Manchester University Press, Manchester, 1992) ch. 10), with the result that the withdrawal of the notice of derogation in February 2001 expressly did not apply to these territories, though the promise was then given to the Secretariat General of the Council of Europe (see http://conventions.coe.int/Treaty/EN/ CadreListeTraites.htm) that 'the Crown Dependencies are actively considering enacting or amending their current Prevention of Terrorism legislation to reflect the changes in the United Kingdom legislation made under the Terrorism Act 2000'. The main problem remains the issue of Article 5(3) and the lack of judicial oversight over detention following arrest or under the port controls. The relevant provisions are: in the Isle of Man, s. 12 of and para. 6 of sch. 5 to the Prevention of Terrorism Act 1990; in Guernsey, s. 12 of and para. 6 of sch. 5 to the Prevention of Terrorism (Bailiwick of Guernsey) Law 1990; in Jersey, art. 13 of and para. 6 of sch. 5 to the Prevention of Terrorism (Jersey) Law 1996. There are significant variations in the Isle of Man model where the maximum extension is for three days and not five days (see Walker, C.P., 'The detention of suspected terrorists in the British Islands' (1992) 12 *Legal Studies* 178), but the absence of judicial oversight is common to all. Therefore, all were specifically notified to the Secretary General of the Council on 12 November 1998. The Isle of Man's Human Rights Act 2001, s. 13 and sch. 2, the Human Rights (Jersey) Law 2000, art. 14 and sch. 2, and the Human Rights Law 2000 of Guernsey preserve the derogation in this respect. Guernsey has also now proposed a new terrorism law based on the UK's Terrorism Act (Billet d'État, XXI, 31 October 2001), as have the Isle of Man (Press Release 34/01, 15 October 2001) and Jersey (Press Release, 15 October 2001).

10.8.2 Coverage

In other respects, the Terrorism Act 2000 has been a less than successful exercise in consolidation, and so a number of closely related laws have not been taken in hand at the same time. Perhaps the most closely related is the Reinsurance (Acts of Terrorism) Act 1993, which paved the way for Government support for the reinsurance sector in the light of the bombs in the City of London in 1992 and 1993.

The other closely related area of law which the Terrorism Act 2000 (aside from ss. 79 and 80) leaves untouched concerns sentencing. The Northern Ireland (Remission of Sentences) Act 1995 and the Northern Ireland (Sentences) Act 1998 have offered substantially accelerated release on licence for prisoners attached to paramilitary groups which are observing a ceasefire and co-operating with decommissioning procedures and the offence was committed before the 10 April 1998. Almost all paramilitary prisoners have been released under these terms. Consequently, the proposals to establish a social reinsertion programme of the kind operated in Spain and Italy, as advocated by Lord Lloyd, to encourage judges to make statement about this mitigating factor and to use their sentencing powers accordingly (Inquiry into Legislation against Terrorism (Cm. 3420, London, 1996), paras 15.4, 15.11), have not been taken up.

A particularly thorny issue has been the use of electronic surveillance evidence in court. Though Lord Lloyd has emphasised the importance both for due process and effectiveness in terrorist prosecutions that this type of evidence should be available in court (Inquiry into Legislation against Terrorism (Cm. 3420, London, 1996), para. 7.25), the Regulation of Investigatory Powers Act 2000, s. 17 seeks to maintain the existing bar (*Interception of Communications in the United Kingdom* (Cm. 4368, London, 1999), ch. 8).

Other relevant issues within domestic legislation might include firearms and explosives regulations (see Walker, C.P., *The Prevention of Terrorism in British Law* (2nd ed., Manchester University Press, Manchester, 1992), ch. 12).

There is also a range of anti-terrorism measures which are based upon international law. Examples include, within the field of extradition and asylum, the Suppression of Terrorism Act 1978. Specific forms of terrorism are dealt with by the Internationally Protected Persons Act 1978, the Taking of Hostages Act 1982, the Nuclear Material (Offences) Act 1983 and the Aviation and Maritime Security Act 1990 (see Walker, C.P., *The Prevention of Terrorism in British Law* (2nd ed., Manchester University Press, Manchester, 1992), ch. 12). The Terrorism Act 2000 might have been an occasion for updating and consolidation. The need for updating was demonstrated by the Anti-terrorism, Crime and Security Act 2001 (see Chapter 9), but a consolidated, accessible statement of law is now even more distant as a result of that legislation.

10.9   FINAL REMARKS

It was asserted in Chapter 1 that the generation of a permanent code responding to terrorism is a worthwhile exercise in practical and ethical terms. Any such code must, nonetheless, comply with the principles set out in Chapter 1, involving a 'rights audit', 'democratic accountability' and 'constitutionalism'.

The Terrorism Act 2000 represents a worthwhile attempt to fulfil the role of a modern code against terrorism, though it fails to meet the desired standards in all respects. There are aspects where rights are probably breached, and its mechanisms to ensure democratic accountability and constitutionalism are even more deficient, as discussed at 10.2 above. It is also a sobering thought, proffered by the Home Affairs Committee, that the result is that 'this country has more anti-terrorist legislation on its statute books than almost any other developed democracy' (Report on the Anti-terrorism, Crime and Security Bill 2001 (2001–02 HC 351), para. 1). But at least that result initially flowed from a solemnly studied and carefully constructed legislative exercise.

The Anti-terrorism, Crime and Security Act 2001 is a much less tolerable item. The advent of what has been called in Chapter 1 'Third Millennium terrorism' — networked rather than nationalist, decentred rather than tightly organised, and based on personality and idealism rather than ideology — does call for reflection in Government and the legislature. But one has the impression of both being, at least for a time, effectively terrorised by the terrorists and willing to try anything.

The whole concept of a 'war against terrorism', admittedly more an American than British concept, risks misconceiving and misrepresenting the threat, with dangerous outcomes for society. The notion that a group like Al Qa'ida, with characteristics as described above, can be treated in a similar fashion to a military-industrial complex, highly organised and precisely located, and can be clearly attacked and defeated by force is absurd. The idea of a war ever being 'won' in these terms is far-fetched, especially if we are to take at face value the warning of the Home Secretary that the greater the military success, the greater the threat, since 'a wounded and cornered tiger is more dangerous than ever' (HC Debs. vol. 375 col. 33, 19 November 2001, David Blunkett). The dismal result of the misconception could be an enduring state of war with a constant threat to extend the conflict into new locations and enduring denials of rights both to combatants and to the general population. The actual response of the Anti-terrorism, Crime and Security Act 2001 is not quite so dire as just painted. It must be recognised that the guts of the Act, Parts V to IX and Part XII, plus several other measures, comprise somewhat technical law reform which was already resting in the out-tray of one or another Government department and would have been enacted in any event, though the emergence of some owes more to opportunism than terrorism. The claim that 'all the measures are designed to enhance intelligence and information gathering, to restrict people suspected of involvement in terrorism, to prevent abuse of asylum and to give law enforcement and security agencies powers to tackle the problems that we face' (HC Debs. vol. 375 col. 113, 19 November 2001, Beverley Hughes) is not sustained by the evidence presented in this book. More candid is the statement of Lord Rooker that:

> I fully admit that, as we prepared the Bill, we trawled Whitehall. . . . We are seeking to close the loopholes and fill the gaps. Frankly, there is no good cause for giving future Home Secretaries extra work when the matter can be dealt with now. (HL Debs. vol. 629 col. 633, 3 December 2001, Lord Rooker)

Other parts, Parts I and II, represent revisions of existing anti-terrorism laws which, in principle, make sense in the light of the more internationalised and networked nature of the threat. Much of the remainder, Parts III, IV, X and XI, had been threatened before but remain no less palatable the second time around.

It was argued in Chapter 1 that a vibrant and inclusive democracy must hold its nerve and vaunt its cherished values in the face of terrorism. Given some failure of nerve and some damage to cherished values in 2001, a test has been set for the Human Rights Act 1998, the judges, Parliament but, above all, for Government to correct the legislative defects in the coming years.

Appendix 1

Terrorism Act 2000

2000 CHAPTER 11

PART I
INTRODUCTORY

PART II
PROSCRIBED ORGANISATIONS

Procedure

Offences

PART III
TERRORIST PROPERTY

Interpretation

PART VIII
GENERAL

Terrorism Act 2000

2000 CHAPTER 11

An Act to make provision about terrorism; and to make temporary provision for Northern Ireland about the prosecution and punishment of certain offences, the preservation of peace and the maintenance of order. [20th July 2000]

BE IT ENACTED by the Queen's most Excellent Majesty, by and with the advice and consent of the Lords Spiritual and Temporal, and Commons, in this present Parliament assembled, and by the authority of the same, as follows:—

PART I
INTRODUCTORY

1. Terrorism: interpretation

(1) In this Act 'terrorism' means the use or threat of action where—

    (a) the action falls within subsection (2),

    (b) the use or threat is designed to influence the government or to intimidate the public or a section of the public, and

    (c) the use or threat is made for the purpose of advancing a political, religious or ideological cause.

(2) Action falls within this subsection if it—

    (a) involves serious violence against a person,

    (b) involves serious damage to property,

    (c) endangers a person's life, other than that of the person committing the action,

    (d) creates a serious risk to the health or safety of the public or a section of the public, or

    (e) is designed seriously to interfere with or seriously to disrupt an electronic system.

(3) The use or threat of action falling within subsection (2) which involves the use of firearms or explosives is terrorism whether or not subsection (1)(b) is satisfied.

(4) In this section—

    (a) 'action' includes action outside the United Kingdom,

    (b) a reference to any person or to property is a reference to any person, or to property, wherever situated,

    (c) a reference to the public includes a reference to the public of a country other than the United Kingdom, and

(d) 'the government' means the government of the United Kingdom, of a Part of the United Kingdom or of a country other than the United Kingdom.

(5) In this Act a reference to action taken for the purposes of terrorism includes a reference to action taken for the benefit of a proscribed organisation.

2. Temporary legislation

(1) The following shall cease to have effect—

(a) the Prevention of Terrorism (Temporary Provisions) Act 1989, and

(b) the Northern Ireland (Emergency Provisions) Act 1996.

(2) Schedule 1 (which preserves certain provisions of the 1996 Act, in some cases with amendment, for a transitional period) shall have effect.

PART II

PROSCRIBED ORGANISATIONS

Procedure

3. Proscription

(1) For the purposes of this Act an organisation is proscribed if—

(a) it is listed in Schedule 2, or

(b) it operates under the same name as an organisation listed in that Schedule.

(2) Subsection (1)(b) shall not apply in relation to an organisation listed in Schedule 2 if its entry is the subject of a note in that Schedule.

(3) The Secretary of State may by order—

(a) add an organisation to Schedule 2;

(b) remove an organisation from that Schedule;

(c) amend that Schedule in some other way.

(4) The Secretary of State may exercise his power under subsection (3)(a) in respect of an organisation only if he believes that it is concerned in terrorism.

(5) For the purposes of subsection (4) an organisation is concerned in terrorism if it—

(a) commits or participates in acts of terrorism,

(b) prepares for terrorism,

(c) promotes or encourages terrorism, or

(d) is otherwise concerned in terrorism.

4. Deproscription: application

(1) An application may be made to the Secretary of State for the exercise of his power under section 3(3)(b) to remove an organisation from Schedule 2.

(2) An application may be made by—

(a) the organisation, or

(b) any person affected by the organisation's proscription.

(3) The Secretary of State shall make regulations prescribing the procedure for applications under this section.

(4) The regulations shall, in particular—

(a) require the Secretary of State to determine an application within a specified period of time, and

(b) require an application to state the grounds on which it is made.

5. Deproscription: appeal

(1) There shall be a commission, to be known as the Proscribed Organisations Appeal Commission.

(2)   Where an application under section 4 has been refused, the applicant may appeal to the Commission.

(3)   The Commission shall allow an appeal against a refusal to deproscribe an organisation if it considers that the decision to refuse was flawed when considered in the light of the principles applicable on an application for judicial review.

(4)   Where the Commission allows an appeal under this section by or in respect of an organisation, it may make an order under this subsection.

(5)   Where an order is made under subsection (4) the Secretary of State shall as soon as is reasonably practicable—

(a)   lay before Parliament, in accordance with section 123(4), the draft of an order under section 3(3)(b) removing the organisation from the list in Schedule 2, or

(b)   make an order removing the organisation from the list in Schedule 2 in pursuance of section 123(5).

(6)   Schedule 3 (constitution of the Commission and procedure) shall have effect.

6.   Further appeal

(1)   A party to an appeal under section 5 which the Proscribed Organisations Appeal Commission has determined may bring a further appeal on a question of law to—

(a)   the Court of Appeal, if the first appeal was heard in England and Wales,

(b)   the Court of Session, if the first appeal was heard in Scotland, or

(c)   the Court of Appeal in Northern Ireland, if the first appeal was heard in Northern Ireland.

(2)   An appeal under subsection (1) may be brought only with the permission—

(a)   of the Commission, or

(b)   where the Commission refuses permission, of the court to which the appeal would be brought.

(3)   An order under section 5(4) shall not require the Secretary of State to take any action until the final determination or disposal of an appeal under this section (including any appeal to the House of Lords).

7.   Appeal: effect on conviction, &c.

(1)   This section applies where—

(a)   an appeal under section 5 has been allowed in respect of an organisation,

(b)   an order has been made under section 3(3)(b) in respect of the organisation in accordance with an order of the Commission under section 5(4) (and, if the order was made in reliance on section 123(5), a resolution has been passed by each House of Parliament under section 123(5)(b)),

(c)   a person has been convicted of an offence in respect of the organisation under any of sections 11 to 13, 15 to 19 and 56, and

(d)   the activity to which the charge referred took place on or after the date of the refusal to deproscribe against which the appeal under section 5 was brought.

(2)   If the person mentioned in subsection (1)(c) was convicted on indictment—

(a)   he may appeal against the conviction to the Court of Appeal, and

(b)   the Court of Appeal shall allow the appeal.

(3)   A person may appeal against a conviction by virtue of subsection (2) whether or not he has already appealed against the conviction.

(4)   An appeal by virtue of subsection (2)—

(a)   must be brought within the period of 28 days beginning with the date on which the order mentioned in subsection (1)(b) comes into force, and

(b)   shall be treated as an appeal under section 1 of the Criminal Appeal Act 1968 (but does not require leave).

(5)   If the person mentioned in subsection (1)(c) was convicted by a magistrates' court—

(a)   he may appeal against the conviction to the Crown Court, and

(b)   the Crown Court shall allow the appeal.

(6)   A person may appeal against a conviction by virtue of subsection (5)—

(a)   whether or not he pleaded guilty,

(b)   whether or not he has already appealed against the conviction, and

(c)   whether or not he has made an application in respect of the conviction under section 111 of the Magistrates' Courts Act 1980 (case stated).

(7)   An appeal by virtue of subsection (5)—

(a)   must be brought within the period of 21 days beginning with the date on which the order mentioned in subsection (1)(b) comes into force, and

(b)   shall be treated as an appeal under section 108(1)(b) of the Magistrates' Courts Act 1980.

(8)   In section 133(5) of the Criminal Justice Act 1988 (compensation for miscarriage of justice) after paragraph (b) there shall be inserted—

'or

(c)   on an appeal under section 7 of the Terrorism Act 2000'.

8.   Section 7: Scotland and Northern Ireland

(1)   In the application of section 7 to Scotland—

(a)   for every reference to the Court of Appeal or the Crown Court substitute a reference to the High Court of Justiciary,

(b)   in subsection (2)(b), at the end insert 'and quash the conviction',

(c)   in subsection (4)—

(i)   in paragraph (a), for '28 days' substitute 'two weeks', and

(ii)   in paragraph (b), for 'section 1 of the Criminal Appeal Act 1968' substitute 'section 106 of the Criminal Procedure (Scotland) Act 1995',

(d)   in subsection (5)—

(i)   for 'by a magistrates' court' substitute 'in summary proceedings', and

(ii)   in paragraph (b), at the end insert 'and quash the conviction',

(e)   in subsection (6), paragraph (c) is omitted, and

(f)   in subsection (7)—

(i)   in paragraph (a) for '21 days' substitute 'two weeks', and

(ii)   for paragraph (b) substitute—

'(b)   shall be by note of appeal, which shall state the ground of appeal,

(c)   shall not require leave under any provision of Part X of the Criminal Procedure (Scotland) Act 1995, and

(d)   shall be in accordance with such procedure as the High Court of Justiciary may, by Act of Adjournal, determine.'

(2)   In the application of section 7 to Northern Ireland—

(a)   the reference in subsection (4) to section 1 of the Criminal Appeal Act 1968 shall be taken as a reference to section 1 of the Criminal Appeal (Northern Ireland) Act 1980,

(b)   references in subsection (5) to the Crown Court shall be taken as references to the county court,

(c)   the reference in subsection (6) to section 111 of the Magistrates' Courts Act 1980 shall be taken as a reference to Article 146 of the Magistrates' Courts (Northern Ireland) Order 1981, and

(d)   the reference in subsection (7) to section 108(1)(b) of the Magistrates' Courts Act 1980 shall be taken as a reference to Article 140(1)(b) of the Magistrates' Courts (Northern Ireland) Order 1981.

9.   Human Rights Act 1998

(1)   This section applies where rules (within the meaning of section 7 of the Human Rights Act 1998 (jurisdiction)) provide for proceedings under section 7(1) of that Act to be brought before the Proscribed Organisations Appeal Commission.

(2)   The following provisions of this Act shall apply in relation to proceedings under section 7(1) of that Act as they apply to appeals under section 5 of this Act—

(a)   section 5(4) and (5),

(b)   section 6,

(c)   section 7, and

(d)   paragraphs 4 to 8 of Schedule 3.

(3)   The Commission shall decide proceedings in accordance with the principles applicable on an application for judicial review.

(4)   In the application of the provisions mentioned in subsection (2)—

(a)   a reference to the Commission allowing an appeal shall be taken as a reference to the Commission determining that an action of the Secretary of State is incompatible with a Convention right, and

(b)   a reference to the refusal to deproscribe against which an appeal was brought shall be taken as a reference to the action of the Secretary of State which is found to be incompatible with a Convention right.

10.   Immunity

(1)   The following shall not be admissible as evidence in proceedings for an offence under any of sections 11 to 13, 15 to 19 and 56—

(a)   evidence of anything done in relation to an application to the Secretary of State under section 4,

(b)   evidence of anything done in relation to proceedings before the Proscribed Organisations Appeal Commission under section 5 above or section 7(1) of the Human Rights Act 1998,

(c)   evidence of anything done in relation to proceedings under section 6 (including that section as applied by section 9(2)), and

(d)   any document submitted for the purposes of proceedings mentioned in any of paragraphs (a) to (c).

(2)   But subsection (1) does not prevent evidence from being adduced on behalf of the accused.

Offences

11.   Membership

(1)   A person commits an offence if he belongs or professes to belong to a proscribed organisation.

(2)   It is a defence for a person charged with an offence under subsection (1) to prove—

(a)   that the organisation was not proscribed on the last (or only) occasion on which he became a member or began to profess to be a member, and

(b)   that he has not taken part in the activities of the organisation at any time while it was proscribed.

(3)   A person guilty of an offence under this section shall be liable—

(a)   on conviction on indictment, to imprisonment for a term not exceeding ten years, to a fine or to both, or

(b)   on summary conviction, to imprisonment for a term not exceeding six months, to a fine not exceeding the statutory maximum or to both.

(4)   In subsection (2) 'proscribed' means proscribed for the purposes of any of the following—

(a)   this Act;

(b)   the Northern Ireland (Emergency Provisions) Act 1996;

(c)   the Northern Ireland (Emergency Provisions) Act 1991;

(d)   the Prevention of Terrorism (Temporary Provisions) Act 1989;

(e)   the Prevention of Terrorism (Temporary Provisions) Act 1984;

(f)   the Northern Ireland (Emergency Provisions) Act 1978;

(g)   the Prevention of Terrorism (Temporary Provisions) Act 1976;

(h)   the Prevention of Terrorism (Temporary Provisions) Act 1974;

(i)   the Northern Ireland (Emergency Provisions) Act 1973.

12. Support

(1)   A person commits an offence if—

(a)   he invites support for a proscribed organisation, and

(b)   the support is not, or is not restricted to, the provision of money or other property (within the meaning of section 15).

(2)   A person commits an offence if he arranges, manages or assists in arranging or managing a meeting which he knows is—

(a)   to support a proscribed organisation,

(b)   to further the activities of a proscribed organisation, or

(c)   to be addressed by a person who belongs or professes to belong to a proscribed organisation.

(3)   A person commits an offence if he addresses a meeting and the purpose of his address is to encourage support for a proscribed organisation or to further its activities.

(4)   Where a person is charged with an offence under subsection (2)(c) in respect of a private meeting it is a defence for him to prove that he had no reasonable cause to believe that the address mentioned in subsection (2)(c) would support a proscribed organisation or further its activities.

(5)   In subsections (2) to (4)—

(a)   'meeting' means a meeting of three or more persons, whether or not the public are admitted, and

(b)   a meeting is private if the public are not admitted.

(6)   A person guilty of an offence under this section shall be liable—

(a)   on conviction on indictment, to imprisonment for a term not exceeding ten years, to a fine or to both, or

(b)   on summary conviction, to imprisonment for a term not exceeding six months, to a fine not exceeding the statutory maximum or to both.

13. Uniform

(1)   A person in a public place commits an offence if he—

(a)   wears an item of clothing, or

(b)   wears, carries or displays an article,

in such a way or in such circumstances as to arouse reasonable suspicion that he is a member or supporter of a proscribed organisation.

(2)   A constable in Scotland may arrest a person without a warrant if he has reasonable grounds to suspect that the person is guilty of an offence under this section.

(3)   A person guilty of an offence under this section shall be liable on summary conviction to—

(a)   imprisonment for a term not exceeding six months,

(b)   a fine not exceeding level 5 on the standard scale, or

(c)   both.

PART III
TERRORIST PROPERTY

Interpretation

14.   Terrorist property

(1)   In this Act 'terrorist property' means—

(a)   money or other property which is likely to be used for the purposes of terrorism (including any resources of a proscribed organisation),

(b)   proceeds of the commission of acts of terrorism, and

(c)   proceeds of acts carried out for the purposes of terrorism.

(2)   In subsection (1)—

(a)   a reference to proceeds of an act includes a reference to any property which wholly or partly, and directly or indirectly, represents the proceeds of the act (including payments or other rewards in connection with its commission), and

(b)   the reference to an organisation's resources includes a reference to any money or other property which is applied or made available, or is to be applied or made available, for use by the organisation.

Offences

15.   Fund-raising

(1)   A person commits an offence if he—

(a)   invites another to provide money or other property, and

(b)   intends that it should be used, or has reasonable cause to suspect that it may be used, for the purposes of terrorism.

(2)   A person commits an offence if he—

(a)   receives money or other property, and

(b)   intends that it should be used, or has reasonable cause to suspect that it may be used, for the purposes of terrorism.

(3)   A person commits an offence if he—

(a)   provides money or other property, and

(b)   knows or has reasonable cause to suspect that it will or may be used for the purposes of terrorism.

(4)   In this section a reference to the provision of money or other property is a reference to its being given, lent or otherwise made available, whether or not for consideration.

16. Use and possession

(1) A person commits an offence if he uses money or other property for the purposes of terrorism.

(2) A person commits an offence if he—

(a) possesses money or other property, and

(b) intends that it should be used, or has reasonable cause to suspect that it may be used, for the purposes of terrorism.

17. Funding arrangements

A person commits an offence if—

(a) he enters into or becomes concerned in an arrangement as a result of which money or other property is made available or is to be made available to another, and

(b) he knows or has reasonable cause to suspect that it will or may be used for the purposes of terrorism.

18. Money laundering

(1) A person commits an offence if he enters into or becomes concerned in an arrangement which facilitates the retention or control by or on behalf of another person of terrorist property—

(a) by concealment,

(b) by removal from the jurisdiction,

(c) by transfer to nominees, or

(d) in any other way.

(2) It is a defence for a person charged with an offence under subsection (1) to prove that he did not know and had no reasonable cause to suspect that the arrangement related to terrorist property.

19. Disclosure of information: duty

(1) This section applies where a person—

(a) believes or suspects that another person has committed an offence under any of sections 15 to 18, and

(b) bases his belief or suspicion on information which comes to his attention in the course of a trade, profession, business or employment.

(2) The person commits an offence if he does not disclose to a constable as soon as is reasonably practicable—

(a) his belief or suspicion, and

(b) the information on which it is based.

(3) It is a defence for a person charged with an offence under subsection (2) to prove that he had a reasonable excuse for not making the disclosure.

(4) Where—

(a) a person is in employment,

(b) his employer has established a procedure for the making of disclosures of the matters specified in subsection (2), and

(c) he is charged with an offence under that subsection,

it is a defence for him to prove that he disclosed the matters specified in that subsection in accordance with the procedure.

(5) Subsection (2) does not require disclosure by a professional legal adviser of—

(a) information which he obtains in privileged circumstances, or

(b)   a belief or suspicion based on information which he obtains in privileged circumstances.

(6)   For the purpose of subsection (5) information is obtained by an adviser in privileged circumstances if it comes to him, otherwise than with a view to furthering a criminal purpose—

(a)   from a client or a client's representative, in connection with the provision of legal advice by the adviser to the client,

(b)   from a person seeking legal advice from the adviser, or from the person's representative, or

(c)   from any person, for the purpose of actual or contemplated legal proceedings.

(7)   For the purposes of subsection (1)(a) a person shall be treated as having committed an offence under one of sections 15 to 18 if—

(a)   he has taken an action or been in possession of a thing, and

(b)   he would have committed an offence under one of those sections if he had been in the United Kingdom at the time when he took the action or was in possession of the thing.

(8)   A person guilty of an offence under this section shall be liable—

(a)   on conviction on indictment, to imprisonment for a term not exceeding five years, to a fine or to both, or

(b)   on summary conviction, to imprisonment for a term not exceeding six months, or to a fine not exceeding the statutory maximum or to both.

20.   Disclosure of information: permission

(1)   A person may disclose to a constable—

(a)   a suspicion or belief that any money or other property is terrorist property or is derived from terrorist property;

(b)   any matter on which the suspicion or belief is based.

(2)   A person may make a disclosure to a constable in the circumstances mentioned in section 19(1) and (2).

(3)   Subsections (1) and (2) shall have effect notwithstanding any restriction on the disclosure of information imposed by statute or otherwise.

(4)   Where—

(a)   a person is in employment, and

(b)   his employer has established a procedure for the making of disclosures of the kinds mentioned in subsection (1) and section 19(2),

subsections (1) and (2) shall have effect in relation to that person as if any reference to disclosure to a constable included a reference to disclosure in accordance with the procedure.

21.   Cooperation with police

(1)   A person does not commit an offence under any of sections 15 to 18 if he is acting with the express consent of a constable.

(2)   Subject to subsections (3) and (4), a person does not commit an offence under any of sections 15 to 18 by involvement in a transaction or arrangement relating to money or other property if he discloses to a constable—

(a)   his suspicion or belief that the money or other property is terrorist property, and

(b)   the information on which his suspicion or belief is based.

(3)   Subsection (2) applies only where a person makes a disclosure—

(a)   after he becomes concerned in the transaction concerned,

(b)   on his own initiative, and

(c)   as soon as is reasonably practicable.

(4)   Subsection (2) does not apply to a person if—

(a) a constable forbids him to continue his involvement in the transaction or arrangement to which the disclosure relates, and

(b) he continues his involvement.

(5) It is a defence for a person charged with an offence under any of sections 15(2) and (3) and 16 to 18 to prove that—

(a) he intended to make a disclosure of the kind mentioned in subsections (2) and (3), and

(b) there is reasonable excuse for his failure to do so.

(6) Where—

(a) a person is in employment, and

(b) his employer has established a procedure for the making of disclosures of the same kind as may be made to a constable under subsection (2),

this section shall have effect in relation to that person as if any reference to disclosure to a constable included a reference to disclosure in accordance with the procedure.

(7) A reference in this section to a transaction or arrangement relating to money or other property includes a reference to use or possession.

22. Penalties

A person guilty of an offence under any of sections 15 to 18 shall be liable—

(a) on conviction on indictment, to imprisonment for a term not exceeding 14 years, to a fine or to both, or

(b) on summary conviction, to imprisonment for a term not exceeding six months, to a fine not exceeding the statutory maximum or to both.

23. Forfeiture

(1) The court by or before which a person is convicted of an offence under any of sections 15 to 18 may make a forfeiture order in accordance with the provisions of this section.

(2) Where a person is convicted of an offence under section 15(1) or (2) or 16 the court may order the forfeiture of any money or other property—

(a) which, at the time of the offence, he had in his possession or under his control, and

(b) which, at that time, he intended should be used, or had reasonable cause to suspect might be used, for the purposes of terrorism.

(3) Where a person is convicted of an offence under section 15(3) the court may order the forfeiture of any money or other property—

(a) which, at the time of the offence, he had in his possession or under his control, and

(b) which, at that time, he knew or had reasonable cause to suspect would or might be used for the purposes of terrorism.

(4) Where a person is convicted of an offence under section 17 the court may order the forfeiture of the money or other property—

(a) to which the arrangement in question related, and

(b) which, at the time of the offence, he knew or had reasonable cause to suspect would or might be used for the purposes of terrorism.

(5) Where a person is convicted of an offence under section 18 the court may order the forfeiture of the money or other property to which the arrangement in question related.

(6) Where a person is convicted of an offence under any of sections 15 to 18, the court may order the forfeiture of any money or other property which wholly or partly, and directly or indirectly, is received by any person as a payment or other reward in connection with the commission of the offence.

(7) Where a person other than the convicted person claims to be the owner of or otherwise interested in anything which can be forfeited by an order under this section, the court shall give him an opportunity to be heard before making an order.

(8) A court in Scotland shall not make an order under this section except on the application of the prosecutor—

    (a) in proceedings on indictment, when he moves for sentence, and

    (b) in summary proceedings, before the court convicts the accused,

and for the purposes of any appeal or review, an order under this section made by a court in Scotland is a sentence.

(9) Schedule 4 (which makes further provision in relation to forfeiture orders under this section) shall have effect.

Seizure of terrorist cash

24. Interpretation

(1) In sections 25 to 31 'authorised officer' means any of the following—

    (a) a constable,

    (b) a customs officer, and

    (c) an immigration officer.

(2) In sections 25 to 31 'cash' means—

    (a) coins and notes in any currency,

    (b) postal orders,

    (c) travellers' cheques,

    (d) bankers' drafts, and

    (e) such other kinds of monetary instrument as the Secretary of State may specify by order.

25. Seizure and detention

(1) An authorised officer may seize and detain any cash to which this section applies if he has reasonable grounds for suspecting that—

    (a) it is intended to be used for the purposes of terrorism,

    (b) it forms the whole or part of the resources of a proscribed organisation, or

    (c) it is terrorist property within the meaning given in section 14(1)(b) or (c).

(2) In subsection (1)(b) the reference to an organisation's resources includes a reference to any cash which is applied or made available, or is to be applied or made available, for use by the organisation.

(3) This section applies to cash which—

    (a) is being imported into or exported from the United Kingdom,

    (b) is being brought to any place in the United Kingdom for the purpose of being exported from the United Kingdom,

    (c) is being brought to Northern Ireland from Great Britain, or to Great Britain from Northern Ireland,

    (d) is being brought to any place in Northern Ireland for the purpose of being brought to Great Britain, or

    (e) is being brought to any place in Great Britain for the purpose of being brought to Northern Ireland.

(4) Subject to subsection (5), cash seized under this section shall be released not later than the end of the period of 48 hours beginning with the time when it is seized.

(5) Where an order is made under section 26 in relation to cash seized, it may be detained during the period specified in the order.

26. Continued detention

(1) An authorised officer or the Commissioners of Customs and Excise may apply to a magistrates' court for an order under this section in relation to cash seized under section 25.

(2) An order under this section—

(a) shall authorise the further detention under section 25 of the cash to which it relates for a period specified in the order,

(b) shall specify a period which ends not later than the end of the period of three months beginning with the date of the order, and

(c) shall require notice to be given to the person from whom the cash was seized and to any other person who is affected by and specified in the order.

(3) An application for an order under this section may be granted only if the court is satisfied—

(a) that there are reasonable grounds to suspect that the cash is cash of a kind mentioned in section 25(1)(a), (b) or (c), and

(b) that the continued detention of the cash is justified pending completion of an investigation of its origin or derivation or pending a determination whether to institute criminal proceedings (whether in the United Kingdom or elsewhere) which relate to the cash.

(4) More than one order may be made under this section in relation to particular cash; but cash shall not be detained by virtue of an order under this section after the end of the period of two years beginning with the date when the first order under this section was made in relation to it.

(5) In Scotland, any application under this section shall be made by the procurator fiscal to the sheriff; and in this section a reference to a magistrates' court shall be taken as a reference to the sheriff.

27. Detained cash

(1) Cash detained under section 25 by virtue of an order under section 26 shall, unless required as evidence of an offence, be held in an interest bearing account; and the interest accruing on the cash shall be added to it on its release or forfeiture.

(2) Any person may apply to a magistrates' court, or in Scotland to the sheriff, for a direction that cash detained under section 25 be released.

(3) A magistrates' court or the sheriff shall grant an application under subsection (2) if satisfied—

(a) that section 26(3)(a) or (b) no longer applies, or

(b) that the detention of the cash is for any other reason no longer justified.

(4) An authorised officer, or in Scotland the procurator fiscal, may release cash detained under section 25 if—

(a) he is satisfied that its detention is no longer justified, and

(b) he has notified the magistrates' court or sheriff who made the order by virtue of which the cash is being detained under section 25.

(5) Cash detained under section 25 shall not be released under this section—

(a) while proceedings on an application for its forfeiture under section 28 have not been concluded, or

(b) while proceedings, whether in the United Kingdom or elsewhere, which relate to the cash have not been concluded.

28. Forfeiture

(1) An authorised officer or the Commissioners of Customs and Excise may apply to a magistrates' court, or in Scotland the procurator fiscal may apply to the sheriff, for an order forfeiting cash being detained under section 25.

(2) A magistrates' court or the sheriff may grant an application only if satisfied on the balance of probabilities that the cash is cash of a kind mentioned in section 25(1)(a), (b) or (c).

(3) Before making an order under this section, a magistrates' court or the sheriff must give an opportunity to be heard to any person—

(a) who is not a party to the proceedings, and

(b) who claims to be the owner of or otherwise interested in any of the cash which can be forfeited under this section.

(4) An order may be made under this section whether or not proceedings are brought against any person for an offence with which the cash is connected.

(5) Proceedings on an application under this section to the sheriff shall be civil proceedings.

29. Forfeiture: appeal

(1) Subject to subsection (2), any party to proceedings in which a forfeiture order is made under section 28 may appeal—

(a) where the order is made by a magistrates' court in England and Wales, to the Crown Court,

(b) where the order is made by the sheriff in Scotland, to the Court of Session, or

(c) where the order is made by a magistrates' court in Northern Ireland, to the county court.

(2) An appeal under subsection (1)—

(a) must be brought before the end of the period of 30 days beginning with the date on which the forfeiture order was made, and

(b) may not be brought by the applicant for the forfeiture order.

(3) On an application by the appellant, a magistrates' court or the sheriff may order the release of so much of the cash to which the forfeiture order applies as it considers appropriate to enable him to meet his reasonable legal expenses in connection with the appeal.

(4) An appeal under subsection (1) shall be by way of a rehearing.

(5) If the court allows the appeal, it may order the release of—

(a) the cash to which the forfeiture order applies together with any interest which has accrued, or

(b) where an order has been made under subsection (3), the remaining cash to which the forfeiture order applies together with any interest which has accrued.

(6) Subsection (7) applies where a successful application for a forfeiture order relies (in whole or in part) on the fact that an organisation is proscribed, and—

(a) a deproscription appeal under section 5 is allowed in respect of the organisation,

(b) an order is made under section 3(3)(b) in respect of the organisation in accordance with an order of the Proscribed Organisations Appeal Commission under section 5(4) (and, if the order is made in reliance on section 123(5), a resolution is passed by each House of Parliament under section 123(5)(b)), and

(c) the forfeited cash was seized under section 25 on or after the date of the refusal to deproscribe against which the appeal under section 5 was brought.

(7) Where this subsection applies an appeal under subsection (1) may be brought at any time before the end of the period of 30 days beginning with the date on which the order under section 3(3)(b) comes into force.

30. Treatment of forfeited cash

Any cash to which a forfeiture order under section 28 applies or accrued interest thereon shall be paid into the Consolidated Fund—

(a) after the end of the period within which an appeal may be brought under section 29(1), or

(b) where an appeal is brought under section 29(1), after the appeal is determined or otherwise disposed of.

31. Rules of court

Provision may be made by rules of court about the procedure on applications or appeals to any court under sections 26 to 29, and in particular as to—

(a) the giving of notice to persons affected by an application or appeal under those provisions;

(b) the joinder, or in Scotland the sisting, of those persons as parties to the proceedings.

PART IV
TERRORIST INVESTIGATIONS

Interpretation

32. Terrorist investigation

In this Act 'terrorist investigation' means an investigation of—

(a) the commission, preparation or instigation of acts of terrorism,

(b) an act which appears to have been done for the purposes of terrorism,

(c) the resources of a proscribed organisation,

(d) the possibility of making an order under section 3(3), or

(e) the commission, preparation or instigation of an offence under this Act.

Cordons

33. Cordoned areas

(1) An area is a cordoned area for the purposes of this Act if it is designated under this section.

(2) A designation may be made only if the person making it considers it expedient for the purposes of a terrorist investigation.

(3) If a designation is made orally, the person making it shall confirm it in writing as soon as is reasonably practicable.

(4) The person making a designation shall arrange for the demarcation of the cordoned area, so far as is reasonably practicable—

(a) by means of tape marked with the word 'police', or

(b) in such other manner as a constable considers appropriate.

34. Power to designate

(1) Subject to subsection (2), a designation under section 33 may only be made—

(a) where the area is outside Northern Ireland and is wholly or partly within a police area, by an officer for the police area who is of at least the rank of superintendent, and

(b) where the area is in Northern Ireland, by a member of the Royal Ulster Constabulary who is of at least the rank of superintendent.

(2) A constable who is not of the rank required by subsection (1) may make a designation if he considers it necessary by reason of urgency.

(3) Where a constable makes a designation in reliance on subsection (2) he shall as soon as is reasonably practicable—

(a) make a written record of the time at which the designation was made, and

(b) ensure that a police officer of at least the rank of superintendent is informed.

(4) An officer who is informed of a designation in accordance with subsection (3)(b)—

(a) shall confirm the designation or cancel it with effect from such time as he may direct, and

(b) shall, if he cancels the designation, make a written record of the cancellation and the reason for it.

35. Duration

(1) A designation under section 33 has effect, subject to subsections (2) to (5), during the period—

(a) beginning at the time when it is made, and

(b) ending with a date or at a time specified in the designation.

(2) The date or time specified under subsection (1)(b) must not occur after the end of the period of 14 days beginning with the day on which the designation is made.

(3) The period during which a designation has effect may be extended in writing from time to time by—

(a) the person who made it, or

(b) a person who could have made it (otherwise than by virtue of section 34(2)).

(4) An extension shall specify the additional period during which the designation is to have effect.

(5) A designation shall not have effect after the end of the period of 28 days beginning with the day on which it is made.

36. Police powers

(1) A constable in uniform may—

(a) order a person in a cordoned area to leave it immediately;

(b) order a person immediately to leave premises which are wholly or partly in or adjacent to a cordoned area;

(c) order the driver or person in charge of a vehicle in a cordoned area to move it from the area immediately;

(d) arrange for the removal of a vehicle from a cordoned area;

(e) arrange for the movement of a vehicle within a cordoned area;

(f) prohibit or restrict access to a cordoned area by pedestrians or vehicles.

(2) A person commits an offence if he fails to comply with an order, prohibition or restriction imposed by virtue of subsection (1).

(3) It is a defence for a person charged with an offence under subsection (2) to prove that he had a reasonable excuse for his failure.

(4) A person guilty of an offence under subsection (2) shall be liable on summary conviction to—

(a) imprisonment for a term not exceeding three months,

(b) a fine not exceeding level 4 on the standard scale, or

(c) both.

Information and evidence

37. Powers
Schedule 5 (power to obtain information, &c.) shall have effect.

38. Financial information
Schedule 6 (financial information) shall have effect.

39. Disclosure of information, &c.
(1) Subsection (2) applies where a person knows or has reasonable cause to suspect that a constable is conducting or proposes to conduct a terrorist investigation.

(2) The person commits an offence if he—

(a) discloses to another anything which is likely to prejudice the investigation, or

(b) interferes with material which is likely to be relevant to the investigation.

(3) Subsection (4) applies where a person knows or has reasonable cause to suspect that a disclosure has been or will be made under any of sections 19 to 21.

(4) The person commits an offence if he—

(a) discloses to another anything which is likely to prejudice an investigation resulting from the disclosure under that section, or

(b) interferes with material which is likely to be relevant to an investigation resulting from the disclosure under that section.

(5) It is a defence for a person charged with an offence under subsection (2) or (4) to prove—

(a) that he did not know and had no reasonable cause to suspect that the disclosure or interference was likely to affect a terrorist investigation, or

(b) that he had a reasonable excuse for the disclosure or interference.

(6) Subsections (2) and (4) do not apply to a disclosure which is made by a professional legal adviser—

(a) to his client or to his client's representative in connection with the provision of legal advice by the adviser to the client and not with a view to furthering a criminal purpose, or

(b) to any person for the purpose of actual or contemplated legal proceedings and not with a view to furthering a criminal purpose.

(7) A person guilty of an offence under this section shall be liable—

(a) on conviction on indictment, to imprisonment for a term not exceeding five years, to a fine or to both, or

(b) on summary conviction, to imprisonment for a term not exceeding six months, to a fine not exceeding the statutory maximum or to both.

(8) For the purposes of this section—

(a) a reference to conducting a terrorist investigation includes a reference to taking part in the conduct of, or assisting, a terrorist investigation, and

(b) a person interferes with material if he falsifies it, conceals it, destroys it or disposes of it, or if he causes or permits another to do any of those things.

PART V
COUNTER-TERRORIST POWERS

Suspected terrorists

40. Terrorist: interpretation
(1) In this Part 'terrorist' means a person who—

(a)   has committed an offence under any of sections 11, 12, 15 to 18, 54 and 56 to 63, or

(b)   is or has been concerned in the commission, preparation or instigation of acts of terrorism.

(2)   The reference in subsection (1)(b) to a person who has been concerned in the commission, preparation or instigation of acts of terrorism includes a reference to a person who has been, whether before or after the passing of this Act, concerned in the commission, preparation or instigation of acts of terrorism within the meaning given by section 1.

41.   Arrest without warrant

(1)   A constable may arrest without a warrant a person whom he reasonably suspects to be a terrorist.

(2)   Where a person is arrested under this section the provisions of Schedule 8 (detention: treatment, review and extension) shall apply.

(3)   Subject to subsections (4) to (7), a person detained under this section shall (unless detained under any other power) be released not later than the end of the period of 48 hours beginning—

(a)   with the time of his arrest under this section, or

(b)   if he was being detained under Schedule 7 when he was arrested under this section, with the time when his examination under that Schedule began.

(4)   If on a review of a person's detention under Part II of Schedule 8 the review officer does not authorise continued detention, the person shall (unless detained in accordance with subsection (5) or (6) or under any other power) be released.

(5)   Where a police officer intends to make an application for a warrant under paragraph 29 of Schedule 8 extending a person's detention, the person may be detained pending the making of the application.

(6)   Where an application has been made under paragraph 29 or 36 of Schedule 8 in respect of a person's detention, he may be detained pending the conclusion of proceedings on the application.

(7)   Where an application under paragraph 29 or 36 of Schedule 8 is granted in respect of a person's detention, he may be detained, subject to paragraph 37 of that Schedule, during the period specified in the warrant.

(8)   The refusal of an application in respect of a person's detention under paragraph 29 or 36 of Schedule 8 shall not prevent his continued detention in accordance with this section.

(9)   A person who has the powers of a constable in one Part of the United Kingdom may exercise the power under subsection (1) in any Part of the United Kingdom.

42.   Search of premises

(1)   A justice of the peace may on the application of a constable issue a warrant in relation to specified premises if he is satisfied that there are reasonable grounds for suspecting that a person whom the constable reasonably suspects to be a person falling within section 40(1)(b) is to be found there.

(2)   A warrant under this section shall authorise any constable to enter and search the specified premises for the purpose of arresting the person referred to in subsection (1) under section 41.

(3)   In the application of subsection (1) to Scotland—

(a)   'justice of the peace' includes the sheriff, and

(b)   the justice of the peace or sheriff can be satisfied as mentioned in that subsection only by having heard evidence on oath.

43. Search of persons

(1) A constable may stop and search a person whom he reasonably suspects to be a terrorist to discover whether he has in his possession anything which may constitute evidence that he is a terrorist.

(2) A constable may search a person arrested under section 41 to discover whether he has in his possession anything which may constitute evidence that he is a terrorist.

(3) A search of a person under this section must be carried out by someone of the same sex.

(4) A constable may seize and retain anything which he discovers in the course of a search of a person under subsection (1) or (2) and which he reasonably suspects may constitute evidence that the person is a terrorist.

(5) A person who has the powers of a constable in one Part of the United Kingdom may exercise a power under this section in any Part of the United Kingdom.

Power to stop and search

44. Authorisations

(1) An authorisation under this subsection authorises any constable in uniform to stop a vehicle in an area or at a place specified in the authorisation and to search—

  (a) the vehicle;

  (b) the driver of the vehicle;

  (c) a passenger in the vehicle;

  (d) anything in or on the vehicle or carried by the driver or a passenger.

(2) An authorisation under this subsection authorises any constable in uniform to stop a pedestrian in an area or at a place specified in the authorisation and to search—

  (a) the pedestrian;

  (b) anything carried by him.

(3) An authorisation under subsection (1) or (2) may be given only if the person giving it considers it expedient for the prevention of acts of terrorism.

(4) An authorisation may be given—

  (a) where the specified area or place is the whole or part of a police area outside Northern Ireland other than one mentioned in paragraph (b) or (c), by a police officer for the area who is of at least the rank of assistant chief constable;

  (b) where the specified area or place is the whole or part of the metropolitan police district, by a police officer for the district who is of at least the rank of commander of the metropolitan police;

  (c) where the specified area or place is the whole or part of the City of London, by a police officer for the City who is of at least the rank of commander in the City of London police force;

  (d) where the specified area or place is the whole or part of Northern Ireland, by a member of the Royal Ulster Constabulary who is of at least the rank of assistant chief constable.

(5) If an authorisation is given orally, the person giving it shall confirm it in writing as soon as is reasonably practicable.

45. Exercise of power

(1) The power conferred by an authorisation under section 44(1) or (2)—

  (a) may be exercised only for the purpose of searching for articles of a kind which could be used in connection with terrorism, and

(b)   may be exercised whether or not the constable has grounds for suspecting the presence of articles of that kind.

(2)   A constable may seize and retain an article which he discovers in the course of a search by virtue of section 44(1) or (2) and which he reasonably suspects is intended to be used in connection with terrorism.

(3)   A constable exercising the power conferred by an authorisation may not require a person to remove any clothing in public except for headgear, footwear, an outer coat, a jacket or gloves.

(4)   Where a constable proposes to search a person or vehicle by virtue of section 44(1) or (2) he may detain the person or vehicle for such time as is reasonably required to permit the search to be carried out at or near the place where the person or vehicle is stopped.

(5)   Where—

(a)   a vehicle or pedestrian is stopped by virtue of section 44(1) or (2), and

(b)   the driver of the vehicle or the pedestrian applies for a written statement that the vehicle was stopped, or that he was stopped, by virtue of section 44(1) or (2), the written statement shall be provided.

(6)   An application under subsection (5) must be made within the period of 12 months beginning with the date on which the vehicle or pedestrian was stopped.

46.   Duration of authorisation

(1)   An authorisation under section 44 has effect, subject to subsections (2) to (7), during the period—

(a)   beginning at the time when the authorisation is given, and

(b)   ending with a date or at a time specified in the authorisation.

(2)   The date or time specified under subsection (1)(b) must not occur after the end of the period of 28 days beginning with the day on which the authorisation is given.

(3)   The person who gives an authorisation shall inform the Secretary of State as soon as is reasonably practicable.

(4)   If an authorisation is not confirmed by the Secretary of State before the end of the period of 48 hours beginning with the time when it is given—

(a)   it shall cease to have effect at the end of that period, but

(b)   its ceasing to have effect shall not affect the lawfulness of anything done in reliance on it before the end of that period.

(5)   Where the Secretary of State confirms an authorisation he may substitute an earlier date or time for the date or time specified under subsection (1)(b).

(6)   The Secretary of State may cancel an authorisation with effect from a specified time.

(7)   An authorisation may be renewed in writing by the person who gave it or by a person who could have given it; and subsections (1) to (6) shall apply as if a new authorisation were given on each occasion on which the authorisation is renewed.

47.   Offences

(1)   A person commits an offence if he—

(a)   fails to stop a vehicle when required to do so by a constable in the exercise of the power conferred by an authorisation under section 44(1);

(b)   fails to stop when required to do so by a constable in the exercise of the power conferred by an authorisation under section 44(2);

(c)   wilfully obstructs a constable in the exercise of the power conferred by an authorisation under section 44(1) or (2).

(2)   A person guilty of an offence under this section shall be liable on summary conviction to—

(a)   imprisonment for a term not exceeding six months,

(b)   a fine not exceeding level 5 on the standard scale, or

(c)   both.

Parking

48. Authorisations

(1)   An authorisation under this section authorises any constable in uniform to prohibit or restrict the parking of vehicles on a road specified in the authorisation.

(2)   An authorisation may be given only if the person giving it considers it expedient for the prevention of acts of terrorism.

(3)   An authorisation may be given—

(a)   where the road specified is outside Northern Ireland and is wholly or partly within a police area other than one mentioned in paragraphs (b) or (c), by a police officer for the area who is of at least the rank of assistant chief constable;

(b)   where the road specified is wholly or partly in the metropolitan police district, by a police officer for the district who is of at least the rank of commander of the metropolitan police;

(c)   where the road specified is wholly or partly in the City of London, by a police officer for the City who is of at least the rank of commander in the City of London police force;

(d)   where the road specified is in Northern Ireland, by a member of the Royal Ulster Constabulary who is of at least the rank of assistant chief constable.

(4)   If an authorisation is given orally, the person giving it shall confirm it in writing as soon as is reasonably practicable.

49. Exercise of power

(1)   The power conferred by an authorisation under section 48 shall be exercised by placing a traffic sign on the road concerned.

(2)   A constable exercising the power conferred by an authorisation under section 48 may suspend a parking place.

(3)   Where a parking place is suspended under subsection (2), the suspension shall be treated as a restriction imposed by virtue of section 48—

(a)   for the purposes of section 99 of the Road Traffic Regulation Act 1984 (removal of vehicles illegally parked, &c.) and of any regulations in force under that section, and

(b)   for the purposes of Articles 47 and 48 of the Road Traffic Regulation (Northern Ireland) Order 1997 (in relation to Northern Ireland).

50. Duration of authorisation

(1)   An authorisation under section 48 has effect, subject to subsections (2) and (3), during the period specified in the authorisation.

(2)   The period specified shall not exceed 28 days.

(3)   An authorisation may be renewed in writing by the person who gave it or by a person who could have given it; and subsections (1) and (2) shall apply as if a new authorisation were given on each occasion on which the authorisation is renewed.

51. Offences

(1)   A person commits an offence if he parks a vehicle in contravention of a prohibition or restriction imposed by virtue of section 48.

(2)   A person commits an offence if—

(a) he is the driver or other person in charge of a vehicle which has been permitted to remain at rest in contravention of any prohibition or restriction imposed by virtue of section 48, and

(b) he fails to move the vehicle when ordered to do so by a constable in uniform.

(3) It is a defence for a person charged with an offence under this section to prove that he had a reasonable excuse for the act or omission in question.

(4) Possession of a current disabled person's badge shall not itself constitute a reasonable excuse for the purposes of subsection (3).

(5) A person guilty of an offence under subsection (1) shall be liable on summary conviction to a fine not exceeding level 4 on the standard scale.

(6) A person guilty of an offence under subsection (2) shall be liable on summary conviction to—

(a) imprisonment for a term not exceeding three months,

(b) a fine not exceeding level 4 on the standard scale, or

(c) both.

52. Interpretation

In sections 48 to 51—

'disabled person's badge' means a badge issued, or having effect as if issued, under any regulations for the time being in force under section 21 of the Chronically Sick and Disabled Persons Act 1970 (in relation to England and Wales and Scotland) or section 14 of the Chronically Sick and Disabled Persons (Northern Ireland) Act 1978 (in relation to Northern Ireland);

'driver' means, in relation to a vehicle which has been left on any road, the person who was driving it when it was left there;

'parking' means leaving a vehicle or permitting it to remain at rest;

'traffic sign' has the meaning given in section 142(1) of the Road Traffic Regulation Act 1984 (in relation to England and Wales and Scotland) and in Article 28 of the Road Traffic Regulation (Northern Ireland) Order 1997 (in relation to Northern Ireland);

'vehicle' has the same meaning as in section 99(5) of the Road Traffic Regulation Act 1984 (in relation to England and Wales and Scotland) and Article 47(4) of the Road Traffic Regulation (Northern Ireland) Order 1997 (in relation to Northern Ireland).

Port and border controls

53. Port and border controls

(1) Schedule 7 (port and border controls) shall have effect.

(2) The Secretary of State may by order repeal paragraph 16 of Schedule 7.

(3) The powers conferred by Schedule 7 shall be exercisable notwithstanding the rights conferred by section 1 of the Immigration Act 1971 (general principles regulating entry into and staying in the United Kingdom).

PART VI

MISCELLANEOUS

Terrorist offences

54. Weapons training

(1) A person commits an offence if he provides instruction or training in the making or use of—

(a) firearms,

(b) explosives, or

(c) chemical, biological or nuclear weapons.

(2) A person commits an offence if he receives instruction or training in the making or use of—

(a) firearms,

(b) explosives, or

(c) chemical, biological or nuclear weapons.

(3) A person commits an offence if he invites another to receive instruction or training and the receipt—

(a) would constitute an offence under subsection (2), or

(b) would constitute an offence under subsection (2) but for the fact that it is to take place outside the United Kingdom.

(4) For the purpose of subsections (1) and (3)—

(a) a reference to the provision of instruction includes a reference to making it available either generally or to one or more specific persons, and

(b) an invitation to receive instruction or training may be either general or addressed to one or more specific persons.

(5) It is a defence for a person charged with an offence under this section in relation to instruction or training to prove that his action or involvement was wholly for a purpose other than assisting, preparing for or participating in terrorism.

(6) A person guilty of an offence under this section shall be liable—

(a) on conviction on indictment, to imprisonment for a term not exceeding ten years, to a fine or to both, or

(b) on summary conviction, to imprisonment for a term not exceeding six months, to a fine not exceeding the statutory maximum or to both.

(7) A court by or before which a person is convicted of an offence under this section may order the forfeiture of anything which the court considers to have been in the person's possession for purposes connected with the offence.

(8) Before making an order under subsection (7) a court must give an opportunity to be heard to any person, other than the convicted person, who claims to be the owner of or otherwise interested in anything which can be forfeited under that subsection.

(9) An order under subsection (7) shall not come into force until there is no further possibility of it being varied, or set aside, on appeal (disregarding any power of a court to grant leave to appeal out of time).

55. Weapons training: interpretation

In section 54—

'biological weapon' means anything to which section 1(1)(b) of the Biological Weapons Act 1974 applies,

'chemical weapon' has the meaning given by section 1 of the Chemical Weapons Act 1996, and

'nuclear weapon' means a weapon which contains nuclear material within the meaning of Article 1(a) and (b) of the Convention on the Physical Protection of Nuclear Material opened for signature at Vienna and New York on 3rd March 1980 (set out in the Schedule to the Nuclear Material (Offences) Act 1983).

56. Directing terrorist organisation

(1) A person commits an offence if he directs, at any level, the activities of an organisation which is concerned in the commission of acts of terrorism.

(2) A person guilty of an offence under this section is liable on conviction on indictment to imprisonment for life.

57. Possession for terrorist purposes

(1) A person commits an offence if he possesses an article in circumstances which give rise to a reasonable suspicion that his possession is for a purpose connected with the commission, preparation or instigation of an act of terrorism.

(2) It is a defence for a person charged with an offence under this section to prove that his possession of the article was not for a purpose connected with the commission, preparation or instigation of an act of terrorism.

(3) In proceedings for an offence under this section, if it is proved that an article—

(a) was on any premises at the same time as the accused, or

(b) was on premises of which the accused was the occupier or which he habitually used otherwise than as a member of the public,

the court may assume that the accused possessed the article, unless he proves that he did not know of its presence on the premises or that he had no control over it.

(4) A person guilty of an offence under this section shall be liable—

(a) on conviction on indictment, to imprisonment for a term not exceeding 10 years, to a fine or to both, or

(b) on summary conviction, to imprisonment for a term not exceeding six months, to a fine not exceeding the statutory maximum or to both.

58. Collection of information

(1) A person commits an offence if—

(a) he collects or makes a record of information of a kind likely to be useful to a person committing or preparing an act of terrorism, or

(b) he possesses a document or record containing information of that kind.

(2) In this section 'record' includes a photographic or electronic record.

(3) It is a defence for a person charged with an offence under this section to prove that he had a reasonable excuse for his action or possession.

(4) A person guilty of an offence under this section shall be liable—

(a) on conviction on indictment, to imprisonment for a term not exceeding 10 years, to a fine or to both, or

(b) on summary conviction, to imprisonment for a term not exceeding six months, to a fine not exceeding the statutory maximum or to both.

(5) A court by or before which a person is convicted of an offence under this section may order the forfeiture of any document or record containing information of the kind mentioned in subsection (1)(a).

(6) Before making an order under subsection (5) a court must give an opportunity to be heard to any person, other than the convicted person, who claims to be the owner of or otherwise interested in anything which can be forfeited under that subsection.

(7) An order under subsection (5) shall not come into force until there is no further possibility of it being varied, or set aside, on appeal (disregarding any power of a court to grant leave to appeal out of time).

Inciting terrorism overseas

59. England and Wales

(1) A person commits an offence if—

(a) he incites another person to commit an act of terrorism wholly or partly outside the United Kingdom, and

(b) the act would, if committed in England and Wales, constitute one of the offences listed in subsection (2).

(2) Those offences are—

(a) murder,

(b) an offence under section 18 of the Offences against the Person Act 1861 (wounding with intent),

(c) an offence under section 23 or 24 of that Act (poison),

(d) an offence under section 28 or 29 of that Act (explosions), and

(e) an offence under section 1(2) of the Criminal Damage Act 1971 (endangering life by damaging property).

(3) A person guilty of an offence under this section shall be liable to any penalty to which he would be liable on conviction of the offence listed in subsection (2) which corresponds to the act which he incites.

(4) For the purposes of subsection (1) it is immaterial whether or not the person incited is in the United Kingdom at the time of the incitement.

(5) Nothing in this section imposes criminal liability on any person acting on behalf of, or holding office under, the Crown.

60. Northern Ireland

(1) A person commits an offence if—

(a) he incites another person to commit an act of terrorism wholly or partly outside the United Kingdom, and

(b) the act would, if committed in Northern Ireland, constitute one of the offences listed in subsection (2).

(2) Those offences are—

(a) murder,

(b) an offence under section 18 of the Offences against the Person Act 1861 (wounding with intent),

(c) an offence under section 23 or 24 of that Act (poison),

(d) an offence under section 28 or 29 of that Act (explosions), and

(e) an offence under Article 3(2) of the Criminal Damage (Northern Ireland) Order 1977 (endangering life by damaging property).

(3) A person guilty of an offence under this section shall be liable to any penalty to which he would be liable on conviction of the offence listed in subsection (2) which corresponds to the act which he incites.

(4) For the purposes of subsection (1) it is immaterial whether or not the person incited is in the United Kingdom at the time of the incitement.

(5) Nothing in this section imposes criminal liability on any person acting on behalf of, or holding office under, the Crown.

61. Scotland

(1) A person commits an offence if—

(a) he incites another person to commit an act of terrorism wholly or partly outside the United Kingdom, and

(b) the act would, if committed in Scotland, constitute one of the offences listed in subsection (2).

(2) Those offences are—

(a)   murder,

(b)   assault to severe injury, and

(c)   reckless conduct which causes actual injury.

(3)   A person guilty of an offence under this section shall be liable to any penalty to which he would be liable on conviction of the offence listed in subsection (2) which corresponds to the act which he incites.

(4)   For the purposes of subsection (1) it is immaterial whether or not the person incited is in the United Kingdom at the time of the incitement.

(5)   Nothing in this section imposes criminal liability on any person acting on behalf of, or holding office under, the Crown.

Terrorist bombing and finance offences

62.   Terrorist bombing: jurisdiction

(1)   If—

(a)   a person does anything outside the United Kingdom as an act of terrorism or for the purposes of terrorism, and

(b)   his action would have constituted the commission of one of the offences listed in subsection (2) if it had been done in the United Kingdom,

he shall be guilty of the offence.

(2)   The offences referred to in subsection (1)(b) are—

(a)   an offence under section 2, 3 or 5 of the Explosive Substances Act 1883 (causing explosions, &c.),

(b)   an offence under section 1 of the Biological Weapons Act 1974 (biological weapons), and

(c)   an offence under section 2 of the Chemical Weapons Act 1996 (chemical weapons).

63.   Terrorist finance: jurisdiction

(1)   If—

(a)   a person does anything outside the United Kingdom, and

(b)   his action would have constituted the commission of an offence under any of sections 15 to 18 if it had been done in the United Kingdom,

he shall be guilty of the offence.

(2)   For the purposes of subsection (1)(b), section 18(1)(b) shall be read as if for 'the jurisdiction' there were substituted 'a jurisdiction'.

64.   Extradition

(1)   The Extradition Act 1989 shall be amended as follows.

(2)   In section 22(2) (international conventions) after paragraph (1) insert—

'(m)   the Convention for the Suppression of Terrorist Bombings, which was opened for signature at New York on 12th January 1998 ("the Terrorist Bombings Convention");

(n)   the Convention for the Suppression of the Financing of Terrorism which was opened for signature at New York on 10th January 2000 ("the Terrorist Finance Convention").'

(3)   In section 22(4) (relevant offences) after paragraph (1) insert—

'(m)   in relation to the Terrorist Bombings Convention, an offence, committed as an act of terrorism or for the purposes of terrorism, under—

(i)   section 2, 3 or 5 of the Explosive Substances Act 1883 (causing explosions, &c.),

    (ii)   section 1 of the Biological Weapons Act 1974 (biological weapons), or

    (iii)   section 2 of the Chemical Weapons Act 1996 (chemical weapons);

    (n)   in relation to the Terrorist Finance Convention, an offence under any of sections 15 to 18 of the Terrorism Act 2000 (terrorist property: offences).'

(4)   After section 24(4) (suppression of terrorism) insert—

'(5)   Subsections (1) and (2) above shall have effect in relation to an offence to which section 22(4)(m) or (n) above applies as they have effect in relation to an offence to which section 1 of the Suppression of Terrorism Act 1978 applies.

(6)   For that purpose subsection (2) applies to a country which is a party to—

    (a)   the Convention for the Suppression of Terrorist Bombings mentioned in section 22(2)(m) above, or

    (b)   the Convention for the Suppression of the Financing of Terrorism mentioned in section 22(2)(n) above.'

(5)   The offences to which an Order in Council under section 2 of the Extradition Act 1870 (arrangements with foreign states) can apply shall include—

    (a)   offences under the provisions mentioned in sections 62(2) and 63(1)(b),

    (b)   conspiracy to commit any of those offences, and

    (c)   attempt to commit any of those offences.

PART VII
NORTHERN IRELAND

Scheduled offences

65. Scheduled offence: interpretation

(1)   In this Part 'scheduled offence' means, subject to any relevant note in Part I or III of Schedule 9, an offence specified in either of those Parts.

(2)   Part II of that Schedule shall have effect in respect of offences related to those specified in Part I.

(3)   The Secretary of State may by order—

    (a)   add an offence to Part I or II of Schedule 9;

    (b)   remove an offence from Part I or II of that Schedule;

    (c)   amend Part I or II of that Schedule in some other way.

66. Preliminary inquiry

(1)   In proceedings before a magistrates' court for a scheduled offence, if the prosecution requests the court to conduct a preliminary inquiry into the offence the court shall grant the request.

(2)   In subsection (1) 'preliminary inquiry' means a preliminary inquiry under the Magistrates' Courts (Northern Ireland) Order 1981.

(3)   Subsection (1)—

    (a)   shall apply notwithstanding anything in Article 31 of that Order,

    (b)   shall not apply in respect of an offence where the court considers that in the interests of justice a preliminary investigation should be conducted into the offence under that Order, and

    (c)   shall not apply in respect of an extra-territorial offence (as defined in section 1(3) of the Criminal Jurisdiction Act 1975)).

(4)   Where a person charged with a scheduled offence is also charged with a non-scheduled offence, the non-scheduled offence shall be treated as a scheduled offence for the purposes of this section.

67. Limitation of power to grant bail

(1) This section applies to a person who—

(a) has attained the age of fourteen, and

(b) is charged with a scheduled offence which is neither being tried summarily nor certified by the Director of Public Prosecutions for Northern Ireland as suitable for summary trial.

(2) Subject to subsections (6) and (7), a person to whom this section applies shall not be admitted to bail except—

(a) by a judge of the High Court or the Court of Appeal, or

(b) by the judge of the court of trial on adjourning the trial of a person charged with a scheduled offence.

(3) A judge may, in his discretion, admit a person to whom this section applies to bail unless satisfied that there are substantial grounds for believing that the person, if released on bail (whether subject to conditions or not), would—

(a) fail to surrender to custody,

(b) commit an offence while on bail,

(c) interfere with a witness,

(d) otherwise obstruct or attempt to obstruct the course of justice, whether in relation to himself or another person, or

(e) fail to comply with conditions of release (if any).

(4) In exercising his discretion in relation to a person under subsection (3) a judge shall have regard to such of the following considerations as he considers relevant (as well as to any others which he considers relevant)—

(a) the nature and seriousness of the offence with which the person is charged,

(b) the character, antecedents, associations and community ties of the person,

(c) the time which the person has already spent in custody and the time which he is likely to spend in custody if he is not admitted to bail, and

(d) the strength of the evidence of his having committed the offence.

(5) Without prejudice to any other power to impose conditions on admission to bail, a judge admitting a person to bail under this section may impose such conditions as he considers—

(a) likely to result in the person's appearance at the time and place required, or

(b) necessary in the interests of justice or for the prevention of crime.

(6) Subsection (7) applies where a person to whom this section applies is a serving member of—

(a) any of Her Majesty's forces, or

(b) the Royal Ulster Constabulary or the Royal Ulster Constabulary Reserve.

(7) Where this subsection applies to a person he may be admitted to bail on condition that he is held in military or police custody if the person granting bail is satisfied that suitable arrangements have been made; and—

(a) bail on that condition may be granted by a judge or a resident magistrate, and

(b) it shall be lawful for the person to be held in military or police custody in accordance with the conditions of his bail.

68. Bail: legal aid

(1) Where it appears to a judge of the High Court or the Court of Appeal—

(a) that a person charged with a scheduled offence intends to apply to be admitted to bail,

(b) that it is desirable in the interests of justice that he should have legal aid, and

(c) that he has not sufficient means to enable him to obtain that aid,

the judge may assign to him a solicitor and counsel, or counsel only, in the application for bail.

(2) If on a question of granting a person free legal aid under this section there is a doubt—

(a) whether his means are sufficient to enable him to obtain legal aid, or

(b) whether it is desirable in the interests of justice that he should have free legal aid,

the doubt shall be resolved in favour of granting him free legal aid.

(3) Articles 32, 36 and 40 of the Legal Aid, Advice and Assistance (Northern Ireland) Order 1981 (statements, payments, rules and stamp duty) shall apply in relation to legal aid under this section as they apply in relation to legal aid under Part III of that Order as if legal aid under this section were given in pursuance of a criminal aid certificate under Article 29 of that Order.

69. Maximum period of remand in custody

(1) The period for which a person charged with a scheduled offence may be remanded in custody by a magistrates' court shall be a period of not more than 28 days beginning with the day following that on which he is remanded.

(2) Subsection (1) has effect—

(a) notwithstanding Article 47(2) and (3) of the Magistrates' Courts (Northern Ireland) Order 1981, and

(b) whether or not a person is also charged with a non-scheduled offence.

70. Young persons: custody on remand, &c.

(1) While a young person charged with a scheduled offence is remanded or committed for trial and not released on bail, he may be held in custody in such prison or other place as may be specified in a direction given by the Secretary of State under this section.

(2) Subsection (1) shall have effect in respect of a person—

(a) notwithstanding the provisions of any enactment, and

(b) whether or not he was remanded or committed for trial at a time when this section was not in force.

(3) The Secretary of State may give a direction under this section in respect of a person if he considers it necessary to make special arrangements as to the place at which the person is to be held in order—

(a) to prevent his escape, or

(b) to ensure his safety or the safety of others.

(4) The Secretary of State may give a direction under this section at any time after the person to whom it relates has been charged.

(5) In this section 'young person' means a person who—

(a) has attained the age of fourteen, and

(b) has not attained the age of seventeen.

71. Directions under section 70

(1) A direction under section 70 shall cease to have effect at the expiry of the period specified in the direction unless—

(a) it has previously ceased to have effect, or

(b) it is continued in force by a further direction.

(2) The specified period shall not end after the end of the period of two months beginning with the date of the direction.

(3) Where—

(a) a person is held in custody in a prison or other place by virtue of a direction, and

(b) the direction ceases to have effect (whether or not by reason of the expiry or cesser of section 70),

it shall be lawful for him to continue to be held in custody in that prison or place until arrangements can be made for him to be held in custody in accordance with the law then applicable to his case.

(4) Nothing in subsection (3) shall be taken as permitting the holding in custody of a person who is entitled to be released from custody.

72. Time limits for preliminary proceedings

(1) The Secretary of State may by regulations make provision, in respect of a specified preliminary stage of proceedings for a scheduled offence, as to the maximum period—

(a) to be allowed to the prosecution to complete the stage;

(b) during which the accused may, while awaiting completion of the stage, be in the custody of a magistrates' court or the Crown Court in relation to the offence.

(2) The regulations may, in particular—

(a) provide for a specified law about bail to apply in relation to cases to which custody or overall time limits apply (subject to any modifications which the Secretary of State considers it necessary to specify in the regulations);

(b) provide for time limits to cease to have effect in cases where the Attorney General for Northern Ireland certifies after the institution of proceedings that an offence is not to be treated as a scheduled offence;

(c) make such provision with respect to the procedure to be followed in criminal proceedings as the Secretary of State considers appropriate in consequence of another provision of the regulations;

(d) make provision which has effect in relation to a non-scheduled offence where separate counts of an indictment allege a scheduled offence and a non-scheduled offence;

(e) enable the Crown Court in specified circumstances to extend or further extend a time limit at any time before it expires.

(3) Subject to subsection (4), where an overall time limit expires before the completion of the stage of proceedings to which the limit applies, the accused shall be treated for all purposes as having been acquitted of the offence to which the proceedings relate.

(4) Regulations under this section which provide for a custody time limit in relation to a preliminary stage shall have no effect where—

(a) a person escapes from the custody of a magistrates' court or the Crown Court before the expiry of the custody time limit,

(b) a person who has been released on bail in consequence of the expiry of a custody time limit fails to surrender himself into the custody of the court at the appointed time, or

(c) a person who has been released on bail in consequence of the expiry of a custody time limit is arrested by a constable in connection with a breach or apprehended breach of a condition of his bail.

(5) If a person escapes from the custody of a magistrates' court or the Crown Court, the overall time limit which applies to the stage which proceedings relating to the person have reached at the time of the escape shall cease to have effect in relation to those proceedings.

(6)   If a person who has been released on bail fails to surrender himself into the custody of the court at the appointed time, the overall time limit which applies to the stage which proceedings relating to the person have reached at the time of the failure shall cease to have effect in relation to those proceedings.

73.   Time limits: supplementary

(1)   Where a person is convicted of an offence, the exercise of power conferred by virtue of section 72(2)(e) in relation to proceedings for the offence shall not be called into question on an appeal against the conviction.

(2)   In the application of section 72 in relation to proceedings on indictment, 'preliminary stage' does not include a stage—

(a)   after the time when the case for the prosecution is opened, or

(b)   if the court accepts a plea of guilty before the case for the prosecution is opened, after the plea is accepted.

(3)   In the application of section 72 in relation to summary proceedings, 'preliminary stage' does not include a stage—

(a)   after the court begins to hear evidence for the prosecution at the trial,

(b)   if the court accepts a plea of guilty before it has begun to hear evidence for the prosecution, after the plea is accepted, or

(c)   after the court begins to consider whether to exercise its power under Article 44(4) of the Mental Health (Northern Ireland) Order 1986 (power to make hospital order without conviction).

(4)   In this section and section 72—

'custody of the Crown Court' includes custody to which a person is committed in pursuance of—

(a)   Article 37 or 40(4) of the Magistrates' Courts (Northern Ireland) Order 1981 (magistrates' court committing accused for trial), or

(b)   section 51(8) of the Judicature (Northern Ireland) Act 1978 (magistrates' court dealing with a person arrested under Crown Court warrant),

'custody of a magistrates' court' means custody to which a person is committed in pursuance of Article 47 or 49 of the Magistrates' Courts (Northern Ireland) Order 1981 (remand),

'custody time limit' means a time limit imposed by regulations in pursuance of section 72(1)(b) or, where a limit has been extended by the Crown Court by virtue of section 72(2)(e), the limit as extended,

'law about bail' means—

(a)   the Magistrates' Courts (Northern Ireland) Order 1981,

(b)   section 67 of this Act,

(c)   any other enactment relating to bail, and

(d)   any rule of law relating to bail, and

'overall time limit' means a time limit imposed by regulations in pursuance of section 72(1)(a) or, where a limit has been extended by the Crown Court by virtue of section 72(2)(e), the limit as extended.

(5)   For the purposes of the application of a custody time limit in relation to a person who is in the custody of a magistrates' court or the Crown Court—

(a)   all periods during which he is in the custody of a magistrates' court in respect of the same offence shall be aggregated and treated as a single continuous period; and

(b)   all periods during which he is in the custody of the Crown Court in respect of the same offence shall be aggregated and treated as a single continuous period.

74. Court for trial

(1)   A trial on indictment of a scheduled offence shall be held only at the Crown Court sitting in Belfast, unless—

(a)   the Lord Chancellor after consultation with the Lord Chief Justice of Northern Ireland directs that the trial, or a class of trials within which it falls, shall be held at the Crown Court sitting elsewhere, or

(b)   the Lord Chief Justice of Northern Ireland directs that the trial, or part of it, shall be held at the Crown Court sitting elsewhere.

(2)   A person committed for trial for a scheduled offence, or for two or more offences at least one of which is a scheduled offence, shall be committed—

(a)   to the Crown Court sitting in Belfast, or

(b)   where a direction has been given under subsection (1) which concerns the trial, to the Crown Court sitting at the place specified in the direction;

and section 48 of the Judicature (Northern Ireland) Act 1978 (committal for trial on indictment) shall have effect accordingly.

(3)   Where—

(a)   a person is committed for trial to the Crown Court sitting in Belfast in accordance with subsection (2), and

(b)   a direction is subsequently given under subsection (1), before the commencement of the trial, altering the place of trial,

the person shall be treated as having been committed for trial to the Crown Court sitting at the place specified in the direction.

75. Mode of trial on indictment

(1)   A trial on indictment of a scheduled offence shall be conducted by the court without a jury.

(2)   The court trying a scheduled offence on indictment under this section shall have all the powers, authorities and jurisdiction which the court would have had if it had been sitting with a jury (including power to determine any question and to make any finding which would, apart from this section, be required to be determined or made by a jury).

(3)   A reference in an enactment to a jury, the verdict of a jury or the finding of a jury shall, in relation to a trial under this section, be construed as a reference to the court, the verdict of the court or the finding of the court.

(4)   Where separate counts of an indictment allege a scheduled offence and a non-scheduled offence, the trial on indictment shall be conducted as if all the offences alleged in the indictment were scheduled offences.

(5)   Subsection (4) is without prejudice to section 5 of the Indictments Act (Northern Ireland) 1945 (orders for amendment of indictment, separate trial and postponement of trial).

(6)   Without prejudice to subsection (2), where the court trying a scheduled offence on indictment—

(a)   is not satisfied that the accused is guilty of the offence, but

(b)   is satisfied that he is guilty of a non-scheduled offence of which a jury could have found him guilty on a trial for the scheduled offence,

the court may convict him of the non-scheduled offence.

(7)   Where the court trying a scheduled offence convicts the accused of that or some other offence, it shall give a judgment stating the reasons for the conviction at or as soon as is reasonably practicable after the time of conviction.

(8)   A person convicted of an offence on a trial under this section without a jury may, notwithstanding anything in sections 1 and 10(1) of the Criminal Appeal (Northern Ireland) Act 1980, appeal to the Court of Appeal under Part I of that Act—

(a)   against his conviction, on any ground, without the leave of the Court of Appeal or a certificate of the judge of the court of trial;

(b)   against sentence passed on conviction, without that leave, unless the sentence is fixed by law.

(9)   Where a person is convicted of an offence on a trial under this section, the time for giving notice of appeal under section 16(1) of that Act shall run from the date of judgment if later than the date from which it would run under that subsection.

76.   Admission in trial on indictment

(1)   This section applies to a trial on indictment for—

(a)   a scheduled offence, or

(b)   two or more offences at least one of which is a scheduled offence.

(2)   A statement made by the accused may be given in evidence by the prosecution in so far as—

(a)   it is relevant to a matter in issue in the proceedings, and

(b)   it is not excluded or inadmissible (whether by virtue of subsections (3) to (5) or otherwise).

(3)   Subsections (4) and (5) apply if in proceedings to which this section applies—

(a)   the prosecution gives or proposes to give a statement made by the accused in evidence,

(b)   prima facie evidence is adduced that the accused was subjected to torture, inhuman or degrading treatment, violence or the threat of violence in order to induce him to make the statement, and

(c)   the prosecution does not satisfy the court that the statement was not obtained in the manner mentioned in paragraph (b).

(4)   If the statement has not yet been given in evidence, the court shall—

(a)   exclude the statement, or

(b)   direct that the trial be restarted before a differently constituted court (before which the statement shall be inadmissible).

(5)   If the statement has been given in evidence, the court shall—

(a)   disregard it, or

(b)   direct that the trial be restarted before a differently constituted court (before which the statement shall be inadmissible).

(6)   This section is without prejudice to any discretion of a court to—

(a)   exclude or ignore a statement, or

(b)   direct a trial to be restarted,

where the court considers it appropriate in order to avoid unfairness to the accused or otherwise in the interests of justice.

77.   Possession: onus of proof

(1)   This section applies to a trial on indictment for a scheduled offence where the accused is charged with possessing an article in such circumstances as to constitute an offence under any of the enactments listed in subsection (3).

(2)   If it is proved that the article—
   (a)   was on any premises at the same time as the accused, or
   (b)   was on premises of which the accused was the occupier or which he habitually used otherwise than as a member of the public,
the court may assume that the accused possessed (and, if relevant, knowingly possessed) the article, unless he proves that he did not know of its presence on the premises or that he had no control over it.

(3)   The following are the offences mentioned in subsection (1)—

The Explosive Substances Act 1883

Section 3, so far as relating to subsection (1)(b) thereof (possessing explosive with intent to endanger life or cause serious damage to property).

Section 4 (possessing explosive in suspicious circumstances).

The Protection of the Person and Property Act (Northern Ireland) 1969

Section 2 (possessing petrol bomb, &c. in suspicious circumstances).

The Firearms (Northern Ireland) Order 1981

Article 6(1) (manufacturing, dealing in or possessing certain weapons, &c.).

Article 17 (possessing firearm or ammunition with intent to endanger life or cause serious damage to property).

Article 18(2) (possessing firearm or imitation firearm at time of committing, or being arrested for, a specified offence).

Article 22(1), (2) or (4) (possession of a firearm or ammunition by a person who has been sentenced to imprisonment, &c.).

Article 23 (possessing firearm or ammunition in suspicious circumstances).

78.   Children: sentence
(1)   This section applies where a child is convicted on indictment of a scheduled offence committed while this section is in force.
(2)   Article 45(2) of the Criminal Justice (Children) (Northern Ireland) Order 1998 (punishment for serious offence) shall have effect with the substitution for the words '14 years' of the words 'five years'.
(3)   In this section 'child' means a person who has not attained the age of 17.

79.   Restricted remission
(1)   The remission granted under prison rules in respect of a sentence of imprisonment passed in Northern Ireland for a scheduled offence shall not, where it is for a term of five years or more, exceed one-third of the term.
(2)   Where a person is sentenced on the same occasion for two or more scheduled offences to terms which are consecutive, subsection (1) shall apply as if those terms were a single term.
(3)   Where a person is serving two or more terms which are consecutive but not all subject to subsection (1), the maximum remission granted under prison rules in respect of those terms taken together shall be arrived at by calculating the maximum remission for each term separately and aggregating the result.

(4)   In this section 'prison rules' means rules made under section 13 of the Prison Act (Northern Ireland) 1953.

(5)   The Secretary of State may by order substitute a different length of sentence and a different maximum period of remission for those mentioned in subsection (1).

(6)   This section applies where—

(a)   the scheduled offence is committed while this section is in force,

(b)   the offence (being a scheduled offence within the meaning of the Northern Ireland (Emergency Provisions) Act 1996) was committed while section 15 of that Act was in force,

(c)   the offence (being a scheduled offence within the meaning of the Northern Ireland (Emergency Provisions) Act 1991) was committed while section 14 of that Act was in force, or

(d)   the offence (being a scheduled offence within the meaning of the Northern Ireland (Emergency Provisions) Act 1978) was committed while section 22 of the Prevention of Terrorism (Temporary Provisions) Act 1989 was in force.

80.   Conviction during remission

(1)   This section applies where—

(a)   a person is sentenced to imprisonment or a term of detention in a young offenders centre for a period exceeding one year,

(b)   he is discharged from prison or the centre in pursuance of prison rules, and

(c)   before his sentence or term would have expired (but for the discharge) he commits, and is convicted on indictment of, a scheduled offence.

(2)   If the court before which he is convicted of the scheduled offence sentences him to imprisonment or a term of detention it shall in addition order him to be returned to prison or a young offenders centre for the period between the date of the order and the date on which the sentence or term mentioned in subsection (1) would have expired but for his discharge.

(3)   No order shall be made under subsection (2) if the sentence imposed by the court is—

(a)   a suspended sentence,

(b)   a sentence of life imprisonment, or

(c)   a sentence of detention during the Secretary of State's pleasure under Article 45(1) of the Criminal Justice (Children) (Northern Ireland) Order 1998.

(4)   An order made under subsection (2) shall cease to have effect if an appeal against the scheduled offence results in—

(a)   the acquittal of the person concerned, or

(b)   the substitution of a sentence other than imprisonment or a term of detention.

(5)   The period for which a person is ordered under this section to be returned to prison or a young offenders centre—

(a)   shall be taken to be a sentence of imprisonment or term of detention for the purposes of the Prison Act (Northern Ireland) 1953 and for the purposes of the Treatment of Offenders Act (Northern Ireland) 1968 other than section 26(2) (reduction for time spent in custody),

(b)   shall not be subject to any provision of prison rules for discharge before expiry, and

(c)   shall be served before, and be followed by, the sentence or term imposed for the scheduled offence and be disregarded in determining the appropriate length of that sentence or term.

(6)　For the purposes of this section a certificate purporting to be signed by the governor or deputy governor of a prison or young offenders centre which specifies—

　　(a)　the date on which a person was discharged from prison or a young offenders centre,

　　(b)　the sentence or term which the person was serving at the time of his discharge, the offence in respect of which the sentence or term was imposed and the date on which he was convicted of that offence, and

　　(c)　the date on which the person would, but for his discharge in pursuance of prison rules, have been discharged from prison or a young offenders centre,
shall be evidence of the matters specified.

(7)　In this section—

　　'prison rules' means rules made under section 13 of the Prison Act (Northern Ireland) 1953,

　　'young offenders centre' has the meaning assigned to it by section 2(a) of the Treatment of Offenders Act (Northern Ireland) 1968.

(8)　For the purposes of subsection (1) consecutive terms of imprisonment or of detention in a young offenders centre shall be treated as a single term and a sentence of imprisonment or detention in a young offenders centre includes—

　　(a)　a sentence or term passed by a court in the United Kingdom or any of the Islands, and

　　(b)　in the case of imprisonment, a sentence passed by a court-martial on a person found guilty of a civil offence within the meaning of the Army Act 1955, the Air Force Act 1955 and the Naval Discipline Act 1957.

(9)　The Secretary of State may by order substitute a different period for the period of one year mentioned in subsection (1).

(10)　This section applies irrespective of when the discharge from prison or a young offenders centre took place but only if—

　　(a)　the scheduled offence is committed while this section is in force,

　　(b)　the offence (being a scheduled offence within the meaning of the Northern Ireland (Emergency Provisions) Act 1996) was committed while section 16 of that Act was in force,

　　(c)　the offence (being a scheduled offence within the meaning of the Northern Ireland (Emergency Provisions) Act 1991) was committed while section 15 of that Act was in force, or

　　(d)　the offence (being a scheduled offence within the meaning of the Northern Ireland (Emergency Provisions) Act 1978) was committed while section 23 of the Prevention of Terrorism (Temporary Provisions) Act 1989 was in force.

Powers of arrest, search, &c.

81.　Arrest of suspected terrorists: power of entry

A constable may enter and search any premises if he reasonably suspects that a terrorist, within the meaning of section 40(1)(b), is to be found there.

82.　Arrest and seizure: constables

(1)　A constable may arrest without warrant any person if he reasonably suspects that the person is committing, has committed or is about to commit—

　　(a)　a scheduled offence, or

　　(b)　a non-scheduled offence under this Act.

(2) For the purpose of arresting a person under this section a constable may enter and search any premises where the person is or where the constable reasonably suspects him to be.

(3) A constable may seize and retain anything if he reasonably suspects that it is, has been or is intended to be used in the commission of—

(a) a scheduled offence, or

(b) a non-scheduled offence under this Act.

83. Arrest and seizure: armed forces

(1) If a member of Her Majesty's forces on duty reasonably suspects that a person is committing, has committed or is about to commit any offence he may—

(a) arrest the person without warrant, and

(b) detain him for a period not exceeding four hours.

(2) A person making an arrest under this section complies with any rule of law requiring him to state the ground of arrest if he states that he is making the arrest as a member of Her Majesty's forces.

(3) For the purpose of arresting a person under this section a member of Her Majesty's forces may enter and search any premises where the person is.

(4) If a member of Her Majesty's forces reasonably suspects that a person—

(a) is a terrorist (within the meaning of Part V), or

(b) has committed an offence involving the use or possession of an explosive or firearm,

he may enter and search any premises where he reasonably suspects the person to be for the purpose of arresting him under this section.

(5) A member of Her Majesty's forces may seize, and detain for a period not exceeding four hours, anything which he reasonably suspects is being, has been or is intended to be used in the commission of an offence under section 93 or 94.

(6) The reference to a rule of law in subsection (2) does not include a rule of law which has effect only by virtue of the Human Rights Act 1998.

84. Munitions and transmitters

Schedule 10 (which confers power to search for munitions and transmitters) shall have effect.

85. Explosives inspectors

(1) An explosives inspector may enter and search any premises for the purpose of ascertaining whether any explosive is unlawfully there.

(2) The power under subsection (1) may not be exercised in relation to a dwelling.

(3) An explosives inspector may stop any person in a public place and search him for the purpose of ascertaining whether he has any explosive unlawfully with him.

(4) An explosives inspector—

(a) may seize any explosive found in the course of a search under this section unless it appears to him that it is being, has been and will be used only for a lawful purpose, and

(b) may retain and, if necessary, destroy it.

(5) In this section 'explosives inspector' means an inspector appointed under section 53 of the Explosives Act 1875.

86. Unlawfully detained persons

(1) If an officer reasonably believes that a person is unlawfully detained in such circumstances that his life is in danger, the officer may enter any premises for the purpose of ascertaining whether the person is detained there.

(2)   In this section 'officer' means—

(a)   a member of Her Majesty's forces on duty, or

(b)   a constable.

(3)   A dwelling may be entered under subsection (1) only by—

(a)   a member of Her Majesty's forces authorised for the purpose by a commissioned officer of those forces, or

(b)   a constable authorised for the purpose by an officer of the Royal Ulster Constabulary of at least the rank of inspector.

87.   Examination of documents

(1)   A member of Her Majesty's forces or a constable who performs a search under a provision of this Part—

(a)   may examine any document or record found in order to ascertain whether it contains information of the kind mentioned in section 58(1)(a) or 103(1)(a), and

(b)   if necessary or expedient for the purpose of paragraph (a), may remove the document or record to another place and retain it there until the examination is completed.

(2)   Subsection (1) shall not permit a person to examine a document or record if he has reasonable cause to believe that it is an item subject to legal privilege (within the meaning of the Police and Criminal Evidence (Northern Ireland) Order 1989).

(3)   Subject to subsections (4) and (5), a document or record may not be retained by virtue of subsection (1)(b) for more than 48 hours.

(4)   An officer of the Royal Ulster Constabulary who is of at least the rank of chief inspector may authorise a constable to retain a document or record for a further period or periods.

(5)   Subsection (4) does not permit the retention of a document or record after the end of the period of 96 hours beginning with the time when it was removed for examination under subsection (1)(b).

(6)   A person who wilfully obstructs a member of Her Majesty's forces or a constable in the exercise of a power conferred by this section commits an offence.

(7)   A person guilty of an offence under subsection (6) shall be liable—

(a)   on conviction on indictment, to imprisonment for a term not exceeding two years, to a fine or to both, or

(b)   on summary conviction, to imprisonment for a term not exceeding six months, to a fine not exceeding the statutory maximum or to both.

88.   Examination of documents: procedure

(1)   Where a document or record is examined under section 87—

(a)   it shall not be photographed or copied, and

(b)   the person who examines it shall make a written record of the examination as soon as is reasonably practicable.

(2)   The record shall—

(a)   describe the document or record,

(b)   specify the object of the examination,

(c)   state the address of the premises where the document or record was found,

(d)   where the document or record was found in the course of a search of a person, state the person's name,

(e)   where the document or record was found in the course of a search of any premises, state the name of a person appearing to the person making the record to be the occupier of the premises or to have had custody or control of the document or record when it was found,

(f)   where the document or record is removed for examination from the place where it was found, state the date and time when it was removed, and

(g)   where the document or record was examined at the place where it was found, state the date and time of examination.

(3)   The record shall identify the person by whom the examination was carried out—

(a)   in the case of a constable, by reference to his police number, and

(b)   in the case of a member of Her Majesty's forces, by reference to his service number, rank and regiment.

(4)   Where a person makes a record of a search in accordance with this section, he shall as soon as is reasonably practicable supply a copy—

(a)   in a case where the document or record was found in the course of a search of a person, to that person, and

(b)   in a case where the document or record was found in the course of a search of any premises, to a person appearing to the person making the record to be the occupier of the premises or to have had custody or control of the document or record when it was found.

89.   Power to stop and question

(1)   An officer may stop a person for so long as is necessary to question him to ascertain—

(a)   his identity and movements;

(b)   what he knows about a recent explosion or another recent incident endangering life;

(c)   what he knows about a person killed or injured in a recent explosion or incident.

(2)   A person commits an offence if he—

(a)   fails to stop when required to do so under this section,

(b)   refuses to answer a question addressed to him under this section, or

(c)   fails to answer to the best of his knowledge and ability a question addressed to him under this section.

(3)   A person guilty of an offence under this section shall be liable on summary conviction to a fine not exceeding level 5 on the standard scale.

(4)   In this section 'officer' means—

(a)   a member of Her Majesty's forces on duty, or

(b)   a constable.

90.   Power of entry

(1)   An officer may enter any premises if he considers it necessary in the course of operations for the preservation of the peace or the maintenance of order.

(2)   In this section 'officer' means—

(a)   a member of Her Majesty's forces on duty, or

(b)   a constable.

91.   Taking possession of land, &c.

If the Secretary of State considers it necessary for the preservation of the peace or the maintenance of order, he may authorise a person—

(a)   to take possession of land or other property;

(b)   to take steps to place buildings or other structures in a state of defence;

(c)   to detain property or cause it to be destroyed or moved;

(d)   to carry out works on land of which possession has been taken by virtue of this section;

(e)   to take any other action which interferes with a public right or with a private right of property.

92.   Road closure: permission

(1)   If he considers it immediately necessary for the preservation of the peace or the maintenance of order, an officer may—
  (a)   wholly or partly close a road;
  (b)   divert or otherwise interfere with a road or the use of a road;
  (c)   prohibit or restrict the exercise of a right of way;
  (d)   prohibit or restrict the use of a waterway.
(2)   In this section 'officer' means—
  (a)   a member of Her Majesty's forces on duty,
  (b)   a constable, or
  (c)   a person authorised for the purposes of this section by the Secretary of State.

93.   Sections 91 and 92: supplementary

(1)   A person commits an offence if he interferes with—
  (a)   works executed in connection with the exercise of powers conferred by virtue of section 91 or 92, or
  (b)   any apparatus, equipment or other thing used in connection with the exercise of those powers.
(2)   It is a defence for a person charged with an offence under this section to prove that he had a reasonable excuse for his interference.
(3)   A person guilty of an offence under this section shall be liable on summary conviction to—
  (a)   imprisonment for a term not exceeding six months,
  (b)   a fine not exceeding level 5 on the standard scale, or
  (c)   both.
(4)   An authorisation to exercise powers under section 91 or 92 may authorise—
  (a)   the exercise of all those powers, or
  (b)   the exercise of a specified power or class of powers.
(5)   An authorisation to exercise powers under section 91 or 92 may be addressed—
  (a)   to specified persons, or
  (b)   to persons of a specified class.

94.   Road closure: direction

(1)   If the Secretary of State considers it necessary for the preservation of the peace or the maintenance of order he may by order direct that a specified road—
  (a)   shall be wholly closed,
  (b)   shall be closed to a specified extent, or
  (c)   shall be diverted in a specified manner.
(2)   A person commits an offence if he interferes with—
  (a)   road closure works, or
  (b)   road closure equipment.
(3)   A person commits an offence if—
  (a)   he executes any bypass works within 200 metres of road closure works,
  (b)   he has in his possession or under his control, within 200 metres of road closure works, materials or equipment suitable for executing bypass works, or

(c) he knowingly permits on land occupied by him the doing or occurrence of anything which is an offence under paragraph (a) or (b).

(4) It is a defence for a person charged with an offence under this section to prove that he had a reasonable excuse for his action, possession, control or permission.

(5) A person guilty of an offence under this section shall be liable on summary conviction to—

(a) imprisonment for a term not exceeding six months,

(b) a fine not exceeding level 5 on the standard scale, or

(c) both.

(6) In this section—

'bypass works' means works which facilitate the bypassing by vehicles of road closure works,

'road closure equipment' means any apparatus, equipment or other thing used in pursuance of an order under this section in connection with the closure or diversion of a road, and

'road closure works' means works executed in connection with the closure or diversion of a road specified in an order under this section (whether executed in pursuance of the order or in pursuance of power under an enactment to close or divert the road).

95. Sections 81 to 94: supplementary

(1) This section applies in relation to sections 81 to 94.

(2) A power to enter premises may be exercised by reasonable force if necessary.

(3) A power to search premises shall, in its application to vehicles (by virtue of section 121), be taken to include—

(a) power to stop a vehicle (other than an aircraft which is airborne), and

(b) power to take a vehicle or cause it to be taken, where necessary or expedient, to any place for the purpose of carrying out the search.

(4) A person commits an offence if he fails to stop a vehicle when required to do so by virtue of this section.

(5) A person guilty of an offence under subsection (4) shall be liable on summary conviction to—

(a) imprisonment for a term not exceeding six months,

(b) a fine not exceeding level 5 on the standard scale, or

(c) both.

(6) In the application to a place or vehicle (by virtue of section 121) of a power to search premises—

(a) a reference to the address of the premises shall be construed as a reference to the location of the place or vehicle together with its registration number (if any), and

(b) a reference to the occupier of the premises shall be construed as a reference to the occupier of the place or the person in charge of the vehicle.

(7) Where a search is carried out under Schedule 10 in relation to a vehicle (by virtue of section 121), the person carrying out the search may, if he reasonably believes that it is necessary in order to carry out the search or to prevent it from being frustrated—

(a) require a person in or on the vehicle to remain with it;

(b) require a person in or on the vehicle to go to and remain at any place to which the vehicle is taken by virtue of subsection (3)(b);

(c) use reasonable force to secure compliance with a requirement under paragraph (a) or (b) above.

(8)   Paragraphs 4(2) and (3), 8 and 9 of Schedule 10 shall apply to a requirement imposed under subsection (7) as they apply to a requirement imposed under that Schedule.

(9)   Paragraph 8 of Schedule 10 shall apply in relation to the search of a vehicle which is not habitually stationary only if it is moved for the purpose of the search by virtue of subsection (3)(b); and where that paragraph does apply, the reference to the address of the premises shall be construed as a reference to the location where the vehicle is searched together with its registration number (if any).

(10)   A member of Her Majesty's forces exercising any power when he is not in uniform shall, if requested to do so by any person at or about the time of exercising the power, produce to that person documentary evidence that he is a member of Her Majesty's forces.

Miscellaneous

96.   Preservation of the peace: regulations

(1)   The Secretary of State may by regulations make provision for promoting the preservation of the peace and the maintenance of order.

(2)   The regulations may authorise the Secretary of State to make orders or give directions for specified purposes.

(3)   A person commits an offence if he contravenes or fails to comply with—

(a)   regulations under this section, or

(b)   an order or direction made or given under regulations made under this section.

(4)   A person guilty of an offence under this section shall be liable on summary conviction to—

(a)   imprisonment for a term not exceeding six months,

(b)   a fine not exceeding level 5 on the standard scale, or

(c)   both.

97.   Port and border controls

(1)   The Secretary of State may by order provide for members of Her Majesty's forces to perform specified functions conferred on examining officers under Schedule 7.

(2)   A member of Her Majesty's forces exercising functions by virtue of subsection (1) shall be treated as an examining officer within the meaning of Schedule 7 for all purposes of this Act except for paragraphs 5 and 6 of Schedule 14.

(3)   The Secretary of State may by order make provision, including provision supplementing or modifying Schedule 7, about entering or leaving Northern Ireland by land.

98.   Independent Assessor of Military Complaints Procedures

(1)   The Secretary of State may appoint a person to be known as the Independent Assessor of Military Complaints Procedures in Northern Ireland.

(2)   A person may be appointed as the Independent Assessor only if—

(a)   he is not a serving member of Her Majesty's forces, and

(b)   he has not been a serving member at any time during the period of 20 years ending with the date of the appointment.

(3)   The Independent Assessor—

(a)   shall keep under review the procedures adopted by the General Officer Commanding Northern Ireland for receiving, investigating and responding to complaints to which this section applies,

(b)   shall receive and investigate any representations about those procedures,

(c)   may investigate the operation of those procedures in relation to a particular complaint or class of complaints,

(d) may require the General Officer Commanding to review a particular case or class of cases in which the Independent Assessor considers that any of those procedures have operated inadequately, and

(e) may make recommendations to the General Officer Commanding about inadequacies in those procedures, including inadequacies in the way in which they operate in relation to a particular complaint or class of complaints.

(4) This section applies to complaints about the behaviour of a member of Her Majesty's forces under the command of the General Officer Commanding Northern Ireland, other than—

(a) a complaint which is referred by the General Officer Commanding to the Royal Ulster Constabulary and which is not remitted by the Royal Ulster Constabulary to the General Officer Commanding to be dealt with by him,

(b) a complaint about a matter in respect of which a claim for compensation has been made under Schedule 12, and

(c) a complaint about a matter which is the subject of proceedings involving a claim for compensation which have been instituted in a court.

(5) The General Officer Commanding Northern Ireland shall—

(a) provide such information,

(b) disclose such documents, and

(c) provide such assistance,

as the Independent Assessor may reasonably require for the purpose of the performance of his functions.

(6) Schedule 11 (which makes supplementary provision about the Independent Assessor) shall have effect.

99. Police and army powers: code of practice

(1) The Secretary of State may make codes of practice in connection with—

(a) the exercise by police officers of any power conferred by this Act, and

(b) the seizure and retention of property found by police officers when exercising powers of search conferred by any provision of this Act.

(2) The Secretary of State may make codes of practice in connection with the exercise by members of Her Majesty's forces of powers by virtue of this Part.

(3) In this section 'police officer' means a member of the Royal Ulster Constabulary or the Royal Ulster Constabulary Reserve.

100. Video recording: code of practice

(1) The Secretary of State shall—

(a) make a code of practice about the silent video recording of interviews to which this section applies, and

(b) make an order requiring the silent video recording of interviews to which this section applies in accordance with the code.

(2) This section applies to—

(a) interviews by police officers of persons detained under section 41 if they take place in a police station (within the meaning of Schedule 8), and

(b) interviews held by police officers in such other circumstances as the Secretary of State may specify by order.

(3) In this section 'police officer' means a member of the Royal Ulster Constabulary or the Royal Ulster Constabulary Reserve.

101. Codes of practice: supplementary

(1) This section applies to a code of practice under section 99 or 100.

(2) Where the Secretary of State proposes to issue a code of practice he shall—

(a) publish a draft,

(b) consider any representations made to him about the draft, and

(c) if he thinks it appropriate, modify the draft in the light of any representations made to him.

(3) The Secretary of State shall lay a draft of the code before Parliament.

(4) When the Secretary of State has laid a draft code before Parliament he may bring it into operation by order.

(5) The Secretary of State may revise the whole or any part of a code of practice issued by him and issue the code as revised; and subsections (2) to (4) shall apply to such a revised code as they apply to an original code.

(6) A failure by a police officer to comply with a provision of a code shall not of itself make him liable to criminal or civil proceedings.

(7) A failure by a member of Her Majesty's forces to comply with a provision of a code shall not of itself make him liable to any criminal or civil proceedings other than—

(a) proceedings under any provision of the Army Act 1955 or the Air Force Act 1955 other than section 70 (civil offences), and

(b) proceedings under any provision of the Naval Discipline Act 1957 other than section 42 (civil offences).

(8) A code—

(a) shall be admissible in evidence in criminal or civil proceedings, and

(b) shall be taken into account by a court or tribunal in any case in which it appears to the court or tribunal to be relevant.

(9) In this section—

'criminal proceedings' includes proceedings in Northern Ireland before a court-martial constituted under the Army Act 1955, the Air Force Act 1955 or the Naval Discipline Act 1957 or a disciplinary court constituted under section 50 of the 1957 Act and proceedings in Northern Ireland before the Courts-Martial Appeal Court, and

'police officer' means a member of the Royal Ulster Constabulary or the Royal Ulster Constabulary Reserve.

102. Compensation

Schedule 12 (which provides for compensation to be paid for certain action taken under this Part) shall have effect.

103. Terrorist information

(1) A person commits an offence if—

(a) he collects, makes a record of, publishes, communicates or attempts to elicit information about a person to whom this section applies which is of a kind likely to be useful to a person committing or preparing an act of terrorism, or

(b) he possesses a document or record containing information of that kind.

(2) This section applies to a person who is or has been—

(a) a constable,

(b) a member of Her Majesty's forces,

(c) the holder of a judicial office,

(d) an officer of any court, or

(e) a full-time employee of the prison service in Northern Ireland.

(3)   In this section 'record' includes a photographic or electronic record.

(4)   If it is proved in proceedings for an offence under subsection (1)(b) that a document or record—

(a)   was on any premises at the same time as the accused, or

(b)   was on premises of which the accused was the occupier or which he habitually used otherwise than as a member of the public,

the court may assume that the accused possessed the document or record, unless he proves that he did not know of its presence on the premises or that he had no control over it.

(5)   It is a defence for a person charged with an offence under this section to prove that he had a reasonable excuse for his action or possession.

(6)   A person guilty of an offence under this section shall be liable—

(a)   on conviction on indictment, to imprisonment for a term not exceeding 10 years, to a fine or to both, or

(b)   on summary conviction, to imprisonment for a term not exceeding six months, to a fine not exceeding the statutory maximum or to both.

(7)   A court by or before which a person is convicted of an offence under this section may order the forfeiture of any document or record containing information of the kind mentioned in subsection (1)(a).

(8)   Before making an order under subsection (7) a court must give an opportunity to be heard to any person, other than the convicted person, who claims to be the owner of or otherwise interested in anything which can be forfeited under that subsection.

(9)   An order under subsection (8) shall not come into force until there is no further possibility of it being varied, or set aside, on appeal (disregarding any power of a court to grant leave to appeal out of time).

104.   Police powers: records
The Chief Constable of the Royal Ulster Constabulary shall make arrangements for securing that a record is made of each exercise by a constable of a power under this Part in so far as—

(a)   it is reasonably practicable to do so, and

(b)   a record is not required to be made under another enactment.

105.   Powers
A power conferred on a person by virtue of this Part—

(a)   is additional to powers which he has at common law or by virtue of any other enactment, and

(b)   shall not be taken to affect those powers or Her Majesty's prerogative.

106.   Private security services
Schedule 13 (private security services) shall have effect.

Specified organisations

107.   Specified organisations: interpretation
For the purposes of sections 108 to 111 an organisation is specified at a particular time if at that time—

(a)   it is specified under section 3(8) of the Northern Ireland (Sentences) Act 1998, and

(b)   it is, or forms part of, an organisation which is proscribed for the purposes of this Act.

108.   Evidence
(1)   This section applies where a person is charged with an offence under section 11.

(2) Subsection (3) applies where a police officer of at least the rank of superintendent states in oral evidence that in his opinion the accused—

(a) belongs to an organisation which is specified, or

(b) belonged to an organisation at a time when it was specified.

(3) Where this subsection applies—

(a) the statement shall be admissible as evidence of the matter stated, but

(b) the accused shall not be committed for trial, be found to have a case to answer or be convicted solely on the basis of the statement.

(4) In this section 'police officer' means a member of—

(a) a police force within the meaning of the Police Act 1996 or the Police (Scotland) Act 1967, or

(b) the Royal Ulster Constabulary.

109. Inferences

(1) This section applies where a person is charged with an offence under section 11.

(2) Subsection (4) applies where evidence is given that—

(a) at any time before being charged with the offence the accused, on being questioned under caution by a constable, failed to mention a fact which is material to the offence and which he could reasonably be expected to mention, and

(b) before being questioned the accused was permitted to consult a solicitor.

(3) Subsection (4) also applies where evidence is given that—

(a) on being charged with the offence or informed by a constable that he might be prosecuted for it the accused failed to mention a fact which is material to the offence and which he could reasonably be expected to mention, and

(b) before being charged or informed the accused was permitted to consult a solicitor.

(4) Where this subsection applies—

(a) the court, in considering any question whether the accused belongs or belonged at a particular time to a specified organisation, may draw from the failure inferences relating to that question, but

(b) the accused shall not be committed for trial, be found to have a case to answer or be convicted solely on the basis of the inferences.

(5) Subject to any directions by the court, evidence tending to establish the failure may be given before or after evidence tending to establish the fact which the accused is alleged to have failed to mention.

110. Sections 108 and 109: supplementary

(1) Nothing in section 108 or 109 shall—

(a) prejudice the admissibility of evidence admissible apart from that section,

(b) preclude the drawing of inferences which could be drawn apart from that section, or

(c) prejudice an enactment providing (in whatever words) that an answer or evidence given by a person in specified circumstances is not admissible in evidence against him or some other person in any proceedings or class of proceedings (however described, and whether civil or criminal).

(2) In subsection (1)(c) the reference to giving evidence is a reference to giving it in any manner (whether by giving information, making discovery, producing documents or otherwise).

111. Forfeiture orders

(1) This section applies if—

(a) a person is convicted of an offence under section 11 or 12, and

(b) at the time of the offence he belonged to an organisation which was a specified organisation.

(2) The court by or before which the person is convicted may order the forfeiture of any money or other property if—

(a) he had it in his possession or under his control at the time of the offence, and

(b) it has been used in connection with the activities of the specified organisation or the court believes that it may be used in that connection unless it is forfeited.

(3) Before making an order under this section the court must give an opportunity to be heard to any person, other than the convicted person, who claims to be the owner of or otherwise interested in anything which can be forfeited under this section.

(4) A question arising as to whether subsection (1)(b) or (2)(a) or (b) is satisfied shall be determined on the balance of probabilities.

(5) Schedule 4 shall apply (with the necessary modifications) in relation to orders under this section as it applies in relation to orders made under section 23.

Duration of Part VII

112. Expiry and revival

(1) This Part shall (subject to subsection (2)) cease to have effect at the end of the period of one year beginning with the day on which it is brought into force.

(2) The Secretary of State may by order provide—

(a) that a provision of this Part which is in force (whether or not by virtue of this subsection) shall continue in force for a specified period not exceeding twelve months;

(b) that a provision of this Part shall cease to have effect;

(c) that a provision of this Part which is not in force (whether or not by virtue of this subsection) shall come into force and remain in force for a specified period not exceeding twelve months.

(3) An order under subsection (2) may make provision with respect to a provision of this Part—

(a) generally,

(b) only in so far as it concerns powers of members of Her Majesty's forces, or

(c) except in so far as it concerns powers of members of Her Majesty's forces.

(4) This Part shall, by virtue of this subsection, cease to have effect at the end of the period of five years beginning with the day on which it is brought into force.

(5) The following provisions shall be treated for the purposes of this section as forming part of this Part of this Act—

(a) paragraphs 36 and 37 of Schedule 4, and

(b) paragraphs 19 to 21 of Schedule 5.

113. Transitional provisions

(1) Where a provision of sections 74 to 77 comes into force by virtue of an order under section 112(2), that shall not affect a trial on indictment where the indictment has been presented before the provision comes into force.

(2) Where a provision of sections 74 to 77 ceases to have effect (whether or not by virtue of an order under section 112(2)), that shall not affect the application of the provision to a trial on indictment where the indictment has been presented before the provision ceases to have effect.

(3) If when section 74(1) comes into force by virtue of an order under section 112(2) a person has been committed for trial for a scheduled offence and the indictment has not been

presented, then on the coming into force of section 74(1) he shall, if he was committed to the Crown Court sitting elsewhere than in Belfast, be treated as having been committed—

(a)   to the Crown Court sitting in Belfast, or

(b)   where a direction is given under section 74(1) which affects the trial, to the Crown Court sitting at the place specified in the direction.

(4)   Where section 74 ceases to have effect (whether or not by virtue of an order under section 112(2)), that shall not affect—

(a)   the committal of a person for trial in accordance with that provision to the Crown Court sitting either in Belfast or elsewhere, or

(b)   the committal of a person for trial which, in accordance with that provision, has taken effect as a committal for trial to the Crown Court sitting elsewhere than in Belfast, in a case where the indictment has not been presented.

(5)   Where section 79 or 80 ceases to have effect (whether or not by virtue of an order under section 112(2)), that shall not affect the operation of the section in relation to an offence committed while it, or a corresponding earlier enactment, was in force.

(6)   Sections 108 and 109 shall not apply to a statement made or failure occurring before 4th September 1998.

(7)   Where section 108 or 109 comes into force by virtue of an order under section 112(2) it shall not apply to a statement made or failure occurring while the section was not in force.

(8)   Section 111 applies where an offence is committed on or after 4th September 1998; and for this purpose an offence committed over a period of more than one day or at some time during a period of more than one day shall be taken to be committed on the last of the days in the period.

(9)   Paragraph 19 of Schedule 9 shall have effect only in relation to an offence alleged to have been committed after the coming into force of that Schedule.

PART VIII
GENERAL

114.   Police powers

(1)   A power conferred by virtue of this Act on a constable—

(a)   is additional to powers which he has at common law or by virtue of any other enactment, and

(b)   shall not be taken to affect those powers.

(2)   A constable may if necessary use reasonable force for the purpose of exercising a power conferred on him by virtue of this Act (apart from paragraphs 2 and 3 of Schedule 7).

(3)   Where anything is seized by a constable under a power conferred by virtue of this Act, it may (unless the contrary intention appears) be retained for so long as is necessary in all the circumstances.

115.   Officers' powers

Schedule 14 (which makes provision about the exercise of functions by authorised officers for the purposes of sections 25 to 31 and examining officers for the purposes of Schedule 7) shall have effect.

116.   Powers to stop and search

(1)   A power to search premises conferred by virtue of this Act shall be taken to include power to search a container.

(2)   A power conferred by virtue of this Act to stop a person includes power to stop a vehicle (other than an aircraft which is airborne).

(3)   A person commits an offence if he fails to stop a vehicle when required to do so by virtue of this section.

(4)   A person guilty of an offence under subsection (3) shall be liable on summary conviction to—

    (a)   imprisonment for a term not exceeding six months,

    (b)   a fine not exceeding level 5 on the standard scale, or

    (c)   both.

117.   Consent to prosecution

(1)   This section applies to an offence under any provision of this Act other than an offence under—

    (a)   section 36,

    (b)   section 51,

    (c)   paragraph 18 of Schedule 7,

    (d)   paragraph 12 of Schedule 12, or

    (e)   Schedule 13.

(2)   Proceedings for an offence to which this section applies—

    (a)   shall not be instituted in England and Wales without the consent of the Director of Public Prosecutions, and

    (b)   shall not be instituted in Northern Ireland without the consent of the Director of Public Prosecutions for Northern Ireland.

(3)   Where it appears to the Director of Public Prosecutions or the Director of Public Prosecutions for Northern Ireland that an offence to which this section applies is committed for a purpose connected with the affairs of a country other than the United Kingdom—

    (a)   subsection (2) shall not apply, and

    (b)   proceedings for the offence shall not be instituted without the consent of the Attorney General or the Attorney General for Northern Ireland.

118.   Defences

(1)   Subsection (2) applies where in accordance with a provision mentioned in subsection (5) it is a defence for a person charged with an offence to prove a particular matter.

(2)   If the person adduces evidence which is sufficient to raise an issue with respect to the matter the court or jury shall assume that the defence is satisfied unless the prosecution proves beyond reasonable doubt that it is not.

(3)   Subsection (4) applies where in accordance with a provision mentioned in subsection (5) a court—

    (a)   may make an assumption in relation to a person charged with an offence unless a particular matter is proved, or

    (b)   may accept a fact as sufficient evidence unless a particular matter is proved.

(4)   If evidence is adduced which is sufficient to raise an issue with respect to the matter mentioned in subsection (3)(a) or (b) the court shall treat it as proved unless the prosecution disproves it beyond reasonable doubt.

(5)   The provisions in respect of which subsections (2) and (4) apply are—

    (a)   sections 12(4), 39(5)(a), 54, 57, 58, 77 and 103 of this Act, and

    (b)   sections 13, 32 and 33 of the Northern Ireland (Emergency Provisions) Act 1996 (possession and information offences) as they have effect by virtue of Schedule 1 to this Act.

119.   Crown servants, regulators, &c.

(1)   The Secretary of State may make regulations providing for any of sections 15 to 23 and 39 to apply to persons in the public service of the Crown.

(2)   The Secretary of State may make regulations providing for section 19 not to apply to persons who are in his opinion performing or connected with the performance of regulatory, supervisory, investigative or registration functions of a public nature.

(3)   Regulations—

  (a)   may make different provision for different purposes,

  (b)   may make provision which is to apply only in specified circumstances, and

  (c)   may make provision which applies only to particular persons or to persons of a particular description.

120.   Evidence

(1)   A document which purports to be—

  (a)   a notice or direction given or order made by the Secretary of State for the purposes of a provision of this Act, and

  (b)   signed by him or on his behalf,

shall be received in evidence and shall, until the contrary is proved, be deemed to have been given or made by the Secretary of State.

(2)   A document bearing a certificate which—

  (a)   purports to be signed by or on behalf of the Secretary of State, and

  (b)   states that the document is a true copy of a notice or direction given or order made by the Secretary of State for the purposes of a provision of this Act,

shall be evidence (or, in Scotland, sufficient evidence) of the document in legal proceedings.

(3)   In subsections (1) and (2) a reference to an order does not include a reference to an order made by statutory instrument.

(4)   The Documentary Evidence Act 1868 shall apply to an authorisation given in writing by the Secretary of State for the purposes of this Act as it applies to an order made by him.

121.   Interpretation

In this Act—

  'article' includes substance and any other thing,

  'customs officer' means an officer commissioned by the Commissioners of Customs and Excise under section 6(3) of the Customs and Excise Management Act 1979,

  'dwelling' means a building or part of a building used as a dwelling, and a vehicle which is habitually stationary and which is used as a dwelling,

  'explosive' means—

    (a)   an article or substance manufactured for the purpose of producing a practical effect by explosion,

    (b)   materials for making an article or substance within paragraph (a),

    (c)   anything used or intended to be used for causing or assisting in causing an explosion, and

    (d)   a part of anything within paragraph (a) or (c),

  'firearm' includes an air gun or air pistol,

  'immigration officer' means a person appointed as an immigration officer under paragraph 1 of Schedule 2 to the Immigration Act 1971,

  'the Islands' means the Channel Islands and the Isle of Man,

  'organisation' includes any association or combination of persons, 'premises' includes any place and in particular includes—

(a) a vehicle,

(b) an offshore installation within the meaning given in section 44 of the Petroleum Act 1998, and

(c) a tent or moveable structure,

'property' includes property wherever situated and whether real or personal, heritable or moveable, and things in action and other intangible or incorporeal property,

'public place' means a place to which members of the public have or are permitted to have access, whether or not for payment,

'road' has the same meaning as in the Road Traffic Act 1988 (in relation to England and Wales), the Roads (Scotland) Act 1984 (in relation to Scotland) and the Road Traffic Regulation (Northern Ireland) Order 1997 (in relation to Northern Ireland), and includes part of a road, and

'vehicle', except in sections 48 to 52 and Schedule 7, includes an aircraft, hovercraft, train or vessel.

122. Index of defined expressions
In this Act the expressions listed below are defined by the provisions specified.

Expression	*Interpretation provision*
Act	Section 121
Action	Section 121
Action taken for the purposes of terrorism	Section 1(5)
Article	Section 121
Authorised officer	Section 24(1)
Cash	Section 24(2)
Cordoned area	Section 33
Customs officer	Section 121
Dwelling	Section 121
Examining officer	Schedule 7, paragraph 1
Explosive	Section 121
Firearm	Section 121
Immigration officer	Section 121
The Islands	Section 121
Organisation	Section 121
Premises	Section 121
Property	Section 121
Proscribed organisation	Section 3(1)
Public place	Section 121
Road	Section 121
Scheduled offence (in Part VII)	Section 65
Terrorism	Section 1
Terrorist (in Part V)	Section 40
Terrorist investigation	Section 32
Terrorist property	Section 14
Vehicle	Section 121
Vehicle (in sections 48 to 51)	Section 52

123. Orders and regulations

(1) An order or regulations made by the Secretary of State under this Act—

   (a) shall be made by statutory instrument,

   (b) may contain savings and transitional provisions, and

   (c) may make different provision for different purposes.

(2) Subject to subsection (3), an order or regulations under any of the following provisions shall be subject to annulment in pursuance of a resolution of either House of Parliament—

   (a) section 4(3);

   (b) section 24(2)(e);

   (c) section 72;

   (d) section 79(5);

   (e) section 80(9);

   (f) section 97(1) or (3);

   (g) section 100(1)(b);

   (h) section 119(1) or (2);

   (i) paragraph 52(1)(a) or (b) of Schedule 4;

   (j) paragraph 17(4) of Schedule 7;

   (k) paragraph 3(1)(b) of Schedule 8;

   (l) paragraph 19 of Schedule 8.

(3) In the cases of—

   (a) the first order to be made under paragraph 17(4) of Schedule 7, and

   (b) the first order to be made under paragraph 19 of Schedule 8,

the order shall not be made unless a draft has been laid before and approved by resolution of each House of Parliament (and subsection (2)(j) or (l) shall not apply).

(4) An order or regulations under any of the following provisions shall not be made, subject to subsection (5), unless a draft has been laid before and approved by resolution of each House of Parliament—

   (a) section 3(3);

   (b) section 53(2);

   (c) section 65(3);

   (d) section 96;

   (e) section 101(4);

   (f) section 112(2);

   (g) paragraph 2(2) of Schedule 1;

   (h) paragraph 6(2) or 7(3) of Schedule 6;

   (i) paragraph 16 of Schedule 7;

   (j) paragraph 3(2) of Schedule 8;

   (k) paragraph 4(4) of Schedule 8;

   (l) paragraph 4(1)(e) of Schedule 14;

   (m) paragraph 7(3) of Schedule 14.

(5) An order or regulations under a provision mentioned in subsection (4), except for paragraph (b), may be made without a draft having been approved if the Secretary of State is of the opinion that it is necessary by reason of urgency; and the order—

   (a) shall contain a declaration of the Secretary of State's opinion, and

   (b) shall cease to have effect at the end of the period of 40 days beginning with the day on which the Secretary of State makes the order, unless a resolution approving the order is passed by each House during that period.

(6) For the purposes of subsection (5)—

(a)   a code of practice or revised code to which an order relates shall cease to have effect together with the order,

(b)   an order's ceasing to have effect shall be without prejudice to anything previously done or to the making of a new order (or the issue of a new code), and

(c)   the period of 40 days shall be computed in accordance with section 7(1) of the Statutory Instruments Act 1946.

(7)   An order under paragraph 8(3) of Schedule 13 shall be laid before Parliament.

(8)   Subsection (1)(a) does not apply to an order made—

(a)   under section 94,

(b)   by virtue of paragraph 36 of Schedule 4, or

(c)   under or by virtue of any of paragraphs 19 to 21 of Schedule 5.

(9)   Subsections (1)(a) and (4)(d) do not apply to an order made under regulations made under section 96.

124.   Directions

A direction given under this Act may be varied or revoked by a further direction.

125.   Amendments and repeals

(1)   Schedule 15 (consequential amendments) shall have effect.

(2)   The enactments listed in Schedule 16 are hereby repealed or revoked to the extent specified.

126.   Report to Parliament

The Secretary of State shall lay before both Houses of Parliament at least once in every 12 months a report on the working of this Act.

127.   Money

The following shall be paid out of money provided by Parliament—

(a)   any expenditure of a Minister of the Crown under or by virtue of this Act, and

(b)   any increase in the sums payable out of money provided by Parliament under any other enactment.

128.   Commencement

The preceding provisions of this Act, apart from sections 2(1)(b) and (2) and 118 and Schedule 1, shall come into force in accordance with provision made by the Secretary of State by order.

129.   Transitional provisions

(1)   Where, immediately before the coming into force of section 2(1)(a), a person is being detained by virtue of a provision of the Prevention of Terrorism (Temporary Provisions) Act 1989—

(a)   the provisions of that Act shall continue to apply to him, in place of the corresponding provisions of this Act, until his detention comes to an end, and

(b)   nothing in paragraph 5 or 8 of Schedule 15 shall have effect in relation to him during his detention.

(2)   Where—

(a)   a person is detained by virtue of a provision of the Northern Ireland (Emergency Provisions) Act 1996 (as continued in force by virtue of Schedule 1 to this Act), and

(b)   the provision ceases to have effect,

he shall be treated as lawfully detained under any corresponding provision of this Act.

(3)   Where this Act repeals and re-enacts a provision of—

(a)   the Prevention of Terrorism (Temporary Provisions) Act 1989, or

(b)   the Northern Ireland (Emergency Provisions) Act 1996,
the repeal and re-enactment shall not, unless the contrary intention appears, affect the continuity of the law.

(4)   A reference in this Act or any other enactment or instrument to a provision of this Act shall (so far as the context permits) be taken to include a reference to a corresponding provision repealed by this Act.

(5)   The repeal by virtue of this Act of section 14 of the Northern Ireland (Emergency Provisions) Act 1996 (young persons convicted of scheduled offences) shall not affect its operation in relation to offences committed while it was in force.

(6)   Any document made, served or issued after the commencement of paragraph (a) or (b) of section 2(1) which contains a reference to an enactment repealed by that paragraph shall, so far as the context permits, be construed as referring to or (as the context may require) including a reference to the corresponding provision of this Act.

(7)   Any document made, served or issued after the commencement of this Act which contains a reference to a provision of this Act shall, so far as the context permits, be construed as referring to or (as the context may require) including a reference to the corresponding provision of—

(a)   the Prevention of Terrorism (Temporary Provisions) Act 1989, or

(b)   the Northern Ireland (Emergency Provisions) Act 1996.

(8)   Section 117 shall apply to the institution of proceedings after commencement of that section whether the offence to which the proceedings relate (which may, by virtue of subsection (4) above, be an offence under a provision repealed by this Act) is alleged to have been committed before or after commencement of that section.

130.   Extent

(1)   Subject to subsections (2) to (6), this Act extends to the whole of the United Kingdom.

(2)   Section 59 shall extend to England and Wales only.

(3)   The following shall extend to Northern Ireland only—

(a)   section 60, and

(b)   Part VII.

(4)   Section 61 shall extend to Scotland only.

(5)   In Schedule 5—

(a)   Part I shall extend to England and Wales and Northern Ireland only, and

(b)   Part II shall extend to Scotland only.

(6)   The amendments and repeals in Schedules 15 and 16 shall have the same extent as the enactments to which they relate.

131.   Short title

This Act may be cited as the Terrorism Act 2000.

SCHEDULES

SCHEDULE 1
NORTHERN IRELAND (EMERGENCY PROVISIONS) ACT 1996

Temporary extension

1.—(1)   This paragraph applies to any of the following if and in so far as it is in force immediately before the passing of this Act by virtue of an order under section 62(3) of the Northern Ireland (Emergency Provisions) Act 1996 (duration)—

(a)   a provision of the Northern Ireland (Emergency Provisions) Act 1996 (other than one mentioned in sub-paragraph (2)),

(b)   a provision of the Prevention of Terrorism (Temporary Provisions) Act 1989, and

(c)   section 4 of the Criminal Justice (Terrorism and Conspiracy) Act 1998 (forfeiture orders).

(2)   This paragraph does not apply to the following provisions of the Northern Ireland (Emergency Provisions) Act 1996—

(a)   section 26(1)(b) (power of entry on authority of Secretary of State),

(b)   section 35 (wearing of hoods), and

(c)   section 50 (explosives factories).

2.—(1)   A provision to which paragraph 1 applies shall continue in force for the period of 12 months starting with the day on which this Act is passed.

(2)   The Secretary of State may by order provide for a provision to which paragraph 1 applies to continue in force for the period of 12 months immediately following the period mentioned in sub-paragraph (1).

3.—(1)   The powers under section 62(3)(a) and (c) of the Northern Ireland (Emergency Provisions) Act 1996 shall continue to be exercisable in relation to a provision to which paragraph 1 applies in respect of any period falling within—

(a)   the period mentioned in paragraph 2(1), or

(b)   a period specified in relation to that provision under paragraph 2(2).

(2)   The power under section 62(3)(b) of the Northern Ireland (Emergency Provisions) Act 1996 shall continue to be exercisable in relation to a provision to which paragraph 1 applies at any time during—

(a)   the period mentioned in paragraph 2(1), or

(b)   a period specified in relation to that provision under paragraph 2(2).

4.   The Secretary of State may by order provide for a provision to which paragraph 1 applies—

(a)   to cease to have effect on a specified day;

(b)   to cease to be capable of being the subject of an order under section 62(3) of the Northern Ireland (Emergency Provisions) Act 1996.

5.   The continuance in force of a provision by virtue of paragraph 2 is subject to any order made by virtue of paragraph 3 or 4.

6.—(1)   A provision of the Northern Ireland (Emergency Provisions) Act 1996 to which paragraph 1 does not apply shall continue to have effect for the purposes of, or in so far it relates to, any provision to which that paragraph does apply.

(2)   While Part I of Schedule 1 to that Act (scheduled offences) has effect by virtue of this Schedule, the following shall also have effect—

(a)   Part III of that Schedule (extra-territorial offences), and

(b)   sections 3, 10 and 11 of that Act so far as they relate to offences which are scheduled offences by virtue of that Part.

Amendments during temporary extension

7.   The provisions of the 1996 Act which continue in force by virtue of this Schedule shall be amended as follows.

8.   In section 19 (arrest and seizure) after subsection (4) insert—

'(5)   The reference to a rule of law in subsection (2) does not include a rule of law which has effect only by virtue of the Human Rights Act 1998.'

9.   In section 20 (search for munitions, &c.) after subsection (5) insert—

'(5A)   The power to extend a period conferred by subsection (5) may be exercised only once in relation to a particular search.'

10.   In section 26 (powers of entry, &c.) after subsection (2) insert—

'(2A)   The Secretary of State may grant an authorisation under subsection (2) only if he considers it necessary for the preservation of the peace or the maintenance of order.'

11.   In section 33 (collection of information, &c.) after subsection (5) insert—

'(5A)   Before making an order under subsection (5) a court must give an opportunity to be heard to any person, other than the convicted person, who claims to be the owner of or otherwise interested in anything which can be forfeited under that subsection.

(5B)   An order under subsection (5) shall not come into force until there is no further possibility of it being varied, or set aside, on appeal (disregarding any power of a court to grant leave to appeal out of time).'

12.—(1)   Part V (private security services) shall have effect subject to the provisions of this paragraph.

(2)   On issuing a certificate under section 39 the Secretary of State may impose a condition if satisfied that it is necessary in order to prevent an organisation within section 39(8) from benefiting from the certificate.

(3)   To the grounds for refusal to issue a certificate and for revocation of a certificate in sections 39(1) and (5) there shall be added the ground that the Secretary of State is satisfied that the applicant for or holder of a certificate has failed to comply with a condition imposed by virtue of sub-paragraph (2) above.

(4)   The applicant for a certificate may appeal to the High Court if—

(a)   the application is refused,

(b)   a condition is imposed on the grant of the certificate, or

(c)   the certificate is revoked.

(5)   Where an appeal is brought under sub-paragraph (4), the Secretary of State may issue a certificate that the decision to which the appeal relates—

(a)   was taken for the purpose of preventing benefit from accruing to an organisation which was within section 39(8), and

(b)   was justified by that purpose.

(6)   If he intends to rely on a certificate under sub-paragraph (5), the Secretary of State shall notify the appellant.

(7)   Where the appellant is notified of the Secretary of State's intention to rely on a certificate under sub-paragraph (5)—

(a)   he may appeal against the certificate to the Tribunal established under section 91 of the Northern Ireland Act 1998, and

(b)   sections 90(3) and (4), 91(2) to (9) and 92 of that Act (effect of appeal, procedure, and further appeal) shall apply.

(8)   Rules made under section 91 or 92 of that Act which are in force immediately before the passing of this Act shall have effect in relation to a certificate under sub-paragraph (5)—

(a)   with any necessary modifications, and

(b)   subject to any later rules made by virtue of sub-paragraph (7)(b).

SCHEDULE 2
PROSCRIBED ORGANISATIONS

The Irish Republican Army.
Cumann na mBan.
Fianna na hEireann.
The Red Hand Commando.
Saor Eire.
The Ulster Freedom Fighters.
The Ulster Volunteer Force.
The Irish National Liberation Army.
The Irish People's Liberation Organisation.
The Ulster Defence Association.
The Loyalist Volunteer Force.
The Continuity Army Council.
The Orange Volunteers.
The Red Hand Defenders.

Note   The entry for The Orange Volunteers refers to the organisation which uses that name and in the name of which a statement described as a press release was published on 14th October 1998.

SCHEDULE 3
THE PROSCRIBED ORGANISATIONS APPEAL COMMISSION

Constitution and administration

1.—(1)   The Commission shall consist of members appointed by the Lord Chancellor.
   (2)   The Lord Chancellor shall appoint one of the members as chairman.
   (3)   A member shall hold and vacate office in accordance with the terms of his appointment.
   (4)   A member may resign at any time by notice in writing to the Lord Chancellor.

2.   The Lord Chancellor may appoint officers and servants for the Commission.

3.   The Lord Chancellor—
   (a)   may pay sums by way of remuneration, allowances, pensions and gratuities to or in respect of members, officers and servants,
   (b)   may pay compensation to a person who ceases to be a member of the Commission if the Lord Chancellor thinks it appropriate because of special circumstances, and
   (c)   may pay sums in respect of expenses of the Commission.

Procedure

4.—(1)   The Commission shall sit at such times and in such places as the Lord Chancellor may direct.
   (2)   The Commission may sit in two or more divisions.
   (3)   At each sitting of the Commission—
   (a)   three members shall attend,
   (b)   one of the members shall be a person who holds or has held high judicial office (within the meaning of the Appellate Jurisdiction Act 1876), and
   (c)   the chairman or another member nominated by him shall preside and report the Commission's decision.

5.—(1) The Lord Chancellor may make rules—

(a) regulating the exercise of the right of appeal to the Commission;

(b) prescribing practice and procedure to be followed in relation to proceedings before the Commission;

(c) providing for proceedings before the Commission to be determined without an oral hearing in specified circumstances;

(d) making provision about evidence in proceedings before the Commission (including provision about the burden of proof and admissibility of evidence);

(e) making provision about proof of the Commission's decisions.

(2) In making the rules the Lord Chancellor shall, in particular, have regard to the need to secure—

(a) that decisions which are the subject of appeals are properly reviewed, and

(b) that information is not disclosed contrary to the public interest.

(3) The rules shall make provision permitting organisations to be legally represented in proceedings before the Commission.

(4) The rules may, in particular—

(a) provide for full particulars of the reasons for proscription or refusal to deproscribe to be withheld from the organisation or applicant concerned and from any person representing it or him;

(b) enable the Commission to exclude persons (including representatives) from all or part of proceedings;

(c) enable the Commission to provide a summary of evidence taken in the absence of a person excluded by virtue of paragraph (b);

(d) permit preliminary or incidental functions to be discharged by a single member;

(e) permit proceedings for permission to appeal under section 6 to be determined by a single member;

(f) make provision about the functions of persons appointed under paragraph 7;

(g) make different provision for different parties or descriptions of party.

(5) Rules under this paragraph—

(a) shall be made by statutory instrument, and

(b) shall not be made unless a draft has been laid before and approved by resolution of each House of Parliament.

(6) In this paragraph a reference to proceedings before the Commission includes a reference to proceedings arising out of proceedings before the Commission.

6.—(1) This paragraph applies to—

(a) proceedings brought by an organisation before the Commission, and

(b) proceedings arising out of proceedings to which paragraph (a) applies.

(2) Proceedings shall be conducted on behalf of the organisation by a person designated by the Commission (with such legal representation as he may choose to obtain).

(3) In paragraphs 5 and 8 of this Schedule a reference to an organisation includes a reference to a person designated under this paragraph.

7.—(1) The relevant law officer may appoint a person to represent the interests of an organisation or other applicant in proceedings in relation to which an order has been made by virtue of paragraph 5(4)(b).

(2) The relevant law officer is—

(a) in relation to proceedings in England and Wales, the Attorney General,

(b) in relation to proceedings in Scotland, the Advocate General for Scotland, and

(c) in relation to proceedings in Northern Ireland, the Attorney General for Northern Ireland.

(3) A person appointed under this paragraph must—

(a) have a general qualification for the purposes of section 71 of the Courts and Legal Services Act 1990 (qualification for legal appointments),

(b) be an advocate or a solicitor who has rights of audience in the Court of Session or the High Court of Justiciary by virtue of section 25A of the Solicitors (Scotland) Act 1980, or

(c) be a member of the Bar of Northern Ireland.

(4) A person appointed under this paragraph shall not be responsible to the organisation or other applicant whose interests he is appointed to represent.

(5) In paragraphs 5 and 8 of this Schedule a reference to a representative does not include a reference to a person appointed under this paragraph.

8.—(1) Section 9(1) of the Interception of Communications Act 1985 (exclusion of evidence) shall not apply in relation to—

(a) proceedings before the Commission, or

(b) proceedings arising out of proceedings to which paragraph (a) applies.

(2) Evidence admitted by virtue of sub-paragraph (1) shall not be disclosed to—

(a) the organisation concerned,

(b) the applicant (where the organisation is not also the applicant), or

(c) any person representing the organisation concerned or the applicant.

SCHEDULE 4
FORFEITURE ORDERS

PART I
ENGLAND AND WALES

Interpretation

1. In this Part of this Schedule—

'forfeiture order' means an order made by a court in England and Wales under section 23, and

'forfeited property' means the money or other property to which a forfeiture order applies.

Implementation of forfeiture orders

2.—(1) Where a court in England and Wales makes a forfeiture order it may make such other provision as appears to it to be necessary for giving effect to the order, and in particular it may—

(a) require any of the forfeited property to be paid or handed over to the proper officer or to a constable designated for the purpose by the chief officer of police of a police force specified in the order;

(b) direct any of the forfeited property other than money or land to be sold or otherwise disposed of in such manner as the court may direct and the proceeds (if any) to be paid to the proper officer;

(c) appoint a receiver to take possession, subject to such conditions and exceptions as may be specified by the court, of any of the forfeited property, to realise it in such manner as the court may direct and to pay the proceeds to the proper officer;

(d)　direct a specified part of any forfeited money, or of the proceeds of the sale, disposal or realisation of any forfeited property, to be paid by the proper officer to a specified person falling within section 23(7).

(2)　A forfeiture order shall not come into force until there is no further possibility of it being varied, or set aside, on appeal (disregarding any power of a court to grant leave to appeal out of time).

(3)　In sub-paragraph (1)(b) and (d) a reference to the proceeds of the sale, disposal or realisation of property is a reference to the proceeds after deduction of the costs of sale, disposal or realisation.

(4)　Section 140 of the Magistrates' Courts Act 1980 (disposal of non-pecuniary forfeitures) shall not apply.

3.—(1)　A receiver appointed under paragraph 2 shall be entitled to be paid his remuneration and expenses by the proper officer out of the proceeds of the property realised by the receiver and paid to the proper officer under paragraph 2(1)(c).

(2)　If and so far as those proceeds are insufficient, the receiver shall be entitled to be paid his remuneration and expenses by the prosecutor.

(3)　A receiver appointed under paragraph 2 shall not be liable to any person in respect of any loss or damage resulting from action—

(a)　which he takes in relation to property which is not forfeited property, but which he reasonably believes to be forfeited property,

(b)　which he would be entitled to take if the property were forfeited property, and

(c)　which he reasonably believes that he is entitled to take because of his belief that the property is forfeited property.

(4)　Sub-paragraph (3) does not apply in so far as the loss or damage is caused by the receiver's negligence.

4.—(1)　In paragraphs 2 and 3 'the proper officer' means—

(a)　where the forfeiture order is made by a magistrates' court, the justices' chief executive for that court,

(b)　where the forfeiture order is made by the Crown Court and the defendant was committed to the Crown Court by a magistrates' court, the justices' chief executive for the magistrates' court, and

(c)　where the forfeiture order is made by the Crown Court and the proceedings were instituted by a bill of indictment preferred by virtue of section 2(2)(b) of the Administration of Justice (Miscellaneous Provisions) Act 1933, the justices' chief executive for the magistrates' court for the place where the trial took place.

(2)　The proper officer shall issue a certificate in respect of a forfeiture order if an application is made by—

(a)　the prosecutor in the proceedings in which the forfeiture order was made,

(b)　the defendant in those proceedings, or

(c)　a person whom the court heard under section 23(7) before making the order.

(3)　The certificate shall state the extent (if any) to which, at the date of the certificate, effect has been given to the forfeiture order.

Restraint orders

5.—(1)　The High Court may make a restraint order under this paragraph where—

(a)　proceedings have been instituted in England and Wales for an offence under any of sections 15 to 18,

(b)   the proceedings have not been concluded,

(c)   an application for a restraint order is made to the High Court by the prosecutor, and

(d)   a forfeiture order has been made, or it appears to the High Court that a forfeiture order may be made, in the proceedings for the offence.

(2)   The High Court may also make a restraint order under this paragraph where—

(a)   it is satisfied that a person is to be charged in England and Wales with an offence under any of sections 15 to 18,

(b)   an application for a restraint order is made to the High Court by the person who the High Court is satisfied will have the conduct of the proposed proceedings for the offence, and

(c)   it appears to the High Court that a forfeiture order may be made in those proceedings.

(3)   A restraint order prohibits a person to whom notice of it is given, subject to any conditions and exceptions specified in the order, from dealing with property in respect of which a forfeiture order has been or could be made in the proceedings referred to in sub-paragraph (1) or (2).

(4)   An application for a restraint order may be made to a judge in chambers without notice.

(5)   In this paragraph a reference to dealing with property includes a reference to removing the property from Great Britain.

6.—(1)   A restraint order shall provide for notice of it to be given to any person affected by the order.

(2)   A restraint order may be discharged or varied by the High Court on the application of a person affected by it.

(3)   In particular, a restraint order shall be discharged on an application under sub-paragraph (2)—

(a)   in the case of an order made under paragraph 5(2), if the proceedings in respect of the offence are not instituted within such time as the High Court considers reasonable, and

(b)   in any case, if the proceedings for the offence have been concluded.

7.—(1)   A constable may seize any property subject to a restraint order for the purpose of preventing it from being removed from Great Britain.

(2)   Property seized under this paragraph shall be dealt with in accordance with the High Court's directions.

8.—(1)   The Land Charges Act 1972 and the Land Registration Act 1925—

(a)   shall apply in relation to restraint orders as they apply in relation to orders affecting land made by the court for the purpose of enforcing judgments or recognizances, and

(b)   shall apply in relation to applications for restraint orders as they apply in relation to other pending land actions.

(2)   Where a restraint order is made under paragraph 5(1) or an application for such an order is made, the prosecutor in the proceedings for the offence shall be treated for the purposes of section 57 of the Land Registration Act 1925 (inhibitions) as a person interested in respect of any registered land to which the restraint order or the application for the restraint order relates.

(3)   Where a restraint order is made under paragraph 5(2) or an application for such an order is made, the person who the High Court is satisfied will have the conduct of the proposed proceedings shall be treated for the purposes of section 57 of that Act as a person interested in respect of any registered land to which the restraint order or the application for the restraint order relates.

Compensation

9.—(1)   This paragraph applies where a restraint order is discharged under paragraph 6(3)(a).

(2)   This paragraph also applies where a forfeiture order or a restraint order is made in or in relation to proceedings for an offence under any of sections 15 to 18 which—

(a)   do not result in conviction for an offence under any of those sections,

(b)   result in conviction for an offence under any of those sections in respect of which the person convicted is subsequently pardoned by Her Majesty, or

(c)   result in conviction for an offence under any of those sections which is subsequently quashed.

(3)   A person who had an interest in any property which was subject to the order may apply to the High Court for compensation.

(4)   The High Court may order compensation to be paid to the applicant if satisfied—

(a)   that there was a serious default on the part of a person concerned in the investigation or prosecution of the offence,

(b)   that the person in default was or was acting as a member of a police force, or was a member of the Crown Prosecution Service or was acting on behalf of the Service,

(c)   that the applicant has suffered loss in consequence of anything done in relation to the property by or in pursuance of the forfeiture order or restraint order, and

(d)   that, having regard to all the circumstances, it is appropriate to order compensation to be paid.

(5)   The High Court shall not order compensation to be paid where it appears to it that proceedings for the offence would have been instituted even if the serious default had not occurred.

(6)   Compensation payable under this paragraph shall be paid—

(a)   where the person in default was or was acting as a member of a police force, out of the police fund out of which the expenses of that police force are met, and

(b)   where the person in default was a member of the Crown Prosecution Service, or was acting on behalf of the Service, by the Director of Public Prosecutions.

10.—(1)   This paragraph applies where—

(a)   a forfeiture order or a restraint order is made in or in relation to proceedings for an offence under any of sections 15 to 18, and

(b)   the proceedings result in a conviction which is subsequently quashed on an appeal under section 7(2) or (5).

(2)   A person who had an interest in any property which was subject to the order may apply to the High Court for compensation.

(3)   The High Court may order compensation to be paid to the applicant if satisfied—

(a)   that the applicant has suffered loss in consequence of anything done in relation to the property by or in pursuance of the forfeiture order or restraint order, and

(b)   that, having regard to all the circumstances, it is appropriate to order compensation to be paid.

(4)   Compensation payable under this paragraph shall be paid by the Secretary of State.

Proceedings for an offence: timing

11.—(1) For the purposes of this Part of this Schedule proceedings for an offence are instituted—

(a) when a justice of the peace issues a summons or warrant under section 1 of the Magistrates' Courts Act 1980 in respect of the offence;

(b) when a person is charged with the offence after being taken into custody without a warrant;

(c) when a bill of indictment charging a person with the offence is preferred by virtue of section 2(2)(b) of the Administration of Justice (Miscellaneous Provisions) Act 1933.

(2) Where the application of sub-paragraph (1) would result in there being more than one time for the institution of proceedings they shall be taken to be instituted at the earliest of those times.

(3) For the purposes of this Part of this Schedule proceedings are concluded—

(a) when a forfeiture order has been made in those proceedings and effect has been given to it in respect of all the forfeited property, or

(b) when no forfeiture order has been made in those proceedings and there is no further possibility of one being made as a result of an appeal (disregarding any power of a court to grant leave to appeal out of time).

Enforcement of orders made elsewhere in the British Islands

12. In the following provisions of this Part of this Schedule—

'a Scottish order' means—

(a) an order made in Scotland under section 23 ('a Scottish forfeiture order'),

(b) an order made under paragraph 18 ('a Scottish restraint order'), or

(c) an order made under any other provision of Part II of this Schedule in relation to a Scottish forfeiture or restraint order;

'a Northern Ireland order' means—

(a) an order made in Northern Ireland under section 23 ('a Northern Ireland forfeiture order'),

(b) an order made under paragraph 33 ('a Northern Ireland restraint order'), or

(c) an order made under any other provision of Part III of this Schedule in relation to a Northern Ireland forfeiture or restraint order;

'an Islands order' means an order made in any of the Islands under a provision of the law of that Island corresponding to—

(a) section 23 ('an Islands forfeiture order'),

(b) paragraph 5 ('an Islands restraint order'), or

(c) any other provision of this Part of this Schedule.

13.—(1) Subject to the provisions of this paragraph, a Scottish, Northern Ireland or Islands order shall have effect in the law of England and Wales.

(2) But such an order shall be enforced in England and Wales only in accordance with—

(a) the provisions of this paragraph, and

(b) any provision made by rules of court as to the manner in which, and the conditions subject to which, such orders are to be enforced there.

(3) On an application made to it in accordance with rules of court for registration of a Scottish, Northern Ireland or Islands order, the High Court shall direct that the order shall, in accordance with such rules, be registered in that court.

(4) Rules of court shall also make provision—

(a)   for cancelling or varying the registration of a Scottish, Northern Ireland or Islands forfeiture order when effect has been given to it, whether in England and Wales or elsewhere, in respect of all or, as the case may be, part of the money or other property to which the order applies;

(b)   for cancelling or varying the registration of a Scottish, Northern Ireland or Islands restraint order which has been discharged or varied by the court by which it was made.

(5)   If a Scottish, Northern Ireland or Islands forfeiture order is registered under this paragraph the High Court shall have, in relation to that order, the same powers as a court has under paragraph 2(1) to give effect to a forfeiture order made by it and—

(a)   paragraph 3 shall apply accordingly,

(b)   any functions of a justices' chief executive shall be exercised by the appropriate officer of the High Court, and

(c)   after making any payment required by virtue of paragraph 2(1)(d) or 3, the balance of any sums received by the appropriate officer of the High Court by virtue of an order made under this sub-paragraph shall be paid by him to the Secretary of State.

(6)   If a Scottish, Northern Ireland or Islands restraint order is registered under this paragraph—

(a)   paragraphs 7 and 8 shall apply as they apply to a restraint order under paragraph 5, and

(b)   the High Court shall have power to make an order under section 33 of the Supreme Court Act 1981 (extended power to order inspection of property, &c.) in relation to proceedings brought or likely to be brought for a Scottish, Northern Ireland or Islands restraint order as if those proceedings had been brought or were likely to be brought in the High Court.

(7)   In addition, if a Scottish, Northern Ireland or Islands order is registered under this paragraph—

(a)   the High Court shall have, in relation to its enforcement, the same power as if the order had originally been made in the High Court,

(b)   proceedings for or with respect to its enforcement may be taken as if the order had originally been made in the High Court, and

(c)   proceedings for or with respect to contravention of such an order, whether before or after such registration, may be taken as if the order had originally been made in the High Court.

(8)   The High Court may also make such orders or do otherwise as seems to it appropriate for the purpose of—

(a)   assisting the achievement in England and Wales of the purposes of a Scottish, Northern Ireland or Islands order, or

(b)   assisting a receiver or other person directed by a Scottish, Northern Ireland or Islands order to sell or otherwise dispose of property.

(9)   The following documents shall be received in evidence in England and Wales without further proof—

(a)   a document purporting to be a copy of a Scottish, Northern Ireland or Islands order and to be certified as such by a proper officer of the court by which it was made, and

(b)   a document purporting to be a certificate for purposes corresponding to those of paragraph 4(2) and (3) and to be certified by a proper officer of the court concerned.

Enforcement of orders made in designated countries

14.—(1)   Her Majesty may by Order in Council make provision for the purpose of enabling the enforcement in England and Wales of external orders.

(2)   An 'external order' means an order—

(a)   which is made in a country or territory designated for the purposes of this paragraph by the Order in Council, and

(b)   which makes relevant provision.

(3)   'Relevant provision' means—

(a)   provision for the forfeiture of terrorist property ('an external forfeiture order'), or

(b)   provision prohibiting dealing with property which is subject to an external forfeiture order or in respect of which such an order could be made in proceedings which have been or are to be instituted in the designated country or territory ('an external restraint order').

(4)   An Order in Council under this paragraph may, in particular, include provision—

(a)   which, for the purpose of facilitating the enforcement of any external order that may be made, has effect at times before there is an external order to be enforced;

(b)   for matters corresponding to those for which provision is made by, or can be made under, paragraph 13(1) to (8) in relation to the orders to which that paragraph applies;

(c)   for the proof of any matter relevant for the purposes of anything falling to be done in pursuance of the Order in Council.

(5)   An Order in Council under this paragraph may also make provision with respect to anything falling to be done on behalf of the United Kingdom in a designated country or territory in relation to proceedings in that country or territory for or in connection with the making of an external order.

(6)   An Order in Council under this paragraph—

(a)   may make different provision for different cases, and

(b)   shall not be made unless a draft of it has been laid before and approved by resolution of each House of Parliament.

PART II
SCOTLAND

Implementation of forfeiture orders

15.   In this Part of this Schedule—

'forfeiture order' means an order made by a court in Scotland under section 23, and

'forfeited property' means the money or other property to which a forfeiture order applies.

16.—(1)   Where a court in Scotland makes a forfeiture order it may make such other provision as appears to it to be necessary for giving effect to the order, and in particular it may—

(a)   direct any of the forfeited property other than money or land to be sold or otherwise disposed of in such manner as the court may direct;

(b)   appoint an administrator to take possession, subject to such conditions and exceptions as may be specified by the court, of any of the forfeited property and to realise it in such manner as the court may direct;

(c)   direct a specified part of any forfeited money, or of the proceeds of the sale, disposal or realisation of any forfeited property, to be paid to a specified person falling within section 23(7).

(2)   A forfeiture order shall not come into force so long as an appeal is pending against the order or against the conviction on which it was made; and for this purpose where an appeal is competent but has not been brought it shall be treated as pending until the expiry of a period of fourteen days from the date when the order was made.

(3)   Any balance remaining after making any payment required under sub-paragraph (1)(c) or paragraph 17 shall be treated for the purposes of section 211(5) of the Criminal Procedure (Scotland) Act 1995 (fines payable to the Treasury) as if it were a fine imposed in the High Court of Justiciary.

(4)   The clerk of court shall, on the application of—

    (a)   the prosecutor in the proceedings in which a forfeiture order is made,

    (b)   the accused in those proceedings, or

    (c)   a person whom the court heard under section 23(7) before making the order,

certify in writing the extent (if any) to which, at the date of the certificate, effect has been given to the order in respect of the money or other property to which it applies.

(5)   In sub-paragraph (1) references to the proceeds of the sale, disposal or realisation of property are references to the proceeds after deduction of the costs of sale, disposal or realisation.

Administrators

17.—(1)   The Court of Session may by rules of court prescribe the powers and duties of an administrator appointed under paragraph 16.

(2)   An administrator appointed under paragraph 16 shall be entitled to be paid his remuneration and expenses out of the proceeds of the property realised by him or, if and so far as those proceeds are insufficient, by the Lord Advocate.

(3)   The accountant of court shall supervise an administrator appointed under paragraph 16 in the exercise of the powers conferred, and discharge of the duties imposed, on him under or by virtue of that paragraph.

(4)   An administrator appointed under paragraph 16 shall not be liable to any person in respect of any loss or damage resulting from action—

    (a)   which he takes in relation to property which is not forfeited property, but which he reasonably believes to be forfeited property,

    (b)   which he would be entitled to take if the property were forfeited property, and

    (c)   which he takes reasonably believing that he is entitled to take because of his belief that the property is forfeited property.

(5)   Sub-paragraph (4) does not apply in so far as the loss or damage is caused by the administrator's negligence.

Restraint orders

18.—(1)   The Court of Session, on an application made by the Lord Advocate, may make a restraint order under this paragraph where—

    (a)   proceedings have been instituted in Scotland for an offence under any of sections 15 to 18,

    (b)   the proceedings have not been concluded, and

    (c)   a forfeiture order has been made, or it appears to the court that a forfeiture order may be made, in the proceedings for the offence.

(2)   The Court of Session may also, on such an application, make a restraint order under this paragraph where—

    (a)   it is satisfied that a person is to be prosecuted in Scotland for an offence under any of sections 15 to 18, and

    (b)   it appears to the Court of Session that a forfeiture order may be made in proceedings for the offence.

(3)   A restraint order prohibits a person to whom notice of it is given, subject to any conditions and exceptions specified in the order, from dealing with property in respect of

which a forfeiture order has been or could be made in the proceedings referred to in sub-paragraph (1) or (2).

(4)　An application for a restraint order may be made ex parte in chambers.

(5)　For the purposes of this paragraph, dealing with property includes removing the property from Great Britain.

19.—(1)　A restraint order shall provide for notice of it to be given to any person affected by the order.

(2)　A restraint order may be recalled or varied by the Court of Session on the application of any person affected by it.

(3)　A restraint order shall be recalled—

　(a)　in the case of an order made under paragraph 18(2), if the proceedings in respect of the offence are not instituted within such time as the Court of Session considers reasonable, or

　(b)　in the case of an order made under paragraph 18(1) or (2), when proceedings for the offence are concluded.

(4)　When proceedings for the offence are concluded the Lord Advocate shall forthwith apply to the Court for recall of the order.

20.—(1)　A constable may seize any property subject to a restraint order for the purpose of preventing it from being removed from Great Britain.

(2)　Property seized under this paragraph shall be dealt with in accordance with the Court's directions.

21.—(1)　On the application of the Lord Advocate, the Court of Session may, in respect of heritable property in Scotland affected by a restraint order (whether such property generally or particular such property) grant warrant for inhibition against any person interdicted by the order.

(2)　Subject to this Part of this Schedule, a warrant under sub-paragraph (1)—

　(a)　shall have effect as if granted on the dependence of an action for debt at the instance of the Lord Advocate against the person and may be executed, recalled, loosed or restricted accordingly;

　(b)　shall have the effect of letters of inhibition and shall forthwith be registered by the Lord Advocate in the register of inhibitions and adjudications.

(3)　Section 155 of the Titles to Land Consolidation (Scotland) Act 1868 (effective date of inhibition) shall apply in relation to an inhibition for which warrant has been granted under sub-paragraph (2)(a) as that section applies to an inhibition by separate letters or contained in a summons.

(4)　The execution of an inhibition under sub-paragraph (2) in respect of property shall not prejudice the exercise of an administrator's powers under or for the purposes of this Part of this Schedule in respect of that property.

(5)　No inhibition executed under sub-paragraph (2) shall have effect once, or in so far as, the restraint order affecting the property in respect of which the warrant for the inhibition has been granted has ceased to have effect in respect of that property, and the Lord Advocate shall—

　(a)　apply for the recall, or as the case may be restriction, of the inhibition or arrestment accordingly; and

　(b)　ensure that recall, or restriction, of an inhibition on such application is reflected in the register of inhibitions and adjudications.

22.—(1) On the application of the Lord Advocate, the court may, in respect of moveable property affected by a restraint order (whether such property generally or particular such property), grant warrant for arrestment if the property would be arrestable if the person entitled to it were a debtor.

(2) A warrant under sub-paragraph (1) shall have effect as if granted on the dependence of an action for debt at the instance of the Lord Advocate against the person and may be executed, recalled, loosed or restricted accordingly.

(3) The execution of an arrestment under sub-paragraph (2) in respect of property shall not prejudice the exercise of an administrator's powers under or for the purposes of this Part of this Schedule in respect of that property.

(4) No arrestment executed under sub-paragraph (2) shall have effect once, or in so far as, the restraint order affecting the property in respect of which the warrant for such arrestment has been granted has ceased to have effect in respect of that property; and the Lord Advocate shall apply to the court for an order recalling, or as the case may be, restricting the arrestment accordingly.

Compensation

23.—(1) This paragraph applies where a restraint order is recalled under paragraph 19(3)(a).

(2) This paragraph also applies where a forfeiture order or a restraint order is made in or in relation to proceedings for an offence under any of sections 15 to 18 which—

(a) do not result in conviction for an offence under any of those sections,

(b) result in conviction for an offence under any of those sections in respect of which the person convicted is subsequently pardoned by Her Majesty, or

(c) result in conviction for an offence under any of those sections which is subsequently quashed.

(3) A person who had an interest in any property which was subject to the order may apply to the Court of Session for compensation.

(4) The Court of Session may order compensation to be paid to the applicant if it is satisfied—

(a) that there was a serious default on the part of a person concerned in the investigation or prosecution of the offence,

(b) that the person in default was a constable of a police force or a constable acting with the powers of such a constable, or was a procurator fiscal or was acting on behalf of the Lord Advocate,

(c) that the applicant has suffered loss in consequence of anything done in relation to the property by or in pursuance of the forfeiture order or the restraint order, and

(d) having regard to all the circumstances, it is appropriate to order compensation to be paid.

(5) The Court of Session shall not order compensation to be paid where it appears to it that the proceedings for the offence would have been instituted even if the serious default had not occurred.

(6) Compensation payable under this paragraph shall be paid—

(a) where the person in default was a constable of a police force, out of the police fund out of which the expenses of that police force are met;

(b) where the person in default was a constable other than is mentioned in paragraph (a) above, but with the powers of such a constable, by the body under whose authority he acts; and

(c) where the person in default was a procurator fiscal or was acting on behalf of the Lord Advocate, by the Lord Advocate.

(7) This paragraph is without prejudice to any right which may otherwise exist to institute proceedings in respect of delictual liability disclosed by such circumstances as are mentioned in paragraphs (a) to (c) of sub-paragraph (2).

24.—(1) This paragraph applies where—

(a) a forfeiture order or a restraint order is made in or in relation to proceedings for an offence under any of sections 15 to 18, and

(b) the proceedings result in a conviction which is subsequently quashed on an appeal under section 7(2) or (5) as applied by section 8(1).

(2) A person who had an interest in any property which was subject to the order may apply to the Court of Session for compensation.

(3) The Court of Session may order compensation to be paid to the applicant if satisfied—

(a) that the applicant has suffered loss in consequence of anything done in relation to the property by or in pursuance of the forfeiture order or restraint order, and

(b) that, having regard to all the circumstances, it is appropriate to order compensation to be paid.

(4) Compensation payable under this paragraph shall be paid by the Secretary of State.

Proceedings for an offence: timing

25.—(1) For the purposes of this Part of this Schedule proceedings for an offence are instituted—

(a) when a person is arrested for the offence,

(b) when a warrant to arrest or cite a person is granted,

(c) when an indictment or complaint is served on a person in respect of the offence.

(2) Where the application of sub-paragraph (1) would result in there being more than one time for the institution of proceedings they shall be taken to be instituted at the earliest of those times.

(3) For the purposes of this Part of this Schedule proceedings are concluded—

(a) when a forfeiture order has been made in those proceedings and effect has been given to it in respect of all the money or other property to which it applies, or

(b) when (disregarding any power of a court to extend the period within which an appeal may be made) there is no further possibility of a forfeiture order being made in the proceedings.

Enforcement of orders made elsewhere in the British Islands

26. In the following provisions of this Part of this Schedule—

'an England and Wales order' means—

(a) an order made in England and Wales under section 23 ('an England and Wales forfeiture order'),

(b) an order made under paragraph 5 ('an England and Wales restraint order'), or

(c) an order made under any other provision of Part I of this Schedule in relation to an England and Wales forfeiture or restraint order;

'a Northern Ireland order' means—

(a) an order made in Northern Ireland under section 23 ('a Northern Ireland forfeiture order'),

(b)   an order made under paragraph 33 ('a Northern Ireland restraint order'), or

(c)   an order made under any other provision of Part III of this Schedule in relation to a Northern Ireland forfeiture or restraint order;

'an Islands order' means an order made in any of the Islands under a provision of the law of that Island corresponding to—

(a)   section 23 ('an Islands forfeiture order'),

(b)   paragraph 18 ('an Islands restraint order'), or

(c)   any other provision of this Part of this Schedule.

27.—(1)   Subject to the provisions of this paragraph, an England and Wales order, Northern Ireland order or Islands order shall have effect in the law of Scotland.

(2)   But such an order shall be enforced in Scotland only in accordance with—

(a)   the provisions of this paragraph, and

(b)   any provision made by rules of court as to the manner in which, and the conditions subject to which, such orders are to be enforced there.

(3)   On an application made to it in accordance with rules of court for registration of an England and Wales order, Northern Ireland order or Islands order, the Court of Session shall direct that the order shall, in accordance with such rules, be registered in that court.

(4)   Rules of court shall also make provision—

(a)   for cancelling or varying the registration of an England and Wales, Northern Ireland or Islands forfeiture order when effect has been given to it, whether in Scotland or elsewhere, in respect of all or, as the case may be, part of the money or other property to which the order applies,

(b)   for cancelling or varying the registration of an England and Wales, Northern Ireland or Islands restraint order which has been discharged or varied by the court by which it was made.

(5)   If an England and Wales, Northern Ireland or Islands forfeiture order is registered under this paragraph the Court of Session shall have, in relation to that order, the same powers as a court has under paragraph 16(1) above in relation to a forfeiture order made by it and paragraphs 16(3) to (5) and 17 apply accordingly.

(6)   If an England and Wales, Northern Ireland or Islands forfeiture order is registered under this paragraph—

(a)   paragraphs 20 and 21 above shall apply as they apply to a restraint order, and

(b)   the Court of Session shall have the like power to make an order under section 1 of the Administration of Justice (Scotland) Act 1972 (extended power to order inspection of documents, &c.) in relation to proceedings brought or likely to be brought for an England and Wales, Northern Ireland or Islands restraint order as if those proceedings had been brought or were likely to be brought in the Court of Session.

(7)   In addition, if an England and Wales order, Northern Ireland order or Islands order is registered under this paragraph—

(a)   the Court of Session shall have, in relation to its enforcement, the same power,

(b)   proceedings for or with respect to its enforcement may be taken, and

(c)   proceedings for or with respect to any contravention of such an order (whether before or after such registration) may be taken,

as if the order had originally been made in the Court of Session.

(8)   The Court of Session may also make such orders or do otherwise as seems to it appropriate for the purpose of—

(a)   assisting the achievement in Scotland of the purposes of an England and Wales order, Northern Ireland order or Islands order, or

(b) assisting any receiver or other person directed by any such order to sell or otherwise dispose of property.

(9) The following documents shall, in Scotland, be sufficient evidence of their contents—

(a) a document purporting to be a copy of an England and Wales order, Northern Ireland order or Islands order and to be certified as such by a proper officer of the court by which it was made, and

(b) a document purporting to be a certificate for purposes corresponding to those of paragraph 16(4) and to be certified by a proper officer of the court concerned.

(10) Nothing in any England and Wales order, Northern Ireland order or Islands order prejudices any enactment or rule of law in respect of the recording of deeds relating to heritable property in Scotland or the registration of interests in such property.

Enforcement of orders made in designated countries

28.—(1) Her Majesty may by Order in Council make provision for the purpose of enabling the enforcement in Scotland of external orders.

(2) An 'external order' means an order—

(a) which is made in a country or territory designated for the purposes of this paragraph by the Order in Council, and

(b) which makes relevant provision.

(3) 'Relevant provision' means—

(a) provision for the forfeiture of terrorist property ('an external forfeiture order'); or

(b) provision prohibiting dealing with property which is subject to an external forfeiture order or in respect of which such an order could be made in proceedings which have been or are to be instituted in the designated country or territory ('an external restraint order').

(4) An Order in Council under this paragraph may, in particular, include provision—

(a) which, for the purpose of facilitating the enforcement of any external order that may be made, has effect at times before there is an external order to be enforced,

(b) for matters corresponding to those for which provision is made by, or can be made under, paragraph 27(1) to (8) in relation to the orders to which that paragraph applies, and

(c) for the proof of any matter relevant for the purposes of anything falling to be done in pursuance of the Order in Council.

(5) An Order in Council under this paragraph may also make provision with respect to anything falling to be done on behalf of the United Kingdom in a designated country or territory in relation to proceedings in that country or territory for or in connection with the making of an external order.

(6) An Order under this paragraph—

(a) may make different provision for different cases, and

(b) shall not be made unless a draft of it has been laid before and approved by resolution of each House of Parliament.

PART III
NORTHERN IRELAND

Interpretation

29. In this Part of this Schedule—

'forfeiture order' means an order made by a court in Northern Ireland under section 23, and 'forfeited property' means the money or other property to which a forfeiture order applies.

Implementation of forfeiture orders

30.—(1)   Where a court in Northern Ireland makes a forfeiture order it may make such other provision as appears to it to be necessary for giving effect to the order, and in particular it may—

(a)   require any of the forfeited property to be paid or handed over to the proper officer or to a member of the Royal Ulster Constabulary designated for the purpose by the Chief Constable;

(b)   direct any of the forfeited property other than money or land to be sold or otherwise disposed of in such manner as the court may direct and the proceeds (if any) to be paid to the proper officer;

(c)   appoint a receiver to take possession, subject to such conditions and exceptions as may be specified by the court, of any of the forfeited property, to realise it in such manner as the court may direct and to pay the proceeds to the proper officer;

(d)   direct a specified part of any forfeited money, or of the proceeds of the sale, disposal or realisation of any forfeited property, to be paid by the proper officer to a specified person falling within section 23(7).

(2)   A forfeiture order shall not come into force until there is no further possibility of it being varied, or set aside, on appeal (disregarding any power of a court to grant leave to appeal out of time).

(3)   In sub-paragraph (1)(b) and (d) a reference to the proceeds of the sale, disposal or realisation of property is a reference to the proceeds after deduction of the costs of sale, disposal or realisation.

(4)   Article 58 of the Magistrates' Courts (Northern Ireland) Order 1981 (disposal of non-pecuniary forfeitures) shall not apply.

31.—(1)   A receiver appointed under paragraph 30 shall be entitled to be paid his remuneration and expenses by the proper officer out of the proceeds of the property realised by the receiver and paid to the proper officer under paragraph 30(1)(c).

(2)   If and so far as those proceeds are insufficient, the receiver shall be entitled to be paid his remuneration and expenses by the prosecutor.

(3)   A receiver appointed under paragraph 30 shall not be liable to any person in respect of any loss or damage resulting from action—

(a)   which he takes in relation to property which is not forfeited property, but which he reasonably believes to be forfeited property,

(b)   which he would be entitled to take if the property were forfeited property, and

(c)   which he reasonably believes that he is entitled to take because of his belief that the property is forfeited property.

(4)   Sub-paragraph (3) does not apply in so far as the loss or damage is caused by the receiver's negligence.

32.—(1)   In paragraphs 30 and 31 'the proper officer' means—

(a)   where the forfeiture order is made by a court of summary jurisdiction, the clerk of petty sessions, and

(b)   where the forfeiture order is made by the Crown Court, the appropriate officer of the Crown Court.

(2)   The proper officer shall issue a certificate in respect of a forfeiture order if an application is made by—

(a)   the prosecutor in the proceedings in which the forfeiture order was made,

(b)   the defendant in those proceedings, or

(c)   a person whom the court heard under section 23(7) before making the order.

(3)   The certificate shall state the extent (if any) to which, at the date of the certificate, effect has been given to the forfeiture order.

(4)   Any balance in the hands of the proper officer after making any payment required under paragraph 30(1)(d) or 31 shall be treated for the purposes of section 20 of the Administration of Justice (Northern Ireland) Act 1954 (application of fines, &c.) as if it were a fine.

Restraint orders

33.—(1)   The High Court may make a restraint order under this paragraph where—

(a)   proceedings have been instituted in Northern Ireland for an offence under any of sections 15 to 18,

(b)   the proceedings have not been concluded,

(c)   an application for a restraint order is made to the High Court by the prosecutor, and

(d)   a forfeiture order has been made, or it appears to the High Court that a forfeiture order may be made, in the proceedings for the offence.

(2)   The High Court may also make a restraint order under this paragraph where—

(a)   it is satisfied that a person is to be charged in Northern Ireland with an offence under any of sections 15 to 18,

(b)   an application for a restraint order is made to the High Court by the person who the High Court is satisfied will have the conduct of the proposed proceedings for the offence, and

(c)   it appears to the High Court that a forfeiture order may be made in those proceedings.

(3)   A restraint order prohibits a person to whom notice of it is given, subject to any conditions and exceptions specified in the order, from dealing with property in respect of which a forfeiture order has been or could be made in the proceedings referred to in sub-paragraph (1) or (2).

(4)   An application for a restraint order may be made to a judge in chambers without notice.

(5)   For the purposes of this paragraph a reference to dealing with property includes a reference to removing the property from Northern Ireland.

34.—(1)   A restraint order shall provide for notice of it to be given to any person affected by the order.

(2)   A restraint order may be discharged or varied by the High Court on the application of a person affected by it.

(3)   In particular, a restraint order shall be discharged on an application under sub-paragraph (2)—

(a)   in the case of an order made under paragraph 33(2), if the proceedings in respect of the offence are not instituted within such time as the High Court considers reasonable, and

(b)   in any case, if the proceedings for the offence have been concluded.

35.—(1)   A constable may seize any property subject to a restraint order for the purpose of preventing it from being removed from Northern Ireland.

(2)   Property seized under this paragraph shall be dealt with in accordance with the High Court's directions.

36.—(1)   The power to make a restraint order under the provisions of paragraph 33 shall be exercisable by the Secretary of State in any case in which it appears to him that the information which it would be necessary to provide in support of an application to the High Court or a judge under those provisions would, if disclosed, be likely to place any person in danger or prejudice the capability of members of the Royal Ulster Constabulary to investigate an offence under any of sections 15 to 18.

(2)   In their application by virtue of sub-paragraph (1) paragraphs 33 to 35 shall have effect with the necessary modifications and as if references to the High Court were references to the Secretary of State.

(3)   An order made by the Secretary of State by virtue of this paragraph may be varied or discharged by the High Court under paragraph 34.

37.—(1)   A person commits an offence if he contravenes a restraint order.

(2)   It is a defence for a person charged with an offence under this paragraph to prove that he had a reasonable excuse for the contravention.

(3)   A person guilty of an offence under this paragraph shall be liable—

(a)   on conviction on indictment, to imprisonment for a term not exceeding 14 years, to a fine or to both, or

(b)   on summary conviction, to imprisonment for a term not exceeding six months, to a fine not exceeding the statutory maximum, or to both.

(4)   Nothing in this paragraph shall be taken to prejudice any power of the High Court to deal with the contravention of a restraint order as a contempt of court.

38.—(1)   The prosecutor shall be treated for the purposes of section 66 of the Land Registration Act (Northern Ireland) 1970 (cautions) as a person interested in respect of any registered land to which a restraint order or an application for such an order relates.

(2)   On the application of the prosecutor, the Registrar of Titles shall, in respect of any registered land to which a restraint order or an application for such an order relates, make an entry inhibiting any dealing with the land without the consent of the High Court.

(3)   Subsections (2) and (4) of section 67 of the Land Registration Act (Northern Ireland) 1970 (inhibitions) shall apply to an entry made on the application of the prosecutor under sub-paragraph (2) as they apply to an entry made on the application of any person interested in the registered land under subsection (1) of that section.

(4)   In this paragraph—

'registered land' has the meaning assigned to it by section 45(1)(a) of the Interpretation Act (Northern Ireland) 1954,

'Registrar of Titles' and 'entry' have the same meanings as in the Land Registration Act (Northern Ireland) 1970, and

'prosecutor' in a case where a restraint order is made under paragraph 33(2) or an application for such an order is made, means the person who the High Court is satisfied has or will have the conduct of the proposed proceedings.

Compensation

39.—(1)   This paragraph applies where a restraint order is discharged under paragraph 34(3)(a).

(2)   This paragraph also apples where a forfeiture order or a restraint order is made in or in relation to proceedings for an offence under any of sections 15 to 18 which—

(a)   do not result in conviction for an offence under any of those sections,

(b) result in conviction for an offence under any of those sections in respect of which the person convicted is subsequently pardoned by Her Majesty, or

(c) result in a conviction for an offence under any of those sections which is subsequently quashed.

(3) A person who had an interest in any property which was subject to the order may apply to the High Court for compensation.

(4) The High Court may order compensation to be paid to the applicant if satisfied—

(a) that there was a serious default on the part of a person concerned in the investigation or prosecution of the offence,

(b) that the person in default was or was acting as a member of the Royal Ulster Constabulary, or was a member of the Office of the Director of Public Prosecutions for Northern Ireland,

(c) that the applicant has suffered loss in consequence of anything done in relation to the property by or in pursuance of the forfeiture order or restraint order, and

(d) that, having regard to all the circumstances, it is appropriate to order compensation to be paid.

(5) The High Court shall not order compensation to be paid where it appears to it that proceedings for the offence would have been instituted even if the serious default had not occurred.

(6) Compensation payable under this paragraph shall be paid—

(a) where the person in default was or was acting as a member of the Royal Ulster Constabulary, out of funds put at the disposal of the Chief Constable under section 10(5) of the Police (Northern Ireland) Act 1998, and

(b) where the person in default was a member of the Office of the Director of Public Prosecutions for Northern Ireland, by the Director of Public Prosecutions for Northern Ireland.

40.—(1) This paragraph applies where—

(a) a forfeiture order or a restraint order is made in or in relation to proceedings for an offence under any of sections 15 to 18, and

(b) the proceedings result in a conviction which is subsequently quashed on an appeal under section 7(2) or (5), as applied by section 8(2).

(2) A person who had an interest in any property which was subject to the order may apply to the High Court for compensation.

(3) The High Court may order compensation to be paid to the applicant if satisfied—

(a) that the applicant has suffered loss in consequence of anything done in relation to the property by or in pursuance of the forfeiture order or restraint order, and

(b) that, having regard to all the circumstances, it is appropriate to order compensation to be paid.

(4) Compensation payable under this paragraph shall be paid by the Secretary of State.

Proceedings for an offence: timing

41.—(1) For the purposes of this Part of this Schedule proceedings for an offence are instituted—

(a) when a summons or warrant is issued under Article 20 of the Magistrates' Courts (Northern Ireland) Order 1981 in respect of the offence;

(b) when a person is charged with the offence after being taken into custody without a warrant;

(c)   when an indictment charging a person with the offence is presented under section 2(2)(c), (e) or (f) of the Grand Jury (Abolition) Act (Northern Ireland) 1969.

(2)   Where the application of sub-paragraph (1) would result in there being more than one time for the institution of proceedings they shall be taken to be instituted at the earliest of those times.

(3)   For the purposes of this Part of this Schedule proceedings are concluded—

(a)   when a forfeiture order has been made in those proceedings and effect has been given to it in respect of all the forfeited property, or

(b)   when no forfeiture order has been made in those proceedings and there is no further possibility of one being made as a result of an appeal (disregarding any power of a court to grant leave to appeal out of time).

Enforcement of orders made elsewhere in the British Islands

42.   In the following provisions of this Part of this Schedule—
'an England and Wales order' means—

(a)   an order made in England and Wales under section 23 ('an England and Wales forfeiture order'),

(b)   an order made under paragraph 5 ('an England and Wales restraint order'), or

(c)   an order made under any other provision of Part I of this Schedule in relation to an England and Wales forfeiture or restraint order;
'a Scottish order' means—

(a)   an order made in Scotland under section 23 ('a Scottish forfeiture order'),

(b)   an order made under paragraph 18 ('a Scottish restraint order'), or

(c)   an order made under any other provision of Part II of this Schedule in relation to a Scottish forfeiture or restraint order;
'an Islands order' means an order made in any of the Islands under a provision of the law of that Island corresponding to—

(a)   section 23 ('an Islands forfeiture order'),

(b)   paragraph 33 ('an Islands restraint order'), or

(c)   any other provision of this Part of this Schedule.

43.—(1)   Subject to the provisions of this paragraph, an England and Wales, Scottish or Islands order shall have effect in the law of Northern Ireland.

(2)   But such an order shall be enforced in Northern Ireland only in accordance with—

(a)   the provisions of this paragraph, and

(b)   any provision made by rules of court as to the manner in which, and the conditions subject to which, such orders are to be enforced there.

(3)   On an application made to it in accordance with rules of court for registration of an England and Wales, Scottish or Islands order, the High Court shall direct that the order shall, in accordance with such rules, be registered in that court.

(4)   Rules of court shall also make provision—

(a)   for cancelling or varying the registration of an England and Wales, Scottish or Islands forfeiture order when effect has been given to it, whether in Northern Ireland or elsewhere, in respect of all or, as the case may be, part of the money or other property to which the order applies;

(b)   for cancelling or varying the registration of an England and Wales, Scottish or Islands restraint order which has been discharged or varied by the court by which it was made.

(5) If an England and Wales, Scottish or Islands forfeiture order is registered under this paragraph the High Court shall have, in relation to that order, the same powers as a court has under paragraph 30(1) to give effect to a forfeiture order made by it and—

(a) paragraph 31 shall apply accordingly,

(b) any functions of the clerk of petty sessions or the appropriate officer of the Crown Court shall be exercised by the appropriate officer of the High Court, and

(c) after making any payment required by virtue of paragraph 30(1)(d) or 31, the balance of any sums received by the appropriate officer of the High Court by virtue of an order made under this sub-paragraph shall be paid into the Consolidated Fund.

(6) If an England and Wales, Scottish or Islands restraint order is registered under this paragraph—

(a) paragraphs 35 and 38 shall apply as they apply to a restraint order under paragraph 33, and

(b) the High Court shall have the like power to make an order under section 21 of the Administration of Justice Act 1969 (extended power to order inspection of property, &c.) in relation to proceedings brought or likely to be brought for an England and Wales, Scottish or Islands restraint order as if those proceedings had been brought or were likely to be brought in the High Court.

(7) In addition, if an England and Wales, Scottish or Islands order is registered under this paragraph—

(a) the High Court shall have, in relation to its enforcement, the same power as if the order had originally been made in the High Court,

(b) proceedings for or with respect to its enforcement may be taken as if the order had originally been made in the High Court, and

(c) proceedings for or with respect to any contravention of such an order, whether before or after such registration, may be taken as if the order had originally been made in the High Court.

(8) The High Court may also make such orders or do otherwise as seems to it appropriate for the purpose of—

(a) assisting the achievement in Northern Ireland of the purposes of an England and Wales, Scottish or Islands order, or

(b) assisting any receiver or other person directed by any such order to sell or otherwise dispose of property.

(9) The following documents shall be received in evidence in Northern Ireland without further proof—

(a) a document purporting to be a copy of an England and Wales, Scottish or Islands order and to be certified as such by a proper officer of the court by which it was made, and

(b) a document purporting to be a certificate for purposes corresponding to those of paragraph 32(2) and (3) and to be certified by a proper officer of the court concerned.

Enforcement of orders made in designated countries

44.—(1) Her Majesty may by Order in Council make provision for the purpose of enabling the enforcement in Northern Ireland of external orders.

(2) An 'external order' means an order—

(a) which is made in a country or territory designated for the purposes of this paragraph by the Order in Council, and

(b) which makes relevant provision.

(3) 'Relevant provision' means—

(a)   provision for the forfeiture of terrorist property ('an external forfeiture order'), or

(b)   provision prohibiting dealing with property which is subject to an external forfeiture order or in respect of which such an order could be made in proceedings which have been or are to be instituted in the designated country or territory ('an external restraint order').

(4)   An Order in Council under this paragraph may, in particular, include provision—

(a)   which, for the purpose of facilitating the enforcement of any external order that may be made, has effect at times before there is an external order to be enforced;

(b)   for matters corresponding to those for which provision is made by, or can be made under, paragraph 43(1) to (8) in relation to the orders to which that paragraph applies;

(c)   for the proof of any matter relevant for the purposes of anything falling to be done in pursuance of the Order in Council.

(5)   An Order in Council under this paragraph may also make provision with respect to anything falling to be done on behalf of the United Kingdom in a designated country or territory in relation to proceedings in that country or territory for or in connection with the making of an external order.

(6)   An Order in Council under this paragraph—

(a)   may make different provision for different cases, and

(b)   shall not be made unless a draft of it has been laid before and approved by resolution of each House of Parliament.

PART IV
INSOLVENCY: UNITED KINGDOM PROVISIONS

General

45.   In this Part of this Schedule—

'ancillary order' means an order made in connection with a forfeiture, other than the forfeiture order,

'forfeiture order' means—

(a)   an order made in England and Wales, Scotland or Northern Ireland under section 23,

(b)   an Islands forfeiture order within the meaning given in paragraph 12, 26 or 42, or

(c)   an external forfeiture order which is enforceable in England and Wales, Scotland or Northern Ireland by virtue of an Order in Council made under paragraph 14, 28 or 44,

'forfeited property' means the money or other property to which a forfeiture order applies, and

'restraint order' means—

(a)   an order made under paragraph 5, 18 or 33,

(b)   an Islands restraint order within the meaning given in paragraph 12, 26 or 42, or

(c)   an external restraint order which is enforceable in England and Wales, Scotland or Northern Ireland by virtue of an Order in Council made under paragraph 14, 28 or 44.

Protection of creditors against forfeiture

46.—(1)   During the period of six months beginning with the making of a forfeiture order, the following shall not be finally disposed of under this Schedule—

(a)   the money to which the order applies, and

(b)   the money which represents any property to which the order applies.

(2)   For the purposes of this paragraph money is finally disposed of under this Schedule when—

(a)   in England and Wales, it is paid to the Lord Chancellor in accordance with section 60 of the Justices of the Peace Act 1997 (application of fines, &c.) or to the Secretary of State in accordance with paragraph 13(5)(c),

(b)   in Scotland, it is paid to the Treasury in accordance with section 211(5) of the Criminal Procedure (Scotland) Act 1995 (as modified by paragraph 16(3)), or

(c)   in Northern Ireland, it is paid into the Consolidated Fund in accordance with paragraph 32(4) or 43(5)(c).

47.—(1)   This paragraph applies where—

(a)   before or after a forfeiture order is made, the commencement of an insolvency occurs in qualifying insolvency proceedings,

(b)   an insolvency practitioner would, but for the forfeiture order, exercise a function in those proceedings in relation to property to which the forfeiture order applies, and

(c)   he gives written notice to the relevant officer of the matters referred to in paragraphs (a) and (b) before the end of the period of six months beginning with the making of the forfeiture order.

(2)   Sub-paragraph (3) shall apply to—

(a)   the property in relation to which the insolvency practitioner would, but for the forfeiture order, exercise a function as described in sub-paragraph (1)(b), and

(b)   the proceeds of sale of that property.

(3)   The property—

(a)   shall cease to be subject to the forfeiture order and any ancillary order, and

(b)   shall be dealt with in the insolvency proceedings as if the forfeiture order had never been made.

(4)   But—

(a)   the property to which sub-paragraph (3) applies is the balance remaining after the relevant officer has exercised his powers under paragraph 50(1), and

(b)   sub-paragraph (3) shall not take effect in respect of property in relation to which the relevant officer, or any person acting in pursuance of an ancillary order, has incurred obligations until those obligations have been discharged.

(5)   In this paragraph 'the commencement of an insolvency' means—

(a)   the making of a bankruptcy order,

(b)   the award of sequestration,

(c)   in England and Wales or in Northern Ireland, in the case of the insolvent estate of a deceased person, the making of an insolvency administration order, or

(d)   in the case of a company, the passing of a resolution for its winding up, or where no such resolution has been passed, the making of an order by the court for the winding up of the company.

48.—(1)   Where by virtue of paragraph 47(3) property falls to be dealt with in insolvency proceedings, the Secretary of State shall be taken to be a creditor in those proceedings to the amount or value of the property.

(2)   Except in a sequestration, his debt—

(a)   shall rank after the debts of all other creditors, and

(b)   shall not be paid until they have been paid in full with interest under the relevant provision.

(3)   In sub-paragraph (2)(b) the 'relevant provision' means—

(a)   in relation to the winding up of a company in England and Wales or Scotland, section 189(2) of the Insolvency Act 1986,

(b)   in relation to a bankruptcy in England and Wales, section 328(4) of that Act,

(c)   in relation to the winding up of a company in Northern Ireland, Article 160(2) of the Insolvency (Northern Ireland) Order 1989, and

(d)   in relation to a bankruptcy in Northern Ireland, Article 300(4) of that Order.

(4)   In a sequestration, his debt shall rank after all of the debts mentioned in section 51(1) of the Bankruptcy (Scotland) Act 1985 and shall not be paid until they have been paid in full.

(5)   Sub-paragraphs (2) to (4) apply notwithstanding any provision contained in or made under any other enactment.

49.—(1)   This paragraph applies to property which ceased to be subject to a forfeiture order by virtue of paragraph 47(3) in consequence of the making of a bankruptcy order or an award of sequestration.

(2)   The property shall again become subject to the forfeiture order and, if applicable, any ancillary order if—

(a)   the bankruptcy order is annulled, or

(b)   the award of sequestration is recalled or reduced.

(3)   Where the property is money or has been converted into money—

(a)   the relevant court shall make an order specifying property comprised in the estate of the bankrupt or debtor to the amount or value of the property, and

(b)   the specified property shall become subject to the forfeiture order, and any applicable ancillary order, in place of the property.

(4)   In sub-paragraph (3) the 'relevant court' means—

(a)   the court which ordered the annulment of the bankruptcy, or

(b)   the court which recalled or reduced the award of sequestration.

Expenses incurred in connection with forfeiture

50.—(1)   Where money or other property falls to be dealt with in accordance with paragraph 47(3), the relevant officer may—

(a)   deduct allowable forfeiture expenses from that money;

(b)   retain so much of that property as he considers necessary for the purpose of realising it and deducting allowable forfeiture expenses from the proceeds of realisation.

(2)   Where property is delivered up in pursuance of paragraph 47(3) and the relevant officer has not made provision under sub-paragraph (1) for all the allowable forfeiture expenses then—

(a)   a person who has incurred allowable forfeiture expenses for which provision has not been made shall have a claim to their value in the insolvency proceedings, and

(b)   the expenses in question shall be treated for the purposes of the insolvency proceedings as if they were expenses of those proceedings.

(3)   In this paragraph 'allowable forfeiture expenses'—

(a)   means expenses incurred in relation to the forfeited property by the relevant officer,

(b)   means expenses incurred in relation to the forfeited property by a receiver, administrator or other person appointed by the relevant officer,

(c)   means expenses incurred in relation to the forfeited property by any person appointed or directed to deal with any property under paragraph 16, and

(d)   includes sums paid or required to be paid under paragraph 2(1)(d), 16(1)(c) or 30(1)(d).

Protection of insolvency practitioners

51.—(1)   This paragraph applies where an insolvency practitioner seizes or disposes of property which is subject to a forfeiture order or a restraint order and—

(a)   he reasonably believes that he is entitled to do so in the exercise of his functions, and

(b)   he would be so entitled if the property were not subject to a forfeiture order or a restraint order.

(2)   The insolvency practitioner shall not be liable to any person in respect of any loss or damage resulting from the seizure or disposal except in so far as the loss or damage is caused by his negligence.

(3)   The insolvency practitioner shall have a lien on the property seized or the proceeds of its sale—

(a)   for such of his expenses as were incurred in connection with the insolvency proceedings in relation to which the seizure or disposal purported to take place, and

(b)   for so much of his remuneration as may be reasonably assigned for his acting in connection with those proceedings.

(4)   Sub-paragraphs (1) to (3) are without prejudice to the generality of any provision contained in the Insolvency Act 1986 or the Bankruptcy (Scotland) Act 1985 or any other Act or the Insolvency (Northern Ireland) Order 1989.

(5)   In this paragraph 'insolvency practitioner', in any part of the United Kingdom, means a person acting as an insolvency practitioner in that or any other part of the United Kingdom.

(6)   For the purpose of sub-paragraph (5) any question whether a person is acting as an insolvency practitioner in England and Wales or in Scotland shall be determined in accordance with section 388 of the Insolvency Act 1986, except that—

(a)   the reference in section 388(2)(a) to a permanent or interim trustee in the sequestration of a debtor's estate shall be taken to include a reference to a trustee in sequestration,

(b)   section 388(5) shall be disregarded, and

(c)   the expression shall also include the Official Receiver acting as receiver or manager of property.

(7)   For the purpose of sub-paragraph (5) any question whether a person is acting as an insolvency practitioner in Northern Ireland shall be determined in accordance with Article 3 of the {/ci} Insolvency (Northern Ireland) Order 1989, except that—

(a)   Article 3(5) shall be disregarded, and

(b)   the expression shall also include the Official Receiver acting as receiver or manager of property.

Insolvency practitioners in the Islands and designated countries

52.—(1)   An order may be made under this paragraph to secure that an Islands or external insolvency practitioner has the same rights under this Part of this Schedule in relation to—

(a)   property situated in England and Wales,

(b)   property situated in Scotland, or

(c)   property situated in Northern Ireland,

as he would have if he were an insolvency practitioner in that part of the United Kingdom.

(2)   The Secretary of State may make an order—

(a)   under sub-paragraph (1)(a) with the concurrence of the Lord Chancellor;

(b)   under sub-paragraph (1)(b).

(3)   An order under sub-paragraph (1)(c)—

(a)   may be made by the Department of Enterprise, Trade and Investment in Northern Ireland,

(b)   shall be a statutory rule for the purposes of the Statutory Rules (Northern Ireland) Order 1979, and

(c)   shall be subject to negative resolution within the meaning of section 41(6) of the Interpretation (Northern Ireland) Act 1954.

(4)   An order under this paragraph may, in particular, include—

(a)   provision which modifies the rights under this Part of this Schedule which are to be conferred under the order;

(b)   provision as to the manner in which the rights conferred under the order are to be exercised;

(c)   provision as to the conditions subject to which those rights are to be exercised, including the obtaining of leave from a court;

(d)   provision for empowering a court granting such leave to impose such conditions as it thinks fit.

(5)   An order under this paragraph may make different provision for different purposes.

(6)   In this paragraph—

'Islands or external insolvency practitioner' means a person exercising under the insolvency law of a relevant country or territory functions corresponding to those exercised by insolvency practitioners under the insolvency law of any part of the United Kingdom,

'insolvency law' has the same meaning as in section 426(10) of the Insolvency Act 1986, except that the reference to a relevant country or territory shall be construed in accordance with this paragraph, and

'relevant country or territory' means—

(a)   any of the Channel Islands,

(b)   the Isle of Man, or

(c)   any country or territory designated as mentioned in paragraph 14, 28 or 44.

Interpretation

53.—(1)   In this Part of this Schedule (other than in paragraph 51) 'insolvency practitioner' means a person acting in any qualifying insolvency proceedings in any part of the United Kingdom as—

(a)   a liquidator of a company or partnership,

(b)   a trustee in bankruptcy,

(c)   the permanent or interim trustee on the debtor's estate,

(d)   an administrator of the insolvent estate of a deceased person, or

(e)   a receiver or manager of any property.

(2)   In this Part of this Schedule 'qualifying insolvency proceedings' means—

(a)   any proceedings under the Insolvency Act 1986 or the Insolvency (Northern Ireland) Order 1989 for the winding up of a company or an unregistered company and includes any voluntary winding up of a company under Part IV of that Act or Part V of that Order,

(b)   any proceedings in England and Wales or Northern Ireland under or by virtue of section 420 of the Insolvency Act 1986 or Article 364 of the Insolvency (Northern Ireland) Order 1989 for the winding up of an insolvent partnership,

(c)   any proceedings in bankruptcy or, in Scotland, any sequestration of a debtor's estate, or

(d)   any proceedings in England and Wales or in Northern Ireland under or by virtue of section 421 of the Insolvency Act 1986 or Article 365 of the Insolvency (Northern Ireland) Order 1989 in relation to the insolvent estate of a deceased person.

(3)   In this Part of this Schedule 'the relevant officer' means in England and Wales and in Northern Ireland—

(a)   where the forfeiture order in question is made by a court in England and Wales, the proper officer within the meaning given in paragraph 4,

(b)   where the forfeiture order in question is made by a court in Northern Ireland, the proper officer within the meaning given in paragraph 32, and

(c)   in any other case, the appropriate officer of the High Court.

(4)   In this Part of this Schedule 'the relevant officer' means in Scotland—

(a)   where the forfeiture order in question is made by a court in Scotland, the clerk of the court,

(b)   in any other case, the Principal Clerk of Session and Justiciary.

(5)   In this Part of this Schedule references to the proceeds of sale or realisation of property are references to the proceeds after deduction of the costs of sale or realisation.

SCHEDULE 5
TERRORIST INVESTIGATIONS: INFORMATION

PART I
ENGLAND AND WALES AND NORTHERN IRELAND

Searches

1.—(1)   A constable may apply to a justice of the peace for the issue of a warrant under this paragraph for the purposes of a terrorist investigation.

(2)   A warrant under this paragraph shall authorise any constable—

(a)   to enter the premises specified in the warrant,

(b)   to search the premises and any person found there, and

(c)   to seize and retain any relevant material which is found on a search under paragraph (b).

(3)   For the purpose of sub-paragraph (2)(c) material is relevant if the constable has reasonable grounds for believing that—

(a)   it is likely to be of substantial value, whether by itself or together with other material, to a terrorist investigation, and

(b)   it must be seized in order to prevent it from being concealed, lost, damaged, altered or destroyed.

(4)   A warrant under this paragraph shall not authorise—

(a)   the seizure and retention of items subject to legal privilege, or

(b)   a constable to require a person to remove any clothing in public except for headgear, footwear, an outer coat, a jacket or gloves.

(5)   Subject to paragraph 2, a justice may grant an application under this paragraph if satisfied—

(a)   that the warrant is sought for the purposes of a terrorist investigation,

(b)   that there are reasonable grounds for believing that there is material on premises specified in the application which is likely to be of substantial value, whether by itself or together with other material, to a terrorist investigation and which does not consist of or include excepted material (within the meaning of paragraph 4 below), and

    (c)   that the issue of a warrant is likely to be necessary in the circumstances of the case.

2.—(1)   This paragraph applies where an application is made under paragraph 1 and—

    (a)   the application is made by a police officer of at least the rank of superintendent,

    (b)   the application does not relate to residential premises, and

    (c)   the justice to whom the application is made is not satisfied of the matter referred to in paragraph 1(5)(c).

(2)   The justice may grant the application if satisfied of the matters referred to in paragraph 1(5)(a) and (b).

(3)   Where a warrant under paragraph 1 is issued by virtue of this paragraph, the powers under paragraph 1(2)(a) and (b) are exercisable only within the period of 24 hours beginning with the time when the warrant is issued.

(4)   For the purpose of sub-paragraph (1) 'residential premises' means any premises which the officer making the application has reasonable grounds for believing are used wholly or mainly as a dwelling.

3.—(1)   Subject to sub-paragraph (2), a police officer of at least the rank of superintendent may by a written authority signed by him authorise a search of specified premises which are wholly or partly within a cordoned area.

(2)   A constable who is not of the rank required by sub-paragraph (1) may give an authorisation under this paragraph if he considers it necessary by reason of urgency.

(3)   An authorisation under this paragraph shall authorise any constable—

    (a)   to enter the premises specified in the authority,

    (b)   to search the premises and any person found there, and

    (c)   to seize and retain any relevant material (within the meaning of paragraph 1(3)) which is found on a search under paragraph (b).

(4)   The powers under sub-paragraph (3)(a) and (b) may be exercised—

    (a)   on one or more occasions, and

    (b)   at any time during the period when the designation of the cordoned area under section 33 has effect.

(5)   An authorisation under this paragraph shall not authorise—

    (a)   the seizure and retention of items subject to legal privilege;

    (b)   a constable to require a person to remove any clothing in public except for headgear, footwear, an outer coat, a jacket or gloves.

(6)   An authorisation under this paragraph shall not be given unless the person giving it has reasonable grounds for believing that there is material to be found on the premises which—

    (a)   is likely to be of substantial value, whether by itself or together with other material, to a terrorist investigation, and

    (b)   does not consist of or include excepted material.

(7)   A person commits an offence if he wilfully obstructs a search under this paragraph.

(8)   A person guilty of an offence under sub-paragraph (7) shall be liable on summary conviction to—

    (a)   imprisonment for a term not exceeding three months,

    (b)   a fine not exceeding level 4 on the standard scale, or

    (c)   both.

Excepted material

4.   In this Part—

(a)   'excluded material' has the meaning given by section 11 of the Police and Criminal Evidence Act 1984,

(b)   'items subject to legal privilege' has the meaning given by section 10 of that Act, and

(c)   'special procedure material' has the meaning given by section 14 of that Act; and material is 'excepted material' if it falls within any of paragraphs (a) to (c).

Excluded and special procedure material: production access

5.—(1)   A constable may apply to a Circuit judge for an order under this paragraph for the purposes of a terrorist investigation.

(2)   An application for an order shall relate to particular material, or material of a particular description, which consists of or includes excluded material or special procedure material.

(3)   An order under this paragraph may require a specified person—

(a)   to produce to a constable within a specified period for seizure and retention any material which he has in his possession, custody or power and to which the application relates;

(b)   to give a constable access to any material of the kind mentioned in paragraph (a) within a specified period;

(c)   to state to the best of his knowledge and belief the location of material to which the application relates if it is not in, and it will not come into, his possession, custody or power within the period specified under paragraph (a) or (b).

(4)   For the purposes of this paragraph—

(a)   an order may specify a person only if he appears to the Circuit judge to have in his possession, custody or power any of the material to which the application relates, and

(b)   a period specified in an order shall be the period of seven days beginning with the date of the order unless it appears to the judge that a different period would be appropriate in the particular circumstances of the application.

(5)   Where a Circuit judge makes an order under sub-paragraph (3)(b) in relation to material on any premises, he may, on the application of a constable, order any person who appears to the judge to be entitled to grant entry to the premises to allow any constable to enter the premises to obtain access to the material.

6.—(1)   A Circuit judge may grant an application under paragraph 5 if satisfied—

(a)   that the material to which the application relates consists of or includes excluded material or special procedure material,

(b)   that it does not include items subject to legal privilege, and

(c)   that the conditions in sub-paragraphs (2) and (3) are satisfied in respect of that material.

(2)   The first condition is that—

(a)   the order is sought for the purposes of a terrorist investigation, and

(b)   there are reasonable grounds for believing that the material is likely to be of substantial value, whether by itself or together with other material, to a terrorist investigation.

(3)   The second condition is that there are reasonable grounds for believing that it is in the public interest that the material should be produced or that access to it should be given having regard—

(a)   to the benefit likely to accrue to a terrorist investigation if the material is obtained, and

(b)   to the circumstances under which the person concerned has any of the material in his possession, custody or power.

7.—(1)   An order under paragraph 5 may be made in relation to—

(a)   material consisting of or including excluded or special procedure material which is expected to come into existence within the period of 28 days beginning with the date of the order;

(b)   a person who the Circuit judge thinks is likely to have any of the material to which the application relates in his possession, custody or power within that period.

(2)   Where an order is made under paragraph 5 by virtue of this paragraph, paragraph 5(3) shall apply with the following modifications—

(a)   the order shall require the specified person to notify a named constable as soon as is reasonably practicable after any material to which the application relates comes into his possession, custody or power,

(b)   the reference in paragraph 5(3)(a) to material which the specified person has in his possession, custody or power shall be taken as a reference to the material referred to in paragraph (a) above which comes into his possession, custody or power, and

(c)   the reference in paragraph 5(3)(c) to the specified period shall be taken as a reference to the period of 28 days beginning with the date of the order.

(3)   Where an order is made under paragraph 5 by virtue of this paragraph, paragraph 5(4) shall not apply and the order—

(a)   may only specify a person falling within sub-paragraph (1)(b), and

(b)   shall specify the period of seven days beginning with the date of notification required under sub-paragraph (2)(a) unless it appears to the judge that a different period would be appropriate in the particular circumstances of the application.

8.—(1)   An order under paragraph 5—

(a)   shall not confer any right to production of, or access to, items subject to legal privilege, and

(b)   shall have effect notwithstanding any restriction on the disclosure of information imposed by statute or otherwise.

(2)   Where the material to which an application under paragraph 5 relates consists of information contained in a computer—

(a)   an order under paragraph 5(3)(a) shall have effect as an order to produce the material in a form in which it can be taken away and in which it is visible and legible, and

(b)   an order under paragraph 5(3)(b) shall have effect as an order to give access to the material in a form in which it is visible and legible.

9.—(1)   An order under paragraph 5 may be made in relation to material in the possession, custody or power of a government department.

(2)   Where an order is made by virtue of sub-paragraph (1)—

(a)   it shall be served as if the proceedings were civil proceedings against the department, and

(b)   it may require any officer of the department, whether named in the order or not, who may for the time being have in his possession, custody or power the material concerned, to comply with the order.

(3)   In this paragraph 'government department' means an authorised government department for the purposes of the Crown Proceedings Act 1947.

10.—(1) An order of a Circuit judge under paragraph 5 shall have effect as if it were an order of the Crown Court.

(2) Crown Court Rules may make provision about proceedings relating to an order under paragraph 5.

(3) In particular, the rules may make provision about the variation or discharge of an order.

Excluded or special procedure material: search

11.—(1) A constable may apply to a Circuit judge for the issue of a warrant under this paragraph for the purposes of a terrorist investigation.

(2) A warrant under this paragraph shall authorise any constable—

    (a) to enter the premises specified in the warrant,

    (b) to search the premises and any person found there, and

    (c) to seize and retain any relevant material which is found on a search under paragraph (b).

(3) A warrant under this paragraph shall not authorise—

    (a) the seizure and retention of items subject to legal privilege;

    (b) a constable to require a person to remove any clothing in public except for headgear, footwear, an outer coat, a jacket or gloves.

(4) For the purpose of sub-paragraph (2)(c) material is relevant if the constable has reasonable grounds for believing that it is likely to be of substantial value, whether by itself or together with other material, to a terrorist investigation.

12.—(1) A Circuit judge may grant an application under paragraph 11 if satisfied that an order made under paragraph 5 in relation to material on the premises specified in the application has not been complied with.

(2) A Circuit judge may also grant an application under paragraph 11 if satisfied that there are reasonable grounds for believing that—

    (a) there is material on premises specified in the application which consists of or includes excluded material or special procedure material but does not include items subject to legal privilege, and

    (b) the conditions in sub-paragraphs (3) and (4) are satisfied.

(3) The first condition is that—

    (a) the warrant is sought for the purposes of a terrorist investigation, and

    (b) the material is likely to be of substantial value, whether by itself or together with other material, to a terrorist investigation.

(4) The second condition is that it is not appropriate to make an order under paragraph 5 in relation to the material because—

    (a) it is not practicable to communicate with any person entitled to produce the material,

    (b) it is not practicable to communicate with any person entitled to grant access to the material or entitled to grant entry to the premises on which the material is situated, or

    (c) a terrorist investigation may be seriously prejudiced unless a constable can secure immediate access to the material.

Explanations

13.—(1) A constable may apply to a Circuit judge for an order under this paragraph requiring any person specified in the order to provide an explanation of any material—

(a)   seized in pursuance of a warrant under paragraph 1 or 11, or

(b)   produced or made available to a constable under paragraph 5.

(2)   An order under this paragraph shall not require any person to disclose any information which he would be entitled to refuse to disclose on grounds of legal professional privilege in proceedings in the High Court.

(3)   But a lawyer may be required to provide the name and address of his client.

(4)   A statement by a person in response to a requirement imposed by an order under this paragraph—

(a)   may be made orally or in writing, and

(b)   may be used in evidence against him only on a prosecution for an offence under paragraph 14.

(5)   Paragraph 10 shall apply to orders under this paragraph as it applies to orders under paragraph 5.

14.—(1)   A person commits an offence if, in purported compliance with an order under paragraph 13, he—

(a)   makes a statement which he knows to be false or misleading in a material particular, or

(b)   recklessly makes a statement which is false or misleading in a material particular.

(2)   A person guilty of an offence under sub-paragraph (1) shall be liable—

(a)   on conviction on indictment, to imprisonment for a term not exceeding two years, to a fine or to both, or

(b)   on summary conviction, to imprisonment for a term not exceeding six months, to a fine not exceeding the statutory maximum or to both.

Urgent cases

15.—(1)   A police officer of at least the rank of superintendent may by a written order signed by him give to any constable the authority which may be given by a search warrant under paragraph 1 or 11.

(2)   An order shall not be made under this paragraph unless the officer has reasonable grounds for believing—

(a)   that the case is one of great emergency, and

(b)   that immediate action is necessary.

(3)   Where an order is made under this paragraph particulars of the case shall be notified as soon as is reasonably practicable to the Secretary of State.

(4)   A person commits an offence if he wilfully obstructs a search under this paragraph.

(5)   A person guilty of an offence under sub-paragraph (4) shall be liable on summary conviction to—

(a)   imprisonment for a term not exceeding three months,

(b)   a fine not exceeding level 4 on the standard scale, or

(c)   both.

16.—(1)   If a police officer of at least the rank of superintendent has reasonable grounds for believing that the case is one of great emergency he may by a written notice signed by him require any person specified in the notice to provide an explanation of any material seized in pursuance of an order under paragraph 15.

(2)   Sub-paragraphs (2) to (4) of paragraph 13 and paragraph 14 shall apply to a notice under this paragraph as they apply to an order under paragraph 13.

(3)   A person commits an offence if he fails to comply with a notice under this paragraph.

(4) It is a defence for a person charged with an offence under sub-paragraph (3) to show that he had a reasonable excuse for his failure.

(5) A person guilty of an offence under sub-paragraph (3) shall be liable on summary conviction to—

(a) imprisonment for a term not exceeding six months,

(b) a fine not exceeding level 5 on the standard scale, or

(c) both.

Supplementary

17. For the purposes of sections 21 and 22 of the Police and Criminal Evidence Act 1984 (seized material: access, copying and retention)—

(a) a terrorist investigation shall be treated as an investigation of or in connection with an offence, and

(b) material produced in pursuance of an order under paragraph 5 shall be treated as if it were material seized by a constable.

Northern Ireland

18. In the application of this Part to Northern Ireland—

(a) the reference in paragraph 4(a) to section 11 of the Police and Criminal Evidence Act 1984 shall be taken as a reference to Article 13 of the Police and Criminal Evidence (Northern Ireland) Order 1989,

(b) the reference in paragraph 4(b) to section 10 of that Act shall be taken as a reference to Article 12 of that Order,

(c) the reference in paragraph 4(c) to section 14 of that Act shall be taken as a reference to Article 16 of that Order,

(d) the references in paragraph 9(1) and (2) to 'government department' shall be taken as including references to an authorised Northern Ireland department for the purposes of the Crown Proceedings Act 1947,

(e) the reference in paragraph 10(2) to 'Crown Court Rules' shall be taken as a reference to county court rules,

(f) the reference in paragraph 17 to sections 21 and 22 of the Police and Criminal Evidence Act 1984 shall be taken as a reference to Articles 23 and 24 of the Police and Criminal Evidence (Northern Ireland) Order 1989, and

(g) references to 'a Circuit judge' shall be taken as references to a county court judge.

19.—(1) The Secretary of State may by a written order which relates to specified premises give to any constable in Northern Ireland—

(a) the authority which may be given by a search warrant under paragraph 1;

(b) the authority which may be given by a search warrant under paragraph 11.

(2) An order shall not be made under this paragraph unless—

(a) it appears to the Secretary of State that the information which it would be necessary to provide to the court in support of an application for a warrant would, if disclosed, be likely to place any person in danger or prejudice the capability of members of the Royal Ulster Constabulary to investigate an offence under any of sections 15 to 18 or under section 56, and

(b) the order is made for the purposes of an investigation of the commission, preparation or instigation of an offence under any of sections 15 to 18 or under section 56.

(3) The Secretary of State may make an order under sub-paragraph (1)(a) in relation to particular premises only if satisfied—

(a)   that there are reasonable grounds for believing that there is material on the premises which is likely to be of substantial value, whether by itself or together with other material, to the investigation mentioned in sub-paragraph (2)(b), and which does not consist of or include excepted material, and

(b)   that the authority of an order is likely to be necessary in the circumstances of the case.

(4)   The Secretary of State may make an order under sub-paragraph (1)(b) in relation to particular premises if satisfied that an order made under paragraph 5 in relation to material on the premises has not been complied with.

(5)   The Secretary of State may also make an order under sub-paragraph (1)(b) in relation to particular premises if satisfied that there are reasonable grounds for believing that—

(a)   there is material on the premises which consists of or includes excluded material or special procedure material but does not include items subject to legal privilege,

(b)   the material is likely to be of substantial value, whether by itself or together with other material, to the investigation mentioned in sub-paragraph (2)(b), and

(c)   an order under paragraph 5 would not be appropriate in relation to the material for the reason mentioned in paragraph 12(4)(a) or (b) or because the investigation mentioned in sub-paragraph (2)(b) might be seriously prejudiced unless a constable can secure immediate access to the material.

(6)   An order under sub-paragraph (1)(b) may not be made except in the circumstances specified in sub-paragraphs (4) and (5).

(7)   A person commits an offence if he wilfully obstructs a search under this paragraph.

(8)   A person guilty of an offence under sub-paragraph (7) shall be liable on summary conviction to—

(a)   imprisonment for a term not exceeding three months,

(b)   a fine not exceeding level 4 on the standard scale, or

(c)   both.

20.—(1)   The Secretary of State may exercise the power to make an order under paragraph 5 in relation to any person in Northern Ireland who is specified in the order.

(2)   An order shall not be made by virtue of this paragraph unless it appears to the Secretary of State that the information which it would be necessary to provide to a county court judge in support of an application for an order under paragraph 5 would, if disclosed—

(a)   be likely to place any person in danger, or

(b)   be likely to prejudice the capability of members of the Royal Ulster Constabulary to investigate an offence under any of sections 15 to 18 or under section 56.

(3)   Paragraphs 5 to 9 shall apply to the making of an order under paragraph 5 by virtue of this paragraph with the following modifications—

(a)   references to a county court judge shall be taken as references to the Secretary of State,

(b)   the references to 'a terrorist investigation' in paragraphs 5(1) and 6(2)(a) shall be taken as references to an investigation of the commission, preparation or instigation of an offence under any of sections 15 to 18 or under section 56, and

(c)   the references to 'a terrorist investigation' in paragraphs 6(2)(b) and 6(3)(a) shall be taken as references to the investigation mentioned in paragraph 6(2)(a).

(4)   Paragraph 10 shall not apply in relation to an order made under paragraph 5 by virtue of this paragraph.

(5)   The Secretary of State may vary or revoke an order made by virtue of this paragraph.

(6)   A person commits an offence if he contravenes an order made by virtue of this paragraph.

(7)   A person guilty of an offence under sub-paragraph (6) shall be liable—

(a)   on conviction on indictment, to imprisonment for a term not exceeding two years, to a fine or to both, or

(b)   on summary conviction, to imprisonment for a term not exceeding six months, to a fine not exceeding the statutory maximum or to both.

21.—(1)   The Secretary of State may by a written order require any person in Northern Ireland who is specified in the order to provide an explanation of any material—

(a)   seized in pursuance of an order under paragraph 19, or

(b)   produced or made available to a constable in pursuance of an order made by virtue of paragraph 20.

(2)   The provisions of paragraphs 13(2) to (4) and 14 shall apply to an order under this paragraph as they apply to an order under paragraph 13.

(3)   The provisions of paragraph 16(3) to (5) shall apply to an order under this paragraph as they apply to a notice under paragraph 16.

PART II
SCOTLAND

Order for production of material

22.—(1)   The procurator fiscal may apply to the sheriff for an order under this paragraph for the purposes of a terrorist investigation.

(2)   An application for an order shall relate to particular material, or material of a particular description.

(3)   An order under this paragraph may require a specified person—

(a)   to produce to a constable within a specified period for seizure and retention any material which he has in his possession, custody or power and to which the application relates;

(b)   to give a constable access to any material of the kind mentioned in paragraph (a) within a specified period;

(c)   to state to the best of his knowledge and belief the location of material to which the application relates if it is not in, and it will not come into, his possession, custody or power within the period specified under paragraph (a) or (b).

(4)   For the purposes of this paragraph—

(a)   an order may specify a person only if he appears to the sheriff to have in his possession, custody or power any of the material to which the application relates, and

(b)   a period specified in an order shall be the period of seven days beginning with the date of the order unless it appears to the sheriff that a different period would be appropriate in the particular circumstances of the application.

(5)   Where the sheriff makes an order under sub-paragraph (3)(b) in relation to material on any premises, he may, on the application of the procurator fiscal, order any person who appears to the sheriff to be entitled to grant entry to the premises to allow any constable to enter the premises to obtain access to the material.

23.—(1)   The sheriff may grant an application under paragraph 22 if satisfied that the conditions in sub-paragraphs (2) and (3) are satisfied in respect of that material.

(2)   The first condition is that—

(a)   the order is sought for the purposes of a terrorist investigation, and

(b)   there are reasonable grounds for believing that the material is likely to be of substantial value, whether by itself or together with other material, to a terrorist investigation.

(3)   The second condition is that there are reasonable grounds for believing that it is in the public interest that the material should be produced or that access to it should be given having regard—

(a)   to the benefit likely to accrue to a terrorist investigation if the material is obtained, and

(b)   to the circumstances under which the person concerned has any of the material in his possession, custody or power.

24.—(1)   An order under paragraph 22 may be made in relation to a person who appears to the sheriff to be likely to have any of the material to which the application relates in his possession, custody or power within the period of 28 days beginning with the date of the order.

(2)   Where an order is made under paragraph 22 by virtue of this paragraph, paragraph 22(3) shall apply with the following modifications—

(a)   the order shall require the specified person to notify a named constable as soon as is reasonably practicable after any material to which the application relates comes into his possession, custody or power,

(b)   the reference in paragraph 22(3)(a) to material which the specified person has in his possession, custody or power shall be taken as a reference to the material referred to in paragraph (a) above which comes into his possession, custody or power, and

(c)   the reference in paragraph 22(3)(c) to the specified period shall be taken as a reference to the period of 28 days beginning with the date of the order.

(3)   Where an order is made under paragraph 22 by virtue of this paragraph, paragraph 22(4) shall not apply and the order—

(a)   may only specify a person falling within sub-paragraph (1), and

(b)   shall specify the period of seven days beginning with the date of notification required under sub-paragraph (2)(a) unless it appears to the sheriff that a different period would be appropriate in the particular circumstances of the application.

25.—(1)   Subject to paragraph 33(1), an order under paragraph 22 shall have effect notwithstanding any obligation as to secrecy or other restriction on the disclosure of the information imposed by statute or otherwise.

(2)   Where the material to which an application under paragraph 22 relates consists of information contained in a computer—

(a)   an order under paragraph 22(3)(a) shall have effect as an order to produce the material in a form in which it can be taken away and in which it is visible and legible, and

(b)   an order under paragraph 22(3)(b) shall have effect as an order to give access to the material in a form in which it is visible and legible.

26.—(1)   An order under paragraph 22 may be made in relation to material in the possession, custody or power of a government department.

(2)   Where an order is made by virtue of sub-paragraph (1)—

(a)   it shall be served as if the proceedings were civil proceedings against the department, and

(b) it may require any officer of the department, whether named in the order or not, who may for the time being have in his possession, custody or power the material concerned, to comply with it.

(3) In this paragraph 'government department' means a public department within the meaning of the Crown Suits Scotland Act 1857 and any part of the Scottish Administration.

27.—(1) Provision may be made by Act of Adjournal as to—
(a) the recall and variation of orders under paragraph 22; and
(b) proceedings relating to such orders.

(2) The following provisions shall have effect pending the coming into force of an Act of Adjournal under sub-paragraph (1)—
(a) an order under paragraph 22 may be recalled or varied by the sheriff on a written application made to him by any person subject to the order;
(b) unless the sheriff otherwise directs on grounds of urgency, the applicant shall, not less than 48 hours before making the application, send a copy of it and a notice in writing of the time and place where the application is to be made to the procurator fiscal on whose application the order was made.

Searches

28.—(1) The procurator fiscal may apply to the sheriff to grant a warrant under this paragraph for the purposes of a terrorist investigation.

(2) A warrant under this paragraph shall authorise any constable—
(a) to enter the premises specified in the warrant,
(b) to search the premises and any person found there, and
(c) to seize and retain any relevant material which is found on a search under paragraph (b).

(3) For the purpose of sub-paragraph (2)(c) material is relevant if the constable has reasonable grounds for believing that it is likely to be of substantial value, whether by itself or together with other material, to a terrorist investigation.

(4) The sheriff may grant an application under this paragraph if satisfied—
(a) that the warrant is sought for the purposes of a terrorist investigation,
(b) that there are reasonable grounds for believing that there is material on premises specified in the application which is likely to be of substantial value to a terrorist investigation, and
(c) that one of the conditions in paragraph 29 is satisfied.

(5) Where a warrant is granted in relation to non-residential premises, the entry and search must be within the period of 24 hours beginning with the time when the warrant is granted.

(6) For the purpose of sub-paragraph (5) 'non-residential premises' means any premises other than those which the procurator fiscal has reasonable grounds for believing are used wholly or mainly as a dwelling.

(7) A warrant under this paragraph may authorise the persons named in the warrant to accompany the constable who is executing it.

29.—(1) The conditions referred to in paragraph 28(4)(c) are—
(a) that an order made under paragraph 28 in relation to material on the premises has not been complied with, or
(b) that for any of the reasons mentioned in sub-paragraph (2) it would not be appropriate to make such an order.

(2) The reasons are—

(a) it is not practicable to communicate with any person entitled to produce the material,

(b) it is not practicable to communicate with any person entitled to grant access to the material or entitled to grant entry to the premises on which the material is situated, or

(c) the investigation for the purposes of which the application is made may be seriously prejudiced unless a constable can secure immediate access to the material.

Explanations

30.—(1) The procurator fiscal may apply to the sheriff for an order under this paragraph requiring any person specified in the order to provide an explanation of any material—

(a) seized in pursuance of a warrant under paragraph 28, or

(b) produced or made available to a constable under paragraph 22.

(2) Without prejudice to paragraph 33(1), an order under this paragraph may require a lawyer to provide the name and address of his client.

(3) A statement by a person in response to a requirement imposed by an order under this paragraph may only be used in evidence against him—

(a) on a prosecution for an offence under section 2 of the False Oaths (Scotland) Act 1933, or

(b) on a prosecution for some other offence where in giving evidence he makes a statement inconsistent with it.

(4) Paragraphs 26 and 27 shall apply to orders under this paragraph as they apply to orders under paragraph 22.

Urgent cases

31.—(1) A police officer of at least the rank of superintendent may by a written order signed by him give to any constable the authority which may be given by a search warrant under paragraph 28.

(2) An order shall not be made under this paragraph unless the officer has reasonable grounds for believing—

(a) that the case is one of great emergency, and

(b) that immediate action is necessary.

(3) Where an order is made under this paragraph particulars of the case shall be notified as soon as is reasonably practicable to the Secretary of State.

32.—(1) If a police officer of at least the rank of superintendent has reasonable grounds for believing that the case is one of great emergency he may by a written notice signed by him require any person specified in the notice to provide an explanation of any material seized in pursuance of an order under paragraph 22.

(2) Sub-paragraphs (2) and (3) of paragraph 30 shall apply to a notice under this paragraph as they apply to an order under that paragraph.

(3) A person commits an offence if he fails to comply with a notice under this paragraph.

(4) It is a defence for a person charged with an offence under sub-paragraph (3) to show that he had a reasonable excuse for his failure.

(5) A person guilty of an offence under sub-paragraph (3) is liable on summary conviction to imprisonment for a term not exceeding six months, to a fine not exceeding level 5 on the standard scale or to both.

Supplementary

33.—(1)   This Part of this Schedule is without prejudice to any rule of law whereby—

(a)   communications between a professional legal adviser and his client, or

(b)   communications made in connection with or in contemplation of legal proceedings and for the purposes of those proceedings,

are in legal proceedings protected from disclosure on the ground of confidentiality.

(2)   For the purpose of exercising any powers conferred on him under this Part of this Schedule a constable may, if necessary, open lockfast places on premises specified in an order under paragraph 22, a warrant under paragraph 28 or a notice under paragraph 32.

(3)   A search of a person under this Part of this Schedule may only be carried out by a person of the same sex.

SCHEDULE 6
FINANCIAL INFORMATION

Orders

1.—(1)   Where an order has been made under this paragraph in relation to a terrorist investigation, a constable named in the order may require a financial institution to provide customer information for the purposes of the investigation.

(2)   The information shall be provided—

(a)   in such manner and within such time as the constable may specify, and

(b)   notwithstanding any restriction on the disclosure of information imposed by statute or otherwise.

(3)   An institution which fails to comply with a requirement under this paragraph shall be guilty of an offence.

(4)   It is a defence for an institution charged with an offence under sub-paragraph (3) to prove—

(a)   that the information required was not in the institution's possession, or

(b)   that it was not reasonably practicable for the institution to comply with the requirement.

(5)   An institution guilty of an offence under sub-paragraph (3) shall be liable on summary conviction to a fine not exceeding level 5 on the standard scale.

Procedure

2.   An order under paragraph 1 may be made only on the application of—

(a)   in England and Wales or Northern Ireland, a police officer of at least the rank of superintendent, or

(b)   in Scotland, the procurator fiscal.

3.   An order under paragraph 1 may be made only by—

(a)   in England and Wales, a Circuit judge,

(b)   in Scotland, the sheriff, or

(c)   in Northern Ireland, a county court judge.

4.—(1)   Crown Court Rules may make provision about the procedure for an application under paragraph 1.

(2)   The High Court of Justiciary may, by Act of Adjournal, make provision about the procedure for an application under paragraph 1.

Criteria for making order

5. An order under paragraph 1 may be made only if the person making it is satisfied that—

   (a)   the order is sought for the purposes of a terrorist investigation,

   (b)   the tracing of terrorist property is desirable for the purposes of the investigation, and

   (c)   the order will enhance the effectiveness of the investigation.

Financial institution

6.—(1)   In this Schedule 'financial institution' means—

   (a)   a person who carries on a business of taking deposits for which he is authorised under the Banking Act 1987,

   (b)   a building society (within the meaning of the Building Societies Act 1986),

   (c)   a credit union (within the meaning of the Credit Unions Act 1979 or the Credit Unions (Northern Ireland) Order 1985),

   (d)   a person carrying on investment business within the meaning of the Financial Services Act 1986,

   (e)   the National Savings Bank,

   (f)   a person who carries out an activity for the purposes of raising money authorised to be raised under the National Loans Act 1968 under the auspices of the Director of National Savings,

   (g)   a European institution carrying on a home regulated activity (within the meaning of the Second Council Directive on the coordination of laws, regulations and administrative provisions relating to the taking up and pursuit of the business of credit institutions),

   (h)   a person carrying out an activity specified in any of points 1 to 12 and 14 of the Annex to that Directive, and

   (i)   a person who carries on an insurance business in accordance with an authorisation pursuant to Article 6 or 27 of the First Council Directive on the coordination of laws, regulations and administrative provisions relating to the taking up and pursuit of the business of direct life assurance.

   (2)   The Secretary of State may by order provide for a class of person—

   (a)   to be a financial institution for the purposes of this Schedule, or

   (b)   to cease to be a financial institution for the purposes of this Schedule.

   (3)   An institution which ceases to be a financial institution for the purposes of this Schedule (whether by virtue of sub-paragraph (2)(b) or otherwise) shall continue to be treated as a financial institution for the purposes of any requirement under paragraph 1 to provide customer information which relates to a time when the institution was a financial institution.

Customer information

7.—(1)   In this Schedule 'customer information' means (subject to sub-paragraph (3))—

   (a)   information whether a business relationship exists or existed between a financial institution and a particular person ('a customer'),

   (b)   a customer's account number,

   (c)   a customer's full name,

   (d)   a customer's date of birth,

   (e)   a customer's address or former address,

   (f)   the date on which a business relationship between a financial institution and a customer begins or ends,

(g) any evidence of a customer's identity obtained by a financial institution in pursuance of or for the purposes of any legislation relating to money laundering, and

(h) the identity of a person sharing an account with a customer.

(2) For the purposes of this Schedule there is a business relationship between a financial institution and a person if (and only if)—

(a) there is an arrangement between them designed to facilitate the carrying out of frequent or regular transactions between them, and

(b) the total amount of payments to be made in the course of the arrangement is neither known nor capable of being ascertained when the arrangement is made.

(3) The Secretary of State may by order provide for a class of information—

(a) to be customer information for the purposes of this Schedule, or

(b) to cease to be customer information for the purposes of this Schedule.

Offence by body corporate, &c.

8.—(1) This paragraph applies where an offence under paragraph 1(3) is committed by an institution and it is proved that the offence—

(a) was committed with the consent or connivance of an officer of the institution, or

(b) was attributable to neglect on the part of an officer of the institution.

(2) The officer, as well as the institution, shall be guilty of the offence.

(3) Where an individual is convicted of an offence under paragraph 1(3) by virtue of this paragraph, he shall be liable on summary conviction to—

(a) imprisonment for a term not exceeding six months,

(b) a fine not exceeding level 5 on the standard scale, or

(c) both.

(4) In the case of an institution which is a body corporate, in this paragraph 'officer' includes—

(a) a director, manager or secretary,

(b) a person purporting to act as a director, manager or secretary, and

(c) if the affairs of the body are managed by its members, a member.

(5) In the case of an institution which is a partnership, in this paragraph 'officer' means a partner.

(6) In the case of an institution which is an unincorporated association (other than a partnership), in this paragraph 'officer' means a person concerned in the management or control of the association.

Self-incrimination

9.—(1) Customer information provided by a financial institution under this Schedule shall not be admissible in evidence in criminal proceedings against the institution or any of its officers or employees.

(2) Sub-paragraph (1) shall not apply in relation to proceedings for an offence under paragraph 1(3) (including proceedings brought by virtue of paragraph 8).

SCHEDULE 7
PORT AND BORDER CONTROLS

Interpretation

1.—(1) In this Schedule 'examining officer' means any of the following—

(a) a constable,

(b)   an immigration officer, and

(c)   a customs officer who is designated for the purpose of this Schedule by the Secretary of State and the Commissioners of Customs and Excise.

(2)   In this Schedule—

'the border area' has the meaning given by paragraph 4,

'captain' means master of a ship or commander of an aircraft,

'port' includes an airport and a hoverport,

'ship' includes a hovercraft, and

'vehicle' includes a train.

(3)   A place shall be treated as a port for the purposes of this Schedule in relation to a person if an examining officer believes that the person—

(a)   has gone there for the purpose of embarking on a ship or aircraft, or

(b)   has arrived there on disembarking from a ship or aircraft.

Power to stop, question and detain

2.—(1)   An examining officer may question a person to whom this paragraph applies for the purpose of determining whether he appears to be a person falling within section 40(1)(b).

(2)   This paragraph applies to a person if—

(a)   he is at a port or in the border area, and

(b)   the examining officer believes that the person's presence at the port or in the area is connected with his entering or leaving Great Britain or Northern Ireland.

(3)   This paragraph also applies to a person on a ship or aircraft which has arrived in Great Britain or Northern Ireland.

(4)   An examining officer may exercise his powers under this paragraph whether or not he has grounds for suspecting that a person falls within section 40(1)(b).

3.   An examining officer may question a person who is in the border area for the purpose of determining whether his presence in the area is connected with his entering or leaving Northern Ireland.

4.—(1)   A place in Northern Ireland is within the border area for the purposes of paragraphs 2 and 3 if it is no more than one mile from the border between Northern Ireland and the Republic of Ireland.

(2)   If a train goes from the Republic of Ireland to Northern Ireland, the first place in Northern Ireland at which it stops for the purpose of allowing passengers to leave is within the border area for the purposes of paragraphs 2 and 3.

5.   A person who is questioned under paragraph 2 or 3 must—

(a)   give the examining officer any information in his possession which the officer requests;

(b)   give the examining officer on request either a valid passport which includes a photograph or another document which establishes his identity;

(c)   declare whether he has with him documents of a kind specified by the examining officer;

(d)   give the examining officer on request any document which he has with him and which is of a kind specified by the officer.

6.—(1)   For the purposes of exercising a power under paragraph 2 or 3 an examining officer may—

    (a)   stop a person or vehicle;

    (b)   detain a person.

(2)   For the purpose of detaining a person under this paragraph, an examining officer may authorise the person's removal from a ship, aircraft or vehicle.

(3)   Where a person is detained under this paragraph the provisions of Part I of Schedule 8 (treatment) shall apply.

(4)   A person detained under this paragraph shall (unless detained under any other power) be released not later than the end of the period of nine hours beginning with the time when his examination begins.

Searches

7.   For the purpose of satisfying himself whether there are any persons whom he may wish to question under paragraph 2 an examining officer may—

    (a)   search a ship or aircraft;

    (b)   search anything on a ship or aircraft;

    (c)   search anything which he reasonably believes has been, or is about to be, on a ship or aircraft.

8.—(1)   An examining officer who questions a person under paragraph 2 may, for the purpose of determining whether he falls within section 40(1)(b)—

    (a)   search the person;

    (b)   search anything which he has with him, or which belongs to him, and which is on a ship or aircraft;

    (c)   search anything which he has with him, or which belongs to him, and which the examining officer reasonably believes has been, or is about to be, on a ship or aircraft;

    (d)   search a ship or aircraft for anything falling within paragraph (b).

(2)   Where an examining officer questions a person in the border area under paragraph 2 he may (in addition to the matters specified in sub-paragraph (1)), for the purpose of determining whether the person falls within section 40(1)(b)—

    (a)   search a vehicle;

    (b)   search anything in or on a vehicle;

    (c)   search anything which he reasonably believes has been, or is about to be, in or on a vehicle.

(3)   A search of a person under this paragraph must be carried out by someone of the same sex.

9.—(1)   An examining officer may examine goods to which this paragraph applies for the purpose of determining whether they have been used in the commission, preparation or instigation of acts of terrorism.

(2)   This paragraph applies to goods which have arrived in or are about to leave Great Britain or Northern Ireland on a ship, aircraft or vehicle.

(3)   In this paragraph 'goods' includes—

    (a)   property of any description, and

    (b)   containers.

(4)   An examining officer may board a ship or aircraft or enter a vehicle for the purpose of determining whether to exercise his power under this paragraph.

10.—(1)   An examining officer may authorise a person to carry out on his behalf a search or examination under any of paragraphs 7 to 9.

(2)   A person authorised under this paragraph shall be treated as an examining officer for the purposes of—

(a)   paragraphs 9(4) and 11 of this Schedule, and

(b)   paragraphs 2 and 3 of Schedule 14.

Detention of property

11.—(1)   This paragraph applies to anything which—

(a)   is given to an examining officer in accordance with paragraph 5(d),

(b)   is searched or found on a search under paragraph 8, or

(c)   is examined under paragraph 9.

(2)   An examining officer may detain the thing—

(a)   for the purpose of examination, for a period not exceeding seven days beginning with the day on which the detention commences,

(b)   while he believes that it may be needed for use as evidence in criminal proceedings, or

(c)   while he believes that it may be needed in connection with a decision by the Secretary of State whether to make a deportation order under the Immigration Act 1971.

Designated ports

12.—(1)   This paragraph applies to a journey—

(a)   to Great Britain from the Republic of Ireland, Northern Ireland or any of the Islands,

(b)   from Great Britain to any of those places,

(c)   to Northern Ireland from Great Britain, the Republic of Ireland or any of the Islands, or

(d)   from Northern Ireland to any of those places.

(2)   Where a ship or aircraft is employed to carry passengers for reward on a journey to which this paragraph applies the owners or agents of the ship or aircraft shall not arrange for it to call at a port in Great Britain or Northern Ireland for the purpose of disembarking or embarking passengers unless—

(a)   the port is a designated port, or

(b)   an examining officer approves the arrangement.

(3)   Where an aircraft is employed on a journey to which this paragraph applies otherwise than to carry passengers for reward, the captain of the aircraft shall not permit it to call at or leave a port in Great Britain or Northern Ireland unless—

(a)   the port is a designated port, or

(b)   he gives at least 12 hours' notice in writing to a constable for the police area in which the port is situated (or, where the port is in Northern Ireland, to a member of the Royal Ulster Constabulary).

(4)   A designated port is a port which appears in the Table at the end of this Schedule.

(5)   The Secretary of State may by order—

(a)   add an entry to the Table;

(b)   remove an entry from the Table.

Embarkation and disembarkation

13.—(1)   The Secretary of State may by notice in writing to the owners or agents of ships or aircraft—

(a)   designate control areas in any port in the United Kingdom;

(b) specify conditions for or restrictions on the embarkation or disembarkation of passengers in a control area.

(2) Where owners or agents of a ship or aircraft receive notice under sub-paragraph (1) in relation to a port they shall take all reasonable steps to ensure, in respect of the ship or aircraft—

(a) that passengers do not embark or disembark at the port outside a control area, and

(b) that any specified conditions are met and any specified restrictions are complied with.

14.—(1) The Secretary of State may by notice in writing to persons concerned with the management of a port in the United Kingdom ('the port managers')—

(a) designate control areas in the port;

(b) require the port managers to provide at their own expense specified facilities in a control area for the purposes of the embarkation or disembarkation of passengers or their examination under this Schedule;

(c) require conditions to be met and restrictions to be complied with in relation to the embarkation or disembarkation of passengers in a control area;

(d) require the port managers to display, in specified locations in control areas, notices containing specified information about the provisions of this Schedule in such form as may be specified.

(2) Where port managers receive notice under sub-paragraph (1) they shall take all reasonable steps to comply with any requirement set out in the notice.

15.—(1) This paragraph applies to a ship employed to carry passengers for reward, or an aircraft, which—

(a) arrives in Great Britain from the Republic of Ireland, Northern Ireland or any of the Islands,

(b) arrives in Northern Ireland from Great Britain, the Republic of Ireland or any of the Islands,

(c) leaves Great Britain for the Republic of Ireland, Northern Ireland or any of the Islands, or

(d) leaves Northern Ireland for Great Britain, the Republic of Ireland or any of the Islands.

(2) The captain shall ensure—

(a) that passengers and members of the crew do not disembark at a port in Great Britain or Northern Ireland unless either they have been examined by an examining officer or they disembark in accordance with arrangements approved by an examining officer;

(b) that passengers and members of the crew do not embark at a port in Great Britain or Northern Ireland except in accordance with arrangements approved by an examining officer;

(c) where a person is to be examined under this Schedule on board the ship or aircraft, that he is presented for examination in an orderly manner.

(3) Where paragraph 27 of Schedule 2 to the Immigration Act 1971 (disembarkation requirements on arrival in the United Kingdom) applies, the requirements of sub-paragraph (2)(a) above are in addition to the requirements of paragraph 27 of that Schedule.

Carding

16.—(1) The Secretary of State may by order make provision requiring a person to whom this paragraph applies, if required to do so by an examining officer, to complete and produce to the officer a card containing such information in such form as the order may specify.

(2) An order under this paragraph may require the owners or agents of a ship or aircraft employed to carry passengers for reward to supply their passengers with cards in the form required by virtue of sub-paragraph (1).

(3) This paragraph applies to a person—

(a) who disembarks in Great Britain from a ship or aircraft which has come from the Republic of Ireland, Northern Ireland or any of the Islands,

(b) who disembarks in Northern Ireland from a ship or aircraft which has come from Great Britain, the Republic of Ireland, or any of the Islands,

(c) who embarks in Great Britain on a ship or aircraft which is going to the Republic of Ireland, Northern Ireland or any of the Islands, or

(d) who embarks in Northern Ireland on a ship or aircraft which is going to Great Britain, the Republic of Ireland, or any of the Islands.

Provision of passenger information

17.—(1) This paragraph applies to a ship or aircraft which—

(a) arrives or is expected to arrive in Great Britain from the Republic of Ireland, Northern Ireland or any of the Islands, or

(b) arrives or is expected to arrive in Northern Ireland from Great Britain, the Republic of Ireland or any of the Islands.

(2) If an examining officer gives the owners or agents of a ship or aircraft to which this paragraph applies a written request to provide specified information, the owners or agents shall comply with the request as soon as is reasonably practicable.

(3) A request to an owner or agent may relate—

(a) to a particular ship or aircraft,

(b) to all ships or aircraft of the owner or agent to which this paragraph applies, or

(c) to specified ships or aircraft.

(4) Information may be specified in a request only if it is of a kind which is prescribed by order of the Secretary of State and which relates—

(a) to passengers,

(b) to crew, or

(c) to vehicles belonging to passengers or crew.

(5) A passenger or member of the crew on a ship or aircraft shall give the captain any information required for the purpose of enabling the owners or agents to comply with a request under this paragraph.

(6) Sub-paragraphs (2) and (5) shall not require the provision of information which is required to be provided under or by virtue of paragraph 27(2) or 27B of Schedule 2 to the Immigration Act 1971.

Offences

18.—(1) A person commits an offence if he—

(a) wilfully fails to comply with a duty imposed under or by virtue of this Schedule,

(b) wilfully contravenes a prohibition imposed under or by virtue of this Schedule, or

(c) wilfully obstructs, or seeks to frustrate, a search or examination under or by virtue of this Schedule.

(2) A person guilty of an offence under this paragraph shall be liable on summary conviction to—

(a) imprisonment for a term not exceeding three months,

(b) a fine not exceeding level 4 on the standard scale, or

(c) both.

TABLE
DESIGNATED PORTS
GREAT BRITAIN

Seaports	*Airports*
Ardrossan	Aberdeen
Cairnryan	Biggin Hill
Campbeltown	Birmingham
Fishguard	Blackpool
Fleetwood	Bournemouth (Hurn)
Heysham	Bristol
Holyhead	Cambridge
Pembroke Dock	Cardiff
Plymouth	Carlisle
Poole Harbour	Coventry
Port of Liverpool	East Midlands
Portsmouth Continental Ferry Port	Edinburgh
Southampton	Exeter
Stranraer	Glasgow
Swansea	Gloucester/Cheltenham (Staverton)
Torquay	Humberside
Troon	Leeds/Bradford
Weymouth	Liverpool
	London-City
	London-Gatwick
	London-Heathrow
	Luton
	Lydd
	Manchester
	Manston
	Newcastle
	Norwich
	Plymouth
	Prestwick
	Sheffield City
	Southampton
	Southend
	Stansted
	Teesside

NORTHERN IRELAND

Seaports	*Airports*
Ballycastle	Belfast City
Belfast	Belfast International
Larne	City of Derry
Port of Londonderry	
Warrenpoint	

SCHEDULE 8
DETENTION

PART I
TREATMENT OF PERSONS DETAINED UNDER SECTION 41
OR SCHEDULE 7

Place of detention

1.—(1) The Secretary of State shall designate places at which persons may be detained under Schedule 7 or section 41.

(2) In this Schedule a reference to a police station includes a reference to any place which the Secretary of State has designated under sub-paragraph (1) as a place where a person may be detained under section 41.

(3) Where a person is detained under Schedule 7, he may be taken in the custody of an examining officer or of a person acting under an examining officer's authority to and from any place where his attendance is required for the purpose of—

(a) his examination under that Schedule,

(b) establishing his nationality or citizenship, or

(c) making arrangements for his admission to a country or territory outside the United Kingdom.

(4) A constable who arrests a person under section 41 shall take him as soon as is reasonably practicable to the police station which the constable considers the most appropriate.

(5) In this paragraph 'examining officer' has the meaning given in Schedule 7.

(6) Where a person is arrested in one Part of the United Kingdom and all or part of his detention takes place in another Part, the provisions of this Schedule which apply to detention in a particular Part of the United Kingdom apply in relation to him while he is detained in that Part.

Identification

2.—(1) An authorised person may take any steps which are reasonably necessary for—

(a) photographing the detained person,

(b) measuring him, or

(c) identifying him.

(2) In sub-paragraph (1) 'authorised person' means any of the following—

(a) a constable,

(b) a prison officer,

(c) a person authorised by the Secretary of State, and

(d) in the case of a person detained under Schedule 7, an examining officer (within the meaning of that Schedule).

(3) This paragraph does not confer the power to take—

(a) fingerprints, non-intimate samples or intimate samples (within the meaning given by paragraph 15 below), or

(b) relevant physical data or samples as mentioned in section 18 of the Criminal Procedure (Scotland) Act 1995 as applied by paragraph 20 below.

Audio and video recording of interviews

3.—(1) The Secretary of State shall—

(a)   issue a code of practice about the audio recording of interviews to which this paragraph applies, and

(b)   make an order requiring the audio recording of interviews to which this paragraph applies in accordance with any relevant code of practice under paragraph (a).

(2)   The Secretary of State may make an order requiring the video recording of—

(a)   interviews to which this paragraph applies;

(b)   interviews to which this paragraph applies which take place in a particular Part of the United Kingdom.

(3)   An order under sub-paragraph (2) shall specify whether the video recording which it requires is to be silent or with sound.

(4)   Where an order is made under sub-paragraph (2)—

(a)   the Secretary of State shall issue a code of practice about the video recording of interviews to which the order applies, and

(b)   the order shall require the interviews to be video recorded in accordance with any relevant code of practice under paragraph (a).

(5)   Where the Secretary of State has made an order under sub-paragraph (2) requiring certain interviews to be video recorded with sound—

(a)   he need not make an order under sub-paragraph (1)(b) in relation to those interviews, but

(b)   he may do so.

(6)   This paragraph applies to any interview by a constable of a person detained under Schedule 7 or section 41 if the interview takes place in a police station.

(7)   A code of practice under this paragraph—

(a)   may make provision in relation to a particular Part of the United Kingdom;

(b)   may make different provision for different Parts of the United Kingdom.

4.—(1)   This paragraph applies to a code of practice under paragraph 3.

(2)   Where the Secretary of State proposes to issue a code of practice he shall—

(a)   publish a draft,

(b)   consider any representations made to him about the draft, and

(c)   if he thinks it appropriate, modify the draft in the light of any representations made to him.

(3)   The Secretary of State shall lay a draft of the code before Parliament.

(4)   When the Secretary of State has laid a draft code before Parliament he may bring it into operation by order.

(5)   The Secretary of State may revise a code and issue the revised code; and sub-paragraphs (2) to (4) shall apply to a revised code as they apply to an original code.

(6)   The failure by a constable to observe a provision of a code shall not of itself make him liable to criminal or civil proceedings.

(7)   A code—

(a)   shall be admissible in evidence in criminal and civil proceedings, and

(b)   shall be taken into account by a court or tribunal in any case in which it appears to the court or tribunal to be relevant.

Status

5.   A detained person shall be deemed to be in legal custody throughout the period of his detention.

Rights: England, Wales and Northern Ireland

6.—(1)   Subject to paragraph 8, a person detained under Schedule 7 or section 41 at a police station in England, Wales or Northern Ireland shall be entitled, if he so requests, to have one named person informed as soon as is reasonably practicable that he is being detained there.

(2)   The person named must be—

(a)   a friend of the detained person,

(b)   a relative, or

(c)   a person who is known to the detained person or who is likely to take an interest in his welfare.

(3)   Where a detained person is transferred from one police station to another, he shall be entitled to exercise the right under this paragraph in respect of the police station to which he is transferred.

7.—(1)   Subject to paragraphs 8 and 9, a person detained under Schedule 7 or section 41 at a police station in England, Wales or Northern Ireland shall be entitled, if he so requests, to consult a solicitor as soon as is reasonably practicable, privately and at any time.

(2)   Where a request is made under sub-paragraph (1), the request and the time at which it was made shall be recorded.

8.—(1)   Subject to sub-paragraph (2), an officer of at least the rank of superintendent may authorise a delay—

(a)   in informing the person named by a detained person under paragraph 6;

(b)   in permitting a detained person to consult a solicitor under paragraph 7.

(2)   But where a person is detained under section 41 he must be permitted to exercise his rights under paragraphs 6 and 7 before the end of the period mentioned in subsection (3) of that section.

(3)   Subject to sub-paragraph (5), an officer may give an authorisation under sub-paragraph (1) only if he has reasonable grounds for believing—

(a)   in the case of an authorisation under sub-paragraph (1)(a), that informing the named person of the detained person's detention will have any of the consequences specified in sub-paragraph (4), or

(b)   in the case of an authorisation under sub-paragraph (1)(b), that the exercise of the right under paragraph 7 at the time when the detained person desires to exercise it will have any of the consequences specified in sub-paragraph (4).

(4)   Those consequences are—

(a)   interference with or harm to evidence of a serious arrestable offence,

(b)   interference with or physical injury to any person,

(c)   the alerting of persons who are suspected of having committed a serious arrestable offence but who have not been arrested for it,

(d)   the hindering of the recovery of property obtained as a result of a serious arrestable offence or in respect of which a forfeiture order could be made under section 23,

(e)   interference with the gathering of information about the commission, preparation or instigation of acts of terrorism,

(f)   the alerting of a person and thereby making it more difficult to prevent an act of terrorism, and

(g)   the alerting of a person and thereby making it more difficult to secure a person's apprehension, prosecution or conviction in connection with the commission, preparation or instigation of an act of terrorism.

(5)   An officer may also give an authorisation under sub-paragraph (1) if he has reasonable grounds for believing that—

(a)   the detained person has committed an offence to which Part VI of the Criminal Justice Act 1988, Part I of the Proceeds of Crime (Scotland) Act 1995, or the Proceeds of Crime (Northern Ireland) Order 1996 (confiscation of the proceeds of an offence) applies,

(b)   the detained person has benefited from the offence within the meaning of that Part or Order, and

(c)   by informing the named person of the detained person's detention (in the case of an authorisation under sub-paragraph (1)(a)), or by the exercise of the right under paragraph 7 (in the case of an authorisation under sub-paragraph (1)(b)), the recovery of the value of that benefit will be hindered.

(6)   If an authorisation under sub-paragraph (1) is given orally, the person giving it shall confirm it in writing as soon as is reasonably practicable.

(7)   Where an authorisation under sub-paragraph (1) is given—

(a)   the detained person shall be told the reason for the delay as soon as is reasonably practicable, and

(b)   the reason shall be recorded as soon as is reasonably practicable.

(8)   Where the reason for authorising delay ceases to subsist there may be no further delay in permitting the exercise of the right in the absence of a further authorisation under sub-paragraph (1).

(9)   In this paragraph 'serious arrestable offence' has the meaning given by section 116 of the Police and Criminal Evidence Act 1984 (in relation to England and Wales) and by Article 87 of the Police and Criminal Evidence (Northern Ireland) Order 1989 (in relation to Northern Ireland); but it also includes—

(a)   an offence under any of the provisions mentioned in section 40(1)(a) of this Act, and

(b)   an attempt or conspiracy to commit an offence under any of the provisions mentioned in section 40(1)(a).

9.—(1)   A direction under this paragraph may provide that a detained person who wishes to exercise the right under paragraph 7 may consult a solicitor only in the sight and hearing of a qualified officer.

(2)   A direction under this paragraph may be given—

(a)   where the person is detained at a police station in England or Wales, by an officer of at least the rank of Commander or Assistant Chief Constable, or

(b)   where the person is detained at a police station in Northern Ireland, by an officer of at least the rank of Assistant Chief Constable.

(3)   A direction under this paragraph may be given only if the officer giving it has reasonable grounds for believing that, unless the direction is given, the exercise of the right by the detained person will have any of the consequences specified in paragraph 8(4) or the consequence specified in paragraph 8(5)(c).

(4)   In this paragraph 'a qualified officer' means a police officer who—

(a)   is of at least the rank of inspector,

(b)   is of the uniformed branch of the force of which the officer giving the direction is a member, and

(c)   in the opinion of the officer giving the direction, has no connection with the detained person's case.

(5)   A direction under this paragraph shall cease to have effect once the reason for giving it ceases to subsist.

10.—(1)   This paragraph applies where a person is detained in England, Wales or Northern Ireland under Schedule 7 or section 41.

(2)   Fingerprints may be taken from the detained person only if they are taken by a constable—

    (a)   with the appropriate consent given in writing, or

    (b)   without that consent under sub-paragraph (4).

(3)   A non-intimate sample may be taken from the detained person only if it is taken by a constable—

    (a)   with the appropriate consent given in writing, or

    (b)   without that consent under sub-paragraph (4).

(4)   Fingerprints or a non-intimate sample may be taken from the detained person without the appropriate consent only if—

    (a)   he is detained at a police station and a police officer of at least the rank of superintendent authorises the fingerprints or sample to be taken, or

    (b)   he has been convicted of a recordable offence and, where a non-intimate sample is to be taken, he was convicted of the offence on or after 10th April 1995 (or 29th July 1996 where the non-intimate sample is to be taken in Northern Ireland).

(5)   An intimate sample may be taken from the detained person only if—

    (a)   he is detained at a police station,

    (b)   the appropriate consent is given in writing,

    (c)   a police officer of at least the rank of superintendent authorises the sample to be taken, and

    (d)   subject to paragraph 13(2) and (3), the sample is taken by a constable.

(6)   An officer may give an authorisation under sub-paragraph (4)(a) or (5)(c) only if—

    (a)   in the case of a person detained under section 41, the officer reasonably suspects that the person has been involved in an offence under any of the provisions mentioned in section 40(1)(a), and the officer reasonably believes that the fingerprints or sample will tend to confirm or disprove his involvement, or

    (b)   in any case, the officer is satisfied that the taking of the fingerprints or sample from the person is necessary in order to assist in determining whether he falls within section 40(1)(b).

(7)   If an authorisation under sub-paragraph (4)(a) or (5)(c) is given orally, the person giving it shall confirm it in writing as soon as is reasonably practicable.

11.—(1)   Before fingerprints or a sample are taken from a person under paragraph 10, he shall be informed—

    (a)   that the fingerprints or sample may be used for the purposes of paragraph 14(4), section 63A(1) of the Police and Criminal Evidence Act 1984 and Article 63A(1) of the Police and Criminal Evidence (Northern Ireland) Order 1989 (checking of fingerprints and samples), and

    (b)   where the fingerprints or sample are to be taken under paragraph 10(2)(a), (3)(a) or (4)(b), of the reason for taking the fingerprints or sample.

(2)   Before fingerprints or a sample are taken from a person upon an authorisation given under paragraph 10(4)(a) or (5)(c), he shall be informed—

    (a)   that the authorisation has been given,

    (b)   of the grounds upon which it has been given, and

    (c)   where relevant, of the nature of the offence in which it is suspected that he has been involved.

(3)   After fingerprints or a sample are taken under paragraph 10, there shall be recorded as soon as is reasonably practicable any of the following which apply—

    (a)   the fact that the person has been informed in accordance with sub-paragraphs (1) and (2),

    (b)   the reason referred to in sub-paragraph (1)(b),

    (c)   the authorisation given under paragraph 10(4)(a) or (5)(c),

    (d)   the grounds upon which that authorisation has been given, and

    (e)   the fact that the appropriate consent has been given.

12.—(1)   This paragraph applies where—

    (a)   two or more non-intimate samples suitable for the same means of analysis have been taken from a person under paragraph 10,

    (b)   those samples have proved insufficient, and

    (c)   the person has been released from detention.

(2)   An intimate sample may be taken from the person if—

    (a)   the appropriate consent is given in writing,

    (b)   a police officer of at least the rank of superintendent authorises the sample to be taken, and

    (c)   subject to paragraph 13(2) and (3), the sample is taken by a constable.

(3)   Paragraphs 10(6) and (7) and 11 shall apply in relation to the taking of an intimate sample under this paragraph; and a reference to a person detained under section 41 shall be taken as a reference to a person who was detained under section 41 when the non-intimate samples mentioned in sub-paragraph (1)(a) were taken.

13.—(1)   Where appropriate written consent to the taking of an intimate sample from a person under paragraph 10 or 12 is refused without good cause, in any proceedings against that person for an offence—

    (a)   the court, in determining whether to commit him for trial or whether there is a case to answer, may draw such inferences from the refusal as appear proper, and

    (b)   the court or jury, in determining whether that person is guilty of the offence charged, may draw such inferences from the refusal as appear proper.

(2)   An intimate sample other than a sample of urine or a dental impression may be taken under paragraph 10 or 12 only by a registered medical practitioner acting on the authority of a constable.

(3)   An intimate sample which is a dental impression may be taken under paragraph 10 or 12 only by a registered dentist acting on the authority of a constable.

(4)   Where a sample of hair other than pubic hair is to be taken under paragraph 10 the sample may be taken either by cutting hairs or by plucking hairs with their roots so long as no more are plucked than the person taking the sample reasonably considers to be necessary for a sufficient sample.

14.—(1)   This paragraph applies to—

    (a)   fingerprints or samples taken under paragraph 10 or 12, and

    (b)   information derived from those samples.

(2)   The fingerprints, samples or information may be used only for the purpose of a terrorist investigation.

(3)   In particular, a check may not be made against them under—

    (a)   section 63A(1) of the Police and Criminal Evidence Act 1984 (checking of fingerprints and samples), or

(b) Article 63A(1) of the Police and Criminal Evidence (Northern Ireland) Order 1989 (checking of fingerprints and samples),
except for the purpose of a terrorist investigation.

(4) The fingerprints, samples or information may be checked, subject to sub-paragraph (2), against—

(a) other fingerprints or samples taken under paragraph 10 or 12 or information derived from those samples,

(b) relevant physical data or samples taken by virtue of paragraph 20,

(c) any of the fingerprints, samples and information mentioned in section 63A(1)(a) and (b) of the Police and Criminal Evidence Act 1984 (checking of fingerprints and samples),

(d) any of the fingerprints, samples and information mentioned in Article 63A(1)(a) and (b) of the Police and Criminal Evidence (Northern Ireland) Order 1989 (checking of fingerprints and samples), and

(e) fingerprints or samples taken under section 15(9) of, or paragraph 7(5) of Schedule 5 to, the Prevention of Terrorism (Temporary Provisions) Act 1989 or information derived from those samples.

(5) This paragraph (other than sub-paragraph (4)) shall apply to fingerprints or samples taken under section 15(9) of, or paragraph 7(5) of Schedule 5 to, the Prevention of Terrorism (Temporary Provisions) Act 1989 and information derived from those samples as it applies to fingerprints or samples taken under paragraph 10 or 12 and the information derived from those samples.

15.—(1) In the application of paragraphs 10 to 14 in relation to a person detained in England or Wales the following expressions shall have the meaning given by section 65 of the Police and Criminal Evidence Act 1984 (Part V definitions)—

(a) 'appropriate consent',
(b) 'fingerprints',
(c) 'insufficient',
(d) 'intimate sample',
(e) 'non-intimate sample',
(f) 'registered dentist', and
(g) 'sufficient'.

(2) In the application of paragraphs 10 to 14 in relation to a person detained in Northern Ireland the expressions listed in sub-paragraph (1) shall have the meaning given by Article 53 of the Police and Criminal Evidence (Northern Ireland) Order 1989 (definitions).

(3) In paragraph 10 'recordable offence' shall have—

(a) in relation to a person detained in England or Wales, the meaning given by section 118(1) of the Police and Criminal Evidence Act 1984 (general interpretation), and

(b) in relation to a person detained in Northern Ireland, the meaning given by Article 2(2) of the Police and Criminal Evidence (Northern Ireland) Order 1989 (definitions).

Rights: Scotland

16.—(1) A person detained under Schedule 7 or section 41 at a police station in Scotland shall be entitled to have intimation of his detention and of the place where he is being detained sent without delay to a solicitor and to another person named by him.

(2) The person named must be—

(a) a friend of the detained person,
(b) a relative, or

(c)   a person who is known to the detained person or who is likely to take an interest in his welfare.

(3)   Where a detained person is transferred from one police station to another, he shall be entitled to exercise the right under sub-paragraph (1) in respect of the police station to which he is transferred.

(4)   A police officer not below the rank of superintendent may authorise a delay in making intimation where, in his view, the delay is necessary on one of the grounds mentioned in paragraph 17(3) or where paragraph 17(4) applies.

(5)   Where a detained person requests that the intimation be made, there shall be recorded the time when the request is—

(a)   made, and

(b)   complied with.

(6)   A person detained shall be entitled to consult a solicitor at any time, without delay.

(7)   A police officer not below the rank of superintendent may authorise a delay in holding the consultation where, in his view, the delay is necessary on one of the grounds mentioned in paragraph 17(3) or where paragraph 17(4) applies.

(8)   Subject to paragraph 17, the consultation shall be private.

(9)   Where a person is detained under section 41 he must be permitted to exercise his rights under this paragraph before the end of the period mentioned in subsection (3) of that section.

17.—(1)   An officer not below the rank of Assistant Chief Constable may direct that the consultation mentioned in paragraph 16(6) shall be in the presence of a uniformed officer not below the rank of inspector if it appears to the officer giving the direction to be necessary on one of the grounds mentioned in sub-paragraph (3).

(2)   A uniformed officer directed to be present during a consultation shall be an officer who, in the opinion of the officer giving the direction, has no connection with the case.

(3)   The grounds mentioned in paragraph 16(4) and (7) and in sub-paragraph (1) are—

(a)   that it is in the interests of the investigation or prevention of crime;

(b)   that it is in the interests of the apprehension, prosecution or conviction of offenders;

(c)   that it will further the recovery of property obtained as a result of the commission of an offence or in respect of which a forfeiture order could be made under section 23;

(d)   that it will further the operation of Part VI of the Criminal Justice Act 1988, Part I of the Proceeds of Crime (Scotland) Act 1995 or the Proceeds of Crime (Northern Ireland) Order 1996 (confiscation of the proceeds of an offence).

(4)   This sub-paragraph applies where an officer mentioned in paragraph 16(4) or (7) has reasonable grounds for believing that—

(a)   the detained person has committed an offence to which Part VI of the Criminal Justice Act 1988, Part I of the Proceeds of Crime (Scotland) Act 1995 or the Proceeds of Crime (Northern Ireland) Order 1996 (confiscation of the proceeds of an offence) applies,

(b)   the detained person has benefited from the offence within the meaning of that Part or Order, and

(c)   by informing the named person of the detained person's detention (in the case of an authorisation under paragraph 16(4)) or by the exercise of the entitlement under paragraph 16(6) (in the case of an authorisation under paragraph 16(7)) the recovery of the value of that benefit will be hindered.

(5)   Where delay is authorised in the exercising of any of the rights mentioned in paragraph 16(1) and (6)—

(a) if the authorisation is given orally, the person giving it shall confirm it in writing as soon as is reasonably practicable,

(b) the detained person shall be told the reason for the delay as soon as is reasonably practicable, and

(c) the reason shall be recorded as soon as is reasonably practicable.

18.—(1) Paragraphs 16 and 17 shall have effect, in relation to a person detained under section 41 or Schedule 7, in place of any enactment or rule of law under or by virtue of which a person arrested or detained may be entitled to communicate or consult with any other person.

(2) But, where a person detained under Schedule 7 or section 41 at a police station in Scotland appears to a constable to be a child—

(a) the other person named by the person detained in pursuance of paragraph 16(1) shall be that person's parent, and

(b) section 15(4) of the Criminal Procedure (Scotland) Act 1995 shall apply to the person detained as it applies to a person who appears to a constable to be a child who is being detained as mentioned in paragraph (b) of section 15(1) of that Act,

and in this sub-paragraph 'child' and 'parent' have the same meaning as in section 15(4) of that Act.

19. The Secretary of State shall, by order, make provision to require that—

(a) except in such circumstances, and

(b) subject to such conditions,

as may be specified in the order, where a person detained has been permitted to consult a solicitor, the solicitor shall be allowed to be present at any interview carried out in connection with a terrorist investigation or for the purposes of Schedule 7.

20.—(1) Subject to the modifications specified in sub-paragraphs (2) and (3), section 18 of the Criminal Procedure (Scotland) Act 1995 (procedure for taking certain prints and samples) shall apply to a person detained under Schedule 7 or section 41 at a police station in Scotland as it applies to a person arrested or a person detained under section 14 of that Act.

(2) For subsection (2) of section 18 there shall be substituted—

'(2) A constable may take from a detained person or require a detained person to provide relevant physical data only if—

(a) in the case of a person detained under section 41 of the Terrorism Act 2000, he reasonably suspects that the person has been involved in an offence under any of the provisions mentioned in section 40(1)(a) of that Act and he reasonably believes that the relevant physical data will tend to confirm or disprove his involvement, or

(b) in any case, he is satisfied that it is necessary in order to assist in determining whether the person falls within section 40(1)(b) of that Act.'

(3) Subsections (3) to (5) shall not apply, but any relevant physical data or sample taken in pursuance of section 18 as applied by this paragraph shall be retained only for the purposes of terrorist investigations.

PART II
REVIEW OF DETENTION UNDER SECTION 41

Requirement

21.—(1) A person's detention shall be periodically reviewed by a review officer.

(2) The first review shall be carried out as soon as is reasonably practicable after the time of the person's arrest.

(3) Subsequent reviews shall, subject to paragraph 22, be carried out at intervals of not more than 12 hours.

(4) No review of a person's detention shall be carried out after a warrant extending his detention has been issued under Part III.

Postponement

22.—(1) A review may be postponed if at the latest time at which it may be carried out in accordance with paragraph 21—

(a) the detained person is being questioned by a police officer and an officer is satisfied that an interruption of the questioning to carry out the review would prejudice the investigation in connection with which the person is being detained,

(b) no review officer is readily available, or

(c) it is not practicable for any other reason to carry out the review.

(2) Where a review is postponed it shall be carried out as soon as is reasonably practicable.

(3) For the purposes of ascertaining the time within which the next review is to be carried out, a postponed review shall be deemed to have been carried out at the latest time at which it could have been carried out in accordance with paragraph 21.

Grounds for continued detention

23.—(1) A review officer may authorise a person's continued detention only if satisfied that it is necessary—

(a) to obtain relevant evidence whether by questioning him or otherwise,

(b) to preserve relevant evidence,

(c) pending a decision whether to apply to the Secretary of State for a deportation notice to be served on the detained person,

(d) pending the making of an application to the Secretary of State for a deportation notice to be served on the detained person,

(e) pending consideration by the Secretary of State whether to serve a deportation notice on the detained person, or

(f) pending a decision whether the detained person should be charged with an offence.

(2) The review officer shall not authorise continued detention by virtue of sub-paragraph (1)(a) or (b) unless he is satisfied that the investigation in connection with which the person is detained is being conducted diligently and expeditiously.

(3) The review officer shall not authorise continued detention by virtue of sub-paragraph (1)(c) to (f) unless he is satisfied that the process pending the completion of which detention is necessary is being conducted diligently and expeditiously.

(4) In sub-paragraph (1)(a) and (b) 'relevant evidence' means evidence which—

(a) relates to the commission by the detained person of an offence under any of the provisions mentioned in section 40(1)(a), or

(b) indicates that the detained person falls within section 40(1)(b).

(5) In sub-paragraph (1) 'deportation notice' means notice of a decision to make a deportation order under the Immigration Act 1971.

Review officer

24.—(1) The review officer shall be an officer who has not been directly involved in the investigation in connection with which the person is detained.

(2) In the case of a review carried out within the period of 24 hours beginning with the time of arrest, the review officer shall be an officer of at least the rank of inspector.

(3) In the case of any other review, the review officer shall be an officer of at least the rank of superintendent.

25.—(1) This paragraph applies where—

(a) the review officer is of a rank lower than superintendent,

(b) an officer of higher rank than the review officer gives directions relating to the detained person, and

(c) those directions are at variance with the performance by the review officer of a duty imposed on him under this Schedule.

(2) The review officer shall refer the matter at once to an officer of at least the rank of superintendent.

Representations

26.—(1) Before determining whether to authorise a person's continued detention, a review officer shall give either of the following persons an opportunity to make representations about the detention—

(a) the detained person, or

(b) a solicitor representing him who is available at the time of the review.

(2) Representations may be oral or written.

(3) A review officer may refuse to hear oral representations from the detained person if he considers that he is unfit to make representations because of his condition or behaviour.

Rights

27.—(1) Where a review officer authorises continued detention he shall inform the detained person—

(a) of any of his rights under paragraphs 6 and 7 which he has not yet exercised, and

(b) if the exercise of any of his rights under either of those paragraphs is being delayed in accordance with the provisions of paragraph 8, of the fact that it is being so delayed.

(2) Where a review of a person's detention is being carried out at a time when his exercise of a right under either of those paragraphs is being delayed—

(a) the review officer shall consider whether the reason or reasons for which the delay was authorised continue to subsist, and

(b) if in his opinion the reason or reasons have ceased to subsist, he shall inform the officer who authorised the delay of his opinion (unless he was that officer).

(3) In the application of this paragraph to Scotland, for the references to paragraphs 6, 7 and 8 substitute references to paragraph 16.

(4) The following provisions (requirement to bring an accused person before the court after his arrest) shall not apply to a person detained under section 41—

(a) section 135(3) of the Criminal Procedure (Scotland) Act 1995, and

(b) Article 8(1) of the Criminal Justice (Children) (Northern Ireland) Order 1998.

(5) Section 22(1) of the Criminal Procedure (Scotland) Act 1995 (interim liberation by officer in charge of police station) shall not apply to a person detained under section 41.

Record

28.—(1) A review officer carrying out a review shall make a written record of the outcome of the review and of any of the following which apply—

  (a) the grounds upon which continued detention is authorised,

  (b) the reason for postponement of the review,

  (c) the fact that the detained person has been informed as required under paragraph 27(1),

  (d) the officer's conclusion on the matter considered under paragraph 27(2)(a),

  (e) the fact that he has taken action under paragraph 27(2)(b), and

  (f) the fact that the detained person is being detained by virtue of section 41(5) or (6).

  (2) The review officer shall—

  (a) make the record in the presence of the detained person, and

  (b) inform him at that time whether the review officer is authorising continued detention, and if he is, of his grounds.

  (3) Sub-paragraph (2) shall not apply where, at the time when the record is made, the detained person is—

  (a) incapable of understanding what is said to him,

  (b) violent or likely to become violent, or

  (c) in urgent need of medical attention.

PART III
EXTENSION OF DETENTION UNDER SECTION 41

Warrants of further detention

29.—(1) A police officer of at least the rank of superintendent may apply to a judicial authority for the issue of a warrant of further detention under this Part.

  (2) A warrant of further detention—

  (a) shall authorise the further detention under section 41 of a specified person for a specified period, and

  (b) shall state the time at which it is issued.

  (3) The specified period in relation to a person shall end not later than the end of the period of seven days beginning—

  (a) with the time of his arrest under section 41, or

  (b) if he was being detained under Schedule 7 when he was arrested under section 41, with the time when his examination under that Schedule began.

  (4) In this Part 'judicial authority' means—

  (a) in England and Wales, the Senior District Judge (Chief Magistrate) or his deputy, or a District Judge (Magistrates' Courts) who is designated for the purpose of this Part by the Lord Chancellor,

  (b) in Scotland, the sheriff, and

  (c) in Northern Ireland, a county court judge, or a resident magistrate who is designated for the purpose of this Part by the Lord Chancellor.

Time limit

30.—(1) An application for a warrant shall be made—

  (a) during the period mentioned in section 41(3), or

  (b) within six hours of the end of that period.

(2)   The judicial authority hearing an application made by virtue of sub-paragraph (1)(b) shall dismiss the application if he considers that it would have been reasonably practicable to make it during the period mentioned in section 41(3).

(3)   For the purposes of this Schedule, an application for a warrant is made when written or oral notice of an intention to make the application is given to a judicial authority.

Notice

31.   An application for a warrant may not be heard unless the person to whom it relates has been given a notice stating—

(a)   that the application has been made,

(b)   the time at which the application was made,

(c)   the time at which it is to be heard, and

(d)   the grounds upon which further detention is sought.

Grounds for extension

32.—(1)   A judicial authority may issue a warrant of further detention only if satisfied that—

(a)   there are reasonable grounds for believing that the further detention of the person to whom the application relates is necessary to obtain relevant evidence whether by questioning him or otherwise or to preserve relevant evidence, and

(b)   the investigation in connection with which the person is detained is being conducted diligently and expeditiously.

(2)   In sub-paragraph (1) 'relevant evidence' means, in relation to the person to whom the application relates, evidence which—

(a)   relates to his commission of an offence under any of the provisions mentioned in section 40(1)(a), or

(b)   indicates that he is a person falling within section 40(1)(b).

Representation

33.—(1)   The person to whom an application relates shall—

(a)   be given an opportunity to make oral or written representations to the judicial authority about the application, and

(b)   subject to sub-paragraph (3), be entitled to be legally represented at the hearing.

(2)   A judicial authority shall adjourn the hearing of an application to enable the person to whom the application relates to obtain legal representation where—

(a)   he is not legally represented,

(b)   he is entitled to be legally represented, and

(c)   he wishes to be so represented.

(3)   A judicial authority may exclude any of the following persons from any part of the hearing—

(a)   the person to whom the application relates;

(b)   anyone representing him.

Information

34.—(1)   The officer who has made an application for a warrant may apply to the judicial authority for an order that specified information upon which he intends to rely be withheld from—

(a) the person to whom the application relates, and

(b) anyone representing him.

(2) Subject to sub-paragraph (3), a judicial authority may make an order under sub-paragraph (1) in relation to specified information only if satisfied that there are reasonable grounds for believing that if the information were disclosed—

(a) evidence of an offence under any of the provisions mentioned in section 40(1)(a) would be interfered with or harmed,

(b) the recovery of property obtained as a result of an offence under any of those provisions would be hindered,

(c) the recovery of property in respect of which a forfeiture order could be made under section 23 would be hindered,

(d) the apprehension, prosecution or conviction of a person who is suspected of falling within section 40(1)(a) or (b) would be made more difficult as a result of his being alerted,

(e) the prevention of an act of terrorism would be made more difficult as a result of a person being alerted,

(f) the gathering of information about the commission, preparation or instigation of an act of terrorism would be interfered with, or

(g) a person would be interfered with or physically injured.

(3) A judicial authority may also make an order under sub-paragraph (1) in relation to specified information if satisfied that there are reasonable grounds for believing that—

(a) the detained person has committed an offence to which Part VI of the Criminal Justice Act 1988, Part I of the Proceeds of Crime (Scotland) Act 1995, or the Proceeds of Crime (Northern Ireland) Order 1996 (confiscation of the proceeds of an offence) applies,

(b) the detained person has benefited from the offence within the meaning of that Part or Order, and

(c) the recovery of the value of that benefit would be hindered, if the information were disclosed.

(4) The judicial authority shall direct that the following be excluded from the hearing of the application under this paragraph—

(a) the person to whom the application for a warrant relates, and

(b) anyone representing him.

Adjournments

35.—(1) A judicial authority may adjourn the hearing of an application for a warrant only if the hearing is adjourned to a date before the expiry of the period mentioned in section 41(3).

(2) This paragraph shall not apply to an adjournment under paragraph 33(2).

Extensions of warrants

36.—(1) A police officer of at least the rank of superintendent may apply to a judicial authority for the extension or further extension of the period specified in a warrant of further detention.

(2) Where the period specified is extended, the warrant shall be endorsed with a note stating the new specified period.

(3) The specified period shall end not later than the end of the period of seven days beginning—

(a) with the time of the person's arrest under section 41, or

(b)   if he was being detained under Schedule 7 when he was arrested under section 41, with the time when his examination under that Schedule began.

(4)   Paragraphs 30(3) and 31 to 34 shall apply to an application under this paragraph as they apply to an application for a warrant of further detention.

(5)   A judicial authority may adjourn the hearing of an application under sub-paragraph (1) only if the hearing is adjourned to a date before the expiry of the period specified in the warrant.

(6)   Sub-paragraph (5) shall not apply to an adjournment under paragraph 33(2).

Detention—conditions

37.   A person detained by virtue of a warrant issued under this Part shall (unless detained in accordance with section 41(5) or (6) or under any other power) be released immediately if the officer having custody of him becomes aware that any of the grounds under paragraph 32(1)(a) and (b) upon which the judicial authority authorised his further detention have ceased to apply.

SCHEDULE 9
SCHEDULED OFFENCES

PART I
SUBSTANTIVE OFFENCES

Common law offences

1.   Murder subject to note 1 below.

2.   Manslaughter subject to note 1 below.

3.   Riot subject to note 1 below.

4.   Kidnapping subject to note 1 below.

5.   False imprisonment subject to note 1 below.

Malicious Damage Act 1861 (c. 97)

6.   Offences under section 35 of the Malicious Damage Act 1861 (interference with railway) subject to note 1 below.

Offences against the Person Act 1861 (c. 100)

7.   Offences under the following provisions of the Offences against the Person Act 1861 subject to note 1 below—
(a)   section 4 (offences relating to murder),
(b)   section 16 (threats to kill),
(c)   section 18 (wounding with intent to cause grievous bodily harm),
(d)   section 20 (causing grievous bodily harm),
(e)   section 29 (causing explosion or sending explosive substance or throwing corrosive liquid with intent to cause grievous bodily harm), and
(f)   section 47 (assault occasioning actual bodily harm).

Explosive Substances Act 1883 (c. 3)

8.   Offences under the following provisions of the Explosive Substances Act 1883 subject to note 1 below—

(a) section 2 (causing explosion likely to endanger life or damage property),

(b) section 3 (intending or conspiring to cause any such explosion, and making or possessing explosive with intent to endanger life or cause serious damage to property), and

(c) section 4 (making or possessing explosives in suspicious circumstances).

Prison Act (Northern Ireland) 1953 (c. 18 (NI))

9. Offences under the following provisions of the Prison Act (Northern Ireland) 1953 subject to note 1 below—

(a) section 25 (being unlawfully at large while under sentence),

(b) section 26 (escaping from lawful custody and failing to surrender to bail),

(c) section 27 (attempting to break prison),

(d) section 28 (breaking prison by force or violence),

(e) section 29 (rescuing or assisting or permitting to escape from lawful custody persons under sentence of death or life imprisonment),

(f) section 30 (rescuing or assisting or permitting to escape from lawful custody persons other than persons under sentence of death or life imprisonment),

(g) section 32 (causing discharge of prisoner under pretended authority), and

(h) section 33 (assisting prisoners to escape by conveying things into prisons).

Theft Act (Northern Ireland) 1969 (c. 16 (NI))

10. Offences under the following provisions of the Theft Act (Northern Ireland) 1969—

(a) section 1 (theft) subject to note 2 below,

(b) section 8 (robbery) subject to notes 1 and 3 below,

(c) section 9 (burglary) subject to note 2 below,

(d) section 10 (aggravated burglary) subject to notes 1 and 3 below,

(e) section 15 (obtaining property by deception) subject to note 2 below, and

(f) section 20 (blackmail) subject to notes 1 and 2 below.

Protection of the Person and Property Act (Northern Ireland) 1969 (c. 29 (NI))

11. Offences under the following provisions of the Protection of the Person and Property Act (Northern Ireland) 1969 subject to note 1 below—

(a) section 1 (intimidation),

(b) section 2 (making or possessing petrol bomb, etc. in suspicious circumstances), and

(c) section 3 (throwing or using petrol bomb, etc.).

Hijacking

12. Offences under section 1 of the Aviation Security Act 1982 (aircraft) subject to note 1 below.

13. Offences in Northern Ireland under section 2 of the Criminal Jurisdiction Act 1975 (vehicles or ships) subject to note 1 below.

Criminal Damage (Northern Ireland) Order 1977 (SI 1977/426 (NI 4))

14. Offences under the following provisions of the Criminal Damage (Northern Ireland) Order 1977 subject to note 1 below—

(a) Article 3(1) and (3) or Article 3(2) and (3) (arson),

(b) Article 3(2) (destroying or damaging property with intent to endanger life),

(c) Article 4 (threats to destroy or damage property), and

(d) Article 5 (possessing anything with intent to destroy or damage property).

Criminal Law (Amendment) (Northern Ireland) Order 1977 (SI 1977/1249 (NI 16))

15. Offences under Article 3 of the Criminal Law (Amendment) (Northern Ireland) Order 1977 (bomb hoaxes) subject to note 1 below.

Firearms (Northern Ireland) Order 1981 (SI 1981/155 (NI 2))

16. Offences under the following provisions of the Firearms (Northern Ireland) Order 1981 subject to note 1 below—

(a) Article 4(1), (2), (3) or (4) (manufacturing, dealing in, repairing, etc, firearm or ammunition without being registered),

(b) Article 5 (shortening barrel of shot gun or converting imitation firearm into firearm),

(c) Article 6(1) (manufacturing, dealing in or possessing certain weapons, etc.),

(d) Article 17 (possessing firearm or ammunition with intent to endanger life or cause serious damage to property),

(e) Article 18 (use or attempted use of firearm or imitation firearm to prevent arrest of self or another etc.),

(f) Article 19 (carrying firearm or imitation firearm with intent to commit indictable offence or prevent arrest of self or another),

(g) Article 20 (carrying firearm, etc. in public place) subject to note 4 below,

(h) Article 22 (possession of firearm or ammunition by person who has been sentenced to imprisonment, etc. and sale of firearm or ammunition to such a person), and

(i) Article 23 (possessing firearm or ammunition in suspicious circumstances).

Taking of Hostages Act 1982 (c. 28)

17. Offences under the Taking of Hostages Act 1982 subject to note 1 below.

Nuclear Material (Offences) Act 1983 (c. 18)

18. Offences under section 2 of the Nuclear Material (Offences) Act 1983 (offences involving nuclear material: preparatory acts and threats) subject to note 1 below.

Computer Misuse Act 1990 (c. 18)

19. Offences under the following provisions of the Computer Misuse Act 1990 subject to note 1 below—

(a) section 1 (unauthorised access to computer material),

(b) section 2 (unauthorised access with intent to commit further offence), and

(c) section 3 (unauthorised modification).

Aviation and Maritime Security Act 1990 (c. 31)

20. Offences under the following provisions of the Aviation and Maritime Security Act 1990 subject to note 1 below—

(a) section 1 (endangering safety at aerodromes),

(b) section 9 (hijacking of ships), and

(c) section 10 (seizing or exercising control of fixed platforms).

Channel Tunnel (Security) Order 1994 (SI 1994/570)

21. Offences under the following provisions of the Channel Tunnel (Security) Order 1994 subject to note 1 below—

(a) Article 4 (hijacking of Channel Tunnel trains), and

(b) Article 5 (seizing or exercising control of the tunnel system).

This Act

22. Offences under the following provisions of this Act—

(a) section 11,

(b) section 12,

(c) section 13,

(d) sections 15 to 19,

(e) section 54,

(f) section 56,

(g) section 57,

(h) section 58,

(i) section 103,

(j) paragraph 37 of Schedule 4,

(k) Schedule 5,

(l) paragraph 10 of Schedule 10 subject to note 1 below, and

(m) paragraphs 2 and 3 of Schedule 13 subject to note 1 below.

Notes

1. Any offence specified in this Part of this Schedule which is stated to be subject to this note is not a scheduled offence in any particular case in which the Attorney General for Northern Ireland certifies that it is not to be treated as a scheduled offence.

2. An offence specified in paragraph 10(a), (c) or (e) is a scheduled offence only where it is charged that the offence was committed in relation to or by means of nuclear material within the meaning of the Nuclear Material (Offences) Act 1983; and the Attorney General for Northern Ireland shall not certify that the offence specified in paragraph 10(f) is not to be treated as a scheduled offence in a case where it is charged that the offence was so committed.

3. An offence specified in paragraph 10(b) or (d) is a scheduled offence only where it is charged—

(a) that an explosive, firearm, imitation firearm or weapon of offence was used to commit the offence, or

(b) that the offence was committed in relation to or by means of nuclear material within the meaning of the Nuclear Material (Offences) Act 1983;

and expressions defined in section 10 of the Theft Act (Northern Ireland) 1969 have the same meaning when used in this note.

4. The offence specified in paragraph 16(g) is a scheduled offence only where it is charged that the offence relates to a weapon other than an air weapon.

PART II
INCHOATE AND RELATED OFFENCES

Each of the following offences, that is to say—

(a)   aiding, abetting, counselling, procuring or inciting the commission of an offence specified in Part I of this Schedule (hereafter in this paragraph referred to as a 'substantive offence'),

(b)   attempting or conspiring to commit a substantive offence,

(c)   an offence under section 4 of the Criminal Law Act (Northern Ireland) 1967 of doing any act with intent to impede the arrest or prosecution of a person who has committed a substantive offence, and

(d)   an offence under section 5(1) of the Criminal Law Act (Northern Ireland) 1967 of failing to give information to a constable which is likely to secure, or to be of material assistance in securing, the apprehension, prosecution or conviction of a person for a substantive offence,

shall be treated for the purposes of Part VII of this Act as if it were the substantive offence.

PART III
EXTRA-TERRITORIAL OFFENCES

Any extra-territorial offence as defined in section 1(3) of the Criminal Jurisdiction Act 1975.

Note

An extra-territorial offence is not a scheduled offence in any particular case in which the Attorney General for Northern Ireland certifies that it is not to be treated as a scheduled offence.

SCHEDULE 10
MUNITIONS AND TRANSMITTERS: SEARCH AND SEIZURE

Interpretation

1.—(1)   In this Schedule 'officer' means—

(a)   a member of Her Majesty's forces on duty, and

(b)   a constable.

(2)   In this Schedule 'authorised officer' means—

(a)   a member of Her Majesty's forces who is on duty and is authorised by a commissioned officer of those forces, and

(b)   a constable who is authorised by an officer of the Royal Ulster Constabulary of at least the rank of inspector.

(3)   In this Schedule—

'munitions' means—

(a)   explosives, firearms and ammunition, and

(b)   anything used or capable of being used in the manufacture of an explosive, a firearm or ammunition,

'scanning receiver' means apparatus (or a part of apparatus) for wireless telegraphy designed or adapted for the purpose of automatically monitoring selected frequencies, or automatically scanning a selected range of frequencies, so as to enable transmissions on any of those frequencies to be detected or intercepted,

'transmitter' means apparatus (or a part of apparatus) for wireless telegraphy designed or adapted for emission, as opposed to reception,

'wireless apparatus' means a scanning receiver or a transmitter, and 'wireless telegraphy' has the same meaning as in section 19(1) of the Wireless Telegraphy Act 1949.

Entering premises

2.—(1)   An officer may enter and search any premises for the purpose of ascertaining—

(a)   whether there are any munitions unlawfully on the premises, or

(b)   whether there is any wireless apparatus on the premises.

(2)   An officer may not enter a dwelling under this paragraph unless he is an authorised officer and he reasonably suspects that the dwelling—

(a)   unlawfully contains munitions, or

(b)   contains wireless apparatus.

3.   If it is necessary for the purpose of carrying out a search under paragraph 2 (including a search of a dwelling) an officer may be accompanied by other persons.

4.—(1)   If the officer carrying out a search of premises under paragraph 2 reasonably believes that it is necessary in order to carry out the search or to prevent it from being frustrated, he may—

(a)   require a person who is on the premises when the search begins, or who enters during the search, to remain on the premises;

(b)   require a person mentioned in paragraph (a) to remain in a specified part of the premises;

(c)   require a person mentioned in paragraph (a) to refrain from entering a specified part of the premises;

(d)   require a person mentioned in paragraph (a) to go from one specified part of the premises to another;

(e)   require a person who is not a resident of the premises to refrain from entering them.

(2)   A requirement imposed under this paragraph shall cease to have effect after the conclusion of the search in relation to which it was imposed.

(3)   Subject to sub-paragraph (4), no requirement under this paragraph for the purposes of a search shall be imposed or have effect after the end of the period of four hours beginning with the time when the first (or only) requirement is imposed in relation to the search.

(4)   An officer of the Royal Ulster Constabulary of at least the rank of superintendent may extend the period mentioned in sub-paragraph (3) in relation to a search by a further period of four hours if he reasonably believes that it is necessary to do so in order to carry out the search or to prevent it from being frustrated.

(5)   The power to extend a period conferred by sub-paragraph (4) may be exercised only once in relation to a particular search.

5.   Section 114(2) has effect for the purposes of this Schedule in relation to a member of Her Majesty's forces as it has effect in relation to a constable.

Stopping and searching persons

6.—(1)   An officer may—

(a)   stop a person in a public place, and

(b)   search him for the purpose of ascertaining whether he has munitions unlawfully with him or wireless apparatus with him.

(2) An officer may search a person who—

(a) is not in a public place, and

(b) whom the officer reasonably suspects to have munitions unlawfully with him or to have wireless apparatus with him.

(3) An officer may search a person entering or found in a dwelling entered under paragraph 2.

Seizure

7.—(1) This paragraph applies where an officer is empowered by virtue of any provision of Part VII of this Act to search premises or a person.

(2) The officer may—

(a) seize any munitions found in the course of the search (unless it appears to him that the munitions are being, have been and will be used only lawfully), and

(b) retain and, if necessary, destroy them.

(3) The officer may—

(a) seize any wireless apparatus found in the course of the search (unless it appears to him that the apparatus is being, has been and will be used only lawfully), and

(b) retain it.

Records

8.—(1) Where an officer carries out a search of premises under this Schedule he shall, unless it is not reasonably practicable, make a written record of the search.

(2) The record shall specify—

(a) the address of the premises searched,

(b) the date and time of the search,

(c) any damage caused in the course of the search, and

(d) anything seized in the course of the search.

(3) The record shall also include the name (if known) of any person appearing to the officer to be the occupier of the premises searched; but—

(a) a person may not be detained in order to discover his name, and

(b) if the officer does not know the name of a person appearing to him to be the occupier of the premises searched, he shall include in the record a note describing him.

(4) The record shall identify the officer—

(a) in the case of a constable, by reference to his police number, and

(b) in the case of a member of Her Majesty's forces, by reference to his service number, rank and regiment.

9.—(1) Where an officer makes a record of a search in accordance with paragraph 8, he shall supply a copy to any person appearing to him to be the occupier of the premises searched.

(2) The copy shall be supplied immediately or as soon as is reasonably practicable.

Offence

10.—(1) A person commits an offence if he—

(a) knowingly fails to comply with a requirement imposed under paragraph 4, or

(b) wilfully obstructs, or seeks to frustrate, a search of premises under this Schedule.

(2) A person guilty of an offence under this paragraph shall be liable—

(a) on conviction on indictment, to imprisonment for a term not exceeding two years, to a fine or to both, or

(b)   on summary conviction, to imprisonment for a term not exceeding six months, to a fine not exceeding the statutory maximum or to both.

11.—(1)   A person commits an offence if he fails to stop when required to do so under paragraph 6.

(2)   A person guilty of an offence under this paragraph shall be liable on summary conviction to a fine not exceeding level 5 on the standard scale.

SCHEDULE 11
INDEPENDENT ASSESSOR OF MILITARY COMPLAINTS PROCEDURES IN NORTHERN IRELAND

Tenure

1.—(1)   The Independent Assessor of Military Complaints Procedures in Northern Ireland shall hold and vacate office in accordance with the terms of his appointment.

(2)   The Independent Assessor shall be appointed for a term not exceeding three years (but may be reappointed).

(3)   The Independent Assessor may at any time resign his office by written notice to the Secretary of State.

(4)   The Secretary of State may remove the Independent Assessor from office—

(a)   if he has failed without reasonable excuse to carry out his duties for a continuous period of six months or more,

(b)   if he has been convicted of a criminal offence,

(c)   if a bankruptcy order has been made against him, his estate has been sequestrated or he has made a composition or arrangement with, or granted a trust deed for, his creditors, or

(d)   if the Secretary of State is satisfied that he is otherwise unable or unfit to perform his functions.

Remuneration

2.—(1)   The Secretary of State shall pay to the Independent Assessor—

(a)   such remuneration, and

(b)   such allowances,

as the Secretary of State may determine.

(2)   The Secretary of State may make payments to or in respect of the Independent Assessor in connection with pensions and gratuities.

Staff

3.—(1)   The Independent Assessor may appoint such number of employees, on such terms and conditions, as he may determine with the approval of the Secretary of State.

(2)   The Secretary of State may make payments to or in respect of persons appointed under this paragraph.

Reports

4.—(1)   The Independent Assessor shall send the Secretary of State an annual report on the performance of his functions.

(2)   Where the Secretary of State receives a report under sub-paragraph (1) he shall—

(a)   publish it, and

(b)   lay it before Parliament.

(3)   The Independent Assessor may report to the Secretary of State on any matter which comes to his attention in the course of the performance of his functions.

Disqualification

5.   In Part III of Schedule 1 to the Northern Ireland Assembly Disqualification Act 1975 (other disqualifying offices) the following entry shall be inserted at the appropriate place—
'Independent Assessor of Military Complaints Procedures in Northern Ireland.'

SCHEDULE 12
COMPENSATION

Right to compensation

1.—(1)   This paragraph applies where under Part VII of this Act—
  (a)   real or personal property is taken, occupied, destroyed or damaged, or
  (b)   any other act is done which interferes with private rights of property.

(2)   Where this paragraph applies in respect of an act taken in relation to any property or rights the Secretary of State shall pay compensation to any person who—
  (a)   has an estate or interest in the property or is entitled to the rights, and
  (b)   suffers loss or damage as a result of the act.

2.   No compensation shall be payable unless an application is made to the Secretary of State in such manner as he may specify.

Time limit

3.—(1)   Subject to sub-paragraphs (2) and (3), an application for compensation in respect of an act must be made within the period of 28 days beginning with the date of the act.

(2)   The Secretary of State may, in response to a request made to him in writing, permit an application to be made—
  (a)   after the expiry of the period mentioned in sub-paragraph (1), and
  (b)   within such longer period, starting from the date of the act and not exceeding six months, as he may specify.

(3)   Where the Secretary of State refuses a request under sub-paragraph (2)—
  (a)   he shall serve a notice of refusal on the person who made the request,
  (b)   that person may, within the period of six weeks beginning with the date of service of the notice, appeal to the county court against the refusal, and
  (c)   the county court may exercise the power of the Secretary of State under sub-paragraph (2).

Determination

4.   Where the Secretary of State determines an application for compensation he shall serve on the applicant a notice—
  (a)   stating that he has decided to award compensation and specifying the amount of the award, or
  (b)   stating that he has decided to refuse the application.

5.—(1)   An applicant may appeal to the county court against—
  (a)   the amount of compensation awarded, or
  (b)   the refusal of compensation.

(2) An appeal must be brought within the period of six weeks beginning with the date of service of the notice under paragraph 4.

6.—(1) This paragraph applies where the Secretary of State considers that in the course of an application for compensation the applicant—
  (a) knowingly made a false or misleading statement,
  (b) made a statement which he did not believe to be true, or
  (c) knowingly failed to disclose a material fact.
(2) The Secretary of State may—
  (a) refuse to award compensation,
  (b) reduce the amount of compensation which he would otherwise have awarded, or
  (c) withhold all or part of compensation which he has awarded.

7. Where the Secretary of State makes an award of compensation he may make a payment to the applicant in respect of all or part of the costs of the application.

Assignment of right

8.—(1) This paragraph applies where—
  (a) a person has made an application for compensation, and
  (b) his right to compensation has passed to another person by virtue of an assignment or the operation of law.
(2) The Secretary of State shall treat the person mentioned in sub-paragraph (1)(b) as the applicant.

Offenders

9.—(1) This paragraph applies where a person has a right to compensation in respect of an act and—
  (a) the act was done in connection with, or revealed evidence of the commission of, a scheduled offence or a non-scheduled offence under this Act, and
  (b) proceedings for the offence are brought against the person.
(2) The person's right to compensation shall not be enforceable while the proceedings have not been concluded.
(3) If the person stands convicted of the offence he shall have no right to compensation.

Notices

10. A notice served under paragraph 3(3)(a) or 4 shall contain particulars of the right of appeal under paragraph 3(3)(b) or 5.

11.—(1) The Secretary of State may serve a notice under this Schedule on an individual—
  (a) by delivering it to him,
  (b) by sending it by post addressed to him at his usual or last-known place of residence or business, or
  (c) by leaving it for him there.
(2) The Secretary of State may serve a notice under this Schedule on a partnership—
  (a) by sending it by post to a partner, or to a person having the control or management of the partnership business, at the principal office of the partnership, or
  (b) by addressing it to a partner or to a person mentioned in paragraph (a) and leaving it at that office.
(3) The Secretary of State may serve a notice under this Schedule on a body corporate—

(a) by sending it by post to the secretary or clerk of the body at its registered or principal office, or

(b) by addressing it to the secretary or clerk of the body and leaving it at that office.

(4) The Secretary of State may serve a notice under this Schedule on any person—

(a) by delivering it to his solicitor,

(b) by sending it by post to his solicitor at his solicitor's office, or

(c) by leaving it for his solicitor there.

Offences

12.—(1) A person commits an offence if he obtains compensation or increased compensation for himself or another person by deception (within the meaning of section 15(4) of the Theft Act (Northern Ireland) 1969).

(2) A person commits an offence if for the purposes of obtaining compensation he—

(a) knowingly makes a false or misleading statement,

(b) makes a statement which he does not believe to be true, or

(c) knowingly fails to disclose a material fact.

(3) A person guilty of an offence under this paragraph shall be liable—

(a) on conviction on indictment, to imprisonment for a term not exceeding five years, to a fine or to both, or

(b) on summary conviction, to imprisonment for a term not exceeding one year, to a fine not exceeding the statutory maximum or to both.

(4) Section 82 shall not apply in relation to an offence under this paragraph.

SCHEDULE 13
PRIVATE SECURITY SERVICES

Security services: interpretation

1. In this Schedule 'security services' means the services of one or more individuals as security guards (whether or not provided together with other services relating to the protection of property or persons).

Unlicensed services: offences

2. A person commits an offence if he provides or offers to provide security services for reward unless he—

(a) holds a licence under this Schedule, or

(b) acts on behalf of someone who holds a licence under this Schedule.

3.—(1) A person commits an offence if he publishes or causes to be published an advertisement for the provision for reward of security services by a person who does not hold a licence under this Schedule.

(2) It is a defence for a person charged with an offence under this paragraph to prove—

(a) that his business is publishing advertisements or arranging for their publication,

(b) that he received the advertisement for publication in the ordinary course of business, and

(c) that he reasonably believed that the person mentioned in the advertisement as the provider of security services held a licence under this Schedule.

4.—(1) A person commits an offence if he pays money, in respect of the provision of security services, to a person who—

(a) does not hold a licence under this Schedule, and

(b) is not acting on behalf of someone who holds a licence under this Schedule.

(2) It is a defence for a person charged with an offence under this paragraph to prove that he reasonably believed that the person to whom he paid the money—

(a) held a licence under this Schedule, or

(b) was acting on behalf of someone who held a licence under this Schedule.

5.—(1) A person guilty of an offence under paragraph 2 or 3 shall be liable—

(a) on conviction on indictment, to imprisonment for a term not exceeding five years, to a fine or to both, or

(b) on summary conviction, to imprisonment for a term not exceeding six months, to a fine not exceeding the statutory maximum or to both.

(2) A person guilty of an offence under paragraph 4 is liable on summary conviction to—

(a) imprisonment for a term not exceeding six months,

(b) a fine not exceeding level 5 on the standard scale, or

(c) both.

Application for licence

6.—(1) An application for a licence under this Schedule shall be made to the Secretary of State—

(a) in such manner and form as he may specify, and

(b) accompanied by such information as he may specify.

(2) The Secretary of State may specify information only if it concerns—

(a) the applicant,

(b) a business involving the provision of security services for reward which is, was or is proposed to be carried on by the applicant,

(c) a person whom the applicant employs or proposes to employ as a security guard,

(d) a partner or proposed partner of the applicant (where the applicant is an individual),

(e) a member or proposed member of the applicant (where the applicant is a partnership),

(f) an officer or proposed officer of the applicant (where the applicant is a body corporate).

(3) A person commits an offence if in connection with an application for a licence he—

(a) makes a statement which he knows to be false or misleading in a material particular, or

(b) recklessly makes a statement which is false or misleading in a material particular.

(4) A person guilty of an offence under sub-paragraph (3) shall be liable—

(a) on conviction on indictment, to imprisonment for a term not exceeding two years, to a fine or to both, or

(b) on summary conviction, to imprisonment for a term not exceeding six months, to a fine not exceeding the statutory maximum or to both.

(5) For the purposes of this paragraph—

(a) a reference to employment or proposed employment by an applicant for a licence shall, where the applicant is a partnership or a member of a partnership, be construed as a reference to employment or proposed employment by the partnership or any of the partners,

(b) 'officer' includes a director, manager or secretary,

(c)   a person in accordance with whose directions or instructions the directors of a body corporate are accustomed to act shall be treated as an officer of that body, and

(d)   the reference to directions or instructions in paragraph (c) does not include a reference to advice given in a professional capacity.

Issue of licence

7.—(1)   The Secretary of State shall grant an application for a licence unless satisfied that—

(a)   an organisation within sub-paragraph (4) would be likely to benefit from the licence (whether or not a condition were imposed under sub-paragraph (2)),

(b)   that the applicant has persistently failed to comply with the requirements of this Schedule, or

(c)   that the applicant has failed to comply with a condition imposed under sub-paragraph (2).

(2)   The Secretary of State may on granting a licence impose a condition if satisfied that it is necessary in order to prevent an organisation within sub-paragraph (4) from benefiting from the licence.

(3)   If the Secretary of State refuses an application for a licence he shall notify the applicant of the refusal.

(4)   An organisation is within this sub-paragraph if—

(a)   it is a proscribed organisation, or

(b)   it appears to the Secretary of State to be closely associated with a proscribed organisation.

(5)   In this paragraph a reference to a benefit is a reference to any benefit—

(a)   whether direct or indirect, and

(b)   whether financial or not.

(6)   In this paragraph a reference to the requirements of this Schedule includes a reference to the requirements of—

(a)   Part V of the Northern Ireland (Emergency Provisions) Act 1991 (private security services), and

(b)   Part V of the Northern Ireland (Emergency Provisions) Act 1996 (private security services).

Duration of licence

8.—(1)   A licence—

(a)   shall come into force at the beginning of the day on which it is issued, and

(b)   subject to sub-paragraph (2), shall expire at the end of the period of 12 months beginning with that day.

(2)   Where a licence is issued to a person who already holds a licence, the new licence shall expire at the end of the period of 12 months beginning with the day after the day on which the current licence expires.

(3)   The Secretary of State may by order substitute a period exceeding 12 months for the period for the time being specified in sub-paragraphs (1)(b) and (2).

Revocation of licence

9.—(1)   The Secretary of State may revoke a licence if satisfied that—

(a)   an organisation within paragraph 7(4) would be likely to benefit from the licence remaining in force,

(b)   the holder of the licence has persistently failed to comply with the requirements of this Schedule, or

(c)   the holder of the licence has failed to comply with a condition imposed under paragraph 7(2).

(2)   The Secretary of State shall not revoke a licence unless the holder—

(a)   has been notified of the Secretary of State's intention to revoke the licence, and

(b)   has been given a reasonable opportunity to make representations to the Secretary of State.

(3)   If the Secretary of State revokes a licence he shall notify the holder immediately.

(4)   Sub-paragraphs (5) and (6) of paragraph 7 shall apply for the purposes of this paragraph.

Appeal

10.   The applicant for a licence may appeal to the High Court if—

(a)   the application is refused,

(b)   a condition is imposed on the grant of the licence, or

(c)   the licence is revoked.

11.—(1)   Where an appeal is brought under paragraph 10, the Secretary of State may issue a certificate that the decision to which the appeal relates—

(a)   was taken for the purpose of preventing benefit from accruing to an organisation which was proscribed or which appeared to the Secretary of State to be closely associated with an organisation which was proscribed, and

(b)   was justified by that purpose.

(2)   If he intends to rely on a certificate under this paragraph, the Secretary of State shall notify the appellant.

(3)   Where the appellant is notified of the Secretary of State's intention to rely on a certificate under this paragraph—

(a)   he may appeal against the certificate to the Tribunal established under section 91 of the Northern Ireland Act 1998, and

(b)   sections 90(3) and (4), 91(2) to (9) and 92 of that Act (effect of appeal, procedure, and further appeal) shall apply.

(4)   Rules made under section 91 or 92 of that Act which are in force immediately before this paragraph comes into force shall have effect in relation to a certificate under this paragraph—

(a)   with any necessary modifications, and

(b)   subject to any later rules made by virtue of sub-paragraph (3)(b).

Change of personnel

12.   Paragraphs 13 and 14 apply to a person who—

(a)   holds a licence, or

(b)   has made an application for a licence which has not yet been determined.

13.—(1)   If a person to whom this paragraph applies proposes to employ a security guard about whom information was not given under paragraph 6, he shall give the Secretary of State such information about the security guard as the Secretary of State may specify.

(2)   The information shall be given not less than 14 days before the employment is to begin.

(3)   For the purposes of this paragraph the provisions of paragraph 6(5) shall have effect in relation to a holder of or an applicant for a licence as they have effect for the purposes of paragraph 6 in relation to an applicant.

14.—(1)   A person to whom this paragraph applies shall give the Secretary of State such information about a relevant change of personnel as the Secretary of State may specify.

(2)   The information shall be given—

(a)   not less than 14 days before the change, or

(b)   if that is not reasonably practicable, as soon as is reasonably practicable.

(3)   A relevant change of personnel is—

(a)   where the application for the licence was made by a partnership or a member of a partnership, a change in the members of the partnership, and

(b)   where the application for the licence was made by a body corporate, a change in the officers of the body (within the meaning of paragraph 6).

(4)   But a change of personnel is not relevant if it was mentioned in the information given under paragraph 6.

15.—(1)   A person commits an offence if he fails to comply with paragraph 13 or 14.

(2)   A person guilty of an offence under this paragraph shall be liable on summary conviction to—

(a)   imprisonment for a term not exceeding six months,

(b)   a fine not exceeding level 5 on the standard scale, or

(c)   both.

Records

16.—(1)   A constable may—

(a)   enter premises where a business involving the provision of security services is being carried on, and

(b)   require records kept there of a person employed as a security guard to be produced for the constable's inspection.

(2)   A constable exercising the power under this paragraph—

(a)   shall identify himself to a person appearing to be in charge of the premises, and

(b)   if the constable is not in uniform, shall produce to that person documentary evidence that he is a constable.

(3)   A person commits an offence if he fails to comply with a requirement under this paragraph.

(4)   It is a defence for a person charged with an offence under sub-paragraph (3) to show that he had a reasonable excuse for his failure.

(5)   A person guilty of an offence under sub-paragraph (3) shall be liable on summary conviction to—

(a)   imprisonment for a term not exceeding six months,

(b)   a fine not exceeding level 5 on the standard scale, or

(c)   both.

17.—(1)   A person who provides security services for reward commits an offence if he makes or keeps a record of a person employed by him as a security guard which he knows to be false or misleading in a material particular.

(2)   A person guilty of an offence under this paragraph shall be liable—

(a) on conviction on indictment, to imprisonment for a term not exceeding two years, to a fine or to both, or

(b) on summary conviction, to imprisonment for a term not exceeding six months, to a fine not exceeding the statutory maximum or to both.

Offence: body corporate

18.—(1) This paragraph applies where an offence under this Schedule committed by a body corporate is proved—

(a) to have been committed with the consent or connivance of an officer of the body corporate, or

(b) to be attributable to neglect on the part of an officer of the body corporate.

(2) The officer, as well as the body corporate, shall be guilty of the offence.

(3) In this paragraph 'officer' includes—

(a) a director, manager or secretary,

(b) a person purporting to act as a director, manager or secretary, and

(c) a member of a body corporate the affairs of which are managed by its members.

Notice

19.—(1) A notice under this Schedule shall be in writing.

(2) Information required to be given to the Secretary of State under this Schedule—

(a) shall be in writing, and

(b) may be sent to him by post.

(3) The Secretary of State may serve a notice under this Schedule on an individual—

(a) by delivering it to him,

(b) by sending it by post addressed to him at his usual or last-known place of residence or business, or

(c) by leaving it for him there.

(4) The Secretary of State may serve a notice under this Schedule on a partnership—

(a) by sending it by post to a partner, or to a person having the control or management of the partnership business, at the principal office of the partnership, or

(b) by addressing it to a partner or to a person mentioned in paragraph (a) and leaving it at that office.

(5) The Secretary of State may serve a notice under this Schedule on a body corporate—

(a) by sending it by post to the secretary or clerk of the body at its registered or principal office, or

(b) by addressing it to the secretary or clerk of the body and leaving it at that office.

(6) The Secretary of State may serve a notice under this Schedule on any person—

(a) by delivering it to his solicitor,

(b) by sending it by post to his solicitor at his solicitor's office, or

(c) by leaving it for his solicitor there.

(7) Sub-paragraphs (3) to (6) do not apply in relation to a notice under paragraph 11.

SCHEDULE 14
EXERCISE OF OFFICERS' POWERS

General

1. In this Schedule an 'officer' means—

(a) an authorised officer within the meaning given by section 24, and

(b)   an examining officer within the meaning of Schedule 7.

2.   An officer may enter a vehicle (within the meaning of section 121) for the purpose of exercising any of the functions conferred on him by virtue of this Act.

3.   An officer may if necessary use reasonable force for the purpose of exercising a power conferred on him by virtue of this Act (apart from paragraphs 2 and 3 of Schedule 7).

Information

4.—(1)   Information acquired by an officer may be supplied—
(a)   to the Secretary of State for use in relation to immigration;
(b)   to the Commissioners of Customs and Excise or a customs officer;
(c)   to a constable;
(d)   to the Director General of the National Criminal Intelligence Service or of the National Crime Squad;
(e)   to a person specified by order of the Secretary of State for use of a kind specified in the order.

(2)   Information acquired by a customs officer or an immigration officer may be supplied to an examining officer within the meaning of Schedule 7.

Code of practice

5.   An officer shall perform functions conferred on him by virtue of this Act in accordance with any relevant code of practice in operation under paragraph 6.

6.—(1)   The Secretary of State shall issue codes of practice about the exercise by officers of functions conferred on them by virtue of this Act.

(2)   The failure by an officer to observe a provision of a code shall not of itself make him liable to criminal or civil proceedings.

(3)   A code—
(a)   shall be admissible in evidence in criminal and civil proceedings, and
(b)   shall be taken into account by a court or tribunal in any case in which it appears to the court or tribunal to be relevant.

(4)   The Secretary of State may revise a code and issue the revised code.

7.—(1)   Before issuing a code of practice the Secretary of State shall—
(a)   publish a draft code,
(b)   consider any representations made to him about the draft, and
(c)   if he thinks it appropriate, modify the draft in the light of any representations made to him.

(2)   The Secretary of State shall lay a draft of the code before Parliament.

(3)   When the Secretary of State has laid a draft code before Parliament he may bring it into operation by order.

(4)   This paragraph has effect in relation to the issue of a revised code as it has effect in relation to the first issue of a code.

SCHEDULE 15
CONSEQUENTIAL AMENDMENTS

Criminal Justice Act 1967 (c. 80)

1.—(1)   The Criminal Justice Act 1967 shall be amended as follows.

(2) In section 67(7)(b) (computation of sentences) for 'section 14 of the Prevention of Terrorism (Temporary Provisions) Act 1989' substitute 'section 41 of the Terrorism Act 2000'.

Treatment of Offenders Act (Northern Ireland) 1968 (c. 29 (NI))

2.—(1) The Treatment of Offenders Act (Northern Ireland) 1968 shall be amended as follows.

(2) In section 26(6)(b) (definition of police detention) for 'section 14 of the Prevention of Terrorism (Temporary Provisions) Act 1989' substitute 'section 41 of the Terrorism Act 2000'.

Suppression of Terrorism Act 1978 (c. 26)

3.—(1) The Suppression of Terrorism Act 1978 shall be amended as follows.

(2) For paragraph 19A of Schedule 1 (list of offences) substitute—

'Financing terrorism

19A. An offence under any of sections 15 to 18 of the Terrorism Act 2000.'

Legal Aid, Advice and Assistance (Northern Ireland) Order 1981 (SI 1981/228 (NI8))

4.—(1) In Schedule 1 to the Legal Aid, Advice and Assistance (Northern Ireland) Order 1981 (proceedings for which legal aid may be given under Part II of that Order) at the end of Part I insert—

'8. Proceedings brought by an individual before the Proscribed Organisations Appeal Commission.'

(2) The amendment made by sub-paragraph (1) is without prejudice to the power to make regulations under Article 10(2) of the Legal Aid, Advice and Assistance (Northern Ireland) Order 1981 amending or revoking the provision inserted by that sub-paragraph.

Police and Criminal Evidence Act 1984 (c. 60)

5.—(1) The Police and Criminal Evidence Act 1984 shall be amended as follows.

(2) For section 30(12)(c) (arrest elsewhere than at a police station) substitute—

'(c) any provision of the Terrorism Act 2000.'

(3) In section 32(10) (search upon arrest) for 'section 15(3), (4) and (5) of the Prevention of Terrorism (Temporary Provisions) Act 1989' substitute 'section 43 of the Terrorism Act 2000'.

(4) For section 51(b) (savings: Part IV) substitute—

'(b) the powers conferred by virtue of section 41 of, or Schedule 7 to, the Terrorism Act 2000 (powers of arrest and detention);'.

(5) For section 56(10) and (11) (application of right to have someone informed) substitute—

'(10) Nothing in this section applies to a person arrested or detained under the terrorism provisions.'

(6) For section 58(12) to (18) (application of right of access to legal advice) substitute—

'(12) Nothing in this section applies to a person arrested or detained under the terrorism provisions.'

(7) For section 61(9)(b) (fingerprinting: disapplication) substitute—

'(b) applies to a person arrested or detained under the terrorism provisions.'

(8) For section 62(12) (intimate samples: disapplication) substitute—

'(12) Nothing in this section applies to a person arrested or detained under the terrorism provisions; and subsection (1A) shall not apply where the non-intimate samples mentioned in that subsection were taken under paragraph 10 of Schedule 8 to the Terrorism Act 2000.'

(9) For section 63(10) (non-intimate samples: disapplication) substitute—

'(10) Nothing in this section applies to a person arrested or detained under the terrorism provisions.'

(10) In section 65 (interpretation) for the definitions of 'the terrorism provisions' and 'terrorism' substitute—

'"the terrorism provisions" means section 41 of the Terrorism Act 2000, and any provision of Schedule 7 to that Act conferring a power of detention; and

"terrorism" has the meaning given in section 1 of that Act.'

(11) In section 116 (definition of serious arrestable offence for the purposes of sections 56 and 58)—

    (a) in subsection (3) for 'subsections (4) and (5)' substitute 'subsection (4)', and

    (b) subsection (5) shall cease to have effect.

(12) For section 118(2)(a) (definition of police detention) substitute—

'(a) he has been taken to a police station after being arrested for an offence or after being arrested under section 41 of the Terrorism Act 2000, or.'

Criminal Justice Act 1988 (c. 33)

6.—(1) The Criminal Justice Act 1988 shall be amended as follows.

(2) In section 71(9)(c)(ii) (offences to which Part VI (confiscation) does not apply) for 'or an offence under Part III of the Prevention of Terrorism (Temporary Provisions) Act 1989' substitute 'or an offence under any of sections 15 to 18 of the Terrorism Act 2000'.

(3) For section 74(2)(d) and (e) (realisable property) substitute—

    '(d) an order under section 23 of the Terrorism Act 2000 (forfeiture orders), or

    (e) an order under section 111 of the Terrorism Act 2000 (forfeiture orders),'.

(4) In section 93E (application to Scotland of sections 93A to 93D)—

    (a) in the definition of offences to which Part VI of the Act applies, for 'Part III of the Prevention of Terrorism Act 1989' substitute 'any of sections 15 to 18 of the Terrorism Act 2000', and

    (b) in the definition of proceeds of criminal conduct, for paragraph (b) substitute—

    '(b) terrorist property within the meaning of section 14 of the Terrorism Act 2000'.

Elected Authorities (Northern Ireland) Act 1989 (c. 3)

7.—(1) The Elected Authorities (Northern Ireland) Act 1989 shall be amended as follows.

(2) In section 6(5) (breach of terms of declaration), in the definition of 'proscribed organisation' for 'section 30 of the Northern Ireland (Emergency Provisions) Act 1996' substitute 'section 3 of the Terrorism Act 2000'.

(3) In Schedule 2 (declaration against terrorism) for 'Schedule 2 to the Northern Ireland (Emergency Provisions) Act 1996' substitute 'Schedule 2 to the Terrorism Act 2000'.

Police and Criminal Evidence (Northern Ireland) Order 1989 (SI 1989/1341 (NI 12))

8.—(1) The Police and Criminal Evidence (Northern Ireland) Order 1989 shall be amended as follows.

(2) In Article 2(2) (interpretation) for the definitions of 'the terrorism provisions' and 'terrorism' substitute—

'"the terrorism provisions" means section 41 of the Terrorism Act 2000, and any provision of Schedule 7 to that Act conferring a power of detention; "terrorism" has the meaning given in section 1 of that Act.'

(3) In Article 2(3) (definition of police detention) for 'section 14 of the Prevention of Terrorism (Temporary Provisions) Act 1989 or under paragraph 6 of Schedule 5 to that Act by an examining officer who is a constable' substitute 'section 41 of the Terrorism Act 2000'.

(4) For Article 4(3)(b) (provisions relating to powers to stop and search) substitute—

'(b) sections 85, 95 and 116 of and Schedule 10 to the Terrorism Act 2000, and'.

(5) In Article 11(3) (special provisions as to access) for 'section 17 of, and Schedule 7 to, the Prevention of Terrorism (Temporary Provisions) Act 1989' substitute 'sections 37 and 38 of, and Schedules 5 and 6 to, the Terrorism Act 2000'.

(6) In Article 30(3) (information to be given on arrest) for 'section 19(2) of the Northern Ireland (Emergency Provisions) Act 1996' substitute 'section 83(2) of the Terrorism Act 2000'.

(7) For Article 32(15)(b) (arrest elsewhere than at a police station) substitute—

'(b) any provision of the Terrorism Act 2000.'

(8) In Article 34(10) (search upon arrest) for 'section 15(3), (4) and (5) of the Prevention of Terrorism (Temporary Provisions) Act 1989' substitute 'section 43 of the Terrorism Act 2000'.

(9) For Article 51(b) (savings: Part V) substitute—

'(b) the powers conferred by virtue of section 41 of, or Schedule 7 to, the Terrorism Act 2000 (powers of arrest and detention);'.

(10) In Article 60 (tape-recording of interviews), omit paragraph (2).

(11) For Article 61(9)(b) (fingerprinting: application) substitute—

'(b) applies to a person arrested or detained under the terrorism provisions'.

(12) For Article 62(12) (intimate samples: application) substitute—

'(12) Nothing in this Article applies to a person arrested or detained under the terrorism provisions; and paragraph (1A) shall not apply where the non-intimate samples mentioned in that paragraph were taken under paragraph 10 of Schedule 8 to the Terrorism Act 2000.'

(13) For Article 63(11) (non-intimate samples: application) substitute—

'(11) Nothing in this Article applies to a person arrested or detained under the terrorism provisions'.

(14) In Article 66 (codes of practice), omit paragraph (12).

(15) In Article 74(9) (confessions) for 'section 12 of the Northern Ireland (Emergency Provisions) Act 1996' substitute 'section 76 of the Terrorism Act 2000'.

(16) In Article 76(2)(b) (exclusion of unfair evidence) for 'subsection (1) of section 12 of the Northern Ireland (Emergency Provisions) Act 1996' substitute 'subsection (1) of section 76 of the Terrorism Act 2000'.

Criminal Justice and Public Order Act 1994 (c. 33)

9. In section 139(11) of the Criminal Justice and Public Order Act 1994 (search powers available on arrests under sections 136 and 137) for 'section 15(3), (4) and (5) of the Prevention of Terrorism (Temporary Provisions) Act 1989' there shall be substituted 'section 43 of the Terrorism Act 2000'.

Drug Trafficking Act 1994 (c. 37)

10.—(1) The Drug Trafficking Act 1994 shall be amended as follows.

(2) In section 6(3) (realisable property)—

(a) in paragraph (d) for 'section 13(2), (3) or (4) of the Prevention of Terrorism (Temporary Provisions) Act 1989' substitute 'section 23 of the Terrorism Act 2000', and

(b) for paragraph (f) there shall be substituted—

'(f) section 111 of the Terrorism Act 2000 (forfeiture orders).'

Proceeds of Crime (Scotland) Act 1995 (c. 43)

11.—(1) The Proceeds of Crime (Scotland) Act 1995 shall be amended as follows.

(2) In subsection (2) of section 1 (offences to which Part I (confiscation) applies), for 'Part III of the 1989 Act' substitute 'any of sections 15 to 18 of the Terrorism Act 2000'.

(3) In subsection (1)(c) of section 42 (reciprocal enforcement of orders), for '1989 Act' substitute 'Terrorism Act 2000'.

(4) In subsection (1) of section 49 (interpretation), the definition of 'the 1989 Act' shall cease to have effect.

Northern Ireland (Remission of Sentences) Act 1995 (c. 47)

12.—(1) The following shall be substituted for section 1(1) and (2) of the Northern Ireland (Remission of Sentences) Act 1995 (release on licence of persons subject to restricted remission)—

'1.—(1) This section applies to persons serving sentences to which section 79 of the Terrorism Act 2000 applies (restricted remission for persons sentenced for scheduled offences).

(2) A person to whom this section applies shall be released on licence for the period (or, where that period has partly elapsed, for the remainder of the period) during which, by reason only of section 79, he is prevented from being discharged in pursuance of prison rules.'

(2) The following shall be substituted for section 1(6) of that Act—

'(6) Section 80 of the Terrorism Act 2000 and Part II of the Treatment of Offenders (Northern Ireland) Order 1976 (conviction within certain period after discharge from prison, &c.) shall apply in relation to a person released on licence under this section as if he had been discharged in pursuance of prison rules.'

Criminal Procedure and Investigations Act 1996 (c. 25)

13.—(1) The Criminal Procedure and Investigations Act 1996 shall, in its application to Northern Ireland (as set out in Schedule 4 to that Act), be amended as follows.

(2) In section 14A(1) (public interest: review for scheduled offences) for 'section 1 of the Northern Ireland (Emergency Provisions) Act 1996' substitute 'section 65 of the Terrorism Act 2000'.

(3) In section 39(3)(a) (start of trial on indictment without a jury) for 'section 11 of the Northern Ireland (Emergency Provisions) Act 1996' substitute 'section 75 of the Terrorism Act 2000'.

Proceeds of Crime (Northern Ireland) Order 1996 (SI 1996/1299 (NI 9))

14.—(1) The Proceeds of Crime (Northern Ireland) Order 1996 shall be amended as follows.

(2) In Article 2(4)(b) (offences to which Order does not apply) for 'Part III of the Prevention of Terrorism (Temporary Provisions) Act 1989' substitute 'any of sections 15 to 18 of the Terrorism Act 2000'.

(3) In Article 5(3) (realisable property) for sub-paragraph (c) substitute—

'(c) section 23 or 111 of the Terrorism Act 2000 (forfeiture orders).'

Northern Ireland Arms Decommissioning Act 1997 (c. 7)

15.—(1) This paragraph applies to a reference in paragraph 9 or 10 of the Schedule to the Northern Ireland Arms Decommissioning Act 1997 (amnesty) to an offence under a provision ('the old provision') of—

(a) the Prevention of Terrorism (Temporary Provisions) Act 1989, or

(b) the Northern Ireland (Emergency Provisions) Act 1996.

(2) The reference shall be taken as a reference to an offence under this Act which is committed in circumstances which would have amounted to the commission of an offence under the old provision before it ceased to have effect.

(3) Sub-paragraph (2) has effect for the purpose of the application of section 4(1) of the Northern Ireland Arms Decommissioning Act 1997 (amnesty) in relation to anything done after the old provision ceases to have effect.

Northern Ireland (Sentences) Act 1998 (c. 35)

16.—(1) The Northern Ireland (Sentences) Act 1998 shall be amended as follows.

(2) In section 5 (fixed term prisoners: special cases)—

(a) in subsection (2) for 'section 16(2) of the Northern Ireland (Emergency Provisions) Act 1996' substitute 'section 80(2) of the Terrorism Act 2000',

(b) in subsection (3)(a) for 'section 16(2) of the 1996 Act' substitute 'section 80(2) of the 2000 Act',

(c) in subsection (4) for 'section 16(2) of the 1996 Act' substitute 'section 80(2) of the 2000 Act', and

(d) at the end of subsection (4)(b) insert ', and

(c) section 16(2) of the Northern Ireland (Emergency Provisions) Act 1996.'

(3) For section 14(3)(a) (inadmissibility of evidence or information in certain proceedings) substitute—

'(a) be admissible in proceedings on applications made under paragraph 1, 2, 5, 11, 13, 22, 28 or 30 of Schedule 5 to the Terrorism Act 2000.'

17.—(1) This paragraph applies to a reference in section 14(2) of the Northern Ireland (Sentences) Act 1998 (inadmissibility of evidence or information in certain proceedings) to an offence under a provision ('the old provision') of—

(a) the Prevention of Terrorism (Temporary Provisions) Act 1989, or

(b) the Northern Ireland (Emergency Provisions) Act 1996.

(2) The reference shall be taken as including a reference to an offence under this Act which is committed in circumstances which would have amounted to the commission of an offence under the old provision before it ceased to have effect.

Criminal Justice (Children) (Northern Ireland) Order 1998 (SI 1998/1504 (NI 9))

18.—(1) The Criminal Justice (Children) (Northern Ireland) Order 1998 shall be amended as follows.

(2) In Article 12(4) (release on bail) for 'section 3 of the Northern Ireland (Emergency Provisions) Act 1996' substitute 'section 67 of the Terrorism Act 2000'.

Access to Justice Act 1999 (c. 22)

19.—(1) In paragraph 2(1) of Schedule 2 to the Access to Justice Act 1999 (Community Legal Service: exceptions to excluded services) after paragraph (h) insert—

'or

(i) the Proscribed Organisations Appeal Commission'.

(2) The amendment made by sub-paragraph (1) is without prejudice to the power to make regulations under section 6(7) of the Access to Justice Act 1999 amending or revoking the provision inserted by that sub-paragraph.

Powers of Criminal Courts (Sentencing) Act 2000 (c. 6)

20.—(1) The Powers of Criminal Courts (Sentencing) Act 2000 shall be amended as follows.

(2) In section 88(2)(b) (meaning of 'remanded in custody') for 'section 14 of the Prevention of Terrorism (Temporary Provisions) Act 1989' substitute 'section 41 of the Terrorism Act 2000'.

(3) In section 101(12)(b) (meaning of 'remanded in custody') for 'section 14 of the Prevention of Terrorism (Temporary Provisions) Act 1989' substitute 'section 41 of the Terrorism Act 2000'.

SCHEDULE 16
REPEALS AND REVOCATIONS

1. ACTS

Chapter	Short title	Extent of repeal
1980 c. 62.	Criminal Justice (Scotland) Act 1980.	Sections 3A to 3D.
1984 c. 60.	Police and Criminal Evidence Act 1984.	Section 1116(5).
1985 c. 73.	Law Reform (Miscellaneous Provisions) (Scotland) Act 1985.	Section 35.
1988 c. 33.	Criminal Justice Act 1988	Section 74(2)(e).
1989 c. 4	Prevention of Terrorism (Temporary Provisions) Act 1989.	The whole Act.
1993 c. 36.	Criminal Justice Act 1993.	Sections 49 to 51. Section 78(11). In Schedule 4, paragraph 4. In Schedule 5, paragraph 15.
1994 c. 33.	Criminal Justice and Public Order Act 1994.	Sections 81 to 83. In Schedule 10, paragraphs 62 (other than sub-paragraph (4)(a) and (b)) and 63.
1995 c. 40.	Criminal Procedure (Consequential Provisions) (Scotland) Act 1995.	In Schedule 4, paragraph 72.
1995 c. 43.	Proceeds of Crime (Scotland) Act 1995.	In section 49(1), the definition of 'the 1989 Act'.

Chapter	Short title	Extent of repeal
1996 c. 7.	Prevention of Terrorism (Additional Powers) Act 1996.	The whole Act.
1996 c. 22.	Northern Ireland (Emergency Provisions) Act 1996.	The whole Act.
1998 c. 9.	Northern Ireland (Emergency Provisions) Act 1998.	The whole Act.
1998 c. 40.	Criminal Justice (Terrorism and Conspiracy) Act 1998.	Sections 1 to 4. Part I of Schedule 1. Part I of Schedule 2.
1999 c. 22.	Access to Justice Act 1999.	In paragraph 2(1) of Schedule 2, the word 'or' after paragraph (f).
1999 c. 33.	Immigration and Asylum Act 1999.	In Schedule 14, paragraph 89.

2. ORDERS

Reference	Title	Extent of revocation
SI 1989/1341 (NI 12).	Police and Criminal Evidence (Northern Ireland) Order 1989.	In Article 54(1) the words 'Subject to paragraph (2)'. Article 54(2). Article 60(2). Article 66(12). In Schedule 2, the entry relating to the Prevention of Terrorism (Temporary Provisions) Act 1989. In Schedule 6, paragraph 18.
SI 1989/2405 (NI 19).	Insolvency (Northern Ireland) Order 1989.	In Schedule 9, paragraph 62.
SI 1995/2993 (NI 17).	Police (Amendment) (Northern Ireland) Order 1995.	Article 10(8). Article 11(7).
SI 1998/1504 (NI 9).	Criminal Justice (Children) (Northern Ireland) Order 1998.	In Schedule 5, paragraphs 39, 47 and 48.

Appendix 2

Anti-terrorism, Crime and Security Act 2001

2001 CHAPTER 24

PART I
TERRORIST PROPERTY

PART II
FREEZING ORDERS

Orders

Interpretation

Orders: procedure etc.

Miscellaneous

PART III
DISCLOSURE OF INFORMATION

PART IV
IMMIGRATION AND ASYLUM

Suspected international terrorists

Refugee Convention

Special Immigration Appeals Commission

Fingerprints

PART V
RACE AND RELIGION

PART VI

WEAPONS OF MASS DESTRUCTION

Amendment of the Biological Weapons Act 1974 and the Chemical Weapons Act 1996

Anti-terrorism, Crime and Security Act 2001

2001 CHAPTER 24

An Act to amend the Terrorism Act 2000; to make further provision about terrorism and security; to provide for the freezing of assets; to make provision about immigration and asylum; to amend or extend the criminal law and powers for preventing crime and enforcing that law; to make provision about the control of pathogens and toxins; to provide for the retention of communications data; to provide for implementation of Title VI of the Treaty on European Union; and for connected purposes. [14th December 2001]

BE IT ENACTED by the Queen's most Excellent Majesty, by and with the advice and consent of the Lords Spiritual and Temporal, and Commons, in this present Parliament assembled, and by the authority of the same, as follows:—

PART I
TERRORIST PROPERTY

1. Forfeiture of terrorist cash

(1) Schedule 1 (which makes provision for enabling cash which—

    (a) is intended to be used for the purposes of terrorism,

    (b) consists of resources of an organisation which is a proscribed organisation, or

    (c) is, or represents, property obtained through terrorism,

to be forfeited in civil proceedings before a magistrates' court or (in Scotland) the sheriff) is to have effect.

(2) The powers conferred by Schedule 1 are exercisable in relation to any cash whether or not any proceedings have been brought for an offence in connection with the cash.

(3) Expressions used in this section have the same meaning as in Schedule 1.

(4) Sections 24 to 31 of the Terrorism Act 2000 (c. 11) (seizure of terrorist cash) are to cease to have effect.

(5) An order under section 127 bringing Schedule 1 into force may make any modifications of any code of practice then in operation under Schedule 14 to the Terrorism Act 2000 (exercise of officers' powers) which the Secretary of State thinks necessary or expedient.

2. Amendments relating to section 1

(1) In Schedule 2 to the Access to Justice Act 1999 (c. 22) (services excluded from the Community Legal Service), paragraph 2 (exclusion of advocacy: exceptions) is amended as follows.

(2)   In paragraph 2(2) (Crown Court), after paragraph (c) insert—
  'or
        (d)   which relate to an order under paragraph 6 of Schedule 1 to the Anti-
  terrorism, Crime and Security Act 2001',
and omit the 'or' at the end of paragraph (b).
(3)   In paragraph 2(3) (magistrates' courts), in paragraph (j), after '1998' insert—
  'or
        (k)   for an order or direction under paragraph 3, 5, 6, 9 or 10 of Schedule 1 to
  the Anti-terrorism, Crime and Security Act 2001',
and omit the 'or' at the end of paragraph (i).
(4)   Schedule 14 to the Terrorism Act 2000 (exercise of officers' powers) is amended as
follows.
(5)   In paragraph 1—
  (a)   in paragraph (a), for 'section 24' substitute 'the terrorist cash provisions', and
  (b)   after paragraph (b) insert—
  'and "the terrorist cash provisions" means Schedule 1 to the Anti-terrorism, Crime
  and Security Act 2001'.
(6)   In paragraphs 2, 3 and 6(1), at the end insert 'or the terrorist cash provisions'.
(7)   In paragraph 5, after 'Act' insert 'or the terrorist cash provisions'.
(8)   In Part I of Schedule 1 to the Legal Aid, Advice and Assistance (Northern Ireland)
Order 1981 (SI 1981/228 (NI 8)) (proceedings for which legal aid may be given under Part
II of the Order), in paragraph 3 (courts of summary jurisdiction) after sub-paragraph (h)
insert—
        '(i)   proceedings under paragraphs 3, 5, 6, 9 and 10 of Schedule 1 to the
  Anti-terrorism, Crime and Security Act 2001'.

3.   Terrorist property: amendments
Schedule 2 contains amendments to the Terrorism Act 2000.

PART II
FREEZING ORDERS

Orders

4.   Power to make order
(1)   The Treasury may make a freezing order if the following two conditions are
satisfied.
(2)   The first condition is that the Treasury reasonably believe that—
  (a)   action to the detriment of the United Kingdom's economy (or part of it) has been
or is likely to be taken by a person or persons, or
  (b)   action constituting a threat to the life or property of one or more nationals of the
United Kingdom or residents of the United Kingdom has been or is likely to be taken by a
person or persons.
(3)   If one person is believed to have taken or to be likely to take the action the second
condition is that the person is—
  (a)   the government of a country or territory outside the United Kingdom, or
  (b)   a resident of a country or territory outside the United Kingdom.
(4)   If two or more persons are believed to have taken or to be likely to take the action
the second condition is that each of them falls within paragraph (a) or (b) of subsection (3);
and different persons may fall within different paragraphs.

5. Contents of order

(1) A freezing order is an order which prohibits persons from making funds available to or for the benefit of a person or persons specified in the order.

(2) The order must provide that these are the persons who are prohibited—

(a) all persons in the United Kingdom, and

(b) all persons elsewhere who are nationals of the United Kingdom or are bodies incorporated under the law of any part of the United Kingdom or are Scottish partnerships.

(3) The order may specify the following (and only the following) as the person or persons to whom or for whose benefit funds are not to be made available—

(a) the person or persons reasonably believed by the Treasury to have taken or to be likely to take the action referred to in section 4;

(b) any person the Treasury reasonably believe has provided or is likely to provide assistance (directly or indirectly) to that person or any of those persons.

(4) A person may be specified under subsection (3) by—

(a) being named in the order, or

(b) falling within a description of persons set out in the order.

(5) The description must be such that a reasonable person would know whether he fell within it.

(6) Funds are financial assets and economic benefits of any kind.

6. Contents: further provisions

Schedule 3 contains further provisions about the contents of freezing orders.

7. Review of order

The Treasury must keep a freezing order under review.

8. Duration of order

A freezing order ceases to have effect at the end of the period of 2 years starting with the day on which it is made.

Interpretation

9. Nationals and residents

(1) A national of the United Kingdom is an individual who is—

(a) a British citizen, a British Dependent Territories citizen, a British National (Overseas) or a British Overseas citizen,

(b) a person who under the British Nationality Act 1981 (c. 61) is a British subject, or

(c) a British protected person within the meaning of that Act.

(2) A resident of the United Kingdom is—

(a) an individual who is ordinarily resident in the United Kingdom,

(b) a body incorporated under the law of any part of the United Kingdom, or

(c) a Scottish partnership.

(3) A resident of a country or territory outside the United Kingdom is—

(a) an individual who is ordinarily resident in such a country or territory, or

(b) a body incorporated under the law of such a country or territory.

(4) For the purposes of subsection (3)(b) a branch situated in a country or territory outside the United Kingdom of—

(a) a body incorporated under the law of any part of the United Kingdom, or

(b) a Scottish partnership,

is to be treated as a body incorporated under the law of the country or territory where the branch is situated.

(5)   This section applies for the purposes of this Part.

Orders: procedure etc.

10.   Procedure for making freezing orders

(1)   A power to make a freezing order is exercisable by statutory instrument.

(2)   A freezing order—

(a)   must be laid before Parliament after being made;

(b)   ceases to have effect at the end of the relevant period unless before the end of that period the order is approved by a resolution of each House of Parliament (but without that affecting anything done under the order or the power to make a new order).

(3)   The relevant period is a period of 28 days starting with the day on which the order is made.

(4)   In calculating the relevant period no account is to be taken of any time during which Parliament is dissolved or prorogued or during which both Houses are adjourned for more than 4 days.

(5)   If the Treasury propose to make a freezing order in the belief that the condition in section 4(2)(b) is satisfied, they must not make the order unless they consult the Secretary of State.

11.   Procedure for making certain amending orders

(1)   This section applies if—

(a)   a freezing order is made specifying by description (rather than by name) the person or persons to whom or for whose benefit funds are not to be made available,

(b)   it is proposed to make a further order which amends the freezing order only so as to make it specify by name the person or persons (or any of the persons) to whom or for whose benefit funds are not to be made available, and

(c)   the Treasury reasonably believe that the person or persons named fall within the description contained in the freezing order and the further order contains a statement of the Treasury's belief.

(2)   This section also applies if—

(a)   a freezing order is made specifying by name the person or persons to whom or for whose benefit funds are not to be made available,

(b)   it is proposed to make a further order which amends the freezing order only so as to make it specify by name a further person or further persons to whom or for whose benefit funds are not to be made available, and

(c)   the Treasury reasonably believe that the further person or persons fall within the same description as the person or persons specified in the freezing order and the further order contains a statement of the Treasury's belief.

(3)   This section also applies if—

(a)   a freezing order is made, and

(b)   it is proposed to make a further order which amends the freezing order only so as to make it specify (whether by name or description) fewer persons to whom or for whose benefit funds are not to be made available.

(4)   If this section applies, a statutory instrument containing the further order is subject to annulment in pursuance of a resolution of either House of Parliament.

12.　Procedure for revoking orders

A statutory instrument containing an order revoking a freezing order (without re-enacting it) is subject to annulment in pursuance of a resolution of either House of Parliament.

13.　De-hybridisation

If apart from this section an order under this Part would be treated for the purposes of the standing orders of either House of Parliament as a hybrid instrument, it is to proceed in that House as if it were not such an instrument.

14.　Orders: supplementary

(1)　Where this Part confers a power to make provision, different provision may be made for different purposes.

(2)　An order under this Part may include supplementary, incidental, saving or transitional provisions.

(3)　Nothing in this Part affects the generality of subsection (2).

Miscellaneous

15.　The Crown

(1)　A freezing order binds the Crown, subject to the following provisions of this section.

(2)　No contravention by the Crown of a provision of a freezing order makes the Crown criminally liable; but the High Court or in Scotland the Court of Session may, on the application of a person appearing to the Court to have an interest, declare unlawful any act or omission of the Crown which constitutes such a contravention.

(3)　Nothing in this section affects Her Majesty in her private capacity; and this is to be construed as if section 38(3) of the Crown Proceedings Act 1947 (c. 44) (meaning of Her Majesty in her private capacity) were contained in this Act.

16.　Repeals

(1)　These provisions shall cease to have effect—

(a)　section 2 of the Emergency Laws (Re-enactments and Repeals) Act 1964 (c. 60) (Treasury's power to prohibit action on certain orders as to gold etc);

(b)　section 55 of the Finance Act 1968 (c. 44) (meaning of security in section 2 of 1964 Act).

(2)　Subsection (1) does not affect a reference which—

(a)　is to a provision referred to in that subsection, and

(b)　is contained in a provision made under an Act.

PART III
DISCLOSURE OF INFORMATION

17.　Extension of existing disclosure powers

(1)　This section applies to the provisions listed in Schedule 4, so far as they authorise the disclosure of information.

(2)　Each of the provisions to which this section applies shall have effect, in relation to the disclosure of information by or on behalf of a public authority, as if the purposes for which the disclosure of information is authorised by that provision included each of the following—

(a)　the purposes of any criminal investigation whatever which is being or may be carried out, whether in the United Kingdom or elsewhere;

(b)   the purposes of any criminal proceedings whatever which have been or may be initiated, whether in the United Kingdom or elsewhere;

(c)   the purposes of the initiation or bringing to an end of any such investigation or proceedings;

(d)   the purpose of facilitating a determination of whether any such investigation or proceedings should be initiated or brought to an end.

(3)   The Treasury may by order made by statutory instrument add any provision contained in any subordinate legislation to the provisions to which this section applies.

(4)   The Treasury shall not make an order under subsection (3) unless a draft of it has been laid before Parliament and approved by a resolution of each House.

(5)   No disclosure of information shall be made by virtue of this section unless the public authority by which the disclosure is made is satisfied that the making of the disclosure is proportionate to what is sought to be achieved by it.

(6)   Nothing in this section shall be taken to prejudice any power to disclose information which exists apart from this section.

(7)   The information that may be disclosed by virtue of this section includes information obtained before the commencement of this section.

18.   Restriction on disclosure of information for overseas purposes

(1)   Subject to subsections (2) and (3), the Secretary of State may give a direction which—

(a)   specifies any overseas proceedings or any description of overseas proceedings; and

(b)   prohibits the making of any relevant disclosure for the purposes of those proceedings or, as the case may be, of proceedings of that description.

(2)   In subsection (1) the reference, in relation to a direction, to a relevant disclosure is a reference to a disclosure authorised by any of the provisions to which section 17 applies which—

(a)   is made for a purpose mentioned in subsection (2)(a) to (d) of that section; and

(b)   is a disclosure of any such information as is described in the direction.

(3)   The Secretary of State shall not give a direction under this section unless it appears to him that the overseas proceedings in question, or that overseas proceedings of the description in question, relate or would relate—

(a)   to a matter in respect of which it would be more appropriate for any jurisdiction or investigation to be exercised or carried out by a court or other authority of the United Kingdom, or of a particular part of the United Kingdom;

(b)   to a matter in respect of which it would be more appropriate for any jurisdiction or investigation to be exercised or carried out by a court or other authority of a third country; or

(c)   to a matter that would fall within paragraph (a) or (b)—

(i)   if it were appropriate for there to be any exercise of jurisdiction or investigation at all; and

(ii)   if (where one does not exist) a court or other authority with the necessary jurisdiction or functions existed in the United Kingdom, in the part of the United Kingdom in question or, as the case may be, in the third country in question.

(4)   A direction under this section shall not have the effect of prohibiting—

(a)   the making of any disclosure by a Minister of the Crown or by the Treasury; or

(b)   the making of any disclosure in pursuance of a Community obligation.

(5) A direction under this section—

(a) may prohibit the making of disclosures absolutely or in such cases, or subject to such conditions as to consent or otherwise, as may be specified in it; and

(b) must be published or otherwise issued by the Secretary of State in such manner as he considers appropriate for bringing it to the attention of persons likely to be affected by it.

(6) A person who, knowing of any direction under this section, discloses any information in contravention of that direction shall be guilty of an offence and liable—

(a) on conviction on indictment, to imprisonment for a term not exceeding two years or to a fine or to both;

(b) on summary conviction, to imprisonment for a term not exceeding three months or to a fine not exceeding the statutory maximum or to both.

(7) The following are overseas proceedings for the purposes of this section—

(a) criminal proceedings which are taking place, or will or may take place, in a country or territory outside the United Kingdom;

(b) a criminal investigation which is being, or will or may be, conducted by an authority of any such country or territory.

(8) References in this section, in relation to any proceedings or investigation, to a third country are references to any country or territory outside the United Kingdom which is not the country or territory where the proceedings are taking place, or will or may take place or, as the case may be, is not the country or territory of the authority which is conducting the investigation, or which will or may conduct it.

(9) In this section 'court' includes a tribunal of any description.

19. Disclosure of information held by revenue departments

(1) This section applies to information which is held by or on behalf of the Commissioners of Inland Revenue or by or on behalf of the Commissioners of Customs and Excise, including information obtained before the coming into force of this section.

(2) No obligation of secrecy imposed by statute or otherwise prevents the disclosure, in accordance with the following provisions of this section, of information to which this section applies if the disclosure is made—

(a) for the purpose of facilitating the carrying out by any of the intelligence services of any of that service's functions;

(b) for the purposes of any criminal investigation whatever which is being or may be carried out, whether in the United Kingdom or elsewhere;

(c) for the purposes of any criminal proceedings whatever which have been or may be initiated, whether in the United Kingdom or elsewhere;

(d) for the purposes of the initiation or bringing to an end of any such investigation or proceedings; or

(e) for the purpose of facilitating a determination of whether any such investigation or proceedings should be initiated or brought to an end.

(3) No disclosure of information to which this section applies shall be made by virtue of this section unless the person by whom the disclosure is made is satisfied that the making of the disclosure is proportionate to what is sought to be achieved by it.

(4) Information to which this section applies shall not be disclosed by virtue of this section except by the Commissioners by or on whose behalf it is held or with their authority.

(5) Information obtained by means of a disclosure authorised by subsection (2) shall not be further disclosed except—

(a) for a purpose mentioned in that subsection; and

(b) with the consent of the Commissioners by whom or with whose authority it was initially disclosed;

and information so obtained otherwise than by or on behalf of any of the intelligence services shall not be further disclosed (with or without such consent) to any of those services, or to any person acting on behalf of any of those services, except for a purpose mentioned in paragraphs (b) to (e) of that subsection.

(6) A consent for the purposes of subsection (5) may be given either in relation to a particular disclosure or in relation to disclosures made in such circumstances as may be specified or described in the consent.

(7) Nothing in this section authorises the making of any disclosure which is prohibited by any provision of the Data Protection Act 1998 (c. 29).

(8) References in this section to information which is held on behalf of the Commissioners of Inland Revenue or of the Commissioners of Customs and Excise include references to information which—

(a) is held by a person who provides services to the Commissioners of Inland Revenue or, as the case may be, to the Commissioners of Customs and Excise; and

(b) is held by that person in connection with the provision of those services.

(9) In this section 'intelligence service' has the same meaning as in the Regulation of Investigatory Powers Act 2000 (c. 23).

(10) Nothing in this section shall be taken to prejudice any power to disclose information which exists apart from this section.

20. Interpretation of Part 3

(1) In this Part—

'criminal investigation' means an investigation of any criminal conduct, including an investigation of alleged or suspected criminal conduct and an investigation of whether criminal conduct has taken place;

'information' includes—

(a) documents; and

(b) in relation to a disclosure authorised by a provision to which section 17 applies, anything that falls to be treated as information for the purposes of that provision;

'public authority' has the same meaning as in section 6 of the Human Rights Act 1998 (c. 42); and

'subordinate legislation' has the same meaning as in the Interpretation Act 1978 (c. 30).

(2) Proceedings outside the United Kingdom shall not be taken to be criminal proceedings for the purposes of this Part unless the conduct with which the defendant in those proceedings is charged is criminal conduct or conduct which, to a substantial extent, consists of criminal conduct.

(3) In this section—

'conduct' includes acts, omissions and statements; and

'criminal conduct' means any conduct which—

(a) constitutes one or more criminal offences under the law of a part of the United Kingdom; or

(b) is, or corresponds to, conduct which, if it all took place in a particular part of the United Kingdom, would constitute one or more offences under the law of that part of the United Kingdom.

PART IV
IMMIGRATION AND ASYLUM

Suspected international terrorists

21. Suspected international terrorist: certification

(1) The Secretary of State may issue a certificate under this section in respect of a person if the Secretary of State reasonably—

(a) believes that the person's presence in the United Kingdom is a risk to national security, and

(b) suspects that the person is a terrorist.

(2) In subsection (1)(b) 'terrorist' means a person who—

(a) is or has been concerned in the commission, preparation or instigation of acts of international terrorism,

(b) is a member of or belongs to an international terrorist group, or

(c) has links with an international terrorist group.

(3) A group is an international terrorist group for the purposes of subsection (2)(b) and (c) if—

(a) it is subject to the control or influence of persons outside the United Kingdom, and

(b) the Secretary of State suspects that it is concerned in the commission, preparation or instigation of acts of international terrorism.

(4) For the purposes of subsection (2)(c) a person has links with an international terrorist group only if he supports or assists it.

(5) In this Part—

'terrorism' has the meaning given by section 1 of the Terrorism Act 2000 (c. 11), and

'suspected international terrorist' means a person certified under subsection (1).

(6) Where the Secretary of State issues a certificate under subsection (1) he shall as soon as is reasonably practicable—

(a) take reasonable steps to notify the person certified, and

(b) send a copy of the certificate to the Special Immigration Appeals Commission.

(7) The Secretary of State may revoke a certificate issued under subsection (1).

(8) A decision of the Secretary of State in connection with certification under this section may be questioned in legal proceedings only under section 25 or 26.

(9) An action of the Secretary of State taken wholly or partly in reliance on a certificate under this section may be questioned in legal proceedings only by or in the course of proceedings under—

(a) section 25 or 26, or

(b) section 2 of the Special Immigration Appeals Commission Act 1997 (c. 68) (appeal).

22. Deportation, removal, &c.

(1) An action of a kind specified in subsection (2) may be taken in respect of a suspected international terrorist despite the fact that (whether temporarily or indefinitely) the action cannot result in his removal from the United Kingdom because of—

(a) a point of law which wholly or partly relates to an international agreement, or

(b) a practical consideration.

(2) The actions mentioned in subsection (1) are—

(a) refusing leave to enter or remain in the United Kingdom in accordance with provision made by or by virtue of any of sections 3 to 3B of the Immigration Act 1971 (c. 77) (control of entry to United Kingdom),

(b)   varying a limited leave to enter or remain in the United Kingdom in accordance with provision made by or by virtue of any of those sections,

(c)   recommending deportation in accordance with section 3(6) of that Act (recommendation by court),

(d)   taking a decision to make a deportation order under section 5(1) of that Act (deportation by Secretary of State),

(e)   making a deportation order under section 5(1) of that Act,

(f)   refusing to revoke a deportation order,

(g)   cancelling leave to enter the United Kingdom in accordance with paragraph 2A of Schedule 2 to that Act (person arriving with continuous leave),

(h)   giving directions for a person's removal from the United Kingdom under any of paragraphs 8 to 10 or 12 to 14 of Schedule 2 to that Act (control of entry to United Kingdom),

(i)   giving directions for a person's removal from the United Kingdom under section 10 of the Immigration and Asylum Act 1999 (c. 33) (person unlawfully in United Kingdom), and

(j)   giving notice to a person in accordance with regulations under paragraph 1 of Schedule 4 to that Act of a decision to make a deportation order against him.

(3)   Action of a kind specified in subsection (2) which has effect in respect of a suspected international terrorist at the time of his certification under section 21 shall be treated as taken again (in reliance on subsection (1) above) immediately after certification.

23. Detention

(1)   A suspected international terrorist may be detained under a provision specified in subsection (2) despite the fact that his removal or departure from the United Kingdom is prevented (whether temporarily or indefinitely) by—

(a)   a point of law which wholly or partly relates to an international agreement, or

(b)   a practical consideration.

(2)   The provisions mentioned in subsection (1) are—

(a)   paragraph 16 of Schedule 2 to the Immigration Act 1971 (c. 77) (detention of persons liable to examination or removal), and

(b)   paragraph 2 of Schedule 3 to that Act (detention pending deportation).

24. Bail

(1)   A suspected international terrorist who is detained under a provision of the Immigration Act 1971 may be released on bail.

(2)   For the purpose of subsection (1) the following provisions of Schedule 2 to the Immigration Act 1971 (control on entry) shall apply with the modifications specified in Schedule 3 to the Special Immigration Appeals Commission Act 1997 (c. 68) (bail to be determined by Special Immigration Appeals Commission) and with any other necessary modifications—

(a)   paragraph 22(1A), (2) and (3) (release),

(b)   paragraph 23 (forfeiture),

(c)   paragraph 24 (arrest), and

(d)   paragraph 30(1) (requirement of Secretary of State's consent).

(3)   Rules of procedure under the Special Immigration Appeals Commission Act 1997 (c. 68)—

(a)   may make provision in relation to release on bail by virtue of this section, and

(b)   subject to provision made by virtue of paragraph (a), shall apply in relation to release on bail by virtue of this section as they apply in relation to release on bail by virtue of that Act subject to any modification which the Commission considers necessary.

25. Certification: appeal

(1)   A suspected international terrorist may appeal to the Special Immigration Appeals Commission against his certification under section 21.

(2)   On an appeal the Commission must cancel the certificate if—

(a)   it considers that there are no reasonable grounds for a belief or suspicion of the kind referred to in section 21(1)(a) or (b), or

(b)   it considers that for some other reason the certificate should not have been issued.

(3)   If the Commission determines not to cancel a certificate it must dismiss the appeal.

(4)   Where a certificate is cancelled under subsection (2) it shall be treated as never having been issued.

(5)   An appeal against certification may be commenced only—

(a)   within the period of three months beginning with the date on which the certificate is issued, or

(b)   with the leave of the Commission, after the end of that period but before the commencement of the first review under section 26.

26. Certification: review

(1)   The Special Immigration Appeals Commission must hold a first review of each certificate issued under section 21 as soon as is reasonably practicable after the expiry of the period of six months beginning with the date on which the certificate is issued.

(2)   But—

(a)   in a case where before the first review would fall to be held in accordance with subsection (1) an appeal under section 25 is commenced (whether or not it is finally determined before that time) or leave to appeal is given under section 25(5)(b), the first review shall be held as soon as is reasonably practicable after the expiry of the period of six months beginning with the date on which the appeal is finally determined, and

(b)   in a case where an application for leave under section 25(5)(b) has been commenced but not determined at the time when the first review would fall to be held in accordance with subsection (1), if leave is granted the first review shall be held as soon as is reasonably practicable after the expiry of the period of six months beginning with the date on which the appeal is finally determined.

(3)   The Commission must review each certificate issued under section 21 as soon as is reasonably practicable after the expiry of the period of three months beginning with the date on which the first review or a review under this subsection is finally determined.

(4)   The Commission may review a certificate during a period mentioned in subsection (1), (2) or (3) if—

(a)   the person certified applies for a review, and

(b)   the Commission considers that a review should be held because of a change in circumstance.

(5)   On a review the Commission—

(a)   must cancel the certificate if it considers that there are no reasonable grounds for a belief or suspicion of the kind referred to in section 21(1)(a) or (b), and

(b)   otherwise, may not make any order (save as to leave to appeal).

(6)   A certificate cancelled by order of the Commission under subsection (5) ceases to have effect at the end of the day on which the order is made.

(7)   Where the Commission reviews a certificate under subsection (4), the period for determining the next review of the certificate under subsection (3) shall begin with the date of the final determination of the review under subsection (4).

27. Appeal and review: supplementary

(1) The following provisions of the Special Immigration Appeals Commission Act 1997 (c. 68) shall apply in relation to an appeal or review under section 25 or 26 as they apply in relation to an appeal under section 2 of that Act—

  (a) section 6 (person to represent appellant's interests),

  (b) section 7 (further appeal on point of law), and

  (c) section 7A (pending appeal).

(2) The reference in subsection (1) to an appeal or review does not include a reference to a decision made or action taken on or in connection with—

  (a) an application under section 25(5)(b) or 26(4)(a) of this Act, or

  (b) subsection (8) below.

(3) Subsection (4) applies where—

  (a) a further appeal is brought by virtue of subsection (1)(b) in connection with an appeal or review, and

  (b) the Secretary of State notifies the Commission that in his opinion the further appeal is confined to calling into question one or more derogation matters within the meaning of section 30 of this Act.

(4) For the purpose of the application of section 26(2) and (3) of this Act the determination by the Commission of the appeal or review in connection with which the further appeal is brought shall be treated as a final determination.

(5) Rules under section 5 or 8 of the Special Immigration Appeals Commission Act 1997 (general procedure; and leave to appeal) may make provision about an appeal, review or application under section 25 or 26 of this Act.

(6) Subject to any provision made by virtue of subsection (5), rules under section 5 or 8 of that Act shall apply in relation to an appeal, review or application under section 25 or 26 of this Act with any modification which the Commission considers necessary.

(7) Subsection (8) applies where the Commission considers that an appeal or review under section 25 or 26 which relates to a person's certification under section 21 is likely to raise an issue which is also likely to be raised in other proceedings before the Commission which relate to the same person.

(8) The Commission shall so far as is reasonably practicable—

  (a) deal with the two sets of proceedings together, and

  (b) avoid or minimise delay to either set of proceedings as a result of compliance with paragraph (a).

(9) Cancellation by the Commission of a certificate issued under section 21 shall not prevent the Secretary of State from issuing another certificate, whether on the grounds of a change of circumstance or otherwise.

(10) The reference in section 81 of the Immigration and Asylum Act 1999 (c. 33) (grants to voluntary organisations) to persons who have rights of appeal under that Act shall be treated as including a reference to suspected international terrorists.

28. Review of sections 21 to 23

(1) The Secretary of State shall appoint a person to review the operation of sections 21 to 23.

(2) The person appointed under subsection (1) shall review the operation of those sections not later than—

  (a) the expiry of the period of 14 months beginning with the day on which this Act is passed;

(b) one month before the expiry of a period specified in accordance with section 29(2)(b) or (c).

(3) Where that person conducts a review under subsection (2) he shall send a report to the Secretary of State as soon as is reasonably practicable.

(4) Where the Secretary of State receives a report under subsection (3) he shall lay a copy of it before Parliament as soon as is reasonably practicable.

(5) The Secretary of State may make payments to a person appointed under subsection (1).

29. Duration of sections 21 to 23

(1) Sections 21 to 23 shall, subject to the following provisions of this section, expire at the end of the period of 15 months beginning with the day on which this Act is passed.

(2) The Secretary of State may by order—

    (a) repeal sections 21 to 23;

    (b) revive those sections for a period not exceeding one year;

    (c) provide that those sections shall not expire in accordance with subsection (1) or an order under paragraph (b) or this paragraph, but shall continue in force for a period not exceeding one year.

(3) An order under subsection (2)—

    (a) must be made by statutory instrument, and

    (b) may not be made unless a draft has been laid before and approved by resolution of each House of Parliament.

(4) An order may be made without compliance with subsection (3)(b) if it contains a declaration by the Secretary of State that by reason of urgency it is necessary to make the order without laying a draft before Parliament; in which case the order—

    (a) must be laid before Parliament, and

    (b) shall cease to have effect at the end of the period specified in subsection (5) unless the order is approved during that period by resolution of each House of Parliament.

(5) The period referred to in subsection (4)(b) is the period of 40 days—

    (a) beginning with the day on which the order is made, and

    (b) ignoring any period during which Parliament is dissolved or prorogued or during which both Houses are adjourned for more than four days.

(6) The fact that an order ceases to have effect by virtue of subsection (4)—

    (a) shall not affect the lawfulness of anything done before the order ceases to have effect, and

    (b) shall not prevent the making of a new order.

(7) Sections 21 to 23 shall by virtue of this subsection cease to have effect at the end of 10th November 2006.

30. Legal proceedings: derogation

(1) In this section 'derogation matter' means—

    (a) a derogation by the United Kingdom from Article 5(1) of the Convention on Human Rights which relates to the detention of a person where there is an intention to remove or deport him from the United Kingdom, or

    (b) the designation under section 14(1) of the Human Rights Act 1998 (c. 42) of a derogation within paragraph (a) above.

(2) A derogation matter may be questioned in legal proceedings only before the Special Immigration Appeals Commission; and the Commission—

    (a) is the appropriate tribunal for the purpose of section 7 of the Human Rights Act 1998 in relation to proceedings all or part of which call a derogation matter into question; and

(b)   may hear proceedings which could, but for this subsection, be brought in the High Court or the Court of Session.

(3)   In relation to proceedings brought by virtue of subsection (2)—

(a)   section 6 of the Special Immigration Appeals Commission Act 1997 (c. 68) (person to represent appellant's interests) shall apply with the reference to the appellant being treated as a reference to any party to the proceedings,

(b)   rules under section 5 or 8 of that Act (general procedure; and leave to appeal) shall apply with any modification which the Commission considers necessary, and

(c)   in the case of proceedings brought by virtue of subsection (2)(b), the Commission may do anything which the High Court may do (in the case of proceedings which could have been brought in that court) or which the Court of Session may do (in the case of proceedings which could have been brought in that court).

(4)   The Commission's power to award costs (or, in Scotland, expenses) by virtue of subsection (3)(c) may be exercised only in relation to such part of proceedings before it as calls a derogation matter into question.

(5)   In relation to proceedings brought by virtue of subsection (2)(a) or (b)—

(a)   an appeal may be brought to the appropriate appeal court (within the meaning of section 7 of the Special Immigration Appeals Commission Act 1997 (c. 68)) with the leave of the Commission or, if that leave is refused, with the leave of the appropriate appeal court, and

(b)   the appropriate appeal court may consider and do only those things which it could consider and do in an appeal brought from the High Court or the Court of Session in proceedings for judicial review.

(6)   In relation to proceedings which are entertained by the Commission under subsection (2) but are not brought by virtue of subsection (2)(a) or (b), subsection (4) shall apply in so far as the proceedings call a derogation matter into question.

(7)   In this section 'the Convention on Human Rights' has the meaning given to 'the Convention' by section 21(1) of the Human Rights Act 1998 (c. 42).

31. Interpretation
A reference in section 22, 23 or 24 to a provision of the Immigration Act 1971 (c. 77) includes a reference to that provision as applied by—

(a)   another provision of that Act, or

(b)   another Act.

32. Channel Islands and Isle of Man
Her Majesty may by Order in Council direct that sections 21 to 31 shall extend, with such modifications as appear to Her Majesty to be appropriate, to any of the Channel Islands or the Isle of Man.

Refugee Convention

33. Certificate that Convention does not apply
(1)   This section applies to an asylum appeal before the Special Immigration Appeals Commission where the Secretary of State issues a certificate that—

(a)   the appellant is not entitled to the protection of Article 33(1) of the Refugee Convention because Article 1(F) or 33(2) applies to him (whether or not he would be entitled to protection if that Article did not apply), and

(b)   the removal of the appellant from the United Kingdom would be conducive to the public good.

(2)   In this section—

'asylum appeal' means an appeal under section 2 of the Special Immigration Appeals Commission Act 1997 (c. 68) in which the appellant makes a claim for asylum (within the meaning given by section 167(1) of the Immigration and Asylum Act 1999 (c. 33)), and

'the Refugee Convention' has the meaning given by that section.

(3)   Where this section applies the Commission must begin its substantive deliberations on the asylum appeal by considering the statements in the Secretary of State's certificate.

(4)   If the Commission agrees with those statements it must dismiss such part of the asylum appeal as amounts to a claim for asylum (before considering any other aspect of the case).

(5)   If the Commission does not agree with those statements it must quash the decision or action against which the asylum appeal is brought.

(6)   Where a decision or action is quashed under subsection (5)—

(a)   the quashing shall not prejudice any later decision or action, whether taken on the grounds of a change of circumstance or otherwise, and

(b)   the claim for asylum made in the course of the asylum appeal shall be treated for the purposes of section 15 of the Immigration and Asylum Act 1999 (interim protection from removal) as undecided until it has been determined whether to take a new decision or action of the kind quashed.

(7)   The Secretary of State may revoke a certificate issued under subsection (1).

(8)   No court may entertain proceedings for questioning—

(a)   a decision or action of the Secretary of State in connection with certification under subsection (1),

(b)   a decision of the Secretary of State in connection with a claim for asylum (within the meaning given by section 167(1) of the Immigration and Asylum Act 1999) in a case in respect of which he issues a certificate under subsection (1) above, or

(c)   a decision or action of the Secretary of State taken as a consequence of the dismissal of all or part of an asylum appeal in pursuance of subsection (4).

(9)   Subsection (8) shall not prevent an appeal under section 7 of the Special Immigration Appeals Commission Act 1997 (appeal on point of law).

(10)   Her Majesty may by Order in Council direct that this section shall extend, with such modifications as appear to Her Majesty to be appropriate, to any of the Channel Islands or the Isle of Man.

34.   Construction

(1)   Articles 1(F) and 33(2) of the Refugee Convention (exclusions: war criminals, national security, &c.) shall not be taken to require consideration of the gravity of—

(a)   events or fear by virtue of which Article 1(A) would or might apply to a person if Article 1(F) did not apply, or

(b)   a threat by reason of which Article 33(1) would or might apply to a person if Article 33(2) did not apply.

(2)   In this section 'the Refugee Convention' means the Convention relating to the Status of Refugees done at Geneva on 28th July 1951 and the Protocol to the Convention.

Special Immigration Appeals Commission

35.   Status of Commission

At the end of section 1 of the Special Immigration Appeals Commission Act 1997 (c. 68) insert—

'(3)   The Commission shall be a superior court of record.

(4)   A decision of the Commission shall be questioned in legal proceedings only in accordance with—

(a)   section 7, or

(b)   section 30(5)(a) of the Anti-terrorism, Crime and Security Act 2001 (derogation).'

Fingerprints

36.   Destruction of fingerprints

(1)   In section 143 of the Immigration and Asylum Act 1999 (c. 33) (destruction of fingerprints)—

(a)   subsections (3) to (8) (requirement to destroy fingerprints on resolution of asylum and immigration cases) shall cease to have effect,

(b)   in subsection (9) (dependants) after 'F' insert '(within the meaning of section 141(7))', and

(c)   subsection (14) (interpretation) shall cease to have effect.

(2)   Subsection (1)—

(a)   shall have effect in relation to fingerprints whether taken before or after the coming into force of this section, and

(b)   in relation to fingerprints which before the coming into force of this section were required by section 143 to be destroyed, shall be treated as having had effect before the requirement arose.

PART V
RACE AND RELIGION

37.   Meaning of racial hatred

In section 17 of the Public Order Act 1986 (c. 64) (racial hatred defined by reference to a group of persons in Great Britain) omit the words 'in Great Britain'.

38.   Meaning of fear and hatred

In Article 8 of the Public Order (Northern Ireland) Order 1987 (SI 1987/463 (NI 7)) in the definition of fear and the definition of hatred (fear and hatred defined by reference to a group of persons in Northern Ireland) omit the words 'in Northern Ireland'.

39.   Religiously aggravated offences

(1)   Part 2 of the Crime and Disorder Act 1998 (c. 37) is amended as set out in subsections (2) to (6).

(2)   In the cross-heading preceding section 28 for 'Racially-aggravated' substitute 'Racially or religiously aggravated'.

(3)   In section 28 (meaning of racially aggravated)—

(a)   in the sidenote and subsection (1) for 'racially aggravated' substitute 'racially or religiously aggravated';

(b)   in subsections (1) and (2) for 'racial group' substitute 'racial or religious group';

(c)   in subsection (3) for the words from 'on' to the end of the subsection substitute 'on any other factor not mentioned in that paragraph.'

(4)   In section 28 after subsection (4) insert—

'(5)   In this section "religious group" means a group of persons defined by reference to religious belief or lack of religious belief.'

(5)   In each of the provisions listed in subsection (6)—

(a)   in the sidenote for 'Racially-aggravated' substitute 'Racially or religiously aggravated';

(b)   in subsection (1) for 'racially aggravated' substitute 'racially or religiously aggravated'.

(6)   The provisions are—

(a)   section 29 (assaults);

(b)   section 30 (criminal damage);

(c)   section 31 (public order offences);

(d)   section 32 (harassment etc.).

(7)   In section 153 of the Powers of Criminal Courts (Sentencing) Act 2000 (c. 6) (increase in sentences for racial aggravation)—

(a)   in the sidenote for 'racial aggravation' substitute 'racial or religious aggravation';

(b)   in subsection (1) for the words from 'racially-aggravated assaults' to the end of the subsection substitute 'racially or religiously aggravated assaults, criminal damage, public order offences and harassment etc).';

(c)   in subsections (2) and (3) for 'racially aggravated' substitute 'racially or religiously aggravated'.

(8)   In section 24(2) of the Police and Criminal Evidence Act 1984 (c. 60) (arrestable offences) in paragraph (p) (offences falling within section 32(1)(a) of the Crime and Disorder Act 1998) for 'racially-aggravated' substitute 'racially or religiously aggravated'.

40.   Racial hatred offences: penalties
In section 27(3) of the Public Order Act 1986 (c. 64) (penalties for racial hatred offences) for 'two years' substitute 'seven years'.

41.   Hatred and fear offences: penalties
In Article 16(1) of the Public Order (Northern Ireland) Order 1987 (SI 1987/463 (NI 7)) (penalties for offences involving stirring up hatred or arousing fear) for '2 years' substitute '7 years'.

42.   Saving
This Part does not apply to anything done before it comes into force.

PART VI
WEAPONS OF MASS DESTRUCTION

Amendment of the Biological Weapons Act 1974 and the Chemical Weapons
Act 1996

43.   Transfers of biological agents and toxins
In section 1 of the Biological Weapons Act 1974 (c. 6) (restriction on development etc. of certain biological agents and toxins and of biological weapons), after subsection (1) insert—

'(1A)   A person shall not—

(a)   transfer any biological agent or toxin to another person or enter into an agreement to do so, or

(b)   make arrangements under which another person transfers any biological agent or toxin or enters into an agreement with a third person to do so,

if the biological agent or toxin is likely to be kept or used (whether by the transferee or any other person) otherwise than for prophylactic, protective or other peaceful purposes and he knows or has reason to believe that that is the case.'

44. Extraterritorial application of biological weapons offences
After section 1 of the Biological Weapons Act 1974 insert—

'1A. Extraterritorial application of section 1
(1) Section 1 applies to acts done outside the United Kingdom, but only if they are done by a United Kingdom person.

(2) Proceedings for an offence committed under section 1 outside the United Kingdom may be taken, and the offence may for incidental purposes be treated as having been committed, in any place in the United Kingdom.

(3) Her Majesty may by Order in Council extend the application of section 1, so far as it applies to acts done outside the United Kingdom, to bodies incorporated under the law of any of the Channel Islands, the Isle of Man or any colony.

(4) In this section "United Kingdom person" means a United Kingdom national, a Scottish partnership or a body incorporated under the law of a part of the United Kingdom.

(5) For this purpose a United Kingdom national is an individual who is—

(a) a British citizen, a British Dependent Territories citizen, a British National (Overseas) or a British Overseas citizen;

(b) a person who under the British Nationality Act 1981 (c. 61) is a British subject; or

(c) a British protected person within the meaning of that Act.

(6) Nothing in this section affects any criminal liability arising otherwise than under this section.'

45. Customs and Excise prosecutions for biological weapons offences
Before section 2 of the Biological Weapons Act 1974 (c. 6) insert—

'1B Customs and Excise prosecutions
(1) Proceedings for a biological weapons offence may be instituted by order of the Commissioners of Customs and Excise if it appears to them that the offence has involved—

(a) the development or production outside the United Kingdom of any thing mentioned in section 1(1)(a) or (b) above;

(b) the movement of any such thing into or out of any country or territory;

(c) any proposal or attempt to do anything falling within paragraph (a) or (b) above.

(2) In this section "biological weapons offence" means an offence under section 1 of this Act or section 50 of the Anti-terrorism, Crime and Security Act 2001 (including an offence of aiding, abetting, counselling, procuring or inciting the commission of, or attempting or conspiring to commit, such an offence).

(3) Any proceedings for an offence which are instituted under subsection (1) above shall be commenced in the name of an officer, but may be continued by another officer.

(4) Where the Commissioners of Customs and Excise investigate, or propose to investigate, any matter with a view to determining—

(a) whether there are grounds for believing that a biological weapons offence has been committed, or

(b) whether a person should be prosecuted for such an offence,

that matter shall be treated as an assigned matter within the meaning of the Customs and Excise Management Act 1979.

(5)   Nothing in this section affects any power of any person (including any officer) apart from this section.

(6)   In this section "officer" means a person commissioned by the Commissioners of Customs and Excise.

(7)   This section does not apply to the institution of proceedings in Scotland.'

46.   Customs and Excise prosecutions for chemical weapons offences
Before section 31 of the Chemical Weapons Act 1996 (c. 6) insert—

'30A.   A Customs and Excise prosecutions

(1)   Proceedings for a chemical weapons offence may be instituted by order of the Commissioners of Customs and Excise if it appears to them that the offence has involved—

(a)   the development or production outside the United Kingdom of a chemical weapon;

(b)   the movement of a chemical weapon into or out of any country or territory;

(c)   any proposal or attempt to do anything falling within paragraph (a) or (b).

(2)   In this section "chemical weapons offence" means an offence under section 2 above or section 50 of the Anti-terrorism, Crime and Security Act 2001 (including an offence of aiding, abetting, counselling, procuring or inciting the commission of, or attempting or conspiring to commit, such an offence).

(3)   Any proceedings for an offence which are instituted under subsection (1) shall be commenced in the name of an officer, but may be continued by another officer.

(4)   Where the Commissioners of Customs and Excise investigate, or propose to investigate, any matter with a view to determining—

(a)   whether there are grounds for believing that a chemical weapons offence has been committed, or

(b)   whether a person should be prosecuted for such an offence,

that matter shall be treated as an assigned matter within the meaning of the Customs and Excise Management Act 1979.

(5)   Nothing in this section affects any power of any person (including any officer) apart from this section.

(6)   In this section "officer" means a person commissioned by the Commissioners of Customs and Excise.

(7)   This section does not apply to the institution of proceedings in Scotland.'

Nuclear weapons

47.   Use etc. of nuclear weapons

(1)   A person who—

(a)   knowingly causes a nuclear weapon explosion;

(b)   develops or produces, or participates in the development or production of, a nuclear weapon;

(c)   has a nuclear weapon in his possession;

(d)   participates in the transfer of a nuclear weapon; or

(e)   engages in military preparations, or in preparations of a military nature, intending to use, or threaten to use, a nuclear weapon,

is guilty of an offence.

(2)   Subsection (1) has effect subject to the exceptions and defences in sections 48 and 49.

(3)   For the purposes of subsection (1)(b) a person participates in the development or production of a nuclear weapon if he does any act which—

(a)   facilitates the development by another of the capability to produce or use a nuclear weapon, or

(b)   facilitates the making by another of a nuclear weapon,

knowing or having reason to believe that his act has (or will have) that effect.

(4)   For the purposes of subsection (1)(d) a person participates in the transfer of a nuclear weapon if—

(a)   he buys or otherwise acquires it or agrees with another to do so;

(b)   he sells or otherwise disposes of it or agrees with another to do so; or

(c)   he makes arrangements under which another person either acquires or disposes of it or agrees with a third person to do so.

(5)   A person guilty of an offence under this section is liable on conviction on indictment to imprisonment for life.

(6)   In this section 'nuclear weapon' includes a nuclear explosive device that is not intended for use as a weapon.

(7)   This section applies to acts done outside the United Kingdom, but only if they are done by a United Kingdom person.

(8)   Nothing in subsection (7) affects any criminal liability arising otherwise than under that subsection.

(9)   Paragraph (a) of subsection (1) shall cease to have effect on the coming into force of the Nuclear Explosions (Prohibition and Inspections) Act 1998 (c. 7).

48. Exceptions

(1)   Nothing in section 47 applies—

(a)   to an act which is authorised under subsection (2); or

(b)   to an act done in the course of an armed conflict.

(2)   The Secretary of State may—

(a)   authorise any act which would otherwise contravene section 47 in such manner and on such terms as he thinks fit; and

(b)   withdraw or vary any authorisation given under this subsection.

(3)   Any question arising in proceedings for an offence under section 47 as to whether anything was done in the course of an armed conflict shall be determined by the Secretary of State.

(4)   A certificate purporting to set out any such determination and to be signed by the Secretary of State shall be received in evidence in any such proceedings and shall be presumed to be so signed unless the contrary is shown.

49. Defences

(1)   In proceedings for an offence under section 47(1)(c) or (d) relating to an object it is a defence for the accused to show that he did not know and had no reason to believe that the object was a nuclear weapon.

(2)   But he shall be taken to have shown that fact if—

(a)   sufficient evidence is adduced to raise an issue with respect to it; and

(b)   the contrary is not proved by the prosecution beyond reasonable doubt.

(3)   In proceedings for such an offence it is also a defence for the accused to show that he knew or believed that the object was a nuclear weapon but, as soon as reasonably practicable after he first knew or believed that fact, he took all reasonable steps to inform the Secretary of State or a constable of his knowledge or belief.

Assisting or inducing weapons-related acts overseas

50. Assisting or inducing certain weapons-related acts overseas

(1) A person who aids, abets, counsels or procures, or incites, a person who is not a United Kingdom person to do a relevant act outside the United Kingdom is guilty of an offence.

(2) For this purpose a relevant act is an act that, if done by a United Kingdom person, would contravene any of the following provisions—

(a)   section 1 of the Biological Weapons Act 1974 (offences relating to biological agents and toxins);

(b)   section 2 of the Chemical Weapons Act 1996 (offences relating to chemical weapons); or

(c)   section 47 above (offences relating to nuclear weapons).

(3) Nothing in this section applies to an act mentioned in subsection (1) which—

(a)   relates to a relevant act which would contravene section 47; and

(b)   is authorised by the Secretary of State;

and section 48(2) applies for the purpose of authorising acts that would otherwise constitute an offence under this section.

(4) A person accused of an offence under this section in relation to a relevant act which would contravene a provision mentioned in subsection (2) may raise any defence which would be open to a person accused of the corresponding offence ancillary to an offence under that provision.

(5) A person convicted of an offence under this section is liable on conviction on indictment to imprisonment for life.

(6) This section applies to acts done outside the United Kingdom, but only if they are done by a United Kingdom person.

(7) Nothing in this section prejudices any criminal liability existing apart from this section.

Supplemental provisions relating to sections 47 and 50

51. Extraterritorial application

(1) Proceedings for an offence committed under section 47 or 50 outside the United Kingdom may be taken, and the offence may for incidental purposes be treated as having been committed, in any part of the United Kingdom.

(2) Her Majesty may by Order in Council extend the application of section 47 or 50, so far as it applies to acts done outside the United Kingdom, to bodies incorporated under the law of any of the Channel Islands, the Isle of Man or any colony.

52. Powers of entry

(1) If—

(a)   a justice of the peace is satisfied on information on oath that there are reasonable grounds for suspecting that evidence of the commission of an offence under section 47 or 50 is to be found on any premises; or

(b)   in Scotland the sheriff is satisfied by evidence on oath as mentioned in paragraph (a),

he may issue a warrant authorising an authorised officer to enter the premises, if necessary by force, at any time within one month from the time of the issue of the warrant and to search them.

(2) The powers of a person who enters the premises under the authority of the warrant include power—

(a) to take with him such other persons and such equipment as appear to him to be necessary;

(b) to inspect, seize and retain any substance, equipment or document found on the premises;

(c) to require any document or other information which is held in electronic form and is accessible from the premises to be produced in a form—

(i) in which he can read and copy it; or

(ii) from which it can readily be produced in a form in which he can read and copy it;

(d) to copy any document which he has reasonable cause to believe may be required as evidence for the purposes of proceedings in respect of an offence under section 47 or 50.

(3) A constable who enters premises under the authority of a warrant or by virtue of subsection (2)(a) may—

(a) give such assistance as an authorised officer may request for the purpose of facilitating the exercise of any power under this section; and

(b) search or cause to be searched any person on the premises who the constable has reasonable cause to believe may have in his possession any document or other thing which may be required as evidence for the purposes of proceedings in respect of an offence under section 47 or 50.

(4) No constable shall search a person of the opposite sex.

(5) The powers conferred by a warrant under this section shall only be exercisable, if the warrant so provides, in the presence of a constable.

(6) A person who—

(a) wilfully obstructs an authorised officer in the exercise of a power conferred by a warrant under this section; or

(b) fails without reasonable excuse to comply with a reasonable request made by an authorised officer or a constable for the purpose of facilitating the exercise of such a power, is guilty of an offence.

(7) A person guilty of an offence under subsection (6) is liable—

(a) on summary conviction, to a fine not exceeding the statutory maximum; and

(b) on conviction on indictment, to imprisonment for a term not exceeding two years or a fine (or both).

(8) In this section 'authorised officer' means an authorised officer of the Secretary of State.

53. Customs and Excise prosecutions

(1) Proceedings for a nuclear weapons offence may be instituted by order of the Commissioners of Customs and Excise if it appears to them that the offence has involved—

(a) the development or production outside the United Kingdom of a nuclear weapon;

(b) the movement of a nuclear weapon into or out of any country or territory;

(c) any proposal or attempt to do anything falling within paragraph (a) or (b).

(2) In this section 'nuclear weapons offence' means an offence under section 47 or 50 (including an offence of aiding, abetting, counselling, procuring or inciting the commission of, or attempting or conspiring to commit, such an offence).

(3) Any proceedings for an offence which are instituted under subsection (1) shall be commenced in the name of an officer, but may be continued by another officer.

(4) Where the Commissioners of Customs and Excise investigate, or propose to investigate, any matter with a view to determining—

(a)   whether there are grounds for believing that a nuclear weapons offence has been committed, or

(b)   whether a person should be prosecuted for such an offence,

that matter shall be treated as an assigned matter within the meaning of the Customs and Excise Management Act 1979 (c. 2).

(5)   Nothing in this section affects any powers of any person (including any officer) apart from this section.

(6)   In this section 'officer' means a person commissioned by the Commissioners of Customs and Excise.

(7)   This section does not apply to the institution of proceedings in Scotland.

54.   Offences

(1)   A person who knowingly or recklessly makes a false or misleading statement for the purpose of obtaining (or opposing the variation or withdrawal of) authorisation for the purposes of section 47 or 50 is guilty of an offence.

(2)   A person guilty of an offence under subsection (1) is liable—

(a)   on summary conviction, to a fine of an amount not exceeding the statutory maximum;

(b)   on conviction on indictment, to imprisonment for a term not exceeding two years or a fine (or both).

(3)   Where an offence under section 47, 50 or subsection (1) above committed by a body corporate is proved to have been committed with the consent or connivance of, or to be attributable to any neglect on the part of—

(a)   a director, manager, secretary or other similar officer of the body corporate; or

(b)   any person who was purporting to act in any such capacity,

he as well as the body corporate shall be guilty of that offence and shall be liable to be proceeded against and punished accordingly.

(4)   In subsection (3) 'director', in relation to a body corporate whose affairs are managed by its members, means a member of the body corporate.

55.   Consent to prosecutions

Proceedings for an offence under section 47 or 50 shall not be instituted—

(a)   in England and Wales, except by or with the consent of the Attorney General;

(b)   in Northern Ireland, except by or with the consent of the Attorney General for Northern Ireland.

56.   Interpretation of Part 6

(1)   In this Part 'United Kingdom person' means a United Kingdom national, a Scottish partnership or a body incorporated under the law of a part of the United Kingdom.

(2)   For this purpose a United Kingdom national is an individual who is—

(a)   a British citizen, a British Dependent Territories citizen, a British National (Overseas) or a British Overseas citizen;

(b)   a person who under the British Nationality Act 1981 (c. 61) is a British subject; or

(c)   a British protected person within the meaning of that Act.

Extension of Part 6 to dependencies

57.   Power to extend Part 6 to dependencies

Her Majesty may by Order in Council direct that any of the provisions of this Part shall extend, with such exceptions and modifications as appear to Her Majesty to be appropriate, to any of the Channel Islands, the Isle of Man or to any British overseas territory.

PART VII
SECURITY OF PATHOGENS AND TOXINS

58. Pathogens and toxins in relation to which requirements under Part 7 apply

(1)   Schedule 5 (which lists the pathogens and toxins in relation to which the requirements of this Part apply) has effect.

(2)   The Secretary of State may by order modify any provision of Schedule 5 (including the notes).

(3)   The Secretary of State may not add any pathogen or toxin to that Schedule unless he is satisfied that the pathogen or toxin could be used in an act of terrorism to endanger life or cause serious harm to human health.

(4)   In this Part 'dangerous substance' means—

(a)   anything which consists of or includes a substance for the time being mentioned in Schedule 5; or

(b)   anything which is infected with or otherwise carries any such substance.

(5)   But something otherwise falling within subsection (4) is not to be regarded as a dangerous substance if—

(a)   it satisfies prescribed conditions; or

(b)   it is kept or used in prescribed circumstances.

59. Duty to notify Secretary of State before keeping or using dangerous substances

(1)   The occupier of any premises must give a notice to the Secretary of State before any dangerous substance is kept or used there.

(2)   Subsection (1) does not apply to premises in respect of which a notice has previously been given under that subsection (unless it has been withdrawn).

(3)   The occupier of any premises in respect of which a notice has been given may withdraw the notice if no dangerous substance is kept or used there.

(4)   A notice under this section must—

(a)   identify the premises in which the substance is kept or used;

(b)   identify any building or site of which the premises form part; and

(c)   contain such other particulars (if any) as may be prescribed.

(5)   The occupier of any premises in which any dangerous substance is kept or used on the day on which this section comes into force must give a notice under this section before the end of the period of one month beginning with that day.

(6)   Where—

(a)   a substance which is kept or used in any premises becomes a dangerous substance by virtue of a modification of Schedule 5, but

(b)   no other dangerous substance is kept or used there,

the occupier of the premises must give a notice under this section before the end of the period of one month beginning with the day on which that modification comes into force.

60. Information about security of dangerous substances

(1)   A constable may give to the occupier of any relevant premises a notice requiring him to give the chief officer of police such information as is specified or described in the notice by a time so specified and in a form and manner so specified.

(2)   The required information must relate to—

(a)   any dangerous substance kept or used in the premises; or

(b)   the measures taken (whether by the occupier or any other person) to ensure the security of any such substance.

(3)   In this Part references to measures taken to ensure the security of any dangerous substance kept or used in any relevant premises include—

(a)   measures taken to ensure the security of any building or site of which the premises form part; and

(b)   measures taken for the purpose of ensuring access to the substance is given only to those whose activities require access and only in circumstances that ensure the security of the substance.

(4)   In this Part 'relevant premises' means any premises—

(a)   in which any dangerous substance is kept or used, or

(b)   in respect of which a notice under section 59 is in force.

61.   Information about persons with access to dangerous substances

(1)   A police officer of at least the rank of inspector may give to the occupier of any relevant premises a notice requiring him to give the chief officer of police a list of—

(a)   each person who has access to any dangerous substance kept or used there;

(b)   each person who, in such circumstances as are specified or described in the notice, has access to such part of the premises as is so specified or described;

(c)   each person who, in such circumstances as are specified or described in the notice, has access to the premises; or

(d)   each person who, in such circumstances as are specified or described in the notice, has access to any building or site of which the premises form part.

(2)   A list under subsection (1) must be given before the end of the period of one month beginning with the day on which the notice is given.

(3)   Where a list under subsection (1) is given, the occupier of the premises for the time being—

(a)   must secure that only the persons mentioned in the list are given the access identified in the list relating to them; but

(b)   may give a supplementary list to the chief officer of police of other persons to whom it is proposed to give access.

(4)   Where a supplementary list is given under subsection (3)(b), the occupier of the premises for the time being must secure that persons mentioned in that list do not have the proposed access relating to them until the end of the period of 30 days beginning with the day on which that list is given.

(5)   The chief officer of police may direct that a person may have such access before the end of that period.

(6)   The Secretary of State may by order modify the period mentioned in subsection (4).

(7)   Any list under this section must—

(a)   identify the access which the person has, or is proposed to have;

(b)   state the full name of that person, his date of birth, his address and his nationality; and

(c)   contain such other matters (if any) as may be prescribed.

62.   Directions requiring security measures

(1)   A constable may give directions to the occupier of any relevant premises requiring him to take such measures to ensure the security of any dangerous substance kept or used there as are specified or described in the directions by a time so specified.

(2)   The directions may—

(a)   specify or describe the substances in relation to the security of which the measures relate; and

(b)   require the occupier to give a notice to the chief officer of police before any other dangerous substance specified or described in the directions is kept or used in the premises.

63. Directions requiring disposal of dangerous substances

(1)   Where the Secretary of State has reasonable grounds for believing that adequate measures to ensure the security of any dangerous substance kept or used in any relevant premises are not being taken and are unlikely to be taken, he may give a direction to the occupier of the premises requiring him to dispose of the substance.

(2)   The direction must—

(a)   specify the manner in which, and time by which, the dangerous substance must be disposed of; or

(b)   require the occupier to produce the dangerous substance to a person specified or described in the notice in a manner and by a time so specified for him to dispose of.

64. Directions requiring denial of access

(1)   The Secretary of State may give directions to the occupier of any relevant premises requiring him to secure that the person identified in the directions—

(a)   is not to have access to any dangerous substance kept or used there;

(b)   is not to have, in such circumstances (if any) as may be specified or described in the directions, access to such part of the premises as is so specified or described;

(c)   is not to have, in such circumstances (if any) as may be specified or described in the directions, access to the premises; or

(d)   is not to have, in such circumstances (if any) as may be specified or described in the directions, access to any building or site of which the premises form part.

(2)   The directions must be given under the hand of the Secretary of State.

(3)   The Secretary of State may not give the directions unless he believes that they are necessary in the interests of national security.

65. Powers of entry

(1)   A constable may, on giving notice under this section, enter any relevant premises, or any building or site of which the premises form part, at a reasonable time for the purpose of assessing the measures taken to ensure the security of any dangerous substance kept or used in the premises.

(2)   The notice must be given to the occupier of the premises, or (as the case may be) the occupier of the building or site of which the premises form part, at least 2 working days before the proposed entry.

(3)   The notice must set out the purpose mentioned in subsection (1).

(4)   A constable who has entered any premises, building or site by virtue of subsection (1) may for the purpose mentioned in that subsection—

(a)   search the premises, building or site;

(b)   require any person who appears to the constable to be in charge of the premises, building or site to facilitate any such inspection; and

(c)   require any such person to answer any question.

(5)   The powers of a constable under this section include power to take with him such other persons as appear to him to be necessary.

66. Search warrants

(1)   If, in England and Wales or Northern Ireland, on an application made by a constable a justice of the peace is satisfied that there are reasonable grounds for believing—

(a)   that a dangerous substance is kept or used in any premises but that no notice under section 59 is in force in respect of the premises, or

(b)   that the occupier of any relevant premises is failing to comply with any direction given to him under section 62 or 63,

and that any of the conditions mentioned in subsection (4) apply, he may issue a warrant authorising a constable to enter the premises, if necessary by force, and to search them.

(2)   If, in Scotland, on an application made by the procurator fiscal the sheriff is satisfied as mentioned in subsection (1), he may issue a warrant authorising a constable to enter the premises, if necessary by force, and to search them.

(3)   A constable may seize and retain anything which he believes is or contains a dangerous substance.

(4)   The conditions mentioned in subsection (1) are—

(a)   that it is not practicable to communicate with any person entitled to grant entry to the premises;

(b)   that it is practicable to communicate with a person entitled to grant entry to the premises but it is not practicable to communicate with any person entitled to grant access to any substance which may be a dangerous substance;

(c)   that entry to the premises will not be granted unless a warrant is produced;

(d)   that the purpose of a search may be frustrated or seriously prejudiced unless a constable arriving at the premises can secure immediate entry to them.

67. Offences

(1)   An occupier who fails without reasonable excuse to comply with any duty or direction imposed on him by or under this Part is guilty of an offence.

(2)   A person who, in giving any information to a person exercising functions under this Part, knowingly or recklessly makes a statement which is false or misleading in a material particular is guilty of an offence.

(3)   A person guilty of an offence under this section is liable—

(a)   on conviction on indictment, to imprisonment for a term not exceeding five years or a fine (or both); and

(b)   on summary conviction, to imprisonment for a term not exceeding six months or a fine not exceeding the statutory maximum (or both).

68. Bodies corporate

(1)   If an offence under this Part committed by a body corporate is shown to have been committed with the consent or connivance of, or to be attributable to any neglect on the part of—

(a)   any officer, or

(b)   any other employee of the body corporate who is in charge of any relevant premises or the access to any dangerous substance kept or used there,

he, as well as the body corporate, is guilty of the offence and liable to be proceeded against and punished accordingly.

(2)   In this section 'officer', in relation to a body corporate, means—

(a)   any director, manager, secretary or other similar officer of the body corporate; or

(b)   any person purporting to act in any such capacity.

(3)   Where the affairs of a body corporate are managed by its members, this section applies in relation to the acts and defaults of a member in connection with his functions of management as if he were a director of the body corporate.

69. Partnerships and unincorporated associations

(1)   Proceedings for an offence alleged to have been committed by a partnership or an unincorporated association must be brought in the name of the partnership or association (and not in that of any of its members).

(2) A fine imposed on the partnership or association on its conviction of an offence is to be paid out of the funds of the partnership or association.

(3) Rules of court relating to the service of documents are to have effect as if the partnership or association were a body corporate.

(4) In proceedings for an offence brought against the partnership or association—

(a) section 33 of the Criminal Justice Act 1925 (c. 86) and Schedule 3 to the Magistrates' Courts Act 1980 (c. 43) (procedure) apply as they do in relation to a body corporate;

(b) sections 70 and 143 of the Criminal Procedure (Scotland) Act 1995 (c. 46) (procedure) apply as they do in relation to a body corporate;

(c) section 18 of the Criminal Justice (Northern Ireland) Act 1945 (c. 15 (NI)) and Schedule 4 to the Magistrates' Courts (Northern Ireland) Order 1981 (SI 1981/1675 (NI 26)) (procedure) apply as they do in relation to a body corporate.

(5) If an offence under this Part committed by a partnership is shown to have been committed with the consent or connivance of, or to be attributable to any neglect on the part of—

(a) a partner or a person purporting to act as a partner, or

(b) any employee of the partnership who is in charge of any relevant premises or the access to any dangerous substance kept or used there,

he, as well as the partnership, is guilty of the offence and liable to be proceeded against and punished accordingly.

(6) If an offence under this Part committed by an unincorporated association is shown to have been committed with the consent or connivance of, or to be attributable to any neglect on the part of—

(a) any officer, or

(b) any employee of the association who is in charge of any relevant premises or the access to any dangerous substance kept or used there,

he, as well as the association, is guilty of the offence and liable to be proceeded against and punished accordingly.

(7) In subsection (6) 'officer', in relation to any association, means—

(a) any officer of the association or any member of its governing body; or

(b) any person purporting to act in such a capacity.

70. Denial of access: appeals

(1) There shall be a commission, to be known as the Pathogens Access Appeal Commission.

(2) Any person aggrieved by directions given under section 64 may appeal to the Commission.

(3) The Commission must allow an appeal if it considers that the decision to give the directions was flawed when considered in the light of the principles applicable on an application for judicial review.

(4) A party to any appeal under this section which the Commission has determined may bring a further appeal on a question of law to—

(a) the Court of Appeal, if the first appeal was heard in England and Wales;

(b) the Court of Session, if the first appeal was heard in Scotland; or

(c) the Court of Appeal in Northern Ireland, if the first appeal was heard in Northern Ireland.

(5) An appeal under subsection (4) may be brought only with the permission of—

(a) the Commission; or

(b) where the Commission refuses permission, the court to which the appeal would be brought.

(6) Schedule 6 (constitution of the Commission and procedure) has effect.

71. Other appeals

(1) Any person who is required to do any act in response to—

(a) any notice under section 60, or

(b) any directions under section 62 or 63,

may appeal to a magistrates' court against the requirement on the ground that, having regard to all the circumstances of the case, it is unreasonable to be required to do that act.

(2) An appeal may not be brought after the end of the period of one month beginning with the day on which the notice or directions were given.

(3) If the magistrates' court allows the appeal, it may—

(a) direct that the required act need not be done; or

(b) make such modification of the requirement as it considers appropriate.

(4) An appeal shall lie to the Crown Court against any decision of the magistrates' court.

(5) Subsections (1) to (3) apply to Scotland with the substitution for references to the magistrates' court of references to the sheriff.

(6) The appeal to the sheriff is by way of summary application.

(7) A further appeal shall lie—

(a) to the sheriff principal from the decision of the sheriff; and

(b) with the leave of the sheriff principal, to the Court of Session from the decision of the sheriff principal.

(8) In the application of this section to Northern Ireland references to a magistrates' court are to a court of summary jurisdiction.

72. Giving of directions or notices

Any direction or notice under this Part may be given by post.

73. Orders and regulations

(1) The power to make an order or regulations under this Part is exercisable by statutory instrument.

(2) A statutory instrument containing an order under section 58 shall not be made unless a draft of it has been laid before and approved by a resolution of each House of Parliament.

(3) A statutory instrument containing—

(a) an order under section 61, or

(b) regulations under section 58, 59 or 61,

shall be subject to annulment in pursuance of a resolution of either House of Parliament.

74. Interpretation of Part 7

(1) In this Part—

'act of terrorism' has the same meaning as in the Terrorism Act 2000 (c. 11);

'chief officer of police' means—

(a) in relation to any premises in Great Britain, the chief officer of police for the area in which the premises are situated; and

(b) in relation to any premises in Northern Ireland, the Chief Constable of the Police Service of Northern Ireland;

'dangerous substance' has the meaning given in section 58;

'direction' means a direction in writing;

'notice' means a notice in writing;

'occupier' includes a partnership or unincorporated association and, in relation to premises that are unoccupied, means any person entitled to occupy the premises;

'prescribed' means prescribed in regulations made by the Secretary of State; and

'relevant premises' has the meaning given in section 60.

(2)   In this Part references to measures taken to ensure the security of any dangerous substance are to be construed in accordance with section 60.

75.   Power to extend Part 7 to animal or plant pathogens, pests or toxic chemicals

(1)   The Secretary of State may, in relation to anything to which this section applies, make an order applying, or making provision corresponding to, any provision of this Part, with or without modifications.

(2)   This section applies to—

    (a)   toxic chemicals (within the meaning of the Chemical Weapons Act 1996 (c. 6));

    (b)   animal pathogens;

    (c)   plant pathogens; and

    (d)   pests.

(3)   The power under this section may be exercised in relation to any chemical only if the Secretary of State is satisfied that the chemical could be used in an act of terrorism to endanger life or cause serious harm to human health.

(4)   The power under this section may be exercised in relation to any pathogen or pest only if the Secretary of State is satisfied that there is a risk that the pathogen or pest is of a description that could be used in an act of terrorism to cause—

    (a)   widespread damage to property;

    (b)   significant disruption to the public; or

    (c)   significant alarm to the public.

(5)   An order under this section may—

    (a)   provide for any reference in the order to an instrument or other document to take effect as a reference to that instrument or document as revised or re-issued from time to time;

    (b)   make different provision for different purposes; and

    (c)   make such incidental, supplementary and transitional provision as the Secretary of State thinks fit.

(6)   A statutory instrument containing an order under this section shall not be made unless a draft of it has been laid before and approved by a resolution of each House of Parliament.

PART VIII

SECURITY OF NUCLEAR INDUSTRY

76.   Atomic Energy Authority special constables

(1)   Section 3 of the Special Constables Act 1923 (c. 11) shall have effect as if all nuclear sites that are not for the time being designated under subsection (2) were premises under the control of the United Kingdom Atomic Energy Authority.

(2)   The Secretary of State may by order made by statutory instrument designate any nuclear sites which appear to him to be used wholly or mainly for defence purposes as premises to which subsection (1) does not apply.

(3)   An AEA constable shall have the powers and privileges (and be liable to the duties and responsibilities) of a constable anywhere within 5 kilometres of the limits of the nuclear sites to which subsection (1) applies.

(4)   An AEA constable shall have the powers and privileges (and be liable to the duties and responsibilities) of a constable anywhere it appears to him expedient to go—

(a)   in order to safeguard any nuclear material which is being carried (or being trans-shipped or stored incidentally to its carriage) before its delivery at its final destination; or

(b)   in order to pursue, arrest, place in the custody of the police, or take to any premises within which the constable was appointed to act, a person who the constable reasonably believes has (or has attempted to) unlawfully remove or interfere with any nuclear material being safeguarded by the constable.

(5)   An AEA constable shall have the powers and privileges (and be liable to the duties and responsibilities) of a constable at any place at which he reasonably believes a particular consignment of nuclear material will be trans-shipped or stored incidentally to its carriage, in order to ensure the security of the nuclear material on its arrival at that place.

(6)   This section has effect in United Kingdom waters adjacent to Great Britain as it applies in Great Britain.

(7)   In this section—

'AEA constable' means a person appointed on the nomination of the United Kingdom Atomic Energy Authority to be a special constable under section 3 of the Special Constables Act 1923;

'nuclear material' means—

(a)   any fissile material in the form of uranium metal, alloy or chemical compound, or of plutonium metal, alloy or chemical compound; or

(b)   any other fissile material which may be prescribed by regulations made by the Secretary of State;

'nuclear site' means premises in respect of which a nuclear site licence (within the meaning of the Nuclear Installations Act 1965 (c. 57)) is for the time being in force; and

'United Kingdom waters' means waters within the seaward limits of the territorial sea.

(8)   An order under subsection (2) shall be laid before Parliament after being made.

(9)   The power to make regulations under subsection (7) is exercisable by statutory instrument subject to annulment in pursuance of a resolution of either House of Parliament.

77.   Regulation of security of civil nuclear industry

(1)   The Secretary of State may make regulations for the purpose of ensuring the security of—

(a)   nuclear sites and other nuclear premises;

(b)   nuclear material used or stored on nuclear sites or other nuclear premises and equipment or software used or stored on such sites or premises in connection with activities involving nuclear material;

(c)   other radioactive material used or stored on nuclear sites and equipment or software used or stored on nuclear sites in connection with activities involving other radioactive material;

(d)   sensitive nuclear information which is in the possession or control of anyone who is (or is expected to be) involved in activities on, or in relation to, any nuclear site or other nuclear premises;

(e)   nuclear material which is being (or is expected to be)—

(i)   transported within the United Kingdom or its territorial sea;

(ii)   transported (outside the United Kingdom and its territorial sea) to or from any nuclear site or other nuclear premises in the United Kingdom; or

(iii)   carried on board a United Kingdom ship;

(f)   information relating to the security of anything mentioned in paragraphs (a) to (e).

(2)   The regulations may, in particular—

(a)   require a person to produce for the approval of the Secretary of State a plan for ensuring the security of anything mentioned in subsection (1) and to comply with the plan as approved by the Secretary of State;

(b)   require compliance with any directions given by the Secretary of State;

(c)   impose requirements in relation to any activities by reference to the approval of the Secretary of State;

(d)   create summary offences or offences triable either way;

(e)   make provision for the purposes mentioned in subsection (1) corresponding to any provision which may be made for the general purposes of Part 1 of the Health and Safety at Work etc. Act 1974 (c. 37) by virtue of section 15(2), (3)(c) and (4) to (8) of that Act (health and safety regulations);

(f)   make provision corresponding to any provision which may be made by virtue of section 43(2) to (5), (8) and (9) of that Act (fees), in connection with the performance by or on behalf of the Secretary of State or any other specified body or person of functions under the regulations; and

(g)   apply (with or without modifications), or make provision corresponding to, any provision contained in sections 19 to 42 and 44 to 47 of that Act.

(3)   An offence under the regulations may be made punishable—

(a)   in the case of an offence triable either way—

(i)   on conviction on indictment, with imprisonment for a term not exceeding two years or a fine (or both); and

(ii)   on summary conviction, with imprisonment for a term not exceeding six months or a fine not exceeding the statutory maximum (or both); or

(b)   in the case of a summary offence, with imprisonment for a term not exceeding six months or a fine not exceeding level 5 on the standard scale (or both).

(4)   The regulations may make—

(a)   provision applying to acts done outside the United Kingdom by United Kingdom persons;

(b)   different provision for different purposes; and

(c)   such incidental, supplementary and transitional provision as the Secretary of State considers appropriate.

(5)   Before making the regulations the Secretary of State shall consult—

(a)   the Health and Safety Commission; and

(b)   such other persons as he considers appropriate.

(6)   The power to make the regulations is exercisable by statutory instrument subject to annulment in pursuance of a resolution of either House of Parliament.

(7)   In this section—

'nuclear material' and 'nuclear site' have the same meaning as in section 76;

'other nuclear premises' means premises other than a nuclear site on which nuclear material is used or stored;

'sensitive nuclear information' means—

(a)   information relating to, or capable of use in connection with, any treatment of uranium that increases the proportion of the isotope 235 contained in the uranium; or

(b)   information relating to activities carried out on or in relation to nuclear sites or other nuclear premises which appears to the Secretary of State to be information which needs to be protected in the interests of national security;

'United Kingdom ship' means a ship registered in the United Kingdom under Part 2 of the Merchant Shipping Act 1995 (c. 21)

(8)   Any sums received by virtue of provision made under subsection (2)(f) shall be paid into the Consolidated Fund.

78. Repeals relating to security of civil nuclear installations

(1)   In Schedule 1 to the Nuclear Installations Act 1965 (c. 57) (security provisions applicable by order under section 2 of that Act), paragraphs 5 and 6 shall cease to have effect.

(2)   In section 19(1) of the Atomic Energy Authority Act 1971 (c. 11) (application of certain security provisions to designated companies), for 'Paragraphs 4 to 6' and 'they apply' substitute respectively 'Paragraph 4' and 'it applies'.

79. Prohibition of disclosures relating to nuclear security

(1)   A person is guilty of an offence if he discloses any information or thing the disclosure of which might prejudice the security of any nuclear site or of any nuclear material—

(a)   with the intention of prejudicing that security; or

(b)   being reckless as to whether the disclosure might prejudice that security.

(2)   The reference in subsection (1) to nuclear material is a reference to—

(a)   nuclear material which is being held on any nuclear site, or

(b)   nuclear material anywhere in the world which is being transported to or from a nuclear site or carried on board a British ship,

(including nuclear material which is expected to be so held, transported or carried).

(3)   A person guilty of an offence under subsection (1) is liable—

(a)   on conviction on indictment, to imprisonment for a term not exceeding seven years or a fine (or both); and

(b)   on summary conviction, to imprisonment for a term not exceeding six months or a fine not exceeding the statutory maximum (or both).

(4)   In this section—

'British ship' means a ship (including a ship belonging to Her Majesty) which is registered in the United Kingdom;

'disclose' and 'disclosure', in relation to a thing, include parting with possession of it;

'nuclear material' has the same meaning as in section 76; and

'nuclear site' means a site in the United Kingdom (including a site occupied by or on behalf of the Crown) which is (or is expected to be) used for any purpose mentioned in section 1(1) of the Nuclear Installations Act 1965 (c. 57).

(5)   This section applies to acts done outside the United Kingdom, but only if they are done by a United Kingdom person.

(6)   Proceedings for an offence committed outside the United Kingdom may be taken, and the offence may for incidental purposes be treated as having been committed, in any place in the United Kingdom.

(7)   Nothing in subsection (5) affects any criminal liability arising otherwise than under that subsection.

80. Prohibition of disclosures of uranium enrichment technology

(1)   This section applies to—

(a)   any information about the enrichment of uranium; or

(b)   any information or thing which is, or is likely to be, used in connection with the enrichment of uranium;

and for this purpose 'the enrichment of uranium' means any treatment of uranium that increases the proportion of the isotope 235 contained in the uranium.

(2)   The Secretary of State may make regulations prohibiting the disclosure of information or things to which this section applies.

(3)   A person who contravenes a prohibition is guilty of an offence and liable—

(a)   on conviction on indictment, to imprisonment for a term not exceeding seven years or a fine (or both); and

(b)   on summary conviction, to imprisonment for a term not exceeding six months or a fine not exceeding the statutory maximum (or both).

(4)   The regulations may, in particular, provide for—

(a)   a prohibition to apply, or not to apply—

(i)   to such information or things; and

(ii)   in such cases or circumstances,

as may be prescribed;

(b)   the authorisation by the Secretary of State of disclosures that would otherwise be prohibited; and

(c)   defences to an offence under subsection (3) relating to any prohibition.

(5)   The regulations may—

(a)   provide for any prohibition to apply to acts done outside the United Kingdom by United Kingdom persons;

(b)   make different provision for different purposes; and

(c)   make such incidental, supplementary and transitional provision as the Secretary of State thinks fit.

(6)   The power to make the regulations is exercisable by statutory instrument.

(7)   The regulations shall not be made unless a draft of the regulations has been laid before and approved by each House of Parliament.

(8)   In this section—

'disclosure', in relation to a thing, includes parting with possession of it;

'information' includes software; and

'prescribed' means specified or described in the regulations.

81.   Part 8: supplementary

(1)   Proceedings for an offence under section 79 or 80 shall not be instituted—

(a)   in England and Wales, except by or with the consent of the Attorney General; or

(b)   in Northern Ireland, except by or with the consent of the Attorney General for Northern Ireland.

(2)   In this Part 'United Kingdom person' means a United Kingdom national, a Scottish partnership or a body incorporated under the law of any part of the United Kingdom.

(3)   For this purpose a United Kingdom national is an individual who is—

(a)   a British citizen, a British Dependent Territories citizen, a British National (Overseas) or a British Overseas citizen;

(b)   a person who under the British Nationality Act 1981 (c. 61) is a British subject; or

(c)   a British protected person within the meaning of that Act.

PART IX

AVIATION SECURITY

82.   Arrest without warrant

(1)   At the end of section 24(2) of the Police and Criminal Evidence Act 1984 (c. 60) (arrest without warrant: particular offences) insert—

'(u)   an offence under section 21C(1) or 21D(1) of the Aviation Security Act
1982 (c. 36) (unauthorised presence in restricted zone or on aircraft);
         (v)   an offence under section 39(1) of the Civil Aviation Act 1982 (c. 16)
(trespass on aerodrome).'

(2)   At the end of Article 26(2) of the Police and Criminal Evidence (Northern Ireland)
Order 1989 (SI 1989/1341 (NI 12)) (arrest without warrant: particular offences) insert—

'(j)   an offence under section 21C(1) or 21D(1) of the Aviation Security Act 1982
(unauthorised presence in restricted zone or on aircraft);
         (k)   an offence under section 39(1) of the Civil Aviation Act 1982 (trespass on
aerodrome).'

(3)   Where, in Scotland, a constable has reasonable grounds for suspecting that a person
has committed—
         (a)   an offence under section 21C(1) or 21D(1) of the Aviation Security Act 1982
(unauthorised presence in restricted zone or on aircraft);
         (b)   an offence under section 39(1) of the Civil Aviation Act 1982 (trespass on
aerodrome),
he may arrest that person without warrant.

(4)   This section shall have effect in relation to an offence committed or alleged to have
been committed after the end of the period of two months beginning with the day on which
this Act is passed.

83.   Trespass on aerodrome: penalty

(1)   In section 39(1) of the Civil Aviation Act 1982 (trespass on aerodrome) for 'level
1 on the standard scale' substitute 'level 3 on the standard scale'.

(2)   This section shall have effect in relation to an offence committed after the end of
the period of two months beginning with the day on which this Act is passed.

84.   Removal of intruder

(1)   At the end of section 21C of the Aviation Security Act 1982 (unauthorised presence
in aerodrome) add—

'(4)   A constable, the manager of an aerodrome or a person acting on his behalf
may use reasonable force to remove a person who fails to comply with a request under
subsection (1)(b) above.'

(2)   At the end of section 21D of that Act (unauthorised presence on aircraft) add—

'(3)   A constable, the operator of an aircraft or a person acting on his behalf may
use reasonable force to remove a person who fails to comply with a request under
subsection (1)(b) above.'

85.   Aviation security services

After section 20 of the Aviation Security Act 1982 (c. 36) (security directions: inspection)
insert—

'20A.   Aviation security services: approved providers

(1)   In this section "aviation security service" means a process or activity carried out
for the purpose of—
         (a)   complying with a requirement of a direction under any of sections 12 to 14, or
         (b)   facilitating a person's compliance with a requirement of a direction under any
of those sections.

(2)   Regulations may provide for the Secretary of State to maintain a list of persons
who are approved by him for the provision of a particular aviation security service.

(3) The regulations may—

(a) prohibit the provision of an aviation security service by a person who is not listed in respect of that service;

(b) prohibit the use or engagement for the provision of an aviation security service of a person who is not listed in respect of that service;

(c) create a criminal offence;

(d) make provision about application for inclusion in the list (including provision about fees);

(e) make provision about the duration and renewal of entries on the list (including provision about fees);

(f) make provision about training or qualifications which persons who apply to be listed or who are listed are required to undergo or possess;

(g) make provision about removal from the list which shall include provision for appeal;

(h) make provision about the inspection of activities carried out by listed persons;

(i) confer functions on the Secretary of State or on a specified person;

(j) confer jurisdiction on a court.

(4) Regulations under subsection (3)(c)—

(a) may not provide for a penalty on summary conviction greater than a fine not exceeding the statutory maximum,

(b) may not provide for a penalty of imprisonment on conviction on indictment greater than imprisonment for a term not exceeding two years (whether or not accompanied by a fine), and

(c) may create a criminal offence of purporting, with intent to deceive, to do something as a listed person or of doing something, with intent to deceive, which purports to be done by a listed person.

(5) A direction under any of sections 12 to 14 may—

(a) include a requirement to use a listed person for the provision of an aviation security service;

(b) provide for all or part of the direction not to apply or to apply with modified effect where a listed person provides an aviation security service.

(6) Regulations under this section—

(a) may make different provision for different cases,

(b) may include incidental, supplemental or transitional provision,

(c) shall be made by the Secretary of State by statutory instrument,

(d) shall not be made unless the Secretary of State has consulted organisations appearing to him to represent persons affected by the regulations, and

(e) shall be subject to annulment in pursuance of a resolution of either House of Parliament.'

86. Detention of aircraft

(1) After section 20A of the Aviation Security Act 1982 (c. 36) (aviation security services) (inserted by section 85)) insert—

'Detention of aircraft

20B. Detention direction

(1) An authorised person may give a detention direction in respect of an aircraft if he is of the opinion that—

(a) a person has failed to comply or is likely to fail to comply with a requirement of a direction under section 12 or 14 of this Act in respect of the aircraft,

(b) a person has failed to comply with a requirement of an enforcement notice in respect of the aircraft,

(c) a threat has been made to commit an act of violence against the aircraft or against any person or property on board the aircraft, or

(d) an act of violence is likely to be committed against the aircraft or against any person or property on board the aircraft.

(2) A detention direction in respect of an aircraft—

(a) shall be given in writing to the operator of the aircraft, and

(b) shall require him to take steps to ensure that the aircraft does not fly while the direction is in force.

(3) An authorised person who has given a detention direction in respect of an aircraft may do anything which he considers necessary or expedient for the purpose of ensuring that the aircraft does not fly while the direction is in force; in particular, the authorised person may—

(a) enter the aircraft;

(b) arrange for another person to enter the aircraft;

(c) arrange for a person or thing to be removed from the aircraft;

(d) use reasonable force;

(e) authorise the use of reasonable force by another person.

(4) The operator of an aircraft in respect of which a detention direction is given may object to the direction in writing to the Secretary of State.

(5) On receipt of an objection to a detention direction under subsection (4) the Secretary of State shall—

(a) consider the objection,

(b) allow the person making the objection and the authorised person who gave the direction an opportunity to make written or oral representations to the Secretary of State or to a person appointed by him,

(c) confirm, vary or cancel the direction, and

(d) give notice of his decision in writing to the person who made the objection and to the authorised person who gave the direction.

(6) A detention direction in respect of an aircraft shall continue in force until—

(a) an authorised person cancels it by notice in writing to the operator of the aircraft, or

(b) the Secretary of State cancels it under subsection (5)(c).

(7) A person commits an offence if—

(a) without reasonable excuse he fails to comply with a requirement of a detention direction, or

(b) he intentionally obstructs a person acting in accordance with subsection (3).

(8) A person who is guilty of an offence under subsection (7) shall be liable—

(a) on summary conviction, to a fine not exceeding the statutory maximum, or

(b) on conviction on indictment, to a fine, to imprisonment for a term not exceeding two years or to both.

(9) A detention direction may be given in respect of—

(a) any aircraft in the United Kingdom, and

(b) any aircraft registered or operating in the United Kingdom.

(10)   A detention direction may be given in respect of a class of aircraft; and for that purpose—

(a)   a reference to "the aircraft" in subsection (1) shall be treated as a reference to all or any of the aircraft within the class, and

(b)   subsections (2) to (9) shall apply as if the direction were given in respect of each aircraft within the class.'

(2)   In section 23 of the Aviation Security Act 1982 (c. 36) (annual report)—

(a)   in subsection (1) after 'enforcement notices' insert 'and detention directions', and

(b)   in subsection (2) for 'and enforcement notices' substitute ', enforcement notices and detention directions'.

(3)   At the end of section 24 of that Act add—

'(9)   Subsections (6) to (8) above shall apply to a detention direction as they apply to an enforcement notice.'

87.   Air cargo agent: documents

After section 21F of the Aviation Security Act 1982 (air cargo agents) insert—

'21FA.   Air cargo agents: documents

(1)   A person commits an offence if with intent to deceive he issues a document which purports to be issued by a person on a list of approved air cargo agents maintained under section 21F(2)(a) of this Act.

(2)   A person guilty of an offence under subsection (1) shall be liable on summary conviction to imprisonment for a term not exceeding six months or to a fine not exceeding level 5 on the standard scale or to both.'

88.   Extent outside United Kingdom

(1)   The powers in section 108(1) and (2) of the Civil Aviation Act 1982 (c. 16) (extension outside United Kingdom) apply to provisions of this Part which amend that Act.

(2)   The powers in section 39(3) of the Aviation Security Act 1982 (extension outside United Kingdom) apply to provisions of this Part which amend that Act.

PART X
POLICE POWERS

Identification

89.   Fingerprinting of terrorist suspects

(1)   Schedule 8 to the Terrorism Act 2000 (c. 11) (persons detained under terrorism provisions) is amended as follows.

(2)   In paragraph 10, at the beginning of sub-paragraph (6) (grounds on which officer may authorise fingerprinting or taking of sample), insert 'Subject to sub-paragraph (6A)'; and after that sub-paragraph insert—

'(6A)   An officer may also give an authorisation under sub-paragraph (4)(a) for the taking of fingerprints if—

(a)   he is satisfied that the fingerprints of the detained person will facilitate the ascertainment of that person's identity; and

(b)   that person has refused to identify himself or the officer has reasonable grounds for suspecting that that person is not who he claims to be.

(6B)   In this paragraph references to ascertaining a person's identity include references to showing that he is not a particular person.'

(3) In paragraph 20(2), for the subsection (2) substituted by way of modification of section 18 of the Criminal Procedure (Scotland) Act 1995 (c. 46) substitute—

'(2) Subject to subsection (2A), a constable may take from a detained person or require a detained person to provide relevant physical data only if—

(a) in the case of a person detained under section 41 of the Terrorism Act 2000, he reasonably suspects that the person has been involved in an offence under any of the provisions mentioned in section 40(1)(a) of that Act and he reasonably believes that the relevant physical data will tend to confirm or disprove his involvement; or

(b) in any case, he is satisfied that it is necessary to do so in order to assist in determining whether the person falls within section 40(1)(b).

(2A) A constable may also take fingerprints from a detained person or require him to provide them if—

(a) he is satisfied that the fingerprints of that person will facilitate the ascertainment of that person's identity; and

(b) that person has refused to identify himself or the constable has reasonable grounds for suspecting that that person is not who he claims to be.

(2B) In this section references to ascertaining a person's identity include references to showing that he is not a particular person.'

(4) For paragraph 20(3) substitute—

'(3) Subsections (3) to (5) shall not apply, but any relevant physical data or sample taken in pursuance of section 18 as applied by this paragraph may be retained but shall not be used by any person except for the purposes of a terrorist investigation or for purposes related to the prevention or detection of crime, the investigation of an offence or the conduct of a prosecution.

(4) In this paragraph—

(a) a reference to crime includes a reference to any conduct which—

(i) constitutes one or more criminal offences (whether under the law of a part of the United Kingdom or of a country or territory outside the United Kingdom); or

(ii) is, or corresponds to, any conduct which, if it all took place in any one part of the United Kingdom, would constitute one or more criminal offences; and

(b) the references to an investigation and to a prosecution include references, respectively, to any investigation outside the United Kingdom of any crime or suspected crime and to a prosecution brought in respect of any crime in a country or territory outside the United Kingdom.'

90. Searches, examinations and fingerprinting: England and Wales

(1) After section 54 of the Police and Criminal Evidence Act 1984 (c. 60) (searches of detained persons) insert—

'54A. Searches and examination to ascertain identity

(1) If an officer of at least the rank of inspector authorises it, a person who is detained in a police station may be searched or examined, or both—

(a) for the purpose of ascertaining whether he has any mark that would tend to identify him as a person involved in the commission of an offence; or

(b) for the purpose of facilitating the ascertainment of his identity.

(2) An officer may only give an authorisation under subsection (1) for the purpose mentioned in paragraph (a) of that subsection if—

(a) the appropriate consent to a search or examination that would reveal whether the mark in question exists has been withheld; or

(b)   it is not practicable to obtain such consent.

(3)   An officer may only give an authorisation under subsection (1) in a case in which subsection (2) does not apply if—

(a)   the person in question has refused to identify himself; or

(b)   the officer has reasonable grounds for suspecting that that person is not who he claims to be.

(4)   An officer may give an authorisation under subsection (1) orally or in writing but, if he gives it orally, he shall confirm it in writing as soon as is practicable.

(5)   Any identifying mark found on a search or examination under this section may be photographed—

(a)   with the appropriate consent; or

(b)   if the appropriate consent is withheld or it is not practicable to obtain it, without it.

(6)   Where a search or examination may be carried out under this section, or a photograph may be taken under this section, the only persons entitled to carry out the search or examination, or to take the photograph, are—

(a)   constables; and

(b)   persons who (without being constables) are designated for the purposes of this section by the chief officer of police for the police area in which the police station in question is situated;

and section 117 (use of force) applies to the exercise by a person falling within paragraph (b) of the powers conferred by the preceding provisions of this section as it applies to the exercise of those powers by a constable.

(7)   A person may not under this section carry out a search or examination of a person of the opposite sex or take a photograph of any part of the body of a person of the opposite sex.

(8)   An intimate search may not be carried out under this section.

(9)   A photograph taken under this section—

(a)   may be used by, or disclosed to, any person for any purpose related to the prevention or detection of crime, the investigation of an offence or the conduct of a prosecution; and

(b)   after being so used or disclosed, may be retained but may not be used or disclosed except for a purpose so related.

(10)   In subsection—

(a)   the reference to crime includes a reference to any conduct which—

(i)   constitutes one or more criminal offences (whether under the law of a part of the United Kingdom or of a country or territory outside the United Kingdom); or

(ii)   is, or corresponds to, any conduct which, if it all took place in any one part of the United Kingdom, would constitute one or more criminal offences; and

(b)   the references to an investigation and to a prosecution include references, respectively, to any investigation outside the United Kingdom of any crime or suspected crime and to a prosecution brought in respect of any crime in a country or territory outside the United Kingdom.

(11)   In this section—

(a)   references to ascertaining a person's identity include references to showing that he is not a particular person; and

(b)   references to taking a photograph include references to using any process by means of which a visual image may be produced, and references to photographing a person shall be construed accordingly.

(12)   In this section "mark" includes features and injuries; and a mark is an identifying mark for the purposes of this section if its existence in any person's case facilitates the ascertainment of his identity or his identification as a person involved in the commission of an offence.'

(2)   In section 61(4) of that Act (grounds on which fingerprinting of person detained at a police station may be authorised)—

(a)   in paragraph (b), after 'his involvement' insert 'or will facilitate the ascertainment of his identity (within the meaning of section 54A), or both';

(b)   after that paragraph insert—

'but an authorisation shall not be given for the purpose only of facilitating the ascertainment of that person's identity except where he has refused to identify himself or the officer has reasonable grounds for suspecting that he is not who he claims to be.'

91.   Searches, examinations and fingerprinting: Northern Ireland

(1)   After Article 55 of the Police and Criminal Evidence (Northern Ireland) Order 1989 (SI 1989/1341 (NI 12)) (searches of detained persons) insert—

'55A.   Searches and examination to ascertain identity

(1)   If an officer of at least the rank of inspector authorises it, a person who is detained in a police station may be searched or examined, or both—

(a)   for the purpose of ascertaining whether he has any mark that would tend to identify him as a person involved in the commission of an offence; or

(b)   for the purpose of facilitating the ascertainment of his identity.

(2)   An officer may only give an authorisation under paragraph (1) for the purpose mentioned in sub-paragraph (a) of that paragraph if—

(a)   the appropriate consent to a search or examination that would reveal whether the mark in question exists has been withheld; or

(b)   it is not practicable to obtain such consent.

(3)   An officer may only give an authorisation under paragraph (1) in a case in which paragraph (2) does not apply if—

(a)   the person in question has refused to identify himself; or

(b)   the officer has reasonable grounds for suspecting that that person is not who he claims to be.

(4)   An officer may give an authorisation under paragraph (1) orally or in writing but, if he gives it orally, he shall confirm it in writing as soon as is practicable.

(5)   Any identifying mark found on a search or examination under this Article may be photographed—

(a)   with the appropriate consent; or

(b)   if the appropriate consent is withheld or it is not practicable to obtain it, without it.

(6)   Where a search or examination may be carried out under this Article, or a photograph may be taken under this Article, the only persons entitled to carry out the search or examination, or to take the photograph, are—

(a)   constables; and

(b)   persons who (without being constables) are designated for the purposes of this Article by the Chief Constable;

and Article 88 (use of force) applies to the exercise by a person falling within sub-paragraph (b) of the powers conferred by the preceding provisions of this Article as it applies to the exercise of those powers by a constable.

(7)   A person may not under this Article carry out a search or examination of a person of the opposite sex or take a photograph of any part of the body of a person of the opposite sex.

(8)   An intimate search may not be carried out under this Article.

(9)   A photograph taken under this Article—

(a)   may be used by, or disclosed to, any person for any purpose related to the prevention or detection of crime, the investigation of an offence or the conduct of a prosecution; and

(b)   after being so used or disclosed, may be retained but may not be used or disclosed except for a purpose so related.

(10)   In paragraph (9)—

(a)   the reference to crime includes a reference to any conduct which—

(i)   constitutes one or more criminal offences (whether under the law of a part of the United Kingdom or of a country or territory outside the United Kingdom); or

(ii)   is, or corresponds to, any conduct which, if it all took place in any one part of the United Kingdom, would constitute one or more criminal offences; and

(b)   the references to an investigation and to a prosecution include references, respectively, to any investigation outside the United Kingdom of any crime or suspected crime and to a prosecution brought in respect of any crime in a country or territory outside the United Kingdom.

(11)   In this Article—

(a)   references to ascertaining a person's identity include references to showing that he is not a particular person; and

(b)   references to taking a photograph include references to using any process by means of which a visual image may be produced, and references to photographing a person shall be construed accordingly.

(12)   In this Article "mark" includes features and injuries; and a mark is an identifying mark for the purposes of this Article if its existence in any person's case facilitates the ascertainment of his identity or his identification as a person involved in the commission of an offence.'

(2)   In Article 61(4) of that Order (grounds on which fingerprinting of person detained at a police station may be authorised)—

(a)   in sub-paragraph (b), after 'his involvement' insert 'or will facilitate the ascertainment of his identity (within the meaning of Article 55A), or both'; and

(b)   after that sub-paragraph insert—

'but an authorisation shall not be given for the purpose only of facilitating the ascertainment of that person's identity except where he has refused to identify himself or the officer has reasonable grounds for suspecting that he is not who he claims to be.'

92.   Photographing of suspects etc.: England and Wales

After section 64 of the Police and Criminal Evidence Act 1984 (c. 60) insert—

'64A.   Photographing of suspects etc.

(1)   A person who is detained at a police station may be photographed—

(a) with the appropriate consent; or

(b) if the appropriate consent is withheld or it is not practicable to obtain it, without it.

(2) A person proposing to take a photograph of any person under this section—

(a) may, for the purpose of doing so, require the removal of any item or substance worn on or over the whole or any part of the head or face of the person to be photographed; and

(b) if the requirement is not complied with, may remove the item or substance himself.

(3) Where a photograph may be taken under this section, the only persons entitled to take the photograph are—

(a) constables; and

(b) persons who (without being constables) are designated for the purposes of this section by the chief officer of police for the police area in which the police station in question is situated;

and section 117 (use of force) applies to the exercise by a person falling within paragraph (b) of the powers conferred by the preceding provisions of this section as it applies to the exercise of those powers by a constable.

(4) A photograph taken under this section—

(a) may be used by, or disclosed to, any person for any purpose related to the prevention or detection of crime, the investigation of an offence or the conduct of a prosecution; and

(b) after being so used or disclosed, may be retained but may not be used or disclosed except for a purpose so related.

(5) In subsection (4)—

(a) the reference to crime includes a reference to any conduct which—

(i) constitutes one or more criminal offences (whether under the law of a part of the United Kingdom or of a country or territory outside the United Kingdom); or

(ii) is, or corresponds to, any conduct which, if it all took place in any one part of the United Kingdom, would constitute one or more criminal offences;
and

(b) the references to an investigation and to a prosecution include references, respectively, to any investigation outside the United Kingdom of any crime or suspected crime and to a prosecution brought in respect of any crime in a country or territory outside the United Kingdom.

(6) References in this section to taking a photograph include references to using any process by means of which a visual image may be produced; and references to photographing a person shall be construed accordingly.'

93. Photographing of suspects etc.: Northern Ireland
After Article 64 of the Police and Criminal Evidence (Northern Ireland) Order 1989 (SI 1989/1341 (NI 12)) insert—

'64A. Photographing of suspects etc.
(1) A person who is detained at a police station may be photographed—

(a) with the appropriate consent; or

(b) if the appropriate consent is withheld or it is not practicable to obtain it, without it.

(2) A person proposing to take a photograph of any person under this Article—

(a)   may, for the purpose of doing so, require the removal of any item or substance worn on or over the whole or any part of the head or face of the person to be photographed; and

(b)   if the requirement is not complied with, may remove the item or substance himself.

(3)   Where a photograph may be taken under this Article, the only persons entitled to take the photograph are—

(a)   constables; and

(b)   persons who (without being constables) are designated for the purposes of this Article by the Chief Constable;

and Article 88 (use of force) applies to the exercise by a person falling within sub-paragraph (b) of the powers conferred by the preceding provisions of this Article as it applies to the exercise of those powers by a constable.

(4)   A photograph taken under this Article—

(a)   may be used by, or disclosed to, any person for any purpose related to the prevention or detection of crime, the investigation of an offence or the conduct of a prosecution; and

(b)   after being so used or disclosed, may be retained but may not be used or disclosed except for a purpose so related.

(5)   In paragraph (4)—

(a)   the reference to crime includes a reference to any conduct which—

(i)   constitutes one or more criminal offences (whether under the law of a part of the United Kingdom or of a country or territory outside the United Kingdom); or

(ii)   is, or corresponds to, any conduct which, if it all took place in any one part of the United Kingdom, would constitute one or more criminal offences;

and

(b)   the references to an investigation and to a prosecution include references, respectively, to any investigation outside the United Kingdom of any crime or suspected crime and to a prosecution brought in respect of any crime in a country or territory outside the United Kingdom.

(6)   References in this Article to taking a photograph include references to using any process by means of which a visual image may be produced; and references to photographing a person shall be construed accordingly.'

94. Powers to require removal of disguises: England and Wales

(1)   After section 60 of the Criminal Justice and Public Order Act 1994 (c. 33) insert—

'60AA. Powers to require removal of disguises

(1)   Where—

(a)   an authorisation under section 60 is for the time being in force in relation to any locality for any period, or

(b)   an authorisation under subsection (3) that the powers conferred by subsection (2) shall be exercisable at any place in a locality is in force for any period,

those powers shall be exercisable at any place in that locality at any time in that period.

(2)   This subsection confers power on any constable in uniform—

(a)   to require any person to remove any item which the constable reasonably believes that person is wearing wholly or mainly for the purpose of concealing his identity;

(b)   to seize any item which the constable reasonably believes any person intends to wear wholly or mainly for that purpose.

(3) If a police officer of or above the rank of inspector reasonably believes—

(a) that activities may take place in any locality in his police area that are likely (if they take place) to involve the commission of offences, and

(b) that it is expedient, in order to prevent or control the activities, to give an authorisation under this subsection,

he may give an authorisation that the powers conferred by this section shall be exercisable at any place within that locality for a specified period not exceeding twenty-four hours.

(4) If it appears to an officer of or above the rank of superintendent that it is expedient to do so, having regard to offences which—

(a) have been committed in connection with the activities in respect of which the authorisation was given, or

(b) are reasonably suspected to have been so committed,

he may direct that the authorisation shall continue in force for a further twenty-four hours.

(5) If an inspector gives an authorisation under subsection (3), he must, as soon as it is practicable to do so, cause an officer of or above the rank of superintendent to be informed.

(6) Any authorisation under this section—

(a) shall be in writing and signed by the officer giving it; and

(b) shall specify—

(i) the grounds on which it is given;

(ii) the locality in which the powers conferred by this section are exercisable;

(iii) the period during which those powers are exercisable;

and a direction under subsection (4) shall also be given in writing or, where that is not practicable, recorded in writing as soon as it is practicable to do so.

(7) A person who fails to remove an item worn by him when required to do so by a constable in the exercise of his power under this section shall be liable, on summary conviction, to imprisonment for a term not exceeding one month or to a fine not exceeding level 3 on the standard scale or both.

(8) The preceding provisions of this section, so far as they relate to an authorisation by a member of the British Transport Police Force (including one who for the time being has the same powers and privileges as a member of a police force for a police area), shall have effect as if references to a locality or to a locality in his police area were references to any locality in or in the vicinity of any policed premises, or to the whole or any part of any such premises.

(9) In this section "British Transport Police Force" and "policed premises" each has the same meaning as in section 60.

(10) The powers conferred by this section are in addition to, and not in derogation of, any power otherwise conferred.

(11) This section does not extend to Scotland.'

(2) In section 60A(1) of that Act (retention of things seized under section 60), after 'section 60' insert 'or 60AA'.

(3) In section 24(2) of the Police and Criminal Evidence Act 1984 (c. 60) (arrestable offences), in paragraph (o), for 'section 60(8)(b)' substitute 'section 60AA(7)'.

95. Powers to require removal of disguises: Northern Ireland

(1) In Part 5 of the Public Order (Northern Ireland) Order 1987 (SI 1987/463 (NI 7)), before Article 24 insert—

'Temporary powers to deal with activities in a locality

23A. Powers to require removal of disguises

   (1) Where—

      (a) an authorisation under paragraph (3) that the powers conferred by paragraph (2) shall be exercisable at any place in a locality is in force for any period, or

      (b) an authorisation under Article 23B is for the time being in force in relation to any locality for any period,

those powers shall be exercisable at any place in that locality at any time in that period.

   (2) This paragraph confers power on any constable in uniform—

      (a) to require any person to remove any item which the constable reasonably believes that person is wearing wholly or mainly for the purpose of concealing his identity;

      (b) to seize any item which the constable reasonably believes any person intends to wear wholly or mainly for that purpose.

   (3) If a police officer of or above the rank of inspector reasonably believes—

      (a) that activities may take place in any locality that are likely (if they take place) to involve the commission of offences, and

      (b) that it is expedient, in order to prevent or control the activities, to give an authorisation under this paragraph,

he may give an authorisation that the powers conferred by this Article shall be exercisable at any place within that locality for a specified period not exceeding twenty-four hours.

   (4) If it appears to an officer of or above the rank of superintendent that it is expedient to do so, having regard to offences which—

      (a) have been committed in connection with the activities in respect of which the authorisation was given, or

      (b) are reasonably suspected to have been so committed,

he may direct that the authorisation shall continue in force for a further twenty-four hours.

   (5) If an officer below the rank of superintendent gives an authorisation under paragraph (3), he must, as soon as it is practicable to do so, cause an officer of or above that rank to be informed.

   (6) Any authorisation under this Article—

      (a) shall be in writing and signed by the officer giving it; and

      (b) shall specify—

         (i) the grounds on which it is given;

         (ii) the locality in which the powers conferred by this Article are exercisable;

         (iii) the period during which those powers are exercisable;

and a direction under paragraph (4) shall also be given in writing or, where that is not practicable, recorded in writing as soon as it is practicable to do so.

   (7) A person who fails to remove an item worn by him when required to do so by a constable in the exercise of his power under this Article shall be liable, on summary conviction, to imprisonment for a term not exceeding one month or to a fine not exceeding level 3 on the standard scale or both.

   (8) The powers conferred by this Article are in addition to, and not in derogation of, any power otherwise conferred.'

   (2) In Article 26(2) of the Police and Criminal Evidence (Northern Ireland) Order 1989 (SI 1989/1341 (NI 12)) (arrestable offences), after sub-paragraph (i) insert—

'(ia)   an offence under Article 23A(7) of the Public Order (Northern Ireland) Order 1987 (SI 1987/463 (NI 7)) (failing to comply to requirement to remove disguise).'

Powers of stop, search and seizure in Northern Ireland

96. Power to stop and search in anticipation of violence

In the Public Order (Northern Ireland) Order 1987 (SI 1987/463 (NI 7)), after Article 23A (which is inserted by section 95) insert—

'23B.   Powers to stop and search in anticipation of violence

(1)   If a police officer of or above the rank of inspector reasonably believes—

(a)   that incidents involving serious violence may take place in any locality, and that it is expedient to give an authorisation under this Article to prevent or control their occurrence, or

(b)   that persons are carrying dangerous instruments or offensive weapons in any locality without good reason,

he may give an authorisation that the powers conferred by this Article are to be exercisable at any place within that locality for a specified period not exceeding twenty-four hours.

(2)   This Article confers power on any constable in uniform—

(a)   to stop any pedestrian and search him or anything carried by him for offensive weapons or dangerous instruments;

(b)   to stop any vehicle and search the vehicle, its driver and any passenger for offensive weapons or dangerous instruments;

and a constable may in the exercise of those powers stop any person or vehicle and make any search he thinks fit whether or not he has any grounds for suspecting that the person or vehicle is carrying weapons or dangerous instruments.

(3)   If it appears to an officer of or above the rank of superintendent that it is expedient to do so, having regard to offences which—

(a)   have been committed in connection with the activities in respect of which the authorisation was given, or

(b)   are reasonably suspected to have been so committed,

he may direct that the authorisation shall continue in force for a further twenty-four hours.

(4)   If an officer below the rank of superintendent gives an authorisation under paragraph (1) he must, as soon as it is practicable to do so, cause an officer of or above that rank to be informed.

(5)   If in the course of a search under this Article a constable discovers a dangerous instrument or an article which he has reasonable grounds for suspecting to be an offensive weapon, he may seize it.

(6)   This Article applies (with the necessary modifications) to ships, aircraft and hovercraft as it applies to vehicles.

(7)   A person who fails to stop or (as the case may be) fails to stop a vehicle when required to do so by a constable in the exercise of his powers under this Article shall be liable on summary conviction to imprisonment for a term not exceeding one month or to a fine not exceeding level 3 on the standard scale or both.

(8)   Any authorisation under this Article—

(a)   shall be in writing and signed by the officer giving it; and

(b)   shall specify—

(i)   the grounds on which it is given;

(ii)   the locality in which the powers conferred by this Article are exercisable;

(iii) the period during which those powers are exercisable;

and a direction under paragraph (3) shall also be given in writing or, where that is not practicable, recorded in writing as soon as it is practicable to do so.

(9)   Where a vehicle is stopped by a constable under this Article the driver shall be entitled to obtain a written statement that the vehicle was stopped under the powers conferred by this Article if he applies for such a statement not later than the end of the period of 12 months from the day on which the vehicle was stopped.

(10)   A person who is searched by a constable under this Article shall be entitled to obtain a written statement that he was searched under the powers conferred by this Article if he applies for such a statement not later than the end of the period of 12 months from the day on which he was searched.

(11)   The powers conferred by this Article are in addition to, and not in derogation of, any power otherwise conferred.

(12)   For the purposes of this Article, a person carries a dangerous instrument or an offensive weapon if he has it in his possession.

(13)   In this Article—

"caravan" has the meaning given by section 25(1) of the Caravans Act (Northern Ireland) 1963 (NI c. 17);

"dangerous instrument" means an instrument which has a blade or is sharply pointed;

"offensive weapon" has the meaning given by Article 22(1);

"vehicle" includes a caravan.'

97.   Seized articles

In the Public Order (Northern Ireland) Order 1987 (SI 1987/463 (NI 7)), after Article 23B insert—

'23C.   Retention and disposal of things seized under Article 23A and 23B

(1)   Anything seized by a constable under Article 23A or 23B may be retained in accordance with regulations made by the Secretary of State under this Article.

(2)   The Secretary of State may make regulations regulating the retention and safe keeping, and the disposal and destruction in prescribed circumstances, of such things.

(3)   Regulations made under this Article shall be subject to annulment in pursuance of a resolution of either House of Parliament in like manner as a statutory instrument and section 5 of the Statutory Instruments Act 1946 (c. 36) shall apply accordingly.'

MoD and transport police

98.   Jurisdiction of MoD police

(1)   Section 2 of the Ministry of Defence Police Act 1987 (c. 4) (jurisdiction of members of the Ministry of Defence Police) is amended as follows.

(2)   In subsection (2) (places where members of Ministry of Defence Police have powers and privileges of constables), omit paragraph (d) (which is superseded by the amendment made by subsection (4) of this section).

(3)   In subsection (3) (circumstances in which members of Ministry of Defence Police have powers and privileges of constables in places in United Kingdom not mentioned in subsection (2)), after paragraph (b) insert—

'(ba)   in connection with offences against persons within paragraph (b) above, with the incitement of such persons to commit offences and with offences under the Prevention of Corruption Acts 1889 to 1916 in relation to such persons;'.

(4)   After that subsection insert—

'(3A)   Where a member of the Ministry of Defence Police has been requested by a constable of—

(a)   the police force for any police area;

(b)   the Police Service of Northern Ireland;

(c)   the British Transport Police Force; or

(d)   the United Kingdom Atomic Energy Authority Constabulary,

to assist him in the execution of his duties in relation to a particular incident, investigation or operation, members of the Ministry of Defence Police shall have the powers and privileges of constables for the purposes of that incident, investigation or operation but subject to subsection (3B) below.

(3B)   Members of the Ministry of Defence Police have the powers and privileges of constables for the purposes of an incident, investigation or operation by virtue of subsection (3A) above—

(a)   if the request was made under paragraph (a) of that subsection by a constable of the police force for a police area, only in that police area;

(b)   if it was made under paragraph (b) of that subsection, only in Northern Ireland;

(c)   if it was made under paragraph (c) of that subsection, only to the extent that those powers and privileges would in the circumstances be exercisable for those purposes by a constable of the British Transport Police Force by virtue of subsection (1A) or, in Scotland, subsection (4) of section 53 of the British Transport Commission Act 1949 (c. xxix); or

(d)   if it was made under paragraph (d) of that subsection, only to the extent that those powers and privileges would in the circumstances be exercisable for those purposes by a constable of the United Kingdom Atomic Energy Authority Constabulary.

(3C)   Members of the Ministry of Defence Police shall have in any police area the same powers and privileges as constables of the police force for that police area, and in Northern Ireland the same powers and privileges as constables of the Police Service of Northern Ireland,—

(a)   in relation to persons whom they suspect on reasonable grounds of having committed, being in the course of committing or being about to commit an offence; or

(b)   if they believe on reasonable grounds that they need those powers and privileges in order to save life or to prevent or minimise personal injury.

(3D)   But members of the Ministry of Defence Police have powers and privileges by virtue of subsection (3C) above only if—

(a)   they are in uniform or have with them documentary evidence that they are members of the Ministry of Defence Police; and

(b)   they believe on reasonable grounds that a power of a constable which they would not have apart from that subsection ought to be exercised and that, if it cannot be exercised until they secure the attendance of or a request under subsection (3A) above by a constable who has it, the purpose for which they believe it ought to be exercised will be frustrated or seriously prejudiced.'

(5)   In subsection (4) (territorial waters)—

(a) for 'to (3)' substitute 'to (3D)', and

(b) for 'subsections (1) and (3)' substitute 'those subsections'.

(6) In subsection (5)—

    (a) after the definition of 'appropriate Gazette' insert—

      ' "British Transport Police Force" means the constables appointed under section 53 of the British Transport Commission Act 1949 (c. xxix);', and

    (b) after the definition of 'service authorities' insert—

      ' "United Kingdom Atomic Energy Authority Constabulary" means the special constables appointed under section 3 of the Special Constables Act 1923 (c. 11) on the nomination of the United Kingdom Atomic Energy Authority;'.

99. Provision of assistance by MoD police

After section 2 of the Ministry of Defence Police Act 1987 (c. 4) insert—

'2A. Provision of assistance to other forces

(1) The Chief Constable of the Ministry of Defence Police may, on the application of the chief officer of any relevant force, provide constables or other assistance for the purpose of enabling that force to meet any special demand on its resources.

(2) Where a member of the Ministry of Defence Police is provided for the assistance of a relevant force under this section—

    (a) he shall be under the direction and control of the chief officer of that force; and

    (b) he shall have the same powers and privileges as a member of that force.

(3) Constables are not to be regarded as provided for the assistance of a relevant force under this section in a case where assistance is provided under section 2 above.

(4) In this section—

"British Transport Police Force" has the same meaning as in section 2 above;

"chief officer" means—

    (a) the chief officer of the police force for any police area;

    (b) the Chief Constable of the Police Service of Northern Ireland;

    (c) the Chief Constable of the British Transport Police Force; or

    (d) the Chief Constable of the United Kingdom Atomic Energy Authority Constabulary;

"relevant force" means—

    (a) the police force for any police area;

    (b) the Police Service of Northern Ireland;

    (c) the British Transport Police Force; or

    (d) the United Kingdom Atomic Energy Authority Constabulary; and

"United Kingdom Atomic Energy Authority Constabulary" has the same meaning as in section 2 above.'

100. Jurisdiction of transport police

(1) Where a member of the British Transport Police Force has been requested by a constable of—

    (a) the police force for any police area,

    (b) the Ministry of Defence Police, or

    (c) the United Kingdom Atomic Energy Authority Constabulary,

('the requesting force') to assist him in the execution of his duties in relation to a particular incident, investigation or operation, members of the British Transport Police Force have for the purposes of that incident, investigation or operation the same powers and privileges as constables of the requesting force.

(2)   Members of the British Transport Police Force have in any police area the same powers and privileges as constables of the police force for that police area—

(a)   in relation to persons whom they suspect on reasonable grounds of having committed, being in the course of committing or being about to commit an offence, or

(b)   if they believe on reasonable grounds that they need those powers and privileges in order to save life or to prevent or minimise personal injury.

(3)   But members of the British Transport Police Force have powers and privileges by virtue of subsection (2) only if—

(a)   they are in uniform or have with them documentary evidence that they are members of that Force, and

(b)   they believe on reasonable grounds that a power of a constable which they would not have apart from that subsection ought to be exercised and that, if it cannot be exercised until they secure the attendance of or a request under subsection (1) by a constable who has it, the purpose for which they believe it ought to be exercised will be frustrated or seriously prejudiced.

(4)   In this section—

'British Transport Police Force' means the constables appointed under section 53 of the British Transport Commission Act 1949 (c. xxix), and

'United Kingdom Atomic Energy Authority Constabulary' means the special constables appointed under section 3 of the Special Constables Act 1923 (c. 11) on the nomination of the United Kingdom Atomic Energy Authority.

101.   Further provisions about transport police and MoD police
Schedule 7 contains amendments relating to the British Transport Police Force and the Ministry of Defence Police.

PART XI
RETENTION OF COMMUNICATIONS DATA

102.   Codes and agreements about the retention of communications data
(1)   The Secretary of State shall issue, and may from time to time revise, a code of practice relating to the retention by communications providers of communications data obtained by or held by them.

(2)   The Secretary of State may enter into such agreements as he considers appropriate with any communications provider about the practice to be followed by that provider in relation to the retention of communications data obtained by or held by that provider.

(3)   A code of practice or agreement under this section may contain any such provision as appears to the Secretary of State to be necessary—

(a)   for the purpose of safeguarding national security; or

(b)   for the purposes of prevention or detection of crime or the prosecution of offenders which may relate directly or indirectly to national security.

(4)   A failure by any person to comply with a code of practice or agreement under this section which is for the time being in force shall not of itself render him liable to any criminal or civil proceedings.

(5)   A code of practice or agreement under this section which is for the time being in force shall be admissible in evidence in any legal proceedings in which the question arises whether or not the retention of any communications data is justified on the grounds that a

failure to retain the data would be likely to prejudice national security, the prevention or detection of crime or the prosecution of offenders.

103. Procedure for codes of practice

    (1) Before issuing the code of practice under section 102 the Secretary of State shall—

        (a) prepare and publish a draft of the code; and

        (b) consider any representations made to him about the draft;

and the Secretary of State may incorporate in the code finally issued any modifications made by him to the draft after its publication.

    (2) Before publishing a draft of the code the Secretary of State shall consult with—

        (a) the Information Commissioner; and

        (b) the communications providers to whom the code will apply.

    (3) The Secretary of State may discharge his duty under subsection (2) to consult with any communications providers by consulting with a person who appears to him to represent those providers.

    (4) The Secretary of State shall lay before Parliament the draft code of practice under section 102 that is prepared and published by him under this section.

    (5) The code of practice issued by the Secretary of State under section 102 shall not be brought into force except in accordance with an order made by the Secretary of State by statutory instrument.

    (6) An order under subsection (5) may contain such transitional provisions and savings as appear to the Secretary of State to be necessary or expedient in connection with the coming into force of the code to which the order relates.

    (7) The Secretary of State shall not make an order under this section unless a draft of the order has been laid before Parliament and approved by resolution of each House.

    (8) The Secretary of State may from time to time—

        (a) revise the whole or any part of the code issued under section 102; and

        (b) issue the revised code.

    (9) The preceding provisions of this section shall apply (with appropriate modifications) in relation to the issue of any revised code under section 102 as they apply in relation to the first issuing of the code.

    (10) Subsection (9) shall not, in the case of a draft of a revised code, require the Secretary of State to consult under subsection (2) with any communications providers who would not be affected by the proposed revisions.

104. Directions about retention of communications data

    (1) If, after reviewing the operation of any requirements contained in the code of practice and any agreements under section 102, it appears to the Secretary of State that it is necessary to do so, he may by order made by statutory instrument authorise the giving of directions under this section for purposes prescribed in section 102(3).

    (2) Where any order under this section is in force, the Secretary of State may give such directions as he considers appropriate about the retention of communications data—

        (a) to communications providers generally;

        (b) to communications providers of a description specified in the direction; or

        (c) to any particular communications providers or provider.

    (3) An order under this section must specify the maximum period for which a communications provider may be required to retain communications data by any direction given under this section while the order is in force.

    (4) Before giving a direction under this section the Secretary of State shall consult—

(a) with the communications provider or providers to whom it will apply; or

(b) except in the case of a direction confined to a particular provider, with the persons appearing to the Secretary of State to represent the providers to whom it will apply.

(5) A direction under this section must be given or published in such manner as the Secretary of State considers appropriate for bringing it to the attention of the communications providers or provider to whom it applies.

(6) It shall be the duty of a communications provider to comply with any direction under this section that applies to him.

(7) The duty imposed by subsection (6) shall be enforceable by civil proceedings by the Secretary of State for an injunction, or for specific performance of a statutory duty under section 45 of the Court of Session Act 1988 (c. 36), or for any other appropriate relief.

(8) The Secretary of State shall not make an order under this section unless a draft of it has been laid before Parliament and approved by a resolution of each House.

105. Lapsing of powers in section 104

(1) Section 104 shall cease to have effect at the end of the initial period unless an order authorising the giving of directions is made under that section before the end of that period.

(2) Subject to subsection (3), the initial period is the period of two years beginning with the day on which this Act is passed.

(3) The Secretary of State may by order made by statutory instrument extend, or (on one or more occasions) further extend the initial period.

(4) An order under subsection (3)—

(a) must be made before the time when the initial period would end but for the making of the order; and

(b) shall have the effect of extending, or further extending, that period for the period of two years beginning with that time.

(5) The Secretary of State shall not make an order under subsection (3) unless a draft of it has been laid before Parliament and approved by a resolution of each House.

106. Arrangements for payments

(1) It shall be the duty of the Secretary of State to ensure that such arrangements are in force as he thinks appropriate for authorising or requiring, in such cases as he thinks fit, the making to communications providers of appropriate contributions towards the costs incurred by them—

(a) in complying with the provisions of any code of practice, agreement or direction under this Part, or

(b) as a consequence of the retention of any communications data in accordance with any such provisions.

(2) For the purpose of complying with his duty under this section, the Secretary of State may make arrangements for the payments to be made out of money provided by Parliament.

107. Interpretation of Part 11

(1) In this Part—

'communications data' has the same meaning as in Chapter 2 of Part 1 of the Regulation of Investigatory Powers Act 2000 (c. 23);

'communications provider' means a person who provides a postal service or a telecommunications service;

'legal proceedings', 'postal service' and 'telecommunications service' each has the same meaning as in that Act;

and any reference in this Part to the prevention or detection of crime shall be construed as if contained in Chapter 2 of Part 1 of that Act.

(2)   References in this Part, in relation to any code of practice, agreement or direction, to the retention by a communications provider of any communications data include references to the retention of any data obtained by that provider before the time when the code was issued, the agreement made or the direction given, and to data already held by that provider at that time.

PART XII
BRIBERY AND CORRUPTION

108.   Bribery and corruption: foreign officers etc.

(1)   For the purposes of any common law offence of bribery it is immaterial if the functions of the person who receives or is offered a reward have no connection with the United Kingdom and are carried out in a country or territory outside the United Kingdom.

(2)   In section 1 of the Prevention of Corruption Act 1906 (c. 34) (corrupt transactions with agents) insert this subsection after subsection (3)—

'(4)   For the purposes of this Act it is immaterial if—

(a)   the principal's affairs or business have no connection with the United Kingdom and are conducted in a country or territory outside the United Kingdom;

(b)   the agent's functions have no connection with the United Kingdom and are carried out in a country or territory outside the United Kingdom.'

(3)   In section 7 of the Public Bodies Corrupt Practices Act 1889 (c. 69) (interpretation relating to corruption in office) in the definition of 'public body' for 'but does not include any public body as above defined existing elsewhere than in the United Kingdom' substitute 'and includes any body which exists in a country or territory outside the United Kingdom and is equivalent to any body described above'.

(4)   In section 4(2) of the Prevention of Corruption Act 1916 (c. 64) (in the 1889 and 1916 Acts public body includes local and public authorities of all descriptions) after 'descriptions' insert '(including authorities existing in a country or territory outside the United Kingdom)'.

109.   Bribery and corruption committed outside the UK

(1)   This section applies if—

(a)   a national of the United Kingdom or a body incorporated under the law of any part of the United Kingdom does anything in a country or territory outside the United Kingdom, and

(b)   the act would, if done in the United Kingdom, constitute a corruption offence (as defined below).

(2)   In such a case—

(a)   the act constitutes the offence concerned, and

(b)   proceedings for the offence may be taken in the United Kingdom.

(3)   These are corruption offences—

(a)   any common law offence of bribery;

(b)   the offences under section 1 of the Public Bodies Corrupt Practices Act 1889 (c. 69) (corruption in office);

(c)   the first two offences under section 1 of the Prevention of Corruption Act 1906 (c. 34) (bribes obtained by or given to agents).

(4)   A national of the United Kingdom is an individual who is—

(a)   a British citizen, a British Dependent Territories citizen, a British National (Overseas) or a British Overseas citizen,

(b)   a person who under the British Nationality Act 1981 (c. 61) is a British subject, or

(c)   a British protected person within the meaning of that Act.

110.   Presumption of corruption not to apply

Section 2 of the Prevention of Corruption Act 1916 (c. 64) (presumption of corruption in certain cases) is not to apply in relation to anything which would not be an offence apart from section 108 or section 109.

PART XIII
MISCELLANEOUS

Third pillar of the European Union

111.   Implementation of the third pillar

(1)   At any time before 1st July 2002, an authorised Minister may by regulations make provision—

(a)   for the purpose of implementing any obligation of the United Kingdom created or arising by or under any third pillar measure or enabling any such obligation to be implemented,

(b)   for the purpose of enabling any rights enjoyed or to be enjoyed by the United Kingdom under or by virtue of any third pillar measure to be exercised, or

(c)   for the purpose of dealing with matters arising out of or related to any such obligation or rights.

(2)   For the purposes of subsection (1), the following are third pillar measures—

(a)   the 1995 Convention drawn up on the basis of Article K.3 of the Treaty on European Union on Simplified Extradition Procedure between the Member States of the European Union,

(b)   the 1996 Convention drawn up on the basis of Article K.3 of the Treaty on European Union relating to Extradition between the Member States of the European Union,

(c)   any framework decision adopted under Article 34 of the Treaty on European Union on the execution in the European Union of orders freezing property or evidence, on joint investigation teams, or on combatting terrorism, and

(d)   the Convention on Mutual Assistance in Criminal Matters between the Member States of the European Union, and the Protocol to that Convention, established in accordance with Article 34 of the Treaty on European Union.

(3)   The provision that may be made under subsection (1) includes, subject to subsection (4), any such provision (of any such extent) as might be made by Act of Parliament.

(4)   The powers conferred by subsection (1) do not include power—

(a)   to make any provision imposing or increasing taxation,

(b)   to make any provision taking effect from a date earlier than that of the making of the instrument containing the provision,

(c)   to confer any power to legislate by means of orders, rules, regulations or other subordinate instrument, other than rules of procedure for a court or tribunal, or

(d)   to create, except in accordance with subsection (6), a criminal offence which is punishable—

(i)   on conviction on indictment, with imprisonment for more than two years, (ii)　on summary conviction, with imprisonment for more than three months,

(iii)　on summary conviction, with a fine (not calculated on a daily basis) of more than level 5 on the standard scale or (for an offence triable either way) more than the statutory maximum, or

(iv)　on summary conviction, with a fine of more than £100 a day.

(5)　Subsection (4)(c) does not preclude the modification of a power to legislate conferred otherwise than under subsection (1), or the extension of any such power to purposes of the like nature as those for which it was conferred, and a power to give directions as to matters of administration is not to be regarded as a power to legislate within the meaning of subsection (4)(c).

(6)　Subsection (4)(d) does not preclude the creation of an offence punishable on conviction on indictment with imprisonment for a term of any length if—

(a)　the offence is one for which a term of that length, a term of at least that length, or a term within a range of lengths including that length, is required for the offence by an obligation created or arising by or under any third pillar measure,

(b)　the offence, if committed in particular circumstances, would be an offence falling within paragraph (a), or

(c)　the offence is not committed in the United Kingdom but would, if committed in the United Kingdom, or a part of the United Kingdom, be punishable on conviction on indictment with imprisonment for a term of that length.

112.　Third pillar: supplemental

(1)　'Authorised Minister' in section 111(1) has the meaning given by subsections (2) and (3).

(2)　The Scottish Ministers are authorised Ministers for any purpose for which powers under section 111(1) are exercisable within devolved competence (within the meaning of the Scotland Act 1998 (c. 46)).

(3)　For any other purpose, the following are authorised Ministers—

(a)　the Secretary of State,

(b)　the Lord Chancellor,

(c)　the Treasury,

(d)　the National Assembly for Wales, if designated under subsection (4),

(e)　the First Minister and deputy First Minister acting jointly, a Northern Ireland Minister or a Northern Ireland department, if the Ministers are, or the Minister or the department is, designated under subsection (4).

(4)　A designation under this subsection may be made by Order in Council in relation to any matter or for any purpose, and is subject to any restriction or condition specified in the Order.

(5)　An Order in Council under subsection (4) is subject to annulment in pursuance of a resolution of either House of Parliament.

(6)　The power to make regulations under section 111(1)—

(a)　in the case of the First Minister and deputy First Minister acting jointly, a Northern Ireland Minister or a Northern Ireland Department, is exercisable by statutory rule for the purposes of the Statutory Rules (Northern Ireland) Order 1979 (SI 1979/1573 (NI 12)),

(b)　in any other case, is exercisable by statutory instrument.

(7)　No regulations may be made under section 111(1) unless a draft of the regulations has been laid before and approved by a resolution of each House of Parliament.

(8)   Subsection (7) has effect, so far as it relates to the exercise of powers under section 111(1) by the Scottish Ministers, as if the reference to each House of Parliament were a reference to the Scottish Parliament.

(9)   Subsection (7) does not apply to a statutory instrument containing regulations made by the National Assembly for Wales unless the statutory instrument contains regulations—

(a)   made by the Secretary of State, the Lord Chancellor or the Treasury (whether or not jointly with the Assembly),

(b)   relating to an English border area, or

(c)   relating to a cross-border body (and not relating only to the exercise of functions, or the carrying on of activities, by the body in or with respect to Wales or a part of Wales); and in this subsection expressions used in the Government of Wales Act 1998 (c. 38) have the same meaning as in that Act.

(10)   Subsection (7) has effect, so far as it relates to the exercise of powers under section 111(1) by the First Minister and deputy First Minister acting jointly, a Northern Ireland Minister or a Northern Ireland department, as if the reference to each House of Parliament were a reference to the Northern Ireland Assembly.

Dangerous substances

113.   Use of noxious substances or things to cause harm and intimidate

(1)   A person who takes any action which—

(a)   involves the use of a noxious substance or other noxious thing;

(b)   has or is likely to have an effect falling within subsection (2); and

(c)   is designed to influence the government or to intimidate the public or a section of the public,

is guilty of an offence.

(2)   Action has an effect falling within this subsection if it—

(a)   causes serious violence against a person anywhere in the world;

(b)   causes serious damage to real or personal property anywhere in the world;

(c)   endangers human life or creates a serious risk to the health or safety of the public or a section of the public; or

(d)   induces in members of the public the fear that the action is likely to endanger their lives or create a serious risk to their health or safety;

but any effect on the person taking the action is to be disregarded.

(3)   A person who—

(a)   makes a threat that he or another will take any action which constitutes an offence under subsection (1); and

(b)   intends thereby to induce in a person anywhere in the world the fear that the threat is likely to be carried out,

is guilty of an offence.

(4)   A person guilty of an offence under this section is liable—

(a)   on summary conviction, to imprisonment for a term not exceeding six months or a fine not exceeding the statutory maximum (or both); and

(b)   on conviction on indictment, to imprisonment for a term not exceeding fourteen years or a fine (or both).

(5)   In this section—

'the government' means the government of the United Kingdom, of a part of the United Kingdom or of a country other than the United Kingdom; and

'the public' includes the public of a country other than the United Kingdom.

114. Hoaxes involving noxious substances or things

(1)   A person is guilty of an offence if he—

(a)   places any substance or other thing in any place; or

(b)   sends any substance or other thing from one place to another (by post, rail or any other means whatever);

with the intention of inducing in a person anywhere in the world a belief that it is likely to be (or contain) a noxious substance or other noxious thing and thereby endanger human life or create a serious risk to human health.

(2)   A person is guilty of an offence if he communicates any information which he knows or believes to be false with the intention of inducing in a person anywhere in the world a belief that a noxious substance or other noxious thing is likely to be present (whether at the time the information is communicated or later) in any place and thereby endanger human life or create a serious risk to human health.

(3)   A person guilty of an offence under this section is liable—

(a)   on summary conviction, to imprisonment for a term not exceeding six months or a fine not exceeding the statutory maximum (or both); and

(b)   on conviction on indictment, to imprisonment for a term not exceeding seven years or a fine (or both).

115. Sections 113 and 114: supplementary

(1)   For the purposes of sections 113 and 114 'substance' includes any biological agent and any other natural or artificial substance (whatever its form, origin or method of production).

(2)   For a person to be guilty of an offence under section 113(3) or 114 it is not necessary for him to have any particular person in mind as the person in whom he intends to induce the belief in question.

Intelligence Services Act 1994

116. Amendments of Intelligence Services Act 1994

(1)   In section 7 of the Intelligence Services Act 1994 (c. 13) (authorisation of acts outside the British Islands), in subsection (3)—

(a)   in paragraphs (a) and (b)(i), after 'the Intelligence Service' insert, in each case, 'or GCHQ'; and

(b)   in paragraph (c), after '2(2)(a)' insert 'or 4(2)(a)'.

(2)   After subsection (8) of that section insert—

'(9)   For the purposes of this section the reference in subsection (1) to an act done outside the British Islands includes a reference to any act which—

(a)   is done in the British Islands; but

(b)   is or is intended to be done in relation to apparatus that is believed to be outside the British Islands, or in relation to anything appearing to originate from such apparatus;

and in this subsection "apparatus" has the same meaning as in the Regulation of Investigatory Powers Act 2000 (c. 23).'

(3)   In section 11(1A) of that Act (prevention and detection of crime to have the same meaning as in Chapter 1 of Part 1 of the Regulation of Investigatory Powers Act 2000), for the words from 'for the purposes of this Act' to the end of the subsection substitute—

'(a)   for the purposes of section 3 above, as it applies for the purposes of Chapter 1 of Part 1 of that Act; and

(b) for the other purposes of this Act, as it applies for the purposes of the provisions of that Act not contained in that Chapter.'

Terrorism Act 2000

117. Information about acts of terrorism

(1) The Terrorism Act 2000 (c. 11) is amended as follows.

(2) After section 38 insert—

'38B. Information about acts of terrorism

(1) This section applies where a person has information which he knows or believes might be of material assistance—

(a) in preventing the commission by another person of an act of terrorism, or

(b) in securing the apprehension, prosecution or conviction of another person, in the United Kingdom, for an offence involving the commission, preparation or instigation of an act of terrorism.

(2) The person commits an offence if he does not disclose the information as soon as reasonably practicable in accordance with subsection (3).

(3) Disclosure is in accordance with this subsection if it is made—

(a) in England and Wales, to a constable.

(b) in Scotland, to a constable, or

(c) in Northern Ireland, to a constable or a member of Her Majesty's forces.

(4) It is a defence for a person charged with an offence under subsection (2) to prove that he had a reasonable excuse for not making the disclosure.

(5) A person guilty of an offence under this section shall be liable—

(a) on conviction on indictment, to imprisonment for a term not exceeding five years, or to a fine or to both, or

(b) on summary conviction, to imprisonment for a term not exceeding six months, or to a fine not exceeding the statutory maximum or to both.

(6) Proceedings for an offence under this section may be taken, and the offence may for the purposes of those proceedings be treated as having been committed, in any place where the person to be charged is or has at any time been since he first knew or believed that the information might be of material assistance as mentioned in subsection (1).'

(3) In section 39(3) (disclosure of information etc.), after '21' insert 'or 38B'.

118. Port and airport controls for domestic travel

(1) Schedule 7 to the Terrorism Act 2000 (port and border controls) is amended as follows.

(2) In paragraph 2(2)(b), at the end insert 'or his travelling by air within Great Britain or within Northern Ireland.'

(3) In paragraph 2(3), for 'in Great Britain or Northern Ireland.' substitute 'at any place in Great Britain or Northern Ireland (whether from within or outside Great Britain or Northern Ireland).'

(4) For paragraph 9(2) substitute—

'(2) This paragraph applies to—

(a) goods which have arrived in or are about to leave Great Britain or Northern Ireland on a ship or vehicle, and

(b) goods which have arrived at or are about to leave any place in Great Britain or Northern Ireland on an aircraft (whether the place they have come from or are going to is within or outside Great Britain or Northern Ireland).'

119. Passenger information

(1) Paragraph 17 of Schedule 7 to the Terrorism Act 2000 (c. 11) (port and border controls: passenger information) is amended as follows.

(2) For sub-paragraph (1) substitute—

'(1) This paragraph applies to a ship or aircraft which—

(a) arrives or is expected to arrive in any place in the United Kingdom (whether from another place in the United Kingdom or from outside the United Kingdom), or

(b) leaves or is expected to leave the United Kingdom.'

(3) In sub-paragraph (4)—

(a) omit the 'or' at the end of paragraph (b), and

(b) after paragraph (c) add—

', or (d) to goods.'

120. Weapons training for terrorists

(1) In section 54(1) and (2) of the Terrorism Act 2000 (weapons training for terrorists), after paragraph (a) insert—

'(aa) radioactive material or weapons designed or adapted for the discharge of any radioactive material,'.

(2) In section 55 of that Act (definitions)—

(a) for the definition of 'biological weapon' substitute—

' "biological weapon" means a biological agent or toxin (within the meaning of the Biological Weapons Act 1974) in a form capable of use for hostile purposes or anything to which section 1(1)(b) of that Act applies,';

(b) after the definition of 'chemical weapon' insert—

' "radioactive material" means radioactive material capable of endangering life or causing harm to human health,'; and

(c) the definition of 'nuclear weapon' shall cease to have effect.

121. Crown Court judges: Northern Ireland

(1) The Terrorism Act 2000 (c. 11) is amended as follows.

(2) In paragraph 18 of Schedule 5 (terrorist investigations: application to Northern Ireland)—

(a) omit paragraph (e);

(b) in paragraph (g) for 'county court judge' substitute 'Crown Court judge'.

(3) In paragraph 20 of that Schedule (powers of Secretary of State), in sub-paragraphs (2) and (3)(a) for 'county court judge' substitute 'Crown Court judge'.

(4) In paragraph 3(c) of Schedule 6 (persons by whom financial information orders may be made) for 'county court judge' substitute 'Crown Court judge'.

PART XIV
SUPPLEMENTAL

122. Review of Act

(1) The Secretary of State shall appoint a committee to conduct a review of this Act.

(2) He must seek to secure that at any time there are not fewer than seven members of the committee.

(3) A person may be a member of the committee only if he is a member of the Privy Council.

(4)   The committee shall complete the review and send a report to the Secretary of State not later than the end of two years beginning with the day on which this Act is passed.

(5)   The Secretary of State shall lay a copy of the report before Parliament as soon as is reasonably practicable.

(6)   The Secretary of State may make payments to persons appointed as members of the committee.

123. Effect of report

(1)   A report under section 122(4) may specify any provision of this Act as a provision to which this section applies.

(2)   Subject to subsection (3), any provision specified under subsection (1) ceases to have effect at the end of the period of 6 months beginning with the day on which the report is laid before Parliament under section 122(5).

(3)   Subsection (2) does not apply if before the end of that period a motion has been made in each House of Parliament considering the report.

124. Consequential and supplementary provision

(1)   A Minister of the Crown may by order make such incidental, consequential, transitional or supplemental provision as he thinks necessary or expedient for the general purposes, or any particular purpose, of this Act or in consequence of any provision made by or under this Act or for giving full effect to this Act or any such provision.

(2)   An order under this section may, in particular, make provision—

    (a)   for applying (with or without modifications) or amending, repealing or revoking any provision of or made under an Act passed before this Act or in the same Session,

    (b)   for making savings, or additional savings, from the effect of any repeal or revocation made by or under this Act.

(3)   Amendments made under this section are in addition, and without prejudice, to those made by or under any other provision of this Act.

(4)   No other provision of this Act restricts the powers conferred by this section.

(5)   An order under this section may make different provision for different purposes.

(6)   An order under this section shall be made by statutory instrument which shall be subject to annulment in pursuance of a resolution of either House of Parliament.

(7)   In this Part, 'Minister of the Crown' has the same meaning as in the Ministers of the Crown Act 1975 (c. 26).

125. Repeals and revocation

The enactments mentioned in Schedule 8 are repealed or revoked to the extent specified in the second column of that Schedule.

126. Expenses

There shall be paid out of money provided by Parliament—

    (a)   any expenditure incurred by a Minister of the Crown by virtue of this Act, and

    (b)   any increase attributable to this Act in the sums payable out of money so provided under any other enactment.

127. Commencement

(1)   Except as provided in subsections (2) to (4), this Act comes into force on such day as the Secretary of State may appoint by order.

(2)   The following provisions come into force on the day on which this Act is passed—

(a)   Parts 2 to 6,

(b)   Part 8, except section 78,

(c)   Part 9, except sections 84 and 87,

(d)   sections 89 to 97,

(e)   sections 98 to 100, except so far as they extend to Scotland,

(f)   section 101 and Schedule 7, except so far as they relate to the entries in respect of the Police (Scotland) Act 1967,

(g)   Part 11,

(h)   Part 13, except section 121,

(i)   this Part, except section 125 and Schedule 8 so far as they relate to the entries—

(i)   in Part 1 of Schedule 8,

(ii)   in Part 5 of Schedule 8, in respect of the Nuclear Installations Act 1965,

(iii)   in Part 6 of Schedule 8, in respect of the British Transport Commission Act 1962 and the Ministry of Defence Police Act 1987, so far as those entries extend to Scotland,

(iv)   in Part 7 of Schedule 8, in respect of Schedule 5 to the Terrorism Act 2000.

(3)   The following provisions come into force at the end of the period of two months beginning with the day on which this Act is passed—

(a)   section 84,

(b)   section 87.

(4)   The following provisions come into force on such day as the Secretary of State and the Scottish Ministers, acting jointly, may appoint by order—

(a)   sections 98 to 100, so far as they extend to Scotland,

(b)   section 101 and Schedule 7, so far as they relate to the entries in respect of the Police (Scotland) Act 1967, and

(c)   section 125 and Schedule 8, so far as they relate to the entries in Part 6 of Schedule 8 in respect of the British Transport Commission Act 1962 and the Ministry of Defence Police Act 1987, so far as those entries extend to Scotland.

(5)   Different days may be appointed for different provisions and for different purposes.

(6)   An order under this section—

(a)   must be made by statutory instrument, and

(b)   may contain incidental, supplemental, consequential or transitional provision.

128.   Extent

(1)   The following provisions do not extend to Scotland—

(a)   Part 5,

(b)   Part 12,

(c)   in Part 6 of Schedule 8, the repeals in the Criminal Justice and Police Order Act 1994 and in the Crime and Disorder Act 1998.

(2)   The following provisions do not extend to Northern Ireland—

(a)   section 76,

(b)   section 100.

(3)   Except as provided in subsections (1) and (2), an amendment, repeal or revocation in this Act has the same extent as the enactment amended, repealed or revoked.

129.   Short title

This Act may be cited as the Anti-terrorism, Crime and Security Act 2001.

SCHEDULES

SCHEDULE 1
FORFEITURE OF TERRORIST CASH

PART I
INTRODUCTORY

Terrorist cash

1.—(1) This Schedule applies to cash ('terrorist cash') which—
    (a) is within subsection (1)(a) or (b) of section 1, or
    (b) is property earmarked as terrorist property.
    (2) 'Cash' means—
    (a) coins and notes in any currency,
    (b) postal orders,
    (c) cheques of any kind, including travellers' cheques,
    (d) bankers' drafts,
    (e) bearer bonds and bearer shares,
found at any place in the United Kingdom.
    (3) Cash also includes any kind of monetary instrument which is found at any place in the United Kingdom, if the instrument is specified by the Secretary of State by order.
    (4) The power to make an order under sub-paragraph (3) is exercisable by statutory instrument, which is subject to annulment in pursuance of a resolution of either House of Parliament.

PART II
SEIZURE AND DETENTION

Seizure of cash

2.—(1) An authorised officer may seize any cash if he has reasonable grounds for suspecting that it is terrorist cash.
    (2) An authorised officer may also seize cash part of which he has reasonable grounds for suspecting to be terrorist cash if it is not reasonably practicable to seize only that part.

Detention of seized cash

3.—(1) While the authorised officer continues to have reasonable grounds for his suspicion, cash seized under this Schedule may be detained initially for a period of 48 hours.
    (2) The period for which the cash or any part of it may be detained may be extended by an order made by a magistrates' court or (in Scotland) the sheriff; but the order may not authorise the detention of any of the cash—
    (a) beyond the end of the period of three months beginning with the date of the order, and
    (b) in the case of any further order under this paragraph, beyond the end of the period of two years beginning with the date of the first order.
    (3) A justice of the peace may also exercise the power of a magistrates' court to make the first order under sub-paragraph (2) extending the period.
    (4) An order under sub-paragraph (2) must provide for notice to be given to persons affected by it.

(5)   An application for an order under sub-paragraph (2)—

(a)   in relation to England and Wales and Northern Ireland, may be made by the Commissioners of Customs and Excise or an authorised officer,

(b)   in relation to Scotland, may be made by a procurator fiscal,

and the court, sheriff or justice may make the order if satisfied, in relation to any cash to be further detained, that one of the following conditions is met.

(6)   The first condition is that there are reasonable grounds for suspecting that the cash is intended to be used for the purposes of terrorism and that either—

(a)   its continued detention is justified while its intended use is further investigated or consideration is given to bringing (in the United Kingdom or elsewhere) proceedings against any person for an offence with which the cash is connected, or

(b)   proceedings against any person for an offence with which the cash is connected have been started and have not been concluded.

(7)   The second condition is that there are reasonable grounds for suspecting that the cash consists of resources of an organisation which is a proscribed organisation and that either—

(a)   its continued detention is justified while investigation is made into whether or not it consists of such resources or consideration is given to bringing (in the United Kingdom or elsewhere) proceedings against any person for an offence with which the cash is connected, or

(b)   proceedings against any person for an offence with which the cash is connected have been started and have not been concluded.

(8)   The third condition is that there are reasonable grounds for suspecting that the cash is property earmarked as terrorist property and that either—

(a)   its continued detention is justified while its derivation is further investigated or consideration is given to bringing (in the United Kingdom or elsewhere) proceedings against any person for an offence with which the cash is connected, or

(b)   proceedings against any person for an offence with which the cash is connected have been started and have not been concluded.

Payment of detained cash into an account

4.—(1)   If cash is detained under this Schedule for more than 48 hours, it is to be held in an interest-bearing account and the interest accruing on it is to be added to it on its forfeiture or release.

(2)   In the case of cash seized under paragraph 2(2), the authorised officer must, on paying it into the account, release so much of the cash then held in the account as is not attributable to terrorist cash.

(3)   Sub-paragraph (1) does not apply if the cash is required as evidence of an offence or evidence in proceedings under this Schedule.

Release of detained cash

5.—(1)   This paragraph applies while any cash is detained under this Schedule.

(2)   A magistrates' court or (in Scotland) the sheriff may direct the release of the whole or any part of the cash if satisfied, on an application by the person from whom it was seized, that the conditions in paragraph 3 for the detention of cash are no longer met in relation to the cash to be released.

(3)   A authorised officer or (in Scotland) a procurator fiscal may, after notifying the magistrates' court, sheriff or justice under whose order cash is being detained, release the

whole or any part of it if satisfied that the detention of the cash to be released is no longer justified.

(4) But cash is not to be released—

(a) if an application for its forfeiture under paragraph 6, or for its release under paragraph 9, is made, until any proceedings in pursuance of the application (including any proceedings on appeal) are concluded,

(b) if (in the United Kingdom or elsewhere) proceedings are started against any person for an offence with which the cash is connected, until the proceedings are concluded.

PART III
FORFEITURE

Forfeiture

6.—(1) While cash is detained under this Schedule, an application for the forfeiture of the whole or any part of it may be made—

(a) to a magistrates' court by the Commissioners of Customs and Excise or an authorised officer,

(b) (in Scotland) to the sheriff by the Scottish Ministers.

(2) The court or sheriff may order the forfeiture of the cash or any part of it if satisfied that the cash or part is terrorist cash.

(3) In the case of property earmarked as terrorist property which belongs to joint tenants one of whom is an excepted joint owner, the order may not apply to so much of it as the court or sheriff thinks is attributable to the excepted joint owner's share.

(4) An excepted joint owner is a joint tenant who obtained the property in circumstances in which it would not (as against him) be earmarked; and references to his share of the earmarked property are to so much of the property as would have been his if the joint tenancy had been severed.

Appeal against forfeiture

7.—(1) Any party to proceedings in which an order is made under paragraph 6 ('a forfeiture order') who is aggrieved by the order may appeal—

(a) in relation to England and Wales, to the Crown Court,

(b) in relation to Scotland, to the Court of Session,

(c) in relation to Northern Ireland, to a county court.

(2) An appeal under sub-paragraph (1) must be made—

(a) within the period of 30 days beginning with the date on which the order is made, or

(b) if sub-paragraph (6) applies, before the end of the period of 30 days beginning with the date on which the order under section 3(3)(b) of the Terrorism Act 2000 (c. 11) referred to in that sub-paragraph comes into force.

(3) The appeal is to be by way of a rehearing.

(4) The court hearing the appeal may make any order it thinks appropriate.

(5) If the court upholds the appeal, it may order the release of the cash.

(6) Where a successful application for a forfeiture order relies (wholly or partly) on the fact that an organisation is proscribed, this sub-paragraph applies if—

(a) a deproscription appeal under section 5 of the Terrorism Act 2000 is allowed in respect of the organisation,

(b) an order is made under section 3(3)(b) of that Act in respect of the organisation in accordance with an order of the Proscribed Organisations Appeal Commission under section 5(4) of that Act (and, if the order is made in reliance on section 123(5) of that Act, a resolution is passed by each House of Parliament under section 123(5)(b)), and

(c)   the forfeited cash was seized under this Schedule on or after the date of the refusal to deproscribe against which the appeal under section 5 of that Act was brought.

Application of forfeited cash

8.—(1)   Cash forfeited under this Schedule, and any accrued interest on it—

(a)   if forfeited by a magistrates' court in England and Wales or Northern Ireland, is to be paid into the Consolidated Fund,

(b)   if forfeited by the sheriff, is to be paid into the Scottish Consolidated Fund.

(2)   But it is not to be paid in—

(a)   before the end of the period within which an appeal under paragraph 7 may be made, or

(b)   if a person appeals under that paragraph, before the appeal is determined or otherwise disposed of.

PART IV
MISCELLANEOUS

Victims

9.—(1)   A person who claims that any cash detained under this Schedule, or any part of it, belongs to him may apply to a magistrates' court or (in Scotland) the sheriff for the cash or part to be released to him.

(2)   The application may be made in the course of proceedings under paragraph 3 or 6 or at any other time.

(3)   If it appears to the court or sheriff concerned that—

(a)   the applicant was deprived of the cash claimed, or of property which it represents, by criminal conduct,

(b)   the property he was deprived of was not, immediately before he was deprived of it, property obtained by or in return for criminal conduct and nor did it then represent such property, and

(c)   the cash claimed belongs to him,

the court or sheriff may order the cash to be released to the applicant.

Compensation

10.—(1)   If no forfeiture order is made in respect of any cash detained under this Schedule, the person to whom the cash belongs or from whom it was seized may make an application to the magistrates' court or (in Scotland) the sheriff for compensation.

(2)   If, for any period after the initial detention of the cash for 48 hours, the cash was not held in an interest-bearing account while detained, the court or sheriff may order an amount of compensation to be paid to the applicant.

(3)   The amount of compensation to be paid under sub-paragraph (2) is the amount the court or sheriff thinks would have been earned in interest in the period in question if the cash had been held in an interest-bearing account.

(4)   If the court or sheriff is satisfied that, taking account of any interest to be paid under this Schedule or any amount to be paid under sub-paragraph (2), the applicant has suffered loss as a result of the detention of the cash and that the circumstances are exceptional, the court or sheriff may order compensation (or additional compensation) to be paid to him.

(5) The amount of compensation to be paid under sub-paragraph (4) is the amount the court or sheriff thinks reasonable, having regard to the loss suffered and any other relevant circumstances.

(6) If the cash was seized by a customs officer, the compensation is to be paid by the Commissioners of Customs and Excise.

(7) If the cash was seized by a constable, the compensation is to be paid as follows—

(a) in the case of a constable of a police force in England and Wales, it is to be paid out of the police fund from which the expenses of the police force are met,

(b) in the case of a constable of a police force in Scotland, it is to be paid by the police authority or joint police board for the police area for which that force is maintained,

(c) in the case of a police officer within the meaning of the Police (Northern Ireland) Act 2000 (c. 32), it is to be paid out of money provided by the Chief Constable.

(8) If the cash was seized by an immigration officer, the compensation is to be paid by the Secretary of State.

(9) If a forfeiture order is made in respect only of a part of any cash detained under this Schedule, this paragraph has effect in relation to the other part.

(10) This paragraph does not apply if the court or sheriff makes an order under paragraph 9.

PART V
PROPERTY EARMARKED AS TERRORIST PROPERTY

Property obtained through terrorism

11.—(1) A person obtains property through terrorism if he obtains property by or in return for acts of terrorism, or acts carried out for the purposes of terrorism.

(2) In deciding whether any property was obtained through terrorism—

(a) it is immaterial whether or not any money, goods or services were provided in order to put the person in question in a position to carry out the acts,

(b) it is not necessary to show that the act was of a particular kind if it is shown that the property was obtained through acts of one of a number of kinds, each of which would have been an act of terrorism, or an act carried out for the purposes of terrorism.

Property earmarked as terrorist property

12.—(1) Property obtained through terrorism is earmarked as terrorist property.

(2) But if property obtained through terrorism has been disposed of (since it was so obtained), it is earmarked as terrorist property only if it is held by a person into whose hands it may be followed.

(3) Earmarked property obtained through terrorism may be followed into the hands of a person obtaining it on a disposal by—

(a) the person who obtained the property through terrorism, or

(b) a person into whose hands it may (by virtue of this sub-paragraph) be followed.

Tracing property

13.—(1) Where property obtained through terrorism ('the original property') is or has been earmarked as terrorist property, property which represents the original property is also earmarked.

(2) If a person enters into a transaction by which—

(a) he disposes of earmarked property, whether the original property or property which (by virtue of this Part) represents the original property, and

(b)   he obtains other property in place of it,
the other property represents the original property.

(3)   If a person disposes of earmarked property which represents the original property, the property may be followed into the hands of the person who obtains it (and it continues to represent the original property).

Mixing property

14.—(1)   Sub-paragraph (2) applies if a person's property which is earmarked as terrorist property is mixed with other property (whether his property or another's).

(2)   The portion of the mixed property which is attributable to the property earmarked as terrorist property represents the property obtained through terrorism.

(3)   Property earmarked as terrorist property is mixed with other property if (for example) it is used—

(a)   to increase funds held in a bank account,

(b)   in part payment for the acquisition of an asset,

(c)   for the restoration or improvement of land,

(d)   by a person holding a leasehold interest in the property to acquire the freehold.

Accruing profits

15.—(1)   This paragraph applies where a person who has property earmarked as terrorist property obtains further property consisting of profits accruing in respect of the earmarked property.

(2)   The further property is to be treated as representing the property obtained through terrorism.

General exceptions

16.—(1)   If—

(a)   a person disposes of property earmarked as terrorist property, and

(b)   the person who obtains it on the disposal does so in good faith, for value and without notice that it was earmarked,
the property may not be followed into that person's hands and, accordingly, it ceases to be earmarked.

(2)   If—

(a)   in pursuance of a judgment in civil proceedings (whether in the United Kingdom or elsewhere), the defendant makes a payment to the claimant or the claimant otherwise obtains property from the defendant,

(b)   the claimant's claim is based on the defendant's criminal conduct, and

(c)   apart from this sub-paragraph, the sum received, or the property obtained, by the claimant would be earmarked as terrorist property,
the property ceases to be earmarked.
In relation to Scotland, 'claimant' and 'defendant' are to be read as 'pursuer' and 'defender'; and, in relation to Northern Ireland, 'claimant' is to be read as 'plaintiff'.

(3)   If—

(a)   a payment is made to a person in pursuance of a compensation order under Article 14 of the Criminal Justice (Northern Ireland) Order 1994 (SI 1994/2795 (NI 15)), section 249 of the Criminal Procedure (Scotland) Act 1995 (c. 46) or section 130 of the Powers of Criminal Courts (Sentencing) Act 2000 (c. 6), and

(b)   apart from this sub-paragraph, the sum received would be earmarked as terrorist property,
the property ceases to be earmarked.

(4)   If—

(a)   a payment is made to a person in pursuance of a restitution order under section 27 of the Theft Act (Northern Ireland) 1969 (c. 16 (NI)) or section 148(2) of the Powers of Criminal Courts (Sentencing) Act 2000 or a person otherwise obtains any property in pursuance of such an order, and

(b)   apart from this sub-paragraph, the sum received, or the property obtained, would be earmarked as terrorist property,
the property ceases to be earmarked.

(5)   If—

(a)   in pursuance of an order made by the court under section 382(3) or 383(5) of the Financial Services and Markets Act 2000 (c. 8) (restitution orders), an amount is paid to or distributed among any persons in accordance with the court's directions, and

(b)   apart from this sub-paragraph, the sum received by them would be earmarked as terrorist property,
the property ceases to be earmarked.

(6)   If—

(a)   in pursuance of a requirement of the Financial Services Authority under section 384(5) of the Financial Services and Markets Act 2000 (c. 8) (power of authority to require restitution), an amount is paid to or distributed among any persons, and

(b)   apart from this sub-paragraph, the sum received by them would be earmarked as terrorist property,
the property ceases to be earmarked.

(7)   Where—

(a)   a person enters into a transaction to which paragraph 13(2) applies, and

(b)   the disposal is one to which sub-paragraph (1) applies,
this paragraph does not affect the question whether (by virtue of paragraph 13(2)) any property obtained on the transaction in place of the property disposed of is earmarked.

PART VI
INTERPRETATION

Property

17.—(1)   Property is all property wherever situated and includes—

(a)   money,

(b)   all forms of property, real or personal, heritable or moveable,

(c)   things in action and other intangible or incorporeal property.

(2)   Any reference to a person's property (whether expressed as a reference to the property he holds or otherwise) is to be read as follows.

(3)   In relation to land, it is a reference to any interest which he holds in the land.

(4)   In relation to property other than land, it is a reference—

(a)   to the property (if it belongs to him), or

(b)   to any other interest which he holds in the property.

Obtaining and disposing of property

18.—(1)   References to a person disposing of his property include a reference—

(a)   to his disposing of a part of it, or

(b)   to his granting an interest in it,

(or to both); and references to the property disposed of are to any property obtained on the disposal.

(2)   If a person grants an interest in property of his which is earmarked as terrorist property, the question whether the interest is also earmarked is to be determined in the same manner as it is on any other disposal of earmarked property.

(3)   A person who makes a payment to another is to be treated as making a disposal of his property to the other, whatever form the payment takes.

(4)   Where a person's property passes to another under a will or intestacy or by operation of law, it is to be treated as disposed of by him to the other.

(5)   A person is only to be treated as having obtained his property for value in a case where he gave unexecuted consideration if the consideration has become executed consideration.

General interpretation

19.—(1)   In this Schedule—

'authorised officer' means a constable, a customs officer or an immigration officer,

'cash' has the meaning given by paragraph 1,

'constable', in relation to Northern Ireland, means a police officer within the meaning of the Police (Northern Ireland) Act 2000 (c. 32),

'criminal conduct' means conduct which constitutes an offence in any part of the United Kingdom, or would constitute an offence in any part of the United Kingdom if it occurred there,

'customs officer' means an officer commissioned by the Commissioners of Customs and Excise under section 6(3) of the Customs and Excise Management Act 1979 (c. 2),

'forfeiture order' has the meaning given by paragraph 7,

'immigration officer' means a person appointed as an immigration officer under paragraph 1 of Schedule 2 to the Immigration Act 1971 (c. 77),

'interest', in relation to land—

(a)   in the case of land in England and Wales or Northern Ireland, means any legal estate and any equitable interest or power,

(b)   in the case of land in Scotland, means any estate, interest, servitude or other heritable right in or over land, including a heritable security,

'interest', in relation to property other than land, includes any right (including a right to possession of the property),

'part', in relation to property, includes a portion,

'property obtained through terrorism' has the meaning given by paragraph 11,

'property earmarked as terrorist property' is to be read in accordance with Part 5,

'proscribed organisation' has the same meaning as in the Terrorism Act 2000 (c. 11),

'terrorism' has the same meaning as in the Terrorism Act 2000,

'terrorist cash' has the meaning given by paragraph 1,

'value' means market value.

(2)   Paragraphs 17 and 18 and the following provisions apply for the purposes of this Schedule.

(3)   For the purpose of deciding whether or not property was earmarked as terrorist property at any time (including times before commencement), it is to be assumed that this Schedule was in force at that and any other relevant time.

(4)   References to anything done or intended to be done for the purposes of terrorism include anything done or intended to be done for the benefit of a proscribed organisation.

(5)   An organisation's resources include any cash which is applied or made available, or is to be applied or made available, for use by the organisation.

(6)   Proceedings against any person for an offence are concluded when—

(a)   the person is convicted or acquitted,

(b)   the prosecution is discontinued or, in Scotland, the trial diet is deserted simpliciter, or

(c)   the jury is discharged without a finding.

SCHEDULE 2
TERRORIST PROPERTY: AMENDMENTS

PART I
ACCOUNT MONITORING ORDERS

1.—(1)   The Terrorism Act 2000 is amended as follows.

(2)   The following section is inserted after section 38—

'38A.   Account monitoring orders

Schedule 6A (account monitoring orders) shall have effect.'

(3)   The following Schedule is inserted after Schedule 6—

'SCHEDULE 6A
ACCOUNT MONITORING ORDERS

Introduction

1.—(1)   This paragraph applies for the purposes of this Schedule.

(2)   A judge is—

(a)   a Circuit judge, in England and Wales;

(b)   the sheriff, in Scotland;

(c)   a Crown Court judge, in Northern Ireland.

(3)   The court is—

(a)   the Crown Court, in England and Wales or Northern Ireland;

(b)   the sheriff, in Scotland.

(4)   An appropriate officer is—

(a)   a police officer, in England and Wales or Northern Ireland;

(b)   the procurator fiscal, in Scotland.

(5)   "Financial institution" has the same meaning as in Schedule 6.

Account monitoring orders

2.—(1)   A judge may, on an application made to him by an appropriate officer, make an account monitoring order if he is satisfied that—

(a)   the order is sought for the purposes of a terrorist investigation,

(b)   the tracing of terrorist property is desirable for the purposes of the investigation, and

(c)   the order will enhance the effectiveness of the investigation.

(2)   The application for an account monitoring order must state that the order is sought against the financial institution specified in the application in relation to information which—

(a)   relates to an account or accounts held at the institution by the person specified in the application (whether solely or jointly with another), and

(b)   is of the description so specified.

(3)   The application for an account monitoring order may specify information relating to—

(a)   all accounts held by the person specified in the application for the order at the financial institution so specified,

(b)   a particular description, or particular descriptions, of accounts so held, or

(c)   a particular account, or particular accounts, so held.

(4)   An account monitoring order is an order that the financial institution specified in the application for the order must—

(a)   for the period specified in the order,

(b)   in the manner so specified,

(c)   at or by the time or times so specified, and

(d)   at the place or places so specified,

provide information of the description specified in the application to an appropriate officer.

(5)   The period stated in an account monitoring order must not exceed the period of 90 days beginning with the day on which the order is made.

Applications

3.—(1)   An application for an account monitoring order may be made ex parte to a judge in chambers.

(2)   The description of information specified in an application for an account monitoring order may be varied by the person who made the application.

(3)   If the application was made by a police officer, the description of information specified in it may be varied by a different police officer.

Discharge or variation

4.—(1)   An application to discharge or vary an account monitoring order may be made to the court by—

(a)   the person who applied for the order;

(b)   any person affected by the order.

(2)   If the application for the account monitoring order was made by a police officer, an application to discharge or vary the order may be made by a different police officer.

(3)   The court—

(a)   may discharge the order;

(b)   may vary the order.

Rules of court

5.—(1)   Rules of court may make provision as to the practice and procedure to be followed in connection with proceedings relating to account monitoring orders.

(2)   In Scotland, rules of court shall, without prejudice to section 305 of the Criminal Procedure (Scotland) Act 1995 (c. 46), be made by Act of Adjournal.

Effect of orders

6.—(1)   In England and Wales and Northern Ireland, an account monitoring order has effect as if it were an order of the court.

(2) An account monitoring order has effect in spite of any restriction on the disclosure of information (however imposed).

Statements

7.—(1) A statement made by a financial institution in response to an account monitoring order may not be used in evidence against it in criminal proceedings.

(2) But sub-paragraph (1) does not apply—

(a) in the case of proceedings for contempt of court;

(b) in the case of proceedings under section 23 where the financial institution has been convicted of an offence under any of sections 15 to 18;

(c) on a prosecution for an offence where, in giving evidence, the financial institution makes a statement inconsistent with the statement mentioned in sub-paragraph (1).

(3) A statement may not be used by virtue of sub-paragraph (2)(c) against a financial institution unless—

(a) evidence relating to it is adduced, or

(b) a question relating to it is asked,

by or on behalf of the financial institution in the proceedings arising out of the prosecution.'

PART II
RESTRAINT ORDERS

2.—(1) Part 1 of Schedule 4 to the Terrorism Act 2000 (c. 11) (forfeiture orders under section 23 of that Act: England and Wales) is amended as follows.

(2) In paragraph 5 (restraint orders) for sub-paragraph (2) substitute—

'(2) The High Court may also make a restraint order under this paragraph where—

(a) a criminal investigation has been started in England and Wales with regard to an offence under any of sections 15 to 18,

(b) an application for a restraint order is made to the High Court by the person who the High Court is satisfied will have the conduct of any proceedings for the offence, and

(c) it appears to the High Court that a forfeiture order may be made in any proceedings for the offence.'

(3) In paragraph 5(3) for 'the proceedings' substitute 'any proceedings'.

(4) In paragraph 5 after sub-paragraph (5) insert—

'(6) In this paragraph "criminal investigation" means an investigation which police officers or other persons have a duty to conduct with a view to it being ascertained whether a person should be charged with an offence.'

(5) For paragraph 6(3) substitute—

'(3) A restraint order made under paragraph 5(1) shall in particular be discharged on an application under sub-paragraph (2) if the proceedings for the offence have been concluded.

(4) A restraint order made under paragraph 5(2) shall in particular be discharged on an application under sub-paragraph (2)—

(a) if no proceedings in respect of offences under any of sections 15 to 18 are instituted within such time as the High Court considers reasonable, and

(b)   if all proceedings in respect of offences under any of sections 15 to 18 have been concluded.'

(6)   In paragraph 8(3) for 'the proposed proceedings' substitute 'any proceedings for an offence under any of sections 15 to 18'.

(7)   In paragraph 9(1) (compensation where restraint order discharged) for 'paragraph 6(3)(a)' substitute 'paragraph 6(4)(a)'.

3.—(1)   Part 2 of Schedule 4 to the Terrorism Act 2000 (c. 11) (forfeiture orders under section 23 of that Act: Scotland) is amended as follows.

(2)   In paragraph 18 (restraint orders) for sub-paragraph (2) substitute—

'(2)   The Court of Session may also make a restraint order on such an application where—

(a)   a criminal investigation has been instituted in Scotland with regard to an offence under any of sections 15 to 18, and

(b)   it appears to the Court of Session that a forfeiture order may be made in any proceedings for the offence.'

(3)   In paragraph 18(3) for 'the proceedings' substitute 'any proceedings'.

(4)   In paragraph 18 after sub-paragraph (5) insert—

'(6)   In this paragraph "criminal investigation" means an investigation which police officers or other persons have a duty to conduct with a view to it being ascertained whether a person should be charged with an offence.'

(5)   For paragraph 19(3) substitute—

'(3)   A restraint order made under paragraph 18(1) shall in particular be recalled on an application under sub-paragraph (2) if the proceedings for the offence have been concluded.

(3A)   A restraint order made under paragraph 18(2) shall in particular be discharged on an application under sub-paragraph (2)—

(a)   if no proceedings in respect of offences under any of sections 15 to 18 are instituted within such time as the Court of Session considers reasonable, and

(b)   if all proceedings in respect of offences under any of sections 15 to 18 have been concluded.'

(6)   In paragraph 23(1) for '19(3)(a)' substitute '19(3A)(a)'.

4.—(1)   Part 3 of Schedule 4 to the Terrorism Act 2000 (forfeiture orders under section 23 of that Act: Northern Ireland) is amended as follows.

(2)   In paragraph 33 (restraint orders) for sub-paragraph (2) substitute—

'(2)   The High Court may also make a restraint order under this paragraph where—

(a)   a criminal investigation has been started in Northern Ireland with regard to an offence under any of sections 15 to 18,

(b)   an application for a restraint order is made to the High Court by the person who the High Court is satisfied will have the conduct of any proceedings for the offence, and

(c)   it appears to the High Court that a forfeiture order may be made in any proceedings for the offence.'

(3)   In paragraph 33(3) for 'the proceedings' substitute 'any proceedings'.

(4)   In paragraph 33 after sub-paragraph (5) insert—

'(6)   In this paragraph "criminal investigation" means an investigation which police officers or other persons have a duty to conduct with a view to it being ascertained whether a person should be charged with an offence.'

(5)   For paragraph 34(3) substitute—

'(3)   A restraint order made under paragraph 33(1) shall in particular be discharged on an application under sub-paragraph (2) if the proceedings for the offence have been concluded.

(4)   A restraint order made under paragraph 33(2) shall in particular be discharged on an application under sub-paragraph (2)—

(a)   if no proceedings in respect of offences under any of sections 15 to 18 are instituted within such time as the High Court considers reasonable, and

(b)   if all proceedings in respect of offences under any of sections 15 to 18 have been concluded.'

(6)   In paragraph 38(4), in the definition of 'prosecutor', for 'the proposed proceedings' substitute 'any proceedings for an offence under any of sections 15 to 18'.

(7)   In paragraph 39(1) (compensation where restraint order discharged) for 'paragraph 34(3)(a)' substitute 'paragraph 34(4)(a)'.

PART III
DISCLOSURE OF INFORMATION

5.—(1)   The Terrorism Act 2000 (c. 11) is amended as follows.

(2)   The following sections are inserted after section 21—

'21A.   Failure to disclose: regulated sector

(1)   A person commits an offence if each of the following three conditions is satisfied.

(2)   The first condition is that he—

(a)   knows or suspects, or

(b)   has reasonable grounds for knowing or suspecting,

that another person has committed an offence under any of sections 15 to 18.

(3)   The second condition is that the information or other matter—

(a)   on which his knowledge or suspicion is based, or

(b)   which gives reasonable grounds for such knowledge or suspicion,

came to him in the course of a business in the regulated sector.

(4)   The third condition is that he does not disclose the information or other matter to a constable or a nominated officer as soon as is practicable after it comes to him.

(5)   But a person does not commit an offence under this section if—

(a)   he has a reasonable excuse for not disclosing the information or other matter;

(b)   he is a professional legal adviser and the information or other matter came to him in privileged circumstances.

(6)   In deciding whether a person committed an offence under this section the court must consider whether he followed any relevant guidance which was at the time concerned—

(a)   issued by a supervisory authority or any other appropriate body,

(b)   approved by the Treasury, and

(c)   published in a manner it approved as appropriate in its opinion to bring the guidance to the attention of persons likely to be affected by it.

(7)   A disclosure to a nominated officer is a disclosure which—

(a)   is made to a person nominated by the alleged offender's employer to receive disclosures under this section, and

(b)   is made in the course of the alleged offender's employment and in accordance with the procedure established by the employer for the purpose.

(8)   Information or other matter comes to a professional legal adviser in privileged circumstances if it is communicated or given to him—

(a)   by (or by a representative of) a client of his in connection with the giving by the adviser of legal advice to the client,

(b)   by (or by a representative of) a person seeking legal advice from the adviser, or

(c)   by a person in connection with legal proceedings or contemplated legal proceedings.

(9)   But subsection (8) does not apply to information or other matter which is communicated or given with a view to furthering a criminal purpose.

(10)   Schedule 3A has effect for the purpose of determining what is—

(a)   a business in the regulated sector;

(b)   a supervisory authority.

(11)   For the purposes of subsection (2) a person is to be taken to have committed an offence there mentioned if—

(a)   he has taken an action or been in possession of a thing, and

(b)   he would have committed the offence if he had been in the United Kingdom at the time when he took the action or was in possession of the thing.

(12)   A person guilty of an offence under this section is liable—

(a)   on conviction on indictment, to imprisonment for a term not exceeding five years or to a fine or to both;

(b)   on summary conviction, to imprisonment for a term not exceeding six months or to a fine not exceeding the statutory maximum or to both.

(13)   An appropriate body is any body which regulates or is representative of any trade, profession, business or employment carried on by the alleged offender.

(14)   The reference to a constable includes a reference to a person authorised for the purposes of this section by the Director General of the National Criminal Intelligence Service.

21B.   Protected disclosures

(1)   A disclosure which satisfies the following three conditions is not to be taken to breach any restriction on the disclosure of information (however imposed).

(2)   The first condition is that the information or other matter disclosed came to the person making the disclosure (the discloser) in the course of a business in the regulated sector.

(3)   The second condition is that the information or other matter—

(a)   causes the discloser to know or suspect, or

(b)   gives him reasonable grounds for knowing or suspecting,

that another person has committed an offence under any of sections 15 to 18.

(4)   The third condition is that the disclosure is made to a constable or a nominated officer as soon as is practicable after the information or other matter comes to the discloser.

(5)   A disclosure to a nominated officer is a disclosure which—

(a)   is made to a person nominated by the discloser's employer to receive disclosures under this section, and

(b)   is made in the course of the discloser's employment and in accordance with the procedure established by the employer for the purpose.

(6)   The reference to a business in the regulated sector must be construed in accordance with Schedule 3A.

(7)   The reference to a constable includes a reference to a person authorised for the purposes of this section by the Director General of the National Criminal Intelligence Service.'

(3)   In section 19 after subsection (1) insert—

'(1A)   But this section does not apply if the information came to the person in the course of a business in the regulated sector.'

(4)   In section 19 after subsection (7) insert—

'(7A)   The reference to a business in the regulated sector must be construed in accordance with Schedule 3A.

(7B)   The reference to a constable includes a reference to a person authorised for the purposes of this section by the Director General of the National Criminal Intelligence Service.'

(5)   In section 20 after subsection (4) insert—

'(5)   References to a constable include references to a person authorised for the purposes of this section by the Director General of the National Criminal Intelligence Service.'

(6)   The following Schedule is inserted after Schedule 3—

'SCHEDULE 3A
REGULATED SECTOR AND SUPERVISORY AUTHORITIES

PART I
REGULATED SECTOR

Business in the regulated sector

1.—(1)   A business is in the regulated sector to the extent that it engages in any of the following activities—

(a)   accepting deposits by a person with permission under Part 4 of the Financial Services and Markets Act 2000 (c. 8) to accept deposits (including, in the case of a building society, the raising of money from members of the society by the issue of shares);

(b)   the business of the National Savings Bank;

(c)   business carried on by a credit union;

(d)   any home-regulated activity carried on by a European institution in respect of which the establishment conditions in paragraph 13 of Schedule 3 to the Financial Services and Markets Act 2000, or the service conditions in paragraph 14 of that Schedule, are satisfied;

(e)   any activity carried on for the purpose of raising money authorised to be raised under the National Loans Act 1968 (c. 13) under the auspices of the Director of Savings;

(f)   the activity of operating a bureau de change, transmitting money (or any representation of monetary value) by any means or cashing cheques which are made payable to customers;

(g)   any activity falling within sub-paragraph (2);

(h)   any of the activities in points 1 to 12 or 14 of Annex 1 to the Banking Consolidation Directive, ignoring an activity described in any of paragraphs (a) to (g) above;

(i)   business which consists of effecting or carrying out contracts of long term insurance by a person who has received official authorisation pursuant to Article 6 or 27 of the First Life Directive.

(2)   An activity falls within this sub-paragraph if it constitutes any of the following kinds of regulated activity in the United Kingdom—

     (a)   dealing in investments as principal or as agent;

     (b)   arranging deals in investments;

     (c)   managing investments;

     (d)   safeguarding and administering investments;

     (e)   sending dematerialised instructions;

     (f)   establishing (and taking other steps in relation to) collective investment schemes;

     (g)   advising on investments.

(3)   Paragraphs (a) and (i) of sub-paragraph (1) and sub-paragraph (2) must be read with section 22 of the Financial Services and Markets Act 2000 (c. 8), any relevant order under that section and Schedule 2 to that Act.

2.—(1)   This paragraph has effect for the purposes of paragraph 1.

(2)   "Building society" has the meaning given by the Building Societies Act 1986.

(3)   "Credit union" has the meaning given by the Credit Unions Act 1979 (c. 34) or the Credit Unions (Northern Ireland) Order 1985 (SI 1985/1205 (NI 12)).

(4)   "European institution" means an EEA firm of the kind mentioned in paragraph 5(b) or (c) of Schedule 3 to the Financial Services and Markets Act 2000 which qualifies for authorisation for the purposes of that Act under paragraph 12 of that Schedule.

(5)   "Home-regulated activity" in relation to a European institution, means an activity—

     (a)   which is specified in Annex 1 to the Banking Consolidation Directive and in respect of which a supervisory authority in the home State of the institution has regulatory functions, and

     (b)   if the institution is an EEA firm of the kind mentioned in paragraph 5(c) of Schedule 3 to the Financial Services and Markets Act 2000, which the institution carries on in its home State.

(6)   "Home State", in relation to a person incorporated in or formed under the law of another member State, means that State.

(7)   The Banking Consolidation Directive is the Directive of the European Parliament and Council relating to the taking up and pursuit of the business of credit institutions (No. 2000/12 EC).

(8)   The First Life Directive is the First Council Directive on the co-ordination of laws, regulations and administrative provisions relating to the taking up and pursuit of the business of direct life assurance (No. 79/267/EEC).

Excluded activities

3.   A business is not in the regulated sector to the extent that it engages in any of the following activities—

     (a)   the issue of withdrawable share capital within the limit set by section 6 of the Industrial and Provident Societies Act 1965 (c. 12) by a society registered under that Act;

(b)   the acceptance of deposits from the public within the limit set by section 7(3) of that Act by such a society;

(c)   the issue of withdrawable share capital within the limit set by section 6 of the Industrial and Provident Societies Act (Northern Ireland) 1969 (NI c. 24) by a society registered under that Act;

(d)   the acceptance of deposits from the public within the limit set by section 7(3) of that Act by such a society;

(e)   activities carried on by the Bank of England;

(f)   any activity in respect of which an exemption order under section 38 of the Financial Services and Markets Act 2000 (c. 8) has effect if it is carried on by a person who is for the time being specified in the order or falls within a class of persons so specified .

PART II
SUPERVISORY AUTHORITIES

4.—(1)   Each of the following is a supervisory authority—

(a)   the Bank of England;

(b)   the Financial Services Authority;

(c)   the Council of Lloyd's;

(d)   the Director General of Fair Trading;

(e)   a body which is a designated professional body for the purposes of Part 20 of the Financial Services and Markets Act 2000.

(2)   The Secretary of State is also a supervisory authority in the exercise, in relation to a person carrying on a business in the regulated sector, of his functions under the enactments relating to companies or insolvency or under the Financial Services and Markets Act 2000.

(3)   The Treasury are also a supervisory authority in the exercise, in relation to a person carrying on a business in the regulated sector, of their functions under the enactments relating to companies or insolvency or under the Financial Services and Markets Act 2000.

PART III
POWER TO AMEND

5.—(1)   The Treasury may by order amend Part 1 or 2 of this Schedule.

(2)   An order under sub-paragraph (1) must be made by statutory instrument subject to annulment in pursuance of a resolution of either House of Parliament.'

PART IV
FINANCIAL INFORMATION ORDERS

6.—(1)   Paragraph 1 of Schedule 6 to the Terrorism Act 2000 (c. 11) (financial information orders) is amended as follows.

(2)   In sub-paragraph (1) after 'financial institution' insert 'to which the order applies'.

(3)   After sub-paragraph (1) insert—

'(1A)   The order may provide that it applies to—

(a)   all financial institutions,

(b)   a particular description, or particular descriptions, of financial institutions, or

(c)   a particular financial institution or particular financial institutions.'

SCHEDULE 3
FREEZING ORDERS

Interpretation

1.   References in this Schedule to a person specified in a freezing order as a person to whom or for whose benefit funds are not to be made available are to be read in accordance with section 5(4).

Funds

2.   A freezing order may include provision that funds include gold, cash, deposits, securities (such as stocks, shares and debentures) and such other matters as the order may specify.

Making funds available

3.—(1)   A freezing order must include provision as to the meaning (in relation to funds) of making available to or for the benefit of a person.

(2)   In particular, an order may provide that the expression includes—

(a)   allowing a person to withdraw from an account;

(b)   honouring a cheque payable to a person;

(c)   crediting a person's account with interest;

(d)   releasing documents of title (such as share certificates) held on a person's behalf;

(e)   making available the proceeds of realisation of a person's property;

(f)   making a payment to or for a person's benefit (for instance, under a contract or as a gift or under any enactment such as the enactments relating to social security);

(g)   such other acts as the order may specify.

Licences

4.—(1)   A freezing order must include—

(a)   provision for the granting of licences authorising funds to be made available;

(b)   provision that a prohibition under the order is not to apply if funds are made available in accordance with a licence.

(2)   In particular, an order may provide—

(a)   that a licence may be granted generally or to a specified person or persons or description of persons;

(b)   that a licence may authorise funds to be made available to or for the benefit of persons generally or a specified person or persons or description of persons;

(c)   that a licence may authorise funds to be made available generally or for specified purposes;

(d)   that a licence may be granted in relation to funds generally or to funds of a specified description;

(e)   for a licence to be granted in pursuance of an application or without an application being made;

(f)   for the form and manner in which applications for licences are to be made;

(g)   for licences to be granted by the Treasury or a person authorised by the Treasury;

(h) for the form in which licences are to be granted;

(i) for licences to be granted subject to conditions;

(j) for licences to be of a defined or indefinite duration;

(k) for the charging of a fee to cover the administrative costs of granting a licence;

(l) for the variation and revocation of licences.

Information and documents

5.—(1) A freezing order may include provision that a person—

(a) must provide information if required to do so and it is reasonably needed for the purpose of ascertaining whether an offence under the order has been committed;

(b) must produce a document if required to do so and it is reasonably needed for that purpose.

(2) In particular, an order may include—

(a) provision that a requirement to provide information or to produce a document may be made by the Treasury or a person authorised by the Treasury;

(b) provision that information must be provided, and a document must be produced, within a reasonable period specified in the order and at a place specified by the person requiring it;

(c) provision that the provision of information is not to be taken to breach any restriction on the disclosure of information (however imposed);

(d) provision restricting the use to which information or a document may be put and the circumstances in which it may be disclosed;

(e) provision that a requirement to provide information or produce a document does not apply to privileged information or a privileged document;

(f) provision that information is privileged if the person would be entitled to refuse to provide it on grounds of legal professional privilege in proceedings in the High Court or (in Scotland) on grounds of confidentiality of communications in proceedings in the Court of Session;

(g) provision that a document is privileged if the person would be entitled to refuse to produce it on grounds of legal professional privilege in proceedings in the High Court or (in Scotland) on grounds of confidentiality of communications in proceedings in the Court of Session;

(h) provision that information or a document held with the intention of furthering a criminal purpose is not privileged.

Disclosure of information

6.—(1) A freezing order may include provision requiring a person to disclose information as mentioned below if the following three conditions are satisfied.

(2) The first condition is that the person required to disclose is specified or falls within a description specified in the order.

(3) The second condition is that the person required to disclose knows or suspects, or has grounds for knowing or suspecting, that a person specified in the freezing order as a person to whom or for whose benefit funds are not to be made available—

(a) is a customer of his or has been a customer of his at any time since the freezing order came into force, or

(b) is a person with whom he has dealings in the course of his business or has had such dealings at any time since the freezing order came into force.

(4)   The third condition is that the information—

(a)   on which the knowledge or suspicion of the person required to disclose is based, or

(b)   which gives grounds for his knowledge or suspicion,

came to him in the course of a business in the regulated sector.

(5)   The freezing order may require the person required to disclose to make a disclosure to the Treasury of that information as soon as is practicable after it comes to him.

(6)   The freezing order may include—

(a)   provision that Schedule 3A to the Terrorism Act 2000 (c. 11) is to have effect for the purpose of determining what is a business in the regulated sector;

(b)   provision that the disclosure of information is not to be taken to breach any restriction on the disclosure of information (however imposed);

(c)   provision restricting the use to which information may be put and the circumstances in which it may be disclosed by the Treasury;

(d)   provision that the requirement to disclose information does not apply to privileged information;

(e)   provision that information is privileged if the person would be entitled to refuse to disclose it on grounds of legal professional privilege in proceedings in the High Court or (in Scotland) on grounds of confidentiality of communications in proceedings in the Court of Session;

(f)   provision that information held with the intention of furthering a criminal purpose is not privileged.

Offences

7.—(1)   A freezing order may include any of the provisions set out in this paragraph.

(2)   A person commits an offence if he fails to comply with a prohibition imposed by the order.

(3)   A person commits an offence if he engages in an activity knowing or intending that it will enable or facilitate the commission by another person of an offence under a provision included under sub-paragraph (2).

(4)   A person commits an offence if—

(a)   he fails without reasonable excuse to provide information, or to produce a document, in response to a requirement made under the order;

(b)   he provides information, or produces a document, which he knows is false in a material particular in response to such a requirement or with a view to obtaining a licence under the order;

(c)   he recklessly provides information, or produces a document, which is false in a material particular in response to such a requirement or with a view to obtaining a licence under the order;

(d)   he fails without reasonable excuse to disclose information as required by a provision included under paragraph 6.

(5)   A person does not commit an offence under a provision included under sub-paragraph (2) or (3) if he proves that he did not know and had no reason to suppose that the person to whom or for whose benefit funds were made available, or were to be made available, was the person (or one of the persons) specified in the freezing order as a person to whom or for whose benefit funds are not to be made available.

(6)   A person guilty of an offence under a provision included under sub-paragraph (2) or (3) is liable—

(a)   on summary conviction, to imprisonment for a term not exceeding 6 months or to a fine not exceeding the statutory maximum or to both;

(b)   on conviction on indictment, to imprisonment for a term not exceeding 2 years or to a fine or to both.

(7)   A person guilty of an offence under a provision included under sub-paragraph (4) is liable on summary conviction to imprisonment for a term not exceeding 6 months or to a fine not exceeding level 5 on the standard scale or to both.

Offences: procedure

8.—(1)   A freezing order may include any of the provisions set out in this paragraph.

(2)   Proceedings for an offence under the order are not to be instituted in England and Wales except by or with the consent of the Treasury or the Director of Public Prosecutions.

(3)   Proceedings for an offence under the order are not to be instituted in Northern Ireland except by or with the consent of the Treasury or the Director of Public Prosecutions for Northern Ireland.

(4)   Despite anything in section 127(1) of the Magistrates' Courts Act 1980 (c. 43) (information to be laid within 6 months of offence) an information relating to an offence under the order which is triable by a magistrates' court in England and Wales may be so tried if it is laid at any time in the period of one year starting with the date of the commission of the offence.

(5)   In Scotland summary proceedings for an offence under the order may be commenced at any time in the period of one year starting with the date of the commission of the offence.

(6)   In its application to an offence under the order Article 19(1)(a) of the Magistrates' Courts (Northern Ireland) Order 1981 (SI 1981/1675 (NI 26)) (time limit within which complaint charging offence must be made) is to have effect as if the reference to six months were a reference to twelve months.

Offences by bodies corporate etc.

9.—(1)   A freezing order may include any of the provisions set out in this paragraph.

(2)   If an offence under the order—

(a)   is committed by a body corporate, and

(b)   is proved to have been committed with the consent or connivance of an officer, or to be attributable to any neglect on his part,
he as well as the body corporate is guilty of the offence and liable to be proceeded against and punished accordingly.

(3)   These are officers of a body corporate—

(a)   a director, manager, secretary or other similar officer of the body;

(b)   any person purporting to act in any such capacity.

(4)   If the affairs of a body corporate are managed by its members sub-paragraph (2) applies in relation to the acts and defaults of a member in connection with his functions of management as if he were an officer of the body.

(5)   If an offence under the order—

(a)   is committed by a Scottish partnership, and

(b)   is proved to have been committed with the consent or connivance of a partner, or to be attributable to any neglect on his part,
he as well as the partnership is guilty of the offence and liable to be proceeded against and punished accordingly.

Compensation

10.—(1) A freezing order may include provision for the award of compensation to or on behalf of a person on the grounds that he has suffered loss as a result of—

(a) the order;

(b) the fact that a licence has not been granted under the order;

(c) the fact that a licence under the order has been granted on particular terms rather than others;

(d) the fact that a licence under the order has been varied or revoked.

(2) In particular, the order may include—

(a) provision about the person who may make a claim for an award;

(b) provision about the person to whom a claim for an award is to be made (which may be provision that it is to be made to the High Court or, in Scotland, the Court of Session);

(c) provision about the procedure for making and deciding a claim;

(d) provision that no compensation is to be awarded unless the claimant has behaved reasonably (which may include provision requiring him to mitigate his loss, for instance by applying for a licence);

(e) provision that compensation must be awarded in specified circumstances or may be awarded in specified circumstances (which may include provision that the circumstances involve negligence or other fault);

(f) provision about the amount that may be awarded;

(g) provision about who is to pay any compensation awarded (which may include provision that it is to be paid or reimbursed by the Treasury);

(h) provision about how compensation is to be paid (which may include provision for payment to a person other than the claimant).

Treasury's duty to give reasons

11. A freezing order must include provision that if—

(a) a person is specified in the order as a person to whom or for whose benefit funds are not to be made available, and

(b) he makes a written request to the Treasury to give him the reason why he is so specified,

as soon as is practicable the Treasury must give the person the reason in writing.

SCHEDULE 4
EXTENSION OF EXISTING DISCLOSURE POWERS

PART I
ENACTMENTS TO WHICH SECTION 17 APPLIES

Agricultural Marketing Act 1958 (c. 47)

1. Section 47(2) of the Agricultural Marketing Act 1958.

Harbours Act 1964 (c. 40)

2. Section 46(1) of the Harbours Act 1964.

Cereals Marketing Act 1965 (c. 14)

3. Section 17(2) of the Cereals Marketing Act 1965.

Agriculture Act 1967 (c. 22)

4.   Section 24(1) of the Agriculture Act 1967.

Trade Descriptions Act 1968 (c. 29)

5.   Section 28(5A) of the Trade Descriptions Act 1968.

Sea Fish Industry Act 1970 (c. 11)

6.   Section 14(2) of the Sea Fish Industry Act 1970.

National Savings Bank Act 1971 (c. 29)

7.   Section 12(2) of the National Savings Bank Act 1971.

Employment Agencies Act 1973 (c. 35)

8.   Section 9(4) of the Employment Agencies Act 1973.

Fair Trading Act 1973 (c. 41)

9.   Section 133(3) of the Fair Trading Act 1973 so far only as it relates to information obtained under or by virtue of any provision of Part 3 of that Act (protection of consumers).

Prices Act 1974 (c. 24)

10.   Paragraph 12(2) of the Schedule to the Prices Act 1974.

Consumer Credit Act 1974 (c. 39)

11.   Section 174(3) of the Consumer Credit Act 1974.

Health and Safety at Work etc. Act 1974 (c. 37)

12.   Section 28(7) of the Health and Safety at Work etc. Act 1974.

Sex Discrimination Act 1975 (c. 65)

13.   Section 61(1) of the Sex Discrimination Act 1975.

Race Relations Act 1976 (c. 74)

14.   Section 52(1) of the Race Relations Act 1976.

Energy Act 1976 (c. 76)

15.   Paragraph 7 of Schedule 2 to the Energy Act 1976.

National Health Service Act 1977 (c. 49)

16.   Paragraph 5 of Schedule 11 to the National Health Service Act 1977.

Estate Agents Act 1979 (c. 38)

17.   Section 10(3) of the Estate Agents Act 1979.

Public Passenger Vehicles Act 1981 (c. 14)

18. Section 54(8) of the Public Passenger Vehicles Act 1981.

Fisheries Act 1981 (c. 29)

19. Section 12(2) of the Fisheries Act 1981.

Merchant Shipping (Liner Conferences) Act 1982 (c. 37)

20. Section 10(2) of the Merchant Shipping (Liner Conferences) Act 1982.

Civil Aviation Act 1982 (c. 16)

21. Section 23(4) of the Civil Aviation Act 1982.

Diseases of Fish Act 1983 (c. 30)

22. Section 9(1) of the Diseases of Fish Act 1983.

Telecommunications Act 1984 (c. 12)

23. Section 101(2) of the Telecommunications Act 1984.

Companies Act 1985 (c. 6)

24. Section 449(1) of the Companies Act 1985.

Airports Act 1986 (c. 31)

25. Section 74(2) of the Airports Act 1986.

Legal Aid (Scotland) Act 1986 (c. 47)

26. Section 34(2) of the Legal Aid (Scotland) Act 1986.

Consumer Protection Act 1987 (c. 43)

27. Section 38(2) of the Consumer Protection Act 1987.

Companies Act 1989 (c. 40)

28. Section 87(1) of the Companies Act 1989.

Broadcasting Act 1990 (c. 42)

29. Section 197(2) of the Broadcasting Act 1990.

Property Misdescriptions Act 1991 (c. 29)

30. Paragraph 7(1) of the Schedule to the Property Misdescriptions Act 1991.

Water Industry Act 1991 (c. 56)

31. Section 206(3) of the Water Industry Act 1991.

Water Resources Act 1991 (c. 57)

32.   Section 204(2) of the Water Resources Act 1991.

Timeshare Act 1992 (c. 35)

33.   Paragraph 5(1) of Schedule 2 to the Timeshare Act 1992.

Railways Act 1993 (c. 43)

34.   Section 145(2) of the Railways Act 1993.

Coal Industry Act 1994 (c. 21)

35.   Section 59(2) of the Coal Industry Act 1994.

Shipping and Trading Interests (Protection) Act 1995 (c. 22)

36.   Section 3(4) of the Shipping and Trading Interests (Protection) Act 1995.

Pensions Act 1995 (c. 26)

37.—(1)   Section 105(2) of the Pensions Act 1995.
  (2)   Section 108(2) of that Act.

Goods Vehicles (Licensing of Operators) Act 1995 (c. 23)

38.   Section 35(4) of the Goods Vehicles (Licensing of Operators) Act 1995.

Chemical Weapons Act 1996 (c. 6)

39.   Section 32(2) of the Chemical Weapons Act 1996.

Bank of England Act 1998 (c. 11)

40.—(1)   Paragraph 5 of Schedule 7 to the Bank of England Act 1998.
  (2)   Paragraph 2 of Schedule 8 to that Act.

Audit Commission Act 1998 (c. 18)

41.   Section 49(1) of the Audit Commission Act 1998.

Data Protection Act 1998 (c. 29)

42.   Section 59(1) of the Data Protection Act 1998.

Police (Northern Ireland) Act 1998 (c. 32)

43.   Section 63(1) of the Police (Northern Ireland) Act 1998.

Landmines Act 1998 (c. 33)

44.   Section 19(2) of the Landmines Act 1998.

Health Act 1999 (c. 8)

45.   Section 24 of the Health Act 1999.

Disability Rights Commission Act 1999 (c. 17)

46.   Paragraph 22(2)(f) of Schedule 3 to the Disability Rights Commission Act 1999.

Access to Justice Act 1999 (c. 22)

47.   Section 20(2) of the Access to Justice Act 1999.

Nuclear Safeguards Act 2000 (c. 5)

48.   Section 6(2) of the Nuclear Safeguards Act 2000.

Finance Act 2000 (c. 21)

49.   Paragraph 34(3) of Schedule 22 to the Finance Act 2000.

Local Government Act 2000 (c. 22)

50.   Section 63(1) of the Local Government Act 2000.

Postal Services Act 2000 (c. 26)

51.   Paragraph 3(1) of Schedule 7 to the Postal Services Act 2000.

Utilities Act 2000 (c. 27)

52.   Section 105(4) of the Utilities Act 2000.

Transport Act 2000 (c. 38)

53.—(1)   Section 143(5)(b) of the Transport Act 2000.
   (2)   Paragraph 13(3) of Schedule 10 to that Act.

PART II
NORTHERN IRELAND LEGISLATION TO WHICH SECTION 17 APPLIES

Transport Act (Northern Ireland) 1967 (c. 37 (NI))

54.   Section 36(1) of the Transport Act (Northern Ireland) 1967.

Sex Discrimination (Northern Ireland) Order 1976 (SI 1976/1042 (NI 15))

55.   Article 61(1) of the Sex Discrimination (Northern Ireland) Order 1976.

Health and Safety at Work (Northern Ireland) Order 1978 (SI 1978/1039 (NI 9))

56.   Article 30(6) of the Health and Safety at Work (Northern Ireland) Order 1978.

Legal Aid, Advice and Assistance (Northern Ireland) Order 1981 (SI 1981/228 (NI 8))

57.   Article 24(1) of the Legal Aid, Advice and Assistance (Northern Ireland) Order 1981.

Agricultural Marketing (Northern Ireland) Order 1982 (SI 1982/1080 (NI 12))

58.   Article 29(3) of the Agricultural Marketing (Northern Ireland) Order 1982.

Companies (Northern Ireland) Order 1986 (SI 1986/1032 (NI 6))

59.   Article 442(1) of the Companies (Northern Ireland) Order 1986.

Consumer Protection (Northern Ireland) Order 1987 (SI 1987 (NI 20))

60.   Article 29(2) of the Consumer Protection (Northern Ireland) Order 1987.

Electricity (Northern Ireland) Order 1992 (SI 1992/231 (NI 1))

61.   Article 61(2) of the Electricity (Northern Ireland) Order 1992.

Airports (Northern Ireland) Order 1994 (SI 1994/426 (NI 1))

62.   Article 49(2) of the Airports (Northern Ireland) Order 1994.

Pensions (Northern Ireland) Order 1995 (SI 1995/3213 (NI 22))

63.—(1)   Article 103(2) of the Pensions (Northern Ireland) Order 1995.
    (2)   Article 106(2) of that Order.

Gas (Northern Ireland) Order 1996 (SI 1996/275 (NI 2))

64.   Article 44(3) of the Gas (Northern Ireland) Order 1996.

Race Relations (Northern Ireland) Order 1997 (SI 1997/869 (NI 6))

65.   Article 50(1) of the Race Relations (Northern Ireland) Order 1997.

Fair Employment and Treatment (Northern Ireland) Order 1998 (SI 1998/3162 (NI 21))

66.   Article 18(1) of the Fair Employment and Treatment (Northern Ireland) Order 1998.

SCHEDULE 5
PATHOGENS AND TOXINS

VIRUSES

Chikungunya virus
Congo-crimean haemorrhagic fever virus
Dengue fever virus
Eastern equine encephalitis virus
Ebola virus
Hantaan virus
Japanese encephalitis virus
Junin virus
Lassa fever virus
Lymphocytic choriomeningitis virus
Machupo virus
Marburg virus
Monkey pox virus
Rift Valley fever virus
Tick-borne encephalitis virus (Russian Spring-Summer encephalitis virus)

Variola virus
Venezuelan equine encephalitis virus
Western equine encephalitis virus
Yellow fever virus

RICKETTSIAE

Bartonella quintana (Rochalimea quintana, Rickettsia quintana)
Coxiella burnetii
Rickettsia prowazeki
Rickettsia rickettsii

BACTERIA

Bacillus anthracis
Brucella abortus
Brucella melitensis
Brucella suis
Burkholderia mallei (Pseudomonas mallei)
Burkholderia pseudomallei (Pseudomonas pseudomallei)
Chlamydophila psittaci
Clostridium botulinum
Francisella tularensis
Salmonella typhi
Shigella dysenteriae
Vibrio cholerae
Yersinia pestis

TOXINS

Aflatoxins
Botulinum toxins
Clostridium perfringens toxins
Conotoxin
Microcystin (Cyanginosin)
Ricin
Saxitoxin
Shiga toxin
Staphylococcus aureus toxins
Tetrodotoxin
Verotoxin

Notes

1.   Any reference in this Schedule to a micro-organism includes—
     (a)   any genetic material containing any nucleic acid sequence associated with the pathogenicity of the micro-organism; and
     (b)   any genetically modified organism containing any such sequence.
2.   Any reference in this Schedule to a toxin includes—
     (a)   any genetic material containing any nucleic acid sequence for the coding of the toxin; and

(b)   any genetically modified organism containing any such sequence.

3.   Any reference in this Schedule to a toxin includes subunits of the toxin.

SCHEDULE 6
THE PATHOGENS ACCESS APPEAL COMMISSION

Constitution and administration

1.—(1)   The Commission shall consist of members appointed by the Lord Chancellor.

(2)   The Lord Chancellor shall appoint one of the members as chairman.

(3)   A member shall hold and vacate office in accordance with the terms of his appointment.

(4)   A member may resign at any time by notice in writing to the Lord Chancellor.

2.   The Lord Chancellor may appoint officers and servants for the Commission.

3.   The Lord Chancellor—

(a)   may pay sums by way of remuneration, allowances, pensions and gratuities to or in respect of members, officers and servants;

(b)   may pay compensation to a person who ceases to be a member of the Commission if the Lord Chancellor thinks it appropriate because of special circumstances; and

(c)   may pay sums in respect of expenses of the Commission.

Procedure

4.—(1)   The Commission shall sit at such times and in such places as the Lord Chancellor may direct.

(2)   The Commission may sit in two or more divisions.

(3)   At each sitting of the Commission—

(a)   three members shall attend;

(b)   one of the members shall be a person who holds or has held high judicial office (within the meaning of the Appellate Jurisdiction Act 1876 (c. 59)); and

(c)   the chairman or another member nominated by him shall preside and report the Commission's decision.

5.—(1)   The Lord Chancellor may make rules—

(a)   regulating the exercise of the right of appeal to the Commission;

(b)   prescribing practice and procedure to be followed in relation to proceedings before the Commission;

(c)   providing for proceedings before the Commission to be determined without an oral hearing in specified circumstances;

(d)   making provision about evidence in proceedings before the Commission (including provision about the burden of proof and admissibility of evidence);

(e)   making provision about proof of the Commission's decisions.

(2)   In making the rules the Lord Chancellor shall, in particular, have regard to the need to secure—

(a)   that decisions which are the subject of appeals are properly reviewed; and

(b)   that information is not disclosed contrary to the public interest.

(3)   The rules may, in particular—

(a)   provide for full particulars of the reasons for denial of access to be withheld from the applicant and from any person representing him;

(b)   enable the Commission to exclude persons (including representatives) from all or part of proceedings;

(c)   enable the Commission to provide a summary of evidence taken in the absence of a person excluded by virtue of paragraph (b);

(d)   permit preliminary or incidental functions to be discharged by a single member;

(e)   permit proceedings for permission to appeal under section 70(5) to be determined by a single member;

(f)   make provision about the functions of persons appointed under paragraph 6;

(g)   make different provision for different parties or descriptions of party.

(4)   Rules under this paragraph—

(a)   shall be made by statutory instrument; and

(b)   shall not be made unless a draft of them has been laid before and approved by resolution of each House of Parliament.

(5)   In this paragraph a reference to proceedings before the Commission includes a reference to proceedings arising out of proceedings before the Commission.

6.—(1)   The relevant law officer may appoint a person to represent the interests of an organisation or other applicant in proceedings in relation to which an order has been made by virtue of paragraph 5(3)(b).

(2)   The relevant law officer is—

(a)   in relation to proceedings in England and Wales, the Attorney General;

(b)   in relation to proceedings in Scotland, the Advocate General for Scotland; and

(c)   in relation to proceedings in Northern Ireland, the Attorney General for Northern Ireland.

(3)   A person appointed under this paragraph must—

(a)   have a general qualification for the purposes of section 71 of the Courts and Legal Services Act 1990 (c. 41) (qualification for legal appointments);

(b)   be an advocate or a solicitor who has rights of audience in the Court of Session or the High Court of Justiciary by virtue of section 25A of the Solicitors (Scotland) Act 1980 (c. 46); or

(c)   be a member of the Bar of Northern Ireland.

(4)   A person appointed under this paragraph shall not be responsible to the applicant whose interests he is appointed to represent.

(5)   In paragraph 5 of this Schedule a reference to a representative does not include a reference to a person appointed under this paragraph.

SCHEDULE 7
TRANSPORT POLICE AND MOD POLICE: FURTHER PROVISIONS

Police (Scotland) Act 1967 (c. 77)

1.   The Police (Scotland) Act 1967 has effect subject to the following amendments.

2.—(1)   Section 11 (aid of one police force by another) is amended as follows.

(2)   In subsection (2), for 'Secretary of State' substitute 'appropriate Minister or Ministers' and after 'he' insert 'or they'.

(3)   In subsection (4), for 'Secretary of State' substitute 'appropriate Ministers'.

(4)   After that subsection insert—

'(5)   This section shall apply in relation to the Strategic Rail Authority and the British Transport Police Force as it applies to a police authority and a police force respectively.

(6)   In subsection (2) "appropriate Minister or Ministers" means—

(a)   in relation to a direction given to the Chief Constable of the British Transport Police Force, the Secretary of State, and

(b)   in any other case, the Scottish Ministers.

(7)   In subsection (4) "appropriate Ministers" means—

(a)   where the police authorities concerned include the Strategic Rail Authority, the Scottish Ministers and the Secretary of State, acting jointly, and

(b)   in any other case, the Scottish Ministers.'

3.—(1)   Section 12 (collaboration agreements) is amended as follows.

(2)   In subsection (3), for 'Secretary of State' substitute 'Scottish Ministers'.

(3)   For subsection (5) substitute—

'(5)   If it appears to the Scottish Ministers that an agreement should be made for the purposes specified in subsection (1), (2) or (4) of this section, they may, after considering any representations made by the parties concerned, direct those parties to enter into such agreement for that purpose as may be specified in the directions.

(6)   For the purposes of this section—

(a)   the British Transport Police Force shall be treated as if it were a police force;

(b)   "police functions" shall include the functions of the British Transport Police Force;

(c)   the British Transport Police Committee shall be treated as if it were the police authority maintaining that Force for the purposes of subsections (1) and (2) of this section and the Strategic Rail Authority shall be so treated for the purposes of subsection (3) of this section; and

(d)   "police area", in relation to the British Transport Police Force and the British Transport Police Committee, means those places where members of the British Transport Police Force have the powers, protection and privileges of a constable under section 53(4) of the British Transport Commission Act 1949 (c. xxix).

(7)   In relation to agreements relating to the British Transport Police Force, any determination under subsection (3) shall be made, and any directions under subsection (5) shall be given, by the Scottish Ministers and the Secretary of State, acting jointly.'

4.—(1)   Section 17 (general functions and jurisdiction of constables) is amended as follows.

(2)   After subsection (4) insert—

'(4A)   A member of the British Transport Police Force who is for the time being required by virtue of section 11 or 12 of this Act to serve with a police force shall—

(a)   have all the powers and privileges of a constable of that police force, and

(b)   be subject to the direction of the chief constable of that force.'

(3)   In subsection (7)(a), after 'first-mentioned force' insert 'or, if he is serving with the British Transport Police Force, the Chief Constable of that Force'.

5.—(1)   Section 42 (causing disaffection) is amended as follows.

(2)   In subsection (1), after 'force' insert 'or of the British Transport Police Force'.

(3)   In subsection (2), after 'constable' insert 'or a member of the British Transport Police Force'.

6.—(1)   Section 43 (impersonation etc.) is amended as follows.

(2)   After subsection (2) insert—

'(2A)   For the purposes of this section—

      (a)   "constable" includes a member of the British Transport Police Force, and

      (b)   any reference to "police" includes a reference to that force.'

(3)   In subsection (3), after 'police authority' insert 'or by the British Transport Police Committee'.

(4)   After that subsection insert—

    '(4)   In its application to articles of British Transport Police Force uniform, subsection (1)(b) has effect as if for the words "without the permission of the police authority for the police area in which he is" there were substituted the words "in circumstances where it gives him an appearance so nearly resembling that of a constable as to be calculated to deceive".'

7.   In section 51 (interpretation), after the definition of 'amalgamation scheme' insert—

'"British Transport Police Force" means the constables appointed under section 53 of the British Transport Commission Act 1949 (c. xxix);'.

Firearms Act 1968 (c. 27)

8.   The Firearms Act 1968 has effect subject to the following amendments.

9.   In section 54 (Crown servants etc.), after subsection (3) insert—

    '(3A)   An appropriately authorised person who is either a member of the British Transport Police Force or an associated civilian employee does not commit any offence under this Act by reason of having in his possession, or purchasing or acquiring, for use by that Force anything which is—

      (a)   a prohibited weapon by virtue of paragraph (b) of section 5(1) of this Act; or

      (b)   ammunition containing or designed or adapted to contain any such noxious thing as is mentioned in that paragraph.

    (3B)   In subsection (3A) of this section—

      (a)   "appropriately authorised" means authorised in writing by the Chief Constable of the British Transport Police Force or, if he is not available, by a member of that Force who is of at least the rank of assistant chief constable; and

      (b)   "associated civilian employee" means a person employed by the Strategic Rail Authority who is under the direction and control of the Chief Constable of the British Transport Police Force.'

10.   In section 57(4), after the definition of 'Article 7 authority' insert—

'"British Transport Police Force" means the constables appointed under section 53 of the British Transport Commission Act 1949;'.

Police and Criminal Evidence Act 1984 (c. 60)

11.   The Police and Criminal Evidence Act 1984 has effect subject to the following amendments.

12.   In section 35 (designated police stations), after subsection (2) insert—

    '(2A)   The Chief Constable of the British Transport Police Force may designate police stations which (in addition to those designated under subsection (1) above) may be used for the purpose of detaining arrested persons.'

13.—(1)   Section 36 (custody officers at designated police stations) is amended as follows.

(2)   In subsection (2), for 'a designated police station' substitute 'a police station designated under section 35(1) above'.

(3)   After that subsection insert—

'(2A)   A custody officer for a police station designated under section 35(2A) above shall be appointed—

(a)   by the Chief Constable of the British Transport Police Force; or

(b)   by such other member of that Force as that Chief Constable may direct.'

14.   In section 118(1), after the definition of 'arrestable offence' insert—

' "British Transport Police Force" means the constables appointed under section 53 of the British Transport Commission Act 1949 (c. xxix);'.

Criminal Justice and Public Order Act 1994 (c. 33)

15.   The Criminal Justice and Public Order Act 1994 has effect subject to the following amendments.

16.—(1)   Section 60 (powers to stop and search) is amended as follows.

(2)   After subsection (9) insert—

'(9A)   The preceding provisions of this section, so far as they relate to an authorisation by a member of the British Transport Police Force (including one who for the time being has the same powers and privileges as a member of a police force for a police area), shall have effect as if the references to a locality in his police area were references to any locality in or in the vicinity of any policed premises, or to the whole or any part of any such premises.'

(3)   In subsection (11)—

(a)   before the definition of 'dangerous instruments' insert—

' "British Transport Police Force" means the constables appointed under section 53 of the British Transport Commission Act 1949;', and

(b)   after the definition of 'offensive weapon' insert—

' "policed premises", in relation to England and Wales, has the meaning given by section 53(3) of the British Transport Commission Act 1949 and, in relation to Scotland, means those places where members of the British Transport Police Force have the powers, protection and privileges of a constable under section 53(4)(a) of that Act (as it relates to Scotland);'.

17.   In section 136(1) and (2) (cross-border enforcement: execution of warrants), after 'country of execution' insert ', or by a constable appointed under section 53 of the British Transport Commission Act 1949,'.

18.   In section 137 (cross-border powers of arrest), after subsection (2) insert—

'(2A)   The powers conferred by subsections (1) and (2) may be exercised in England and Wales and Scotland by a constable appointed under section 53 of the British Transport Commission Act 1949.'

19.   In section 140 (reciprocal powers of arrest), after subsection (6) insert—

'(6A)   The references in subsections (1) and (2) to a constable of a police force in Scotland, and the references in subsections (3) and (4) to a constable of a police force in England and Wales, include a constable appointed under section 53 of the British Transport Commission Act 1949 (c. xxix).'

Police Act 1996 (c. 16)

20.   The Police Act 1996 has effect subject to the following amendments.

21.   In section 23 (collaboration agreements between police forces), after subsection (7) insert—

'(7A)   For the purposes of this section—

(a)   the British Transport Police Force shall be treated as if it were a police force,

(b)   the Chief Constable of that Force shall be treated as if he were the chief officer of police of that Force,

(c)   "police functions" shall include the functions of the British Transport Police Force, and

(d)   the British Transport Police Committee shall be treated as if it were the police authority maintaining that Force for the purposes of subsections (1), (2) and (7) and the Strategic Rail Authority shall be so treated for the purposes of subsection (3).'

22.   In section 24 (aid of one police force by another), after subsection (4) insert—

'(4A)   This section shall apply in relation to the Strategic Rail Authority, the British Transport Police Force and the Chief Constable of that Force as it applies to a police authority, a police force and a chief officer of police respectively, and accordingly the reference in subsection (3) to section 10(1) shall be construed, in a case where constables are provided by that Chief Constable, as including a reference to the scheme made under section 132 of the Railways Act 1993 (c. 43).'

23.   In section 25 (provision of special services), after subsection (1) insert—

'(1A)   The Chief Constable of the British Transport Police Force may provide special police services at the request of any person, subject to the payment to the Strategic Rail Authority of charges on such scales as may be determined by that Authority.'

24.   In section 30 (jurisdiction of constables), after subsection (3) insert—

'(3A)   A member of the British Transport Police Force who is for the time being required by virtue of section 23 or 24 to serve with a police force maintained by a police authority shall have all the powers and privileges of a member of that police force.'

25.   In section 90(4) (impersonation etc.), before the word 'and' at the end of paragraph (a) insert—

'(aa)   "member of a police force" includes a member of the British Transport Police Force,'.

26.   In section 91(2) (causing disaffection), after 'applies to' insert 'members of the British Transport Police Force and'.

27.   In section 101(1), before the definition of 'chief officer of police' insert—

'"British Transport Police Force" means the constables appointed under section 53 of the British Transport Commission Act 1949 (c. xxix);'.

28.   In section 105(2) (extent), after the entry relating to section 21 insert 'section 25(1A);'.

Terrorism Act 2000 (c. 11)

29.   The Terrorism Act 2000 has effect subject to the following amendments.

30.—(1)   Section 34 (power of superintendent for police area to designate cordoned area in the police area) is amended as follows.

(2)   In subsection (1), for 'subsection (2)' substitute 'subsections (1A), (1B) and (2)'.

(3)   After that subsection insert—

'(1A)   A designation under section 33 may be made in relation to an area (outside Northern Ireland) which is in, on or in the vicinity of any policed premises by a member of the British Transport Police Force who is of at least the rank of superintendent.

(1B)   A designation under section 33 may be made by a member of the Ministry of Defence Police who is of at least the rank of superintendent in relation to an area outside or in Northern Ireland—

(a)   if it is a place to which subsection (2) of section 2 of the Ministry of Defence Police Act 1987 (c. 4) applies,

(b)   if a request has been made under paragraph (a), (b) or (d) of subsection (3A) of that section in relation to a terrorist investigation and it is a place where he has the powers and privileges of a constable by virtue of that subsection as a result of the request, or

(c)   if a request has been made under paragraph (c) of that subsection in relation to a terrorist investigation and it is a place in, on or in the vicinity of policed premises.

(1C)   But a designation under section 33 may not be made by—

(a)   a member of the British Transport Police Force, or

(b)   a member of the Ministry of Defence Police,

in any other case.'

31.   In section 44 (power to authorise stopping and searching), after subsection (4) insert—

'(4A)   In a case (within subsection (4)(a), (b) or (c)) in which the specified area or place is in, on or in the vicinity of policed premises, an authorisation may also be given by a member of the British Transport Police Force who is of at least the rank of assistant chief constable.

(4B)   In a case in which the specified area or place is a place to which section 2(2) of the Ministry of Defence Police Act 1987 applies, an authorisation may also be given by a member of the Ministry of Defence Police who is of at least the rank of assistant chief constable.

(4C)   But an authorisation may not be given by—

(a)   a member of the British Transport Police Force, or

(b)   a member of the Ministry of Defence Police,

in any other case.'

32.   In section 121—

(a)   after the definition of 'article' insert—

'"British Transport Police Force" means the constables appointed under section 53 of the British Transport Commission Act 1949 (c. xxix),', and

(b)   after the definition of 'organisation' insert—

'"policed premises", in relation to England and Wales, has the meaning given by section 53(3) of the British Transport Commission Act 1949 and, in relation to Scotland, means those places where members of the British Transport Police Force have the powers, protection and privileges of a constable under section 53(4)(a) of that Act (as it relates to Scotland).'

33.   In section 122—

(a)   after the entry relating to the expression 'Authorised officer' insert—

'British Transport Police Force Section 121'

and

(b)   after the entry relating to the expression 'organisation' insert—
'Policed premises Section 121'.

SCHEDULE 8
REPEALS AND REVOCATION

PART I
TERRORIST PROPERTY

Short title and chapter	Extent of repeal
Access to Justice Act 1999 (c. 22)	In Schedule 2, in paragraph 2(2), the 'or' at the end of paragraph (b), and in paragraph 2(3) the 'or' at the end of paragraph (i).
Terrorism Act 2000 (c. 11)	Sections 24 to 31. In section 122, the entries for 'Authorised officer' and 'Cash'.

PART II
FREEZING ORDERS

Short title and chapter	Extent of repeal
Emergency Laws (Re-enactments and Repeals) Act 1964 (c. 60)	Section 2. In section 7(1) the words ', and any general direction given under section 2 of this Act,'. In section 14(1) and (2) the words 'or direction' and ', section 2'.
Finance Act 1968 (c. 44)	Section 55.

These repeals have effect subject to section 16(2).

PART III
IMMIGRATION AND ASYLUM

Short title and chapter	Extent of repeal
Immigration and Asylum Act 1999 (c. 33)	In section 143, subsections (3) to (8) and (14).

PART IV
RACE AND RELIGION

Short title and chapter	Extent of repeal or revocation
Public Order Act 1986 (c. 64)	In section 17 the words 'in Great Britain'.
Public Order (Northern Ireland) Order 1987 (SI 1987/463 (NI 7))	In Article 8 in the definition of fear and the definition of hatred the words 'in Northern Ireland'.

This repeal and this revocation have effect subject to section 42.

PART V
CIVIL NUCLEAR SECURITY

Short title and chapter	Extent of repeal
Nuclear Installations Act 1965 (c. 57)	In Schedule 1, paragraphs 5 and 6.
Atomic Energy Authority (Special Constables) Act 1976 (c. 23)	Section 3. In section 4(2), the definitions of 'specified body corporate' and 'designated company'.

PART VI
POLICE POWERS

Short title and chapter	Extent of repeal
British Transport Commission Act 1962 (c. xlii)	Section 43(3).
Ministry of Defence Police Act 1987 (c. 4)	In section 2, subsection (2)(d), in subsection (3), the words ', but only' and, in subsection (4), the words 'as they have effect in the United Kingdom'.
Criminal Justice and Public Order Act 1994 (c. 33)	In section 60, subsection (4A) and, in subsection (8), paragraph (b) and the word 'or' immediately preceding it.
Crime and Disorder Act 1998 (c. 37)	Section 25(1).

PART VII
MISCELLANEOUS

Short title and chapter	Extent of repeal
Terrorism Act 2000 (c. 11)	In section 55, the definition of 'nuclear weapon'. In Schedule 5, paragraph 18(e). In Schedule 7, in paragraph 17(4) the 'or' at the end of paragraph (b).

Bibliography

These listings concentrate upon contemporary terrorism and legislation. For readings about previous incarnations of anti-terrorism legislation, see: Walker, C.P., *The Prevention of Terrorism in British Law* (2nd ed., Manchester University Press, Manchester, 1992).

Adams, J., *The Financing of Terrorism* (New English Library, London, 1986)

Alexander, Y., and Swetnam, M., *Usama bin Laden's al-Qaida* (Transnational Publishers, Ardsley NY, 2001)

Bice, W.B., 'British government reinsurance and acts of terrorism' (1994) 15 *University of Pennsylvania Journal of International Business Law*, 441

Bishop, P., and Mallie, E., *The Provisional I.R.A.* (Heinemann, London, 1987)

Bonner, D., 'Combating terrorism in the 1990s' [1989] *Public Law* 440

Bonner, D., *Emergency Powers in Peacetime* (Sweet & Maxwell, London, 1985)

Bowyer Bell, J., *The I.R.A. 1968-2000* (Frank Cass, London, 2000)

Brown, D., *Detention under the Prevention of Terrorism Act* (Home Office Research and Planning Unit paper 75, London, 1993)

Bruce, S., *The Red Hand* (Oxford University Press, Oxford, 1992)

Bucke, T., and Brown, D., *In Police Custody* (Home Office Research Study No.174, London, 1997)

Campbell, C., 'Two steps backwards' [1999] *Criminal Law Review* 941

Clare, P.K., *Racketeering in Northern Ireland* (OICJ, Chicago, 1989)

Committee on the Administration of Justice, *No Emergency, No Emergency Law* (Belfast, 1995)

Coogan, T.P., *The I.R.A.* (3rd ed., Fontana Books, Isle of Man, 1987)

Coogan, T.P., *The Troubles* (Arrow Books, London, 1996)

Cusak, J., and Holland, H., *UVF* (Poolbeg, Dublin, 1997)

Denning, D.E., *Information Warfare and Security* (ACM Press, Addison-Wesley, New York, 1999)

Dillon, M., *25 Years Of Terror: The IRA's War Against The British* (Bantam, London, 1996)

Dillon, M., *The Dirty War* (Hutchinson, London, 1990)

Dillon, M., *The Enemy Within* (Doubleday, London, 1994)

Donoghue, L.K., *Counter-Terrorism Law* (Irish Academic Press, Dublin, 2001)

Douglas-Scott, S., and Kimbell, J.A., 'The Adams exclusion order case' [1994] *Public Law* 516

Edge, P., 'Religious organisations and the prevention of terrorism legislation' (1999) 4 *Journal of Civil Liberties* 194

Finn, J.E., *Constitutions in Crisis* (Oxford University Press, Oxford, 1991)

Finnie, W., 'Anti-terrorist legislation and the European Convention on Human Rights' (1991) 54 *Modern Law Review* 288

Finnie, W., 'Fourth bite at the cherry' 1989 *Scottish Law Times* 329

Finnie, W., 'Old wine in new bottles?' 1990 *Juridical Review* 1

Flaherty, M., 'Human rights violations against defence lawyers: the case of Northern Ireland' (1994) 7 *Harvard Human Rights Journal* 87

Flaherty, M.S., 'Interrogation, legal advice and human rights in Northern Ireland' (1997) 27 *Columbia Human Rights Law Review* 1

Gearty, C., (ed.), *Terrorism* (Dartmouth, Aldershot, 1996)

Gearty, C., 'Finding an enemy' (1999) *London Review of Books* 15 April 23

Gearty, C., 'Terrorism and human rights' (1999) 19 *Legal Studies* 366

Gearty, C., 'The cost of human rights' (1994) 47 *Current Legal Problems* 19

Gearty, C., 'Turning point' (2001) 145 *Solicitors' Journal* 426

Gearty, C., and Kimbell, J.A., *Terrorism and the Rule of Law* (King's College London, 1995)

Gearty, C., *Terror* (Faber & Faber, London, 1991)

Greer, S.C., and White A., *Abolishing the Diplock Courts* (Cobden Trust, London, 1986)

Greer, S.C, *Supergrasses* (Clarendon Press, Oxford, 1995)

Henshaw, D., *Animal Warfare* (Fontana, London, 1989)

Hickman, L., 'Press freedom and new legislation' (2001) 151 *New Law Journal* 716

Higgins, R., and Flory, M., (eds), *Terrorism and International Law* (Routledge, London, 1997)

Hillyard, P., *Suspect Community* (Pluto Press, London, 1993)

Hogan, G., and Walker C., *Political Violence and the Law in Ireland* (Manchester University Press, Manchester, 1989)

Holland, D., *The INLA* (TORC, Dublin, 1992)

Hunt, A., 'Terrorism and reasonable suspicion by "proxy"' (1997) 113 *Law Quarterly Review* 540

Hunt, P., and Dickson, B., 'Northern Ireland's emergency laws and international human rights' (1993) *Netherlands Quarterly on Human Rights* 173

Jackson, J.R., 'Curtailing the right to silence' [1991] *Criminal Law Review* 407

Jackson, J.R., and Doran, S, 'Conventional trials in unconventional times' (1993) 4 *Criminal Law Forum* 503

Jackson, J.R., and Doran, S, 'Diplock and the presumption against jury trial' [1992] *Criminal Law Review* 755

Jackson, J.R., and Doran, S., *Judge without Jury* (Clarendon Press, Oxford, 1995)

Jackson, J.R., Quinn, K., and O'Malley, T., 'The jury system in contemporary Ireland' (1999) 62 *Law & Contemporary Problems* 203

Jason-Lloyd, L., 'The Prevention of Terrorism (Additional Powers) Act 1996 — a commentary', (1996) 160 *Justice of the Peace* 503

Jennings, A., (ed.), *Justice Under Fire* (2nd ed., Pluto Press, London, 1990)

Kassimeris, G., 'Europe's last red terrorists: the Revolutionary Organization 17 November 1975-2000' (2001) 13(2) *Terrorism & Political Violence* 67

Kent, K., 'Basic rights and anti-terrorism legislation' (2000) 33 *Vanderbilt Journal of Transnational Law* 221

Klip, A., and Mackarel, M., 'The Lockerbie trial' (1999) 70 *Revue Internationale de Droit Penal* 777

Kushner, H.W., *The Future of Terrorism* (Sage, Thousand Oaks, 1998)

Laquer, W., *The New Terrorism: Fanaticism and the Arms of Mass Destruction* (Oxford University Press, Oxford, 1999)

Livingstone, S., 'The House of Lords and the Northern Ireland conflict' (1994) 57 *Modern Law Review* 333

Mallie, E., and McKittrick, D., *The Fight for Peace* (Heinemann, London, 1996)

Marks, S., 'Civil liberties at the margins' (1995) 15 *Oxford Journal of Legal Studies* 69

Monaghan, R., 'Terrorism in the name of animal rights' (1999) 11(4) *Terrorism & Political Violence* 159

Mullin, C., *Error of Judgment* (Revised ed., Poolbeg Press, Dublin, 1990)

Murphy, M.R., 'Northern Ireland policing reform and the intimidation of defense lawyers' (2000) 68 *Fordham Law Review* 1877

Murray, R., *The S.A.S. in Ireland* (Mercier, Dublin, 1990)

Nelson, S., *Ulster's Uncertain Defenders* (Appletree Press, Belfast, 1984)

New Zealand Law Commission Report No. 12, *First Report on Emergencies* (Wellington, 1990); Report No. 22, *Final Report on Emergencies* (Wellington, 1991)

Ni Aolain, F., 'The fortification of an emergency regime' (1996) 59 *Albany Law Review* 1353

Ni Aolain, F., *The Politics of Force* (Blackstaff, Belfast, 2000)

Norman, P., 'The Terrorist Finance Unit and the Joint Action Group on Organised Crime' (1998) 37 *Howard Journal* 375

Post, J.M., Ruby, K.G., and Shaw, E.D., 'From car bombs to logic bombs' (2000) 12(2) *Terrorism & Political Violence* 97

Raufer, X., 'New world disorder and new terrorism' (1999) 11(4) *Terrorism & Political Violence* 30

Reid, K., 'Businesses and the Prevention of Terrorism (Additional Powers) Act 1996' (1997) 4(3) *Journal of Financial Crime* 245

Reid, K., 'Prevention of Terrorism (Additional Powers) Act 1996' (1996) 4 *Web Journal of Current Legal Issues*

Reinares, F., (ed.), *European Democracies Against Terrorism* (Ashgate, Aldershot, 2000)

Rowe, J.J., 'The Terrorism Act 2000' [2000] *Criminal Law Review* 527

Srivastava, A., 'Regulating money laundering to combat terrorism' (2001) 151 *New Law Journal* 1466

Taylor, M., and Horgan, J., 'Future developments of political terrorism in Europe' (1999) 11(4) *Terrorism & Political Violence* 83

Taylor, P., *Loyalists* (Bloomsbury, London, 2000)

Taylor, P., *Provos: The IRA and Sinn Fein* (Bloomsbury, London, 1997)

Thomas, P., 'Emergency terrorist legislation' (1998) 3 *Journal of Civil Liberties* 240

Vercher, A., *Terrorism in Europe: An International Comparative Legal Analysis*, (Clarendon Press, Oxford, 1992)

Wadham, J., and Chakrabarti, S., 'Indefinite Detention Without Trial' (2001) 151 *New Law Journal* 1564

Walker, C., and Fitzpatrick, B., 'Holding Centres in Northern Ireland, the Independent Commissioner and the rights of detainees' [1999] *European Human Rights Law Review* 27

Walker, C., and Fitzpatrick, B., 'The Independent Commissioner for the Holding Centres: a review' [1998] *Public Law* 106

Walker, C., 'Anti-terrorism laws for the future' (1996) 146 *New Law Journal* 586, 657

Walker, C., 'Army special powers on parade' (1989) 40 *Northern Ireland Legal Quarterly* 1

Walker, C., 'Briefing on the Terrorism Act 2000' (2000) 12(2) *Terrorism & Political Violence* 1

Walker, C., 'Constitutional governance and special powers against terrorism' (1997) 35 *Columbia Journal of Transnational Law* 1

Walker, C., 'Military aid in civil emergencies: lessons from New Zealand' (1998) 27 *Anglo American Law Review* 133

Walker, C., 'Paramilitary displays and the PTA' 1992 *Juridicial Review* 90

Walker, C., 'Police and community in Northern Ireland' (1990) 41 *Northern Ireland Legal Quarterly* 105

Walker, C., 'The bombs in Omagh and their aftermath: the Criminal Justice (Terrorism and Conspiracy Act 1998)' (1999) 62 *Modern Law Review* 879

Walker, C., 'The commodity of justice in states of emergency' (1999) 50 *Northern Ireland Legal Quarterly* 164

Walker, C., 'The role and powers of the Army in Northern Ireland' in Hadfield, B., (ed.), *Northern Ireland and the Constitution* (Open University Press, 1992)

Walker, C., and McGuinness, M., Risk, political violence and policing the City of London' in Crawford, A., (ed.), *Crime, Insecurity, Safety and the New Governance* (Willan Publishing, 2002)

Walker, C., and Reid, K., 'The offence of directing terrorist organisations' [1993] *Criminal Law Review* 669

Walker, C., and Starmer, K., *Miscarriages of Justice* (Blackstone Press, London, 1999)

Walker, C., 'Terrorism' in Bridge, J.W., *et al*, *UK Law in the Mid-1990s* (UK Comparative Law Series, UK National Committee of Comparative Law, London, 1994) 170

Walker, C., 'The detention of suspected terrorists in the British Islands' (1992) 12 *Legal Studies* 178

Walker, C., 'The governance of special powers' in Gearty, C., and Tomkins, A, *Understanding Human Rights* (Mansell, London, 1996) 611-643

Walker, C., *The Prevention of Terrorism in British Law* (2nd ed., Manchester University Press, Manchester, 1992)

Walsh, D., *Bloody Sunday and the Rule of Law in Northern Ireland* (Gill & MacMillan, Dublin, 2000)

Wardlaw, G., *Political Terrorism* (2nd ed., Cambridge University Press, Cambridge, 1989)

Wheatley, D., 'Guilty . . . said the Red Queen?' (1989) 139 *New Law Journal* 499

Whitty, N., Murphy, T., and Livingstone, S., *Civil Liberties Law* (Butterworths, London, 2001) chap. 3, 'Terrorism: rhetoric and reality'

Wilkinson, P., *Terrorism versus Democracy* (Frank Cass, London, 2000)

Parliamentary debates on the Terrorism Act 2000

House of Commons, First reading: vol. 340 col. 443 2 December 1999; Second reading: vol. 341 col. 152 14 December 1999; Committee stage: Standing Committee D; Report stage vol. 346 col. 329 15 March 2000; Third reading vol. 346 col. 445 15 March 2000; Lord amendments vol. 353 col. 353 10 July 2000

House of Lords, First reading: vol. 611 col. 9 6 April 2000; Second reading: vol. 611 col. 1427 6 April 2000; Committee stage: vol. 613 col. 214 16 May 2000; Report stage vol. 614 col. 159 20 June 2000; Third reading vol. 614 col. 1442 4 July 2000

Parliamentary debates on the Anti-terrorism, Crime and Security Act 2001

House of Commons, First reading: vol. 374 col. 571 12 November 2001; Second reading: vol. 375 col. 21 19 November 2001; Committee stage: vol. 375 col. 342 21 and 26 November 2001; Third reading vol. 375 col. 801 26 November 2001; Lords amendments vol. 376 col. 841 12 and 13 December 2001

House of Lords, First reading: vol. 629 col. 130 26 November 2001; Second reading: vol. 629 col. 142 27 November 2001; Committee stage: vol. 629 col. 301 28 and 29 November, 3 and 4 December 2001; Report stage vol. 629 col. 949 6 and 10 December 2001; Third reading vol. 629 col. 1238 11 December 2001; Commons amendments vol. 629 col. 1420 13 December 2001

Reports from official sources

Baker Report, Review of the Operation of the Northern Ireland (Emergency Provisions) Act 1978 (Cmnd. 9222, London, 1984)

Bennett Report, Report of the Committee of Inquiry into Police Interrogation Procedures in Northern Ireland (Cmnd. 9497, London, 1979)

Bowen Report, Report on Procedures for the Arrest, Interrogation and Detention of Suspected Terrorists in Aden (Cmnd. 3165, London, 1966)

Cameron Report, Disturbances in Northern Ireland. Report of the Commission appointed by the Governor of Northern Ireland (Cmd. 532, Belfast, 1969)

Caddy Report, Assessment and Implications of Centrifuge Contamination in the Trace Explosive Section of the Forensic Explosives Laboratory at Fort Halstead (Cm.3491, London, 1996)

Colville Report, Review of the Operation of the Prevention of Terrorism (Temporary Provisions) Act 1984 (Cm. 264, London, 1987)

Colville Annual Reports on the PTA, Reports on the Operation in 1986-92 of the Prevention of Terrorism (Temporary Provisions) Acts (Home Office)

Colville Report on the EP Acts, Review of the Northern Ireland (Emergency Provisions) Acts 1978 and 1987 (Cm. 1115, London, 1990)

Colville Annual Reports on the EPA, Reports on the Operation in 1987-92 of the Northern Ireland (Emergency Provisions) Acts (Northern Ireland Office)

Compton Report, Report of an Enquiry into allegations against the security forces of physical brutality in Northern Ireland arising out of arrests on the 9 August 1971 (Cmnd. 4828, London, 1972)

Defence Select Committee, The Ministry of Defence Police: Changes in Jurisdiction Proposed under the Anti-Terrorism, Crime and Security Bill 2001 (2001-02 HC 382) and Government Response (2001-02 HC 621)

Defence Select Committee, The Threat from Terrorism (2001-02 HC 348-I)

Delegated Powers and Regulatory Reform Select Committee, Report on the Anti-terrorism, Crime and Security Bill (2001-02 HL 45)

Diplock Report, Report of the Commission to consider legal procedures to deal with terrorist activities in Northern Ireland (Cmnd. 5185, London, 1972)

Gardiner Report, Report of a Committee to consider, in the context of civil liberties and human rights, measures to deal with terrorism in Northern Ireland (Cmnd. 5847, London, 1975)

Home Affairs Select Committee, Report on the Anti-terrorism, Crime and Security Bill 2001 (2001-02 HC 351)

Home Office Circulars (applicable also in Northern Ireland and Scotland), Home Office Circular No. 3/2001: Terrorism Act 2000; Home Office Circular 7/2002: Guidance for the police and public on the implementation of section 89; sections 113-115; sections 117-120 and section 121 of the Anti-Terrorism, Crime and Security Act 2001

Home Office Consultation Paper, Home Office and Northern Ireland Office, Legislation against Terrorism (Cm.4178, London, 1998)

Home Office Regulatory Impact Assessments, Home Office, Anti-terrorism, Crime and Security Bill, Aviation Security, Retention of Communications Data, Security of Nuclear Industry, Security of Pathogens and Toxins, Terrorism Act

2000 Passenger Information, Terrorism Property, all at http://www.homeoffice. gov.uk/oicd/antiterrorism/ria—antiterrorism.htm, 2001

House of Commons Library, House of Commons Library, The Anti-Terrorism, Crime and Security Bill (Research Papers 01/101 (Introduction and Summary); 01/99 (Parts I, II, VIII, IX & XIII: Property, Security & Crime); 01/98 (Parts III & XI: Disclosure and Retention of Information); 01/96 (Parts IV & V: immigration, asylum, race and religion); 01/94 (Parts VI & VII: Pathogens, Toxins and Weapons of Mass Destruction); 01/97 (Part X: Police Powers))

Independent Assessor of Military Complaints Procedures in Northern Ireland, Annual Reports (1993-4 HC 369) and onwards

Independent Commissioner for the Holding Centres, Annual Reports (Northern Ireland Office, Belfast, 1994 and onwards)

Jellicoe Report, Review of the Operation of the Prevention of Terrorism (Temporary Provisions) Act 1976 (Cmnd. 8803, London, 1983)

Joint Committee on Human Rights, Reports on the Anti-terrorism, Crime and Security Bill (2001-02 HL 37, HC 372) and (2001-02 HL 51, HC 420)

Lloyd Report, Lord Lloyd and Sir John Kerr, Inquiry into Legislation against Terrorism (Cm.3420, London, 1996)

May Inquiry, May, Sir John, Report of the Inquiry into the circumstances surrounding the convictions arising out of the bomb attacks in Guildford and Woolwich in 1974, Interim Report (1989-90 H.C. 556), Second Report (1992-93 H.C. 296), Final Report (1993-94 H.C. 449)

Mitchell Report, Report of the International Body on Decommissioning (http://www.britainUSA.com/nireland/law&order.asp, 1996)

Northern Ireland Office Diplock Review, Diplock Review: Report (Belfast, 2000)

Patten Report, The Independent Commission on Policing for Northern Ireland, A New Beginning: Policing in Northern Ireland (Northern Ireland Office, Belfast, 1999)

Philips Annual Reports on the PTA, Reports on the Operation in 1984-85 of the Prevention of Terrorism (Temporary Provisions) Acts (Home Office)

Rowe Report on the EP Act, Review of the Northern Ireland (Emergency Provisions) Act 1991 (Cm.2706, London, 1995)

Rowe Annual Reports on the EP Acts, Reports on the Operation in 1992-99 of the Northern Ireland (Emergency Provisions) Acts (Northern Ireland Office)

Rowe Annual Reports on the PTA, Reports on the Operation in 1993-99 of the Prevention of Terrorism (Temporary Provisions) Acts (Home Office)

S.A.C.H.R., Standing Advisory Commission on Human Rights for Northern Ireland, Annual Reports, 1973-99 (for the final report, see (1998-99 HC 265)

Scarman Report, Government of Northern Ireland. Violence and Civil Disturbance in Northern Ireland in 1969. Report of a Tribunal of Inquiry (Cmd. 566, Belfast, 1972)

Shackleton Report, Review of the Operation of the Prevention of Terrorism (Temporary Provisions) Acts 1974 and 1976 (Cmnd. 7324 London, 1978)

Widgery Report, Report of the Tribunal appointed to inquire into the events on Sunday 30 January 1972 which led to loss of life in connection with the procession in Londonderry on that day (1971-72 H.C. 220)

Web sources

Center for Democracy and Technology, http://www.cdt.org/policy/terrorism/
Committee on the Administration of Justice (Northern Ireland),
    http://www.caj.org.uk/
Conflict Archive on the Internet (Northern Ireland), http://cain.ulst.ac.uk/
Counter-Terrorism Home Page, http://www.counterterrorism.com
Cyborg Anarchy, www.geocities.com/cyborg_anarchy/downloads.html
Electronic Frontier Foundation,
    http://www.eff.org/pub/Privacy/Terrorism_militias/
Electronic Privacy Information Center, http://www.epic.org/privacy/terrorism
Emergency Response Guide to Terrorism, http://www.emergency.com/cntrterr.htm
ERRI Counter-Terrorism Archive, http://www.emergency.com/cntrterr.htm
Federation of American Scientists, http://www.fas.org/irp/world/para/
Home Office, http://www.homeoffice.gov.uk/atoz/terrorists.htm
Home Office, http://www.homeoffice.gov.uk/terrorism/index.htm
Infowar.Com, http://www.infowar.com/
International Policy Institute for Counter-Terrorism, http://www.ict.org.il/
Law Library Resource Xchange, 9-11-2001 News and Legal Resources,
    Information and Related Services, http://www.llrx.com/newstand/wtc_i.htm
Lockerbie Trial Briefing, http://www.ltb.org.uk/
Lockerbie Trial, http://www.thelockerbietrial.com/
National Security Institute, http://nsi.org/terrorism.html
Pan-Am 103 Crash website,
    http://www.geocities.com/CapitolHill/5260/headpage.html
Pat Finucane Centre, http://www.iol.ie/~pfc/policing/pta.html
PBS, Behind the mask — the IRA and Sinn Fein,
    http://www.pbs.org/wgbh/pages/frontline/shows/ira
Policestop.org, http://www.policestop.org.uk/Anti_Terrorist.html
Political Science Resources: Terrorism, http://www.psr.keele.ac.uk/sseal/terror.htm
Political Terrorism Database, http://polisci.home.mindspring.com/ptd/
Queen's University Law School States of Emergency Database,
    http://143.117.33.157/emergency/emerghome.html
Ralph Smyth's website, http://www.blagged.freeserve.co.uk/ta2000/fhome.htm
Rand Corporation, http://www.rand.org/hot/newslinks.html
South Asia Terrorism Portal, http://www.satp.org/
St Andrews Centre for the Study of Terrorism and Political Violence,
    http://www.st-and.ac.uk/academic/intrel/research/cstpv/
Terrorism Research Center, http://www.terrorism.com/welcome.htm
UK Civil Contingencies Committee and Secretariat,
    http://www.co-ordination.gov.uk/terrorism.htm

UN Dag Hammarskjöld Library,
   http://www.un.org/Depts/dhl/resources/terrorism/index.html
US Counter-Terrorism Rewards Program,
   http://www.heroes.net/pub/heroes/index.html
US Department of Defence, http://www.defenselink.mil/other_info/terrorism.html
US Department of State Counter-Terrorism Office, http://www.state.gov/s/ct/
US Department of State Patterns of Global Terrorism Reports,
   http://www.state.gov/www/global/terrorism/gt_index.html
US National Commission on Terrorism, http://w3.access.gpo.gov/nct/
US Naval Postgraduate School, http://web.nps.navy.mil/~library/tgp/tgpmain.htm

Index